THE ROUTLEDGE HISTORY HANDBOOK OF MEDIEVAL REVOLT

*Edited by Justine Firnhaber-Baker
with Dirk Schoenaers*

LONDON AND NEW YORK

First published 2017
by Routledge
2 Park Square, Milton Park, Abingdon, Oxon OX14 4RN

and by Routledge
711 Third Avenue, New York, NY 10017

Routledge is an imprint of the Taylor & Francis Group, an informa business

© 2017 selection and editorial matter, Justine Firnhaber-Baker with Dirk Schoenaers; individual chapters, the contributors

The right of the editors to be identified as the authors of the editorial matter, and of the authors for their individual chapters, has been asserted in accordance with sections 77 and 78 of the Copyright, Designs and Patents Act 1988.

All rights reserved. No part of this book may be reprinted or reproduced or utilised in any form or by any electronic, mechanical, or other means, now known or hereafter invented, including photocopying and recording, or in any information storage or retrieval system, without permission in writing from the publishers.

Trademark notice: Product or corporate names may be trademarks or registered trademarks, and are used only for identification and explanation without intent to infringe.

British Library Cataloguing in Publication Data
A catalogue record for this book is available from the British Library

Library of Congress Cataloging in Publication Data
Names: Firnhaber-Baker, Justine, editor of compilation. | Schoenaers, Dirk, editor of compilation.
Title: The Routledge history handbook of medieval revolt / edited by Justine Firnhaber-Baker with Dirk Schoenaers.
Other titles: History handbook of medieval revolt
Description: Milton Park, Abingdon, Oxon ; New York, NY : Routledge, 2017. | Includes bibliographical references and index.
Identifiers: LCCN 2016019411| ISBN 9781138952225 (hardback : alkaline paper) | ISBN 9781315542423 (ebook)
Subjects: LCSH: Europe–Politics and government–476-1492. | Middle Ages. | Revolutions–Europe–History–To 1500. | Social conflict–Europe–History–To 1500. | Violence–Europe–History–To 1500. | Europe–Social conditions–To 1492. | Europe–History–476-1492.
Classification: LCC D131 .R68 2017 | DDC 355.02/180940902–dc23
LC record available at https://lccn.loc.gov/2016019411

ISBN: 978-1-138-95222-5 (hbk)
ISBN: 978-1-315-54242-3 (ebk)

Typeset in Bembo
by Wearset Ltd, Boldon, Tyne and Wear

Printed and bound in Great Britain by
TJ International Ltd, Padstow, Cornwall

CONTENTS

Figures, maps, and tables   *viii*
Notes on contributors   *ix*
Preface   *xii*
List of abbreviations   *xiii*

Introduction: medieval revolt in context   1
Justine Firnhaber-Baker

PART I
Conceptualising revolt: then and now   **17**

1 Writing revolt in the early Roman empire   19
   Myles Lavan

2 *Takehan, Cokerulle,* and *Mutemaque*: naming collective action in the later medieval Low Countries   39
   Jan Dumolyn and Jelle Haemers

3 The eponymous Jacquerie: making revolt mean some things   55
   Justine Firnhaber-Baker

4 'Great and horrible rumour': shaping the English revolt of 1381   76
   Andrew Prescott

5 'United we stand?' Representing revolt in the historiography of Brabant and Holland (fourteenth to fifteenth centuries)   104
   Dirk Schoenaers

6 An exemplary revolt of the central Middle Ages? Echoes of the first
   Lombard League across the Christian world around the year 1200   130
   Gianluca Raccagni

PART II
Socio-political contexts: identity, motivation, and mobilisation   **153**

7 Looking forward: peasant revolts in Europe, 600–1200   155
   Chris Wickham

8 Invoking and constructing legitimacy: rebels in the late medieval
   European and Islamic worlds   168
   Patrick Lantschner

9 Rebellion and the law in fifteenth-century English towns   189
   Eliza Hartrich

10 Women in revolt in medieval and early modern Europe   208
   Samuel Cohn, Jr.

11 Popular movements and elite leadership: exploring a late medieval
   conundrum in cities of the Low Countries and Germany   220
   Justine Smithuis

12 Revolts and wars, corporations and leagues: remembering and
   communicating urban uprisings in the medieval Empire   236
   Gisela Naegle

PART III
Communication: language, performance, and violence   **265**

13 A dossier of peasant and seigneurial violence   267
   Paul Freedman

14 Violence as a political language: the uses and misuses of violence in
   late medieval French and English popular rebellions   279
   Vincent Challet

15 Developing strategies of protest in late medieval Sicily   292
   Fabrizio Titone

16 Cultures of surveillance in late medieval English towns: the monitoring
   of speech and the fear of revolt   311
   Christian D. Liddy

17	Interpreting large-scale revolts: some evidence from the War of the Communities of Castile *Hipólito Rafael Oliva Herrer*	330
18	Prophetic rebellions: radical urban theopolitics in the era of the Reformations *Phillip Haberkern*	349
	Conclusion *John Watts*	370
Index		381

FIGURES, MAPS, AND TABLES

Figures

3.1	Peasant house in Beauvais, built c.1410	65
3.2	Montépilloy, castle attacked by the Jacques	66
13.1	Frontispiece from *Die auffrur so geschehen ist im Ungerlandt* ... Nuremberg, 1514	269
13.2	Frontispiece from Johann Christian Engel, *monumenta Ungrica*, Vienna, 1809	270

Maps

3.1	Geographic extent of the Jacquerie	61
4.1	Some places in Southern England which experienced disturbances during the English rising of 1381	86
4.2	Some places in Northern England which experienced disturbances during the English rising of 1381	90
15.1	Sicily	295
17.1	The scope of the War of the Communities	333

Tables

5.1	Regional historiography in the vernacular before the Burgundian integration of Brabant and Holland	107
5.2	Regional historiography in the vernacular after the Burgundian integration of Brabant and Holland	108

CONTRIBUTORS

Vincent Challet is Assistant Professor in Medieval History at the University of Montpellier. After a PhD on the revolt of the Tuchins in Languedoc, he directed a research programme on the urban chronicle of Montpellier (online edition: thalamus.huma-num.fr) and currently works on the political culture of urban and rural communities of Southern France.

Samuel Cohn, Jr. is Professor of Medieval History at the University of Glasgow, an Honorary Fellow of the Institute for Advanced Studies in Humanities (University of Edinburgh), and a Fellow of the Royal Society of Edinburgh. Over the past 15 years he has focused on the history of popular unrest in late medieval and early modern Europe and on the history of disease and medicine. His latest books include: *The Black Death Transformed: Disease and Culture in Early Renaissance Europe*; *Popular Protest in Late Medieval Europe: Italy, France, and Flanders*; *Lust for Liberty: The Politics of Social Revolt in Medieval Europe, 1200–1425*; *Cultures of Plague: Medical Thinking at the End of the Renaissance*; and *Popular Protest in Late Medieval English Towns*. He is presently on leave funded by a three-year 'Major Research Fellowship' from the Leverhulme Trust on the project, 'Epidemics: Waves of Disease, Waves of Hate from the Plague of Athens to AIDS'.

Jan Dumolyn is a Senior Lecturer in Medieval History (with special research assignment) at Ghent University. He publishes on the social, political, and cultural history of the later medieval Low Countries.

Justine Firnhaber-Baker is Lecturer in Late Mediaeval History at the University of St Andrews. She has published *Violence and the State in Languedoc, 1250–1400* on 'private' wars and royal government and *Difference and Identity in Francia and Medieval France*, an essay collection co-edited with art historian Meredith Cohen, as well as other articles. She is currently writing a book on the Jacquerie of 1358.

Paul Freedman is the Chester D. Tripp Professor of History at Yale University where he has taught since 1997. From 1979 until 1997 he was at Vanderbilt University. He has written on topics related to medieval European history, especially with regard to Catalonia, the Church, and peasants. His *Images of the Medieval Peasant* (1999) received the Haskins Medal from the Medieval Academy of America. Another book, *Out of the East: Spices and the Medieval Imagination* (2008), considers the desire for spices in the Middle Ages and how it led to European exploration and conquest.

Contributors

Phillip Haberkern is an Assistant Professor of History at Boston University. His research focuses on the Bohemian and German reformations, with particular attention to the role of history and memory in justifying religious change. He is the author of *Patron Saint and Prophet: Jan Hus in the Bohemian and German Reformations* (2016), and his work has also appeared in *German History* and *History Compass*.

Jelle Haemers is a Senior Lecturer at the Department of History at the University of Leuven (KU Leuven). His publications include *For the Common Good: State Power and Urban Revolts in the Reign of Mary of Burgundy, 1477–1482* (2009), and *De strijd om het regentschap over Filips de Schone: Opstand, facties en geweld in Brugge, Gent en Ieper, 1482–1488* (2014).

Eliza Hartrich is a Fellow-by-Examination (JRF) at Magdalen College, Oxford. Her work focuses on urban political culture in later medieval England, examining the ways in which towns and civic culture affected national politics. She was awarded a DPhil from Oxford for her dissertation 'Town, Crown, and Urban System: The Position of Towns in the English Polity, 1413–71', currently being revised for publication. She has published articles on London's role in Henry of Lancaster's 1328 rebellion and on urban councils in fifteenth-century England.

Patrick Lantschner is a Lecturer at University College London. He works and teaches on Europe and the Islamic world in the later Middle Ages. He has published on medieval cities in Europe and the Islamic world, and is broadly interested in societies in which the state is but one of a number of players. He takes a keen interest in comparative and transnational history, and has worked with scholars from anthropology, law, and oriental studies.

Myles Lavan is a historian of the Roman empire and a Senior Lecturer at the University of St Andrews. His first monograph, *Slaves to Rome: Paradigms of Empire in Roman Culture*, explored how the Roman imperial project is conceptualised and debated in Latin literature. He is currently working on the spread of Roman citizenship, further studies of the language of imperialism in Latin, and the historian Tacitus.

Christian D. Liddy is Senior Lecturer in the Department of History at the University of Durham. He has written several articles on urban revolt and has a particular interest in the relationship between ideas of citizenship and practices of resistance. His recent research, which will culminate in a forthcoming Oxford University Press monograph, has been on the multiple and, sometimes, conflicting meanings of citizenship in late medieval English towns.

Gisela Naegle studied history, Romance philology, and law in Germany and France. She was awarded a PhD in medieval history from the University of Giessen in Germany with a thesis on the relations of French towns and the king at the end of the Middle Ages, which was published in 2002. Her work has a special focus on comparative medieval European and urban history. In addition to numerous scientific articles and reviews in German and French, she edited a collection of essays on peace and defence in late medieval Western Europe (*Frieden schaffen und sich verteidigen im Spätmittelalter/ Faire la paix et se defender à la fin du Moyen Âge*) published in 2012.

Hipólito Rafael Oliva Herrer is Senior Lecturer in the University of Sevilla. He has published widely both on medieval peasants and on popular political culture, including the making of popular ideologies and forms of popular protest.

Contributors

Andrew Prescott is Professor of Digital Humanities at the University of Glasgow. He was formerly a Curator of Manuscripts at the British Library, and has also held posts at the University of Sheffield, King's College London, and University of Wales Lampeter. He is currently Theme Leader Fellow for the 'Digital Transformations' theme of the Arts and Humanities Research Council.

Gianluca Raccagni is Chancellor's Fellow in History at the School of History, Classics and Archaeology of the University of Edinburgh. His research focuses on political culture in the central Middle Ages. His book *The Lombard League (1167–1225)* was published in 2010.

Dirk Schoenaers (PhD: University of Liverpool) wrote his dissertation on the Middle Dutch translation of Froissart's *Chroniques* (2010). He later held post-doctoral positions at University College London and at the University of St Andrews. His principal research interests are manuscript studies, translation, transcultural contact, and how historiographical narratives (particularly in the medieval duchy of Brabant) construe and confirm social identities. Schoenaers's current research focuses on Jean d'Enghien's *Livre des cronicques* (Brabant, *c*.1470) and includes a collaborative book project on the history of translation in the Low Countries (with colleagues in London, Utrecht, and Amsterdam).

Justine Smithuis studied at the University of Leiden, specialising in late medieval urban history. She has published articles on urban politics and violence in late medieval Utrecht and on collective identity in medieval Frisia.

Fabrizio Titone is the Ramón y Cajal Researcher at Universidad del País Vasco and the author of many publications in the field of urban history. His early research pertained to Sicily's urban institutions and society in the late Middle Ages. More recently, he has expanded his analysis and included the intersection between written and oral memory, emotion, gender history, and forms of dissent in high and late medieval Sicily analysed in the broader Mediterranean context and beyond. He also approaches these themes through an analysis of rites of passage, particularly marriages. Since September 2014 he has been the coordinator of the research project 'Policies of disciplined dissent in the western Mediterranean in the twelfth to the early sixteenth centuries'.

John Watts is Professor of Later Medieval History at the University of Oxford and a fellow of Corpus Christi College. He has written a number of books and articles about later medieval political life, including *Henry VI and the Politics of Kingship* (1996) and *The Making of Polities: Europe, 1300–1500* (2009). He is currently working on a book for the New Oxford History of England series, entitled *Renaissance England, 1461–1547*.

Chris Wickham is Chichele Professor of Medieval History at the University of Oxford (2005–16); prior to that, he taught at the University of Birmingham. He has published numerous books on the history of Italy and of Europe, up to 1200.

PREFACE

This volume comes out of a multi-year collaborative project that began, as many things do, with a conversation at the Leeds International Medieval Congress. Delighted at the revived interest in medieval revolts, Justine Firnhaber-Baker and Patrick Lantschner agreed that it would be useful and interesting to gather together scholars working on the subject to see how new approaches might develop out of putting regional specialisms into a comparative framework. Justine set out to make this happen, organising the first of these gatherings in April 2013 with the support of the St Andrews Institute of Mediaeval Studies and the School of History. From the beginning, the focus was on collecting a broad spectrum of view-points, in terms of specialism, methodology, and career stage, and on encouraging discussion and debate. This approach blossomed in 2014 and 2015, when two more conferences were held in St Andrews, this time with the support of a British Arts and Humanities Research Council Early Career Fellowship awarded to Justine. (It was with AHRC support, too, that Dirk Schoenaers joined the project in 2015 as a post-doctoral research fellow.) Every paper was followed by friendly but intense discussion, ranging from the interpretation of particular words to the road network in medieval Flanders. It is fair to say that no one left with views unchanged, or at least unchallenged. The essays that are collected here reflect those discussions and hopefully capture some of the energy that buoyed those meetings. We hope that the volume will continue to drive discussion, spark debate, and move the conversation forward.

St Andrews, Scotland,
April 2016

ABBREVIATIONS

AN	Paris, Archives nationales de France
BIHR	*Bulletin of the Institute of Historical Research*
BL	London, British Library
BN	Paris, Bibliothèque nationale de France
CCR	*Calendar of the Close Rolls Preserved in the Public Record Office*, 45 vols, London: Her Majesty's Stationery Office, 1892–1945
EcHR	*Economic History Review*
EHR	*English Historical Review*
JMH	*Journal of Medieval History*
MGH	Monumenta Germaniae Historica
Const.	Constitutiones et acta publica imperatorum et regum
CPR	*Calendar of the Patent Rolls Preserved in the Public Record Office, 1377–1477*, 20 vols, London: Her Majesty's Stationery Office, 1895–1911
DD	Diplomata
DD Mer.	Diplomata regum francorum e stirpe merovingica
Epp.	Epistolae
SS rer. Germ.	Scriptores rerum Germanicarum in usum scholarum separatim editi
SS rer. Germ., N. S.	Scriptores rerum Germanicarum, Nova series
SS rer. Merov	Scriptores rerum Merovingicarum
SS	Scriptores (in folio)
P&P	*Past & Present*
RIS	Rerum Italicarum Scriptores
TNA	Kew, The National Archives of Britain
TRHS	*Transactions of the Royal Historical Society*

INTRODUCTION
Medieval revolt in context

Justine Firnhaber-Baker

This anthology is part of an emerging body of historiography devoted to late medieval uprisings and to popular politics more generally that has developed since the turn of the millennium. These topics, hotly contested in the 1970s and 1980s, had fallen out of vogue in the previous decade, as attention shifted from classical social and political history to new kinds of cultural history. The renewed attention to medieval revolts reflects the return of political history to the fore since the new millennium but in a very different way, as our understanding of the state and violence has undergone a thorough revision and as the insights of the cultural turn have transformed how we read the events that made up a rebellion and the sources that report them. Continental scholars, often in the earlier stages of their careers, have been particularly prominent producers of new work on medieval revolt, publishing a series of inter-related essay collections.[1] The 2006 publication of Samuel K. Cohn, Jr.'s *Lust for Liberty: The Politics of Social Revolt in Medieval Europe* has also galvanised much scholarship, particularly among Anglophones.[2] The fruit of this work, often pursued collaboratively, has rapidly pushed the study of revolt in a number of new directions, which we hope not only to showcase here, but also to drive forward by bringing together work from a dynamic group of historians (plus a classicist and a literary scholar) from continental Europe, North America, and the UK.

The aims of our work in this volume are heuristic and exploratory rather than definitive. There is an overall consensus among the authors here that our approach to medieval uprisings must take account of their actors' agency within their historically specific societies, but also that our access to those actors and societies is mediated – and often obscured – by the texts that report them. From these agreed methodological starting points, our investigations move in a variety of directions and work to raise questions, as well as to answer them. Drawing on instances of revolt from Ireland to Syria and from periods to either side of the later Middle Ages as well as the core centuries from 1250 to 1500, contributors think about how uprisings worked, why they happened, whom they implicated, what they meant to contemporaries, and how we might understand them now.

I have divided the volume into three parts, each focused on a particular area of inquiry, though aspects of these themes are common to nearly every essay. The first group of essays is particularly concerned with the conceptualisation of revolt in both modern and medieval thinking.[3] Fundamentally, what are we studying and how do we know that the events and actions we group together as a revolt should be categorised as such? This is partly a problem of language and sources, due to the documents' semantic variability, the imperfect approximation of modern categories with medieval ones, and the authorial programmes of medieval writers. The problem also stems from how medieval 'states' worked differently from our own governments, a difference that drives the book's Part II, on the relationship between revolt and the institutions, ideas, and practices that structured society. In the modern West, where there is a clear distinction between the apparatus of the state and the society it governs and where the state has a monopoly on legitimate violence, revolt can be identified as collective violence by non-state actors making claims that implicates the state, even when they are not directed at it.[4] But medieval polities were considerably more fragmented than modern states. 'Revolt' in such a context might not have been construed as such by contemporaries. The role of violence is key, for it served not only strategic goals but also as a means of communication in this highly gestural society. Communication, through acts and signs, as well as words, is thus the third theme of the volume. The repertoires, models, and media through which rebels made their aims known and through which they effected their protests give us a window on to the political culture of rebels and the wider society. At the same time, problems of reception, memorialisation (or its opposite), and propagandistic intent return us to the interpretative questions that underlie Part I.

These themes reflect areas of inquiry fundamental to current scholarship on medieval revolt, but they also arise out of and benefit from a long historiographical tradition. The new medieval political history of the last decade has made a major impact on the approaches taken here, but many of the fundamental questions and problems that shaped our inquiries have been stable features of the scholarship for a long time, however novel our proposed solutions. The following introduction thus not only draws together the themes of this book, but also shows how recent work, including our own in this and other publications, has extended and developed – as well as revised – the contributions of older approaches. This volume embodies a particular historiographical moment. We hope it will provide a resource for students and a foundation for revolutionary studies in the future.

The age of revolt through the ages of revolution

Interest in the uprisings of the later Middle Ages, a period once called 'the age *par excellence* of "popular revolutions"', has waxed and waned with historical circumstances, particularly political ones.[5] Despite medieval chroniclers' fascination with the uprisings of their day, historians in Europe's *anciens régimes* were basically uninterested in them. Modern historians first turned their attention to medieval revolts during the Age of Revolution that began in 1789 (or 1776), that witnessed the great tumults of 1848, and that gave rise to Marxism. The first studies of what might be thought of (however unjustly) as the canonical medieval revolts – the 1358 French Jacquerie, the 1378 Florentine Ciompi revolt, and the 1381 English Rising – were written in more or less conscious reaction to the political upheavals of their own day.[6] Siméon Luce, author of the first study of the Jacquerie, wrote in 1859 that the politics of the Parisian rebel leader Étienne Marcel 'contained the seed of the principles of 1789'.[7] The first modern treatment of the Ciompi, written by Jean Charles Léonard de Sismondi in the early nineteenth century and revised in 1840, fitted the uprising into the author's liberal but anti-democrat vision of bourgeois political freedom; the rebels themselves he characterised as 'enemies of the republic … incapable of liberal feelings'.[8] The English Rising, as Barrie Dobson wrote, only 'ceased to be regarded as primarily "A Warnyng to Be Ware" after the publication of Thomas Paine's *The Rights of Man* in 1792'. Its historiography first flourished after the advent of Marxism and the social tumult of the 1880s when André Réville discovered the vast extent of the archival records.[9]

The anachronism of nineteenth-century writers may seem overwhelming to us now, but twentieth- and twenty-first-century historiography on medieval revolt has tracked contemporary political circumstances with remarkable coincidence. A major wave of interest in the topic arose in the early 1970s, concomitant with the social and political unrest that had begun in the previous decade. A cluster of books – Mollat and Wolff's *Ongles bleus*, Fourquin's *Les soulèvements populaires au Moyen Âge*, and Hilton's *Bond Men Made Free* – was published nearly simultaneously and stood as the essential works, especially in Anglophone historiography, until very recently.[10] The current generation's reassessment of late medieval polities that became visible at the turn of the millennium no doubt owes something to the rearrangement of global politics in the post-Cold War era and the rise of 'non-state actors'.[11] The subsequent prominence of 'popular movements', ranging from protests at World Trade Organization meetings to the 'Arab Spring' to the 2011 London Riots, has neatly coincided with the revitalisation of interest in revolt and medieval 'popular politics'.[12]

That historiography is shaped by the historical context in which it is written does not necessarily mean that its arguments are wrong, even if we sometimes find them infelicitously phrased. We cannot help but see things from our own vantage, and different perspectives reveal different aspects of the past in different lights. But it is worth unpacking those influences to understand how they have worked in relation with other intellectual currents to create particular views of the historical past, which we now build upon, modify, or utterly eschew. For the study of medieval revolt, it is notable that although the past two centuries have seen major shifts in method and interpretation, some central problems have remained surprisingly constant. The relationship between revolt and the state (however conceptualised), attention to social dynamics and non-elite groups (even if sometimes unfavourable), and a profound concern for language, sources, and source criticism are threads that have run through the scholarship since the beginning of the nineteenth century.

The state and the perimeters of 'revolt'

Studies of medieval revolt have almost invariably organised themselves around the concept of the state as the arena within which revolts take place and take on meaning. For nineteenth-century historians, who saw medieval uprisings as disruptive eruptions and deviations from normal politics, revolts were directed against the state by constituencies outside it who opposed its power. Twentieth-century historians, too, understood revolt as an expression of opposition to the state, especially to the growth of royal governments. Mollat and Wolff, for example, argued that fourteenth-century revolts erupted in protest against 'the invasion of society by the State', particularly in terms of tax demands.[13] Even in 2006, the rise of the late medieval state was portrayed as something that rebels organised themselves to oppose as an encroachment on 'liberty', understood in the modern sense as freedom from hierarchic control.[14]

As should already be clear, most of the essays in this volume envisage the state in a different and more multi-dimensional way than was the case for earlier historians, and this reassessment of the state necessarily entails the reconceptualisation of late medieval revolt. Nevertheless, the relationship between uprisings and their institutional political context remains central in current writing. Indeed, the political ramifications of revolt are perhaps more important to current historiography than they have ever been before. New historiography on late medieval politics has revised the view that the remarkable growth of government in the later Middle Ages was an inherently antagonistic process imposed upon an unwilling population, which was thus primed for rebellion. Historians have increasingly shown that 'the rise of the state' was a dialogic process in which the governed had considerable agency, often clamouring for *more* government rather than less. People employed the infrastructure and even the ideology of late medieval authorities to their own ends, not just accidentally benefiting from the expansion of government but actively abetting and encouraging it.[15]

In this light, popular protest can often be understood to reflect not unease with the growing reach of government, but dissatisfaction with its limitations. As John Watts's 2009 book on late medieval polities put it 'the development of government and its associated politics helped to create and advertise a set of political expectations among the governed', which created opposition when disappointed.[16] It was not just the state's fulfilment of its ambitions that engendered criticism, but also its failures to live up to its promises. Analyses of the ubiquitous late medieval discourse of the common good, including those of Hartrich, Titone, and Oliva Herrer in this volume, have repeatedly shown how rebels employed the government's own language of *bonum commune* (common good), *res publica* (republic or 'public thing'), or 'common weal' to criticise authorities and to advance their own programmes.[17] Indeed, Watts has argued elsewhere that this kind of language actually necessitated intervention by common people in late medieval English politics.[18]

A related shift has been the move to view 'the state' not as a monolithic entity in contrast to or opposition with 'society', but rather as a collection of institutions, practices, and ideas indistinct from the people and structures it purported to govern. Watts's book pointed to the ways through which late medieval states 'generated structures and resources which smaller powers could use to consolidate their influence or jurisdiction locally'.[19] In cities, where most medieval revolts took place, these resources included not only 'public' governmental bodies as we would now think of them, such as royal representatives or the town council, but also such 'private' institutions as craft guilds, confraternities, neighbourhood associations, and long-established factions, such as the Florentine Guelf Party.[20] In a comparative study of Bruges and York, Jelle Haemers and Christian Liddy pointed to the ways that major revolts in both cities were not only organised by the craft guilds but also employed long-established venues for and methods of complaint to pursue their aims.[21] Patrick Lantschner took this argument further, showing how this fragmentary and multi-centric nature of medieval government meant that, especially in urban contexts, groups could marshal resources from a variety of power bases to pursue their claims.[22]

Conflict was a normal part of this process, and so, as Lantschner writes, 'revolts were not, in general at least, an antithesis, subversion or pathology of the political order', but rather 'intensifications of existing processes of negotiation that were ordinarily taking place around the multiple nodes and layers of the city's political structure'.[23] In this light, Samuel Cohn's remarkable finding in *Lust for Liberty* that over 1,000 popular uprisings took place between 1250 and 1425 not only seems plausible, but appears to be a logical outcome of the make-up of late medieval cities. While the German lands of the Empire were outside Cohn's purview, the hundreds of civic revolts that Gisela Naegle's essay discusses reflect the same phenomenon. The essays in this volume show that such rebellions were usually (though not exclusively) made possible by insurgents' mobilisation of pre-existing structures rather than the invention of novel forms. They illustrate that rebellion could function as one extreme of a continuum of normal political processes in late medieval contexts as different as those of Damascus and the English Midlands.

That changes in our view of the state have necessarily resulted in changes in our understanding of revolt is related to a shift in thinking about what violence meant and how it functioned in medieval society. For modern historians whose view of the state was bounded by their experience of the state's '*monopoly* of the *legitimate* use of physical force in the enforcement of its order', violence by what we might call 'non-state' (usually meaning 'non-royal') actors was inherently a disorderly usurpation of governmental prerogatives.[24] But as it has become clearer that 'the state' in the late Middle Ages was much more polycentric, multi-layered, and diffuse than modern Western governments, there has been a consequent move to understand some kinds of violence not as crime but as politics.[25] This kind of reassessment is behind Justine Smithuis's provocative sketch of the relationship between violence and elite leadership of revolt, and it is central, too, to my suggestion that there are lights in which the Jacquerie might be better seen as a military undertaking than as a revolt.

If authority for legitimate violence was a contested question – or simply an open one – this makes the identification of 'revolt' a more uncertain exercise. That violence (real or threatened) should be a key marker seems at least implicit in nearly all of the essays here.[26] But that this violence be direct against 'the state' presents a more problematic requirement. As Lantschner has argued, many of the groups and institutions involved in rebel coalitions not only had access to the infrastructure of warfare, such as weapons, troops, and banners, but could also make a reasonable legal claim to exercise violence legitimately either on the basis of their institutional ties or because of medieval ideas about justified resistance to tyranny.[27] The legalistic concerns that seem ubiquitous in late medieval society were fundamental to many rebellions and are at the forefront of contributions by Lantschner, Hartrich, Smithuis, and Challet, and are touched on by most others.[28] What constituted a revolt for medieval contemporaries, and what should constitute a revolt for historians now, therefore depends partly on one's perspective, as the essays in Part I of this book illustrate and explore.

Social dynamics and non-elites

Alongside an emphasis on politics in a relatively strict sense, our enquiries have been shaped by a social historical programme whose roots again reach back to the subject's earliest historiography. Nineteenth-century studies of medieval revolt were strongly influenced by the period's radically democratic developments, which turned historians' attention not just to the dramatic episodes of revolt, but also to the role of non-elites as historical actors in a broader way. We may have little time for Augustin Thierry's obviously anachronistic characterisation in 1827 of the 1112 Laon commune's revolt as the direct ancestor of the French Revolution.[29] On the other hand, his opposition to historiography 'in which the broad mass of the nation disappears under mantles of the court' strikes a sympathetic chord with more recent efforts to rescue ordinary people 'from the enormous condescension of posterity'.[30] Twentieth-century historiography 'from below', itself partly driven by the major social changes of the 1960s, was fundamental to the studies of medieval revolt that appeared in the 1970s and 1980s.[31]

While the cultural turn moved many historians' interests away from social history in the later 1980s and 1990s, the turn of the millennium brought renewed attention to how 'little people' and their social networks shaped history.[32] The study of medieval revolts stands separate from this larger historiographical field, but it both benefits from and contributes to it a great deal. Medieval sources, which were almost exclusively produced by and for elites, usually have little to say about ordinary people. Except, that is, when they were rebelling. Such exceptional glimpses must be treated very cautiously, with due attention to authorial programmes and audience reception, semantics and philology, as well as the obvious fact that they describe acute episodes, not everyday existence. Indeed, Myles Lavan suggests that in the early Roman empire, the social reality of revolt is irretrievable from elite sources written for the purpose of confirming imperial agendas. The medievalists are more optimistic, but still careful. Paul Freedman's contribution, on the interplay of peasant and seigneurial violence as portrayed in written and visual sources, is particularly mindful of the interpretive gaps between what the sources intended to tell their audiences, what those audiences might have understood, and what we as historians want to know.[33]

The social world of non-elites as revealed – however partially – through the lens of revolt was one whose inhabitants often show a surprising capacity for political action, though its extent was more varied than misleadingly homogeneous terms like the 'masses', 'commoners', or 'little people' convey.[34] As Gianluca Raccagni shows, although recent emphasis on aristocrats in the central Middle Ages has obscured Northern Italy's communal institutions and culture, the political participation of non-elites was key to civic life, even in extramural political struggles. The range of terms that Jan Dumolyn and Jelle Haemers's contribution identifies for collective actions in the Low Countries speaks to the variety of ways that urban workers could seek to influence their political and economic fates, even if their bosses and rulers denigrated their efforts. Yet, as Justine Smithuis's essay reminds us, when a group of non-elites banded together, they nonetheless often had to make 'vertical' alliances with their social betters for strategic reasons. And as Eliza Hartrich points out, how a person 'revolted' in late medieval England depended a great deal on his or her particular social context: for an unfree English peasant, a lawsuit outside seigniorial jurisdiction might actually be just as effectively 'rebellious' in its implications as an armed uprising.

How revolt worked in different social and political contexts is one of the major heuristic dynamics of this book. While the recent re-imagination of the relationship between revolt and the state has been especially focused on urban environments in the late Middle Ages, many of the essays in this book cross those borders, looking at revolts that took place in the countryside and/or in periods outside the core late medieval centuries. Patrick Lantschner's chapter shows that his model can work for Islamic cities, as well as Western ones, but he is clear here, as elsewhere, that not all configurations of urban government were equally productive of uprisings.[35] Lavan's discussion certainly suggests that in an autocratic polity like that of imperial Rome, conflict was the very antithesis of how politics and government were thought ideally to work. Early medieval political configurations based on rural lordship may have been less productive of revolt, as Chris Wickham argues, though the idea of 'bad lordship' served as a galvanising criticism in the twelfth- and thirteenth-century Lombard Leagues' struggle with the Emperor, as Raccagni outlines. In the early modern cities of Haberkern's chapter, the kinds of infrastructure available to rebels were similar to those employed by their late medieval predecessors, but the advent of new kinds of religious struggle – not to mention printing – made for different types of leaders and processes of mobilisation.

The question of differences in revolt between rural and urban settings, once a major historiographical focus, has been less urgent in recent years as historians have emphasised relationships between town and country and even partnerships between urban and rural rebels.[36] Cohn's survey of mostly narrative sources produced a surprisingly meagre harvest of rural revolts, putting paid to Marc Bloch's famous claim that 'peasant revolts were as natural to traditional Europe as strikes are today'.[37] It seems possible that there were more rural revolts of varying size and importance than we know about, particularly given that they are more likely to be found in under-exploited archival sources than in the chronicles upon which Cohn's survey depended.[38] The countryside had a rich social and political landscape of communities and institutions, and it is certain that peasants and rural artisans had knowledge and opinions about politics.[39] Rural people may have been hit hardest by the economic and demographic pressures of the period, especially in the decades following the Black Death (from 1347), though there is far from a consensus on this point, let alone on how such factors might have affected revolt.[40] (Contrast, for example, Cohn's argument, that the Black Death's effects galvanised a spirit of liberty leading to revolt, with that of Mollat and Wolff, for whom the post-plague revolts were those of desperation.) But if country dwellers had socio-political infrastructure and ideologies to draw upon in pursuit of their grievances, they had fewer of these tools – not to mention relative wealth and population density – than were available to their urban counterparts.

The fact that social position conditioned how one might engage in revolt is nowhere clearer than with regard to gender. Yet, with the exception of a classic article on the English Rising, work on the intersection of gender and social structure in medieval Europe has little discussed women's involvement in popular politics or protest.[41] This may well be because medieval revolt was a particularly masculine undertaking. One of Cohn's remarkable findings in *Lust for Liberty* was that, contrary to received wisdom and historiographic tradition, women did not dominate late medieval popular movements. Indeed, they were almost entirely absent from them. In this volume, Cohn reprises that research but contrasts it with the situation in the early modern centuries, when women seem to have been more active. This may be one of the areas in which England differed from the continent.[42] But even regarding continental rebellions, not all observers agree with the negative assessment; it may be necessary to look more closely, again especially at archival sources.[43]

Women do make cameo appearances in some of the chapters here besides Cohn's. Raccagni notes a few instances of women acting in support of their cities against the emperor, and Prescott, Titone, and Oliva Herrer also mention participation by the occasional woman in episodes from their uprisings. Gender, though less so the experiences of actual women (or so we think), is addressed in my own piece and that of Vincent Challet. As we both argue, the sources' charges of rebel violence against women may have had more to do with their literary efforts to portray rebels as aliens to normal social practice than with the realities of revolt. It is clear that women were on the whole less prominent as public agents of insurgency in medieval revolts than were men. Whether women might have had a greater role to play in private and how those 'private' roles related to 'public' action are questions that probably require much more research into workers' and peasants' households and family lives than has currently been done, as well as a more thorough reconceptualisation of the intersections between the 'public', the 'private', and the 'personal' in the lives of medieval common people.[44]

Communicative strategies

A final area of emphasis in this collection, arising out of a shared concern for rigorous source criticism, is that of language and communication. Advances in manuscript studies and philology were central to the nineteenth-century historical professionalisation and archival training programmes that enabled early revolt historians like Luce and Réville to discover and exploit the historical records that had lain forgotten for centuries. Technical mastery and empirical discovery remain fundamental to the research presented here, much of which is based on unpublished sources. We are also greatly indebted to new ways of reading sources and new areas of investigation brought to prominence by the linguistic and cultural turns of the 1980s and 1990s.[45] Insights from literary theory, from sociology, and from anthropology have transformed how we analyse rebels' reported speech, their banners, badges, and rituals, and the variety of responses with which they were met.[46] The resultant focus on how language, signs, and acts constructed meaning – and therefore power – both during the revolts themselves and in the sources that report them has led to some of the most interesting efforts to recover how and why medieval people rebelled.

As Jan Dumolyn and Jelle Haemers assert in this volume, 'The history of medieval contentious politics cannot be reduced to political quarrels or armed confrontations; it is also a history of discursive conflicts.' The names and works by which rebellions were recorded were important sites of this struggle. As Vincent Challet has shown elsewhere, the names given to rebels or to their movements were often employed to deprive them of legitimacy, a strategy that Prescott also describes in his essay on the English Rising in this volume.[47] Revolts in German-speaking imperial lands also went by a variety of names that frequently conveyed fear, derision, or suspicion, as Naegle's chapter shows. But as Dumolyn and Haemers demonstrate here as elsewhere, folk naming and official labelling could be interwoven.[48] My own chapter suggests that rebels themselves might have contested the derogatory implications of such names and re-appropriated them as positive markers.

The naming of a revolt was part of the larger process of shaping its memory and meaning, a process that we can partially access through the creation and transmission of historical records. These records are fraught with interpretive difficulties: they followed generic conventions with implications for interpretation, and they were also instruments through which their creators consciously sought to control an uprising's reception and posterity. Chronicles – stylised stories written almost exclusively by and for social elites – and judicial documents – stereotyped accounts representing victorious authority – used revolts to draw moral or historical lessons, when they did not try to suppress their memory altogether.[49] Such programmes might be entirely successful at obscuring rebel voices and perspectives, as Lavan fears for the Roman imperial case. Those who work on later periods must carefully consider the insights he has gleaned from work on discourses of modern counter-insurgency, and Freedman's essay goes a long way towards this. But in contrast to imperial Roman sources, those of the late Middle Ages are more numerous and more varied in type and in terms of the discourses of power in which they participated. They sometimes betray evidence of confusion, contradiction, or even open ideological contestation.[50] Here, we try to exploit these cracks, not necessarily in the hope of finding out 'what really happened' – for our view will always be partial in both senses of that term – but rather to access other ways that these events might have been imagined and understood.

Far preferable to looking at what was said about rebels after the fact, of course, is to focus on what they themselves said at the time. Whether rebels (reportedly) cried, 'Long live the king!', 'For our common good and profit!', or 'Death to the treacherous governor!' when they stormed a palace or a grain silo gives us insights into their specific grievances and their wider socio-political culture. Our evidence here, of course, is obviously mediated by the same sources and consequently subject to the same interpretative problems as that of the memorialisation of revolt. As Christian Liddy's chapter discusses, the surveillance and suppression of rebellious discourse was a major preoccupation of English authorities, but their efforts were often unsuccessful. We know that bill-casting, pamphleteering, and the distribution of circular letters took place, as well as the composition of sermons, songs, and even visual art.[51] Gisela Naegle is able to trace some networks of communication in the medieval Empire, while Philip Haberkern's evidence allows him to examine how the leaders of early modern religious rebellions manipulated a variety of media, including print, before and during uprisings. For earlier rebellions, we sometimes have the petitions or complaints submitted by rebels, but the literary production of most revolts was either immediately destroyed or has proved too ephemeral for the centuries. The sources as we have them sometimes present the rebels as almost speechless (though they frequently also consider them noisy), but in many cases, especially urban ones, they give us a surprising amount of evidence about what the rebels supposedly said.

Recent analyses of these utterances have argued that rebels' words were based upon an established and deeply meaningful linguistic repertoire.[52] Here and there, we may catch glimpses of the 'hidden transcripts' of workers' and peasants' resistance to the hegemonic ideologies of exploitative regimes that the anthropologist James Scott has taught us to look for.[53] But, even allowing for the sources' normalising agendas, much rebellious speech was not drawn from now obscure idioms of non-elite culture. Rather, their language usually reflected a discourse of values commonly held: peace, justice, profit, liberty, and, as discussed above, the common good. Christian humility, spiritual equality, and holy poverty were also normative values that shaped the rebels' language and social imagination, much as they did those of their enemies.[54]

Shared discourses, however, did not necessarily mean that popular political visions were conservative or anodyne. As Titone's essay on 'disciplined dissent' in Sicily shows, rebels might strategically adopt the language of obedience to princely authority in order to advance programmes whose socio-political implications were actually rather radical. In England and Flanders, the valorisation of the 'commonwealth', combined with the inclusion of the 'commons' in politics, meant that political discourse was not always hegemonic or resistance hidden. Rather, dissent was integral to civic political life, as Watts, Lantschner, and Haemers and Liddy have emphasised elsewhere, and as Hartrich expands upon in this book.[55]

In addition to the written and spoken word, rebellion and its repression were also articulated and pursued through signs, including clothing, banners, flags, and badges, as well as rituals of many types. The passions that flag-burning or Nazi salutes provoke in our own times perhaps give us some insight into the potentially powerful effects that signs might produce, a power that must have been much greater in the mostly non-literate (or para-literate) societies of the Middle Ages. Research into the semiotic life of medieval societies, often inspired by anthropological work, has shown the rich language of signs and rituals that groups employed to express and to effect their objectives, including those of rebellion.[56] Flags and banners were used to rally followers, as has been particularly well documented in Italy.[57] Bells sounded throughout cities and countryside alike to call inhabitants to rebellion.[58] In Flanders, guildsmen gathered under their banners and in arms in the market squares, a practice evocatively called the *waepening*, to signal their revolt.[59] In the neighbouring Northern French cities, it has been argued, street theatre and revolt might blend seamlessly into one another.[60]

Rituals are one place we might look for the 'non-rational' features of revolts, especially in terms of carnivalesque or 'popular religious' elements and their emotional impact. The folkloric or ludic aspects of rebellion are central to some classic works of medieval and early modern historiography on revolt,[61] but these topics are mostly absent here. As Dumolyn and Haemers note, some of the names given to Flemish revolts may have associations with liturgical feasts or popular celebrations. There are also some reports of apparently festive behaviour in the English Rising, and the names given to it such as 'the rifling time' emphasised this characteristic, but Prescott observes that we must consider whether and how the sources' authors used this aspect to discredit the Rising.[62] This point is all the more salient given the interplay discussed in Freedman's chapter between the reports of gruesome and ritualistic violence in rebellions and that of their suppression and punishment by the authorities. Festive behaviour may be less central to medieval revolts than was once thought – indeed I know of only two possible examples in the Jacquerie[63] – but its appearances in the sources require the most sensitive of readings.

Apocalypticism, prophecy, spiritual experience, and even religious language are also sparsely in evidence in this volume, again despite seminal work in the field.[64] When such subjects do appear, they are in contexts different from those examined in most other chapters. Lantschner shows that Islam, as a legal framework as well as a religious one, was central to revolt in Damascus to a much greater extent than Christianity was in Bolognese revolts, while prophecy and preaching were major media of rebellion in the fifteenth- and sixteenth-century landscapes explored by Philip Haberkern.[65] But as Oliva Herrer notes in his chapter, the millenarianism once ascribed to rural rebels during the War of the Communities of Castile has, at best, a doubtful evidentiary basis. It is true that if we had been able to include essays on heresy and popular crusade, these kinds of topics would have been more in evidence.[66] (It is particularly regrettable that John Arnold was unable to include his conference contribution on remembering heresy and rebellion in Southern France in the volume.) Still, that these topics are not a major theme of discussion reflects the fact that the types of conflict that we have concentrated on simply did not evince major elements of religious structures or spiritual experiences.

The emphases in this volume may thus suggest an inattention to their affective implications for rebels and their targets. Our relative reserve on this topic partly reflects an unwillingness to copy the sources' ascription of irrational and/or excessively emotional motives to medieval insurgents, particularly as the sources seem very selective about what they do tell us of rebels' affective experience. While *hilaria* (joy or fun) is mentioned at least once in the Flemish sources discussed by Dumolyn and Haemers, our sources are generally much more expansive about the rebels' anger – perhaps because *ira* was a mortal sin – and their targets' fear. Moreover, as Freedman's chapter stresses, we cannot know what medieval audiences found 'fun' or 'funny'. It is difficult enough to access such responses in the sources produced by elites for themselves,[67] and their description of rebels' feelings is at best second-hand, when not fantastical and/or programmatically biased. The growing body of scholarship on the historicity of emotions will no doubt expand our understanding of the role that affective experience and emotive language played in revolts and their records,[68] but many of the essays here do note such affective expressions, at least in passing. My own chapter makes clear that terror was essential not only to many contemporaries' experience of the Jacquerie – including those who were allegedly forced to participate in it – but also to efforts to shape its memory afterwards.

Fear's centrality to the mechanisms of revolt and its reception is also implicit in the attention that we pay to violence, a theme that runs throughout this collection. As discussed above, new insights into the multi-polar nature of political authority in the late Middle Ages have taken place in step with a more positive re-evaluation of the role of violence in medieval society. Here, we understand violence and the threat thereof as a strategic tool for the accomplishment of rebellion and its suppression – that is, as physical force causing destruction, pain, and terror – but we also consider it as a form of communication. In the absence of recorded speech, which the sources often ignored or suppressed and which they always mediate with some effect, such violence may be our only entrée to rebels' mental architecture.[69] For historians of medieval violence more generally, anthropology has been fundamental to understanding violence as a complex phenomenon whose form, use, and meaning are highly dependent upon socio-political and cultural context.[70] For the study of revolt in particular, this approach has meant a re-evaluation of what medieval chroniclers often represented as the savagery of rebellions. Drawing also upon sociological research, historians of revolt increasingly think about violent acts as part of a 'repertoire' of actions with established meanings and social functions that rebels consciously employed in significant ways.[71]

The essays in this book show that what violence meant was entirely context specific and subject to change. Challet speaks in terms of a 'grammar of violence' whose vocabulary was nonetheless geographically (and presumably, chronologically) specific. Violence was often carefully targeted and limited, as Titone shows in Sicily, and indeed could backfire if it exceeded limits, as Challet argues. It could serve not only materially strategic ends, such as the destruction of opponents' fortresses, jails, or archives, but also a means of communicating specific grievances or even as social commentary. As Paul Freedman demonstrates, the brutal repression of revolt might draw upon long-established tropes and stereotypes, but audiences' interpretation of those acts could vary tremendously, sometimes in ways alien to our own seemingly intuitive (but actually culturally conditioned) reactions. What was most 'violent' in medieval eyes might not be a murder or a housebreaking but rather a lawsuit, as Hartrich argues, or even, as Challet suggests, a handshake.

Historians have only recently begun to appreciate fully just how much the revolts of the later Middle Ages can tell us about the people, practices, and ideas that constituted historical society. How we understand the relationship between legal authority, violence, and politics has undergone a transformation in recent years. Building on those insights and attentive to the critical role of language and performance in shaping revolts and their sources, we hope to have provided a more complex but also more satisfying reading of a variety of revolts in a range of geographic and chronological contexts. None of us would claim to have definitive answers to the questions we have asked, or even to have asked all the questions we ought to have done. The full potential of the study of medieval revolts for medieval historiography is long from being realised. What we aim to have done in this volume is to have moved the conversation forward. If the evidence we have found and the arguments in which we employ it start more debates than they settle, we will have accomplished our most important objective.

Notes

1 Collections include M. T. Fögen (ed.), *Ordnung und Aufruhr im Mittelalter. Historische und juristische Studien zur Rebellion*, Frankfurt am Main: Klostermann, 1995; M. Bourin, G. Cherubini, and G. Pinto (eds), *Rivolte urbane e rivolte contadine nell'Europa del Trecento: Un conforto*, Florence: Firenze University Press, 2008; G. Brunel and S. Brunet (eds), *'Haro sur le seigneur!': Les luttes anti-seigneuriales dans l'Europe médiévale et moderne*, Toulouse: Presses Universitaires du Mirail, 2009; H. R. Oliva Herrer, V. Challet, J. Dumolyn, and M. A. Carmona Ruiz (eds), *La comunidad medieval como esfera pública*, Seville: Universidad de Sevilla, 2014; J. Dumolyn, J. Haemers, H. R. Oliva Herrer, and V. Challet (eds), *The Voices of the People in Late Medieval Europe: Communication and Popular Politics*, Turnhout: Brepols, 2014; J. A. Solórzano Telechea, B. Arízaga Bolumburu, and J. Haemers (eds), *Los grupos populares en la ciudad medieval europea*, Logroño: Instituto de Estudios Riojanos, 2014.
2 S. K. Cohn, Jr., *Lust for Liberty: The Politics of Social Revolt in Medieval Europe, 1200–1450: Italy, France, and Flanders*, Cambridge, MA: Harvard University Press, 2006. Cohn also published a source reader for teaching: *Popular Protest in Late Medieval Europe: Italy, France, and Flanders*, Manchester: Manchester University Press, 2004, and a comparative study on England: *Popular Protest in Late Medieval English Towns*, Cambridge: Cambridge University Press, 2013.
3 All authors carefully consider the problems of historical identification and sources' languages but spend little time making distinctions between modern categories like 'revolt', 'rebellion', 'uprising', etc., which do not seem useful given the sources' own semantic variability (discussed below and at length throughout the volume). Cf. Dumolyn and Haemers's essay, who prefer the sociologist Charles Tilly's term 'contentious politics'.
4 For example, D. L. Horowitz, *The Deadly Ethnic Riot*, Berkeley: California University Press, 2001; C. Tilly and S. Tarrow, *Contentious Politics*, Boulder, CO: Paradigm, 2007; D. Frost and R. Phillips (eds), *Liverpool '81 Remembering the Riots*, Liverpool: Liverpool University Press, 2011; and see n. 11, below.
5 Quote from M. Mollat and P. Wolff, *The Popular Revolutions of the Late Middle Ages*, trans. A. L. Lytton-Sells, London: George Allen & Unwin Ltd, 1973, p. 11.
6 On the Ciompi, see P. Lantschner, 'The "Ciompi Revolution" constructed: modern historians and the nineteenth-century paradigm of revolution', *Annali di Storia di Firenze*, 4, 2009, pp. 277–97. Spanish *comunero* historiography has some similarities, discussed in H. R. Oliva Herrer's essay in this volume.
7 S. Luce, *Histoire de la Jacquerie d'après des documents inédits*, 1st edn, Paris: A. Durand, 1859, pp. 147–8; new edn, Paris: Honoré Champion, 1894, pp. 127–8.
8 J. C. L. S. de Sismondi, *Histoire des républiques italiennes du Moyen Âge*, new edn, 10 vols, Paris: Furne et ce., 1840 [1809–18], 4: 455.
9 R. B. Dobson, *The Peasants' Revolt of 1381*, 2nd edn, London: Macmillan, 1983, pp. xliii–xliv. Similarly, see A. Wood, *The 1549 Rebellions and the Making of Early Modern England*, Cambridge: Cambridge University Press, 2007, pp. 257–64. A. Réville, *Le soulèvement des travailleurs d'Angleterre en 1381*, Paris: A. Picard et fils, 1898.
10 M. Mollat and P. Wolff, *Ongles bleus, Jacques et Ciompi: Les révolutions populaires en Europe aux XIVe et XVe siècles*, Paris: Calman-Lévy, 1970, trans. as Mollat and Wolff, *Popular Revolutions*; G. Fourquin, *Les soulèvements populaires au Moyen Âge*, Paris: Presses universitaires de France, 1972, trans. A. Chesters as *The Anatomy of Popular Rebellion in the Middle Ages*, Oxford: North-Holland, 1978; R. H. Hilton, *Bond Men Made Free: Medieval Peasant Movements and the English Rising of 1381*, New York, Viking Press, 1973. See also P. Blickle (ed.), *Revolte und Revolution in Europa*, Munich: Oldenbourg, 1975; P. Blickle and C. Catt, 'Peasant revolts in the German empire in the late Middle Ages', *Social History*, 4, 1979, pp. 223–39.
11 For the way that the concept of 'revolution' has run into difficulties in recent history, see J. Foran, D. Lane, and A. Zivkovic (eds), *Revolution in the Making of the Modern World: Social Identities, Globalization, and Modernity*, Abingdon and New York: Routledge, 2008, pt 4.

12 For the influence of recent events on studies of medieval revolt, see J. Haemers, 'A victorious state and defeated rebels? Historians' views of violence and urban revolts in medieval Flanders', in D. Nicholas, B. S. Bachrach, and J. M. Murray (eds), *Comparative Perspectives on History and Historians: Essays in Memory of Bryce Lyon (1920–2007)*, Kalamazoo: Medieval Institute Publications, 2012, pp. 112–13 and the conclusion to A. Prescott, '"Great and horrible rumour": shaping the English Revolt of 1381', in this volume. I also wish to thank my student S. Monaghan for her thoughtful essay 'Making sense of madness: writing about rebels and rioters in 1381 and 2011' written for ME3425 'The Age of Revolt', University of St Andrews, 2014.

13 Mollat and Wolff, *Popular Revolutions*, p. 283.

14 Cohn, *Lust for Liberty*, ch. 10.

15 For example, G. Harriss, *Shaping the Nation: England, 1360–1461*, Oxford: Oxford University Press, 2005; D. L. Smail, *The Consumption of Justice: Emotions, Publicity, and Legal Culture in Marseille, 1264–1423*, Ithaca, NY: Cornell University Press, 2003; J. Watts, *The Making of Polities: Europe, 1300–1500*, Cambridge: Cambridge University Press, 2009; J. Firnhaber-Baker, *Violence and the State in Languedoc, 1250–1400*, Cambridge: Cambridge University Press, 2014; P. Lantschner, *The Logic of Political Conflict in Late Medieval Cities: Italy and the Southern Low Countries, 1370–1440*, Oxford: Oxford University Press, 2015.

16 Watts, *The Making of Polities*, p. 273.

17 E. Lecuppre-Desjardin and A.-L. van Bruaene (eds), *De Bono Communi: The Discourse and Practice of the Common Good in the European City (13th–16th C.)*, Turnhout: Brepols, 2010. See also (among many others) P. Blickle, 'Der Gemeine Nutzen. Ein kommunaler Wert und seine politische Karriere', in H. Münkler and H. Bluhm (eds), *Gemeinwohl und Gemeinsinn. Historische Semantiken politischer Leitbegriffe*, Berlin: Akademie Verlag, 2001, pp. 85–107; V. Challet, 'Political *topos* or community principle? *Res publica* as a source of legitimacy in the French peasants' revolts of the late Middle Ages', in W. Blockmans, A. Holenstein, J. Mathieu, and D. Schläppi (eds), *Empowering Interactions: Political Cultures and the Emergence of the State in Europe 1300–1900*, Farnham and Burlington, VT: Ashgate, 2009, pp. 205–18; J. Dumolyn, '"Our land is only founded on trade and industry": economic discourses in fifteenth-century Bruges', *JMH*, 36, 2010, 374–89; and essays by C. Fletcher, 'What makes a political language? Key terms, profit and damage in the Common Petition of the English Parliament, 1343–1422', J. Watts, 'Popular voices in England's War of the Roses, *c*.1445–*c*.1485', and A. Stella, '"Racconciare la terra": à l'écoute des voix des "Ciompi" de Florence en 1378', in Dumolyn *et al.* (eds), *Voices of the People*, pp. 91–106, 107–22, and 139–47, and by M. Asenjo González, 'Ambición política y discurso: el "común" en Segovia y Valladolid (1480–1520)', J. Haemers, 'Governing and gathering about the common welfare of the town: the petitions of the craft guilds of Leuven, 1378', H. R. Oliva Herrer, '¡Viva el rey y la comunidad! Arqueología del discurso político de la Comunidades', and J. Firnhaber-Baker, '*À son de cloche*: the interpretation of public order and legitimate authority in Northern France 1355–1358' in Oliva Herrer *et al.* (eds), *La comunidad*, pp. 73–105, 153–69, 315–55, 357–76.

18 J. Watts, 'Popular voices in England's War of the Roses, *c*.1445–*c*.1485', in Dumolyn *et al.* (eds), *Voices of the People*, 107–22.

19 Watts, *The Making of Polities*, p. 275.

20 On the relative frequency of urban to rural revolts see Cohn, *Lust for Liberty*, ch. 2 and contributions by Prescott, Firnhaber-Baker, Wickham, and Oliva Herrer in this volume, as well as further discussion below. The English case may have differed from that of continental societies: S. K. Cohn, Jr., 'Revolts of the late Middle Ages and the peculiarities of the English', in R. Goddard, J. Langdon, and M. Müller (eds), *Survival and Discord in Medieval Society: Essays in Honour of Christopher Dyer*, Turnhout: Brepols, 2010, pp. 269–85.

21 J. Haemers and C. Liddy, 'Popular politics in the late medieval city: York and Bruges', *EHR*, 128, 2013, pp. 771–805; and see J. Haemers, 'Governing and gathering about the common welfare of the town: the petitions of the craft guilds of Leuven, 1378', in Oliva Herrer *et al.* (eds), *La comunidad*, pp. 153–69.

22 P. Lantschner, 'Revolts and the political order of cities in the late Middle Ages', *P&P*, 225, 2014, pp. 5–11; Lantschner, *The Logic of Political Conflict*.

23 Lantschner, 'Revolts and the political order', p. 4.

24 M. Weber, *The Theory of Social and Economic Organization*, ed. and trans. A. M. Henderson and T. Parsons, New York: Oxford University Press, 1947, p. 154.

25 This revision has taken place in dialogue with developments in the scholarship on 'feud': e.g. P. C. Maddern, *Violence and Social Order: East Anglia, 1422–1442*, Oxford: Clarendon Press, 1992; H. Zmora, *State and Nobility in Early Modern Germany: The Knightly Feud in Franconia, 1440–1567*, Cambridge: Cambridge

University Press, 1997; H. Kaminsky, 'The noble feud in the later Middle Ages', *P&P*, 177, 2002, pp. 55–83; A. Zorzi, '*Fracta est civitas magna in tres* partes: conflitto e costitutizione nell'Italia communale', *Scienza e politica*, 39, 2008, pp. 61–87; works by Harriss and Firnhaber-Baker cited in n. 15, above; and seminally, if problematically, O. Brunner, *Land und Herrschaft. Grundfragen der territorialen Verfassungsgeschichte Südostdeutschlands im Mittelalter*, 1st edn, Baden bei Wien: Rohrer, 1939, trans. (of the 4th edn) H. Kaminsky and J. Van Horn Melton as *Land and Lordship: Structures of Governance in Medieval Austria*, Philadelphia: University of Pennsylvania Press, 1992.

26 As Haemers and Liddy put it, 'What separated revolt and rebellion from other kinds of collective action was the threat (not necessarily the reality) of physical force and the refusal to submit to the wishes of the authorities' ('Popular politics', p. 785). Cf. Liddy in this volume and Cohn, *Lust for Liberty*, p. 4.

27 Lantschner, 'Revolts and the political order', pp. 37–44.

28 See also A. Wood, 'Collective violence, social drama and rituals of rebellion in late medieval and early modern England', in S. Carroll (ed.), *Cultures of Violence: Interpersonal Violence in Historical Perspective*, Basingstoke: Palgrave Macmillan, 2007, pp. 101–4; Haemers and Liddy, 'Popular politics', esp. p. 800.

29 A. Thierry, *Lettres sur l'histoire de France, pour servir d'introduction à l'étude de cette histoire*, Paris: Sautelet, 1827, pp. 270–312.

30 Thierry, *Lettres sur l'histoire de France*, p. 4, quoted in P. den Boer, 'Historical writing in France, 1800–1914', in S. Macintyre, J. Maiguaschca, and A. Pók (eds), *The Oxford History of Historical Writing*, vol. 4: *1800–1945*, Oxford: Oxford University Press, 2011, pp. 187–8. 'Condescension': E. P. Thompson, *The Making of the English Working Class*, London: V. Gollancz, 1963, p. 12.

31 On history from below, see E. P. Thompson, 'History from below', *Times Literary Supplement*, 7 April 1966, pp. 279–80; J. Sharpe, 'History from below', in P. Burke (ed.), *New Perspectives on Historical Writing*, 2nd edn, Cambridge: Polity Press, 2001, ch. 2. On the implications of social changes in the Anglo-American academy, see G. M. Spiegel, *The Past as Text: The Theory and Practice of Medieval Historiography*, Baltimore, MD: Johns Hopkins University Press, 1997, pp. 71, 78–9 and E. R. Leach, 'Glimpses of the unmentionable in the history of British social anthropology', *Annual Review of Anthropology*, 13, 1984, pp. 1–23.

32 For example, works cited in n. 39, below; P. Freedman, *Images of the Medieval Peasant*, Stanford, CA: Stanford University Press, 1999; P. Freedman and M. Bourin (eds), *Forms of Servitude in Northern and Central Europe: Decline, Resistance, and Expansion*, Turnhout: Brepols, 2005; P. Boglioni, R. Delort, and C. Gauvard (eds), *Le petit peuple dans l'Occident medieval: Terminologies, perceptions, réalitiés*, Paris: Publications de la Sorbonne, 2002; for the early Middle Ages, C. Wickham, *Framing the Middle Ages: Europe and the Mediterranean, 400–800*, Oxford: Oxford University Press, 2005, pt 3. Work on English rural commoners remained robust through the end of the millennium. Important books since 2000 include P. R. Schofield, *Peasant and Community in Medieval England, 1200–1500*, Basingstoke: Palgrave Macmillan, 2003; C. Briggs, *Credit and Village Society in Fourteenth-Century England*, Oxford: Oxford University Press, 2009; Goddard *et al.* (eds), *Survival and Discord*.

33 See also S. Greenblatt, 'Murdering peasants: status, genre, and the representation of rebellion', *Representations*, 1, 1983, pp. 1–29 and P. Strohm, '"A revelle!": chronicle evidence and the rebel voice', in *Hochon's Arrow: The Social Imagination of Fourteenth-Century Texts*, Princeton, NJ: Princeton University Press, 1992, ch. 2.

34 V. Challet and I. Forrest, 'The masses', in C. Fletcher, J.-P. Genet, and J. Watts (eds), *Government and Political Life in England and France, c.1300–c.1500*, Cambridge: Cambridge University Press, 2015, pp. 279–316; J. Watts, 'Public or plebs: the changing meaning of "the commons", 1381–1549', in H. Pryce and J. Watts (eds), *Power and Identity in the Middle Ages: Essays in Memory of Rees Davies*, Oxford: Oxford University Press, 2007, pp. 242–60.

35 Lantschner, 'Revolts and the political order', pp. 5, 33–4.

36 W. H. TeBrake, *A Plague of Insurrection: Popular Politics and Peasant Revolt in Flanders, 1323–1328*, Philadelphia University of Pennsylvania Press, 1993; V. Challet, 'La révolte des Tuchins: banditisme social ou sociabilité villageoise?', *Médiévales*, 17, 1998, pp. 101–12; S. K. Cohn, Jr., *Creating the Florentine State: Peasants and Rebellion, 1348–1434*, Cambridge: Cambridge University Press, 1999; and see essays by Prescott, Oliva Herrer, and Firnhaber-Baker in this volume. For older views, see R. H. Hilton, 'Révoltes rurales et révoltes urbaines au Moyen Âge', in F. Gambrelle and M. Trebitsch (eds), *Révolte et société, Actes du IVe colloque d'histoire au présent*, 2 vols, Paris: Publications de la Sorbonne, 1989, 2, pp. 25–33.

37 M. Bloch, *French Rural History: An Essay on its Basic Characteristics*, trans. J. Sondheimer, London: Routledge & Kegan Paul, 1966 [French edn, 1931], p. 170. (1931 was a 'today' of more, and much more radical, labour strikes than we are accustomed to in our own 'today'.)

38 V. Challet, 'Un village sans histoire? La communauté de Villeveyrac en Languedoc', in Dumolyn *et al.* (eds), *Voices of the People*, pp. 123–38.
39 R. Faith, 'The "Great Rumour" of 1377 and peasant ideology', in R. H. Hilton and T. H. Aston (eds), *The English Rising of 1381*, Cambridge: Cambridge University Press, 1984, pp. 43–73; D. A. Carpenter, 'English peasants in politics, 1258–1267', *P&P*, 136, 1992, pp. 3–42; C. Gauvard, 'Rumeur et stéréotypes à la fin du Moyen Âge', in *La circulation des nouvelles au Moyen Âge*, Rome: École française de Rome, 1994, pp. 157–77; J. Watts, 'The pressure of the public on later medieval politics', in C. Carpenter and L. Clark (eds), *The Fifteenth Century IV: Political Culture in Late Medieval Britain*, Woodbridge: Boydell, 2004, pp. 159–80; J. Dumolyn, 'The vengeance of the commune: sign systems of popular politics in medieval Bruges', in Oliva Herrer *et al.* (eds), *La comunidad*, pp. 259, 268–9.
40 T. H. Aston and C. H. E. Philpin (eds), *The Brenner Debate: Agrarian Class Structure and Economic Development in Pre-industrial Europe*, Cambridge: Cambridge University Press, 1985; B. M. S. Campbell (ed.), *Before the Black Death: Studies in the 'Crisis' of the Early Fourteenth Century*, Manchester: Manchester University Press, 1991; C. Dyer, *Making a Living in the Middle Ages: The People of Britain, 850–1520*, New Haven, CT, and London: Yale University Press, 2002, pp. 228–97.
41 S. Federico, 'The imaginary society: women in 1381', *Journal of British Studies*, 40, 2001, pp. 159–83. On gender in depictions of 1381 see W. M. Ormrod, 'In bed with Joan of Kent: the king's mother and the Peasants' Revolt', in J. Wogan-Browne (ed.), *Medieval Women: Texts and Contexts in Late Medieval Britain: Essays for Felicity Riddy*, Turnhout: Brepols, 2000, pp. 277–92. Regarding the failure of gender historians and social historians of early modern England to engage intensively with one another's work, see A. Wood, 'History from below and early modern social history', https://manyheadedmonster.wordpress.com/2013/08/21/andy-wood-history-from-below-and-early-modern-social-history/.
42 Cohn, *Popular Protest . . . English Towns*, p. 7.
43 Challet, 'Un village sans histoire?', p. 133.
44 Federico, 'The imaginary society', pp. 182–3. Useful starting points include M. C. Howell, *Women, Production, and Patriarchy in Late Medieval Cities* Chicago, IL: University of Chicago Press, 1986; P. J. P. Goldberg, 'The public and the private: women in the pre-plague economy', in P. R. Coss and S. D. Lloyd (eds), *Thirteenth Century England* III, Woodbridge: Boydell, 1991, pp. 75–89; Freedman, *Images of the Medieval Peasant*, ch. 7; S. A. Farmer, *Surviving Poverty in Medieval Paris: Gender, Ideology, and the Daily Lives of the Poor*, Ithaca, NY: Cornell University Press, 2002. For masculinity of king and commoners in English politics, see the work of C. Fletcher, particularly 'Manhood, kingship, and the public in late medieval England', *Edad media, revista de historia*, 13, 2012, pp. 123–42.
45 Justice, *Writing and Rebellion*, pp. 5–8; Dumolyn, 'The vengeance of the commune', pp. 252–6.
46 For example, the influence of Clifford Geertz on P. J. Arnade, *Realms of Ritual: Burgundian Ceremony and Civic Life in Late Medieval Ghent*, Ithaca, NY: Cornell University Press, 1996; of James C. Scott on C. Wickham, 'Gossip and resistance among the medieval peasantry', *P&P*, 160, 1998, pp. 3–24 and Justice, *Writing and Rebellion*; of Victor Turner on Wood, 'Collective violence'; and of sociologists and linguists on Dumolyn and Haemers.
47 V. Challet, 'L'exclusion par le nom: réflexions sur la dénomination des révoltés à la fin du Moyen-Âge', in N. Gonthier (ed.), *L'exclusion au Moyen Âge*, Lyon: Centre d'histoire médiévale, Université Jean Moulin Lyon 3, 2007, pp. 373–88; A. Stella, '"Ciompi . . . gens de la plus basse condition . . . crasseux et dépenaillés": désigner, inférioriser, exclure', in Boglioni *et al.* (eds), *Le petit peuple*, pp. 145–52.
48 J. Dumolyn and J. Haemers, '"A bad chicken was brooding": subversive speech in late medieval Flanders', *P&P*, 214, 2012, pp. 45–86.
49 V. Challet, 'Peasants' revolts memories: *damnatio memoriae* or hidden memories', in L. Doležalová (ed.), *The Making of Memory in the Middle Ages*, Leiden: Brill, 2010, pp. 397–413.
50 See also, Strohm, '"A revelle!"' and A. Stella, '"Racconciare la terra": À l'écoute des voix des "Ciompi" de Florence en 1378', in Dumolyn *et al.* (eds), *Voices of the People*, pp. 139–47.
51 W. Scase, '"Strange and wonderful bills": bill-casting and political discourse in late medieval England', in R. Copeland, D. Lawton, and W. Scase (eds), *New Medieval Literatures* II, Oxford: Clarendon, 1998, pp. 225–47; E. Lecuppre-Desjardin, 'Des portes qui parlent: placards, feuilles volantes et communication politique dans les villes des Pays-Bas à la fin du Moyen Âge', *Bibliothèque de l'École des Chartes*, 168, 2010, pp. 151–72; M. K. Perett, 'Vernacular songs as "oral pamphlets": the Hussites and their propaganda campaign', *Viator*, 42, 2011, pp. 371–92; C. Liddy, 'Bill casting and political communication: a public sphere in late medieval English towns?', in J. A. Solórzano Telechea and B. Arizaga Bolúmburu (eds), *La gobernanza de la ciudad europea en la Edad Media*, Logroño: Instituto de Estudios Riojanos, 2011,

pp. 447–61; J. Dumolyn and J. Haemers, 'Political poems and subversive songs: the circulation of "public poetry" in the late medieval Low Countries', *Journal of Dutch Literature*, 5, 2014, pp. 1–22.
52 Dumolyn, '"Our land is only founded on trade and industry"'; A. Gamberini, J.-P. Genet, and A. Zorzi (eds), *The Languages of Political Society: Western Europe, 14th–17th Centuries*, Rome: Viella, 2011; and see blog contributions to the 2015 online symposium 'Voices of the people' focused on early modern and modern history, https://manyheadedmonster.wordpress.com/voices-of-the-people/.
53 J. C. Scott, *Weapons of the Weak: Everyday Forms of Peasant Resistance*, New Haven, CT: Yale University Press, 1985; J. C. Scott, *Domination and the Arts of Resistance: Hidden Transcripts*, New Haven, CT: Yale University Press, 1990.
54 Freedman, *Image of the Medieval Peasant*, ch. 11; J. H. Arnold, 'Religion and popular rebellion, from the Capuciati to Niklashausen', *Cultural and Social History*, 6, 2009, pp. 149–69.
55 Watts, 'Popular voices', pp. 114–16; Liddy and Haemers, 'Popular protest'.
56 C. de Merindol, 'Mouvements sociaux et troubles politiques à la fin du Moyen Âge: essai sur la symbolique des villes', in *Violence et contestation au Moyen Âge: Actes du 144e congrès des societies savantes (Paris, 1989), section d'histoire médiévale et de philologie*, Paris: C.T.H.S., 1990, pp. 267–302; Wood, 'Collective violence'; E. J. Hutchison, 'Partisan identity in the French civil war, 1405–1418: reconsidering the evidence on livery badges', *JMH*, 33, 2007, pp. 250–74.
57 Cohn, *Lust for Liberty*, ch. 8; R. C. Trexler, 'Follow the flag: the Ciompi Revolt seen from the streets', *Bibliothèque d'Humanisme et Renaissance*, 46, 1984, pp. 357–92. For flags in Northern European revolts, see Haemers and Dumolyn, Firnhaber-Baker, and Smithuis in this volume.
58 S. K. Cohn, 'Enigmas of communication: Jacques, Ciompi, and the English', in Oliva Herrer *et al.* (eds), *La comunidad*, pp. 227–47; Dumolyn, 'Vengeance of the commune'; Firnhaber-Baker, '*À son de cloche*'; J. H. Arnold and C. Goodson, 'Resounding community: the history and meaning of medieval church bells', *Viator*, 43, 2012, pp. 99–130.
59 J. Haemers, 'A moody community? Emotion and ritual in late medieval urban revolts', in E. Lecuppre-Desjardin and A.-L. Van Bruaene (eds), *Emotions in the Heart of the City (14th–16th century)*, Turnhout: Brepols, 2005, pp. 63–81.
60 H. Skoda, *Medieval Violence: Physical Brutality in Northern France, 1270–1330*, Oxford: Oxford University Press, 2013, pp. 164–9; and more generally on performance and the medieval public sphere, C. Symes, *A Common Stage: Theater and Public Life in Medieval Arras*, Ithaca, NY: Cornell University Press, 2007.
61 N. Z. Davis, 'The reasons of misrule', in *Society and Culture in Early Modern France: Eight Essays*, London: Duckworth, 1975, ch. 4; R. Darnton, 'Workers revolt: the great cat massacre of the rue Saint-Séverin', in *The Great Cat Massacre and Other Episodes in French Cultural History*, New York: Basic Books, 1984, ch. 2; Y.-M. Bercé, *Histoire des Croquants*, Paris: Seuil, 1986, trans. A. Whitmore as *History of Peasant Revolts: The Social Origins of Rebellion in Early Modern France*, Cambridge: Polity, 1990.
62 See also M. Aston, '*Corpus christi* and *corpus regni*: heresy and the Peasants' Revolt', *P&P*, 143, 1994, pp. 3–47.
63 That the Jacques dressed themselves and their wives up in the nobles' clothes (J. de Venette, *Chronique dite de Jean de Venette*, ed. C. Beaune, Paris: Le Livre de Poche, 2011, p. 176) and that an assembly featured music and dancing (AN JJ 86, no. 265, fol. 89r, ed. in Luce, *Histoire de la Jacquerie*, no. 34).
64 N. Cohn, *The Pursuit of the Millennium: Revolutionary Millenarians and Mystical Anarchists of the Middle Ages*, rev. edn, Oxford: Oxford University Press, 1970 [1957].
65 On prophecy as a medium for popular politics in medieval England and France, see Challet and Forrest, 'The masses', pp. 291–4.
66 For popular crusade, see D. Nirenberg, *Communities of Violence: Persecution of Minorities in the Middle Ages*, Princeton, NJ: Princeton University Press, 1996, ch. 2–4.
67 Greenblatt, 'Murdering peasants'.
68 For example, Haemers, 'A moody community?' and other essays in Lecuppre-Desjardin and Van Bruaene (eds), *Emotions in the Heart of the City*; Challet and Forrest, 'The masses', pp. 294–7.
69 Stella, '"Racconciare la terra"'; B. Bommersbach, 'Gewalt in der Jacquerie von 1358', in N. Bulst, I. Gilcher-Holtey, and H.-G. Haupt (eds), *Gewalt im politischen Raum. Fallanalysen vom Spätmittelalter bis ins 20. Jahrhundert*, Frankfurt: Campus Verlag, 2008, pp. 46–81.
70 For some guide to the vast scholarship, see the works cited in n. 25, above.
71 C. Tilly, 'Contentious repertoires in Great Britain, 1758–1834', *Social Science History*, 17, 1993, pp. 253–80; C. Tilly, *Contentious Performances*, Cambridge: Cambridge University Press, 2008.

PART I

Conceptualising revolt

Then and now

1

WRITING REVOLT IN THE EARLY ROMAN EMPIRE

Myles Lavan

If the later Middle Ages are emerging ever more clearly as an age of revolt, the Roman empire of the first and second centuries CE has long seemed an age of order.[1] There were a few large-scale provincial rebellions, but they were mostly limited to peripheral areas and to the immediate aftermath of conquest. The thousands of cities in the empire offer only scattered evidence for urban revolts; slave revolts appear few and minor; peasant revolt is virtually invisible. It has even been suggested that banditry all but disappeared for much of the period.[2] For many scholars, the remarkable thing about revolt in the early Roman empire is its rarity. On one reading, this picture is explained by the Roman state's success in securing the consent of the governed, its provision of mechanisms of dispute resolution that were relatively predictable, rational, and autonomous from local interests and thus worked to reduce the frequency with which aggrieved groups turned to violence, and perhaps also its ability to constrain predatory behaviour by local magnates through the ever present threat of Roman intervention in the case of unrest.[3] On a more cynical interpretation, the Roman empire appears peaceful not because rational Roman government worked to limit the causes of conflict, but because the threat of retaliation by Rome deterred the disadvantaged from attempting to use violence to address their grievances. Stability was a product of an unusually neat alignment of interests between the imperial state and local elites, with Roman power underwriting highly unequal distributions of wealth, privilege, and political power in the provinces.[4]

But the image of the Pax Romana has not gone unquestioned. One approach has been to assemble the scattered evidence for revolt into a coherent picture. Thomas Pekáry, for example, set out to critique the prevailing view that the Roman empire was highly successful at keeping the peace by cataloguing every instance of 'unrest and revolt' that he could find. Producing a list of more than 100 examples, he concluded that minor disturbances of the peace were a feature of life in the empire even during peaceful periods.[5] At the macro-level, it has become evident not just that large-scale revolts requiring a major military response were frequent during the first generations after incorporation into the empire, but also that there were regions where they continued sporadically through the second century – notably Britain and Mauretania, as well as the obvious case of Judea.[6] At the micro-level, banditry can now be seen more clearly as a ubiquitous structural consequence of the uneven penetration of the Roman state.[7]

Equally important work has highlighted the unreliability of the literature produced by the Roman elite and civic epigraphy – our two most important sources – as evidence for revolt.[8]

There are several revealing examples of major episodes that we know of from some texts that are ignored or suppressed by other texts. A famous speech by the emperor Claudius delivered in the senate in 48 CE praised the 'unswerving faith and obedience' of the Gauls during the hundred years since their conquest by Julius Caesar, wilfully ignoring a major revolt as recently as 21 CE.[9] Talmudic sources reveal endemic banditry in Judea that is largely invisible in Latin and Greek sources.[10] Archaeology is also revealing evidence of military installations in some supposedly peaceful areas.[11] It thus seems likely that our sources significantly under-report both the incidence and scale of disturbance. Their myopia may be partly strategic, aiming to limit the circulation of knowledge about instability, but it is probably predominantly ideological. The Roman elite were so deeply invested in convincing their subjects and themselves of their success in creating peace that they were likely to ignore or trivialise discordant events.[12] The Roman world was surely less peaceful than it appears. But that does not necessarily mean that it was not, in comparative perspective, an age of order. Sympathetic as I am to projects of compilation, it remains unclear how many instances we would need to find in order to conclude that revolt or was not relatively rare, given that the object of study is a vast and diverse imperial state encompassing tens of millions of inhabitants distributed across 2,000–3,000 largely autonomous local communities.

The considerable uncertainty about the frequency of revolt is compounded by the paucity of information about most of the events that we do know of. In many cases, the sum total of the evidence available to us is 10 to 20 words in one or two texts – often much less. In these circumstances, there is probably little that the study of the early Roman empire can contribute to the social history of revolt in other periods – though the exchange can be very profitable for Roman historians; indeed most of the best work has leant heavily on the comparative method.[13] But the Roman empire is a useful context in which to think through some of the methodological difficulties involved in moving from a textual record to a social history of revolt. Our ability to identify and understand past revolts is necessarily constrained by our sources' operations of classification (what they consider a revolt) and selection (their threshold for taking notice of relevant events) and the conceptual apparatus they deploy to explain and describe episodes of revolt, which may not be particularly accurate and is unlikely to be disinterested. These are problems that beset any history of revolt, but they appear in particularly sharp relief in the case of the early Roman empire. Hence I focus on the Roman discourse on revolt and the ways in which it continues to shape our understanding of the social processes it describes.[14]

The most obvious problem is our dependence on sources written by the literate, propertied classes – especially the administrative elite and their social circle. The best analysis of this predicament known to me is Ranajit Guha's study of peasant insurgency in colonial India, which ought to be the starting point for any history of revolt in an imperial context.[15] Guha foregrounds the problem of reliance on elitist evidence, which 'has a way of stamping the interests and outlook of the rebels' enemies on every account of our peasant rebellions'.[16] 'The historical phenomenon of insurgency', he writes, 'meets the eye for the first time as an image framed in the prose, hence the outlook, of counter-insurgency.'[17] The distortions of elitist discourse on peasant revolt – what Guha calls the 'prose of counter-insurgency' – include not just the obvious rhetorics of barbarism, criminality, and immorality, which deny legitimacy to the rebels, but also more subtle tropes, such as spontaneity or hysteria, which deny them agency and rationality. These distortions pervade not just the communications of colonial administrators but also the private writings of elites in the periphery and the metropole, even those writing at some emotional distance from events and with some sympathy for the rebels. They continue to shape modern historiography, however sympathetic it may be:

> It is still very common for many [historians] to let their source material, almost invariably of an administrative nature, command their view of peasant revolt both in fact and judgement. The reliance on official evidence cannot be helped in most cases because of the absence or inadequacy of information of any other kind. But for a modern scholar to vitiate his work with the subjectivity of the guardian of law and order is to renounce the advantage he has over any contemporary witness of an event.[18]

He is scathing in his dismissal of historians who have denied peasant rebels the possibility of agency and rationality merely because they are denied them by elitist sources. Guha insists that the historian must acknowledge the peasant as 'the maker of his own rebellion'. His solution to the problem of dependence on elitist evidence is to assume, plausibly enough for his period, that political discourse is necessarily dialogic: 'counter-insurgency can hardly afford a discourse that is not fully and compulsively involved with the rebel and his activities'. Starting from the observation that the prose of counter-insurgency is pervaded by terms 'designed primarily to indicate the immorality, illegality, undesirability, barbarity, etc of insurgent practice', he argues that it is possible to recover the real history of peasant insurgency by inverting those tropes to recover the practices they delegitimised.[19] For reasons I will return to, I doubt that Guha's methodology of inversion will work for my period, but his insights into what an adequate history of revolt should look like and into the need to interrogate the tropes of elitist discourse on revolt have profoundly shaped this chapter.

This chapter offers a close analysis of the Roman discourse on revolt, exploring the key terms in the Latin vocabulary of revolt (*seditio, rebellio, motus, tumultus, latrocinium*) and the conceptual models that Latin texts use to explain and narrate revolt. I show *inter alia* that the categories employed by Roman writers tend to conflate many different types of conflict, that Roman writers draw on a relatively limited repertoire of quite simplistic narrative models to explain revolt, and that their choices of which revolts to mention and how to describe them were often governed by larger agendas – all of which complicates our attempts to write histories of revolt. I finish with some discussion of discursive history of revolt as a supplement, or even alternative to, social history of revolt. The chapter is largely philological, even literary, in its approach, because that is what the sources for the period require. We are disproportionately dependent on narrative histories – ambitious and sophisticated texts that need to be understood on their own terms before we can redeploy them for our purposes. This chapter emerges from a revolution in the study of Roman historical writing, in which the chief *turbator* was Tony Woodman, which has destabilised realist readings of the key texts on which much Roman history is based.[20] For pragmatic reasons, I focus on Latin texts and the West of the empire. This means excluding the single most substantial revolt narrative from the period, Josephus's *Jewish War*. Covering the East would require analysis of material in Greek and hence engagement with the related but distinct Greek tradition of writing revolt, not to mention the additional complexities of Greek authors' self-positioning in relation to Roman power, which would be impractical here. In any case, it is the lexicon, imagery, and narrative models of Latin texts that have the most significant afterlife in medieval discourses on revolt.

Seeing like an empire

'Revolt', 'rebellion', 'insurgency', and their like do not denote a natural category. These terms are intimately bound up with ongoing processes of state formation. Our lexicon of revolt stands at the end of a discursive tradition that can be traced back to the earliest states and which developed in tandem with the efforts of states to deny legitimacy to groups that challenged their supremacy.[21]

Though these terms are now regularly invoked in emancipatory histories of those groups, they are not particularly helpful as analytical categories. This is a particular problem in a context as complex as the Roman empire, which presents us with a fractured landscape of many types of revolt. The social historian is necessarily impelled to try to isolate specific phenomena, e.g. challenges to the reigning emperor by members of the imperial elite, 'native revolts' against Roman rule, social conflict within communities, banditry, or the persistence of 'non-state space' within the empire.[22] But the evidence provided by our sources is rarely granular enough to draw such distinctions with any real confidence. And the exercise may be misguided insofar as the complexities of alliance formation in an imperial context are likely to have blurred these distinctions in many individual cases. In any case, it is not my intention to delineate any analytical categories here. Instead my focus is on the Latin analogue to our underdetermined and ideologically laden category of 'revolt' – what a Roman would most likely have termed 'disturbance' (using the nouns *motus* or *tumultus* or related metaphors). The Roman discourse on disturbance is characteristically imperial, indiscriminately conflating a wide range of disruptions to the Roman order.

Studies of lexical fields in Latin are often highly subjective. To lend this exercise some degree of rigour, I began by constituting a corpus of revolt narratives (defined minimally as any notice in a Latin text of an episode we might classify as a revolt) in order to identify the most important lexemes and analyse their usage. My starting point was Thomas Pekáry's useful catalogue of episodes of 'unrest and revolt', expanded to cover some omissions.[23] A survey of the 100 years following Augustus's death in CE 14, produced a corpus of 65 texts describing 52 discrete episodes of revolt. One important caveat is that 49 of those 65 texts all come from a single author, the second-century senatorial historian Cornelius Tacitus, our most important source for this period. Any analysis of revolt narratives in the early empire is largely an analysis of revolt narratives in Tacitus. The most important nouns used to denote the events in this corpus are *seditio* (15×), *motus* (10×), *rebellio* (9×), *defectio* (6×), and *tumultus* (5×). The network of nouns are undergirded by a common structure of metaphors, most notably the tropes of motion (17×) and disturbance (11×) and complementary tropes which represent the suppression of revolt as forcibly restraining movement (17×), imposing stillness (7×), or putting things back in place (7×). The counts given – based on frequency in the corpus – are just intended as a crude metric of relative importance. These terms and tropes are connected by being used in similar contexts and often together (e.g. a revolt in Gaul in CE 21 is variously termed *rebellio*, *motus*, *defection*, and *tumultus* by Tacitus at *Ann.* 3.40–7). Rather than being employed as specialised terms each specific to a particular domain of conflict, they tend to be used as near synonyms, all capable of embracing a broad range of types of conflict with at most some subtle difference in connotative meaning.

The most generic terms are *motus* (literally 'movement') and *tumultus* ('upheaval'), which we might gloss as revolt-as-disturbance. *Tumultus* has a technical sense as a state of emergency short of war. The senate could declare a *tumultus*, facilitating the mobilising of citizen forces by *inter alia* suspending public business and enabling ad hoc conscription.[24] But the term could also be used in a looser sense as a near synonym of *motus*, describing a disturbance as serious without necessarily implying that a formal *tumultus* had been declared. In both cases, the emphasis seems to be on the scale of the threat to the Roman order while its nature is left underdetermined. *Motus* is a common label for rebellions by subject peoples against Roman rule, but it is also applied to incursions by barbarian tribes beyond the frontier and even to revolts by provincial governors aiming at displacing the emperor. It can also be used in very general terms to describe a situation of turmoil, such as followed the death of Nero. The *tumultus* identified by my sources are similarly varied, including disturbances in the city of Rome, slave revolts, mutinies in the Roman army, barbarian incursions, and revolts by provincial governors. The two substantives are at the centre of a much larger complex of metaphors of motion and disturbance that pervade

Roman revolt narratives. Barbarian incursions, native revolts, conflicts between communities, and mutinies are all described as originating with peoples being set in motion (the verbs *concire* and *commouere* are particularly common). Tropes of disturbance – notably the verb *turbare*, noun *turbatio*, and adjective *turbidus* – are similarly widespread, featuring in accounts of everything from civil war and mutiny through social conflict within communities to native revolts, with the rebels described as a source of disturbance or as themselves disturbed.

Seditio (revolt-as-disobedience) is the most prominent term in my corpus and only slightly less capacious than *motus*. It is the *mot propre* for disruption arising from within the Roman citizen body – riots and other disturbances in the city and mutinies in the army (it being the standard term for a mutiny in Latin). It has a double aspect, being capable of denoting division on both horizontal and vertical lines – both dissension within a group and disobedience to legitimate authority – and often both simultaneously. It is a word that tropes disobedience as dissension and vice versa. Derived from *sed* in its original meaning of 'by oneself' and *itio* (going), its root meaning is 'going apart', as Cicero observed ('dissension among citizens is called *seditio* because some go apart from the others', Cic. *Rep.* 6.1) and it is sometimes used as a synonym of *discordia* and *dissensio* to denote strife, dissension, or quarrelling within a group. It is also the legal term for collective insubordination to a magistrate, an offence which fell under the remit of several laws including the *lex Cornelia de sicariis*, the *lex Iulia de maiestate*, and the *lex Iulia de vi*.[25] It enjoys wide currency in early imperial Latin, being used of mutinies in the army and urban disturbances both in Rome and elsewhere in the empire – their severity ranging from a crowd pelting a governor with turnips (Tac. *Ann.* 1.77.2) to a riot in which soldiers were killed (Vell. 2.12) – and even conflicts between communities, such as a riot between the populations of the Campanian cities of Pompeii and Nuceria (Tac. *Ann* 14.17.2) or the forcible occupation by one Sardinian community of land belonging to another (*Inscriptiones Latinae Selectae* 5947). It thus seems to be a master-term for defiance of the Roman state's authority, encompassing everything short of full-scale war. Its centrality to the rhetoric of imperial order made it a powerful term that could be appropriated in other contexts. We find it, for example, somewhat incongruously in the regulations of a private association which provide for the punishment of members who cause *seditio* by changing seats during the dinner (*Inscriptiones Latinae Selectae* 7212). The only context in which it is not normally used is large-scale revolts in the provinces, perhaps because it seemed inappropriate to their scale – though it and its cognates are sometimes extended to those contexts (e.g. Tac. *Hist.* 4.14.2 and *Ann.* 3.40.3).

Large-scale provincial revolts tend rather to be referred to as *rebelliones* or *defectiones* – if not just called disturbances (*motus*, *tumultus*). *Defectio* (revolt-as-betrayal), from *deficere* ('to desert'), connotes a breach of faith. In Republican Latin, *defectio* and *seditio* were mutually exclusive: *seditio* was the act of citizens; *defectio* that of allies and subjects.[26] By the imperial period, however, that distinction had been lost. As well as being used to describe provincial revolts (e.g. Tac. *Ann*, 12.39.3 and 14.30.3), *defectio* is the offence of a Roman soldier who deserts to or otherwise aids the enemy (*Digest* 4.5.5.1); it is also used to describe revolts by provincial governors aiming at ousting the reigning emperor (e.g. Suet. *Nero* 42 and 47). *Rebellio* (revolt-as-renewal-of-war) literally means 'fighting again' or 'fighting back' (the prefix *re-* conveying a sense of repeated action and/or opposition) and normally denotes a renewal of warfare, usually by the defeated party. In my corpus, it is used exclusively of conflict in the periphery of the empire (not just provincial revolts but also incursions from outside the empire), never of social conflict in the city of Rome or other communities of the empire – or of senatorial revolts against the emperor. It can be used in a pejorative sense to delegitimise or trivialise resistance as *rebellio* rather than true *bellum* (e.g. Livy 34.13.8–9). But the distinction should not be exaggerated, since the terms *rebellio* and *bellum* tend to be used almost interchangably and rebels are more often termed *hostes* ('enemies') than *rebelles* ('rebels'). In any case *rebellio* seems to convey slightly more information than the other terms I have discussed, both about the scale of the conflict (outright warfare) and the identity of the rebels (who are marked as foreign).

One surprising absence from my corpus is *latrocinium* (banditry) and its cognates. These terms are one of the most common and powerful ways of delegitimising violence or opposition in Latin texts – performing very similar work to the language of 'terrorism' today. The literature of the Roman civil wars, for example, is littered with accusations of banditry thrown by both sides. There is some evidence that Roman law of the imperial period used the category of *latrocinium* to delegitimise non-state violence. The second-century jurist Sextus Pomponius defined 'enemies' (*hostes*) as 'those who have publicly declared war on us or on whom we have done so. Others are "bandits" [*latrones*] or "robbers" [*praedones*]' (*Digest* 50.16.118). One might thus expect the imperial elite to dismiss popular protest or native revolts as *latrocinium*. But there are no such examples among my corpus of narratives. Instead, Tacitus and other writers are quite prepared to describe provincial revolts in the language of *bellum* and refer to the rebels as *hostes*. This speaks to a perhaps surprising lack of anxiety about revolt, something that will emerge as a characteristic feature of these texts. I will return to it at the end of the chapter.

A dizzying array of different types of conflict – mutinies in the Roman army, native revolts against Roman rule, barbarian incursions, slave revolts, unrest in the city of Rome, various kinds of internal conflict in the cities of Italy and the provinces, conflicts between neighbouring communities, and revolts by provincial governors with imperial ambitions – are conflated by the language of disturbance (*motus*, *tumultus*, and the whole network of related metaphors) and *seditio*. *Rebellio* and *defectio* are somewhat more circumscribed in their range of meaning, but still capable of eliding distinctions we might think important. Latin texts confront us with an imperial perspective which blurs all social and political specificity and sees only a shared antagonism to the Roman order, troped variously as disturbance, disobedience, treachery, or defiance. This tendency to conflate a wide range of threats to the Roman order is a particular problem because so many episodes of revolt are known only from a brief notice in narrative history, passing mention in another literary work or allusion in civic epigraphy. If all we have is a mention of a *seditio*, *motus*, or *tumultus*, there is little or nothing that we can infer with confidence about the nature of the conflict denoted. Our view is limited by the low resolution of the imperial gaze.

Revolt narratives

Lexemes are only the smallest building blocks of the Latin discourse on revolt. There is a higher order of patterning at the level of whole narratives. Here it is possible to draw some clearer distinctions between types of revolt – though I will suggest that the resulting typology may well be misleading. I outline here three recurring types of revolt narrative – 'eruptions of discord', 'unruly landscapes', and 'rebellions by subject peoples'. My aim is to illustrate the predictability of these accounts and the inadequacy of their explanations. I follow them with one anomalous outlier, Tacitus's account of a revolt in Gaul in 21 CE, which illustrates by contrast the limitations of most other revolt narratives. I eschew providing historical bibliography because my focus is on the structure of the texts themselves, rather than the events which they describe.

Eruptions of discord

My first type barely deserves the label narrative. It consists of notices of disturbances within the empire that are characterised by extreme brevity and minimal explanation. Conflict is attributed to discord (*discordia* or *dissensio*) and/or the lack of self-control (*licentia* or *lasciuia*) of the population.

Discord becomes a quasi-natural force, always threatening to break out if not kept under check. The model has broad application, being used to 'explain' all sorts of disturbances within the empire – riots and popular protest in the city of Rome, social strife within other communities in Italy and the provinces, and also conflicts between neighbouring communities.

I start with two parallel accounts of a riot in the theatre in Rome in 15 CE. Tacitus writes:

> The lawlessness [*licentia*] in the theatre which had begun in the previous year broke out [*erupit*] more seriously. Those killed included not just some of the plebs but also soldiers and a centurion, and a tribune of the Praetorian Guard was wounded, while they were trying to suppress the abuse of magistrates and the antagonisms [*dissension*] of the crowd. The sedition [*seditio*] was discussed in the senate.
>
> *(Tac. Ann. 1.77.1)*

The only attempt at explanation is an allusion to the presence of *licentia* (lawlessness, disorder, lack of self-control) which suddenly burst out (*erupit*) like some natural force. Suetonius records the same event:

> As for disturbances by the populace [*populares tumultus*], Tiberius repressed [*coercuit*] them with the utmost severity when they arose [*ortos*], and worked diligently to prevent them arising. When discord [*discordia*] led to murder being committed in the theatre, he banished the leaders of the factions and the actors, who were the cause of the divisions.
>
> *(Suet. Tib. 37.2)*

He gives a little more circumstantial detail, concerning the existence of theatre factions, but only as an aside. His brief narrative reifies *discordia* as the cause of the violence and his language (the noun *tumultus* and the verbs *orior* and *coercere*) implies the existence of an eruptive force that needs to be kept under tight control. A third example is Tacitus's notice of some conflict, the nature of which is left obscure, between or within the cities of Campania in 70 CE (in the aftermath of the civil wars of 68–69):

> At the same time, Lucilius Bassus was sent with lightly armed cavalry to put Campania in order [*ad componendam Campaniam*]. The cause was more the towns being at variance [*discordes*] with each other than recalcitrance [*contumacia*] towards the emperor. When the soldiers appeared there was quiet [*quies*] and impunity for the lesser cities; Capua saw the third legion installed to winter there and noble houses suffered.
>
> *(Tac. Hist. 4.3.1)*

Again *discordia* is presented as a sufficient explanation for the disturbance that Bassus has to settle.

These notices revert to the same, simplistic model for explaining conflict. There is little attempt to specify the lines of division and no engagement with the agenda of the actors – indeed they are largely denied any agency at all. All of this makes them unpromising material for social history, which is unfortunate since notices like these are often our only evidence for episodes of what might be popular protest or revolt. One significant corollary of the minimalist explanation is a relatively neutral moral tone. There is no obvious attempt to condemn the actors involved and delegitimise their agenda, e.g. by using the language of *latrocinium*. Instead the outbreaks are represented as part of the natural order. This raises questions that I will return to below.

Unruly landscapes

A second recurring narrative type similarly forgoes deeper explanation, but it invokes the natural unruliness and un-governability of certain peoples and landscapes rather than *discordia* as the cause of revolt. Challenges to the Roman order in marginal areas are represented as spontaneous and unprovoked. Describing wilderness landscapes and the uncivilised character of their inhabitants becomes a substitute for any consideration of the motivations of the rebels. A good example is Tacitus's short notice of a revolt in Isauria (on the south coast of Anatolia) in 52 CE:

> Shortly afterwards, the tribes of wild [*agrestes*] Cilicians called the Cietae, who had been disturbed [*commotae*] on many previous occasions, now under the leadership of Troxobor occupied the rugged mountains with forts. Descending on the coasts or cities, they had the temerity to use violence against the farmers and townspeople and especially the merchants and shipmasters.
>
> (*Tac. Ann. 12.55.1*)

No explanation is given for the Cilicians' actions. Apparently none was necessary. Marking the Cietae as wild (*agrestes*), situating them among steep hills (*montes asperi*) and contrasting them with figures of civilisation (*cultores*, *oppidani*, *mercatores*, and *navicularii*) all makes their behaviour unremarkable. Indeed, we are told that they are regularly 'disturbed' or 'agitated' (*commotae*). The agentless passive leaves little scope for rebel agency. Revolt is again reduced to an almost natural phenomenon.

A slightly more complex example is a revolt in Thrace in 26 CE:

> In the consulship of Lentulus Gaetulicus and C. Calvisius, triumphal honours were decreed to Poppaeus Sabinus for having crushed Thracian tribes who lived on mountain heights without civilisation and so all the more savagely [*montium editis inculti atque eo ferocius agitabant*]. The cause of the disturbance [*motus*], besides the people's character [*hominum ingenium*], was that they refused to suffer the levy and to give all their strongest men to our army, being unaccustomed to obey even kings except at their own whim – or, if they did send military support, being used to appointing their own leaders and only waging war against neighbours. A rumour had arisen that they would be split up, mixed in with other peoples and dragged off to distant lands. Before they took to arms, they sent a delegation.
>
> (*Tac. Ann. 4.45.1–2*)

Tacitus does grant the Thracians a concrete grievance, namely the levying of troops for the Roman army. But the explanation that follows implies that this was a problem only because they were a people unaccustomed to obedience. Moreover Tacitus suggests that it was only a trigger; the underlying cause was the Thracians' natural character (*hominum ingenium*). The Thracians are characterised by *ferocia* ('wildness' or 'savagery'), a trait regularly associated with and often used to explain barbarian revolt. That *ferocia* is in turn explained by their way of life (*inculti*) and ultimately their environment (*montium editis*): they 'lived on mountain heights without civilisation and so all the more savagely'. The wilderness landscape pervades the rest of the narrative, with recurring details about high crags, mountain passes, narrow ridges, and savage winters. This is a world where rebellion needs little explanation.

Rebellions by subject peoples

The narratives of my third type tend to be much longer than the other models discussed here – as much as ten times their length – because they captured the imagination of ancient historians. As an inevitable result, they also dominate modern scholarship on 'revolt' in the Roman empire. These narratives present rebellions by whole peoples, rising organically in a bid for freedom from Roman rule. The revolts are invariably explained as the result of provincial grievances, some related to the structures of Roman rule (levying men for the Roman army, taxation, or the census), others resulting from the personal vices of Roman rulers (typically greed, lust, and cruelty), with the emphasis tending to fall on the latter. Those grievances are normally reinforced by a positive desire for freedom (*libertas*) and scorn for enslavement to Rome.

One example is Tacitus's first and shorter account of the Boudiccan revolt in Britain in 61 CE:

> Relieved of their fear by the absence of the governor, the Britons were discussing the evils of slavery [*mala seruitutis*], comparing injustices [*iniuriae*] and aggravating them with their own interpretations. Nothing was gained through compliance, they said, except that heavier burdens were imposed on them as if they would bear them easily. In the old days they had one king each; now two kings were imposed on them, a governor to savage their bodies and a procurator to savage their property. Concord and discord between the rulers were equally fatal to the subjects. Their instruments, centurions and slaves respectively, mixed violence and insult. There was no limit to their greed, no limit to their lust. In war it is the stronger who carries off the spoils; now it was mostly cowards and weaklings who were stealing homes, taking children and imposing conscription on men who seemed to be prepared to die for anything except their own fatherland.... [There follow some arguments that rebellion was likely to be successful] Inspiring each other with such words ... they all took up arms [*sumpsere bellum*].
>
> (Tac. Ag. 15–16)

This revolt is motivated by grievances, which are enumerated in a passage of indirect speech giving voice to the rebel complaints in emotive language (a striking and recurring feature of these narratives). The grievances focus on Roman vices rather than the structures of Roman rule. There are references to the expropriation of land and the levying of troops (the *dilectus*), but the emphasis is on greed (*cupiditas*), cruelty (*saeuitia*), and lust (*libido*) – a triad of vices that recur again and again in these narratives.

Tacitus revisited the revolt at greater length in a later work, giving a rather different account of its causes:

> While Suetonius was thus engaged, he received word that the province had suddenly defected [*defectio*]. Prasutagus, king of the Iceni and famous for his long wealth, had made the emperor and his own two daughters his heirs. He thought that such obedience would protect his kingdom and family from injustice. But events proved otherwise, to the point that his kingdom was plundered by centurions and his household by slaves, as if they had been taken in war. First, his wife Boudicca was punished with the whip and his daughters were violated by rape. Then, as if the Romans had received the whole country as a gift, the most prominent of the Iceni were stripped of their ancestral property and the king's retainers were treated like slaves. Because of that outrage, and out of fear of worse to come after they had been reorganised as a province, they rushed

to arms. They stirred [*commouere*] to revolt [*rebellatio*] the Trinovantes and whatever other peoples had not yet been broken by enslavement and had pledged with secret oaths to take back their freedom. Their most bitter hatred was directed at the veterans. For the men recently settled at the colony of Camulodunum were forcing Britons from their homes and driving them from their fields, calling them captives and slaves. The army encouraged the veterans' lawlessness because they had a similar way of life and because they looked forward to taking the same liberties themselves. There was also the sight of the temple dedicated to the Divine Claudius which seemed a citadel of eternal mastery. Under the pretext of religion, the whole fortunes of those chosen as priests were being squandered.

(Tac. Ann. 14.30–1)

The details of the explanation are quite different: no mention of the *dilectus*, instead a description of the abuse of the property and family of Prasutagus (though the depredations of the veterans settled at Camulodunum/Colchester does correspond to the vague references to expropriation in the earlier account). But the focus remains on abuses by Roman officials and soldiers rather than the structures of Roman rule, with the same triad of greed, cruelty, and lust visible in the references to expropriation, physical violence and rape.

A third example is a revolt by the Frisii in 28 CE:

In the same year, the Frisians, a people living beyond the Rhine, threw off the peace [*pacem exuere*]. The cause was more our greed [*auaritia*] than their inability to tolerate obedience. Drusus [i.e. the Roman commander who first conquered them] had fixed a modest tribute for them in proportion to their poverty, the payment of ox-hides for military use. No one had specified their strength or dimension until Olennius, a senior centurion installed to rule the Frisii, chose the hides of aurochs as the model for what was acceptable. What would have been onerous even for other peoples was all the more untolerable for the Germans, who have forests teeming with massive beasts but only small cattle at home. They handed over first their oxen, then their land, and eventually the bodies of their wives and children to slavery. There was anger and complaint and – when there came no relief – they sough remedy in war.

(Tac. Ann. 4.72)

Again Tacitus blames the revolt on Roman vice, specifically greed (*auaritia*) – though it is worth noting that his reference to an inability to tolerate obedience (*obsequii impatientes*) recalls the 'unruly landscapes' type. The particular instantiation of Roman greed is described in detail, ending in a telling reference to the bodies of their wives and children – another allusion to Roman lust.

A final example, necessarily truncated, is Tacitus's account of the outbreak of the so-called 'Batavian revolt', an uprising by several German and northern Gallic tribes under the leadership of the Batavian noble Julius Civilis during the Roman civil war of 69–70 CE:

Having resolved to revolt [*desciscere*], concealing his ulterior plan for the moment and ready to adjust his other plans as events required, Civilis began fomenting revolution [*nouare res*]. On the instructions of Vitellius, the young men of the Batavians were being summoned to a levy. Grievous enough in itself, it was exacerbated by the greed and luxury of the officials responsible, who hunted out the old and infirm, so in order to extract a fee for granting them exemption. Meanwhile the young and attractive (most of the Batavians being unusually tall in boyhood) were dragged off to be raped [*ad stuprum*]. This caused resentment, and the leaders of the revolt [*seditio*], which had already been arranged, persuaded the Batavians to refuse the levy. Civilis summoned the tribe's nobility and the most energetic of the commoners to a sacred grove on the pretext of a feast. Once he saw that night and revelry had heated their blood, he began to speak of the distinction and glory of their tribe and then enumerated the injustices and depredations and the other evils of enslavement. They were no longer treated like allies, he said, but like chattel. Where was the governor? He might be accompanied by an oppressive and arrogant retinue, but at least he had authority. Instead they were handed over to prefects and centurions. As soon as they had their fill of treasure and blood [*spoliis et sanguine*], they were replaced by others who sought out new pockets to plunder and new pretexts for doing so. Now a levy was upon them, by which children would be separated from parents, brothers from brothers, as if by death.... [Civilis goes on to assert the likelihood of victory] His words were received with a great affirmation and he bound them all with a barbarian rite and ancestral oaths.

(*Tac. Hist. 4.14–15*)

Civilis's ulterior motives are a distinctive feature of this narrative, which I will return to in a later section. The other features are entirely familiar. The *dilectus* features again, both in Tacitus's explanation and in Civilis's speech. But the real focus is still on Roman vice, the familiar triad of greed (*auaritia* and the abuse of the *dilectus* for self-enrichment), cruelty ('satiated with blood'), and lust (children dragged away *ad stuprum*).

All but the first of these examples contain at least one concrete detail that gives the revolt a distinct identity and establishes Tacitus's authority as a narrator: the abuse of the Prasutagus's household and the violence of Roman colonists in Britain, the tribute in ox-hides paid by the Frisii, the abuse of the *dilectus* among the Batavians. Put together, however, what is striking is the conventionality of Tacitus's explanations. The one or two specific details are always embedded in more generic analysis and made to illustrate one or two aspects of the same triad of vices: greed, cruelty, and lust. In every case, the same Roman vices lead to administrative abuses which provoke the provincials to reject subjection as enslavement and seek to recover their lost freedom.

Two obvious limitations of the implicit sociology of revolt are worth emphasising. First, is the way in which it severely restricts the scope for rebel agency and rationality. Except in the last case, which is exceptional for reasons I will return to, it is always Roman vice that is the driving force, provoking the provincials to action. This is revolt as reflex. There is no suggestion of long-term planning or alliance formation on the side of the rebels. Nor are they allowed any more than the crudest of goals – the pursuit of freedom. There is no space for the possibility that they might have taken up arms to achieve anything short of total independence.[27] Second, the lines of rupture are far too neat. In each case, a subject people rises in its entirety against their Roman oppressors. There is a clean division along ethnic lines and no hint of social or other divisions within the rebel community or of collusion by any colonial elements, whether administrators, soldiers, traders, or other settlers. We must wait a book after Tacitus's account of a revolt in Gaul in 21 CE, which unambiguously pits Gauls against Romans (Tac. *Ann.* 3.40–7, discussed below), to learn that two Roman governors were later accused of complicity in the revolt (*Ann.* 4.18.1 and 4.28.2). Whatever the truth of the charges (and it suits Tacitus's representation of the then emperor Tiberius to make them seem false), they illustrate that it was at least plausible that the alliances underlying the revolt were more complex than Tacitus's earlier narrative suggests.

It is also worth noting that this narrative type shares with the other two their lack of any obvious strategies of delegitimisation. The language of *latrocinium*, for example, is again notably absent (except when it is applied to *Roman* abuses). On the contrary, the rebels are credited with real grievances arising out of abuses by Roman officials, their plight is represented sympathethically as a struggle for freedom against metaphorical enslavement to Rome, and they are even allowed a voice in the rhetorically powerful passages of direct or indirect speech that are a hallmark of this narrative type.

The Florus-Sacrovir revolt

It would be easy to delineate other types of revolt narrative, such as arise in the context of slave revolts, mutinies, or attempts at usurpation by Roman aristocrats in Rome and in the provinces. But these three examples should be enough to illustrate the relatively limited repertoire of highly schematic models that Tacitus and other writers draw on to explain internal conflict. Not the least problem is that the distinctions between these types are suspiciously neat. This is illustrated by a few examples that prove hard to categorise. Perhaps the most interesting example is Tacitus's account of a revolt in Gaul in 21 CE.

> In the same year the peoples of the Gauls began a rebellion [*rebellio*] because of the immensity of debt [*aes alienum*]. The sharpest goading came from Iulius Florus among the Treviri and Iulius Sacrovir among the Aedui. They could both boast of nobility and ancestral achievements and hence the long possession of Roman citizenship, granted when it was rare and only bestowed as a reward for valour. They held secret meetings, recruited all the fiercest men [*ferocissimus quisque*] and those who had the greatest need to do wrong [*maxima peccandi necessitudo*] due to destitution [*egestas*] and fear born of past crimes [*flagitia*]. They agreed that Florus would incite [*concire*] the Belgae and Sacrovir the nearer Gauls. In small meetings and gatherings, they spread seditious talk [*seditiosa*] about the endlessness of tribute, the weight of debt [*faenus*], the cruelty [*saeuitia*] and arrogance of the governors. The army, they said, was divided by news of Germanicus' death; it was an excellent time to regain their freedom, if in their strength they would just realise how weak Italy was, how unwarlike the city's population – and that all that was strong in the army was foreign. Scarcely a single people was untouched by the seeds of that disturbance [*motus*]. But it was the Andecavi and Turoni who broke out [*erupere*] first.
>
> *(Tac. Ann. 3.40–1)*

Some elements here are familiar from the 'rebellion by subject peoples' type: the complaints about tribute and about Roman vices and the aspiration to freedom (*libertas*). But there are some unusual additions, notably the headline reference to debt ('the Gauls began a rebellion *because of the immensity of debt*'), echoed in the later complaint about the weight of debt and the references to destitution (*egestas*) and social discontent. The theme is continued later in the narrative when the rebels recruit their army from debtors (4.42.2). The references to debt and destitution are also embedded in a language of criminality and moral outrage (*peccandi necessitudo, flagitia*) that was notably absent from the other narratives.

The attention to the economic and social context of revolt looks promising at first sight. The prominent role of debt seems particularly plausible given what we know about Roman lending in conquered provinces. Indeed this narrative is one of the pillars on which Stephen Dyson built his theory of a second wave of native revolts sparked by debt.[28] But the analysis here is in fact no less conventional, and hence just as problematic, as that found in other revolt narratives. The nexus of debt, criminality, guilt, and revolution is a topos of the history of civil strife in the Roman republic.[29] Compare Cicero's claims about there being elements in the population always ready to support revolution:

> In so large a citizen body there is a great mass of men who look for upheaval [*noui motus*] and revolution, fearing punishment for the wrongs [*peccata*] that weigh on their consciences, or who feed on civil discord [*discordiae ciuium*] and unrest [*seditio*] because of a certain ingrained distemper, or who, when their finances are in shambles [*implicatio rei familiaris*], prefer to go up in the flames of a general conflagration than burn all on their own.
>
> (*Pro Sestio* 99, trans. Kaster)

The paradigmatic literary exemplar of this distinctly aristocratic sociology of social conflict was Sallust's *Bellum Catilinae*, his single-book history of the Catilinarian conspiracy in Rome in 63 BCE. Debt (*aes alienum*) plays a central role. One of the key circumstances that prompts Catiline to embark on his revolutionary course is the fact 'that there was great debt [*aes alienum ... ingens*] throughout the entire world' (*Cat.* 16.4); debt features repeatedly in descriptions of his supporters (*Cat.* 14.2, 24.3, 40.1, 41.2) and in their rhetoric (*Cat.* 20.13, 33.2). In fact Tacitus's account of the outbreak of the Gallic revolt is closely modelled on Sallust. The first men recruited by Florus and Sacrovir were '[i] all the fiercest men and [ii] those who had the greatest need to do wrong because of destitution and fear born of past crimes' (*ferocissimo quoque adsumpto aut quibus ob egestatem ac metum ex flagitiis maxima peccandi necessitudo*). This is a careful reworking of Sallust's description of Catiline's co-conspirators at their first meeting: 'he assembled all those who [i] [faced] the greatest necessity and [ii] had the most recklessness' (*in unum omnis convocat, quibus maxuma necessitudo et plurumum audaciae inerat*, *Cat.* 17.2).

Both descriptions are bipartite. Tacitus's second element repeats the three words in Sallust's first (*quibus maxuma necessitudo*) and expands on them (*quibus ... maxima peccandi necessitudo*).[30] The parallel is all the more striking because of the studied use of *necessitudo* in the sense of *necessitas* ('necessity', 'compulsion'), rather than its ordinary language meaning ('a bond of kinship'). Sallust strained language further with the absolute use of *necessitudo*, with necessity standing by metonymy for the circumstances that produced it (it is often translated as 'poverty' here), and the zeugma with *inerat* (where *necessitudo* needs to be construed with a verb like *erat*). Tacitus has unpacked Sallust's compression, explaining both the nature of the compulsion (by appending the gerund *peccandi*) and its source (by adding the explanatory adverbial phrase *ob egestatem ac metum ex flagitiis*). The latter phrase itself reworks an earlier passage in the *Bellum Catilinae*, where Sallust sums up a list of the types of person Catiline associated with in his youth: 'in short, everyone hounded by crime, destitution or a guilty conscience' (*postremo omnes quos flagitium, egestas, conscius animus exagitabat*). Tacitus repeats *flagitium* (changing singular to plural) and *egestas* but substitutes *metus* (*ex flagitiis*) for *conscius animus* and changes the order to clarify the relationship between the three terms.

Tacitus's first element (*ferocissimo quoque*) balances Sallust's second (*quibus ... plurumum audaciae inerat*) with varied wording and grammatical structure. *Audacia* is replaced by *ferocia*, a near-synonym with equal Sallustian pedigree, which is more apposite here because of its association with barbarians.[31] Sallust's complex construction with *plurimum* and partitive genitive of an abstract noun (*quibus plurimum audaciae inerat*) has been replaced by a simple superlative adjective (*ferocissimus*), while *quisque* plus adjective substitutes for *omnes* plus relative clause.

This combination of repetition, variation, and explication is characteristic of the formidably learned allusive practice of Latin literature. An educated reader would recognise Catiline's followers in those of Florus and Sacrovir.[32] The echoes of Sallust's Catilinarian conspiracy in Tacitus's Gallic revolt are entirely typical of Roman historical writing. The studied reworking of earlier writers was one key way in which Roman writers situated themselves within a literary tradition, in historiography no less than in other genres.[33] It also reflects a different vision of what persuasive history looks like: 'A man's own experience might seem less attractive and convincing than what stood in literary tradition, guaranteed by time and famous names.'[34] Syme was writing about ethnography and geography, but his insight is equally applicable to the task of explaining revolt. At a more profound level it embodies a deep attention to patterning in history, a tendency to see and emphasise parallels between past and present, such that 'history becomes "a knot of different times" in which theoretically unique, non-recurrent events are built from other episodes, other stories'.[35]

Putting this revolt back in its literary context reframes the problem of its divergence from Tacitus's other provincial revolts such as those of the Britons and Frisii discussed above. Rather than seeking to explain the differences as reflecting a different social and economic context (as Dyson did), we should see it first and foremost as a choice by the writer. Rather than a different kind of revolt, it is a different kind of revolt narrative, one produced by the fusion of two distinct literary traditions. Of course it should now also be clear that the normal disjunction between narratives of rebellion and narratives of civil strife is just as stylised as their conflation here. It is striking that our other source for Boudicca's revolt, the third-century historian Cassius Dio, makes debt the prime cause of that revolt (Dio 62[62].2.1). This tradition must have been known to Tacitus, yet he makes no mention of it in either of his two accounts of the revolt. The exclusion of any mention of debt allows him to dissociate those revolts from the history of civil strife in Rome, where rebellion is inextricably linked with criminality and moral degeneration. I will return to his motivations for doing so.

The question then becomes why Tacitus might have decided to situate the Florus-Sacrovir revolt within a different literary tradition, and what he achieves by doing so. This is obviously the realm of speculation but two explanations spring to mind. This revolt was not in the periphery of the empire, as were the revolts in Britain and on the Rhine, but in Gaul, which was by Tacitus's time well integrated into the Roman imperial network, increasingly urbanised, and supplying equestrians and even senators to the imperial elite. Indeed Tacitus himself may have been from Southern Gaul.[36] The simplistic model of a foreign people rising up against their Roman rulers may have seemed inadequate to describe this upheaval much closer to the centre. This might explain why Tacitus reached out to a different tradition in Latin historical writing in order to construct this revolt as a hybrid between native revolt and Roman civil strife – which is another way of saying that he represented it as blurring the distinction between the two.

The Gallic rebellion of 21 CE was also important insofar as it anticipated the revolt of Julius Vindex (another Gallic Julius, this time a senator and provincial governor) under Nero in 68 CE. This famous revolt must have been narrated at the end of the *Annals* (which presumably ended with the death of Nero), though the transmitted text cuts off in 66 CE. Given both the general tendency of Roman historiography to see repetition in history and Tacitus's particular attention to such responsion across the five-and-a-half decades covered by the *Annals*, it is highly likely that the revolt of 21 CE was constructed as a precursor to that of 68 CE.[37] The nature of the latter revolt, whether a 'national' uprising against Rome or merely an attempt by a senatorial governor to oust an unpopular emperor, has generated heated debate out of all proportion to the meagre supply of ancient evidence.[38] If Tacitus's account of the revolt of 21 CE is any guide to how he narrated Vindex's revolt, it suggests that he may have explored similar issues, in his own more subtle manner.

Larger agendas

In a Latin revolt narrative, a reference to debt is not just a circumstantial detail. For the educated reader, it evokes a long tradition of writing about social strife at Rome. Tacitus seems to have made debt central to his account of the Florus-Sacrovir revolt precisely in order to establish that connection. Conversely, he apparently suppressed any mention of debt in his accounts of the Boudiccan revolt, presumably to keep those narratives of northern barbarians fighting for freedom against Roman greed, cruelty, and lust uncontaminated by the moral judgements embedded in the other tradition. This is a powerful illustration of the extent to which our understanding of the nature of these revolts is shaped by choices made by the writers on whom we depend for our information. This is a particular problem for Roman historians, because so much of our knowledge is mediated by highly sophisticated texts that have their own complex agendas.

Similar processes of selection explain the massive discrepancy in scale between the extended narratives of 'native revolts' and the brief notices of internal social conflict which I noted above. Large-scale uprisings in the provinces were clearly of much more interest than rioting in an Italian or provincial city or even in the city of Rome. That is partly a reflection of the opportunities they offered for writing in the grand manner, with battle narratives and the like. But it is also because Roman writers – particularly Tacitus – found provincial revolt 'good to think with'. It is well established that Tacitus's presentation of provincial revolts, particularly revolts by northern barbarians is intimately bound up with his overarching subject, the state of the Roman *res publica*. To give just one instance, his shorter account of Boudicca's revolt in the *Agricola* (the first exemplar of my 'rebellion by subject peoples' type) is embedded in a work that is not just an encomiastic biography of an expansionist governor of Britain (which would already complicate any representation of British revolts in the text), but also a profound meditation on what autocracy means for an aristocratic elite. Its central subject is the difficulty of finding an honourable middle way between futile defiance and servile submission. The British revolts are integral to the analysis. An elaborate complex of lexical, structural, and thematic parallels establishes a homology between the position of the British under Rome and that of senators under the emperor. With their rousing rhetoric of freedom, their defiant confrontation with Roman arms, and most importantly their end in total defeat, the British rebels provide a powerful illustration of both the attractions and the futility of the policy of outright defiance from which Tacitus seeks to dissuade his readers.[39] The imperative of establishing this homology governs much of the presentation of revolt in Britain.

Another good example of the considerations governing the inclusion and presentation of revolts is the 'Batavian revolt' of 69–70 CE. It dominates a book-and-a-half of Tacitus's *Histories*.[40] Yet it is almost entirely ignored by our other principal source for the period, Cassius Dio's *Roman History*: 'There were other revolts against the Romans in Germany, which are in my opinion not worth mentioning' (Dio 65[66].3.1). The explicit dismissal may be that of the epitomator, Xiphilinus, rather than Dio himself, but it is clear from the summary of the book that Dio did not discuss the revolt at length.[41] The much more extensive treatment in Tacitus is proportionate to the revolt's thematic importance for his work. It allowed him to craft a narrative in which subjects reject their state of enslavement and succeed in throwing off their oppressors only to find themselves unable to cope with their new found freedom; duped by duplicitous, self-serving leaders and riven by *discordia*, they eventually have to resign themselves to return to subjection and to being satisfied with at least choosing their master.[42] They neatly illustrate the dilemma of the Roman senate as diagnosed at the start of the *Histories*: 'they can endure neither total enslavement nor total freedom' (*nec totam seruitutem pati possunt nec totam libertatem*, *Hist.* 1.16.5). This is another instance where a revolt narrative has been carefully crafted in order to shed light on Tacitus's real concern, the principate itself. We can only deduce from the limited coverage of the same revolt in Dio's history that he found it less useful for his purposes.

It is no accident that we are particularly well informed about small-scale internal conflict during the period covered by the *Histories*. The surviving four-and-a-half books, covering 69 and 70 CE (the 'year of four emperors' and its aftermath), take their place alongside Lucan's *Bellum Civile* and Statius's *Thebaid* as one of the most profound meditations on civil war in Latin literature.[43] In Tacitus's telling, the civil wars that followed the death of Nero revealed not just a lack of cohesion and shared identity among Roman citizens, but an empire fractured everywhere by deep-running antipathies. Besides the familiar topoi of civil war – citizens killing citizens, fathers killing sons – Tacitus presents a series of vignettes in which the larger civil war is mirrored in miniature in strife between and within the individual communities of the provinces. His narrative is thus key evidence for conflicts between neighbouring communities in the provinces, including a long-running antagonism between the neighbouring cities of Lugdunum and Vienna in Gaul which erupted into armed conflict (*Hist.* 1.65–6), bad blood between the cities of Oea and Lepcis Magna in Africa which escalated from raiding to outright warfare (*Hist.* 4.50.4), and strife between or within the cities of Campania which required military intervention (*Hist.* 4.3.1). The *Histories* also offers a rare example of what seems to be a small popular revolt, perhaps even a peasant revolt, in the territory of the Gallic Aedui, which was quickly put down by the local propertied classes with the support of Roman troops (*Hist.* 2.61). This was certainly an exceptional time and it is entirely plausible that provincials took advantage of the distraction of provincial governors to escalate local disagreements. But that is not a sufficient explanation for the inclusion of these minor provincial disturbances in a grand narrative of Roman history. They are there because they illustrated a central theme of Tacitus's narrative. It is an open question how many similar episodes in other periods were passed over by other authors and texts because they were not as relevant to their agendas.

Towards a discursive history of revolt

The historical record for all kinds of revolt in the early empire is thin and patchy. Many episodes are attested by only 10 to 20 words in one or two texts, sometimes less. The labels used by Roman authors are vague and their analyses generic, giving us little insight into the nature of the movements described. When we do have fuller accounts, they are invariably embedded in works of historiography, highly sophisticated texts with their own complex agendas which often determine the inclusion and treatment of particular revolts. All of this raises profound questions about the sort of history this record can support. The prospect of an adequate social history of revolt, particularly popular revolt, seems to me ever more illusory.

One alternative is to take an oblique approach, focusing on the textual record itself. There is clearly a need for a literary history of revolt narratives, which is the primary context in which most of these texts must be understood. We also need at least a crude history of the broader discourse on revolt in which they were originally embedded. Historiographical accounts of revolt were originally only one small component of a much larger discursive formation, though the vagaries of survival have obliterated most of the rest. A discursive history of this sort is, at a minimum, a prerequisite for any social history. It is also an important project in its own right.

Seen in comparative perspective, one of the most remarkable features of the Latin discourse on revolt is the lack of strategies of delegitimisation, such as the rhetoric of moral outrage or the language of *latrocinium*. Most of the texts I have discussed appear to show a remarkable lack of anxiety about the conflicts they describe. This is a surprising characteristic that demands some explanation. The most obvious explanation is that outbreaks were relatively rare and no real threat to the Roman order and so could be described with relative equanimity. Hence the confidence of writers like Tacitus might be taken as indirect confirmation that the early empire was indeed as peaceful as Roman writers and many modern scholars have suggested. But there are other possible explanations that keep open the possibility that it was not. The vast majority of our evidence for revolt in the first century derives from historians writing at some remove from the events they described. Tacitus and Suetonius were writing early in the second century, Cassius Dio a century later. That historical distance, combined with the distancing effect of writing a work intended to circulate as literature, may have enabled them to write about these events with more objectivity than contemporaries caught up in the course of events could have mustered. In the terminology of Guha, the discourse we have is entirely *secondary*, shorn of the immediacy and connection to action that characterises the *primary* discourse of administrators and others caught up in the course of events – a discourse which is entirely lost to us.[44] The limited geographic representation of the imperial elite of this period may also be a factor. The circle of senators and office-holding equestrians in which men like Tacitus and Suetonius moved was not yet the trans-regional aristocracy it would become by the third century. Although it was no longer exclusively Italian, Italians were disproportionately represented (and probably still a majority in the senate) and most of the exceptions came from a small number of highly urbanised areas in the provinces, notably Southern Gaul and South-eastern Iberia.[45] The imperial elite had relatively few personal ties to large swathes of imperial territory. Disruptions in peripheral provinces were not a direct threat to their wealth or social pre-eminence and so could be recorded with dispassion or outright ignored.

The apparent self-confidence of the imperial elite also seems to reflect a particular vision of the imperial project – the work that they thought Roman power was doing in the world. The metaphors of movement and disturbance that pervade accounts of the outbreak of revolts are balanced by a set of complementary tropes for the re-imposition of order which appear again and again at the end of revolt narratives. The metaphors of motion are complemented by tropes of stillness – *quies* ('rest') and its cognates and verbs like *considere* and *residere* (both meaning 'to settle'). Also important are metaphors of ordering, notably the verbs *componere* ('to put in place') and *ordinare* ('to put in order', in the literal sense of place in a row), the counterpart to the tropes of disturbance and confusion. Most prominent of all is a complex of strikingly physical metaphors evoking the forcible restraint of movement including the verbs *coercere* ('restrain') and various compounds of the verb *premere* ('exert pressure'), notably *comprimere* ('hold in', 'constrict') and *opprimere* ('hold down', 'crush').

These metaphors of constriction are central to the imagination of the Roman elite. Consider three honorific inscriptions from the late first and early second centuries CE, enumerating the details of a senatorial or equestrian career with the brevity characteristic of the genre: 'To Tiberius Plautius Silvanus, son of Marcus, tribe Aniensis ... pro-praetorian legate of Moesia, in which ... he crushed [*comprimere*] an incipient disturbance [*motus*] by/among the Sarmatians' (epitaph of a former governor of Moesia, late first century CE, *Inscriptiones Latinae Selectae* 986); 'Sextus Sentius Caecilianus, son of Sextus, tribe Quirina, pro-praetorian imperial legate for ordering [*ordinare*] both Mauretanias' (from a patronage 'contract' between the African city of Banasa and the governor of Mauretania in 75 CE, *L'Année Epigraphique* 1941, 79); 'To Caius Velius Rufus ... commander of the African and Mauretanian army tasked with crushing [*comprimere*] the tribes which are in Mauretania' (honorific inscription from Baalbek in Syria, late first century CE, *Inscriptiones Latinae Selectae* 9200).

It is worth noting that none of these texts tells us anything about the nature of the disturbance – though they are in each case the only evidence for the episode to which they refer.

They focus entirely on the forcible re-imposition of order by the agents of the Roman state. It is also clear from the conventions of the genre that the latter two texts are citing the terms of the men's appointments. The tropes of constriction are not a literary conceit; they were firmly entrenched in the language of the imperial administration. They embody a distinctively Roman conception of the imperial project as a difficult, almost physical task of holding a dynamic world in unnatural stillness. That project presupposed the presences of disruptive forces as part of the natural order. They expected dynamic forces to break out; and they were confident in their ability to restrain them. Far from being a challenge to Roman legitimacy, continued revolts were a precondition for it.

Paradoxically, the relative equanimity with which Tacitus and other Roman historians recorded revolt makes it all the more difficult to write an adequate social history. Strategies of inversion – tropes 'designed primarily to indicate the immorality, illegality, undesirability, barbarity, etc of insurgent practice' – were central to Guha's revisionist history of peasant revolt in colonial India. The problem with the Roman sources is that it is hard to see any so obvious attempt to delegitimise the revolts they describe. On the contrary, in the case of provincial rebellions Roman historians are quite happy to attribute grievances and aspirations to the rebels, which seem if anything to legitimise their revolts. But we cannot assume that this is an authentic representation of the rebels' aims. Writers like Tacitus ventriloquised through their rebels in the pursuit of their own agendas. The absence of any attempt to engage with and counter rebel discourse makes it extremely difficult to recover the aspirations and consciousness of any of the groups that challenged the Roman order.

Notes

1 Ancient texts are abbreviated as per P. Glare (ed.), *Oxford Latin Dictionary*, Oxford: Oxford University Press, 1982, pp. ix–xx. Thanks to Antti Lampinen and Chris Whitton for penetrating comments on an early draft, to Greg Woolf for inspiration and to Justine Firnhaber-Baker and the other participants in the conferences in which this book originated for providing a stimulating context in which to revisit these problems.
2 R. MacMullen, *Enemies of the Roman Order*, Cambridge, MA: Harvard University Press, 1966, p. 194.
3 For the thesis that the 'quietude and obedience' of Rome's subjects is best explained by their acceptance of Roman claims to rule rationally, see above all C. Ando, *Imperial Ideology and Provincial Loyalty in the Roman Empire*, Berkeley: University of California Press, 2000. On dispute resolution, see e.g. A. Z. Bryen, *Violence in Roman Egypt: A Study in Legal Interpretation*, Philadelphia: University of Pennsylvania Press, 2013, ch. 5.
4 A case made most strongly by G. E. M. de Ste Croix, *The Class Struggle in the Ancient Greek World: From the Archaic Age to the Arab Conquests*, London: Duckworth, 1981. See also C. F. Noreña, *Imperial Ideals in the Roman West: Representation, Circulation, Power*, Cambridge: Cambridge University Press, 2011, ch. 1.
5 T. Pekáry, 'Seditio. Unruhen und Revolten im römischen Reich von Augustus bis Commodus', *Ancient Society*, 18, 1987, pp. 133–50.
6 The best synthesis remains S. Dyson, 'Native revolt patterns in the Roman Empire', *Aufstieg und Niedergang der römischen Welt* II 3, 1975, pp. 138–75. See also S. Dyson, 'Native revolts in the Roman empire', *Historia*, 20, 1971, pp. 239–74; M. Goodman, 'Opponents of Rome: Jews and others', in L. Alexander (ed.), *Images of Empire*, Sheffield: Sheffield Academic Press, 1991, pp. 222–38; M. Goodman, 'Enemies of Rome', in P. Garnsey and R. P. Saller (eds), *The Roman Empire: Economy, Society and Culture*, London and New York: Bloomsbury, 2014, pp. 55–67.
7 B. D. Shaw, 'Bandits in the Roman empire', *P&P*, 105, 1984, pp. 3–51; see also B. Isaac, *The Limits of Empire: The Roman Imperial Army in the East*, Oxford: Oxford University Press, 1992, pp. 68–99 and B. D. Shaw, 'Rebels and outsiders', in A. K. Bowman, P. Garnsey, and D. Rathbone (eds), *The Cambridge Ancient History, Volume XI*, Cambridge: Cambridge University Press, 2000, pp. 361–403, at 387–8.
8 See especially G. Woolf, 'Roman peace', in J. Rich and G. Shipley (eds), *War and Society in the Roman World*, London: Routledge, 1993, pp. 171–94 and also G. Gambash, *Rome and Provincial Resistance*, New York and London: Routledge, 2015, ch. 4.

9 *Inscriptiones Latinae Selectae* 212; the revolt of CE 21 is discussed later in this chapter. See further Woolf, 'Roman peace', pp. 187–8 and Dyson, 'Native revolt patterns', p. 141.
10 Isaac, *Limits of Empire*, pp. 68–99, esp. 87–9.
11 Woolf, 'Roman peace'; Isaac, *Limits of Empire*; P. Le Roux, *L'armée romaine et l'organisation des provinces ibériques d'Auguste a l'invasion de 409*, Paris: Boccard, 1983.
12 Strategic: Gambash, *Rome and Provincial Resistance*, ch. 4. Ideological: Woolf, 'Roman peace'. On the ambition of Roman claims of peace-making, see M. Lavan, 'Peace and empire: *pacare, pacatus* and the language of Roman imperialism', in E. P. Moloney and M. S. Williams (eds), *Peace and Reconciliation in the Classical World*, Farnham and Burlington, VT: Ashgate, forthcoming.
13 See e.g. Dyson, 'Native revolt patterns'; Shaw, 'Bandits in the Roman empire'.
14 As such this chapter builds on moves by Greg Woolf to shift our focus from revolt to discourse about revolt: 'Provincial revolts in the early Roman empire', in M. Popović (ed.), *The Jewish Revolt against Rome: Interdisciplinary Perspectives*, Leiden: Brill, 2011 and 'Roman peace'.
15 R. Guha, 'The prose of counter-insurgency', in *Subaltern Studies II: Writings on South Asian History and Society*, Delhi, Oxford, and New York: Oxford University Press, 1983, pp. 45–85; R. Guha, *Elementary Aspects of Peasant Insurgency in Colonial India*, Durham, NC: Duke University Press, 1999.
16 Guha, *Elementary Aspects*, p. 14.
17 Ibid., p. 333.
18 Ibid., p. 106.
19 Ibid., pp. 15–17.
20 See especially A. J. Woodman, *Rhetoric in Classical Historiography*, London: Croom Helm, 1988 and A. J. Woodman (ed.), *Tacitus Reviewed*, Oxford: Oxford University Press, 1998.
21 For Mesopotamian discourses on revolt in the second and first millennia BCE, see S. Richardson, 'Writing rebellion back into the record: a methodologies toolkit', in *Rebellions and Peripheries in the Cuneiform World*, New Haven, CT: American Oriental Society, 2010, pp. 1–27 and the other essays in that volume.
22 Revolts by members of the imperial elite: E. Flaig, *Den Kaiser herausfordern. Die Usurpation im römischen Reich*, Frankfurt: Campus Verlag, 1992; R. MacMullen, 'How to revolt in the Roman empire', *Rivista storica dell'antichità*, 15, 1985, pp. 67–76, reprinted in *Changes in the Roman Empire*, Princeton, NJ: Princeton University Press, 1990, pp. 198–203. 'Native'/'provincial' revolts: see n. 6 above and also Woolf, 'Provincial revolts in the early Roman empire' and Gambash, *Rome and Provincial Resistance*. Social conflict within communities is a subject for which the early empire has proved fallow ground, but see e.g. A. Zuiderhoek, *The Politics of Munificence in the Roman Empire*, Cambridge: Cambridge University Press, 2009, pp. 66–70. Banditry: see n. 7 above. 'Non-state space': P. Thonemann, 'Phrygia: an anarchist history, 950 BC–AD 100', in *Roman Phrygia: Culture and Society*, Cambridge: Cambridge University Press, 2013, pp. 1–41, building on the ideas of J. C. Scott, *The Art of Not Being Governed: An Anarchist History of Upland Southeast Asia*, New Haven, CT: Yale University Press, 2009; see also the work of Shaw in n. 7 above.
23 Pekáry, 'Seditio'.
24 W. Kunkel, *Staatsordnung und Staatspraxis der Römischen Republik*, Munich: Beck, 1995, pp. 228–9.
25 T. Mommsen, *Römisches Strafrecht*, Leipzig: Duncker & Humblot, 1899, pp. 562–5.
26 W. Hoben, *Terminologische Studien zu den Sklavenerhebungen der römischen Republik*, Wiesbaden: Steiner, 1978, pp. 21–5.
27 See e.g. Goodman, 'Opponents of Rome: Jews and others', p. 227 for a more generous reading of the goals of some of these revolts.
28 Dyson, 'Native revolt patterns', pp. 156–8.
29 A. J. Woodman (ed.), *Velleius Paterculus: The Caesarian and Augustan Narrative (2.41–93)*, Cambridge: Cambridge University Press, 1983, p. 273.
30 The difference between *maxuma* and *maxima* is purely one of orthography (*maxuma*, the original spelling, being displaced by *maxima* by the imperial period). Tacitus always uses the new form.
31 A. J. Woodman and R. H. Martin, *The Annals of Tacitus: Book 3*, Cambridge: Cambridge University Press, 1996 *ad loc.* rightly note that *ferocia* is characteristic of barbarians, but exaggerate the contrast with the Sallustian language of criminality ('the quintessentially barbarian representatives contrast with the penurious and criminal elements' that follow). *Ferocia* is in fact a key characteristic of Sallust's Catiline. He is described as having an *animus ferox* in the famous character sketch (5.7) and again in his death scene where his face retains the *ferocia animi* it had in life (61.4). Note also the *ferocia* of his followers at 38.1, 43.4, and 52.18.

32 So already B. Walker, *The Annals of Tacitus: A Study in the Writing of History*, Manchester: Manchester University Press, 1951, p. 209, n. 8 ('Sacrovir's rebellion, joined by men like Catiline's followers') and Woodman and Martin, *Annals 3*, pp. 330–1. There are other echoes of Sallust in the narrative. The opening reference to a revolt begun *ob magnitudinem aeris alieni* recalls a speech by one of Catiline's co-conspirators (*propter magnitudinem aeris alieni, Cat.* 33.2).
33 J. Marincola, *Authority and Tradition in Ancient Historiography*, Cambridge: Cambridge University Press, 1997, pp. 12–19, especially 19: 'the appeal to tradition [through creative imitation] is itself a part of the historian's authority, for it is a shorthand used by the historian to identify his interests, approach and alliances'; D. S. Levene, *Livy on the Hannibalic War*, Oxford: Oxford University Press, 2010, ch. 2.
34 R. Syme, *Tacitus*, Oxford: Oxford University Press, 1958, p. 126.
35 C. S. Kraus, *Livy Ab Urbe Condita Book VI*, Cambridge: Cambridge University Press, 1994, p. 16, quoting Michel Serres.
36 A. R. Birley, 'The life and death of Cornelius Tacitus', *Historia*, 49, 2000, pp. 230–47.
37 Woodman and Martin, *Annals 3*, p. 329.
38 Contrast P. A. Brunt, 'The revolt of Vindex and the fall of Nero', *Latomus*, 18, 1960, pp. 531–59, reprinted in *Imperial Themes*, Oxford University Press: Oxford, 1990, pp. 9–32; and Dyson, 'Native revolt patterns', pp. 158–61.
39 J. H. W. G. Liebeschuetz, 'The theme of liberty in the *Agricola* of Tacitus', *Classical Quarterly*, 16, 1966, pp. 126–39; M. Lavan, 'Slavishness in Britain and Rome in Tacitus' *Agricola*', *Classical Quarterly*, 61, 2011, pp. 294–305.
40 Comment attributed to at 3.46.1, the Batavian revolt occupies almost two-thirds of Book 4 (4.12–37 and 54–79, 52 of 86 chapters) and half of what survives of Book 5 (5.14–26, where the transmitted text breaks off).
41 Comment attributed to Xiphilinus: U. P. Boissevain (ed.), *Cassii Dionis Cocceiani Historiarum Romanarum quae supersunt*, Leipzig: Weidmann, 1895–1901 *ad loc*. The brief note at 65(66).3.1–3 accounts for just half a page out of the 16 pages of text allocated to Book 65(66) in ibid.
42 See further E. Keitel, 'Speech and narrative in *Histories* 4', in T. J. Luce and A. J. Woodman (eds), *Tacitus and the Tacitean Tradition*, Princeton, NJ: Princeton University Press, 1993, pp. 39–58, at 41–3. This explains the unusual attention to Civilis's ulterior motives at the beginning of the narrative, which I noted above.
43 E. O'Gorman, 'Shifting ground: Lucan, Tacitus and the landscape of civil war', *Hermathena*, 158, 1995, pp. 117–31.
44 Guha, 'The prose of counter-insurgency'.
45 See especially S. Panciera, *Atti del Colloquio internazionale AIEGL su Epigrafia e ordine senatorio, Roma, 14–20 maggio 1981*, Rome: Ed. di storia e letteratura, 1982 and W. Eck, 'Die Struktur der Städte in den nordwestlichen Provinzen und ihr Beitrag zur Administration des Reiches', in W. Eck and H. Galsterer (eds), *Die Stadt in Oberitalien und in den nordwestlichen Provinzen des romischen Reiches*, Cologne: Philipp von Zabern, 1991, pp. 73–84 and A. Chastagnol, *Le sénat romain a l'époque imperiale: recherches sur la composition de l'assemblée et le statut de ses membres*, Paris: Les Belles Lettres, 1992, ch. 11.

2
TAKEHAN, COKERULLE, AND *MUTEMAQUE*

Naming collective action in the later medieval Low Countries

Jan Dumolyn and Jelle Haemers[1]

After 1280, the year in which a general wave of revolts struck the textile-producing cities of the Southern Low Countries and Northern France, two enigmatic and colourful proper nouns suddenly appear in the sources: *Cokerulle* and *Moerlemaye*. They refer to instances of collective action in Ypres and Bruges respectively.[2] Although historians and linguists have reached a consensus neither on the precise meanings of these names nor on their etymology, the most plausible explanation seems to be that they were derived from the shouts and gestures collectively produced by rebels during their turbulent meetings, strikes, and demonstrations. A comital inquiry, held on 3 April 1281, used the term *fait d'Ippre* (the event of Ypres), and the more general terms *li esmuete* (the mutiny) and *le meskeanche* (the bad handling), to refer to the Cokerulle rising, while in a letter written by the count dated two days earlier it was again described more generally as *mout de grief chas et de fais oribles ki selonc Dieu et raison ne doivent demorer sans etre amendei* (many serious cases and horrible facts which according to God and reason cannot remain unpunished). In a charter dated October 1283, however, Count Guy de Dampierre of Flanders refers to the revolt as *lequeil grief fait on apela et apele là meismes Cokerulle* (the grave event which was and is called Cokerulle in the place itself). 'Cokerulle' was supposedly a cry the rebels uttered as they were running through the streets, although the first source to state this explicitly is the jurist Filips Wielant's *Recueil des Antiquitéz de Flandre*, a text written two centuries later. It has been suggested that the word was related to the verb *kokerillen*, translated by the sixteenth-century linguist Cornelis Kiliaan as *celebrare hilaria* (cheerfully celebrating) which implies a sort of popular revelry possibly associated with Shrove Tuesday. Other philologists, however, have claimed either that the term was a bastardisation of *Kyrie Eleison*, meant to denote a popular song, which would also imply some sort of connection with carnivalesque behaviour and popular processions or, in our view less credibly, that it was derived from *coterelus*, meaning 'ruffian' or 'evildoer'.[3]

The term *Moerlemaeye*, *Mourlemai*, or *Muerlemaye* makes only two appearances within Middle French documents, in 1296 and 1297, and there is only one reference in Middle Dutch, in the form of a 1331 charter from Bruges itself. Contemporary city accounts simply refer to it as a *ceditio* (sedition) while the first comital inquiry of 1281 called it the *fait de Bruges* (the event of Bruges). Charters from 1280, the year of the rebellion itself, speak in general terms about *griefs, outrages, conspiracions, alliances* (griefs, outrages, conspiracies, and alliances) and *meffais* (misdeeds).

It seems plausible, however, that the name Moerlemaeye, like Cokerulle, also dates from the time of the event and was used either by those who participated in the revolt or by their adversaries. According to one historian it may be derived from the combination of *moerlen* or *moerelen* (shouting out loud) and *mayen* (fiercely waving one's arms), invoking the image of an agitated and noisy mob. Another scholar, however, interpreted *moerlen* or *morrelen* as a frequentative of *morren* (to mutter) while *maye* (or *mye* in a variant spelling) was supposedly a suffix to substantivise this verb. According to that etymology Moerlemaye would mean 'the muttering', as a *pars pro toto* for the entire revolt. Indeed, from an etymological point of view, the most plausible option seems to be that the Dutch *murmelen* (to mutter) was substantivised into *murmelye* (the muttering) and subsequently resulted in *murlemye* as a result of 'adjacent metathesis' (a linguistic phenomenon in which two contiguous sounds are switched).[4]

Moreover, the proper noun Moerlemaeye, which originally only referred to the Bruges rising of 1280–1, later clearly evolved into a common noun to denote popular collective action in general. Thus a fifteenth-century copy of a charter dealing with a revolt in Bruges in 1319–20 has the word *Moerlemaye* as its title, and the early fifteenth-century chronicle *Flandria Generosa C*, referring to the peasant rising of Cassel in 1429, uses the *groot moorlemay* (a Middle Dutch expression within this Latin chronicle) as a synonym for 'revolt' in general, while a Dutch elaboration of this Latin chronicle calls the revolt of Geraardsbergen in 1430 *vele moerlemaeys* (many moerlemaeys). Interestingly, there is no mention in this chronicle tradition of the Bruges Moerlemaeye of 1280–1 itself, suggesting that the name was remembered better than the event it originally denoted. But its origins were also not entirely forgotten two centuries later. In the early sixteenth century, Wielant, who gives an otherwise confused account of the Bruges revolt and wrongly dates it to 1282, also uses the name *Morlamay* (or in another manuscript of the text: *Moerlamay*). By now however, *moerlemaeye* (and its variants) had also become a generic term, and perhaps this was also the case for *cockarulle*, as suggested by an early sixteenth-century satirical text called 'The Confession of the Fool of Ypres', in which the word seems to denote a carnivalesque or 'charivari'-like procession of fools.[5] Even if, as a result of the infrequency of their attestations, full philological clarity eludes us with regard to these two fascinating terms they clearly appear to have a 'popular' origin. The words suggest links with the gestures, movements, and verbal utterances produced by an unruly urban populace, and perhaps also with the carnivalesque sentiment of 'the world turned upside down', features obviously not uncommon to medieval popular collective action in general.[6]

These two specific names do not stand alone. Between the thirteenth and sixteenth centuries, in the Southern Low Countries, a great variety of common nouns or 'generic terms' (*muete, roeringhe*...) were used to denote various forms of collective action, as were proper nouns, or 'personal names', for specific events (as well as Cockerulle and Moerlemaeye there was also *Good Friday, Hard Monday, Good Tuesday, the Terrible Wednesday of Pentecost,* the *Mal Saint-Martin*...).[7] Some of these signifiers described subversive speech acts and illegal gatherings (*murmuracie, ongheoorloofde verghaderinghe*...), others denoted types of public mobilisation (*loepe, wapeninghe*...), while others still derive from the context of labour conflicts (*takehan, ledichganck*...). Of course, the Low Countries are not the only regions where specific collective actions were sometimes given proper names. In England and Wales, for instance, insurgency was sometimes remembered by its leaders, as in the so-called 'Jack Cade rebellion' or the 'revolt of Owain Glyn Dŵr', both in the fifteenth century.[8] For France, Challet has shown that three revolts which took place at the same time around 1382 were named in different ways: in one the name of the rebel group itself provided a pejorative (the 'Tuchins' in the South), another evoked the popular cries ('La Harelle' in Rouen, but this term was also used elsewhere, derived from the rallying cry 'Haro'), and a third was named after the main weapons of the rebels (the

'Maillotins', in fact originally the 'Maillets' or mauls).[9] Lyon was known for its *Rebeynes* (apparently directly derived from *rebellionem*) and Angers for the *Tricoterie* (from *tricot* or 'club'). In 1477 a revolt in Dijon was named the *Mutemaque*, a term, interestingly, derived from the Middle Dutch *mute maecken* or 'to set up a mutiny'.[10] Rioting in the German-speaking world would also often be remembered by the names of participants, such as the *Knochenhauer* rebellion in Lübeck in the 1380s, which made reference to the butchers rising against the aldermen, and even the shabby shoes they wore, such as the *Bundschuh* in Baden and its surroundings around 1500.[11]

These signifiers, denoting popular collective action, are onomastic, etymological, and historical-anthropological sources in themselves. In many cases they can provide insight not only into how rebels experienced such events, how they distinguished between different types of mobilisation, and how they were judged by elites, but also into how they were later remembered in official memories and counter-memories. Most modern terms, such as rebellion (derived from *bellum* or war) or revolt (a 'turnover'), do not adequately reflect the actions and motives of medieval protesters. Yet if we consider terms such as 'revolt' and 'rebellion' to be part of social-scientific discourse, deprived of bias or connotations, these words can still be used to refer to political conflict. There are perhaps, however, better alternatives in the contemporary social sciences. In the context of medieval Europe, the term 'contentious politics', in the sense given to it by Charles Tilly and others, encompasses both violent protest, such as 'rebellions' or 'riots', and other 'collective actions', such as labour strikes or indeed any popular social and political action considered by the authorities as illegal.[12] Even so, there remains an inevitably artificial distinction between such categories on the one hand and the peaceful assembly of citizens and the legal or semi-legal utterance of grievances, such as petitioning, on the other. All protests, whether unlawful or authorised, were part of the same process of claim-making which the authorities may or may not have considered to be justified on any given occasion.[13] The 'legitimacy' of any collective action ultimately depended upon the balance of forces, the willingness of rulers to give in, the deliberations taking place during the events or afterwards, the final result of the action, and the ideas and memories of those who composed the available sources.

Even if we agree to use 'collective action' or 'contentious politics' in their broadest senses, as contemporary terms for that which we are dealing with in the present contribution, there still remain additional methodological problems in discussing the 'original' words and names for collective actions. Many of the proper names given to revolts are later inventions, like the so-called English 'Peasants Revolt' of 1381 which, as is now generally acknowledged, certainly did not only include peasants. The term itself is a product of Victorian historiography but earlier chronicle descriptions of the great rising had also referred to carnivalesque behaviour and 'rumours'.[14] Thus, many names or terms used to denote collective action clearly changed over time, modified by the mechanisms of oral transmission, by the more literarily inspired interventions of chroniclers and copyists, or sometimes also consciously to reframe the events by using terms with different connotations serving contemporary ideological purposes. The 'Bruges Matins' of 18 May 1302, for example, during which the Bruges rebels drove out the French occupying troops and killed many of them, received this name during the Romantic period in analogy with the name given to the so-called 'Sicilian Vespers' and was actually originally called the 'Good Friday' revolt.[15] Other names, including perhaps the most famous one, the *Jacquerie*, developed from a proper noun into a common noun, itself in all likelihood derived from 'Jacques Bonhomme', the archetypal peasant. It became a generic term for a rebellion, in this case any 'peasant revolt' (even though the Jacquerie was also not only a 'peasant revolt').[16]

Here we will prioritise names and terms found in documents which are contemporary with the events they describe, or in sources written shortly afterwards, but we shall also consider how changing names might offer some insight into the meaning of popular contentious politics. We focus on fourteenth- and fifteenth-century documents written in the vernacular (Dutch and French), but of course we realise that some of these terms are derived from a wide range of Latin words already present in the Bible, juridical documents, and clerical texts from earlier days. For instance, when writing about social upheaval, clerical authors in the High Middle Ages used words such as *commotio*, *seditio*, and *tribulatio*, often also referring to an existing discourse on disease (plague and epidemics), meteorological phenomena or natural disasters (storm, inundation, eruptions...), or biblical stories (on the Sins or the Devil).[17] Also treatises in the vernacular contained a more learned discourse, sometimes based on Latin manuscripts. For instance, by the late fourteenth century Jean Boutillier, a clerk of the city of Tournai, compiled the first custumal in the Low Countries which systematically listed and distinguished forms of political conflict: *sédition* involved violently plotting with others against a lord or his people, *monopole* concerned assemblies and strikes amongst the people themselves, and *conspiration* happened when similar such assemblies were organised in opposition to a prince. Revealingly, the son of one of the insurgents in Tournai in 1423 (Tassart Savary) owned a copy of this manuscript.[18] Yet our survey makes clear that far from all expressions were lent from learned discourse. Urban elites in the Low Countries developed a language on social conflict of their own, while the rebels themselves were also very creative in naming seditious events, as was true in other regions and languages. We will start with an analysis of the discursive register used by urban authorities to describe political protest in some of the main principalities of the Southern Low Countries. These are the counties of Flanders, Hainaut, Loon, Namur; the duchies of Brabant, Limburg, Luxemburg; the prince-bishopric of Liège; and the cities (and surroundings) of Mechelen and Tournai. The remarkable nomenclature of rebellion in these regions mostly had a pejorative connotation because the protest was described as harmful to the urban community in general and the ruling elite in particular. However, as we have shown in other publications, the popular classes of the late medieval Low Countries also maintained a lively memorial culture of rebellion that praised the subversive deeds of the past.[19] This 'counter-memory' of political subversion was used to legitimise rebellion, define group solidarity, and people identified with rebel heroes. So, both a pejorative and a euphemist discourse on collective action can be distinguished; much depended of course on the reason which the author of a source had for writing about the event.

Terms relating to legal repression and moral condemnation

Unsurprisingly, contemporary elite sources employ a consistently negative discourse in relation to collective action. This was inspired both by legal discourse and by a general medieval political ideology informed by theology, Aristotelian philosophy, 'mirrors for princes', and other normative texts. These elite discourses looked down upon the lower social orders who had to know their place in society and were denied political agency.[20] One interesting term, used in a Flemish literary source from the end of the fourteenth century, is *Kerels* (Churls). The Bruges song 'We want to sing of the Churls' depicts these men as primitive and dangerous ruffians who must be slain by the *ruters*, the mounted soldiers (as in the Middle French *routiers*). At first it was presumed that the term *Kerels* referred to the peasant rebels of the revolt of Maritime Flanders of 1323–8, in a similar fashion to the French *Jacques*. It has recently been suggested, however, that Kerels instead referred to urban rebels during the later revolt of 1379–85.[21] At any rate, in the song the rebels are also mocked as people who eat 'curd, whey, bread and cheese' (*wronglen, wey, broot ende caas*), the diet of the common people. This stereotype brings to mind the name of another revolt in the Netherlands, which took place in Haarlem, other smaller towns, and their surrounding area in Holland in 1491–2, during which the 'People of Cheese and Bread' (*tKasenbroots volck, commocie van Casenbroot, rebellichheyt genoemt tcaes ende broot*) carried with them depictions of these foodstuffs, protesting against their declining standard of living. They could now eat only bread, and no longer the dairy product essential to the diet of the working class.[22]

In examining the terminology used to denote collective action in chronicles and archival sources, we find that some terms have a moral as well as a legal dimension. 'Uproar' is one such (the English term is in fact a loan translation from the Middle Dutch *oproer*), while 'tumult' (Ghent, 1340)[23] 'troubles' (*beroerten*: Leuven, 1477),[24] and 'slander, discontent and sorrow' ('s-Hertogenbosch, 1450) all also emphasise the alleged bad intentions of the people and their unwillingness to behave properly.[25] A revolt in Limburg (the main city of the eponymous duchy to the east of Liège) in 1446 was called an 'insubordination', *en grant desrision de ceulx de la dicte loy* (in great contempt of the magistrate).[26] A document condemning the rising of the weavers of Bruges in 1360 manages to mention no fewer than ten terms which criminalised their deeds.[27] These terms all had the same purpose: justifying punishment and criminalising subversive or rebellious behaviour. Rebellious actions of this kind were 'misdeeds' (as they were called in Antwerp in 1435), 'bad adventures' (Brussels, 1306), or 'excesses and abuses against the highness and lordship' of the duke of Brabant (again in Brussels, 1446).[28] The meetings of the apprentices of Mechelen in 1361 and 1379 were denoted as a 'bad upset or quarrel' (*quaet opset ochte werringhe*).[29] A *conspiration*, another typical term, took place in Ypres in 1369, while *commocion* and *monopole* were also commonly used by chroniclers to describe protests or other collective actions against decisions made by urban or higher authorities which were considered to be unjust.[30] In short, there existed an extensive generic vocabulary to denote conflict, troubles, disobedience, and riots, terms which in many cases also developed a clear legal meaning, though with great variations in time and place rather than as a well-defined legal terminology. Of course, this is a widespread pattern in late medieval Europe.[31]

The predominant political ideal of medieval society was always one of harmony and unanimity under a just ruler while the political reality was often one of division and conflict between lords, social groups, factions, and parties, a phenomenon often closely intertwined with popular collective action.[32] For instance, typical terms in Flanders to describe factions included *convenances* (agreements), *bendes* (bands), *sects* (sections), or *partijlichede* (partiality), while general states of political discord were often described as *ghescille* (differences, conflicts), *werringhen* (feuds), *hayne* (hatred), *divisions et parcialitez* or *rancunes et divisions* (ill-will and divisions).[33] Also in other regions in the Low Countries, they spoke of 'unrest and factionalism' (*onrast ende partijscap*),[34] feuds (*feden*),[35] or 'wars of friends' (*guerres d'amys*) when factions took up weapons to fight each other.[36] In 1459 in the County of Hainaut, the Burgundian duke promulgated an ordinance forbidding the wearing of factional clothing. Unruly armed bands in the service of noblemen robbing and killing the people were also considered to be guilty of *meutemacquerie* or *mutemaque* (literally 'making mutiny'), the same Middle Dutch term as used in Dijon in 1477 and in some other French-speaking towns, who must clearly have been inspired to adopt this name by the frequency of collective actions in the Dutch-speaking cities of Flanders.[37] The terminology which described rebellion and factionalism was indeed quite similar and both were also close to the vocabulary of war. The violent factional struggle between the noble lineages of the Amans and the Waroux in Liège at the beginning of the fourteenth century, for instance, was described as 'the time of wars', or 'the time of feuds' (*le temps des werres*) by chronicler Jacques de Hemricourt. The term *werre* is derived from the Latinised Germanic word *werra* (also the root of the French *guerre* and English 'war'), and the distinction between the private feuds which took place between clans and families and the more 'political' factional struggles was a fine one.[38] Other chroniclers spoke about the *partialitatés* between these *partes dissidentes* who fought each other with their 'friends and kin' (*prismes et amis, amicis et consanguineis*).[39] This discourse, which identified rebellion with warfare and hatred, is perhaps most prominent between 1465 and 1467, when the future duke of Burgundy, Charles the Bold, faced violent opposition following his interference in the County of Loon and the Prince Bishopric of Liège. He described the military opposition to his reign as a 'war and rebellion' (*oorloghe ende rebelheden*), as one chronicler noted.[40] Similarly, in December 1465, 13 cities under the authority of Liège had to hand over their privileges because of the *guerres, divisions, et debatz* (wars, divisions, and conflicts) which had taken place *par l'ennort et seduction d'aucunes gens de mauvaise voulenté* (at the instigation and by the seduction of some ill-willed people). The cities were warned not 'to arm themselves or to incite to war' against the prince any longer.[41] Likewise in 1478 the citizens of Luxembourg who refused to accept the Burgundian dynasty as rightful heirs of the title of 'Duke of Luxemburg' were called *rebelles* and the *ennemis du pays* (enemies of the country). The term *rebellen* in Middle Dutch is less frequent, although it was, for instance, used in Bruges in 1360 to denote the weavers who had risen against the city government.[42]

Terms relating to dangerous speech acts, sounds, and bodily movements

As the proper nouns Cokerulle and certainly Moerlemaye would tend to suggest, many common nouns used for subversive political actions could also refer to speech acts. Verbal violence and rebellious speech were general features of the politics of the towns in the Low Countries.[43] A narrative on the Ghent revolt of 1452, for instance, mentions 'rumours' and 'agitation' which were 'produced among the people every day' as the craft guilds publicly questioned the policy of Duke Philip the Good.[44] Likewise, chronicler Wein van Cotthem, the continuator of the *Brabantsche Yeesten* chronicle, commented (around 1430, so some time after the event) that in the Brabantine city of 's-Hertogenbosch in 1386 the 'commonality started to mutter' (*murmureren*), as 'commoners within a city rarely remain calm for a long time'.[45] In Liège, chroniclers regularly complained about the *murmures* and *rumores* of the people, and the revolt in Bruges of 1488 was accompanied with 'shouting and crying in all the streets' (*roepinghen ende crijsschingen ... in allen straten*).[46] In 1477 in Leuven, rebels were punished because they 'had spoken out against those who had the regiment in the town'.[47] Fourteenth-century urban ordinances in Bruges and Antwerp forbade citizens to 'speak badly' about the governors and mention 'calumnies' which should not take place between members of guild communities.[48] A similar by-law was promulgated in Liège after the repression of a revolt by Bishop Adolf de la Marck in 1331. The people called it the *Loi de Murmure* as it forbade any inhabitant to 'move people to sedition by acts or words'.[49] Guilds were still allowed to meet and to discuss their business during their meetings, but no longer without prior consent of the urban authorities.[50]

Meetings where ordinary people communicated on matters of public interest in more organised or institutionalised ways were also often considered to be immoral and illegal.[51] In fifteenth-century Hainaut, 'alliances' (*alliancez*), 'oath-swearing' (*sermens*), 'assemblies' (*assamblees, verghaderinghe*), and, as we have seen above, wearing factional liveries which could divide the community, were not allowed. Of course, the fact that such restrictions were regularly repeated outlines that their effect was only limited.[52] Illicit 'gathering' was also a common term to describe unlawful meetings of artisans. In 1415, because of the recent upheaval which had taken place in Geraardsbergen, Duke John the Fearless forbade the inhabitants of this small textile centre, and its craftsmen in particular, to organise *aucunes assemblees ou convocacions quelxconques* (whatever kind of assemblies or meetings) without the consent of the authorities.[53] Similarly, any group of people organising for political objectives without the permission of the authorities could be accused of 'making alliances'. The Moerlemaye rebels of Bruges in 1280 were punished because 'they had made an alliance against the honour of the lord', and again in Bruges in 1386, the weaver Jan Groeninc was sentenced to death because, undoubtedly with some exaggeration, he 'had made an alliance, congregation and meeting in order to form an army to destroy all the good people'.[54] Aggravating circumstances included being armed or organising a meeting with a high level of secrecy. The revolt of the town of Limburg in 1446 was described as a 'bond' or 'league', set up by a 'gathering of a big commonality', which had not been disbanded after an initial warning by the authorities. The league had allegedly formed 'by force' and 'with violence' and this political crime was punished severely by the prince.[55] There were also other terms with the same meaning. Some of these implied an 'out in the open' character while others seem to have been of a more conspiratorial nature. In 1379 the weavers of Ghent had made a 'league and ratification' (*tverbind ende bezeghelte*), indicating a typical oath sworn to engage in political action.[56] While they were planning to go on strike in 1524, 'deliberated upset and illicit meetings' of the fullers and the weavers of Mechelen (*gedelibereerden opstel ende onbehoirlicke vergaderinge*) were prohibited. An earlier but similar 'secret conspiracy' (*heimelijc opset*) by the craftsmen of Leuven in 1360 was also strongly denounced by Wein van Cotthem in his above mentioned continuation of the history of Brabant.[57]

Justifying collective action

In contrast, in the letters, petitions, and occasional small chronicle fragments composed by the artisans or their guilds themselves, gatherings of craftsmen were considered to be legitimate actions. Their own vocabulary to describe meetings and rallies, although often overlapping with that of the authorities, always referred to customary law and to the rights and privileges they had obtained earlier. In a petition of 1378, for instance, the guildsmen of Leuven asked the duke of Brabant for the ratification of their 'right to gather' because it had been questioned by the urban elite after a rising. Just as they had done in a letter of alliance composed in 1360, the craftsmen called their actions simply a 'gathering' (*verghaderinghe*), unaccompanied by adjectives with a pejorative meaning such as 'illicit'.[58] Indeed, 'to assemble' seems to have been the most common verb by which protesters defined their collective actions, and in their own discourse this practice was often closely associated with notions like 'common consent' and 'unity'. In Ghent, in 1449, for instance, the assembled artisans stated that they had 'advised, deliberated and concluded unitedly' to hand over certain petitions to the authorities.[59] Also in Ypres (1369) and Bruges (1436) rebels focused on the fact that they had organised legitimate collective meetings and deliberations before complaining about the government of their cities.[60]

Another non-violent collective action undertaken by the guildsmen of the Low Countries which frightened the authorities was the so-called 'run' (*loop, gheloop, lopinghe,* or *uploop* or *oploepe doen* in Middle Dutch, and *course* and its variants in Middle French). This action was one of bodily movement rather than subversive speech; 'running through the town' or 'organising a run' meant demonstrating in order to reclaim urban space and its central symbolic places, whether in an orderly fashion similar to a procession or entry ceremony or in the more unruly manner of carnivalesque revellers.[61] Thus, as a *pars pro toto*, the revolt in Limburg in 1446 was referred to as the *lopinghe*.[62] During the so-called 'Bad Wednesday' (*Quade Woensdach*) of 4 August 1311, several craftsmen organised such a 'run' in Ghent, ending in a fight killing sympathisers of the Count. The comital charter which followed the event forbade the people from Ghent to organise a 'run with or without banners' again (*gheloepe dat nu gheweest hevet met banieren of sonder banieren*).[63] Banners were a common feature of popular collective action throughout medieval Europe, and in Ypres in 1380 they were unfolded everywhere as craftsmen ran towards the market square 'with open banners' (*met opener banieren*).[64] In 1401 a much smaller-scale attempt was made to cause a riot, but it was nevertheless considered dangerous. Antwerp citizen Lippyn de Keysere was forced to go on a pilgrimage to Santiago de Compostella because he had 'behaved badly in a tavern and elsewhere, and had run against the good men of town with fierce words'.[65] In this context it is worth remembering that 'mutiny' or 'commotion', and hence also typical medieval terms like *esmeute* in French or *meute* in Dutch, contain a strong element of 'movement' in their etymology as well as their 'emotional' component of 'stirring up the people'.[66] These variants are among the most common terms for collective action. For instance *moyeterien* took place in Mechelen in 1389, while the Brussels revolt of the weavers and butchers in 1360 was again described as a *meutemaquerie* by the fifteenth-century court chronicler Jean de Wauquelin.[67]

The terms used for more specific types of collective action usually referred to certain characteristics, such as the use of banners, the armaments of guild militias, the ringing of bells, or the way in which a labour strike was organised. The act of gathering in the central square of the city was known as an 'armament' (a *wapeninghe*). These armed gatherings in which rebel artisans would occupy a central place within their city, usually an important market square, normally started with a shout (a *roep* or *roepinghe*), as in the case of the *wapeninghe* at the Corn Market in the city of Ghent in 1353. Sound was also an important element of this armed assembly, with the rebels shouting 'Down with the thirteen aldermen', and 'Abolish the tax on the Ghent beer'.[68] The related term *auweet*, from the French *au guet* ('stand guard') was also used in Ghent, Bruges, and other cities to refer to episodes in the turbulent history of the town in which craftsmen had assembled in arms.[69] Terms like 'bell ringing' (*clockenslagen*) in Veurne in 1324, *beckergeslach* (hitting on cymbals) in a Leuven revolt in 1360, or 'running with the banner' in Ghent in 1479 were all words and expressions associated with popular sounds and movements, each again serving as a *pars pro toto* to denote an uprising.[70]

Strikes and *takehans*

The *leechganc* or *ledichganck*, which literally means 'going idle' in the sense of collectively withholding productive labour from the community, was a general term used to describe a strike action, such as that in Bruges in 1344, or in Ghent in 1366.[71] Workers collectively leaving the city was even more serious. This type of action was called an *uutganck*, literally a 'walkout'. At the beginning of the sixteenth century, for instance, such walkouts were organised by the fullers in Mechelen and Hasselt in response to the introduction of fulling mills in these cities. In Mechelen, they typically assembled in taverns outside the city to discuss further plans.[72] Labour strikes, however, were already a common feature of urban politics by the mid-thirteenth century, when artisan and guild actions are first clearly recorded in the Southern Low Countries and Northern France. In this context, undoubtedly the most intriguing term is the word *takehan*, alternatively spelt *taskehem*, *taquehein*, *taquehan*, or *taquehain*. It first appears in Douai (1244), and shortly afterwards in other industrial cities like Arras and Abbeville; it is mentioned in Paris (1286), Rouen (1290), and during the fourteenth century is also found in the Champagne region, apparently spreading towards other regions in France. This rather mysterious term has traditionally been thought to describe a tumultuous and illegal assembly of workers, a conspiracy against their employers and the city government. Du Cange also understood it as a *conventus illicitus*, *conspiratio*, or *turba* (illicit meeting, conspiracy, or turmoil). In this sense a takehan is a secret meeting or any gathering during which the artisans collectively decided to stop working until the authorities gave in.[73] A *conspirationem sive taquehanum* against the aldermen and mayors of Arras in 1285 was described in the registers of the *Parlement de Paris*, the central royal court of France. The guilds, which from 1253 onwards had lost the right autonomously to organise themselves, defied the authorities and their bad management of the city, and ran through the town with their standards, a forbidden act of self-organisation as they had no right to use these banners without the town government's authorisation. They also symbolically seized a reliquary chest in which a candle of the Blessed Mary was kept. With good reason, Carol Symes has emphasised the principles of equal association and mutual support displayed in this type of collective action.[74] A takehan was clearly not a spontaneous riot; it was a well-organised action of artisans who asserted their material and symbolic power within the town.

But how should the word itself be explained? The internal letter -h- suggests a Germanic origin of the word but it has not been preserved in any Middle Dutch texts. The earlier explanation by Von Wartburg, according to which takehan refers to the gesture and sound of clapping one's hands (the related French word *taquin* means *frappeur*), may be considered colourful but far-fetched. In a later contribution Wartburg suggested that it was instead derived from the Germanic form *taken* (to take something violently) and *Han* for 'John', giving a comic name for a man of the lower classes, similar to *Jaques Bonhomme*.[75] More careful analysis of the historical documents in which this word appears may shed new light upon the philological debate. Although the origins of the term remain obscure, most historians implicitly agree that *takehan* means a 'labour strike', as this is clearly the context in which it appears. In his *Coutumes de Beauvaisis* (1283), the contemporary Northern French jurist Philippe de Beaumanoir describes such *aliances fetes contre seigneur ou contre le commun pourfit* (alliances made against the lord or against the common profit). Participants in this alliance agreed no longer to work for lower salaries than they had had before, trying instead to increase their wages, and yet the term takehan, although a contemporary one, is not employed in this text.[76] In January 1245, the city government of Douai mandated a fine of 60 pounds and one year's banishment from the city for whoever *face takehan*, be it a man or a woman. Furthermore, it was also forbidden to organise an *asanlée encontre le vile, de quel mestier ke ce fust* (an assembly against the city, by whichever craft guild).[77] In another urban ordinance of Douai, dated around 1250, a distinction was made between [faire] *takehan*, [faire] *asanlée* and someone who *laisce oevre* or impedes the work of others, in other words someone who strikes.[78] Finally, another ordinance by the aldermen of Douai strictly outlawed the giving of help or advice to people who organised a *takehan* or an *assanlée ki fust contre le vile*, or to those who obstructed or disturbed the work of others. Perpetrators would be fined 50 pounds and banished for a year.[79]

These juxtapositions seem to imply that a takehan was something other than merely an unauthorised gathering or a labour strike. All scholars who have mentioned the takehan seem to agree that this word, which is first used in sources from the French-speaking area of Flanders and its neighbouring regions, seems to have spread from there to Northern and Central France in general, and is of Germanic, probably Dutch origin. Indeed, there is an Old Dutch verb *takan* which means 'to take'. Similarly, a later Middle Dutch form *taecke* means a measure, a part, or portion which one takes, as in a 'tax'. A *taecke* can also be a measure of wine, and a *takecanne* is a jug which contains such a measure.[80] A fourteenth-century bylaw enacted by the aldermen of Béthune forbids the textile workers *que nul ne faiche ban ne taskehem ne autre assise de sen mesthier* (so nobody would organise a levy, or a takehan or any other taxation of his craft guild).[81] This passage suggests that a *taskehem* was a kind of *assise* or tax. A charter from Charles V of France, in 1375, confirms earlier rights given to the communes of Meulan and Les Mureaux (on the Seine, near Paris). These towns had abandoned their commune to their lord, the Count of Evreux, in exchange for payment of their debts, but they still explicitly retained many privileges, among which was the right to *se pourront assembler pour eulx conseiller et tailler senz ce quil puist estre dit Taquehan* (assemble in order to consult among themselves and gather money, without this being called a takehan).[82]

Within the context of thirteenth-century textile workers, such a contribution was probably an internal tax to build up a charity fund or 'box'. In later Middle Dutch sources these 'mutuality boxes' belonging to the craft guilds are called *bussen* and it is clear that they were also used as potential strike funds. This was the reason that urban governments were always very suspicious of this practice. An ordinance issued by the so-called *huit hommes* or *eswardeurs* of the Douai weavers, dated between 1261 and 1287, does not explicitly mention the term takehan but it does forbid *assanler le kemun ne por rouver deniers ne por prendre deniers* (to assemble the commoners neither to ask for money nor to take it) without the permission of the aldermen.[83] This document also points to the practice of making voluntary or forced contributions to a strike fund, or at least to that of gathering money in preparation for any potential collective action. All the evidence considered, it seems right to conclude that the take in takehan means exactly that: a tax within a trade, agreed by an alliance, from which everyone contributed his 'portion' of the solidarity fund. But the word can also refer to socio-economic collective action in general. In addition to the sources associated with workers in the artisanal industries, the *Dictionnaire du Moyen Français* also includes references to merchants, who *eussent fait taquehan ensemble* (made takehan together), suggesting a meaning related to monopole, in the sense of a cartel to agree on prices. This is something both artisans and merchants could establish.[84] Meetings of the innkeepers of Lille in 1434 were also called 'monopoles'. The latter had met and taken advice on the procedure for handing over a petition, when in fact they were prohibited from doing so.[85] Yet another etymological possibility (in the *lectio difficilior*-principle in textual criticism according to which the most difficult reading is the strongest one) is that takehan it is a composed word from both Romanesque and Germanic origin. The Old Picard *tasque* (later take and modern French *tâche*) is the amount of work someone needs to carry out, literally one's 'task' and thus can also be associated with a 'working class organisation' while the Germanic root *hemmen*, common to different old Germanic languages, means 'to obstruct'. Takehan would thus be a hybrid form alluding to a strike.[86] The term takehan should perhaps be simultaneously associated both with an illegal gathering, 'alliance', or 'monopoly' and with the money gathered in such meetings. Or is there another explanation for the suffix -*han*? Could this be derived, as Wartburg suggested, from the given name Han (Jan or John) which was the most common forename in the medieval Low Countries and perhaps denoted 'a common man', in a connection similar to that between the French name Jacques and the *Jacquerie* rising? Were Pirenne and Espinas right in associating it with 'hands'? Or does -*han* only denote a derived meaning, as in 'the gathering of the tax'? At any rate, the evidence and the various etymological hypotheses seem to suggest that 'takehan' refers to any 'alliance', any collective action with a primarily socio-economic goal, including setting up strikes, other forms of workers' solidarity, and gathering money for that purpose. By the fourteenth century it had become a general French term but after that it again disappeared.

Parallels can be drawn here with the word 'guild', which is derived from the West Germanic *geld* – the sum paid to join the guild – and also with the merchant *hanse* or *hansa*, which can mean both the subscription fee and the organisation itself. Such associations emerged in the twelfth and thirteenth centuries in the Low Countries, such as the *Hanse* of Bruges, or the *Gilde* of Leuven and Mechelen, three associations of cloth merchants trading on long distance.[87] Though these were elites gathering for economic purposes, these associations can also be considered as conspiracies (in the meaning of *conjuratio*), referring to the names given to the twelfth-century communes on the one hand, and rebel gatherings in the later Middle Ages on the other. Indeed, each of these movements had the same purpose: assembling people with a common background and collective claims. Unsurprisingly, fourteenth-century urban craftsmen would use the same linguistic register to describe their associations in the decades of their political awareness. Just as their fellow citizens some centuries earlier, they used words as *gild* when referring to practices of money gathering for collective purposes. For instance, in 1255, the *decani guldarum*, the deans of the guilds, took over the urban government in Sint-Truiden (a town in the prince-bishopric of Liège) in a successful attempt to destroy the political and economic monopoly of the wealthy merchants. The fullers, shearers, and weavers clearly assembled money within these *guldes* since 1237, which they spent for charity though not without interference of the main abbey in the town. The rebellion of 1255 freed them of this paternalism.[88] In 1280, the Bruges aldermen had ordered 'all citizens who had collected money in commonality' to hand these sums over to the authorities.[89] Clearly, the ordinance referred to the artisans who had participated in the Moerlemaye, mentioned earlier in this text. The Dutch word which the artisans used for 'commonality' was *meentucht*, a loan translation of the Latin *communitas*. Indeed, in the 1280s but also in the centuries to come, the craftsmen regularly would use the terminology of *meentucht* and *gemeente* to describe themselves. As we have shown elsewhere, on such occasions the 'commoners' used the discourse on the 'commune' with the aim to participate in the government of town.[90]

Conclusion

The history of medieval contentious politics cannot be reduced to political quarrels or armed confrontations; it is also a history of discursive conflicts. To paraphrase Pierre Bourdieu, naming and classifying social upheaval is always a permanent struggle between groups who are unequally equipped to attain absolute vision. The symbolic power of naming creates social and even legal power; it either maintains the social order or subverts it.[91] The discursive struggles between 'rebels' and the authorities about the name of a collective action was not only a struggle about definitions, but also one about political recognition and dominance. Perhaps, gaining the upper hand in such a conflict was as important as a military victory, because those who were victorious could decide the name given to the event. The denotations and connotations of these common and proper nouns would influence opinions and memories in the near future, and indirectly either justified and inspired collective action in the following centuries or condemned it as illegal and immoral. Naming conflicts was an essential feature of late medieval popular politics. As a result, names and words referring to collective actions were certainly not chosen arbitrarily. They were coloured by the opinion and beliefs of the people participating in the rebellion *or* the authorities suppressing it. Yet, both the authorities and their opponents used a common discursive register to legitimise their respective political actions. 'Takehan', 'guild', 'gathering' etc. referred to the associations which both elite citizens and the urban commoners made to express wishes and claims, while names like Cokerulle and Moerlemaye or a term like 'loepe' seem to have denoted the speech acts and bodily movements they used in mobilising for action. Surely, both the rebels as well as the authorities had a very different opinion on the nomenclature of these forms of collective action. While the latter would describe an armed assembly of artisans as 'mutiny', the 'mutineers' themselves would speak of a 'gathering' and would certainly not consider their political action 'illegal'. A more linguistically oriented history of medieval revolts to a large degree remains to be written. This short overview of names and terms used to denote revolts in the Low Countries should perhaps be geographically extended to come to a general comparative overview for medieval Europe to analyse if, apart from the names and terms imposed 'from above', similar patterns occur whereby specific names refer to particular speech acts or bodily movements or to forms of solidarity and organisation from below.

J. Dumolyn and J. Haemers

Notes

1 We dedicate this chapter to Daniel Lievois (1940–2014), historian of medieval Ghent. We thank Claire Hawes for correcting our English, professor emeritus Luc De Grauwe for his very helpful etymological suggestions, and Justine Firnhaber-Baker and Dirk Schoenaers for their very useful comments on the first version of this chapter.
2 F. Hooghe, 'De Cokerulle (1280–1285): een conflict tussen Ieper en zijn hinterland over de lakennijverheid', *Handelingen van het Genootschap voor Geschiedenis*, 143, 2006, pp. 393–443; M. Boone, 'Social conflicts in the cloth industry of Ypres (late 13th–early 14th centuries): the Cockerulle reconsidered', in M. Dewilde, A. Ervynck, and A. Wielemans (eds), *Ypres and the Medieval Cloth Industry in Flanders: Archaeological and Historical Contributions*, Zellik: Instituut voor het Archeologisch Patrimonium, 1998, pp. 147–55; A. Bardoel, 'The urban uprising at Bruges, 1280–81: some new findings about the rebels and the partisans', *Revue belge de philologie et d'histoire*, 72, 1994, pp. 761–91.
3 R. De Keyser, 'Cokerulle en Moerlemaye', *Verslagen en mededelingen van de Koninklijke Vlaamse Academie voor Taal- en Letterkunde*, 1965, pp. 369–78; H. Eymael, 'Kokerellen', *Tijdschrift voor Nederlandse Taal- en Letterkunde*, 11, 1892, pp. 82–92; G. Doudelez 'La révolution communale de 1280 à Ypres', *Revue des questions historiques*, 133, 1939, p. 26; G. Espinas and H. Pirenne (eds), *Recueil de documents relatifs à l'histoire de l'industrie drapière en Flandre*, 7 vols, Brussels: Kiessling et Imbreghts, 1906–66, vol. 3, pp. 102–4, 679, 691; J. J. De Smet (ed.), *Corpus chronicorum Flandriae*, Brussels: Hayez, 1865, vol. 4, p. 289: *et coururent avant la vile arengiez par longues renges et crians 'covela ville'* (or 'cockerulle' in ms. B). See also G. Hendrix, 'Cokerulle – Kyrie Eleison – coterel', *Biekorf*, 67, 1966, pp. 153–5; A. Viaene, 'Moerlemaye en Cokerulle: in het museum van onze historienamen', *Biekorf*, 70, 1969, pp. 299–303; L. Warnkoenig and A. Gheldolf, *Histoire de la Flandre et de ses institutions civiles et politiques jusqu'à l'année 1305*, Brussels: Hayez, 1864, vol. 5, p. 68.
4 The adjacent-metathesis hypothesis seems to be the most credible one. We thank Luc De Grauwe for his expert opinion on this matter.
5 C. Wyffels, 'Nieuwe gegevens betreffende de 13de eeuwse "demokratische" stedelijke opstand: de Brugse "Moerlemaye" (1280–1281)', *Bulletin de la Commission royale d'histoire*, 132, 1966, pp. 39–40, 109, 128–37; De Keyser, 'Cokerulle en Moerlemaye', pp. 381–2; De Smet, *Corpus chronicorum*, vol. 1, p. 160. This is also the case in some of the Middle Dutch elaborations of this chronicle, the *Excellente Cronike van Vlaenderen*, see for instance Bruges, Public Library, Ms. 436, fol. 167r and J.-J. Lambin (ed.), *Dits de cronike ende genealogie van den prinsen ende graven van den foreeste van buc, dat heet Vlaenderlant*, Ypres: Lambin, 1839, pp. 307–10 (but not in another version of the same text: Ms. 437, fol. 268r); Douai, Bibliothèque Municipale, Ms. 1110, fol. 170r; De Smet, *Corpus chronicorum*, vol. 4, p. 290; I. Diegerick, 'Le fou d'Ypres', *Annales de la Société d'Emulation pour l'étude de l'histoire et des antiquités de la Flandre*, 15, 1857–61, pp. 143–6.
6 See also H. Skoda, *Medieval Violence: Physical Brutality in Northern France, 1270–1330*, Oxford: Oxford University Press, 2013, pp. 181–92.
7 We will elaborate on these names which specifically denote revolts by using chronological and liturgical elements in a forthcoming publication.
8 I. Harvey, 'Was there popular politics in fifteenth-century England?', in R. Britnell and A. Pollard (eds), *The McFarlane Legacy*, New York: St Martin's Press, 1997, pp. 167–8. See for instance, I. Harvey, *Jack Cade's Rebellion of 1450*, Oxford: Clarendon Press, 1991; R. Davies, *The Revolt of Owain Glyn Dŵr*, Oxford: Oxford University Press, 1995.
9 V. Challet, 'L'exclusion par le nom: réflexions sur la dénomination des révoltés à la fin du Moyen-Âge', in N. Gonthier (ed.), *L'exclusion au Moyen Âge*, Lyon: Université Jean Moulin, 2007, pp. 373–88; F. Chauvau and P. Prétou (eds), *Clameur publique et émotions judiciaires de l'Antiquité à nos jours*, Rennes: Presses universitaires, 2014, pp. 13–14; M. Mollat and P. Wolf, *Ongles bleus, Jacques et Ciompi: les révolutions populaires en Europe aux XIVe et XVe siècles*, Paris: Calmann-Lévy, 1970.
10 M. Tournier, 'Émotion populaire: petite note lexicologique', *Mots: Les langages du politique*, 75, 2004, pp. 121–5; M. Tournier, *Propos d'étymologie sociale*, Lyon: ENS, 2002, vol. 1, pp. 33–66; A. Voisin, 'La "mutemaque" du 26 juin 1477: notes sur l'opinion à Dijon au lendemain de la réunion', *Annales de Bourgogne*, 7, 1935, pp. 337–56.
11 A. von Brandt, 'Die Lübecker Knochenhaueraufstände von 1380–84 und ihre Voraussetzungen. Studien zur Sozialgeschichte Lübecks in der zweiten Hälfte des 14. Jahrhunderts', in K. Friedland and R. Sprandel (eds), *Lübeck, Hanse, Nordeuropa. Gedächtnisschrift für Ahasver von Brandt*, Köln: Böhlau, 1979, pp. 129–208; P. Blickle and A. Thomas (eds), *Bundschuh. Untergrombach 1502, das unruhige Reich und die Revolutionierbarkeit Europas*, Stuttgart: Steiner, 2004.

12 C. Tilly, *Contentious Performances*, Cambridge: Cambridge University Press, 2008.
13 S. K. Cohn, Jr., *Popular Protest in Late Medieval English Towns*, Cambridge: Cambridge University Press, 2013, pp. 27–33; P. Lantschner, 'Revolts and the political order of cities in the late Middle Ages', *P&P*, 225, 2014, pp. 3–46.
14 See the chapter by Andrew Prescott in the present volume.
15 A. Viaene, 'De Brugse Metten als historienaam', *Biekorf*, 53, 1952, pp. 90–2: it was J. Kervyn de Lettenhove, *Histoire de Flandre*, Brussels: Beyaert-Defoort, 1847, vol. 2, pp. 448, 454, who invented this term which has, unjustifiably, become the standard name for the event in the historiography.
16 N. Bulst, '"Jacquerie" und "Peasant's Revolt" in der französischen und englischen Chronistik', in H. Patze (ed.), *Geschichtsschreibung und Geschichtsbewusstsein im späten Mittelalter*, Sigmaringen: Thorbecke, 1987, pp. 791–819 and see J. Firnhaber-Baker, in this volume.
17 Examples in C. Mauntel, *Gewalt in Wort und Tat. Praktiken und Narrative im spätmittelalterlichen Frankreich*, Stuttgart: Thorbecke, 2014, p. 226.
18 A discussion of the text in P. Lantschner, *The Logic of Political Conflict in Medieval Cities: Italy and the Southern Low Countries, 1370–1440*, Oxford: Oxford University Press, 2015, pp. 25–7. The text of Jean Boutillier (*Somme rurale ou le gran coustumier général de practique civil et canon*) was printed in 1603; see G. Van Dievoet, *Jehan Boutillier en de Somme rurale*, Leuven: Leuvense Universitaire Uitgeverij, 1951. Furthermore, Boutillier's text was printed in Bruges by Colard Mansion in 1479 (during a period of turmoil).
19 J. Haemers, 'Social memory and rebellion in fifteenth-century Ghent', *Social History*, 36, 2011, pp. 443–63; J. Dumolyn and J. Haemers, 'Let each man carry on with his trade and remain silent: middle-class ideology in the urban literature of the late medieval Low Countries', *Cultural and Social History*, 10, 2013, pp. 169–89.
20 See on this the introduction to J. Dumolyn, J. Haemers, H. R. Oliva Herrer, and V. Challet (eds), *The Voices of the People in Late Medieval Europe: Communication and Popular Politics*, Turnhout: Brepols, 2014.
21 H. Brinkman, 'Een lied van hoon en weerwraak: "Ruters" contra "Kerels" in het Gruuthusehandschrift', *Queeste*, 11, 2004, pp. 1–43.
22 J. Scheurkogel, 'Het kaas- en broodspel', *Bijdragen en Mededelingen betreffende de Geschiedenis der Nederlanden*, 94, 1979, p. 190.
23 N. De Pauw (ed.), *De voorgeboden der stad Gent in de XIVe eeuw (1337–1382)*, Ghent: Annoot-Braeckman, 1885, p. 35.
24 R. Van Uytven, '1477 in Brabant', in W. Blockmans (ed.), *1477. Het algemene en de gewestelijke privilegiën van Maria van Bourgondië voor de Nederlanden*, Kortrijk: UGA, 1985, p. 257.
25 *Smaden, ongenuechten ende verdriete* (P. Godding (ed.), *Ordonnances de Philippe le Bon pour les duchés de Brabant et de Limbourg et les pays d'Outre-Meuse, 1430–1467*, Brussels: Service public fédéral justice, 2005, p. 293).
26 *Wederspennige' and 'beruerte, ongehoirsaamheit ende hanteringe* (Godding (ed.), *Ordonnances de Philippe le Bon*, pp. 254 and 257).
27 *Gescillen, discorden, niden, viantscepen, mesdaden, manslachten, quetsinghen, scaden ende verliesen, beroerten* (J. Mertens, 'Woelingen te Brugge tussen 1359 en 1361', in *Album Carlos Wyffels*, Brussels: [n. n.], 1987, p. 330).
28 *Misdaet, misdaen ende mesgrepen* (Godding (ed.), *Ordonnances de Philippe le Bon*, p. 140), *quade avonturen* (H. Vandecandelaere, 'Een opstand in "zeven aktes": Brussel, 1303–1306', *Cahiers Bruxellois*, 40, 2009, p. 61), *grans exces et abus par eulx commis et perpetrez contre nostre haulteur et seignourie* (Godding (ed.), *Ordonnances de Philippe le Bon*, p. 244).
29 R. Joossen, 'Recueil de documents relatifs à l'histoire de l'industrie drapière à Malines (des origines à 1384)', *Bulletin de la Commission royale d'histoire*, 101, 1935, p. 450.
30 R. Verbruggen, *Geweld in Vlaanderen: Macht en onderdrukking in de Vlaamse steden tijdens de veertiende eeuw*, Bruges: Van de Wiele, 2005, p. 69.
31 Comparable terms such as *concursus, conjuratio, aufrure, crieg, zweyung, twidracht, missehel, geschelle, stozze, ufflauf, samelung, bannerlop, wapenlop* etc. were used in German-speaking territories of the Holy Roman Empire: A. Haverkamp, '"Innerstädtische Auseinandersetzungen" und überlokale Zusammenhänge in deutschen Städten während der ersten Hälfte des 14. Jahrhunderts', in R. Elze and G. Fasoli (eds), *Stadtadel und Bürgertum in den italienischen und deutschen Städten des Mittelalters*, Berlin: Duncker & Humbolt, 1991, p. 100; B. Hergemöller, *Uplop – Seditio. Innerstädtische Unruhen des 14. und 15. Jahrhunderts im engeren Reichsgebiet*, Hamburg: Kovac, 2012, *passim*; P. Monnet, *Villes d'Allemagne au Moyen Âge*, Paris: Picard, 2004, pp. 157–61.

32 P. Strohm, *Hochon's Arrow: The Social Imagination of Fourteenth-Century Texts*, Princeton, NJ: Princeton University Press, 1992, p. 31.
33 J. Braekevelt, F. Buylaert, J. Dumolyn, and J. Haemers, 'The politics of factional conflict in late medieval Flanders', *Historical Research*, 85, 2012, p. 17.
34 Brussels in the 1440s (Godding (ed.), *Ordonnances de Philippe le Bon*, pp. 190, 241, 280).
35 Luxemburg, 1481 (when the party of the Behaingnons fought against Maximilian of Austria, see R. Petit, 'Le Luxembourg et le recul du pouvoir central après la mort de Charles le Téméraire', in Blockmans (ed.), *1477*, p. 433).
36 Namur, 1477 (C. Douxchamps-Lefevre, 'Le privilège de Marie de Bourgogne pour le comté de Namur (mai 1477)', in Blockmans (ed.), *1477*, p. 239); Tournai, 1424 (Lantschner, 'Revolts and the political order', p. 39).
37 *Plusieurs grans seigneurs s'efforchoient ou dit pays de avoir grant cantité de compaignons portans leurs robes de livrees et devises, et tellement que par manière de grant compaignie et meutemacquerie, les dis compaignons se assambloient en festes et en ducasses, attoient et decoppoient gens.*
(J.-M. Cauchies, *La Legislation princière pour le Hainaut, ducs de Bourgogne et premiers Habsbourg (1427–1506)*, Brussels: Service public fédéral justice, 1982, p. 497).
38 For concrete examples, see the publication quoted in n. 33. A similar consideration can be found in the introduction of J. B. Netterstrøm and B. Poulsen (eds), *Feud in Medieval and Early Modern Europe*, Aarhus: Aarhus University Press, 2007.
39 C. Masson, 'La guerre des Awans et des Waroux: une "vendetta" en Hesbaye liégeoise (1297–1335): deuxième partie', *Le Moyen Âge*, 119, 2013, p. 695; G. Xhayet, 'Lignages et conscience lignagère au pays de Liège pendant la guerre des Awans et des Waroux (ca. 1295–1335)', *Actes du 4e congrès des Cercles francophones d'Histoire et d'Archéologie*, 2 vols, Liège, 1994, vol. 2, pp. 319–33.
40 *Dits die Excellente Cronike van Vlaenderen*, Antwerp: W. Vorsterman, 1531, fol. 216r.
41 *Item, que lesdis de Liege et pays ne pourront jamais eulx armer ne mouvoir guerre ... a l'encontre de mon dit seigneur*. This concerned the cities of Tongeren, Sint-Truiden, Thuin, Fosses, Couvin, Borgloon, Hasselt, Herk-de-Stad, Maaseik, Bree, Bilzen, Beringen, and Dilsen-Stokkem (S. Bormans (ed.), *Recueil des ordonnances de la principauté de Liège*, Brussels: Gobbaerts, 1878, pp. 591 and 594).
42 L. Gilliodts-Van Severen, *Inventaire des archives de la ville de Bruges*, Bruges: Gailliard, 1877, vol. 3, p. 233. For Luxemburg, see Petit, 'Le Luxembourg', pp. 424–5.
43 J. Dumolyn and J. Haemers, '"A bad chicken was brooding": subversive speech in late medieval Flanders', *P&P*, 214, 2012, pp. 45–86.
44 *Dewelke zeere veele remours ende onleede maecten daeghelijcs onder tfolc* (*Kronyk van Vlaenderen van 580 tot 1467*, P. Blommaert and C. P. Serrure (eds), Ghent: Annoot-Braeckman, 1840, vol. 2, p. 112).
45 *Ende die ghemeinte op die heren begonden vaste te murmureren ... want die ghemeinte die can selden lange stille geliggen op een stat* (J.-F. Willems (ed.), *De Brabantsche Yeesten of Rymkronyk van Braband*, 3 vols, Brussels: Hayez, 1839–69, vol. 2, p. 279).
46 I. Diegerick, *Correspondance des magistrats d'Ypres députés à Gand et à Bruges pendant les troubles de Flandre sous Maximilien, duc d'Autriche, roi des Romains*, Bruges: Vandecasteele-Werbrouck, 1853, p. 86. For Liège in 1320 and 1408, see G. Xhayet, *Réseaux de pouvoir et solidarités de parti à Liège au Moyen Âge (1250–1468)*, Geneva: Droz, 1997, pp. 341–3.
47 *Der gemeynten woorde te spreken jegen dieghoene die dbewyndt hadden* (Van Uytven, '1477 in Brabant', p. 264).
48 *Die enen andren oploep dade met worden ende qualec toesprake omme eeneghe saken die hi vore den here sochte ochte begherde in rechte* (C. Serrure, *Dit sijn de coren van der stad Antwerpen*, Ghent: Annoot-Braeckman, 1852, p. 7); *Dat ... zy elcandren paisible laten zullen zonder eeneghe upsprake of uploop te doene in eenigher manieren* (Gilliodts-Van Severen, *Inventaire des archives*, vol. 2, p. 330).
49 Bormans (ed.), *Recueil des ordonnances*, p. 217; C. Masson, 'La Paix de Fexhe, de sa rédaction à la fin de la principauté de Liège', *Bulletin de la Commission royale des anciennes lois et ordonnances de la Belgique*, 47, 2006, p. 200.
50 *Quiconcques metterat le communalteit delle citeit de Liege ensemblez sens mandement especial ou commandement exprez dez mestiers ou dez conseilhiers deseur dis, parlerat d'aultre chose que cheu pour quoy on l'arat assemblee, et ilhe ne se taise tantoist* (Bormans (ed.), *Recueil des ordonnances*, p. 219).
51 Dumolyn and Haemers, '"A bad chicken"', p. 37.
52 Such ordinances were promulgated in 1435, 1437, 1440, 1442, 1447, and 1463 (J.-M. Cauchies (ed.), *Ordonnances de Philippe le Bon pour le comté de Hainaut, 1425–1467*, Brussels: Service public fédéral justice, 2010, pp. 138, 156, 176, 203, 246, 368).

53 J.-M. Cauchies (ed.), *Ordonnances de Jean sans Peur, 1405–1419*, Brussels: Service public fédéral justice, 2001, p. 385.
54 1280: *vous aieis fait alience contre leneur mon seigneur . . . et vous soieis mesfait* (C. Wyffels, 'Nieuwe gegevens', p. 107); 1386: *une alianche, congregacion et asanblee pour faire une armée afijn k'yl peust destrure toute bonne gens* (J. Mertens, 'Twee weversopstanden te Brugge (1387–1391)', *Annales de la Société d'emulation de Bruges*, 110, 1973, p. 8).
55 *Beruerten ende versamingen van groten menichten van hen, verbonde ende opsetten om bij malcanderen te bliven ende nyet te scheyden makende, forche, mit gewalt* (Godding (ed.), *Ordonnances de Philippe le Bon*, pp. 254–5).
56 Espinas and Pirenne (eds), *Recueil des documents*, vol. 2, p. 560.
57 G. Willemsen, 'La grève des foulons et des tisserands en 1524–1525, et le règlement général de la draperie Malinoise de 1544', *Bulletin du Cercle archéologique, littéraire et artistique de Malines*, 20, 1910, pp. 118–20; Willems (ed.), *Brabantsche Yeesten*, vol. 2, verse 7074.
58 J. Haemers, 'Governing and gathering about the common welfare of the town: the petitions of the craft Guilds of Leuven, 1378', in R. Oliva Herrer, V. Challet, J. Dumolyn, and M. A. Carmona Ruiz (eds), *La comunidad medieval como esfera publica*, Seville: Secretariado de publicaciones Universidad de Sevilla, 2014, pp. 153–69.
59 *Ghemeenlic vergadert zynde . . . hebben eendrachtelic gheadvyseert, ghedelibereert, overeenghedreghen ende ghecon-clueert* (V. Fris (ed.), *Dagboek van Gent van 1447 tot 1470, met een vervolg van 1477 tot 1515*, 2 vols, Ghent: Annoot-Braeckman, 1901–4, vol. 1, p. 72).
60 Verbruggen, *Geweld in Vlaanderen*, p. 69; J. Dumolyn, '"Rebelheden ende vergaderinghen": twee Brugse documenten uit de grote opstand van 1436–1438', *Bulletin de la Commission royale d'histoire*, 162, 1996, p. 300.
61 M. Boone, 'Armes, coursses, assemblees et commocions: les gens de métiers et l'usage de la violence dans la société urbaine flamande à la fin du Moyen Âge', *Revue du Nord*, 87, 2005, pp. 1–33. *Courses* is also used in French sources in general and in Italy as well *correre la città* was a metaphor for urban turmoil, see R. Trexler, 'Correre la terra: collective insults in the late Middle Ages', *Mélanges de l'Ecole française de Rome. Moyen Âge, Temps Modernes*, 96, 1984, pp. 872–91.
62 Godding (ed.), *Ordonnances de Philippe le Bon*, p. 256.
63 J. Vuylsteke, *Uitleggingen tot de Gentsche stads- en baljuwsrekeningen, 1280–1315*, Ghent: Annoot-Braeckman, 1906, p. 188. *Bannerlop* and *wappenlop* were also general terms used in German chronicles to denote revolts, see P. Monnet, 'Les révoltes urbaines en Allemagne aux XIVe siècle: un état de la question', in M. Bourin, G. Cherubini, and G. Pinto (eds), *Rivolte urbane e rivolte contadine nell'Europa del Trecento: un confronto*, Florence: Firenze University Press, 2008, p. 111.
64 Verbruggen, *Geweld in Vlaanderen*, p. 114; see on the use of banners in Flanders: J. Haemers, 'A moody community? Emotion and ritual in late medieval urban revolts', in E. Lecuppre-Desjardin and A.-L. Van Bruaene (eds), *Emotions in the Heart of the City (14th–16th century)*, Turnhout: Brepols, 2005, pp. 63–81.
65 *Onredelic ghewandelt heeft in tavernen ende eldere, ende goeden lieden oploep ghedaen heeft met fellen woerden* (J. van den Branden, 'Clementynboek (1288–1414)', *Bulletin des Archives d'Anvers*, 25, 1920, p. 369).
66 Tournier, 'Émotion populaire', p. 121. See also B. Chevalier, *Les bonnes villes de France du XIVe au XVIe siècle*, Paris: Aubier Montaigne, 1982, p. 299.
67 See, respectively, L. Maes, *Vijf eeuwen stedelijk strafrecht: Bijdrage tot de rechts- en cultuurgeschiedenis der Nederlanden*, Antwerp: De Sikkel, 1947, p. 322; *Chronique des ducs de Brabant par Edmond de Dynter (avec la traduction française de Jehan Wauquelin)*, P. De Ram (ed.), Brussels: Hayez, 1854, vol. 2, p. 569.
68 'De XIII schepenen af'; 'Of de XII miten van den Gentsche biere' (V. Fris, 'Les origines de la réforme constitutionnelle de Gand de 1360–1369', *Annales du XXe congrès de la fédération archéologique et historique de la Belgique*, 3, 1907, p. 440). On the phenomenon of the *roep* to start a collective action, see J. Dumolyn, '"Criers and shouters": the discourse on radical urban rebels in late medieval Flanders', *Journal of Social History*, 42, 2008, pp. 111–35.
69 For instance in 1346: *Ten aweyten ende ten wapeninghen* (N. De Pauw and J. Vuylsteke, *De rekeningen der stad Gent: Tijdvak van Jacob van Artevelde, 1336–1349*, 3 vols, Ghent: Annoot-Braeckman, 1874–1885, vol. 3, p. 120). About Bruges: J. Haemers and E. Lecuppre-Desjardin, 'Conquérir et reconquérir l'espace urbain: le triomphe de la collectivité sur l'individu dans le cadre de la révolte brugeoise de 1488', in C. Deligne and C. Billen (eds), *Voisinages, coexistences, appropriations: Groupes sociaux et territoires urbains du Moyen Age au 16e siècle*, Turnhout: Brepols, 2007, pp. 119–43.
70 Veurne: Verbruggen, *Geweld in Vlaanderen*, p. 103; Leuven: A. Schayes, *Analectes archéologiques, historiques, géographiques et statistiques concernant principalement la Belgique*, Antwerp: Buschmann, 1857,

p. 364; Ghent: *ende liepen met hueren bannieren uut haren huusen* (Fris (ed.), *Dagboek van Gent*, vol. 2, p. 254), see also V. Fris, 'L'émeute de Gand en février 1479', *Bulletin de la Société d'histoire et d'archéologie de Gand*, 17, 1909, pp. 184–97.

71 J. Dumolyn, 'The vengeance of the commune: sign systems of popular politics in late medieval Bruges', in Oliva Herrer *et al.* (eds), *La comunidad medieval*, p. 283; D. Nicholas, *The Metamorphosis of a Medieval City: Ghent in the Age of the Arteveldes, 1302–1390*, Lincoln: Nebraska University Press, 1987, p. 130. See also J. Haemers, 'Ad petitionem burgensium: petitions and peaceful resistance of craftsmen in late medieval Flanders and Mechelen, 13th–16th centuries', in J. Solorzano Telechea, B. Arizaga Bolumburu, and J. Haemers (eds), *Los grupos populares en la ciudad medieval Europea*, Logroño: Instituto de Estudios Riojanos, 2014, pp. 371–94.

72 See for the *uutganc* of the fullers of Mechelen in 1524: Willemsen, 'La grève des foulons', p. 117; and the *uutgenge van den volres* of Hasselt in 1508: J. Gessler, 'Die Pierts. Topografische, taal- en geschiedkundige aanteekeningen over en om het Peertshuis in de Peertsdemerstraat te Hasselt', *Verslagen en mededelingen van de Koninklijke Vlaamse Academie voor Taal- en Letterkunde*, 1922, p. 150. The context in R. Van Uytven, 'The fulling mill: dynamic of the revolution in industrial attitudes', *Acta Historiae Neerlandica*, 5, 1971, p. 10.

73 G. Espinas, *La vie urbaine de Douai au Moyen Âge*, 4 vols, Paris: Picard, 1913, vol. 1, pp. 226–69.

74 C. Symes, *A Common Stage: Theatre and Public Life in Medieval Arras*, Ithaca, NY: Cornell University Press, 2007, pp. 200–4.

75 W. von Wartburg, 'Glanures étymologiques', *Revue de linguistique romane*, 24, 1960, pp. 292–3.

76 P. de Beaumanoir, *Coutumes de Beauvaisis*, A. Salmon (ed.), 2 vols, Paris: Picard, 1899–1900, vol. 1, p. 446. See also Tournier, *Propos d'étymologie sociale*, vol. 1, p. 24.

77 Espinas and Pirenne (eds), *Recueil des documents*, vol. 1, p. 22.

78 Ibid., pp. 92–3.

79 Ibid., p. 109.

80 See the lemmas 'takan' and 'taken' in both dictionaries, available online on http://gtb.inl.nl.

81 Espinas and Pirenne (eds), *Recueil des documents*, vol. 1, p. 315.

82 E. de Laurière and D. F. Secousse (eds), *Ordonnances des rois de France de la troisième race*, 22 vols, Paris: Imprimerie royale, 1723–1849, vol. 6, p. 139.

83 Espinas and Pirenne (eds), *Recueil des documents*, vol. 1, p. 104.

84 It refers to a mention in *Le Compte des recettes et dépenses du roi de Navarre en France et en Normandie de 1367 à 1370*, E. Izarn (ed.), Paris: Picard, 1885, p. 172.

85 *Que eulx taverniers se avoient assemblé en certain lieu* and *tenu leurs conseils et monopoles* (G. Espinas, *Les origines du droit d'association dans les villes de l'Artois et de la Flandre française jusqu'au début du XVIe siècle*, 2 vols, Lille: Raoust, 1941–2, vol. 2, p. 387).

86 This is the opinion of Professor emeritus Luc De Grauwe whom we again thank for his advice.

87 J.-P. Peeters, 'Het verschijnsel der gilden en hanzen in de middeleeuwse steden in de Nederlanden', *Revue belge de philologie et d'histoire*, 62, 1984, pp. 271–88.

88 In 1237, the fullers and shearers already gathered money for charity in Sint-Truiden (for this and the revolt of 1255, see J. Charles, *La ville de Saint-Trond au Moyen Âge: Des origines à la fin du XIVe siècle*, Paris: Belles Lettres, 1965, pp. 228, 296). Similar examples for other towns of the Low Countries can be found in C. Wyffels, *De oorsprong der ambachten in Vlaanderen en Brabant*, Brussels: Koninklijke Vlaamse academie voor wetenschappen, letteren en schone kunsten van België, 1951, pp. 97–9.

89 *Lieden die ghelt ghegadert hebben in meentuchten* (Wyffels, 'Nieuwe gegevens', p. 103).

90 J. Dumolyn and J. Haemers, 'Reclaiming the common sphere of the city: the revival of the Bruges commune in the late thirteenth century', in J.-P. Genet (ed.), *La légitimité implicite*, 2 vols, Paris: Publications de la Sorbonne, 2015, vol. 2, pp. 161–88. Also in late medieval German and Spanish towns, the 'commune' would remain a point of reference for insurgents, see G. Naegle and J. Solorzano Telechea, 'Geschlechter und Zünfte, prinçipales und común. Städtische Konflikte in Kastilien und dem spätmittelalterlichen Reich', *Zeitschrift für Historische Forschung*, 41, 2014, pp. 574–5.

91 P. Bourdieu, 'The social space and the genesis of groups', *Theory and Society*, 14, 1985, pp. 732–3.

3
THE EPONYMOUS JACQUERIE
Making revolt mean some things[1]

Justine Firnhaber-Baker

Labelling an activity makes it mean something. The decision to term a group of actions a 'revolt' or an 'uprising' today has profound implications for interpretation, just as calling them 'rumours' or 'takehan' went to the very heart of the perception and reception of contentious political acts 600 years ago. The word 'jacquerie' is no exception. In English, as in French, the word has meant 'a peasant revolt, especially a very bloody one' since the nineteenth century.[2] But what the modern term's medieval eponym, the French Jacquerie of May–June 1358, actually meant to its observers and participants is a curiously underexplored subject. Only one scholarly monograph, published in the nineteenth century, has ever been written, and since then fewer than a dozen articles have appeared, the most cogent of them written by Raymond Cazelles over 30 years ago.[3]

In the intervening decades, historians' understanding of later medieval uprisings has changed considerably. While earlier scholars saw events like the Jacquerie as explosions of economic misery, social hatreds, or millenarian mania,[4] there has been a general shift to interpreting popular protests as rational and as predominantly political in their objectives and organisation. So for Samuel Cohn, Jr. the impetus for rebellions after the Black Death was political liberty, while John Watts and Patrick Lantschner have shown that much of what we might now view as abnormal and disorderly behaviour against authority can actually be reimagined as continuations of normal political processes by people who were not so much opposed to the state as critical of its weaknesses or hungry for a piece of the action.[5] This tight focus on the political dimension may ultimately have to be broadened, particularly as the negotiation of power in the Middle Ages encompassed realms of activity and thought habitually excluded from modern politics.[6] Still, these reassessments have produced a robust and profound reorientation of scholarly interpretation: rather than assume we know what a revolt is based on our own (or at any rate more modern) experiences of authority and dissent, we must actively interrogate the meaning that contemporaries ascribed to their actions.[7]

That the Jacquerie has not benefited from this kind of methodological and conceptual reassessment partly stems from the vividness of the received picture of it as a bloody, spontaneous uprising that needs no explanation: i.e. a *jacquerie*. The problem is also empirical: the disposition of the sources and the complex historical circumstances surrounding the uprising have meant that scholarship has been almost exclusively dedicated to the basic problem of figuring out what happened. The sources mainly consist of five chronicle groups, all available in modern editions, and around 200 letters of royal pardon (*lettres de rémission*) for participants in the revolt, most of which are only available in manuscript at the Archives nationales de France.[8] The narratives sources offer an aggregated overview of the event, but they do not always accord with one another or even with themselves, as I will discuss below. The remissions, on the other hand, frequently contain a narrative portion detailing the recipient's crimes, which gives a granular picture of the revolt but which also requires extensive geographical and prosopographical work in order to make sense of the narrative. Still, these difficulties would hardly present an intractable problem, were it not for the fact that the Jacquerie came at a particularly confused moment in French history.

Two years earlier, the English had defeated the French army at the Battle of Poitiers and captured King John II.[9] As a result, a power vacuum arose in the capital, which the young Dauphin Charles mishandled. The government of the realm fell to the assemblies of the three estates (the clergy, the nobles, and the burghers) known as the Estates General (*États généraux*), which were dominated by the Parisian merchant, Étienne Marcel, and the bishop of Laon, Robert le Coq. King Charles II of Navarre's presence in and around Paris further complicated the situation. Possessing a large army, a reasonable claim to the French throne, and a sizeable grudge against King John, he was a valuable ally to the Parisian rebels but a dangerous entity in his own right. On 22 February 1358, Marcel led a mob to the Dauphin's private chambers, where they killed two of the Dauphin's marshals, and by the late spring of 1358, the Prince, now allied with the Northern French nobility, had mobilised to retake Paris by force. He garrisoned fortresses at Meaux on the Marne River and Montereau on the Seine, which cut off Paris' supply lines, and he began recruiting an army. It was at this point that the Jacquerie broke out. Scholarship on it has thus always been divided between two camps: one that sees it as the result of collusion between the Jacques and the Parisians and one that holds that the Jacques acted independently.

These empirical problems have hampered more methodologically sophisticated investigations, but, ironically, they are essentially insoluble without the kind of methodological reassessment of the meaning of revolt that recent historiography offers. Past interpretations of the Jacquerie have all started from the assumption that the revolt had *a* meaning that we can excavate from the documentation, assume from the social position of the perpetrators, and/or infer from the historical context. But as social scientists and our own experiences tell us, the motivations and perceptions of those involved in any large-scale collective action are multiple and mutable.[10] The Jacquerie was an event experienced and shaped by tens of thousands of people; its interpretation necessarily differed from person to person and from community to community. Nor were these interpretations fixed, but rather developed and changed during the rebellion and through the acts of repression and memory and forgetting that followed.[11] But this does not mean that those meanings were limitless or that they are impossible to investigate. The language of the sources, the organisation and objectives of the rebellion, and the violence itself all offer clues to the significance that contemporaries ascribed to the revolt. These windows on to the Jacquerie roughly correspond to the perspectives of the social classes in play: the nobles, the townspeople, and the Jacques themselves. None of them necessarily tells us the 'truth' about the Jacquerie. Rather they illustrate the multiplicity of meanings that the Jacquerie could have had and the dangers of sublimating those meanings to a single explanation.

Language and narrative: after the fact

The search for meaning ought naturally to begin with language, but it is important to recognise that in a sense language is where the Jacquerie itself ended, for we only get sources after the revolt had been put down. We have no documents from the Jacquerie itself: no letters of the type Steven Justice analysed for the English Rising of 1381, no songs or poems of the kind we have for the Hussites.[12] In fact, almost everything dates from after the Dauphin retook Paris in August 1358, that is to say, almost a month after the end of the Jacquerie, and many sources, particularly the narrative ones, were written years or decades later than that. Only the chronicle of Jean le Bel may be contemporaneous, but it is still the product of some distance and reflection. Produced after the fact, the documents are nearly unanimous in describing the Jacquerie in emotional and social terms as a disorganised terror unleashed against the nobility by country dwellers.

Let us begin with the remissions, these letters of pardon issued by the crown for participants in the revolt and its suppression. The words chosen to label the Jacquerie suggest that the royal chancery perceived and presented the Jacquerie as an event whose import was more affective than political. The word *Jacquerie* turns up very early, noting the contents of a letter of remission (*Chartre de Jacquerie*) in a royal register from 1360, but the example is unique to my knowledge.[13] *Jacques*, used for the participants, comes up somewhat more frequently and earlier, in a remission from October 1358 (*pluseurs des Jaques de la dite ville*).[14] In neither of these cases is the word defined, though a remission of December 1358 says that the *Jacques* were people from the countryside (*les gens du plat pais nommez Jaques*).[15] Words with political connotations, like *rebellion* and *esmeute*, do appear occasionally (in 7 and 4 per cent of documents, respectively), but in the overwhelming preponderance of cases, the chancery preferred either *commotions* or *effroiz*. Thirty-seven per cent of the remissions use the word *commotions*, 53 per cent use *effroiz*, and 13 per cent employ both words, often together with other terms like *monopoles*, *comspirations*, or *assemblees*.[16]

These words were both relatively rare in normal chancery usage, and both had strong emotional valences. *Commotions* means violent physical shocks, and its Latin root *commotio* was used not only for uprisings but also for earthquakes.[17] The word *effroiz* means fears or terrors. In Middle French, the word had connotations of noise and disarray, as well as military associations similar to its English relative 'affray'.[18] *Le Robert dictionnaire historique* identifies its Latin root as *exfridare*, to exit from peace, though DuCange thought it came from *efferare*, meaning to make savage or brutal.[19] The apolitical, social, and emotional nature of the Jacquerie that is apparent from word-choice is also emphasised in the formula that is employed in about a third of the remissions: The first part of this formula describes the supplicant's crime as that of 'having been with others of the neighbouring countryside in the terrors which were recently committed by the people of the countryside against the nobles of the realm' (*aient este avec plusieurs autres du pais danviron aus effroiz qui derrainement & nagaires ont este faiz par les diz genz du dit plait pais contre les nobles du dit Royaume*).[20]

The affective language used for the Jacquerie stands in contrast to that used for the Parisian rebellion led by Marcel and le Coq against the Dauphin. Letters of remission issued to their partisans portray their activities exclusively in political terms as treason, *lèse-majesté*, and an attack on the crown. The formula often employed in remissions for Parisian partisans states that the supplicant was implicated in 'great treasons, rebellions, conspiracies, armies, cavalcades, attacks and disobediences ... by committing public force and the crime of lèse-majesté against our lord [King John II], us [the Dauphin], and the crown of France' (*grans traisons, rebellions, conspirations, armees, chevauchees, invasions & dessobeissances ... en commettant force publique & crime de leze mageste envers & contre nostre dit seigneur nous & la couronne de France*).[21] Those remissions do sometimes use emotional language, but they do so in order to describe the interior political state of the supplicant, who had always been 'a good Frenchman' (*bon & loyal francois*) in his 'heart and mind' (*en cuer et en pensee*) despite his misdeeds, rather than to evoke the project's madness or its victims' terror.[22]

Chronicle accounts, our other main source for the Jacquerie, echo the emotional tone adopted by remissions for the Jacques. The chronicles are broadly in agreement: the Jacques acted cruelly and irrationally against their target, the nobles, who were terrified. The most famous narrative accounts, those of the chivalric chroniclers Froissart and his source, Jean le Bel, describe the nobles fleeing the Jacques in terror, dressed only in their shirts and carrying their children piggy-back, the women in Froissart's tale being particularly overcome with fear (*moult ... effraées*).[23] The emotional language is amplified by their reportage that the Jacques had no prior organisation or leadership (they were *san chief*) and their account of the Jacques' deeds, which in their telling include killing children, gang-raping women, and roasting a knight on a spit. The English Anonimalle chronicler took this theme yet farther, accusing 'Jak Bonehomme' of revelling in the blood of foetuses torn from their mothers' wombs and so forth.[24] But even less overwrought writers, such as the stolid Norman chronicler, emphasised that the Jacques acted cruelly and without mercy (*moult cruelement, sanz pitié*).[25] The Picard peasant turned monk usually identified as Jean de Venette, often considered the Jacques' most sympathetic reporter, nevertheless characterised the rising as a monstrous business, an unheard of thing, and vile and evil works (*negotium monstruosum, casus inauditus, opera vilia et nefanda*).[26] The chroniclers attribute the rising to the Jacques' wickedness or insanity: Jean le Bel and Froissart blamed insanity (*rage* or *forsenerie*), while the royal chronicler attributed the Jacquerie to demonic inspiration (*mauvais esprit*).[27] Again, these are interior, affective explanations, rather than political or circumstantial ones.

It is an obvious point but an important one that the chronicles' language is at least as indicative of their contexts of composition and the perceptions of literate elites as it is of the realities of the Jacquerie. Marie-Thérèse de Medeiros argued that Jean le Bel and especially Froissart's stories about the Jacques were strongly influenced by their chivalric ethos, not to mention their aesthetic objectives.[28] Less widely noted but no less critical to interpretation is the way that Jean de Venette fitted the Jacquerie's inversion of social order into an overarching narrative of miracles, wonders, and portents; the entry for 1358, for example, begins 'new marvels [*mirabilia*] were piled atop old'.[29] Nor are the archival sources necessarily any more transparent.[30] The lawyers and the chancery clerks who produced the remissions did not have the kind of elaborately considered narrative programmes of the chroniclers, but they did have their own compositional conventions. And as Natalie Davis has shown, those who came before the crown to beg for remission were just as interested as Froissart in story-telling, perhaps all the more so when their lives and goods hung in the balance.[31]

In both the chronicles and the remissions, though, there are places where the stories break down. If we look at that handful of royal documents related to the Jacquerie that were issued before the Dauphin retook Paris at the beginning of August and started granting remissions in large number, we do not seem to be dealing with quite the same event as the noisy Terror against the nobles (*effroiz contre les nobles*) familiar from later on. There are two remissions issued in July, both for noblemen involved in suppressing the Jacques. One, issued for the lords of Grancy and Saint-Dizier alleges that the 'communes' of the Perthois and Champagne had conspired to kill them, as well as other noblemen and their wives and children, but non-nobles, as well as nobles are said to have got together to put down this conspiracy; the letter mentions the non-nobles' participation several times.[32] The second remission, for two squires in Picardy, presents the crown as a target of the revolt alongside the nobles, characterising the people of the countryside who had attacked nobles as 'enemies and rebels of our lord [king] and us' (*ennemis et rebelles de nostre dit seigneur et de nous*).[33] In addition to these remissions, in June and July the Dauphin issued two donations of Jacques' property to noblemen serving in his army and granted a market franchise to a knight who had been victimised by the revolt. These grants also identify the crown as a target of the Jacques, and they speak of the uprising in terms similar to those used for the Parisian rebellion, as an attack on and even a war (*guerra*) against the royal majesty.[34]

But once the Dauphin retook Paris, the language changed. Possibly this happened because better information became available, or possibly the Dauphin and/or the chancery made a decision to portray the Jacquerie's relation to the crown and the nobles differently.[35] Once victorious, the Dauphin issued a general remission for all the crimes committed in Paris, during the Jacquerie, and during the wave of noble vengeance that had followed.[36] In individual remissions issued from August onward the crown is represented as an arbiter between the nobles and the Jacques, attempting to reconcile them after their discord. The formula which follows the description of the Jacquerie as *effroiz contre les nobles* states that the nobles now hated the country dwellers and wanted to hurt them, and that the Dauphin, having returned to Paris and remitted the crimes on both sides, requires them to forgive one another (*avons ordenne que touz les diz nobles remettent & pardonnent aus diz genz du plait pais, et aussi les dites genz aus diz nobles*).[37] The crown thus removed itself from the conflict, which was thenceforth portrayed as a binary confrontation between the country dwellers (*les gens du plat pays*) and the nobles. The documents that precede that effort, though, suggest that there was a time when other narratives were possible, when the crown might have understood the Jacquerie as something other than a terror against the nobility and might have seen itself as equally targeted.

We can also see change in meaning over time in the chronicles of Jean le Bel and Froissart. As is well known, Froissart incorporated much of Jean le Bel's chronicle into his work, but there is a significant gap between their compositions. Jean le Bel was writing more or less contemporaneously with events in 1358, while Froissart probably produced this part of his chronicle at least 30 years later.[38] Their accounts of the Jacquerie are very similar, in some places word for word, but there are places where they differ. Both writers portrayed the Jacques as a leaderless, frenetic mob, but towards the end of his account, Jean le Bel offers several attempts at explanation that are at odds with this picture, explanations which Froissart decided to omit. Having narrated the Jacques' atrocities at some length, Jean le Bel says 'It is hard to see how these horrid people in far-flung places came to act together at the same time' (*On se doibt bien esmerveillier dont ce courage vint à ces meschans gens en divers pays loing l'ung de l'aultre et tout en ung mesme temps*).[39] He speculates that perhaps it was the fault of tax collectors who were frustrated that peace with England meant they were out of a job, though he also says that people suspected that Étienne Marcel, Robert le Coq, and Charles of Navarre were behind it. He then goes on to talk about the revenge the nobles took against the Jacques, but at the very end of the chapter he returns to the problem of organisation in a passage whose multiple changes of direction make it difficult to translate:

> One can hardly believe that such people would have dared to undertake such devilry without the help of some others, especially in the kingdom of France. In the same manner [as nobles discussed in the previous passage] the Lord of Coucy summoned people from wherever he could get them; thus he attacked his neighbours and destroyed them and hanged and killed them in such a horrible way as it would be terrible to remember; and these bad people had a captain called Jacques Bonhomme, who was a complete hick [*parfait villain*] and who tried to claim that the bishop of Laon had urged him to do this, for he was one of his men. The Lord of Coucy also did not like that bishop.[40]

Gerald Nachtwey has argued that Froissart's omission of these passages stems from his efforts to explain the Jacquerie as a symptom of a systematic social malaise, a challenge to chivalry in which the aristocrats eventually triumph.[41] This seems self-evidently true, but his explanation for Jean le Bel's original inclusion of these passages is less convincing. Nachtwey argues that being closer to the terrifying events of the Jacquerie, Jean le Bel needed someone to blame and structured his narrative to point the finger at particular individuals, but the passages do not read as if they are part of a considered narrative framework. Rather, they appear more like afterthoughts or interruptions where the chronicler realised he had something he did not fully understand, but being committed to the truth he had to include anyway.[42] The first passage is sandwiched between his accounts of the Jacquerie's outbreak and the nobles' revenge, and the second is simply tacked on to the end of the chapter and moves back and forth in a few lines between different topics, first talking about organisation, then describing the response of the Lord of Coucy, then suddenly mentioning this captain Jacques Bonhomme who was connected to Robert le Coq. There is a half-realised effort to link this in narratively by saying that there was also no love lost between Robert le Coq and Coucy, but the transition is very rough. The confusion of this passage suggests that this is another moment in the creation of a narrative, similar to that of the early remissions and grants, in which the story is not yet fixed.[43] Despite the affecting depiction of noble terror and rural insanity in Jean le Bel and the uses that Froissart will put that to in his far more influential work, the earlier chronicle – again, this is the earliest chronicle – suggests that the Jacquerie might once have meant something other than, or perhaps something *as well as*, an emotional and social commotion.

Organisation and objectives

Many historians have, of course, agreed with Jean le Bel that 'it's hard to believe that such people would dare undertake such actions without help'. The geographic extent of Jacquerie alone makes it clear that the Jacques could not have risen as a spontaneous mob, but rather must have made prior arrangements. Over 150 localities, most of them villages, were implicated in the uprising (Map 3.1). It is possible that they did not all rise quite simultaneously, but even if not, the timing was very close. The first incidents took place on 28 May, and by Corpus Christi on 31 May, the whole countryside north and east of Paris was up in arms.[44] Siméon Luce noted many incidents of communication and coordination among the Jacques and between the Jacques and Paris in his book, and, more recently, Samuel Cohn, Jr. has shown that there is copious evidence of planning and long-distance coordination in many large-scale revolts, including the Jacquerie as well as the Ciompi, and the English Rising.[45] Indeed, if we set aside, at least temporarily, the idea of the Jacquerie as a shapeless social terror, it is easily possible to build up a picture of it that bears less resemblance to a *jacquerie* than to a planned military venture with political aims similar to acts of war under state authority.

Some observers clearly thought the thing had a distinctly military air. One remission speaks of the Jacques as a host or battalion (*ost & bataille*), and there are at least two references to the Jacquerie as war (*guerra*).[46] The redaction of Froissart's chronicle now housed at Chicago's Newberry Library also speaks of the Jacques as a *hoost* and of their *logeis*, or military encampments.[47] The Norman chronicler, who was probably a military man himself, reported that they arranged themselves 'in good military order' (*en belle ordonnance*) before combat with the nobles near Poix.[48] The *Chronique des quatres premiers Valois* gives this more flesh, noting that before their battle with the king of Navarre outside Clermont the Jacques formed two battalions of 2,000 men on foot, with the archers in front and the baggage forming a barrier before them, and another battalion of 600 men on horse. He goes on to say that the Jacques faced off against the nobles 'in formation, blowing horns and trumpets and loudly crying *Mont Joye* and bearing many flags painted with the fleur-de-lys'.[49] The detail about the flag is important, for raised banners were a legal indication of warfare in the fourteenth century, and other sources corroborate the presence of flags (*vexilla* or *bannières*) among the Jacques.[50]

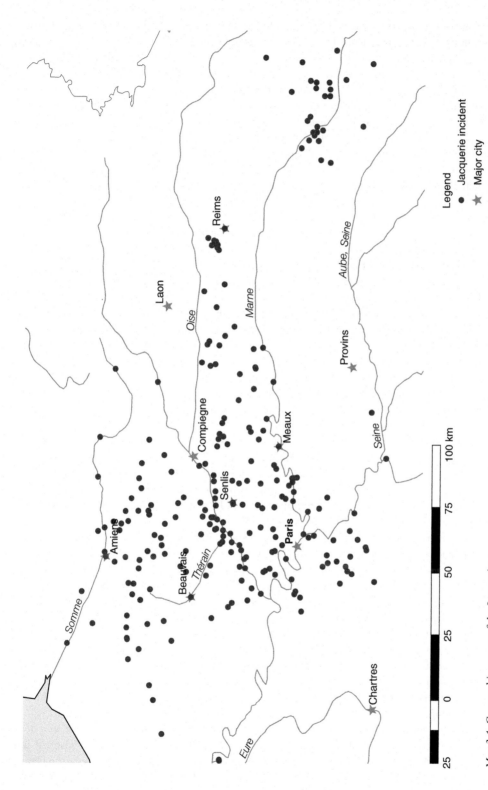

Map 3.1 Geographic extent of the Jacquerie.

Organisationally, the Jacques also look more like an army than a mob.[51] Details gleaned from remissions show that they had a hierarchical command structure governed by captains.[52] At the apex of command was the 'general captain of the countryside' or 'great captain of the non-nobles' mentioned in several remissions, and identified in two of them as the famous Guillaume Calle.[53] Calle is also named as the leader of the Jacquerie in several chronicles, though some remissions speak of him in more limited terms as the leader of the Jacques in the Beauvaisis.[54] Several remissions mention the *captains* (plural) of the countryside who forced the recipients' participation, and one remission speaks of these captains as being 'sovereign' over the lesser captains in command of villages.[55] The great captain had at least one lieutenant, mentioned without a name in a remission from 1363.[56] This lieutenant may be identified with Germain de Révillion, who commanded the Jacques whilst Calle was besieging Ermenonville, or with Archat of Bulles, styled in one remission as the 'then [*lors*] captain of the people of the countryside of Beauvaisis', who may have served in Calle's absence or after his execution on 10 June.[57] The *Chronique des ... Valois* also mentions a certain hospitaller as Calle's co-commander, but he has never been identified.[58]

Below this top layer of command, there were individual captains at the village level. We know of nearly 20 individuals serving in this capacity. At least some of them had sub-officers and coherent companies under their orders. The captain of Jaux, for example, had a lieutenant and at least one *dizanier* (probably in charge of a contingent of ten men), while the captain of Bessencourt had a counsellor, and the captain of Chambly commanded a company of eight men on horse and 16 on foot.[59] There were also captains in charge of several villages or areas, and at least one who commanded a company entrusted with a specific, long-distance mission.[60] This suggests that there was a middle layer between the great captain or sovereign captains and those in charge of individual communities. And while the evidence for the highest level of command is restricted to the Beauvaisis, the evidence for the middle and communal layers comes from almost every area implicated in the uprising.[61]

Thinking about the Jacquerie as a military undertaking, begs the question in the service of what or whom? This returns us to the empirical problem that has bedevilled the scholarship: Why did the Jacquerie occur and what was the relationship between it and the rebellion in Paris? The preponderance of evidence is on the side of collaboration between the Parisians and the Jacques. In separate instances, both Pope Innocent IV and the Dauphin himself claimed that the Parisians had orchestrated the Jacquerie.[62] Many remissions also indicate collusion: some issued to Parisians state that Marcel had usurped the government not just of Paris, but of the countryside around it, and that he 'had given people to believe that the Dauphin intended to allow the cities and the countryside to be pillaged by soldiers' (*audit peuple donnoient entendre que nous les voulions destruire & faire pillier par noz genz d'armes*).[63] Some for individual Jacques speak of orders from Marcel to destroy all fortresses and houses prejudicial to the town of Paris and the countryside and to assemble together in arms and follow the commands of his commissioners.[64] There is evidence of combined Parisian and Jacques forces in attacks at Ermenonville, Gonesse, and Meaux, and possibly also at Montépilloy and Palaiseau.[65] Marcel himself, of course, denied that the uprising had begun with his knowledge and consent in letters he wrote in July, after the Jacquerie had ended, but his denial was couched in narrow terms, and even there he admitted having authority over the Jacques, claiming he told them not to kill women and children, at least, so long as they were not enemies of Paris.[66]

There is substantial support for Raymond Cazelles's speculation that the Jacquerie was not just used by the Parisians after it had broken out 'spontaneously' but had been planned in advance by Marcel and le Coq in cooperation with the revolt's leaders as a response to the Dauphin's military efforts against Paris.[67] We could certainly read the Jacques' attack on *les nobles* not as (or not just as) an attack on a social group but rather on a party allied with the Dauphin against the reform party that orchestrated the revolt.[68] In the spring of 1358, *les nobles*, that is, the second estate, had withdrawn from the Estates General, where Marcel held sway, and opposed his reform programme. It was *les nobles*, particularly those of Champagne, who had been mostly deeply offended by the murder of the marshals and who used that incident to turn the Dauphin against the Parisians. According to the royal chronicler, the Dauphin had initially accepted Marcel's explanation for the murders, pardoned the murderers, and expressed his wish to be good friends with the Parisians.[69] The break only came when the Dauphin went to Champagne in April and was taken aside by some noblemen who questioned him about his acquiescence. He admitted some doubts about the men's guilt and promised to stand with the *champenois* nobility.[70] On the morrow of this encounter, he headed to the fortress of Montereau and sent a garrison to Meaux, blockading the river traffic to Paris on the Seine and the Marne, and he began to recruit his army – mostly made up of the regional nobility – to take back the capital.[71] An attack on the nobility was thus an attack on the Dauphin's allies.

The Parisian's concerns are clearly reflected in the first identifiable episode in the Jacquerie, the murder of a nobleman named Raoul de Clermont-Nesle and eight others at the village of Saint-Leu d'Esserent on 28 May, an event attested in several chronicles and two letters of remission.[72] The village, as Cazelles observed, was vital to the Dauphin's blockade of Paris because it had an important bridge over the Oise River, the only river still open after his occupation of Meaux and Montereau.[73] Saint-Leu was also a quarry town that produced high quality building stone, again key to royal efforts to dominate the countryside by re-fortifying the castles.[74] The control of rivers and building seems to have been a central objective for the Jacquerie as a whole, especially in the Beauvaisis. A line of villages implicated in the revolt runs along the Oise and its tributary the Thérain (see Map 3.1), and the other three villages identified by some chronicles as cradles of the Jacquerie were also quarry towns.[75] These foci dovetail neatly with events in Paris, where the day after the violence at Saint-Leu, the townsmen executed the crown's master carpenter and its master of the bridge, who was responsible for traffic on the Seine.[76]

The events in Saint-Leu were freighted with political as well as military significance for the conflict between Paris and the Dauphin and his noble allies. The murder of Raoul de Clermont-Nesle and his company was not an irrelevant coincidence, but rather a calculated shot across the Dauphin's bow. Raoul was the nephew of Robert de Clermont, who was one of the marshals murdered by Marcel's mob in the Dauphin's presence in February,[77] the act that irrevocably alienated the nobility and eventually the Dauphin from the Parisians and thus set in motion the military confrontation now coming to a head. The symbolic impact of Raoul's death at the hands of commoners could hardly have been greater, perhaps all the more so as he was the great-nephew and namesake of King Philip the Fair's constable Raoul de Clermont, who had also been killed by commoners at that great defeat of the French nobility, the Battle of Courtrai in 1302.[78] The remission that describes these events in most detail notes Raoul's relationship to the murdered marshal, as well as the family's long history of service to the French crown.[79] Raoul's death was no accident. Everybody knew what it meant.

Violence and the social order

Or did they? For if we can deduce clerics' and aristocrats' interpretations of the Jacquerie from their words and those of the Parisians from its aims and organisation, understanding how the *gens du plat pays* themselves thought about things is much more difficult. I have elsewhere concurred with Luce and Cazelles that many of them may have understood the Jacquerie as a defensive measure against predatory soldiers, and that this move might even have been legally defensible given promulgations issued by the Estates General in the king's name that authorised communal violence against such depredations.[80] There are indications that the Jacquerie's leadership may have fostered this impression that the violence was licensed. One of the captains who had been a royal sergeant, for example, was allegedly forced to give commands as if they were from the king or the Dauphin (*de par nostre dit seigneur & de par nous*).[81] But not all Jacques necessarily participated in this understanding (however valid it might have been). If we look at the Jacques' violence itself, which Bettina Bommersbach has characterised as their 'means of communication', there is much about their actions that cannot be explained solely by military or narrowly political circumstances, but which reflects and was perhaps even productive of a social and emotional aspect of the uprising for the participants themselves.[82]

The Jacques' reputation for violence is fearsome, but their actual deeds seem to have been far less extreme than the term *jacquerie* now suggests or as Jean le Bel and Froissart claimed. There was certainly some interpersonal violence. About half of the remissions say that noblemen were killed, and seven also report interpersonal violence against noblewomen or noble children.[83] In addition to Raoul de Clermont-Nesle, we know of at least 12 named noblemen and one woman whom the Jacques killed, and there are also some unnamed victims.[84] Still, we are very far here from a mindless massacre of gentlemen, let alone of their dependants. There is even less documentary evidence of sexual violence. Several chronicles report rape, but there is only a single remission that records an accusation of what was probably rape (*raptus*).[85] None of the few specific noblewomen reportedly victimised by the Jacques was raped, and the only archival document I know of that mentions both the Jacquerie and the rape of a specific noblewoman presents the rape and the revolt as separate, unrelated incidents.[86] Even in Froissart's chronicle, the non-specificity of the sexual violence is striking. He says that women were raped, but when we get to specific women, it is the fear of rape that we hear about, rather than its actuality.[87]

This is not to say that dastardly deeds did not take place – Luce found some corroborating evidence for the famous story in Jean le Bel that the Jacques roasted a nobleman, for instance[88] – but the bulk of the Jacques' violence was not directed against nobles' bodies. Rather, it was focused on the destruction of their fortresses, homes, and goods. Jean le Bel/Froissart reported that the Jacques destroyed more than 140 houses and castles. From other sources, we can identify over 30 castles, fortresses, or towers and 20 houses attacked or destroyed, as well as more than two dozen other places in which the type of building is not specified. These attacks were intended to destroy the buildings; the verb most often used is *abattre*, to tear down, closely followed by *ardoir*, to burn. The Jacques were also keen to destroy what was in these buildings. *Dissiper leurs biens* (to destroy their goods) is how the remissions' formula puts it. Again mostly they did this by burning. There was also a fair amount of looting. Lawsuits over the property lost or damaged in this way continued well into the 1370s.[89]

What did this violence mean? Attacking castles obviously had a strategic aim consonant with the Parisians' needs. The Dauphin's control of the rivers was complemented by his control of the castles, which were in the hands of his allies, *les nobles*, and the demolition of their domiciles served as a diversionary tactic, pulling them away from the prince's planned assault on Paris. There may also have been a judicial element, as the destruction of noxious individuals' houses or castles was a common punishment.[90] But the Jacques' attacks on castles can also be read in social rather than or even as well as military (or judicial) terms, for the Jacques seem to have had an antipathy towards castles per se. With the possible exception of the great castle at Creil, there is not a single example of a fortress that the Jacques occupied rather than attacked.[91] This may be because fourteenth-century castles' military uses were inherently odious to the *gens du plat pays*. Castles' offensive use as strong points from which to raid the surrounding countryside was obviously upsetting to the countryfolk: it was they who were raped and ransomed, their livestock and grain that was taken, and their houses and fields that were burned.[92] But castles' defensive use as refuges was – perhaps surprisingly – not that much more popular, primarily because it was expensive and inconvenient.[93] In many ways, the local fortress was just another place in which countryfolk paid seigneurial exactions.

Of course, the social meaning of castles, fortresses, and manor houses went beyond their military value and their fiscal burden. Many of these places, at least according to their owners, were beautiful (*pulchra*) and must have been quite different from most of the dwellings of their common-born neighbours (Figures 3.1 and 3.2).[94] The nobles' things were also nicer.[95] We get

Figure 3.1 Peasant house in Beauvais, built *c.*1410.
Source: author's photograph.

Figure 3.2 Montépilloy, castle attacked by the Jacques.

Source: 'Château de Montépilloy' by Chatsam, licensed under Creative Commons Attribution-Share Alike 3.0 Unported License.

some sense of this aesthetic difference from a remark in Jean de Venette's chronicle that is usually translated to mean that the Jacques and their wives got dressed up in the nobles' clothing and paraded around in their finery.[96] This is not to say, of course, that there was always an insuperable social and economic distance between the nobles and the non-nobles: nobles and non-nobles intermarried, their children played together, and there were non-nobles who held fortresses and fiefs.[97] But the distinction does seem to have been important to the Jacques: a non-noble whose wife was noble was attacked by the Jacques for that reason; a youths' rough game turned actually violent when a commoner teased his noble playmate about the Jacques' exploits; and a commoner's *châteaux et heritages* did not keep him from joining those who 'made themselves adversaries of the realm's nobles'.[98]

The link between this social meaning of nobility and its political/fiscal and in turn military implications is inextricable. The reason nobles lived in fortresses was because they could physically coerce the peasants into handing over their surplus (whilst they themselves remained often exempt from royal taxation), and the reason they could do that was because they were a warrior aristocracy who lived in fortresses. This is an oversimplification of the complex and changing situation of the late medieval French nobility,[99] but this nexus of economic, political, and military privilege inherent in *noblesse* seems nonetheless to have been at the heart of the Jacquerie for its rank and file participants. Their attack on the nobles was not about the weight of local lordship per se, but about the entire system of social difference based on violence (real or threatened) against commoners' bodies and their property. The Jacques did not primarily attack their own lords. The sources describe their targets in the aggregate as 'the nobles' (*les nobles*), not 'the lords' (*les seigneurs*), and it is notable that ecclesiastical lordships were left untouched.[100] The importance of nobility to ordinary Jacques, whatever their commanders' orders, can be seen in the inhabitants of Gonesse's objection to the attack on Pierre d'Orgemont's property that 'Pierre was not a noble' (*Petrum non esse nobilem*) and the mercy shown by other Jacques to Robert de Lorris when he renounced his nobility (*regnia gentillesse*).[101]

There are cases in which we know that Jacques attacked targets in their own villages, including their own lords.[102] But many Jacques travelled, first assembling elsewhere and then attacking in combination with other villages, sometimes in concert with local inhabitants, as happened in Saint-Leu. Under 15 per cent of the localities from which Jacques originated also experienced attacks from them, and GIS analysis shows that the geographic centre of Jacquerie hometowns was over 26 km away from the geographic centre of attacks.[103] Far from taking vengeance against their subjects, a number of lords intervened on their behalf after the Jacquerie, petitioning the king for their remission and complaining about their victimisation by other nobles or royal commissioners.[104] Nor were local inhabitants always entirely enthusiastic about the revolt. The villagers of Épieds, for example, claimed that they only participated in the attack on a local knight's manors because 'a great number of country dwellers came to the village and forced them to do it … which displeased them' (*grant nombre des genz du plat pays vinrent en la dite ville & par contrainte furent avec eulz a faire les diz malefices … dont il leur desplaisoit forment*).[105] Obviously their testimony was self-serving, but it does give a sense, confirmed by other indications, that local, individual relationships were not always as key to mobilising violence as opposition to more generalised social relations.

But was this attack on the social system always *the* or at least *a* fundamental meaning of the uprising for its participants? Most historians of the Jacques are certain that it was, that whatever the spark that ignited the Jacquerie, it landed upon the driest of tinder. For some, that hatred was the product of centuries, finally bursting forth at this moment.[106] Others point to more recent complaints about the nobility's failure to protect first the king at Poitiers and then the country dwellers afterward.[107] We can find elements of this sort of moral economy argument in most of the chronicles, even in Froissart/le Bel where the Jacquerie begins with the Jacques' accusation that the nobles had shamed and pillaged the realm (*les nobles … honissoient et gastoient le royaume*), and there are echoes of it in some remissions.[108] Nor is this moral economy argument necessarily incompatible with the strategic military explanation: as the Norman chronicler explains, the Dauphin had allowed the nobles to pillage their own people so that they could victual the castles enabling them to blockade Paris, which led the peasants to say that 'the knights who ought to have protected them had colluded to take all their goods'. He adds, 'For this reason, they revolted' (*Pour ce fait s'esmeurent*).[109]

It is also possible, though, that the social aspect of the revolt might have developed or become sharpened during the course of the rebellion. The non-nobles' experience of committing violence against nobles, the very act of challenging the military aspect of their dominance, may have led them inevitably to question the social structure. In a parallel case from the twelfth-century Auvergne, John Arnold has argued that the movement of the *capuciati*, which began as a peace-keeping association against mercenaries, underwent a transformation, becoming an anti-noble movement not only for their terrified elite observers but possibly also for the *capuciati* themselves who 'having usurped the lords' ability to command the battlefield' may also have found 'the necessary confidence to express a radical challenge to the existing hierarchy'.[110] The brevity of the Jacquerie in comparison to that movement, which lasted several years, and the *post facto* nature of the Jacquerie documentation, makes it harder to isolate that development here, but Jean de Venette's chronicle does offer us a glimmer of this hypothetical process. Explaining the origin of the name *Jacques Bonhomme*, he says it began as a derisive term that the nobles gave to the countryfolk (the *rustici*), but he says 'in the year that the countryfolk "rustically" carried their arms into battle they took up this name for themselves [*nomen … acceperunt*] and abandoned the name *rustici*'.[111] Jean de Venette's story relates to peasants who went to war in 1356 against the English, not to the Jacquerie itself, but it does intimate that the act of taking up arms transformed the rustics and enabled them to appropriate their nickname, transforming it from one of ridicule to one of threat. The Jacquerie may not have been originally planned as a social rebellion, but when the countryfolk marched across the countryside in their battalions, under their banners, burning down the infrastructure of noble domination, they may have started to think about themselves and their relationship to the nobility differently from how they had before.

Conclusion

What the Jacquerie meant to its participants and observers was varied and fluid. Recovering those meanings from the sources requires thinking about how and why people made their interpretative moves, as well as how their interpretations might change over time. As John Arnold observes, 'The successful motivation of large groups to collective action both requires and inspires acts of imagination; to ask which comes first is perhaps to miss the messy, partly aleatory, nature of such events.'[112] There were many acts of imagination that made the Jacquerie mean something – or some things – for its contemporaries. Penetrating that thicket of beliefs, hopes, intentions, fears, and lies presents difficulties, but we can penetrate it. We do not need to pare it back to a single, immutable interpretation. We can unpack the sources' language of social and emotional chaos that obscures the Jacquerie's connection to the Parisian rebellion, but we need not reduce the revolt to its leaders' strategic objectives any more than we should define it by the chancery's talk of terror. As much in the eyes of its protagonists as of its victims, the Jacquerie was *also* a war of non-nobles against nobles and an inherent challenge to the social order. These interpretations are not contradictory, or even necessarily complementary. The Jacquerie simply meant different things to different people at different times.

It is tempting to generalise this insight to revolts at large, especially as similarities can be found elsewhere in this volume in discussions of the English Rising of 1381 and the sixteenth-century War of the Communities of Castile. I would urge some caution, though, at least in degree. All large-scale, collective actions must have some 'fuzzy edges', but this indefinite quality may be especially pronounced in these kinds of very big revolts with major rural components, which though famous, were relatively rare.[113] By contrast with their rustic counterparts, urban rebels had long traditions of 'contentious politics' and very complex systems of internal governance and social differentiation. They could employ pre-existing infrastructure and rhetoric, as well as an established repertoire of provocative acts, including the production of documents, for staking their claims.[114] Rural rebels, of course, were not without socio-political infrastructure or traditions stemming from practices as diverse as cooperative agriculture, the maintenance of the parish church, or collective legal action.[115] The Jacques clearly employed existing village organisation, and they might well have remembered earlier uprisings, such as a revolt outside Laon in 1338, the great Flemish Maritime Revolt of 1323–8 and its antecedents, or a number of thirteenth-century fiscal uprisings south of Paris about which we know too little.[116] The Jacquerie had echoes in later rural rebellions, even far away or long in the future.[117] But neither the Jacques themselves nor their immediate ancestors had ever really done this before. What it meant was open to interpretation.

Notes

1. This work was undertaken with the support of a British Arts and Humanities Research Council Early Career Fellowship (grant reference AH/K006843/1). My thanks to John Arnold, Chris Fletcher, James Palmer, Andrew Prescott, and John Watts for comments on earlier drafts.
2. English definition taken from *The American Heritage Dictionary*, 2011 edn. *Le Robert Dictionnaire historique de la langue française*, 1998 edn, entry *Jacques* cites the first French usage in a general sense in 1821. The *Oxford English Dictionary* notes the first instance in English in 1882.
3. S. Luce, *Histoire de la Jacquerie d'ápres des documents inédits*, new edn, Paris: Honoré Champion, 1894; J. Flammermont, 'La Jacquerie en Beauvaisis', *Revue historique*, 9, 1879, pp. 123–43; R. Cazelles, 'La Jacquerie: fut-elle un mouvement paysan?', *Académie des inscriptions et belles lettres. Comptes rendus*, 122, 1978, pp. 654–66; R. Cazelles, 'The Jacquerie', in R. H. Hilton and T. H. Aston (eds), *The English Rising of 1381*, Cambridge and New York: Cambridge University Press, 1984, pp. 74–83; P. Durvin, 'Les origines de la Jacquerie à Saint-Leu-d'Esserent en 1358', *Actes du 101e congrès national des Sociétés savantes (Lille – 1976)*, Paris: Bibliothèque nationale de France, 1978, pp. 365–74; M.-T. de Medeiros, *Jacques et chroniqueurs: Une étude comparée des récits contemporains relatant la Jacquerie de 1358*, Paris: Honoré Champion, 1979; D. Bessen, 'The Jacquerie: class war or co-opted rebellion', *JMH*, 11, 1985, pp. 43–59; N. Bulst, ' "Jacquerie" und "Peasants' Revolt" in der französischen und englischen Chronistik', in H. Patze (ed.), *Geschichtsschreibung und Geschichtsbewußtsein im späten Mittelalter*, Sigmaringen: Thorbecke, 1987, pp. 791–819; D. Aiton, ' "Shame on him who allows them to live": the Jacquerie of 1358', PhD thesis, Glasgow University, 2007; B. Bommersbach, 'Gewalt in der *Jacquerie* von 1358', in N. Bulst, I. Gilcher-Holtey, and H.-G. Haupt (eds), *Gewalt im politischen Raum. Fallanalysen vom Spätmittelalter bis ins 20. Jahrhundert*, Frankfurt: Campus Verlag, 2008, pp. 46–81; J. Firnhaber-Baker, '*À son de cloche*: the interpretation of public order and legitimate authority in northern France, 1355–1358', in H. R. Oliva Herrer, V. Challet, J. Dumolyn, and M. A. Carmona Ruiz (eds), *La comunidad medieval como esfera pública*, Seville: Universidad de Sevilla, 2014, pp. 357–76; J. Firnhaber-Baker, 'Soldiers, villagers, and politics: the role of mercenaries in the Jacquerie of 1358', in G. Pépin, F. Laine, and F. Boutoulle (eds), *Routiers et mercenaires pendant la guerre de Cent ans*, Bordeaux: Ausonius, 2016, pp. 101–14.
4. N. Cohn, *The Pursuit of the Millennium: Revolutionary Millenarians and Mystical Anarchists of the Middle Ages*, rev. edn, Oxford: Oxford University Press, 1970 [1957]; G. Fourquin, *The Anatomy of Popular Rebellion in the Middle Ages*, trans. A. Chesters, Oxford: North-Holland, 1978 (French edn, 1972); M. Mollat and P. Wolff, *The Popular Revolutions of the Late Middle Ages*, trans. A. L. Lytton-Sells, London: George Allen & Unwin Ltd, 1973 (French edn, 1970); R. H. Hilton, *Bond Men Made Free: Medieval Peasant Movements and the English Rising of 1381*, New York, Viking Press, 1973.
5. S. K. Cohn, Jr., *Lust for Liberty: The Politics of Social Revolt in Medieval Europe, 1200–1425*, Cambridge, MA: Harvard University Press, 2006; J. Watts, *The Making of Polities: Europe, 1300–1500*, Cambridge: Cambridge University Press, 2009, pp. 270–86; P. Lantschner, 'Revolts and the political order of cities in the late Middle Ages', *P&P*, 225, 2014, pp. 3–46.
6. J. Arnold, 'Religion and popular rebellion, from the Capuciati to Niklashausen', *Cultural and Social History*, 6, 2009, pp. 149–69.
7. P. Lantschner, 'The "Ciompi Revolution" constructed: modern historians and the nineteenth-century paradigm of revolution', *Annali di storia di Firenze*, 4, 2009, pp. 277–97; Arnold, 'Religion and popular rebellion'; G. Brunel and S. Brunet, 'Introduction', in *Haro sur le seigneur!: Les luttes anti-seigneuriales dans l'Europe médiévale et moderne*, Toulouse: Presses universitaires du Mirail, 2009, pp. 7–18.
8. Luce, *Histoire*, published excerpts from the chronicles and several dozen of the remissions. S. K. Cohn, Jr. translated much of this material: *Popular Protest in Late Medieval Europe: Italy, France, and Flanders*, Manchester: University of Manchester Press, 2004, pt 3. I have also located several dozen previously unknown or unexploited documents from civil cases in the Parlement court (AN X1a series) and in the records of settlements between parties (AN X1c).
9. F. Autrand, *Charles V, le Sage*, Paris: Fayard, 1994, chs 10–14, J. Sumption, *The Hundred Years War*, 4 vols, Philadelphia and London: University of Pennsylvania Press and Faber & Faber, 1990–2015, vol. 2, chs 5–7.
10. See especially, D. Snow, E. Burke Rochford, Jr., S. K. Worden, and R. D. Benford, 'Frame alignment processes, micromobilization, and movement participation', *American Sociological Review*, 51, 1986, pp. 464–81 and C. McPhail, *The Myth of the Madding Crowd*, New York: Aldine de Gruyter,

1991, esp. pp. 162–3 and ch. 6; J. Berejikian, 'Revolutionary collective action and the agent–structure problem', *American Political Science Review*, 86, 1992, pp. 647–57; D. McAdam, S. Tarrow, and C. Tilly, 'Towards an integrated perspective on social movements and revolution', in M. I. Lichbach and A. S. Zuckerman (eds), *Comparative Politics: Rationality, Culture, and Structure*, Cambridge: Cambridge University Press, 1997, pp. 142–72.

11 Comparatively, A. Wood, *The 1549 Rebellions and the Making of Early Modern England*, Cambridge, Cambridge University Press, 2007, ch. 6.

12 S. Justice, *Writing and Rebellion: England in 1381*, Berkeley: University of California Press, 1994; T. A. Fudge (ed. and trans.), *The Crusade against Heretics in Bohemia, 1418–1437: Sources and Documents for the Hussite Crusades*, Aldershot and Burlington, VT: Ashgate, 2002.

13 AN JJ 88, no. 43, fol. 29v. The registry entry only mentions the letter without transcribing it.

14 AN JJ 86, no. 430, fol. 151r. About a dozen other instances including, AN JJ 88, no. 9, fol. 7r; AN JJ 89, no. 377, fol. 159; AN JJ 90, no. 354, fol. 182, ed. Luce, *Histoire*, no. 49; AN JJ 90, no. 488, fol. 244r, ed. Luce, *Histoire*, no. 50; AN JJ 145, no. 498, fols 229v–30r; next note.

15 AN JJ 87, no. 117, fols 80v–1r.

16 The use of *effroiz* is almost entirely restricted to remissions. In contrast, Parlement documents almost exclusively employ *commotions*.

17 J. F. Niermeyer and C. Van de Kieft, *Mediae latinitatis lexicon minus*, rev. edn J. W. J. Burgers, 2 vols, Leiden: Brill 2002, entry *commotio*.

18 Online Dictionnaire du Moyen Français, entry *effrayer, -oyer*. www.atilf.fr/dmf/definition/effrayer.

19 C. du Fresne du Cange, *Glossaire françois*, new edn, 2 vols, Niort: Typographie de L. Favre, 1879, entry *effroy*.

20 AN JJ 86, no. 205, fol. 67r, granted in August 1358, appears to be the earliest letter with this formula.

21 For example, AN JJ 86, no. 289, fols 96v–7r. On the contrast with the Jacquerie remissions, see Aiton, '"Shame"', pp. 38–40.

22 AN JJ 86, no. 216, fols 70v–1r; AN JJ 86, no. 220, fol. 72v; AN JJ 86, no. 271, fol. 91r, among others.

23 J. le Bel, *Chronique de Jean le Bel*, ed. J. Viard and E. Déprez, 2 vols, Paris: H. Laurens, 1904–5, vol. 2, pp. 256–7, followed by J. Froissart, *Chroniques de Jean Froissart*, ed. S. Luce, G. Raynaud, and L. Mirot, 15 vols, Paris: Mme. Ve. Jules Renouard and others, 1869–1919, vol. 5, pp. 100–1, 105.

24 *The Anonimalle Chronicle, 1333 to 1381, from a MS. written at St Mary's Abbey, York*, ed. V. H. Galbraith, Manchester: University of Manchester Press, 1970, p. 42.

25 *Chronique normande du XIVe siècle*, ed. A. Molinier and E. Molinier, Paris: Librarie Renouard, 1882, p. 128.

26 J. de Venette, *Chronique dite de Jean de Venette*, ed. C. Beaune, Paris: Le Livre de Poche, 2011, pp. 174, 176. The identity of the chronicler is disputed, but the controversy is not material here.

27 J. le Bel, *Chronique*, ed. Viard and Déprez, vol. 2, p. 257; Froissart, *Chroniques*, ed. Luce *et al.*, vol. 5, pp. 100, 105; *Chronique des règnes de Jean II et Charles V: Les grandes chroniques de France*, ed. R. Delachenal, 2 vols, Paris: Librarie Renouard, 1910–20, 1: 178. For similar language used for other revolts, see C. Gauvard, *Violence et ordre public au Moyen Âge*, Paris: Picard, 2005, pp. 208–10 and discussion in V. Challet's chapter in this volume.

28 De Medeiros, *Jacques et chroniqueurs*, ch. 2. On Froissart's approach to facts and aesthetics, see G. T. Diller, 'Froissart's 1389 travel to Béarn: a voyage narration to the center of the *Chroniques*', in D. Maddox and S. Sturm-Maddox (eds), *Froissart across the Genres*, Gainesville, FL: University Press of Florida, 1998, pp. 56–8.

29 J. de Venette, *Chronique*, ed. Beaune, p. 162.

30 See A. Prescott, 'Writing about rebellion: using the records of the Peasants' Revolt of 1381', *History Workshop Journal*, 45, 1998, pp. 1–27.

31 N. Z. Davis, *Fiction in the Archives: Pardon Tales and their Tellers in Sixteenth-Century France*, Stanford, CA: Stanford University Press, 1987.

32 AN JJ 86, no. 142, fol. 49, ed. Luce, *Histoire*, no. 21.

33 AN JJ 86, no. 165, fol. 54v, ed. Luce, *Histoire*, no. 20.

34 [P]luribus habitatoribus patrie Belvacensis & nonullorum aliorum qui guerram, controversiam seu monopolium contra regis maiestatem, nobiles & fideles dicti Regni machinaverant (AN JJ 86, no. 152, fol. 51v); genz du plat pays de Beauvoisis & d'ailleurs qui naguieres soy rendoient adversaires des nobles du dit Royaume et Rebelles de la coronne de france, de monsire & de nous (AN JJ 86, no. 153, fol. 51v); par les communes & habitanz d'environ leur pais Rebelles a nostre dit seigneur & a nous & ennemis de touz nobles du dit Royaume (AN JJ 86, no. 173, fol. 56r).

35 Cf. V. Challet, 'Peasants' revolts memories: *damnatio memoriae* or hidden memories', in L. Doležalová (ed.), *The Making of Memory in the Middle Ages*, Brill: Leiden, 2010, pp. 399–405.
36 AN JJ 86, no. 241, fol. 80, ed. Luce, *Histoire*, no. 23.
37 For example, AN JJ 86, no. 205, fol. 67r.
38 For the *Chroniques*' composition see G. Croenen, 'A "re-found" manuscript of Froissart revisited: Newberry MS F.37', *French Studies Bulletin*, 31, 2010, pp. 56–60, which addresses some of the difficulties laid out in J. J. N. Palmer, 'Book I (1325–78) and its sources', in *Froissart: Historian*, Woodbridge: Boydell, 1981, pp. 7–24.
39 J. le Bel, *Chronique*, ed. Viard and Déprez, vol. 2, p. 258.
40 *Comment eust on poeu penser que telles gens eussent osé encommencier celle dyablerie, sans le confort d'aucuns aultres certainement, il est à croire mesmement ou royaume de France. Par semblable maniere manda le sire de Coussy gens partout où il le poeut avoir; si courut sus ses voisins, et le destruit, et en pendi, et fist morir de male mort tant que merveille seroit à recorder; et avoient ces meschans gens ung chappitaine qu'on appelloit Jaque Bonhomme, qui estoit un parfait vilain et vouloit adeviner que l'evesque de Laon l'avoit enhorté a ce faire, car il estoit des ses hommes. Le seigneur de Coussy aussy n'amoit pas ledit evesque.*
(Jean le Bel, *Chronique*, ed. Viard and Déprez, vol. 2, pp. 259–60)
The passage is smoothed out in The True Chronicles of Jean le Bel, 1290–1360, trans. N. Bryant, Woodbridge: Boydell, 2011, p. 237.
41 G. Nachtwey, 'Scapegoats and conspirators in the Chronicles of Froissart and Jean le Bel', *Fifteenth-Century Studies*, 36, 2011, pp. 103–25.
42 Diana Tyson has argued repeatedly for Jean le Bel's earnest veracity: D. B. Tyson, 'Jean le Bel: portrait of a chronicler', *JMH*, 12, 1986, pp. 315–32; D. B. Tyson, 'Jean le Bel, annalist or artist? A literary appraisal', in S. Burch North (ed.), *Studies in Medieval French Language and Literature Presented to Brian Woledge in Honour of his 80th Birthday*, Geneva: Droz, 1988, pp. 217–26. Cf. N. Chareyron, *Jean le Bel: Le Maître de Froissart, grand imagier de la guerre de Cent Ans*, Brussels: De Boeck Université, 1996.
43 De Medeiros speculates on the *rédaction hâtive* of this passage (*Jacques et chroniqueurs*, p. 42). For tension between Coucy and Robert le Coq see Laon, archives départementales de l'Aisne G 69. On the interpretative possibilities of chroniclers' 'slips', see Justice, *Writing*, pp. 4–8, *passim* and P. Strohm, *Hochon's Arrow: The Social Imagination of Fourteenth-Century Texts*, Princeton, NJ: Princeton University Press, 1992, ch. 2.
44 Flammermont, 'La Jacquerie', 130, n. 2; *la feste du saint Sacrement l'an mil ccc lviii ou environ que ladite commotion commenca* (AN JJ 100, no. 478, fol. 148r). See also AN JJ 86, no. 387, fols 133v–4r, ed. Luce, *Histoire*, no. 37; AN JJ 90, no. 148, fols 79v–80r; AN X1c 32, no. 31.
45 S. K. Cohn, 'Enigmas of communication: Jacques, Ciompi, and the English', in Oliva Herrer *et al.* (eds), *La comunidad*, pp. 227–47.
46 AN JJ 89, no. 377, fol. 159; *Guerra*: AN JJ 86, no. 152, fol. 51v; AN X2a 7, fol. 213r.
47 Chicago, Newberry Library, MS F.37, fol. 168v; see n. 38, above. A transcription is available from the online Froissart, www.hrionline.ac.uk/onlinefroissart.
48 *Chronique normande*, ed. Molinier and Molinier, p. 129.
49 *Chronique des quatre premiers Valois (1327–1393)*, ed. S. Luce, Paris: Mme Ve Jules Renouard, 1862, p. 73.
50 AN JJ 89, no. 481, fol. 242v; J. de Venette, *Chronique*, ed. Beaune, p. 174. The Parisians also carried unfurled flags (*bannières desploiées*) when attacking Meaux (AN JJ 105, no. 91, fols 57–8r, ed. Luce, *Histoire*, no. 19) and Étienne Marcel had his own standard (*vexillum seu penuncellum*) (AN JJ 86, no. 321, fol. 107v). For raised banners as a legal sign of war, see M. H. Keen, 'Treason trials under the law of arms: the Alexander Prize essay', *TRHS*, 5th ser., 12, 1962, pp. 93–5; R. W. Jones, *Bloodied Banners: Martial Display on the Medieval Battlefield*, Woodbridge: Boydell, 2010, ch. 2.
51 The military activities of French countryfolk are poorly understood, though participation in village watches and even seigneurial and/or royal expeditions is attested: P. Contamine, *Guerre, État et société à la fin du Moyen Âge: Études sur les armées des rois de France, 1337–1494*, 2 vols, Paris: École Pratique des Hautes Études et Mouton & Co, 1972, vol. 1, pp. 35–8, 53–6; X. Hélary, *L'armée du roi de france: La guerre de Saint Louis à Philippe le Bel*, Paris: Perrin, 2012, pp. 56–60; and works cited in n. 115, below. For the use of English village military organisation in later revolts, see M. Bohna, 'Armed force and civic legitimacy in Jack Cade's Revolt, 1450', *EHR*, 118, 2003, pp. 563–82 and A. Wood, 'Collective violence, social drama and rituals of rebellion in late medieval and early modern England', in S. Carroll (ed.), *Cultures of Violence: Interpersonal Violence in Historical Perspective*, Basingstoke and New York: Palgrave, 2007, pp. 101–4.

52 Aiton, '"Shame"', pp. 217–45 discusses the importance of captains, while denying hierarchy.
53 *Guillaume Cale, soi portant general capitaine dudit plat païs* (AN JJ 86, no. 365, fols 124v–5r, ed. Luce, *Histoire*, no. 35); *Guillaume Calle, lors capitainne dez dictes gens du plat pays* (AN JJ 98, no. 252, fol. 80, ed. Luce, *Histoire*, no. 63); *magno capitaneo dictorum innobilium* (AN JJ 94, no. 4, fol. 3v, ed. Luce, *Histoire*, no. 61); *ex parte Capitanei plane seu plate patrie tunc electi vel deputati* (AN JJ 86, no. 606, fols 223v–4r).
54 He is mentioned as the leader of the Jacques in J. de Venette (*Chronique*, ed. Beaune, p. 174), *Chronique des règnes*, ed. Delachenal, vol. 1, p. 178, and the *Chronique des . . . Valois*, ed. Luce, pp. 71–4. Remissions: *feu Guillaume Calle nagaires esleu Capitaine du pueple & commun de beauvoisiz* (AN JJ 86, no. 391, fol. 136r); *Guillaume Calle, soy portant capitaine du dit païs de Beauvoisin* (AN JJ 86, no. 387, fols 133v–4r, ed. Luce, *Histoire*, no. 37); 'pueple [*sic*] du pais de Beauvoisiz, du quel Guill[aum]e Calle estoit capitaine' (AN JJ 86, no. 392, fol. 136).
55 *[L]es Capitaines du dit pais contraindrent* (AN JJ 90, no. 148, fols 79v–80r); *par la contrainte et enortement des capitaines du dit plat pais* (AN JJ 86, no. 345, fol. 117); *du mandement de plusieurs capitaines du plat pais* (AN JJ 86, no. 437, fol. 154, ed. V. de Beauvillé, *Histoire de la ville de Montdidier*, 2nd edn, 3 vols, Paris: Imprimerie de J. Claye, 1875, vol. 1, pp. 112–14); *ait este Capitaine subget des souverains capitaines du plat pais* (AN JJ 86, no. 344, fols 116v–17r).
56 AN JJ 94, no. 4, fol. 3v, ed. Luce, *Histoire*, no. 61.
57 Germain de Réveillon: AN JJ 86, no. 309, fol. 103, ed. Luce, *Histoire*, no. 29. Archat de Bulles: AN JJ 90, no. 294, fol. 150, ed. Luce, *Histoire*, no. 48.
58 *Chronique des . . . Valois*, ed. Luce, p. 71.
59 Jaux: AN JJ 86, nos 361–2, fols 123–4r; Bessancourt: AN X1a 19, fols 348v–50r; Chambly: AN JJ 90, no. 354, fol. 182, ed. Luce, *Histoire*, no. 49.
60 Philippe Poignant (royal sergeant and guardian of the bishop of Beauvais and the monks of St-Denis) was captain of four towns between the Oise and the Thérain Rivers (AN JJ 90, no. 148, fols 79v–80r); Simon Doublet, captain of three towns in Picardy (AN JJ 86, no. 392, fol. 136); Jean Flagelot, captain of several towns in the Perthois (AN JJ 90, no. 292, fols 149v–50r, ed. Luce, *Histoire*, no. 46), and Jaquin de Chenevières, captain of the lands of Montmorency (AN JJ 86, no. 207, fol. 67v, ed. Luce, *Histoire*, no. 25). Particular mission: AN JJ 90, no. 294, fol. 150, ed. Luce, *Histoire*, no. 48.
61 The possible exception is the region south of Paris, where we have only Jean Charroit, named individually in a communal remission for the villages of Boissy and Egly, which may indicate he had a leadership role (AN JJ 86, no. 215, fol. 70).
62 *Parisienses et quamplurimi aliarum communitatum aliarum partium de regno Francie populi contra nonnullos ipsarum partium nobiles* (H. Denifle with E. Chatelain (eds), *Chartularium universitatis Parisiensis*, 4 vols, Paris: Delalain, 1889–97, vol. 4, no. 1239); *d'avoir esmeu les gens du plat païs de France, de Beauvoisins, de Champaigne et d'autres lieux, contre les nobles du dit royaume* (Kervyn de Lettenhove (ed.), *Oeuvres de Froissart*, 25 vols, Brussels: V. Devaux, 1867–7, vol. 6, p. 474, also published by M. F. Combes, *Lettre inédite du dauphin Charles sur la conjuration d'Étienne Marcel et du roi de Navarre addressée aux comtes de Savoie (31 août 1358)*, Paris: Imprimerie nationale, 1889, pp. 2–3). On this letter, see J. d'Avout, *Le meurte d'Étienne Marcel, 31 juillet 1358*, Paris: Gallimard, 1960, pp. 259–62.
63 AN JJ 86, no. 282, fol. 94 among others. This language was borrowed from the general letter of remission issued for the Parisians on 10 August 1358 (AN JJ 86, no. 240, fols 79–80r, ed. in E. de Laurière, D.-F. Secousse, L. G. de Villevault, L. G. O. F. de Bréquigny, C. E. J. P. de Pastoret, and J. M. Pardessus (eds), *Les ordonnances des rois de la troisième race . . .*, 21 vols, Paris: Imprimerie royale and others, 1723–1849, vol. 4, pp. 346–8).
64 AN JJ 86, no. 207, fol. 67v, ed. Luce, *Histoire*, no. 25; AN JJ 86, no. 231, fols 75v–6r, ed. Luce, *Histoire*, no. 30; AN X1a 19, fols 348v–50r. See also AN JJ 90, no. 288, fol. 148r, ed. Luce, *Histoire*, no. 24.
65 Ermenonville: AN JJ 86, no. 391, fol. 136r; AN JJ 86, no. 309, fol. 103, ed. Luce, *Histoire*, no. 29; *Chronique des règnes*, ed. Delachenal, vol. 1, p. 178; *Chronique normande*, ed. Molinier and Molinier, p. 130. Gonesse: AN X1a 14, fols 476–7, ed. Luce, *Histoire*, no. 57; AN X1a 19, fols 348v–50r; Luce, *Histoire*, no. 18 (erroneously citing AN X1a 14, fol. 249). Meaux: AN JJ 86, no. 286, fol. 95v, ed. Luce, *Histoire*, no. 27; AN JJ 86, no. 606, fols 223v–4r; Luce, *Histoire*, no. 18; *Chronique normande*, ed. Molinier and Molinier, p. 131. Montépilloy: AN X1a 18, fol. 63. Palaiseau: AN JJ 86, no. 252, fol. 84v; *Chronique normande*, ed. Molinier and Molinier, p. 128.
66 Ed. in d'Avout, *Le meurtre*, pp. 304–10.
67 Cazelles, 'La Jacquerie'; R. Cazelles, *Société politique, noblesse et couronne sous Jean le Bon et Charles V*, Geneva and Paris: Droz, 1982, pp. 324–9.

68 Cf. Bessen, 'The Jacquerie', p. 56. For peasants' potentially sophisticated opinions on high politics see C. Gauvard, 'Rumeur et stéréotypes à la fin du Moyen Âge', in *La circulation des nouvelles au Moyen Âge*, Rome: École française de Rome, 1994, pp. 157–77 and F. Boutoulle, '"il y un meilleur roi que le roi d'Angleterre": Note sur la diffusion et la fonction d'une rumeur dans la paysannerie du Bordelais au XIIIe siècle', in M. Billoré and M. Soria (eds), *La rumeur au Moyen Âge: du mépris à la manipulation (Ve–XVe siècle)*, Rennes: Press Universitaires de Rennes, 2011, pp. 279–90.
69 *Chronique des règnes*, ed. Delachenal, vol. 1, p. 151.
70 Ibid., vol. 1, pp. 165–7.
71 R. Delachenal, *Histoire de Charles V*, 5 vols, Paris: A. Picard & fils, 1909–31, vol. 1, pp. 383–5.
72 *Chronique des règnes*, ed. Delachenal, vol. 1, p. 177; J. de Venette, *Chronique*, ed. Beaune, p. 174; *Chronique des ... Valois*, ed. Luce, p. 71; AN JJ 90, no. 356, fol. 183v; AN JJ 92, no. 227, fol. 55v, ed. de Beauvillé, *Histoire de Montdidier*, vol. 1, pp. 516–17.
73 Cazelles, 'La Jacquerie', pp. 663–5.
74 Durvin, 'Les origines'.
75 See also AN JJ 90, no. 148, fols 79v–80r and AN JJ 86, no. 207, fol. 67v, ed. Luce, *Histoire*, no. 25 for rivers.
76 *Chronique des règnes*, ed. Delachenal, vol. 1, pp. 178–80; *Chronique normande*, ed. Molinier and Molinier, p. 126; AN JJ 86, no. 240, fols 79–80r, ed. Secousse, *Les ordonnances*, vol. 4, pp. 346–8; AN JJ 86, no. 390, fol. 135.
77 Luce, *Histoire*, pp. 69–70.
78 *Annales gandenses*, ed. F. Funck-Brentano, new edn, Paris: Alphonse Picard et fils, 1896, p. 32, n. 3; F. Funck-Brentano, *Les origines de la guerre de Cent Ans: Philippe le Bel en Flandres*, Paris: Honoré Champion, 1896, p. 409.
79 AN JJ 92, no. 227, fol. 55v, ed. de Beauvillé, *Histoire de Montdidier*, vol. 1, pp. 516–17.
80 Firnhaber-Baker, '*À son de cloche*'.
81 He claims to have refused (AN JJ 90, no. 148, fols 79v–80r). See also AN X1a 19, fols 476–7, ed. Luce, *Histoire*, no. 57 at p. 318; Cazelles, 'La Jacquerie', pp. 657, 662.
82 Bommersbach, 'Gewalt'. See also A. Stella, '"Racconciare la terra": à l'écoute des voix des "Ciompi" de Florence en 1378', in J. Dumolyn, J. Haemers, H. R. Oliva Herrer, and V. Challet (eds), *The Voices of the People in Late Medieval Europe: Communication and Popular Politics*, Turnhout: Brepols, 2014, pp. 139–47.
83 AN JJ 86, no. 142, fol. 49, ed. Luce, *Histoire*, no. 21; AN JJ 86, no. 207, fol. 67v, ed. Luce, *Histoire*, no. 25; AN JJ 86, no. 241, fol. 80, ed. Luce, *Histoire*, no. 23; AN JJ 88, no. 1, fols 1–2; AN JJ 90, no. 425, fols 212v–13r; AN JJ 90, no. 556, fols 275v–6r (the only one to report actual violence – drowning – against a specific, named woman); and AN JJ 108, no. 86, fol. 55.
84 For example, the eight noblemen who accompanied Raoul de Clermont-Nesle at St-Leu; *plusieurs autres* who fell in a battle in Ponthieu (AN JJ 89, no. 377, fol. 159); an unidentified squire killed near Compiègne (AN JJ 86, no. 444, fol. 156, ed. Luce, *Histoire*, no. 39); and an unnamed nobleman killed near Pontpoint when it was discovered that he was a spy (AN JJ 96, no. 425, fol. 145; ed. Luce, *Histoire*, no. 62).
85 Froissart, Jean le Bel, and Jean de Venette report rape, the *Chronique des règnes*, *Chronique normande*, and *Chroniques des ... Valois* do not. Remission: *pro suspicione plurium & diversorum homicidiorum, incendiorum, raptorum* (AN JJ 88, no. 1, fols 1–2, lost until now because erroneously cited as AN JJ 87, no. 1 in Luce, *Histoire*). On the absence of rape from the remissions, see Aiton, '"Shame"', pp. 180–3. Rape was generally a pardonable crime in fourteenth-century France (C. Gauvard, '*De grace especial*': *Crime, État, et société en France à la fin du Moyen Âge*, 2 vols, Paris: Publications de la Sorbonne, 1991, vol. 1, pp. 308, 330–9, vol. 2, pp. 813–17), though under Marcel and le Coq the Estates General had attempted to forbid the crown from remitting it in 1357 (Secousse (ed.), *Les ordonnances*, vol. 3, pp. 128–9).
86 AN JJ 95, no. 121, fols 47–8r.
87 The most illuminating story in this regard is that of Mahieu de Roye's family, which appears only in Chicago, Newberry Library, MS F.37, vol. 2, fols 168–9r (transcribed at www.hrionline.ac.uk/onlinefroissart). I am grateful to Godfried Croenen for drawing my attention to this story. For Froissart's narrative use of rape see de Medeiros, *Jacques et chroniqueurs*, ch. 2.
88 Dijon, AD de la Côte-d'Or B 1451, fol. 85v (recording a donation of one franc made in 1377 by the duke of Burgundy to *une povre dame de Peronne qui eust son filz Rosti par les Jaques*). I am grateful to the AD Côte-d'or for providing me with an image of the document.

89 For example, In 1364, a squire sued a Jacques for damages of 300 *écus* incurred during the *commotio gentium de plana patria* when he and other *nonnobiles* burned the squire's house (*hospicius*) and stole his goods (AN X1a 18, fol. 204r).
90 A *droit d'arsin* authorised Flemish communities to destroy the homes and castles of publicly offensive individuals: A. Delcourt, *La vengeance de la commune: l'arsin et l'abattis de maison en Flandre et en Hainaut*, Lille: É. Raoust, 1930. Many Northern French communities also had this right (ibid., pp. 20–3), and French royal courts sometimes meted out this punishment to violent nobles, e.g. AN X1a 12, fols 239v–40r. J. Dumolyn sees this as a keystone of communal mobilisation in Flemish rebellions: 'The vengeance of the commune: sign systems of popular politics in medieval Bruges', in Oliva Herrer *et al.* (eds), *La comunidad*, pp. 251–89. See also Challet's chapter in this volume.
91 J. le Bel, *Chronique*, ed. Viard and Déprez, vol. 2, p. 259 reports that the nobles went to Creil because they thought the Jacques were based there. He does not say whether they were right. One Jacques repaired to the fortress of Cramoisy, but this was after (*depuis*) the revolt (AN JJ 90, no. 378, fol. 239).
92 G. Algazi, 'The social use of private war: some late medieval views reviewed', *Tel Aviver Jahrbuch für Deutsche Geschichte*, 22, 1993, pp. 253–73; H. Zmora, *State and Nobility in Early Modern Germany: The Knightly Feud in Franconia, 1440–1567*, Cambridge: Cambridge University Press, 1997, pp. 102–11; J. Firnhaber-Baker, 'Techniques of seigneurial war in the fourteenth century', *JMH*, 36, 2010, pp. 94–8.
93 N. Wright, *Knights and Peasants: The Hundred Years War in the French Countryside*, Woodbridge: Boydell, 1998, pp. 98–100; P.-C. Timbal, *La guerre de Cent Ans vue à travers les registres du parlement (1337–1369)*, Paris: CNRS, 1961, pp. 149–65. For 1358: AN X1c 11, no. 9.
94 For example, AN X1a 19, fols 348v–50r, 407v. Extant medieval peasant houses in France have not been catalogued to my knowledge, but many surviving English peasant houses from the period are substantial, two-story buildings (N. Alcock and D. Miles, *The Medieval Peasant House in Midland England*, Oxford: Oxbow, 2012; C. Dyer, *An Age of Transition? Economy and Society in England in the Later Middle Ages*, Oxford: Oxford University Press, 2005, pp. 51–6).
95 P. Mane, 'Le paysan dans ses meubles', in E. Mornet (ed.), *Campagnes médiévales: L'homme et son espace: Études offertes à Robert Fossier*, Paris: Publications de la Sorbonne, 1995, pp. 247–60.
96 [B]*ona reperta rapiebant, se ipsos et uxores suas rusticanas curiosius vestientes*, facing page translation as *Il se livrèrent au pillage; eux et leurs femmes revêtirent avec une curiosité indue l'habit des nobles* (*Chronique*, ed. Beaune, pp. 176–7). Translated into English as 'carried off such property as they found, wherewith they clothed themselves and their peasant wives luxuriously', in J. de Venette, *The Chronicle of Jean de Venette*, trans. J. Birdsall, New York: Columbia University Press, 1953, p. 77.
97 Marriage: AN JJ 90, no. 476, fols 238v–9r, ed. Luce, *Histoire*, no. 52; playing: AN JJ 99, no. 480, fols 149v–50r; castles: AN JJ 86, no. 153, fol. 51v regarding the man discussed in AN JJ 86, no. 365, fols 124v–5r.
98 Ibid. See C. Tilly, *The Politics of Collective Violence*, Cambridge and New York: Cambridge University Press, 2003, esp. pp. 75–80 on the activation of latent social boundaries in the mobilisation of violence.
99 P. Contamine, 'Noblesse française, *nobility* et *gentry* anglaises à la fin du Moyen Âge: une comparaison', *Cahiers de recherches médiévales et humanistes*, 13, 2006, pp. 105–31; P. Contamine, *La noblesse au royaume de France de Philippe le Bel à Louis XII: essai de synthèse*, 2nd edn, Paris: Presses universitaires de France, 1997.
100 Three remissions for villages in Champagne say that the Jacquerie was directed against both clerics and nobles, but this was not a general feature of the revolt (AN JJ 86, no. 357, fol. 122, ed. Luce, *Histoire*, no. 31, confirmed at AN JJ 95, no. 19, fols 9v–10r; AN JJ 90, no. 271, fols 139v–40r; and AN JJ 95, no. 22, fols 10v–11r). On clerical participation, see Luce, *Histoire*, pp. 64–5.
101 AN X1a 14, fols 476–7, ed. Luce, *Histoire*, no. 57; *Chronique normande*, ed. Molinier and Molinier, p. 130.
102 For example, AN X1c 32a, nos 30–1, an accord between the lord of Vez and his subjects.
103 My thanks to H. Ward for analysing my data as part of module SG4228 at the University of St Andrews.
104 AN JJ 86, no. 346, fols 117v–18r; AN JJ 86, no. 357, fol. 122, ed. Luce, *Histoire*, no. 31; AN JJ 86, nos 377–9, fols 129–30r; AN JJ 90, no. 564, fol. 279r; AN JJ 95, no. 22, fols 10v–11r; AN JJ 107, no. 185, fol. 87.
105 AN X1c 11, nos 61–2.

106 Flammermont, 'La Jacquerie', p. 129.
107 Luce, *Histoire*; Cazelles, 'The Jacquerie', pp. 81–2; Hilton, *Bond Men*, pp. 114–19; Bommersbach, 'Gewalt', pp. 50–62; Firnhaber-Baker, '*À son de cloche*'; but cf. Firnhaber-Baker, 'Soldiers, villagers, and politics' for lack of pillage in the Jacquerie heartlands.
108 For example, AN JJ 86, no. 585, fol. 212 and AN JJ 86, no. 267, fols 89v–90r, ed. Luce, *Histoire*, no. 36.
109 *Chronique normande*, ed. Molinier and Molinier, pp. 127–8.
110 Arnold, 'Religion and popular rebellion', p. 161. See also Snow *et al*. 'Frame alignment', pp. 477–8 on 'frame transformation'.
111 *Tunc temporis [1356] nobiles, derisiones de rusticis et simplicibus facientes, vocabant eos* Jaque Bonne homme. *Unde illo anno qui in bellis rusticaliter missi portabant arma sua, trufati et spreti ab aliis, hoc nomen* Jaque Bonne homme *acceperunt, et nomen rustici perdiderunt.*
(J. de Venette, *Chronique*, ed. Beaune, p. 144)
112 Arnold, 'Religion and popular rebellion', p. 159.
113 Cohn, *Lust for Liberty*, ch. 2.
114 For example, M. Boone, 'The Dutch revolt and the medieval tradition of urban dissent', *Journal of Early Modern History*, 11, 2007, pp. 351–75; J. Dumolyn and J. Haemers, 'Patterns of urban rebellion in medieval Flanders', *JMH*, 31, 2005, pp. 369–93; Lantschner, 'Revolts and the political order'.
115 R. Fossier, *La terre et les hommes en Picardie jusqu'à la fin du XIIIe siècle*, Paris: Béatrice-Nauwelaerts, 1968; G. Fourquin, *Les campagnes de la région parisienne à la fin du Moyen Âge (du milieu du XIIIe siècle au début du XVIe siècle)*, Paris: Presses Universitaires de France, 1964; A. Chédeville, *Chartres et ses campagnes, XIe–XIIIe siècles*, Paris: Editions Klincksieck, 1973, pp. 331–92; G. Brunel, 'Seigneurs et paysans en Soissonnais et Valois aux XIe–XIIIe siècles', in *Seigneurs et seigneurie au Moyen Âge*, Paris: CTHS, 1993, pp. 289–306; G. Brunel, 'Les hommes de corps du chapitre cathédral de Laon (1200–1460): continuité et crises de la servitude dans une seigneurie ecclésiastique', in P. Freedman and M. Bourin (eds), *Forms of Servitude in Northern and Central Europe: Decline, Resistance, and Expansion*, Turnhout: Brepols, 2005, pp. 131–77. The Jacquerie's Picard heartlands had witnessed a rural communal movement in the thirteenth century, which lapsed or was even suppressed in the fourteenth: R. Fossier, 'Les "communes rurales" au Moyen Âge', *Journal des savants*, 1992, pp. 235–76; Brunel, 'Les hommes de corps', pp. 171, 175.
116 Village organisation: Wright, *Knights and Peasants*, chs 4–5; Cohn, 'Enigmas'. Laon: Brunel, 'Les hommes de corps' pp. 171–5. Flanders: W. H. TeBrake, *A Plague of Insurrection: Popular Politics and Peasant Revolt in Flanders, 1323–1328*, Philadelphia: University of Pennsylvania Press, 1993; B. J. P. van Bavel, 'Rural revolts and structural change in the Low Countries, thirteenth–early fourteenth centuries', in R. Goddard, J. Langdon, and M. Müller (eds), *Survival and Discord in Medieval Society: Essays in Honour of Christopher Dyer*, Turnhout: Brepols, 2010, pp. 249–68; thirteenth century: Fourquin, *Les campagnes*, pp. 167–8, 171–2.
117 Justice, *Writing and Rebellion*, p. 222, n. 103; Y.-M. Bercé, *History of Peasant Revolts: The Social Origins of Rebellion in Early Modern France*, trans. A. Whitmore, Cambridge: Polity, 1990, p. 100.

4

'GREAT AND HORRIBLE RUMOUR'

Shaping the English revolt of 1381

Andrew Prescott

A commission issued in the name of the young King Richard II to the Mayor of London and others on 15 June 1381 described how unprecedented events had convulsed England.[1] Groups of persons 'largely of middling and lesser status' such as labourers, servants, and craftsmen had gathered in armed multitudes in Essex, Kent, Surrey, Sussex, and Middlesex, and, prompted by the devil, used threats of beheading and of the burning of houses and goods to compel knights or other free men to join them. Many faithful subjects of the king had been killed and beheaded and their houses demolished or burnt. These disturbances had spread to London and its suburbs, and the palace of John of Gaunt, the king's uncle, known as the Savoy Palace, and the Priory of the Hospital of St John of Jerusalem at Clerkenwell had been inhumanly burnt and devastated. Regardless of the fear of God or the reverence owed to the king's personal presence, Simon Sudbury, the Archbishop of Canterbury and Chancellor of England, and Robert Hales, the Prior of the Hospitallers and Treasurer of England, together with others found within the city had been beheaded and killed. The king denounced these treasonable actions and declared that they would not go unpunished.

This is the earliest account of what is now known as the English Peasants' Revolt. At this time, perhaps within hours of the death of the rebel leader Wat Tyler at Smithfield, the king and his councillors were probably not yet fully aware of the scale of the disturbances in East Anglia and elsewhere. Nevertheless, this commission established at the outset one of the chief features of narrative descriptions of 1381, namely the prominence given to the disturbances in London and the assumption that the city was the chief target of the rebels. This is epitomised by John Gower's description of the rising in his poem *Vox Clamantis* which portrays London, the New Troy, 'powerless as a widow', with

> a thousand wolves and bears approaching with the wolves determined to go out of the woods to the homes of the city ... And so the savage throngs approached the city like the waves of the sea and entered it by violence.[2]

The image of bands of peasants from Kent and Essex, enraged by clumsy attempts to enforce payment of the poll tax, marching on London to demand freedom from the king, has become one of the most familiar in British history – the Edwardian historical novelist G. A. Henty called his novel on the Peasants' Revolt *A March on London*.[3]

A London-focused event?

The assumption that the focus of the revolt was London and that its significance derives from the events there is entrenched in scholarly discussion of the rising. Sir Charles Oman in 1906 noted that the disturbances in East Anglia were as intense as those in South-east England, but concluded that 'their history was not intimately connected with that of the main rebellion'.[4] For Oman, the epicentre of the revolt was London, with disturbances elsewhere 'no more than the ground-swell moving outward from the central disturbance which had burst so tempestuously upon London'.[5] More recently, Rodney Hilton emphasised how 'the focus of the rising was London, the administrative and political capital of the country'[6] with the efforts of rebels in Essex and Kent 'directed on London in the hope of exerting pressure on the king to obtain satisfaction of their demands'.[7] While acknowledging the importance of the rising in East Anglia, Hilton dismissed the disturbances in towns like York as irrelevant and 'not part of the peasants' revolt'.[8] For Caroline Barron, the aim of the rebels was 'to march on London to find King Richard and the redress of their grievances'.[9] Barron declares that 'Had London been more strongly and effectively governed, the Peasants' Revolt might have melted away in the city suburbs'.[10] Paul Freedman argues that the rebels in London had a clear political agenda and distinguishes the rebels in London from those in other parts of the country whose aims were 'not so different from that of previous movements that had aimed at restoring a supposed earlier just relation between lords and men without eliminating lordship altogether'.[11]

Perhaps the most extreme proponent of a London-centric view of the revolt is Nicholas Brooks, who argued that all the disturbances outside Kent and Essex were opportunistic, declaring that

> Any attempt to understand the revolt needs to distinguish clearly the rising of the men of Essex and Kent, who moved simultaneously on London and sought to dictate their terms to the king and his government, from the sympathetic movements of local unrest that only occurred when news of the successes of the main rising had spread.[12]

In Brooks's view, even the Hertfordshire rebels who witnessed the burning of the Hospitallers' property or the Suffolk insurgents who beheaded the Chief Justice of the King's Bench were not part of the core rebellion.[13]

The fault is not wholly one of historians. Those literary scholars such as Paul Strohm, Steven Justice, Sylvia Federico, and Lynn Arner who have recently made an important contribution to discussion of the revolt have also often privileged London in their accounts. Steven Justice sets the northern boundary of the revolt at Derby, and declares that the urban risings in York, Scarborough, and Beverley were 'not obviously connected with that was happening in the south'.[14] Justice largely ignores events in Norfolk even though he suggests that one of the rebel letters which are the focus of his study is in a Norfolk dialect.[15]

The dramatic nature of the events in London has meant that insufficient attention has been given to the wide geographical extent of the revolt. The way in which the disturbances in 1381 spread north to Lincolnshire and Yorkshire, south to Sussex and Hampshire, and west to Gloucester and Somerset is just as remarkable and significant as the events in London. Moreover, an interpretation of the revolt which focuses only on London and the south-east of England and regards the disturbances elsewhere as secondary creates a partial and distorted picture of the nature and significance of the rising, since it omits the bulk of rebel activity. By insisting that the disturbances outside the Home Counties were mere aftershocks of the events in London, much scholarship on the revolt has diminished the achievement of the rebels. There is a need for a view of the rising which embraces its complexity by exploring more fully its spatial characteristics, taking account of its wide geographical spread and seeking to understand better how all the various disturbances fitted together.

When the revolt is viewed in its entirety, rather than simply through the narrow lens of the events in London, it emerges as a much more multi-layered event. Nicholas Brooks was concerned that a more rounded view of the revolt which emphasised its scale and complexity would give the impression that the 'revolt developed almost unintentionally and that rural smallholders, bondsmen and artisans were not capable of the elaborate planning necessary to realise their radical social and political aspirations'.[16] This is not the case. A geographically wider view of the rising shows that the coordination and communication between the rebels was even more sophisticated and extensive than suggested by Brooks. There is an important comparison here with the historiography of the French Jacquerie. As Justine Firnhaber-Baker discusses elsewhere in this volume, historians have hitherto presented the Jacquerie as chaotic and dispersed, but closer analysis suggests a more coherent pattern of protest and greater level of organisation. By contrast, the historiography of the English Peasants' Revolt has over-simplified its shape and structure by focusing on events in London, and there is a need to embrace more fully its complex spatial and social character.

When we start to examine the regional revolt more closely, it quickly becomes apparent that incidents in towns like Bridgwater, Salisbury, and York formed an integral part of the rising and were not mere isolated outliers. Moreover, the complex intertwining of local, regional, and national issues that is evident in these towns can also be found in events in London – the suggestion that the events in London and the south-east somehow represented a 'purer' form of revolt is not viable. The principal objection of some historians to treating the regional disturbances on a similar basis to those in London is that these events do not form part of a 'true' Peasants' Revolt. But the term 'Peasants' Revolt' was not used by contemporaries. Indeed, 'Peasants' Revolt' only began to be commonly used to describe the events of 1381 in the nineteenth century. In the fourteenth century, the revolt was described in much vaguer terms, suggesting that contemporaries saw the event as much more diffuse and dispersed than modern scholars.

Naming the revolt

It has long been recognised that 'Peasants' Revolt' is an unhelpful designation for the English Rising of 1381.[17] Not only did towns like St Albans, Cambridge, Bury St Edmunds, Ipswich, Maidstone, and Canterbury play a significant role in the rising,[18] but many of the rural insurgents were artisans such as carpenters, masons, tailors, weavers, skinners, and cobblers.[19] A number of chaplains and lower clergy took a prominent part in the rising,[20] and in some places attacks were led by members of the gentry such as Bertram Wilmington of Wye in Kent[21] and Roger Bacon of Baconsthorpe who had recently been retained to take part as a captain in an expedition to Brittany.[22] The use of the term 'Peasants' Revolt' to describe the rising of 1381 is of extremely recent origin. It was popularised by John Richard Green who included a chapter called 'Peasant Revolt' in his 1874 *Short History of the English People*.[23]

No such succinct designation as 'Peasants' Revolt' was used in the fourteenth century. Although chroniclers used a wide range of rhetorical devices to vilify the rebels and denigrate their status, the rising itself was described in very vague terms, such as Froissart's 'great mischief and rebellion of moving of the common people'.[24] Royal orders for the punishment of rebels referred to insurrections, risings, and congregations.[25] Indictments in East Anglia described acts committed by rebels as taking place 'in the time of rising in a warlike fashion'.[26] One particularly popular term for the rising in indictments from East Anglia and Essex was 'rumour'. John Snell was said to have gone to St Osyth in Essex, 'in the time of the said rumour', and encouraged the people to rise by ringing the bell.[27] The Suffolk rebel leader John Wraw was described as 'the procurer and instigator of all the evils and rumours done and perpetrated by the commons in the towns of Melford and Cavendish'.[28] An order in French from the Court of King's Bench referred to 'the great and horrible rumour and insurrection lately traitorously made in the kingdom'.[29] Indictments from Essex referred to the 'company of rumour' (*compaignie del rumour*) and also to 'the last rumour' (*darrein rumour*).[30] John of Gaunt's butler also referred in his accounts to the seizure of wine 'by the common rebels in the time of the great rumour'.[31] The use of the term 'rumour' to describe the events of 1381 suggests that many contemporaries saw continuities between 1381 and an earlier 'great rumour', a protest movement by rural tenants in Southern England during 1377.[32]

A number of other vague and ominous terms were used in the Middle Ages to refer to the revolt. Continuations to the *Brut* chronicle from the early fifteenth century onwards state that the rebels described the 1381 rising as 'hurling time', referring to a rough game of village football.[33] Thomas Howes, the chaplain of Sir John Fastolf, in writing to Fastolf in 1447, recalled how the Norfolk lawyer Reginald Eccles was beheaded 'in the Rifling tyme', a term for the revolt also recorded in Norfolk by Blomefield and equating the revolt with robbery and plunder.[34] Such terms as 'hurling' and 'rifling' may be seen as another expression of the carnivalesque revelry of 1381 which was evident in the ghoulish pantomime with the heads of the Chief Justice and the Prior of St Edmunds at Bury, the boisterous play of the rebels on the bed of Joan of Kent, or the cries of 'A Revell, A Revell' which the Westminster chronicler claimed the rebels made as they ransacked Lambeth Palace.[35] However, chroniclers emphasised such features of the revolt in order to present the rebels as boorish rustics, and terms like 'hurling' or 'rifling' were also intended to denigrate the rebels and formed part of the development of a tradition by which town chroniclers in cities like London and Norwich sought to distance themselves from the memory of 1381.[36]

During the fifteenth century, the names of the leaders of the revolt, particularly Jack Straw and Wat Tyler, increasingly came to be used to designate the revolt, diminishing sense of its scale and complexity. As is well known, Chaucer refers to 'Jakke Straw, and his meynee' when directly mentioning the rising.[37] In 1407, William Chestershire, Henry Gylle, and other inhabitants of Packington, who were threatened with excommunication as a result of an attack on property of the Prior of Kenilworth, posted bills written in English and sealed with red wax to the doors of the church and the manor house which were signed 'Per Johan Strawe et ses compaignouns'.[38] A 1413 indictment from Uckfield in Sussex declared that a group who seized land at Seaford as part of a dispute there was so large that it resembled the 'late company of John Rakestrawe'.[39] In 1452, Kentish protesters wanted to return to customs from 'the time of Jack Straw'.[40] This identification of the 1381 revolt with its leaders was a pronounced feature of early modern depictions, such as the Elizabethan play *The Life and Death of Jack Straw* (1594) or in John Cleveland's 1642 *Idol of the Clownes or Insurrection of Wat Tyler*[41] — indeed the revolt was mostly commonly referred to as the Insurrection of Wat Tyler during the eighteenth and nineteenth centuries before Green popularised 'Peasants' Revolt'.[42]

The political and personal in narratives of revolt

The use of words like 'rumour', 'hurling', and 'rifling' to describe the events of 1381 recalls the way in which the term 'commotion time' was used by contemporaries to describe the disturbances of 1549, which recent historiography has emphasised were much more extensive than the rising led by Robert Kett in Norfolk and, like 1381, involved disturbances from Somerset in the west to Yorkshire in the north.[43] Andy Wood has argued that the contraction by historians of the events of 1549 into 'Kett's Rebellion' was caused by the need to try and accommodate a complex and mysterious phenomenon into an integrated political narrative.[44] We can see a similar process in the way in which historians have sought to oversimplify the structure of the 1381 rising by repackaging it into a 'Peasants' Revolt'. Wood notes how 'the sudden intrusion of rebellious plebeians into conventional histories of government and court factions ruptures the assumption that politics stemmed from the central state and the "political" nation of the gentry and nobility'.[45] Likewise, the events of 1381 represent for many historians a rude interruption to the high politics of Richard II's court, suddenly bringing to the fore such issues as labour services, wages, popular access to justice, and the growth of new social elites in town and country which are usually safely tucked away in such *longue durée* fields as economic, social, and legal history. Events like that of 1381 confirm the comment of Heide Wunder that 'peasants ... only turn up in political history when they attempt rebellions or peasant wars'.[46]

As scholars have sought smoothly to integrate the revolt of 1381 into the political history of Richard II's reign, they have distorted its character and misrepresented its significance. This process of incorporating the revolt of 1381 into a political narrative can be traced back as far as David Hume who in the eighteenth century saw the rising as an inevitable consequence of an inequitable method of taxation, drawing parallels with the poll tax levied by Constantine the Great which he thought fatally weakened the Roman Empire.[47] Likewise, many modern political historians such as Nigel Saul present the rising as a unique passing episode 'highly political in character', which was 'a movement of the more ambitious and assertive in society' who were frustrated by the failure of the government to respond to their aspirations.[48] If the rising is regarded primarily as a political movement and assessed chiefly on the extent to which it changed policy on matters such as tax or land tenure, its achievements will inevitably be seen as limited. Although no attempt was made to levy another poll tax, the letters of manumissions granted during the rising were quickly cancelled. Mark Bailey's recent detailed case studies suggest that the conversion of villain tenure to copyhold and leasehold was already well advanced by the time of the revolt, and his analysis suggests that the Peasants' Revolt was not a major factor in this process, illustrating the difficulty of pinpointing concrete political achievements of the rising.[49]

Although literary scholars such as Steven Justice, Andrew Galloway, Sylvia Federico, and Lynn Arner have shown how the events of 1381 cast a profound cultural shadow over late fourteenth-century England,[50] nevertheless historians seeking concrete outcomes from the revolt have often dismissed it as a meaningless or pointless event. Notoriously, Barrie Dobson concluded that the 1381 revolt was 'a historically unnecessary catastrophe',[51] echoing the view expressed by the historian of the medieval economy Michael Postan that the rising was a 'passing episode in the social history of the late Middle Ages'.[52] So long as we view events like the rising of 1381 solely from the perspective of their impact on the central government and assess their success in terms of the political achievements of the rebels, it is inevitable that such pessimistic assessments should prevail.[53] As Andy Wood declares, 'a different interpretative approach is demanded: one that emphasizes the shifting place of rebellion within pre-existent popular cultures'.[54] A similar point has been made from a different perspective by Sylvia Federico, who notes how modern scholarship makes a false distinction between the political and the 'merely' personal, and emphasises that 'the evidence ... clearly shows that the political revolt of 1381 was often characterized and motivated by domestic, bodily, sexual, and personal grievances'.[55]

Chronicle accounts of the revolt

The 1381 rising spawned a remarkable crop of narrative chronicle descriptions, and these literary narratives have generally been given priority by scholars. One of the chief obstacles in understanding the widespread and complex nature of the rising is the preoccupation of these chroniclers with London. In particular, modern historians have treated with exaggerated respect a description of the rising inserted in a French continuation of the *Brut* chronicle compiled at St Mary's York known as the *Anonimalle* (that is, anonymous) chronicle from a description by a sixteenth-century antiquary.[56] Even such a cautious historian as Barrie Dobson declared that the *Anonimalle* chronicle, 'although by no means a completely artless piece of historical narrative, clearly deserves its reputation as the one chronicle source at considerable pains to anticipate Ranke's objective of "finding out how things actually occurred"'.[57]

The description of the revolt in the *Anonimalle* chronicle was apparently compiled in London and is one of two extended narratives which the *Anonimalle* chronicle borrows from elsewhere, the other being a remarkably detailed description of the Good Parliament of 1376.[58] It has been assumed that the accounts of the Good Parliament and the Peasants' Revolt in the *Anonimalle* chronicle were taken from the same source, and one reason why historians give such credence to the *Anonimalle* chronicle's description of the Peasants' Revolt is that the account of the Good Parliament is so rich in first-hand circumstantial information. However, it has recently been suggested that the *Anonimalle* report of the Good Parliament was issued as a separate pamphlet similar to Favent's account of the Merciless Parliament, which would mean that the account of the revolt is not necessarily from the same source.[59] Indeed, stylistic differences between the accounts of the Good Parliament and the revolt in the *Anonimalle* chronicle indicate that they are probably not by the same person.

The *Anonimalle* chronicle is not such an authoritative account of the revolt as many historians have assumed. It provides a detailed description of the outbreak of the revolt, but the recorded movements of key figures such as Robert Bealknapp and Simon Burley during May and early June 1381 do not correspond with the information given in the *Anonimalle* chronicle, suggesting that the details in the *Anonimalle* chronicle may not be reliable.[60] Moreover, the sequence of events in the *Anonimalle* chronicle at such important moments as the meeting between the king and the rebels at Mile End on 14 June 1381 differs fundamentally from other chronicle accounts, and it is by no means clear from other records that the *Anonimalle* chronicle is right at these points. While the author of the *Anonimalle* chronicle's description of the rising undoubtedly witnessed some of the events described, the *Anonimalle* chronicle highlights incidents which were prominent in legal proceedings arising from the revolt, and it seems likely that this account of the revolt was in part compiled from legal and administrative documents used in the prosecution of the rebels.[61] This makes it historiographically interesting, but maybe less worthy of the enormous prestige it has been often accorded.

Another reason why the *Anonimalle* chronicle account of the revolt has been accorded such respect by historians is that, by focusing on events in London and truncating the description of the unrest in other parts of the country, the *Anonimalle* chronicle provides a narrative which can be easily assimilated into political history. While the *Anonimalle* chronicle gives a balanced account of events outside London, referring to the disturbances at Huntingdon, the activities of John Wraw in Suffolk and the massacre of Norfolk rebels by Bishop Despenser, these are presented as a brief tailpiece to the dramatic events in London. The first editor of the *Anonimalle* chronicle, V. H. Galbraith, thought that this shortened account of events outside London was a good thing:

> For the chronicler, the core and meaning of the revolt are to be found in the march on London, under the leadership of Wat Tyler. To events elsewhere – what we should call today the 'sympathetic strikes' connected with the rising – he devotes no more than two short paragraphs.[62]

Other narrative accounts of the rising, such as those by Henry Knighton and the *Westminster Chronicle*,[63] share with the *Anonimalle* chronicle this preoccupation with events in London. While Froissart attempted to deal more extensively with the rising outside London, he was hampered by his defective grasp of English geography. He provides a bravura, romanticised description of the killing of Robert Salle at Norwich, but claims that the rebels at Norwich came from Stafford, King's Lynn, Cambridge, Bedford, and Yarmouth.[64] Froissart wrongly assumed that the rebels in Norfolk were heading for London and that the key aim of all the rebels was to seize London: 'if we be first lords of London and have the possession of the riches that is therein, we shall not repent us'.[65] The most geographically balanced account of the rising is that of Walsingham, which gives events in Suffolk and Norfolk almost equal prominence to those in London and provides in his account of events in St Albans the most detailed report of a local rising.[66] However, in doing so, Walsingham emphasised the links between regional rebels and those in London, thus subordinating events elsewhere to those in London.

Legal records of the revolt

A prominent feature of recent historical research into the revolt has been the process of identifying and recording the hundreds of legal prosecutions made after the rising. The legal records not only document the names of hundreds of rebels and their victims but also paint a picture of the revolt which contrasts with that in the chronicles, documenting the multi-layered and geographically dispersed character of the disturbances.[67] The first judicial proceedings after the revolt were undertaken by special commissions sent to the most badly affected areas, which were often given exceptional military powers to chastise and punish the rebels.[68] The Court of King's Bench, under its new chief justice Robert Tresilian, took a prominent part in the legal proceedings arising from the revolt, hearing presentations concerning the disturbances by juries from Middlesex and summoning cases from other courts, particularly in connection with the processing of pardons.[69] Many private actions for trespass were also brought in relation to the rising in both the Court of Commons Pleas and the plea side of the King's Bench.[70] Most of these private actions did not come to trial and are only recorded in brief notes on the plea roll, but can be identified by their reference to such characteristic actions of the rebels as the burning of records.

The first historian to draw attention to the scale of the surviving legal records was the French scholar André Réville whose posthumously published work in 1898 revealed the scale and complexity of the disturbances in East Anglia, using chiefly the records of a commission into the disturbances in Norfolk and Suffolk and King's Bench records.[71] Réville also showed that the disturbances in Hertfordshire were more widespread than previously supposed,[72] and noted references to disturbances in a number of towns whose involvement in the revolt was previously unsuspected, ranging from Kingston-upon-Thames to Scarborough.[73] At the same time, another pioneer of the study of these records, Edgar Powell, produced the first detailed account of the rising in Cambridgeshire, drawing on information in a plea roll of a commission under William de la Zouche.[74]

These studies of the legal and administrative records enabled Sir Charles Oman to include detailed accounts of the disturbances in East Anglia in his 1906 book on the revolt. However,

Oman was perplexed by the information about the dozens of violent incidents in East Anglia described in legal records. The nature of the sources encouraged Oman to portray many of the events there as opportunistic violence. Discussing events in west Norfolk, for example, he declared:

> From the bulky rolls of indictments which compose the epitaph of the rising we draw a picture of half a county given over for ten days to mere objectless pillage ... Evidently we are dealing with an outburst of village ruffianism, not with a definite social or political propaganda.[75]

Oman was similarly baffled by Réville's revelations about events in towns such as York, which he dismissed as a 'squalid and obscure municipal quarrel'.[76] However, the detailed picture of local disturbances provided by the legal records shows that they were much more closely integrated into the mainstream of the rising than Oman suggests.

A case study in regional revolt: Bridgwater

The character of these regional disturbances and their dense network of connections to a range of local and national interests are illustrated by the records describing the participation in the revolt of the town of Bridgwater in Somerset.[77] During 1380, there was popular resentment in Bridgwater over the ownership of the advowson of the church of Bridgwater by the Master and brethren of the Augustinian Hospital of St John.[78] The Master of the Hospital complained that townsfolk had attacked the Hospital and excluded the brethren from the church.[79] This dispute was connected with wider factional issues in the town. William la Zouche, one of the lords of Bridgwater, alleged that the Master of the Hospital, with the aid of John Sydenham, one of the most prominent and wealthy burgesses who had been steward of the guild merchant of Bridgwater, had prevented him holding courts in the town.[80] A chaplain called Nicholas Frompton obtained a papal provision to the vicarage of Bridgwater[81] and the Master's attempts to exclude Frompton from the vicarage led to further violent incidents.[82] This conflict resulted in a series of lawsuits,[83] and, when the rising broke out in 1381, Nicholas Frompton together with Thomas Engleby, a leading inhabitant of Bridgwater who had served as MP for the town in 1368 and as warden of the chantry of the Blessed Virgin in Bridgwater church,[84] were pursuing this litigation in London and witnessed the arrival of the insurgents there.[85]

Frompton and Engleby rushed back to Somerset, where they assembled the townsfolk who, bearing the banner of St George in emulation of their comrades in London, forced the Master of the Hospital to admit Frompton to the rectory and pay the townsfolk a fine.[86] The Bridgwater insurgents burnt down houses belonging to John Sydenham and to Thomas Duffield, a leading lawyer in the town who had acted in the consistory court in cases concerning Bridgwater church and was the executor of Robert Plympton, a powerful burgess of Bridgwater.[87] The Bridgwater insurgents then made excursions beyond the town, attacking further property of John Sydenham at Sydenham, where they burnt documents including court rolls belonging to John Cole, another prominent burgess. Moving on to the village of Chilton Polden, they beheaded Walter Baron, another supporter of the Hospital. Finally, Engleby led his men to Ilchester, where they broke into the county gaol and seized Hugh Lavenham, the former keeper of the gaol who had recently been imprisoned for felony there. The Bridgwater rebels forced another local merchant, John Bursy of Long Sutton, to behead Lavenham. The heads of both Baron and Lavenham were carried back to Bridgwater on lances and displayed as traitors' heads on the bridge there. Trespass actions afterwards brought by John Sydenham show how the insurgents in Bridgwater were drawn from a wide range of the town's population, including not only prominent merchants such as John Henton who had been nominated as provost and was afterwards an MP, but also tailors, tanners, weavers, and minor officials such as wardens of the wards of the borough.[88]

It is difficult to see how events in Bridgwater can be construed as disconnected from the mainstream of the rising. The dispute between local townsfolk and a prominent local ecclesiastical institution recalls the way in which similar conflicts in St Albans, Bury St Edmunds, and Cambridge fed into the rising. The attacks on Sydenham suggest that, as in other towns in 1381, there was resentment in Bridgwater at the growth of new urban elites. Like the insurgents in St Albans, the rebels in Bridgwater were in direct contact with the rising in London. The Bridgwater insurgents adopted such characteristic actions of the 1381 rebels as the use of the banner of St George, the burning of manorial records, the beheading of alleged traitors, and the display of the heads of their victims. Above all, the Bridgwater insurgents signalled their solidarity with the rebels in London by seeking letters of manumission in exactly the same form as was granted by the king to the men of Kent and Hertfordshire at Mile End.[89] The manumission from all forms of bondage granted by these letters would have been of little value to the Bridgwater insurgents, but their attempt to secure such letters shows that the terms of this grant provided a shared programme whose value was recognised by inhabitants of both town and country as far afield as Kent, Hertfordshire, and Somerset.

Cross-currents of the rising in London

The legal records not only illustrate that the geographical extent of the rising was greater than has been allowed, but they also show how events in London itself, far from representing a 'purer' more politically focused insurgency, combined local, regional, and national concerns in a way similar to that in towns like Bridgwater. This is illustrated by the complex and confusing circumstances surrounding the meeting between Richard II and the rebels at Mile End on 14 June. The *Anonimalle* chronicle describes this meeting as an orderly and respectful negotiation.[90] According to the *Anonimalle* chronicle, as the king arrived with a party of nobles, the rebels knelt and declared their loyalty to him. Carrying banners and pennants, Tyler presented the rebel demands, and the king asked the rebels to form up in two lines as he proclaimed that they should be free and that their demands would be granted.

This description of the events of 14 June in the *Anonimalle* chronicle contrasts with the more chaotic picture presented in petitions by Margery Tawney, the widow of Thomas Tawney, one of the Poor Knights of St George's Chapel in Windsor Castle.[91] Thomas Tawney had died in about 1379,[92] and Margery alleged that the Warden of St George's Chapel had retained money bequeathed to her. Margery described how on 13 June 1381 during the rising, a proclamation was made that everyone with grievances over old debts and inheritances should go with their evidence to the king in the Tower of London, where justice would be done. On 14 June 1381,[93] Margery went to the Tower, accompanied by her son John Thorp, to press her case. Her petition suggests a tumultuous scene in the Tower as many suitors attempted to present their grievances to the king. Margery did not manage to give the king her document, presumably because of the large crowds, but presented her bill to Richard in the Great Wardrobe the following day, before the meeting at Smithfield. However, some of the people who Margery said owed her money accused her son John of participating in the execution of Simon Sudbury because of his presence in the Tower of London at that time. These enemies of Margery arranged for John Thorp to be violently arrested and thrown into Newgate prison, where he subsequently died from the injuries inflicted during his arrest.

The events of Friday 14 June 1381 were not an orderly political negotiation but a chaotic series of demands for justice by many petitioners, so that, as the *Anonimalle* chronicle describes, it was necessary for chancery clerks 'to write out charters, patents, and letters of protection, granted to the commons in consequence of the matters before mentioned, without taking any fines for the sealing or transcription'.[94] The people demanding concessions were not restricted to the men of Kent and Essex. They included, for example, representatives of the Mayor and commonalty of Oxford, who secured a grant to fortify the town with a huge ditch, 200 feet wide, presumably intended to help the town in its dispute with the Augustinian House of St Frideswide.[95] This grant was afterwards 'cancelled by command of the King because granted and sealed at the time of the insurrection of the commons'.[96] The welter of demands and grievances at Mile End on 14 June 1381 readily spilled over into violence. For example, Thomas Furness alleged that Isabella Chapman entered his property at Mile End on 14 June 1381, imprisoning his servants for three days, in what appears to be an example of one aggrieved litigant resorting to self-help.[97]

The revolt in Southern England

As more and more legal records relating to the revolt have been discovered, the wide extent of the revolt has been revealed. A new geography of the revolt has emerged which shows how the revolt spread across England from Yorkshire to Somerset and enables us to trace the way in which rebel bands communicated and rapidly moved to places as varied as Guildford, Winchester, Salisbury, Cambridge, Great Yarmouth, and beyond.

In Southern England, the rising was not limited to Essex and Kent and there were serious disturbances in many other counties.[98] A commission led by the Earl of Arundel against insurgents in Surrey and Sussex arrested so many suspected rebels that the gaol of Guildford Castle could not hold them all.[99] Unfortunately, the records of Arundel's commission have not survived, but there are indictments relating to riots at Kingston upon Thames in Surrey where, on 15 June, John Bonefaunt, William Osborne, and many others carried flaming torches to the house of John Hunt and threatened to burn it. Hunt was compelled to give Bonefaunt 8s 4d on pain of being beheaded.[100] Two insurgents from Havering in Essex who had taken part in the destruction of the Savoy, went to Clandon in Surrey and extorted money by declaring that the rebel company at Kingston would soon follow them to Clandon.[101] In Sussex, private litigation shows that there was a major attack on Lewes Castle on 16 June 1381,[102] while at Bexhill the house of a local justices of the peace was attacked and records burnt, apparently part of a series of disturbances in this area.[103] There was close contact between the insurgents in Sussex and those in Western Kent, with Sussex insurgents said to have been responsible for the destruction of a house in Yalding.[104]

In Hampshire, there had been disturbances in Winchester in 1380 led by the bailiff of the commons, William Wygge, a member of one of the town's most prominent families.[105] It seems that Wygge may have gone to London at the time of the 1381 revolt. On 17 June 1381, Thomas Falconer arrived in Winchester declaring that there was a great company of the commons at Guildford and said that anyone who put a grievance before the company would receive justice. He persuaded a group of townsfolk to accompany him as far as Farnham, where they met Wygge returning from London. They returned to Winchester, where they rang the bell and blew the horn to raise the town. On 18 June, Wygge and his followers broke into the king's staple, seized the records and burnt them in the high street. They also executed Walter Hogyn, who may have been the staple clerk. The disturbances in Winchester found a sympathetic response in nearby Romsey, where at least one rebel was afterwards beheaded and seven others had fled after the revolt.[106]

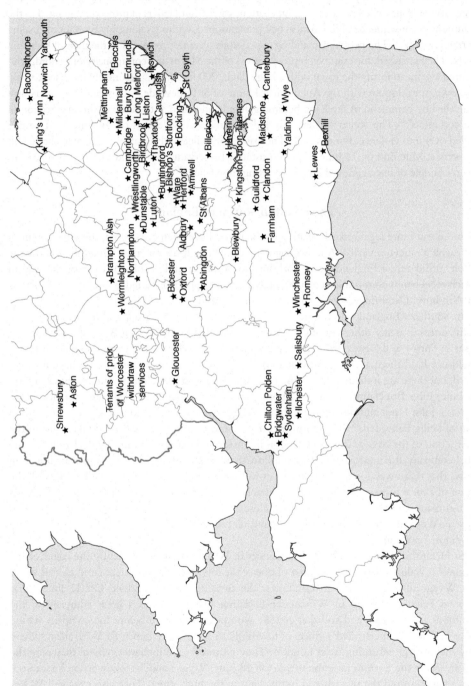

Map 4.1 Some places in Southern England which experienced disturbances during the English rising of 1381.

In Wiltshire, Salisbury seems to have suffered serious unrest, but its exact nature is obscure. There had been disturbances there in March 1381, with the entrances to the city blocked and a defensive ditch recently started was destroyed, presumably because of resentment at the cost of the work.[107] John Hawkwood of Salisbury was accused of leading a rising of the commons of the city and seeking to deny and undermine the king's laws, presumably the labour legislation. Hawkwood was said to have made proclamations in the marketplace in Salisbury and elsewhere in Wiltshire declaring that anyone who disobeyed his commands would be beheaded. Although Hawkwood was found not guilty, it is evident there had been very violent protests at the time of the revolt in Salisbury and its suburbs.[108] The situation in Hampshire and Wiltshire was sufficiently alarming for the king personally to order in late June 1381 that a large group of soldiers under Sir Peter de Veel and Sir Robert Passelowe who had been mustered in Dartmouth for an expedition in France should take action against rebels in Hampshire and Wiltshire. This force stayed in Hampshire and Wiltshire for some time.[109]

In Berkshire, a commission on 28 June 1381 ordered the arrest of a number of men from Abingdon who were said to have rebelled against the king, indicating that the conflict between the town and abbey of Abingdon had flared up again during the rising.[110] A further remarkable Berkshire case vividly illustrates how various threads of grievance and dispute became intertwined during the revolt.[111] In 1376, Edward III had presented William Salisbury to the Salisbury prebend of Blewbery, whose prebendal manor lay in Berkshire between Reading and Oxford.[112] Another clerk called David Calveley obtained a papal provision to the prebend and began action against Salisbury in the church courts, in contravention of the *praemunire* legislation restricting the use of papal provisions.[113] Calveley was a relative of the well-known military commander Sir Hugh Calveley and he had already been involved with members of Sir Hugh's retinue in violent incidents in pursuit of a claim to the Deanery of St Asaph in North Wales.[114] Because of his breach of the *praemunire* legislation in the Blewbery case, Calveley was arrested but released on bail of 1,000 pounds for his good behaviour. Nevertheless Calveley and other malefactors seized William and took him as far away as Newcastle-under-Lyme in Staffordshire.[115] For this breach of his bail, Calveley was arrested again and imprisoned in the Marshalsea prison in Southwark, where he was languishing when the revolt broke out.

When the Marshalsea prison was burnt down by 'Jacke Straw and his fellow traitors', Calveley managed to escape.[116] He joined in the attack on the Savoy and it was alleged that Calveley, Robert Attwood of Kent, John Ferrour of Rochester, and his wife Johanna together seized a chest from the Savoy containing 1,000 pounds, placed it in a boat, and took it back across the Thames to Southwark, where they divided the money amongst themselves.[117] Calveley then gathered a rebel band together and headed out of London to Berkshire where they seized the prebendal manor and took goods worth 200 pounds belonging to Salisbury.[118] Salisbury was forced to bring a chancery action to try and recover the benefice and have Calveley re-arrested.[119] Calveley was eventually pardoned in 1385.[120]

The revolt in Western England

The rising in the south-west of England was not confined to Bridgwater and Somerset. From the perspective of the king and council, the rising in the south-west was not a mere aftershock but a serious and immediate threat. In early July, Thomas of Woodstock, Earl of Buckingham, who had been leading a commission against the rebels in Essex and slaughtered many rebels at Billericay, was dispatched to Gloucester,[121] even though Essex was still unsettled at that time.[122] Buckingham undertook a show of strength as he moved from Essex to Gloucester. Arriving at Llanthony Priory on 13 July, Buckingham held a court at Gloucester two days later at which five leading burgesses of the town were accused of rebellion and representatives of the county were enjoined to fulfil their obligations as serfs and customary tenants. The nature of the disputes in Gloucester remains unclear but may have involved conflicts with the men of the Forest of Dean and antagonism towards the royal servants in Gloucester Castle. Buckingham's commission covered Gloucestershire, Worcestershire, and Shropshire, and there was probably unrest in all these counties. The tenants of the Priory of Worcester withdrew their labour at the time of the rising,[123] while it is difficult to believe that there was no resurgence during the rising of the troubles at Shrewsbury which had caused a complete breakdown of town government in March 1381.[124] The manorial records of Aston, suggest that tenants of Shrewsbury Abbey there attempted to seize the abbot's woods.[125]

In the far south-west, Sir Ralph Carmynowe complained that he had been attacked by sympathisers of the rebels in Cornwall. A jury at Lostwithiel declared that on 26 June 1381, Sir William Botriaux, hearing about the actions of the rebels in London, arose with 80 others and broke into Sir Ralph's manor at Boconnoc, where they seized livestock and killed Carmynowe's servants.[126] It was also alleged that Richard Eyr and others had raised a band of 300 men in Cornwall in imitation of the rebels in Kent and Essex and attacked Bodmin Priory. However, William Botriaux's wife Elizabeth countered with a petition pointing out that her husband was on the king's service in Portugal. She explained that Botriaux had legitimately recovered a manor from Carmynowe's men by legal action, and had installed Richard Eyr as his tenant. After William had left for Portugal, Carmynowe's men had expelled Eyr and occupied the manor once again. Under the pretext that they had been attacked in the rising, Carmynowe and his associates had falsely obtained the commission of inquiry and maliciously procured the indictments against Sir William, Eyr, and others.

A number of historians have taken these allegations against Botriaux at face value as evidence of disturbances in Cornwall.[127] However, it seems that these indictments were procured maliciously and that the information in them is unreliable. This is shown not only by Elizabeth Botriaux's petition but also by the way in which some of the indictments concerning these alleged incidents in Cornwall were quashed because they had been made *before* the incidents described.[128] While there is no firm evidence that the gentry in Cornwall took advantage of the revolt to pursue their own vendettas, they certainly sought to manipulate the proceedings against the rebels. Although the evidence for disturbances in Cornwall is unreliable, there are however other tantalising hints that there may have been disturbances west of Somerset. In particular, two rolls describing disturbances in Devon during the rising were reported to have existed in the English public records in 1860 but have subsequently disappeared.[129]

The revolt in the Midlands

Part of the reason why the full extent of the revolt has not hitherto been evident is the patchy survival of records of commissions against the rebels. So far, records of commissions against the rebels have only been traced for Suffolk, Norfolk, Cambridgeshire, Essex, and Kent. It seems that, like the medieval peace rolls, enrolled proceedings of the rebels were only prepared when summoned by Chancery or King's Bench.[130] Private litigation relating to the revolt can often only be traced from references to known victims of the revolt or the use of distinctive forms of action, and it is difficult to identify private prosecutions relating to the revolt in areas where no commission records survive. It is likely that there are some areas which suffered major disturbances during the rising which we do not know about because records have not survived. This is illustrated by the Midlands, where it is clear that there was serious unrest, but few records relating to these events have survived.

For example, it is evident that men from Oxfordshire were actively engaged in the rising. The earliest recorded attack on a poll tax collector took place in Oxfordshire between Bicester and Woodstock in April 1381, when a collector of the clerical poll tax was assaulted,[131] and representatives of the city of Oxford were present at the meeting at Mile End,[132] but otherwise we have little detailed information about the involvement of that county in the revolt. In Warwickshire, an indictment taken by local justices of the peace accused John Butcher of Wormleighton of going to St Albans on 1 July 1381 to persuade the insurgents there to visit Warwickshire.[133] In anticipation of their arrival, he had removed all his goods from the county. There was major unrest in Bedfordshire, but details are sketchy: the townsfolk of Dunstable tried to secure a charter from the Prior there,[134] while at Luton escheators' records reveal that textile workers rose up[135] and there was an attack on the property of Sir William Crosier at Wrestlingworth on the Cambridgeshire border on 17 June 1381.[136]

An indictment called into King's Bench provides the only information about the attempts of William Napton to incite a rising in Northampton against the mayor and other leading citizens.[137] Another intriguing stray indictment from Northamptonshire describes how John Semper, who had previously escaped from the gaol in Northampton castle, went at the beginning of June 1381 to Brampton Ash and other places in the county, and, claiming that he was John Philpot, the famous London merchant, tried to persuade the local people to rise up. Semper successfully managed to escape these charges by pleading benefit of clergy.[138] Again, a number of passing references attest that there were major disturbances in Lincolnshire in the summer of 1381. On 18 June faithful subjects of the king were ordered to resist insurgents in Lincolnshire,[139] but the only information which survives about these events is that tenants of the Hospitallers in Lincolnshire withdrew their services.[140]

In Derbyshire, the Stahum family had a long-standing dispute with John of Gaunt over the manor of Morley. On 18 June 1381, hearing about the revolt, the Stahums and their supporters killed tenants of Gaunt in Morley and attacked the Augustinian Priory of Breadsall, which also held property in Morley. The Stahums and their supporters besieged the prior in the church and raised the banner of St George over the gatehouse. The Stahums also attacked Horston Castle which was held by Gaunt's chamberlain Sir Robert Swillington. On 20 June, one of Gaunt's knights, retaliated by attacking property of the Stahum family.[141] While these events in Derbyshire might seem merely opportunistic, the use of such signals as the raising of the banner of St George indicates a conscious alignment with the rebels in London. Much of the wider antipathy to Gaunt seems to have been fostered by local disputes of this kind, often encouraged by the gentry.

The revolt in Yorkshire

The Yorkshire disturbances in Scarborough, Beverley, and York have frequently been dismissed as having little to do with the mainstream of the revolt, but this is far from being the case. Indeed, closer analysis of these northern disturbances is the key to understanding the character of the revolt as a whole. The revolt in York, Scarborough, and Beverley was driven by the same tensions about the fiscal and other demands of the crown which fed the insurgency in Southern England.[142] As Christian Liddy has shown, this is particularly evident from the disturbances in York, which had their origins in the forcible removal of John Gisburn as mayor in 1380 and his replacement by Simon Quixlay.[143] As mayor of the staple in York, Gisburn had profited enormously from the export of wool and cloth and had secured huge loans for the crown. He used these financial connections with the crown to secure profitable offices and concessions, at a time when the city found the cost of supporting and maintaining ships to support the war in France burdensome.

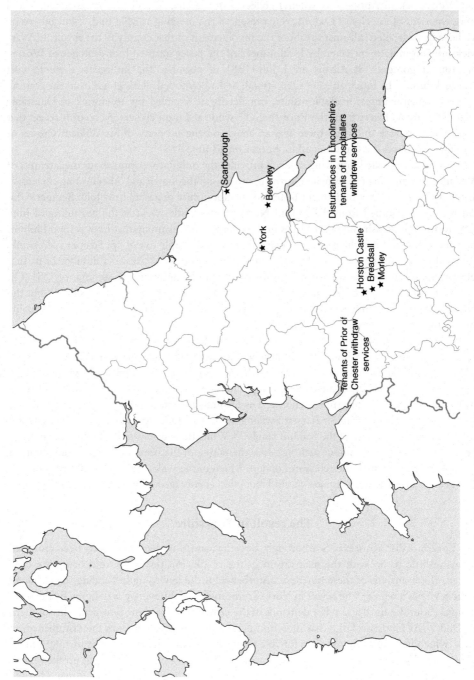

Map 4.2 Some places in Northern England which experienced disturbances during the English rising of 1381.

Gisburn was said to have used his connections with the royal mint in York to profit from the conversion of 10,000 pounds of English money into lighter Scotch coin. Gisburn's use of the ships expensively maintained by the city when they were not wanted against the French particularly rankled. Gisburn served as mayor four times between 1371 and 1380 and appeared to be creating an oligarchy supported by the crown which was excluding other merchants such as Quixlay. The animosity against Gisburn in York, far from being a 'squalid and obscure municipal quarrel', does not appear very different from the motives which drove the inhabitants of London and other towns such as Cambridge, Bury, St Albans, and Canterbury to take part in the revolt. It reflects a wider resentment at the way in which the fiscal and military demands of the crown seemed to be promoting new elites and oligarchies.

If we see events in Yorkshire and Derbyshire in 1381 as part of the mainstream of the revolt, the persistent unrest in those counties over the next ten years, which prompted the King's Bench to hold special judicial hearings in those counties in 1392 and 1393, becomes more significant.[144] Some of the cases heard by King's Bench at that time, including one concerning the proclamation of English verses expressing a determination to resist injustice, date back to the period immediately after the revolt and suggest that its spirit still lingered in Northern England.[145] The persistence of disturbances in Northern England challenges the received view that the revolt quickly collapsed.

As our awareness of the geographically dispersed nature of the rising increases, previous views of the temporal span of the rising as a sharply defined and short-lived event are also challenged. The idea that the disturbances rapidly subsided after the death of Tyler, with equilibrium being rapidly restored by the wise concession of a general pardon, is Whiggish wishful thinking, challenged by the persistent unrest in Northern England.[146] The scale of the revolt meant that its suppression was brutal and bloody, with military commissions executing suspects on the basis of hearsay evidence, Flemish widows allowed to behead the murderers of their husbands in Cheapside, and suspected rebels violently beaten in prison. The judicial proceedings against the rebels were manipulated to pursue private vendettas and a moratorium on private prosecutions had to be introduced. The general amnesty sought to draw a line under a judicial process which was out of control. The revolt was not an isolated passing episode but a traumatic event which overshadowed England for a generation.

As we develop a view of the revolt which emphasises both its geographical scale and its persistence, it ceases to seem so short term and self-contained, and suggestions emerge of continuities between the revolt and later events further afield. For example, it is perhaps significant that the rising tensions in Wales during the years leading up to the rising of Owain Glyn Dŵr in 1400 were fuelled by disputes about the performance of labour services and that there was a wholesale withdrawal of these services in the first stages of Glyn Dŵr's rising.[147] A contemporary observer described Glyn Dŵr's revolt as 'a rising of the Welsh commons',[148] suggesting that it was in its early stages as much a social revolt as a national rebellion, and that it may have been influenced by memories of the disturbances in 1381 along the Welsh borders in places such as Chester, Shrewsbury, and Gloucester and the involvement in the 1381 revolt of men with Welsh connections such as David Calveley.[149]

The composition of the rebel bands in London and the south-east

If we see the revolt as more geographically dispersed than has hitherto been allowed, then how should our view of the events in London change? It seems that, just is in other parts of the country, the disturbances in London were multi-layered, linking together local, regional, and national grievances in a complex fashion. A letter written on 17 June 1381 by the Hanseatic

Kontor at the Steelyard in London to a senior official of the Order of the Teutonic Knights in Prussia described how the arrival of groups from Kent and Essex had precipitated a rising by 'a great multitude from the city of London' and lays the blame for many of the events on the Londoners themselves.[150] A similar picture emerges from trespass actions brought by John of Gaunt over the sacking of the Savoy Palace which provide the names of hundreds of participants in this attack.[151] We do not know how Gaunt and his officials got their information about the rebels, but it is striking that the majority of those identified come from London and its hinterland. There had previously been an attempt by Londoners to attack the Savoy during the aftermath of the reversal of the actions of the Good Parliament when Gaunt had protected John Wyclif.[152] The resentment against Gaunt in London and elsewhere was fed by long-standing grievances such as these. As Caroline Barron observes, 'It was a deeply divided and factious city which confronted the rebels in June 1381 … The city was in the throes of constitutional experiment and of intense and deeply-felt political debate.'[153] The revolt in London was just as much driven by local conflicts and antagonism as those in Bridgwater or York (and, conversely, the rebels in Bridgwater and York were just as concerned with national politics as those in London).

The way in which participation in the rising blended local, regional, economic, religious, and political concerns is illustrated by the small bands from Hertfordshire and Essex identified in Gaunt's prosecutions as joining with Londoners in the destruction of the Savoy. The largest of these groups was from Ware in Hertfordshire. There was intense rivalry between Ware and Hertford as ports of the River Lea, with Hertford seeking unsuccessfully to stifle the growth of Ware by trying to have its bridge destroyed and taking judicial action against its market. Hertford also protested against the growth of dying and tanning in Ware and in 1356 Hertford citizens used the labour legislation to prosecute dyers and tanners in Ware.[154] It seems that the Ware townsfolk encouraged agitation against the labour legislation, and in 1356 the Vicar of Aldbury and a hermit were tried at Ware for preaching against the laws controlling labourers.[155] The rivalry between Hertford and Ware was complicated by the fact that Hertford Castle belonged to John of Gaunt and was one of his favourite residences.[156]

The involvement of Ware in the revolt of 1381 was apparently precipitated by the appearance there of a small group from Thaxted, where labour legislation had recently been used to prevent farmers from offering generous wages in hiring additional help.[157] The arrival of insurgents from Thaxted led to a general rising of a cross-section of the population of Ware, including the Vicar of Ware, the clerk of the church, some former bailiffs of the town, and prominent members of the Guild of Corpus Christi which held property in the town.[158] The intersection between local and national grievances of rebel groups such as these is illustrated by the way in which the Ware insurgents lost no time in organising an attack on Hertford and sacked Gaunt's castle there.[159] Rebels from Ware helped spread the rebellion through Hertfordshire, participating for example in an attack on the Abbot of Westminster's property in Amwell.[160]

The Ware and Thaxted band then moved rapidly down the Lea valley towards London, and participated in an attack on the Bishop of London's prison at Bishop's Stortford.[161] Indeed, one indictment suggests that John Ball was released from Bishop's Stortford rather than Maidstone prison, which would associate Ball with the Ware band rather than the Kent rebels at Blackheath, a suggestion which as Juliet Barker has recently pointed out is not implausible.[162] The motives for the prominence of the Ware band in the attack on the Savoy were thus mixed, including resentment against Gaunt for his association with their hated rival of Hertford, discontent with the labour legislation, and the influence of radical preaching.

Although the Ware band left London after the Mile End meeting, they did not return peaceably. As they went back along the Lea valley, they captured William Patrick who had been among those responsible for the use of labour legislation to prosecute Ware artisans 30 years earlier and beheaded him.[163] The Vicar of Ware took some of those who had been with him in London to North-east Hertfordshire to incite fresh disturbances in his former parish of Aspenden. Within the parish lay the small market town of Buntingford which had grown rapidly since the 1360s and whose inhabitants were fiercely protective of their independence from local manorial control of their market.[164] Recurrent disputes about Buntingford's market apparently prompted the Vicar to lead some of its inhabitants in an attack on the houses of John Quenyld, a former justice of the peace and member of parliament for Hertfordshire.[165]

Networks of insurgency in Essex and East Anglia

The Thaxted and Ware insurgents epitomise the way in which we should think of the structure of the revolt – small bands motivated by a mixture of grievances moving very quickly through the countryside and sparking further disturbances in their wake. We have already seen how similar small groups of messengers and agitators prompted risings in towns like Winchester and Bridgwater. Indeed, the pattern apparent in Winchester, where a small band bringing news of the rising led to riots by local townsfolk fuelled by long-standing grievances, seems to have been repeated on a much larger scale in London. Previous interpretations of the structure of the revolt have imagined hordes of peasants descending on London. It appears that rather we should imagine rebel bands criss-crossing the country, from Surrey to Hampshire, Southwark to Berkshire, and Essex to Cambridgeshire and Suffolk.

However, although the rising was complex and diffuse in its structure, this does not mean that it was unplanned and undirected. The activities of messengers like Thomas Falconer in Surrey and Hampshire, or John Snell raising rebellion by ringing the bell in St Osyth, suggest concerted and coordinated efforts to spread the rising. The large meeting held at Bocking in Essex on 2 June at which a large group swore to be of one mind 'to destroy divers lieges of the king and his common laws and all lordship' or 'to destroy divers lieges of the lord king and to have no law in England except those they themselves moved to be ordained' looks very much like a meeting at which the course of an insurrection might be plotted,[166] especially since the indictments state that the rebels at Bocking afterwards sent letters to many villages urging them to join the rising. However, it does not follow from this that the aim was then to capture London. Rather it appears that there was a concerted attempt to spread the rebellion as far as possible.

The rebel leader whose movements can be reconstructed in most detail at this time is the Suffolk chaplain John Wraw, and he does not seem to have seen London as his primary target.[167] Wraw was in close contact with the group who swore the oath at Bocking, joining with them in an attack on a manor of Richard Lyons at Liston on the Essex–Suffolk border on 12 June. Wraw afterwards went into Cambridgeshire where he attacked a manor of the local sheriff at Birdbrook, an event which triggered the rising in Cambridgeshire. Wraw himself then headed into Suffolk, where he precipitated the riots in Bury. Taking a large force to Mildenhall, Wraw seized the Prior of Bury and brought him back to Bury where he and another monk were beheaded. Wraw then moved to North-east Suffolk, where he stormed the Earl of Suffolk's castle at Mettingham Castle and beheaded a corrupt official, Geoffrey Southgate, at Beccles. Thomas Walsingham alleged that Wraw met Wat Tyler in London and had taken instructions from him.[168] While this seems unlikely, since Wraw was already participating in the revolt before Tyler entered London, Wraw was no opportunist; he had been connected with a key group of insurgents in Essex from the earliest stage of the revolt.

Wraw's focus was on spreading the revolt in East Anglia and he was the chief link between the different groups of insurgents there. He helped precipitate the revolt in Cambridgeshire and was in close contact with rebels in Norfolk. After Roger Bacon, acting under Geoffrey Lister's orders, seized the controversial charter granting the town of Yarmouth extensive powers over the sale of the staple food of herring, he tore it in two, sending one part to Lister and the other to John Wraw,[169] an illustration of the prestige enjoyed by Wraw in East Anglia. The activities of both Wraw and Lister suggest that the political aims of the rebels were more sophisticated than a simple march to London to take control of the king. Lister in particular seems to have been more interested in establishing a regional power base.[170] He held quasi-judicial sessions in which bills were heard and issued proclamations concerning the collection of customs. Thomas Walsingham claimed that Lister seized five members of the local gentry and forced them to ride with him, obliging them to kneel to him in deference and to taste his food and drink.[171] Clearly, Lister was more than a village ruffian, and had some sophisticated political and social ideas.

Reshaping the revolt

One reason why scholars have failed fully to appreciate the complexity of the revolt of 1381 is that they have imposed on the revolt modern preconceptions about the nature and character of revolutions. Just as the structures of political power were more complex and dispersed in the Middle Ages than in modern societies, so likewise the dynamics of conflict and protest were different in the Middle Ages and do not accord with modern assumptions. Patrick Lantschner has stressed the problems caused by analysing the Ciompi as if it was a modern political conflict: '1378 was often analysed almost as if it concerned 1789, 1830 or 1848'.[172] The same difficulties occur in studies of the English rising of 1381. As Lantschner observes:

> Our notion of conflict is intrinsically bound up with particular concepts of state, class and revolution that are particularly geared to the explanation of modern political phenomena. Our understanding of a revolution is shaped by modern paradigms ranging from the French Revolution to the 1979 Iranian Revolution, assuming that a revolution must be a "antithesis, subversion or pathology of the political order".[173]

Scholarly discussion of 1381 has been shaped by implicit comparisons with modern revolutions and uses anachronistic criteria in assessing the character and significance of the rising.

The insistence of many scholars on a distinction between the events in London in 1381 and 'secondary actions' elsewhere is paralleled by the way in which some recent sociological literature on revolutions focuses on central state structures in explaining revolts, playing down the significance of local regional movements. The 'statist' approach of recent theoretical discussions of revolutions is epitomised by the work of Theda Skocpol who argued that revolutions were not primarily 'bottom-up' movements but were generated by weaknesses within the state itself leading to conflict between elites.[174] This structural approach to revolutions was summarised by Skocpol's student Jack Goldstone as 'a top-down view in which a state crisis of authority, when abetted by elite alienation and popular mobilization potential, creates a revolutionary situation'.[175] Such top-down interpretations of revolutions were questioned following the Iranian Revolution of 1979 and the revolutions in Eastern Europe in 1989. Contrary to Skocpol's prognosis, the Iranian Revolution 'occurred in a state that was powerful and wealthy and had experienced no major financial or international crisis',[176] and was led by Islamic revivalists. In Eastern Europe, the relationship between movements such as Solidarity and changes in Soviet policy was more complex than the statist models of Skocpol and Goldstone predicted.

A number of commentators have urged that in analysing revolts and resistance we should focus less on the state and more on wider popular cultures, an approach that seems particularly appropriate to discussion of medieval revolts. Culturalists such as Eric Selbin have argued in favour of 'Bringing Culture Back In' and 'Bringing Agency Back In', using examples from Latin America to emphasise the complexity of revolutions as phenomena and insisting on the importance of taking into account a multiplicity of factors.[177] Paul Routledge in his description of the Nepal Revolution of 1990 describes how 'resistances take diverse forms, they move in different dimensions (of the family, community, region, etc.), they create unexpected networks, connections, and possibilities'.[178] Nevertheless, Routledge emphasises that

> the practices and discourse of such resistance require some form of co-ordination and communication ... In order to effect this resistance, actants [that is, the various collective entities engaged in resistance] must establish (however temporarily) social spaces and socio-spatial networks that are insulated from control or resistance.[179]

Historians of 1381 have been nervous of suggesting that the revolt was dispersed or complex in structure for fear of appearing to impugn the leadership ability and political vision of the rebels, but events like the Nepal Revolution show how revolts often have a complex spatial and social structure.

The Arab uprisings of 2011 and their aftermath provide many examples of protest movements which, just like the 1381 uprisings, are dispersed and multi-layered in their structure. Marc Lynch observes that 'The Arab upheavals of 2011 require a dynamic model of political contention that takes into account the interaction of diverse actors across multiple levels of analysis'.[180] The distinctive features of the Arab risings identified by Lynch can also be seen in the events of 1381 in England: they were massive, surprising, fast, and driven by new actors with a pronounced regional identity. Just as with medieval revolts, the Arab uprisings were characterised by dispersed spatial structures of protest with strong regional networks.

In one of the first analyses of the social geography of the rising in Tunisia in 2011, Habeb Ayeb emphasised the apparent lack of leadership and ideology, and argued that interlocking regional tensions largely shaped the revolt.[181] In Egypt, Maha Abdelrahman has described how

> protests were multilayered, cutting across different social groups in society, while also exposing the basis of a falsely conceived dichotomy between groups organised around 'political' demands on one hand and those struggling to achieve supposedly 'non-political', economic demands on the other.[182]

Koenraad Bogaert has noted how discussion of the 2011 protests in Morocco ignores regional disturbances in areas such as the phosphate mining region of Khouribga.[183] Just as in 1381, the widespread local disturbances in Morocco at this time are 'are usually left out of political analysis or at best considered as local symptoms on the margins – as if this kind of protest were only second to the civil democratic struggle'.[184] The distinctions made between metropolitan revolts and regional disturbances derive from the assumption that there is a difference between more politically focused constitutional revolts and regional socio-economic protests. Drawing on Rosa Luxemburg, Abdelrahman and Bogaert argue that these distinctions make little sense in events like those in Morocco where regional protests were just as important as those in capital cities. A similar analysis is also applicable to the events of 1381 in England, where regional protests have not been given the prominence they deserve.

It would of course be just as dangerous to take the Arab Spring as a paradigm for medieval revolts as it is to rely on the example of the French Revolution or 1848. The post-colonial dimensions of the Arab uprisings for example make them very different from medieval insurgency.

Nevertheless events like those in Morocco illustrate that risings and movements can have complex spatial structures with strong local movements without diminishing their political, social, or cultural sophistication. The anxiety of historians like Brooks and Hilton to demonstrate that the rebels of 1381 were highly organised and possessed a coherent political agenda is in itself an expression of anachronistic statist assumptions – Tyler is seen as a potential Robespierre, Lenin, or Mao, and judged by his ability to match up to these protean figures.

The striking thing about local conflicts in 1381 in towns like Bridgwater, Winchester, Oxford, and Ware is how they embraced many different arenas: the church, local religious houses, the gild merchant, the county community and officials, as well as contact with royal courts, customs, and other agencies. This reflects the way in which political life in medieval towns was distributed across many different associations and jurisdictions.[185] The persistent urban unrest in England, as in other parts of Europe, reflected the dynamics between these different political, ecclesiastical, and jurisdictional units. Moreover, these multiple bases of political and communal organisation were not only a feature of town life but were also a feature of rural society: parish, fraternity, manor all made their own demands for attention and shaped communal life. At many points during the rising of 1381, the intersection between these urban and rural agencies became evident, as for example when rural insurgents attacked Yarmouth's monopolies over the herring trade. These alliances were not temporary phenomena arising from the events of the revolt but rather an expression of the way in which the social structures of town and countryside were deeply intertwined.[186] One reason why the rising in 1381 assumed such a great size and posed such a threat was the way in which urban and rural coalitions were so rapidly formed, so that the Bridgwater insurgents did not simply express their grievances about the town's government but also pressed for the grant of charters of manumission from manorial services.

Medieval revolts differed in aims, character, and structure from modern revolutions because medieval politics and society were different, with their own power and elite structures. The cross-currents that fed and shape medieval revolts reflect the complex layerings of communal and associational structures of medieval society. In studying medieval revolts, our concern should not be to anachronistically reconfigure the event in order to distinguish 'true' rebellion from 'aftershocks', but rather to examine the way in which the different threads of conflict and dissent lock together.

Notes

1 TNA, C 66/310 m. 4d. Extracts from the full text of this commission are printed in A. Réville, *Le soulèvement des travailleurs d'Angleterre en 1381*, Paris: École des Chartes, 1898, pp. 235–6, and it is summarised at *CPR 1381–5*, 23. All records cited in this chapter are in TNA unless otherwise cited. I am very grateful to Lynn Arner, Caroline Barron, Sylvia Federico, Justine Firnhaber-Baker, Elizabeth Robertson, Susan Mitchell Sommers, and Paul Strohm for their incisive comments on drafts of this chapter. As ever, responsibility for errors is mine. An earlier version of this chapter was given in the Medieval and Tudor London seminar convened by Caroline Barron and Vanessa Harding at the Institute of Historical Research.
2 E. W. Stockton, *The Major Latin Works of John Gower*, Seattle, WA: University of Washington Press, 1962, p. 69.
3 London, Blackie, 1898.
4 C. Oman, *The Great Revolt of 1381*, 2nd edn, Oxford: Oxford University Press, 1969, p. 99.
5 Ibid., p. 90.
6 R. Hilton, *Bond Men Made Free: Medieval Peasant Movements and the English Rising of 1381*, 2nd edn, London: Routledge, 2003, p. 174.
7 Ibid., p. 139.

8 Ibid., p. 142.
9 C. Barron, *Revolt in London: 11th to 15th June 1381*, London: Museum of London, 1981, p. 1.
10 Ibid., p. 9.
11 P. Freedman, *Images of the Medieval Peasant*, Stanford, CA: Stanford University Press, 1999, p. 260.
12 N. Brooks, 'The organization and achievements of the peasants of Kent and Essex in 1381', in H. Mayr-Harting and R. I. Moore (eds), *Studies in Medieval History Presented to R. H. C. Davis*, London: Hambledon Press, 1985, p. 248.
13 There are some dissenting voices among this London-centric scholarly consensus, most notably P. Strohm, 'A "Peasants' Revolt"?', in S. J. Harris and B. L. Grigsby (eds), *Misconceptions about the Middle Ages*, New York and London: Routledge, 2008, pp. 197–203, and D. Watts, 'Popular disorder in southern England 1250–1450', in B. Stapleton (ed.), *Conflict and Community in Southern England*, Stroud: Alan Sutton, 1992, pp. 2–15.
14 S. Justice, *Writing and Rebellion: England in 1381*, Berkeley: University of California Press, 1994, p. 2.
15 Ibid., p. 21.
16 Brooks, 'Organization of the peasants in 1381', p. 249.
17 Strohm, 'A "Peasants' Revolt"?', pp. 197–203.
18 Hilton, *Bond Men Made Free*, pp. 198–207; S. K. Cohn, Jr., *Popular Protest in Late Medieval English Towns*, Cambridge: Cambridge University Press, 2013, p. 324.
19 Hilton, *Bond Men Made Free*, p. 179.
20 Ibid., pp. 207–13; Cohn, *Popular Protest in Late Medieval English Towns*, p. 325.
21 D. de Saxe, 'The Hundred of Wye and the Great Revolt of 1381', *Archaeologia Cantiana*, 177, 2007, pp. 143–61.
22 J. Barker, *England Arise: The People, the King and the Great Revolt of 1381*, London: Little, Brown, 2014, pp. 333, 340–3, 351–2, 357.
23 R. Dobson, 'Remembering the Peasants' Revolt, 1381–1981', in W. Liddell and R. Wood (eds), *Essex and the Great Revolt of 1381*, Chelmsford: Essex Record Office, 1982, p. 16; Strohm, 'A "Peasants' Revolt"?', pp. 201–2. The term was also used by P. Lorimer in his translation of G. V. Lechler, *John Wiclif and his English Precursors*, 2 vols, London: Kegan Paul, 1878, vol. 2, p. 229. S. R. Gardiner in his *Outline of English History: First Period BC 55 – AD 1603*, London: Longmans Green, 1881, pp. 98–9 refers to the 'insurrection of the peasants', but by 1890 in his *Students' History of England*, 2 vols, London: Longmans Green, 1890–1, vol. 1, pp. 268–9, Gardiner uses the term 'Peasants' Revolt', thereby further popularising it. Following its use by N. Neilson in *Economic Conditions on the Manors of Ramsey Abbey*, Philadelphia, PA: Sherman, 1898, p. 73, the term 'Peasants' Revolt' was widely adopted by specialist historians of the Middle Ages. A possible source of inspiration for Green's use of the term 'Peasants' Revolt' may perhaps have been the way in which it was used to draw parallels between the revolt of 1381 and the work of Joseph Arch in forming a trade union for agricultural workers, for example by the journalist E. Goadby, 'The Peasants' Revolt', *New Monthly Magazine*, 4, 1873, pp. 36–40.
24 R. B. Dobson, *The Peasants' Revolt of 1381*, 2nd edn, London: Macmillan, 1983, p. 370.
25 For example, on 20 June 1381, Robert Ashton, constable of Dover Castle and warden of the Cinque Ports, John de Clynton and others were ordered to make proclamations against *insurrectiones levaciones et congregaciones*: C 66/310 m. 4d (*CPR 1381–5*, 23); an order in August 1381 for the arrest of John Goodgroom of Brenchley in Kent stated that he had taken part *in insurrectione per communitatem regni nostri Anglie contra pacem nostram*: C 66/311, m. 24d (*CPR 1381–5*, 78).
26 E. Powell, *The Rising in East Anglia in 1381*, Cambridge: Cambridge University Press, 1896, pp. 127–30.
27 KB 145/3/6/1 (unnumbered membranes).
28 KB 145/3/5/1 (unnumbered membranes).
29 *[L]a grant et horrible rumor et insurrection nadgairs treterousement faitz dans le roialme encontre la paix la corone et le dignite nostre dit seigneur le Roi*, order requiring details of proceedings against Thomas Farringdon and Richard Dell who had been excluded from the pardon: KB 145/3/6/1 (unnumbered membranes).
30 KB 145/3/6/1 (unnumbered membranes).
31 R. Somerville, *History of the Duchy of Lancaster*, vol. 1, London: Duchy of Lancaster, 1953, p. 63, n. 1.
32 R. Faith, 'The "Great Rumour" of 1377 and peasant ideology', in R. Hilton and T. Aston (eds), *The English Rising of 1381*, Cambridge: Cambridge University Press, 1984, pp. 43–73.

33 F. Brie (ed.), *The Brut or the Chronicles of England*, 2 vols, London: Kegan Paul, Trench, Trübner for the Early English Text Society, 1906–1908, vol. 2, p. 336. Mary-Rose McLaren suggests that the term may have been first used in a London chronicle of the late fourteenth century: M. McLaren, *The London Chronicles of the Fifteenth Century: A Revolution in English Writing*, Cambridge: D. S. Brewer, 2002, p. 22.
34 R. Beadle and C. Richmond (eds), *Paston Letters and Papers of the Fifteenth Century*, 3 vols, Oxford: Oxford University Press, 2005, vol. 3, pp. 53, 55; F. Blomefield, *An Essay Towards a Topographical History of the County of Norfolk*, 11 vols, London: W. Miller, 1805–10, vol. 3, p. 106.
35 P. Strohm, *Hochon's Arrow: The Social Imagination of Fourteenth-Century Texts*, Princeton, NJ: Princeton University Press, 1992, pp. 33–56.
36 I have discussed this process in an unpublished paper given at the Harlaxton Medieval Symposium in 2004, 'Theatres of Rebellion: Representations of the Peasants' Revolt in London's Civic Culture 1381–1981'.
37 P. Strohm, *Social Chaucer*, Cambridge, MA: Harvard University Press, 1989, pp. 64–5.
38 KB 9/196/2, m. 10; I. W. M. Harvey, 'Was there popular politics in fifteenth-century England?', in R. H. Britnell and A. J. Pollard (eds), *The McFarlane Legacy: Studies in Late Medieval Politics and Society*, Stroud: Alan Sutton, 1995, p. 168.
39 KB 27/650 *rex* m. 2.
40 Harvey, 'Was there popular politics?', p. 168.
41 S. Longstaffe, *A Critical Edition of the Life and Death of Jack Strawe, 1594*, Lewiston: Edwin Mellen Press, 2002; Dobson, 'Remembering the Peasants' Revolt', pp. 11–12.
42 For example, a textbook such as E. Willard, *Universal History in Perspective*, 2nd edn, New York: A. S. Barnes, 1845, p. 265 asked students to 'Give an account of the Insurrection of Wat Tyler'.
43 A. Wood, *The 1549 Rebellions and the Making of Early Modern England*, Cambridge: Cambridge University Press, 2007, pp. 40–69.
44 A. Wood, *Riot, Rebellion and Popular Politics in Early Modern England*, Basingstoke: Palgrave, 2002, pp. 5–48.
45 Ibid., p. 49.
46 H. Wunde, 'The mentality of rebellious peasants: the Samland Peasant Rebellion of 1525', in B. Scribner and G. Benecke (eds), *The German Peasant War of 1525: New Viewpoints*, London: George Allen & Unwin, 1979, p. 144.
47 C. Schmidt, *David Hume: Reason in History*, University Park: Pennsylvania State University Press, 2003, pp. 308–9.
48 N. Saul, *Richard II*, New Haven, CT and London: Yale University Press, 1997, pp. 56–7, 59, 61.
49 M. Bailey, *The Decline of Serfdom in Late Medieval England: From Bondage to Freedom*, Woodbridge: Boydell, 2014, pp. 309–11.
50 Justice, *Writing and Rebellion*; A. Galloway, 'Gower in his most learned role and the Peasants' Revolt of 1381', *Mediaevalia*, 16, 1993, pp. 329–47; A. Galloway, 'Making history legal: *Piers Plowman* and the rebels of fourteenth-century England', in K. Hewett-Smith, *William Langland's Piers Plowman: A Book of Essays*, New York and London: Routledge, 2001, pp. 7–40; A. Galloway, 'Communities, crowd theory and mob theory in late fourteenth-century English history, writing and poetry', in N. van Deusen and L. M. Koff (eds), *Mobs: An Interdisciplinary Enquiry*, Leiden: Brill, 2012, pp. 141–64; S. Federico, *New Troy: Fantasies of Empire in Late Middle Ages*, Minneapolis: University of Minnesota Press, 2003; S. Federico, 'The imaginary society: women in 1381', *Journal of British Studies*, 40, 2001, pp. 159–83; L. Arner, *Chaucer, Gower and the Vernacular Rising: Poetry and the Problem of the Populace after 1381*, University Park: University of Pennsylvania Press, 2013.
51 Dobson, *Peasants' Revolt*, p. 28.
52 M. Postan, 'Medieval agrarian society in its prime: England', in M. Postan (ed.), *Agrarian Life of the Middle Ages*, Cambridge Economic History of Europe from the Decline of the Roman Empire 1, Cambridge: Cambridge University Press, 1966, p. 610.
53 J. A. Raftis, 'Social change versus revolution: new interpretations of the Peasants' Revolt of 1381', in F. Newman (ed.), *Social Unrest in the Middle Ages*, Binghamton: State University of New York, 1986, pp. 3–22, argues that difficulties in interpreting the rising arise from comparison with modern political revolutions. Nevertheless, Raftis concludes (p. 19) that the revolt was 'a mere ripple on the troubled surface of peasant life in late fourteenth-century England'.
54 Wood, *Riot, Rebellion and Popular Politics*, p. 49.
55 Federico, 'The imaginary society', p. 182.

56 V. H. Galbraith (ed.), *The Anonimalle Chronicle 1333 to 1381*, Manchester: Manchester University Press, 1927, pp. 133–51 (Dobson, *Peasants' Revolt*, pp. 123–31, 155–68, 235–7, 305–6).
57 Dobson, 'Remembering the Peasants' Revolt', p. 7.
58 Galbraith, *Anonimalle Chronicle*, pp. xxx–xlv. For a detailed assessment of the quality of the report of the Good Parliament in the *Anonimalle* chronicle, see J. Taylor, 'The Good Parliament and its sources', in J. Taylor and W. Childs (eds), *Politics and Crisis in Fourteenth-Century England*, Gloucester: Alan Sutton, 1990, pp. 88–91.
59 C. Oliver, *Parliament and Political Pamphleteering in Fourteenth-Century England*, York: York Medieval Press, 2010, pp. 29–55.
60 A. J. Prescott, 'The judicial records of the Rising of 1381', PhD thesis, University of London, 1984, pp. 128–9 (available online at ethos.ac.uk).
61 J. Taylor suggested that other parts of the *Anonimalle* chronicle were compiled by someone with access to administrative and legal records: J. Taylor, 'The origins of the *Anonimalle* chronicle', *Northern History*, 31, 1995, pp. 61–2.
62 V. H. Galbraith, 'Thoughts about the Peasants' Revolt', in F. Du Boulay and C. Barron (eds), *The Reign of Richard II*, London: Athlone Press, 1971, p. 53.
63 G. Martin (ed.), *Knighton's Chronicle 1337–1396*, Oxford: Clarendon Press, 1995, pp. 207–31; L. Hector and B. Harvey (eds), *The Westminster Chronicle 1381–1394*, Oxford: Clarendon Press, 1982, pp. 2–21; Dobson, *Peasants' Revolt*, pp. 135–7, 181–7, 199–204, 237–8, 277–9.
64 Dobson, *Peasants' Revolt*, p. 262.
65 Ibid., p. 194.
66 J. Taylor, W. Childs, and L. Watkiss (eds), *The St Albans Chronicle: The Chronica Maiora of Thomas Walsingham*, 2 vols, Oxford: Clarendon Press, 2003–11, vol. 1, pp. 411–563; D. Preest and J. Clark (eds), *The Chronica Maiora of Thomas Walsingham*, Woodbridge: Boydell, 2005, pp. 120–67; Dobson, *Peasants' Revolt*, pp. 131–4, 168–81, 243–8, 256–61, 269–77, 306–13, 363–9.
67 A survey of these records is Prescott, 'Judicial records'. On the textuality of these documents, see further A. Prescott, 'Writing about rebellion: using the records of the Peasants' Revolt of 1381', *History Workshop Journal*, 45, 1998, pp. 1–27, and A. Prescott, 'The imaging of historical documents', in M. Greengrass and L. Hughes (eds), *The Virtual Representation of the Past*, Farnham: Ashgate, 2008, pp. 15–21.
68 Prescott, 'Judicial records', pp. 30–87.
69 Ibid., pp. 194–252.
70 Ibid., pp. 253–91.
71 Réville, *Soulèvement des Travailleurs*, pp. 58–128, 175–82.
72 Ibid., pp. 3–49.
73 Ibid., pp. 223, 254–6.
74 Powell, *Rising in East Anglia*, pp. 41–56, 136–8. This roll, now JUST 1/103, was printed by W. Palmer in what he himself admitted was an 'extraordinary mixture' of unreliable Latin transcription and ambiguous English abridgement: 'Records of the Villein Insurrection in Cambridgeshire', *East Anglian*, n.s., 6, 1896, pp. 81–4, 97–102, 135–9, 167–72, 209–12, 234–7.
75 Oman, *Great Revolt*, pp. 112–13.
76 Ibid., p. 146.
77 T. B. Dilks, 'Bridgwater and the insurrection of 1381', *Proceedings of Somerset Archaeological and Natural History Society*, 73, 1927, pp. 57–69; Prescott, 'Judicial records', pp. 221–4, 271–2.
78 *CPR 1377–81*, pp. 458, 466.
79 *CPR 1377–81*, p. 567.
80 *CPR 1377–81*, p. 570. The allegations suggest that the Master was attempting with the support of a faction led by Sydenham to exercise seigneurial rights in the town. This incident is noted in Cohn, *Popular Protest*, p. 197, but its wider context is not indicated. The reissue on 15 February 1381 to the burgesses of Bridgwater of King John's charter granting borough status is presumably connected with this dispute: *CPR 1377–81*, p. 597.
81 Frompton is described as being the provisor to the vicarage in petitions brought after the rising: SC 8/102/5051.
82 *CCR 1377–81*, p. 505. An indictment in the court of the bailiffs of Bridgwater taken on 9 January 1381 alleged that on the night of 28 October 1380 William Yafford of Sydenham and others lay in wait for John Sydenham in order to kill him. It was also claimed that on 24 April 1380 at Sandford in North Somerset Yafford had assaulted Walter Baron and tried to blind him: KB 145/3/5/1 (unnumbered membranes).

83 KB 27/483 m. 43.
84 T. B. Dilks (ed.), *Bridgwater Borough Archives*, 5 vols, London: Somerset Record Society, 1933–71, vol. 1, p. xxxiii, 179, 200.
85 C. Given-Wilson, P. Brand, S. Phillips, M. Ormrod, G. Martin, A. Curry, and R. Horrox (eds), *Parliament Rolls of Medieval England 1275–1504*, 16 vols, Woodbridge: Boydell Press, 2010, vol. 6, p. 229; SC 8/102/5051.
86 The events in Bridgwater are described in Engleby's pardon, translated in Dobson, *Peasants' Revolt*, pp. 280–2; in allegations brought by Richard Clyvedon against Sir William Coggan in parliament in November 1381: *Parliament Rolls of Medieval England*, vol. 6, pp. 229–30 (another version of Clyvedon's allegations is SC 8/102/5051); and in an indictment against Nicholas Frompton in the King's Bench files: KB 145/5/3/1 (unnumbered membranes).
87 Dilks, *Bridgwater Borough Archives*, vol. 1, p. 168, 216, 228. Duffield also acted as an agent of the guild merchant in repairs to the town bridge: ibid., p. 222. Engleby had been associated with Plympton and Duffield in witnessing land transactions in the town in the 1370s: ibid., pp. 205, 211.
88 The trespass actions by Sydenham are: CP 40/490 m. 495d; CP 40/491 mm. 261, 433, 476, 281d; CP 40/492 m. 151; CP 40/493 mm. 218, 278d. For Henton, see Dilks, *Bridgwater Borough Archives*, vol. 2, pp. xv, 48, *CCR 1381–5*, p. 108 and J. S. Roskell, L. Clarke, and C. Rawcliffe (eds), *The House of Commons 1386–1421*, 4 vols, Stroud: Alan Sutton, 1992, vol. 3, p. 510. For Thomer, see Roskell et al., *House of Commons*, vol. 4, pp. 585–6. Another prominent merchant named by Sydenham was the vintner John Sopham, who had been in April 1381 one of the assessors of the profits of the borough court and on his death in 1386 left land to establish an obit in the church: Dilks, *Bridgwater Borough Archives*, vol. 1, p. 145, vol. 2, pp. 49, 130, 175–8. Among minor officials named by Sydenham were John Canon, sheather, keeper of the northern highway, 1380; Richard Lange, keeper of Orlove Street, 1373; Andrew Skinner, keeper of the northern highway, 1380; John Kelly, keeper within the church and bridge, 1379–80; John Godred, keeper of Dameyete, 1378–9; and John Forthred, keeper of St Mary Street, 1379–80.
89 B. Harvey, 'Draft letters patent of manumission and pardon for the men of Somerset in 1381', *EHR*, 80, 1965, pp. 89–91. A copy of the text of the letters of manumission for the commons of Kent is preserved in BL, Cotton Ch. IV. 51. This is in exactly the same form as the letters for Hertfordshire and Somerset.
90 Galbraith, *Anonimalle Chronicle*, pp. 144–5 (Dobson, *Peasants' Revolt*, pp. 160–2. All translations are taken from Dobson, unless otherwise stated).
91 Tawney had become a Poor Knight before 1376: E. H. Fellowes, *The Military Knights of Windsor 1352–1944*, Windsor: St George's Chapel, 1944, p. 1.
92 *CPR 1381–5*, p. 354.
93 The online calendar entry for SC8/103/5111 states wrongly that Margery and John went to the Tower on the Wednesday after Corpus Christi, but the text of the petition is clear that they went there on 14 June – *Et vendirdy prochain ensuant* – and this is confirmed by the accusation made that John had participated in the killing of Simon Sudbury.
94 Galbraith, *Anonimalle Chronicle*, p. 146 (Dobson, *Peasants' Revolt*, pp. 162–3).
95 *CPR 1381–5*, p. 16; Cohn, *Popular Protest in Late Medieval English Towns*, pp. 234–5.
96 *CPR 1381–5*, p. 16.
97 KB 27/486 m. 69d. The involvement of Margery Tawney and Isabella Chapman in the events of 14 June illustrate the difficulty in assessing the role of women in the revolt of 1381. Cf. Federico, 'The imaginary society', p. 162: 'Women did not … play solely one particular sort of role or another but, rather, many – and interpreting this plurality is as challenging as defining "men's roles" in the Rising'.
98 A point emphasised by Watts, 'Popular disorder'.
99 *CPR 1381–5*, p. 73.
100 KB 27/482 *rex* m. 46d; KB 27/488 *rex* m. 19; KB 27/484 *rex* mm. 14–14d; Réville, *Soulèvement des Travailleurs*, p. 223.
101 KB 27/483 *rex* m. 25; E. Powell and G. Trevelyan, *The Peasants' Rising and the Lollards*, London: Longman, Green, 1899, pp. 17–18.
102 CP 40/491 mm. 81d, 539d; CP 40/492 mm. 407, 410; CP 40/493 m. 25d.
103 CP 40/490 m. 516; CP 40/491 mm. 12, 60d; CP 40/493 m. 109.
104 Powell and Trevelyan, *Peasants' Rising and the Lollards*, p. 12.
105 H. Hinck, 'The Rising of 1381 in Winchester', *EHR*, 125, 2010, pp. 112–26.

106 Ibid., pp. 116, 126.
107 *CPR 1381–5*, p. 631.
108 KB 27/492 *rex* m. 13, printed in J. Bellamy, *The Law of Treason in England in the Later Middle Ages*, Cambridge: Cambridge University Press, 1970, p. 94, n. 1. The indictment against Hawkwood is dated 4 September 1380, but the phraseology of the indictment and the fact that it describes Hawkwood's actions as treasonable are all more appropriate to June 1381. Hawkwood obtained a pardon in 1382, renewed in 1384, for any treasons or felonies committed by him during the late insurrection (*CPR 1381–5*, p. 399), indicating that he was concerned about being prosecuted as a rebel. As Réville, *Soulèvement des Travailleurs*, pp. 280–1, suggests, there may have been a scribal error in the date or (more likely) the indictment was manipulated so that Hawkwood could not use his pardon.
109 G. Sayles, 'Richard II in 1381 and 1399', *EHR*, 94, 1979, pp. 821–2.
110 *CPR 1381–5*, p. 72.
111 D. Lepine, *Brotherhood of Canons Serving Good: English Secular Cathedrals in the Middle Ages*, Woodbridge: Boydell, 1995, pp. 39–40.
112 *CPR 1374–7*, p. 248.
113 *CPR 1377–81*, p. 379.
114 P. Morgan, *War and Society in Medieval Cheshire 1277–1403*, Manchester: Chetham Society, 1987, p. 138; SC 8/103/5103. Calveley was confirmed in the estate of Dean of St Asaph in 1380: *CPR 1377–81*, p. 583.
115 *CPR 1377–81*, p. 632; SC8/140/6955.
116 SC8/140/6955.
117 KB 27/482 *rex* m. 39d; KB 27/485 *rex* m. 30d; KB 27/487 *rex* m. 19d (Réville, *Soulèvement des Travailleurs*, pp. 199–200).
118 SC 8/140/6955.
119 *CPR 1381–5*, p. 75.
120 *CPR 1381–5*, p. 481.
121 R. Holt, 'Thomas of Woodstock and events at Gloucester in 1381', *BIHR*, 58, 1985, pp. 237–42.
122 At the end of June, attempts were being made to raise rebel companies in Tendring Hundred and the Abbot of St Osyth had been threatened with death because of the execution of John Preston for presenting a petition repeating the demands made at Mile End: Prescott, 'Judicial records', p. 141.
123 Dobson, *Peasants' Revolt*, pp. 299–300.
124 Cohn, *Popular Protest in Late Medieval English Towns*, pp. 105–6.
125 E. B. Fryde, 'Peasant rebellion and discontents', in J. Thirsk and H. P. R. Finberg (eds), *The Agrarian History of England and Wales*, 11 vols, Cambridge: Cambridge University Press, 1967–2000, vol. 3, p. 778.
126 SC8/277/13837; *Calendar of Inquisitions Miscellaneous, 1377–88*, London: Her Majesty's Stationery Office, 1957, no. 176; KB 27/516 *rex* m. 14.
127 For example, Dobson, *Peasants' Revolt*, p. xxv; Hannes Kleineke, 'Why the West was wild: law and disorder in fifteenth-century Cornwall and Devon', in L. Clark (ed.), *The Fifteenth Century 3: Authority and Subversion*, Woodbridge: Boydell & Brewer, 2003, p. 77; Sayles, 'Richard II in 1381 and 1399'.
128 KB 27/516 *rex* m. 14.
129 W. Flaherty, 'The great rebellion in Kent of 1381 illustrated from the public records', *Archaeologia Cantiana*, 3, 1860, p. 66, n. 1; Prescott, 'Judicial records', pp. 91–2.
130 J. Post, 'Some limitations of the medieval peace rolls', *Journal of the Society of Archivists*, 4, 1973, p. 634; Prescott, 'Judicial records', pp. 88–91.
131 Barker, *England, Arise*, p. 144.
132 *CPR 1381–5*, 16.
133 JUST 3/167 m. 48; JUST 3/67/4 mm. 6, 19.
134 H. Luard (ed.), 'Annales Prioraratus de Dunstaplia', in *Annales Monastici*, 5 vols, London, Longman, Green, 1864–9, vol. 3, pp. 417–19.
135 E 153/451 m. 2; Réville, *Soulèvement des Travailleurs*, p. 276.
136 CP 40/493 m. 164d; CP 40/495 m. 340.
137 KB 27/486 *rex* m. 30; Réville, *Soulèvement des Travailleurs*, pp. 276–7.
138 JUST 3/52/7 m. 8; JUST 3/52/8 m. 8.
139 BL, Harley Charter 43.E.34. This letter does not appear on either the patent or close rolls.
140 *CPR 1381–5*, p. 75.

141 D. Crook, 'Derbyshire and the English Rising of 1381', *BIHR*, 60, 1987, pp. 9–23; Prescott, 'Judicial records', p. 339.
142 The only overview of these Yorkshire disturbances is R. Dobson, 'The risings in York, Beverley and Scarborough 1380–81', in Hilton and Aston (eds), *English Rising of 1381*, pp. 112–42.
143 C. Liddy, 'Urban conflict in late fourteenth-century England: the case of York in 1380–1', *EHR*, 118, 2003, pp. 1–32.
144 S. Walker, *Political Culture in Later Medieval England*, Manchester: Manchester University Press, p. 98.
145 A. Prescott, 'The Yorkshire partisans and the literature of popular discontent', in E. Treharne and G. Walker (eds), *The Oxford Handbook of Medieval Literature in English*, Oxford: Oxford University Press, 2010, pp. 321–52.
146 A. Prescott, '"The hand of God": the suppression of the Peasants' Revolt of 1381', in N. Morgan (ed.), *Prophecy, Apocalypse and the Day of Doom*, Donington: Shaun Tyas, 2004, pp. 317–41.
147 R. Davies, *The Revolt of Owain Glyn Dŵr*, Oxford: Oxford University Press, 1995, pp. 70–6, 214–17.
148 Davies, *Revolt of Owain Glyn Dŵr*, p. 217.
149 For Calveley, see above, p. 87.
150 F. Pedersen, 'The German Hanse and the Peasants' Revolt of 1381', *BIHR*, 57, 1984, pp. 92–8.
151 A. Prescott, 'Londoners in the Peasants' Revolt: a portrait gallery', *London Journal*, 7, 1981, pp. 126–30; Prescott, 'Judicial records', pp. 292–333.
152 G. Holmes, *The Good Parliament*, Oxford: Clarendon Press, 1975, pp. 189–90; Barron, *Revolt in London*, pp. 16–19.
153 Barron, *Revolt in London*, p. 9.
154 Prescott, 'Judicial records', pp. 304–8.
155 G. Sayles (ed.), *Select Cases in the Court of King's Bench*, 6, Selden Society, London: B. Quaritch, 1965, pp. 110–11.
156 A. Goodman, *John of Gaunt: The Exercise of Princely Power in Fourteenth-Century Europe*, London: Longman, 1992, pp. 302–3.
157 E. Fryde, *Peasants and Landlords in Later Medieval England*, Stroud: Alan Sutton Publishing, 1996, pp. 39, 118.
158 Prescott, 'Judicial records', pp. 304–8; Cohn, *Popular Protest in Late Medieval English Towns*, p. 326; D. Perman, *A New History of Ware, its People and its Buildings*, Ware: Rockingham Press, 2010, pp. 59–61.
159 CP 40/490 m. 489.
160 CP 40/490 m. 517; CP 40/491 m. 68d; CP 40/492 m. 165; B. Harvey, *Westminster Abbey and its Estates in the Middle Ages*, Oxford, Clarendon Press, 1975, pp. 269, 285.
161 KB 145/3/6/1 (unnumbered membranes).
162 Barker, *England, Arise*, pp. 212–13; A. Prescott, 'Ball, John (d. 1381)', *Oxford Dictionary of National Biography*, Oxford: Oxford University Press, 2004; online edn, May 2008, www.oxforddnb.com/view/article/1214.
163 KB 27/482 *rex* m. 438; KB 27/484 *rex* m. 23.
164 M. Bailey, 'A tale of two towns: Buntingford and Standon in the later Middle Ages', *JMH*, 19, 1993, pp. 351–71.
165 CP 40/485 mm. 338, 1858; CP 40/486 mm. 56, 3618; CP 40/489 m. 350; CP 40/492 m. 2798. On Quenyld, see *CCR 1377–81*, pp. 106, 221, 497; *CPR 1361–4*, pp. 64, 66, 293.
166 Brooks, 'Organization of the peasants in 1381', p. 252.
167 Prescott, 'Judicial records', pp. 150–60.
168 Taylor *et al.*, *The St Albans Chronicle*, vol. 1, pp. 480–1; Preest, *Chronica Maiora*, p. 142; Dobson, *Peasants' Revolt*, p. 244.
169 Barker, *England Arise*, pp. 341–2.
170 A. Prescott, 'Lister, Geoffrey (d. 1381)', *Oxford Dictionary of National Biography*, Oxford: Oxford University Press, 2004; online edn, January 2008, www.oxforddnb.com/view/article/16776.
171 Taylor *et al.*, *The St Albans Chronicle*, vol. 1, pp. 488–91; Preest, *Chronica Maiora*, pp. 144–5; Dobson, *Peasants' Revolt*, pp. 257–9.
172 P. Lantschner, 'Revolts and the political order of cities in the late Middle Ages', *P&P*, 225, 2014, p. 7.
173 Lantschner, 'Revolts and the political order of cities', p. 4.

174 T. Skocpol, *States and Social Revolutions: A Comparative Analysis of France, Russia and China*, Cambridge: Cambridge University Press, 1979.
175 J. Goldstone, 'Predicting revolutions: why we could (and should) have foreseen the revolutions of 1989–1991 in the U.S.S.R. and Eastern Europe', in N. Keddie (ed.), *Debating Revolutions*, New York: New York University Press, 1995, p. 54.
176 Keddie (ed.), *Debating Revolutions*, p. ix.
177 J. Wasserstrom, 'Bringing culture back in and other caveats: a critique of Jack Goldstone's recent essays on revolution', in Keddie (ed.), *Debating Revolutions*, pp. 168–9; E. Selbin, 'Bringing agency in', in J. Foran (ed.), *Theorizing Revolutions*, London: Routledge, 1997, p. 133.
178 P. Routledge, 'A spatiality of resistances: theory and practice in Nepal's revolution of 1990', in S. Pike and M. Keith (eds), *Geographies of Resistance*, London and New York: Routledge, p. 69.
179 Routledge, 'Spatiality of resistances', pp. 70–1.
180 M. Lynch, 'Introduction', in *The Arab Uprisings Explained: New Contentious Politics in the Middle East*, New York: Columbia University Press, 2014, p. 3.
181 H. Ayeb, 'Social and political geography of the Tunisian revolution: the alfa grass revolution', *Review of African Political Economy*, 38, 2011, pp. 467–79.
182 M. Abdelrahman, 'A hierarchy of struggles? The "economic" and the "political" in Egypt's revolution', *Review of African Political Economy*, 39, 2012, p. 616.
183 K. Bogaert, 'The revolt of small towns: the meaning of Morocco's history and the geography of social protests', *Review of African Political Economy*, 42, 2015, pp. 124–40.
184 Bogaert, 'Revolt of small towns', p. 125.
185 Lantschner, 'Revolts and the political order of cities', p. 9.
186 A. Butcher, 'English urban society and the Revolt of 1381', in Hilton and Aston (eds), *English Rising of 1381*, p. 110.

5

'UNITED WE STAND?'

Representing revolt in the historiography of Brabant and Holland (fourteenth to fifteenth centuries)

Dirk Schoenaers

In summer or autumn 1316, Jan van Boendale, magistrate's clerk in Antwerp, finished a first version of his *Brabantsche yeesten* (*Gesta* of Brabant). His first *magnum opus* was an ambitious dynastic history of the duchy written in Dutch verse. In the following years and decades, up to *c.*1351, Boendale continued to update his chronicle and to each redaction he added the latest information about recent events.[1] In the opening chapters of the fifth and final book, he commemorated the untimely death of Duke John I, who had been mortally wounded at a tournament in Bar-le-Duc (3 May 1294). Immediately thereafter, he versified the memorable events that had occurred during the reign of John's son and successor. No more than five lines into the rule of John II (1294–1312), Boendale paused to reflect on a long-drawn-out conflict between Philip IV of France and his Flemish subjects. In the final decades of the thirteenth century, the relations between the Flemish and their lawful sovereign had gone sour over the county's cross-Channel contacts and the French king's centralising politics. In January 1297, Count Guy of Dampierre cut all ties with his French liege and officially allied himself with Philip's adversary, King Edward I of England. The dispute had divided the people of Flanders into two opposing factions: the supporters of the king of France (*leliaards*, named after the French *fleur de lis*) and those who remained loyal to the count and the rampant lion of Flanders (*liebaerts*, later also *klauwaerts*). Boendale did not explain the origins of the conflict, but instead focused on the famous battle of the Golden Spurs (Courtrai, 11 July 1302). In this massacre, a militia of 'fullers and weavers' had thoroughly shamed the superior French and allied forces, among whom, according to Boendale, were some of the most accomplished knights in Christendom.[2] At the end of his report, the clerk/chronicler directly addressed his readers and stated that he would 'no longer dwell upon this war, since it does not belong to our subject matter'.[3] There is an obvious explanation for the fact that Boendale did not want to spend too many words on the Flemish conflict. He wrote in the neighbouring duchy of Brabant over a decade after the events. Moreover, Boendale imagined his chronicle as a memory space for 'all things ducal' and therefore had called it the *Brabantsche yeesten* or 'the deeds of Brabant'.[4] Since Duke John II was not directly involved in the confrontation at Courtrai, the Flemish bloodbath was *in stricto sensu* of no consequence to his narrative.

Cross-border accounts of revolt

In his introduction to *From Mutual Observation to Propaganda War*, a collection of essays devoted to transnational representations of premodern revolt, Malte Griesse hypothesised 'that many descriptions of uprisings in *foreign* countries were at the same time, or at least to some extent, reflections on analogous phenomena at home'. He further suggested that as far as revolts were concerned, 'foreign observers, [although they were] less familiar with political and cultural specificities of the country they were writing about, were freer in their interpretation and in their quest for explanations'. For reasons of loyalty, local reporters had little leeway in articulating politically divergent opinions about domestic uprisings.[5] Consequently, when it came to local seditions, their narratives often agreed with the perspective of the dominating elites. Quite plausibly, chroniclers intentionally sidestepped the risk of antagonising municipal, regional, or national regimes, who, for their part, made every attempt to frame the disruptions according to their own needs and purposes or to erase the upheaval from public memory altogether (*damnatio memoriae*). This might explain, at least in part, why relatively few extant reports of domestic revolts tell the events from a rebels' perspective or express sympathy with the insurgents' point of view. Reports of foreign uprisings could circulate more openly and therefore were also suited to transmit covertly information about the organisation and management of dissidence 'at home'. Although Griesse's observations are mostly grounded in examples from early modern Europe, there is little reason to believe that they are not also transferrable to representations of revolt in the late medieval period.

In the same volume, Helmut Hinck and Bettina Bommersbach proposed that, in general, two very basic factors, 'attention' and 'interest', governed the transnational coverage of revolts. A first prerequisite was that foreign reporters had access to information about the incident (e.g. as an eye-witness, through various information networks or written documentation) and that they were sufficiently impressed not to 'dismiss [the uprising] without further consideration'. Second, whether or not an uprising made international headlines depended on its narrative or explanatory potential and the local implications for audiences abroad.[6] Their analysis of cross-Channel reports of revolts in France and England during the Hundred Years War further confirmed the findings of Neithard Bulst, who had previously suggested that representations of these revolts came in regional variants. The accounts of French chroniclers tended to be stereotypical and focused on the atrocity of the events, while their English equivalents were more concerned with exploring the deeper motives behind the disturbances.[7] Interestingly, besides the perhaps obvious observation that it was not uncommon for authors to take sides and reports were potentially biased, it also appeared that some transnational reports of rebellion were construed as a *critique* of foreign adversaries.[8]

Transnational representations of revolt in the Burgundian conglomerate

Not unlike their colleagues in France and England, historiographers in the Low Countries regularly inserted accounts of foreign revolt into their narratives. This was not only the case in undertakings with an international scope (e.g. Froissart's *Chroniques*), but also when the history of the home region or dynasty was at the heart of the project (e.g. Boendale's aforementioned *gesta* of Brabant). News of social unrest easily crossed regional borders, through rumours, official memos, or rebel propaganda. In his *Boec vander wraken* ('Book of Vengeance'), Boendale tells us at two separate occasions that he was in Antwerp when he heard the news (*mare*) of violent confrontations between the communality of Liège and Englebert III de la Marck, the newly elected bishop. The first time, he had been writing (*Ende dichte ter selver stat*), which suggests that word of the Liège rebellion reached him 'on the job', probably via the city's official communication network.[9] In both instances, it was immediately clear that the incidents in Liège were an ideal fit for his most recent project, 'because it [was] called the *Book of Vengeance*'.[10] In April 1452, insurgents from Flanders sent messages to urban administrations all over Holland, in an attempt to convince prospective sympathisers in the North that the Ghent resistance against ducal tax policy (the Second Ghent War, 1447–53) was a matter of common interest. Philip the Good, as count of Flanders and Holland, had already issued an official report of the conflict and expressly forbidden all contact with the Ghent rebels. After copies of the seditious letters had been forwarded to the regional Council, messengers from Ghent, among them also exiles from Holland, were outlawed; their treacherous rumours (*brieven van mompelyen ende conspiracien*) were publicly refuted.[11] Both examples show that rebels and regime could reach potential allies in foreign territories via various channels. The second example also demonstrates that competing representations of disruptive events were simultaneously disseminated across regional borders and illustrates the efforts ruling elites would go through in order to deprecate rebel propaganda. More importantly, that Philip the Good governed rebellious Flanders as well as most surrounding principalities suggests that Griesse's hypothesis may fall short in explaining the function of transnational reports of revolt in composite states with a strong centralising government, like the Burgundian Low Countries. How could representations of 'foreign' uprisings circumvent *damnatio memoriae* and avoid giving offence to the prince when the latter ruled at both sides of the border and actively tried to prevent contagion in his other, neighbouring territories?

In this respect, the international coverage of social unrest in the Low Countries becomes even more interesting after *c*.1430. In spite of the fact that the previous decade had been marked by political turbulence, Philip the Good finally succeeded to add Holland-Zeeland-Hainault (1428/33) and Brabant-Limbourg (1430) to his northern possessions. Previously, after the death of his father in 1419, the duke had already inherited the counties of Flanders and Artois in the Southern Low Countries and in 1429 he had purchased the county of Namur from margrave John III.[12] Philip's accession in all core territories of the region, did not, however, substantially change their individual status. In his monograph on Burgundian state formation, Robert Stein emphasised that 'essentially, the union remained an amalgamation of semi-sovereign principalities' and that the regional Estates, urban administrations, and local elites openly opposed certain aspects of the duke's centralisation policy (e.g. in the field of jurisdiction).[13] On the same note, Wim Blockmans designated the history of the Burgundian Low Countries as a

> long-drawn-out struggle between, on the one hand, the princes' tendency to homogenize administrative and jurisdictional practice and impose centralized procedures, and, on the other, the resistance of centres of power that had been established before the accession of the [Burgundian] dynasty.

He further characterised the Burgundian lands in the North as 'an empire consisting of a large number of provinces' which in reality maintained their own 'institutional practices and clearly distinct collective identities'. Blockmans also questioned 'the extent to which the unifying ambitions of the princes and their entourage had succeeded in penetrating society'. Nonetheless, city administrations in Flanders, Hainault, and Brabant made substantial efforts to win the duke's favour and secure the economic advantages associated with the presence of his court.[14] It is obvious that with relation to the Burgundian Low Countries, Griesse's explanation for the international coverage of social unrest is problematic. The most important reason for this is that in this conglomerate the distinction between 'domestic' and 'foreign' was not as much defined by administrative unity as by individual institutional tradition, locally anchored collective identities, and historically shaped understandings of territory.

In the following, I will explore how and why chroniclers from the Low Countries portrayed uprisings in foreign territories. Although I occasionally refer to scholarship on the representation of revolts in Flanders, the main focus of this chapter is the historiography of Brabant and Holland.

I will primarily discuss texts that were traditionally categorised as regional or urban historiography, first, because in this type of narrative, references to external revolts seem all the more out of place (see Tables 5.1 and 5.2). More importantly, however, in these texts, transnational representations of revolt are embedded in locally negotiated versions of a shared past, which suggests that these accounts of foreign events also actively contributed to the construction of local or regional collective identities.[15] Most of the accounts selected here were written in the local vernacular and thus could, at least in principle, be read or heard by a broader laymen's audience. Although it would certainly be useful also to examine how accounts of social unrest in the remote past were reframed to suit new political configurations better, I will limit my discussion to reports of (near-) contemporaneous events. In order to evaluate effectively the potential differences between internal and external representations of revolt, I will first consider how chroniclers portrayed social unrest in their home region. In a second part of this essay, I explore how the incorporation of the Low Countries into a larger personal union affected the way in which foreign reporters wrote about uprisings in neighbouring territories. To this purpose, I compare cross-border representations of revolt that were composed before and after the Burgundian integration.

Finally, I also devote some attention to the prologues of two texts that were written in Brabant during the reign of Charles the Bold and during or shortly after the regency of Maximilian of Austria. Elements in both introductions suggest that, after Brabant's incorporation into the Burgundian composite state, the perceived lack of revolt was deployed in a strategy the main purpose of which was to make the home region stand out from its neighbours.

Urban pride and prejudice: framing domestic revolt in the Low Countries

In her study of the Ghent memorial books (*Gentse memorieboeken*), Anne-Laure Van Bruaene showed that in surviving fifteenth-century copies, annotators frequently talked about uprisings and intramural urban conflict. However, the descriptions in these local collections of annalistic notes also remained very matter-of-fact and 'at the level of the event'. They left little room for

Table 5.1 Regional historiography in the vernacular before the Burgundian integration of Brabant and Holland

Title	Author	Date	Location/context
Rijmkroniek van Holland ('Rhymed Chronicle of Holland')	Anonymous Melis Stoke	c.1280 c.1301–14, several continuations and revised versions	Holland (comital court)
Brabantsche yeesten ('*Gesta* of Brabant')	Jan van Boendale	c.1316–17 At least five more updated redactions in the period c.1350	Brabant (Antwerp magistrate)
Cornicke van Brabant ('Chronicle of Brabant')	Hennen van Merchtenen	Two redactions 1415 and shortly after	Brabant (Brussels? Ducal court?)
Oude gesten seggen ons ('Old *gesta* tell us')	Anonymous	Shortly after 1306? Fifteenth century?	Brabant (Brussels?)
Hollantsche cronyke ('Chronicle of Holland')	Bavaria herald (Claes Heynenzoon)	Two redactions c.1405–9	Holland (comital court)

Table 5.2 Regional historiography in the vernacular after the Burgundian integration of Brabant and Holland

Title	Author	Date	Location/context
Continuatie van de Brabantsche yeesten ('Continuation of the *Gesta of Brabant*')	Anonymous (possibly Wein van Cotthem)	In four phases between c.1430 to before 1457?	Brabant (Brussels magistrate; comital court)
Die cronyke of die hystorie van hollant, etc. – *Gouds kroniekje* ('Histories of Holland', so-called 'Gouda chronicle')	Three anonymous authors	c.1436 c.1456 c.1468	Holland (Delft?)
Chroniques des pays de Hollande, Zellande et aussy em partie de Haynnau ('Chronicle of Holland, Zeeland and in part also Hainault')	Anonymous translator, based on Dutch text by Hendrik van Heessel?	Shortly after 1456?	Court of the dukes of Burgundy?
Cronyke van Brabant int prose int corte ('Short prose chronicle of Brabant')	Anonymous	c.1468 One manuscript with continuation until 1479	Brabant
Kroniek van Rotterdam ('Chronicle of Rotterdam')	Jan Allertsz. Cornelis Jansz.	c.1462–89 c.1494–9	Holland (Rotterdam)
Die alder excellenste cronyke van Brabant ('The most excellent chronicle of Brabant')	Anonymous	Printed 1497	Brabant (Antwerp?)
Cronijck van Hollant (I) ('Chronicle of Holland')	Jan van Naaldwijk	c.1514	Holland
Divisiekroniek ('Division chronicle')	Cornelius Aurelius (?)	Printed 1517	Holland (Leiden?)
Cronijck van Hollant (II) ('Chronicle of Holland')	Jan van Naaldwijk	c.1520	Holland
Prose annals of Brabant	Various authors and continuators	c.1506/25? c.1469? c.1437? c.1565? c.1455?	Brabant (Rooklooster) Brabant (Brussels) Brabant (Breda) Brabant (Antwerp) Guelders (ducal court)

explanation and authors rarely discussed the concrete reasons for revolt. Most accounts were primarily concerned with the realities of the incidents: locations, the course of rebellious action, sometimes also the immediate consequences. Van Bruaene also noticed that the annotators mostly supported princely policy and that the sovereign was never held personally accountable for the outbreak of conflict, even if there were some instances of shrouded criticism. Generally, lower class social groups were regarded with disdain. In some cases, the intentional selection of events pointed into the direction of urban pride.[16] Other Flemish sources offer a similar 'elite' perspective on contemporary revolt. Two near-contemporaneous reports of the First Ghent War (1379–85), one in French, the other in Dutch, were presumably written by partisans of Count Louis of Male and the duke of Burgundy. Both authors may have been eye-witnesses of the civil war and promoted an unfavourable image of the insurgents in the Flemish cities.[17] A third, shorter, and hitherto unnoticed account written in Dutch verse *c.*1431 is somewhat ambiguous, since it eulogises the rebel leader Jan Yoens from a Ghent perspective, but at the same time is wary of the rebels' actions.[18] Even if recent scholarship has brought to light a number of narratives that relate the events from the rebels' point of view, these 'counter-memories' appear to be rare, especially outside Flanders. In Brabant, the short verse chronicle *Oude gesten seggen ons* ('Old *gesta* tell us') gives a uniquely critical account of ducal interference in the Brussels uprising of 1303–6. However, it is still unclear if this report was written shortly after the events or, alternatively, was based on Hennen van Merchtenen's far more 'mainstream' account composed *c.*1415 discussed below.[19] A short chronicle written in an eastern dialect of Middle Dutch which gives a local perspective on the Liège wars of the second half of the fifteenth century, is clearly biased in favour of the insurgents and counterbalances the official 'Burgundian' version repeated in most chronicles from Brabant and Holland (cf. *infra*).[20]

In broad lines, Van Bruaene's observations also hold for the historiography of other regions in the Low Countries. The same factual tone is found in a group of related prose annals composed in Brabant.[21] The absence of motivations and value judgements is probably connected to the brevity of these texts and the conventions of the *annales* genre, which typically was not concerned with further explaining the exact causes of events.[22] Given that many of these texts were locally anchored and appear to have circulated in municipal councils, authors may have felt that their future audiences would also consist of fellow townsmen who would be sufficiently informed about contemporary local politics. With relation to Holland, Peter Hoppenbrouwers studied the narrative representation of late medieval peasant revolts and concluded that contemporary historiographers 'seemed far more preoccupied with the values of the ruling elite and its ideas about how society ought to work than with the deeper motives behind rural unrest'. Chroniclers generally portrayed the insurgents 'in a predominantly negative way, stressing their stupidity, disloyalty and adherence to dangerous revolutionary ideas'. Out of four case studies, only one author sympathised to some degree with the rebels' cause and legitimated the revolt with legally acceptable reasons.[23]

I will further examine two strategies that historiographers from Brabant and Holland repeatedly used to frame urban uprisings. First, as was also noted by Van Bruaene and Hoppenbrouwers, historiographers usually distanced themselves and their intended audiences from the insurgents and their 'inconceivable' actions. This approach to the rebels can be interpreted as a form of 'othering', a concept that is usually associated with colonial discourse. Second, authors were intentionally selective in their representation of revolts and frequently 'camouflaged' domestic uprisings. In this view, the lacunae in their narratives are as informative as their actual descriptions of revolt, or even more so. Both framing strategies actively contributed to the creation of social identities, which, as I will argue below, is also important for how we should interpret the transnational accounts of foreign revolts in these regional chronicles.

'Othering' the dissidents

The discursive strategies used in elite representations of revolt essentially amount to the 'othering' of dissident social groups. First coined in postcolonial theory, 'othering' describes 'the various ways in which colonial discourse produces its subject'. In imperial narratives, the 'mastered subject' is characterised as 'other' through marginalising discourses such as 'primitivism' and 'cannibalism', while at the same time 'the naturalness and primacy of the colonizing culture and world view is asserted'. Since the identity of the colonising subject is established simultaneously with that of the subjected colonised, othering can be described as a dialectical process.[24] In the framework of popular revolts, the non-conforming dissident easily takes the place of the colonised 'other'.[25] Moreover, like imperial narratives, the historiographical texts under consideration here were for the most part discourses of power. While the available information for many writers is limited or entirely non-existent, most of the identified authors were employed at princely courts (e.g. Melis Stoke, Hendrik van Heessel) or in urban chanceries (e.g. Jan van Boendale, Jan Allertsz., and Cornelis Jansz.). Other projects were initiated by influential members of courtly administrations and/ or the city magistrate (e.g. the *Brabantsche yeesten* and its continuation),[26] potentially as relation gifts with an eye to forging or reinforcing alliances between the involved urban governments and their sovereign.[27] Although it is surely too rash to conclude that these clerks, secretaries, and heralds were 'penny-a-liners' who routinely reverberated their superiors' opinions, in their accounts of uprisings they mostly sided with the dominant elites. While some representations are more nuanced (cf. *infra*), it is noteworthy that insurgents were frequently portrayed as senseless, primitive, and easily deceived. In historiographical accounts, the rebels' motives and behaviour were minimised, ridiculed, or vilified. On the other hand, urban elites were cast in the role of victims and chroniclers tended to underline the excess and cruelty of the rebels' actions.

In chronicle representations from the Northern Low Countries, Hoppenbrouwers identified three recurrent motifs:

> firstly rebels were disloyal to their lawful lord; secondly, that the rebels were stupid, simply because any serious defiance of either lawful lords or the existing social order was doomed to fail; and thirdly, that sometimes the rebels were perhaps not so much stupid as misled by temporary allies, especially other powerful lords.[28]

As will become clear below, these elite discourses also rhetorically debased and disempowered rebellious social groups, by denying them the rational faculties and political agency that was generally associated with the dominant class. This negative labelling of rebels is particularly present in Jan van Boendale's reports of urban uprisings in Malines and Brussels. According to Boendale, the rebels behaved like the devil and his companions (*Oft die duvel uten hellen/Hadde gheweest ende sine gesellen*),[29] or were *overmoedich ende pijllijc* (haughty and harmful)[30] and caused *grote confuse* (great scandal).[31]

The rebels' actions were repeatedly categorised as *overdaet* (excess).[32] When Boendale stated that rebellious commoners behaved like madmen (*recht oft sinloes waer*), running around from pillar to post, he probably referred to the *loepe* (runs), a common feature of medieval revolts.[33] In general, Boendale did not explicitly call the craftsmen 'stupid' (however, v. 448: *domme liede*), but rather judged them to be unfit for executive office. Without proper guidance (*ombedwonghen*), commoners lost all modesty (*alder scamelheit es ontspronghen*).[34] Their *onbesceidenheit* (rudeness, lack of civilisation, or transgression) and *ongeraectheit* (ignorance, inexperience, or lack of skill) was so overwhelming, that eventually they fell flat in the dirt (*datse weder in dassche vallen*) and were more oppressed (*versmaden*) than ever before.[35]

Circa 1430, an anonymous author continued Boendale's chronicle, probably at the request of the Brussels city magistrate.[36] In this continuation, the guildsmen who revolted in Brussels and Louvain *c*.1360 were pictured as 'fools, dazzled and disorderly' (*dwase lieden/Als volc beraest ende onbestiert*),[37] intent on 'taking down the city's magistrate' (*Si die heeren van der stat/vernielen wouden al te samen*).[38] They plotted secretly and illicitly (*Mids overbrekeghe dinge/Der ghemeinten gederinge*) and were not shy of using excessive force.[39] In accordance with his predecessor, the continuator judged that commoners were not equipped to govern: they ruled as they saw fit, shamefully abused the seal of Louvain, and mismanaged the city's finances, for instance by selling rents without end. Most evocative, however, is his description of a rebellious mob in Louvain in 1378.[40] Violence had escalated after mayor Wouter van der Leyden and some of his companions (*sinen cnapen*) were brutally murdered in Brussels. The communality gathered in front of city hall and furiously demanded the defenestration of the city's plutocrats. Clearly outraged by the cruelty of the insurgents' actions, the anonymous chronicler referred to the enraged populace as 'rude and filthy peasants' (*Die onbesnedenen vul gheboere*).[41] He pictured them 'shouting and booing, acting shamefully' (*Met roepen, met yoyten, met vulre voere*).[42] The notables who had hidden inside town hall, were thrown out of the windows, caught on the insurgents' pikes and clubbed to death. The filthy churls (*menich vuul kalant*) were covered in blood up to their elbows, as if they had just slaughtered an ox.[43] Their excess was labelled as an *ondaet* (heinous deed or crime), as *ontellike overdaden* (unspeakable transgressions), and *vreeselike onghenade* (horrible cruelties).[44]

The motivations behind the rebels' (supposedly) savage or unintelligible actions were designated as simplistic, naive, and ungrounded. Rather than associating the uprisings with the economic or political context in which they came about, e.g. (financial) mismanagement or demands for representation, many chroniclers quoted monocausal or incidental explanations, personal conflicts, or underlined the harmful consequences of secret, illicit gatherings, rumours, and gossip. In a general comment on the wave of uprisings *c*.1300, Jan van Boendale asserted that in those days the commoners would attack patricians *om een clein ocsuun* (for trivial reasons).[45] Elsewhere, he claimed that the rebels took revenge for every unkindness (*haerthede*) that had ever been afflicted on them or their forefathers.[46] According to the *Brabantsche yeesten*, the principal motivation for the uprising in Malines in 1301 was that the commoners 'wounded' (*wonden*) a patrician (*Enen goeden man van der stat*).[47] Likewise, in 1303 the wounding of a *knecht* (apprentice) had triggered a riot of guildsmen in Brussels.[48]

Other popular explanatory factors for the derailment of violence were personal ambition and dishonesty. Deception took centre stage in Melis Stoke's report of the Westfrisian uprising in 1297.[49] Stoke directly accused Willem Berthout, bishop of Utrecht, of having pressed the Frisians into rebellion, thus damaging (*scaden*) and calling down calamity (*noet*) over the Frisian people. Stoke wondered what the bishop could have gained by supporting these traitors (*verradere*). To the contrary, he should have acted like a father to the new count (*die met rechte vadre/Des graven soude hebben ghesijn*)![50] According to Boendale's continuator, two decades of social unrest in Louvain (1360–82), which also caused outbreaks of uproar in Brussels, could be retraced to the personal ambitions of one man, the town's sheriff, Pieter Couthereel, to the deception of a malicious and gossiping informant (*quaet knecht*; *clappaert*), and to the deceptive counsel of one of the duke's confidants. The principal actors in this story had become entangled in a web of vicious rumour, malignant advice, and conflicts of interest after a fish merchant with cart-trouble had been unfairly accused of horse-theft. The author's assertion that *van cleinen dinghe comt dicwijls nose* (small things often lead to harm) surely was an understatement.[51]

In certain instances it seems as if chroniclers intentionally minimised the causes for revolt. Among the principal reasons for the outbreak of factional conflict in Leiden in 1445, the author of the *Divisiekroniek* (printed in 1517) listed a personal dispute between Floris van Boschuysen and Boudewijn van Zwieten about a burial plot.[52] A second argument between Van Boschuysen and Simon Vrerix about the local sheriff's office (*scoutambocht*) had aggravated the situation. However, hostilities had not escalated until Jan Danelsz., a relative of Floris van Boschuysen had crossed Boeckel Heerman, a partisan of Simon Vreric, and, in passing, broke wind (*Ende int verbygaen ontghinc hem een wint van afteren*). Heerman had taken this insult badly and vowed revenge ('*Doet ghi dat tot spijt ende scande van mi?! Ic gelove u, dat ic salt u verghelden!*'). On 1 July, the conflict had gone off the rails and representatives of the regional council had come to appease the hostilities. In the end, Danelsz. was executed along with two other agitators: Jan van Haesbroeck and Meynaert Aerntsz.[53] The *Gouda chronicle*, which described the Leiden conflict shortly after the events, is vague about the exact reasons for the confrontations.[54] According to the judicial registers, the conflict begun on 16 May, when Vrerix, a Cod, was attacked by Haesbroeck and Aerntsz. The council negotiated an armistice which was to last until 24 August. However, in the meantime Heerman (Cod) and Danelsz. (Hook) got into a fight, the origin of which was not recorded. Danelsz. shot at Heerman's window and hit target. The next day, the factions assembled and the president and council got involved 'to resolve the dispute, to hear the concerned parties and to do justice by all'. The Hooks had refused to listen to reason, argued they had no business with the president and called out 'improper slogans in opposition of our graceful lord and sovereign'. In the end, they were overpowered, Danelsz., Haesbroeck, and Aerntsz. were accused of treason and 'brought to justice by the sword'.[55] To modern eyes it surely seems as if the author of the *Divisiekroniek* intentionally ridiculed the reasons for this outburst of party-strife. Did Heerman's (accidental?) bowel movement really lead to his execution and that of two fellow party members? Although there is no conclusive answer to this question, this local conflict between members of the two factions should clearly be read against the background of the more general turmoil that had risen after Stadtholder Guillaume de Lalaing had given preferential treatment to the Hooks for almost five years.

By picturing the rebels as inferior and cruel, these narratives also constructed a positive shared identity for the dominant in-group and thus reinforced the status quo. The social identity of a victimised 'us', whose main concern was the common welfare of the city, was positively reaffirmed and differentiated from a violent and rebellious 'they', who, partially because of their haughtiness, posed an imminent threat to society. Astonished by the uprisings at the beginning of the fourteenth century, Boendale confirmed that the lords had been forced to give way to shoemakers, fullers, weavers, butchers, bakers, etc. and were excluded from positions in municipal government.[56] Elsewhere, he claimed that the commoners desired nothing more than to cool their anger on the patricians, to murder or at least banish them.[57] At every outbreak of popular revolt, the oligarchs feared for their lives and abandoned their townhouses,[58] which, as soon as they left, were demolished by the insurgents.[59] Not open to reason, the rebels mercilessly attacked or killed whoever opposed them.[60] Additionally, chroniclers put the rebels' opposition in a positive light. For instance, citing Orosius, Boendale claimed that 'when the commoners are agitated, one should fear the land is lost' (*Als die gemeente wert in rueren/salmen altoes duchten des/Dat lant verloren es*), and sided with the aristocracy (*ridderen ende knapen*), who took up arms for the region's welfare (*dat orbaer es des lants*).[61] In the elegy that precedes the report of the 1303–6 uprising in Brussels in Hennen van Merchtenen's *Cornicke*, Duke John II was portrayed as noble, courageous, and an excellent warrior.[62] But there are also exceptions to this positive portrayal.

Hennen van Merchtenen's representation of events was, for instance, challenged in the related chronicle *Oude gesten seggen ons* which, in a corresponding passage, claimed that the duke treated the commoners 'cruelly and callously like an animal and held them in low esteem'.[63] For the anonymous author of this account it was absolutely clear that on 1 May 1306 the rebellious commune had left Brussels, dressed in linen garments, with the intent to beg for mercy. Nonetheless, the duke had ruthlessly charged into their peaceful march (cf. *infra*).[64] Other reports, Van Merchtenen's included, surmised that John II was confused by the procession, had erred on the side of safety, and presumed that the attack was the best defence. Similarly, the continuator's account of the aforementioned uprisings in Louvain (1360–82) is not entirely biased in favour of the patricians (or even the duke for that matter).[65] After the clans were reinstated in 1362, they had received rents as reimbursement for their losses during the rebellion. In 1378, the patricians had decided to cash in on these rents and thus called down further catastrophe on the community, which already was on the verge of bankruptcy, partially because with every change of government, the duke and his administration had been offered substantial bribes. In this respect, the continuator acknowledged that both the rebellious craftsmen and the patriciate had been to blame for the financial hangover that followed two decades of social unrest. His position may have been inspired by the changed political circumstances in many cities of Brabant at the time of writing.

Brabant in the fifteenth century: mixed representations, mixed feelings

At the end of the fourteenth and the beginning of the fifteenth century, the participation of guild representatives in the urban governments of the four principal cities of Brabant was increasingly formalised. In Louvain, for instance, the charter of 1378 regulated the representation of the guilds in the outer council (*brede raad*) which had an advisory and supervisory role. Ever since 1360, the ten nations each had been entitled to a representative in the city council. In Brussels, the guilds had been awarded a similar consultative role after they had assisted in the coup of regent Philip of Saint-Pol in January 1421. Henceforth, ten patricians (seven aldermen, two stewards or treasurers, and a mayor) and nine non-patricians (six aldermen, two stewards or treasurers, and a mayor) were entrusted with the daily government of the city in a plutocratic regime called the *Weth* (Law). Duke John IV confirmed the reform that same year on 15 July.[66]

The developments in the organisation of urban governments also left their mark on the representation of popular revolts in regional historiography. Many of these texts, or subsequent copies thereof, were connected with urban magistrates. Jan van Boendale wrote his chronicle at the request of Willem Bornecolve, an important official in Antwerp. The continuation of his *Brabantsche yeesten* was probably commissioned by the Brussels city magistrate. Evidence suggests that additional texts, such as the short verse chronicle *Oude gesten seggen ons* and the Brussels prose annal *Een daet rolie* (c.1469?) also circulated in the Brussels city council.[67] Historiographical texts and the manuscripts thereof had an important political dimension. According to Hannes Lowagie, texts of urban historiography should be seen as 'political instruments rather than, as many have done before, merely cultural products'. The primary objectives of these texts were 'to communicate a certain political message', 'be used as a tool that could assist in political negotiations', and to 'promote a region, city or social group'.[68] Boendale's chronicle, for instance, was repeatedly used to adduce evidence in political discussions.[69] One of the manuscripts of this chronicle and its continuation, now kept in the Royal Library in Brussels (cf. *infra*), was in fact copied at the request of the Brussels municipal government and could be consulted in the magistrate's *Librije* (archives).[70] Since these texts and manuscripts functioned in different contexts, it was not uncommon that their contents were altered to suit better the specific requirements of the situation in which they were used. With relation to an example from Flanders, the *Diary of Ghent*, Lowagie demonstrated that the selection of documents inserted into the historiographical narrative was influenced by the political opinions of the (rebellious) urban administration in which it was composed.[71] Likewise, in Brabant, the installation of mixed municipal governments, in which the patriciate and the guilds were officially represented, even if in unequal measure, affected historiographical texts and manuscripts, for instance with relation to the portrayal of urban uprisings and rebellious craftsmen.

The manuscript of Boendale's chronicle and its continuation, which was ordered by the Brussels city magistrate, was completed on 15 May 1444. At the request of his patrons, probably in the person of the town's pensionary Petrus de Thimo, scribe Henricus van den Damme repeatedly intervened in the text of Boendale's *yeesten*.[72] It is, for instance, very likely that the two final chapters of Book Five, which were not transcribed in the Brussels manuscript, were in fact present in Van den Damme's exemplar.[73] At any rate, the scribe or, better, the commissioning party, had good reasons to omit these parts of the text. For instance, in the first deleted chapter, *Van der ghemeinten* (About the commoners), Boendale strongly condemned the erratic behaviour of rebellious guildsmen and underlined their inability to govern a city (cf. *supra*). This message did, of course, no longer resonate with the composition of the city magistrate that had ordered the manuscript and also the continuation of Boendale's chronicle. In this respect, it seems hardly a coincidence that, while the continuator was highly dismissive of the uprisings in Brussels and Louvain in the second half of the fourteenth century, his account of more recent troubles in Brussels in 1420–1 was far more nuanced and put the rebels in a more positive light.[74] The main achievement of the 1421 uprising had been the installation of the mixed council, in which the rebellious guildsmen were officially represented. Quite plausibly, the recently installed form of government also distorted the continuator's account of the fourteenth-century upheaval in Louvain. In spite of the fact that the chronicler was aware of the craftsmen's grievances (e.g. financial mismanagement, abuse of the city's seal), he misrepresented the relation between the rebellious administration and the patriciate. The revolt was thus framed as a binary opposition between guildsmen (*ghemein*) and the dominant clans (*geslechten*), which was finally resolved by the installation of a mixed form of representation, like the one recently adopted in Brussels.

The short verse chronicle *Oude gesten seggen ons* is another perfect fit for this new political context. Wim van Anrooij has argued that this text, which ends with the subduction of the Malines revolt in 1306, was not written shortly after the Brussels insurrection of 1303–6 as had previously been assumed, but was an adaptation of Hennen van Merchtenen's *Cornicke van Brabant* (1415–18).[75] If this is indeed the case, the text's critical evaluation of the oligarchical urban government in Brussels that was (re)introduced in 1306 may have been composed not long after the uprising in 1421 when the old regime dominated by seven clans had been reformed and ducal power was feeble and contested. The author's dismissive report of Duke John II's involvement in the pacification of the revolt (cf. *supra*) also points in this direction. Finally, the aforementioned *Een daet rolie*, composed (or continued) in Brussels, possibly *c.*1469, only mentions that in 1420, *werden te Bruesel borchmeesters ende raetslieden gemaect* (mayors and councillors were installed in Brussels) and, seemingly unrelated, on 6 June 1421 'all the lords in Brussels were decapitated'.[76]

The influence of these mixed-mode urban councils also left its mark on *Die alder excellenste cronyke van Brabant*, which was printed in Antwerp in 1498 and probably also written there.[77] In his prosification of Boendale's narrative, the compiler frequently omitted condescending remarks directed at the rebellious guildsmen. Additionally, he did not eschew openly supporting mixed city councils, and conceded that some of the grievances (e.g. poor government and financial mismanagement) that surfaced after the death of Charles the Bold were in fact legitimate reasons for insurgency.[78] However, ultimately the compiler adhered to the old idea, already advertised in Boendale's chronicle, that commoners were intellectually unequipped for executive office, stating that 'it is much to everyone's disadvantage when the communality riots, because they do not have the skills to govern wisely, which inevitably leads to deplorable events and discord'. By means of consensus, the compiler advocated a system in which urban authorities were selected from the 'whole body of the city', like in Louvain. With reference to the general uproar after the death of Charles the Bold, the compiler stated that 'Brussels had always chosen their seven aldermen from the seven clans, with the result that they were stuck with inept administrators, badly running the city'. For some time the people of Brussels had been allowed to elect representatives from the entire (male and probably also wealthy) population, like in Louvain. The newly elected administrators had put the city back on the rails. Discontent with the altered situation, the lords and clans had contrived to ensure that everything returned to the old ways, and, again, they ruled inadequately.[79] Potentially, the compiler's insistence on mixed representation could be read against the background of Maximilian's decision in November 1486 to reform the urban government in Antwerp and replace the aldermen of the crafts by patricians. In 1477, the guilds had supplied two-thirds of the total number of aldermen, in 1480 half.[80]

In view of his aforementioned understanding for the rebels' objectives, it may seem contradictory that the compiler categorised the uprisings following the deaths of Charles the Bold and Mary of Burgundy as 'wars and tribulations' (*orloghen ende tribulaciën*), portrayed rebels as 'mutineers' (*muytmakers*), and designated their actions as *dolinge* (errant ways), *groote fortse ende excesse* (violent abuse of power and excess), and utterly illegal (*teghen alle goede rechten*). This difference between his representation of political turmoil within the city and the protests against the prince probably followed from a perceived, be it somewhat artificial, distinction between intramural conflict (the so-called 'Little Tradition of Revolt') and revolt against the lawful sovereign (the 'Great Tradition of Revolt'). In spite of the fact that these two Traditions were intertwined, in concrete situations, contemporary historiographers and their audiences may nonetheless have felt the need to distinguish between local uprisings and open rebellion against the prince.[81] Since the compiler wrote sometime after 1486 and his text may have been revised before printing in 1498, at a time when relations with Maximilian were slowly getting normal, it is not surprising that *Die alder excellenste cronyke* promoted a message of pacification and also condemned the rebellious actions of previous years and decades.[82]

'Don't mention the war': camouflaging conflict

According to Anne-Laure van Bruane, the unwillingness of the Ghent annotators to talk about the revolt against Philip the Good in 1447–53 was probably inspired by 'mixed feelings of urban shame and pride'. Particularly the *amende honorable*, the public humiliation before the duke, was something they would rather forget.[83] This kind of 'selective appropriation' was a widely used strategy in the representation of social unrest. Many chroniclers cherry-picked events and camouflaged incidents that did not fit the desired picture, for instance because of their shameful nature. With relation to the 'Verse chronicle of Holland' (*Rijmkroniek van Holland*), Jan Burgers observed that Melis Stoke conveniently covered up the 'less than glorious story' of the Kennemer revolt of 1274, when a peasant militia had cornered Florent V.[84] Stoke's professional activities sufficiently explain the author's concern for the count's reputation. He wrote his parts of the rhymed chronicle between c.1301 and 1314, while he was employed as a clerk in the chancery of Holland, in all likelihood in support of Florent's successors, the Avesnes Counts John II (1299–1304) and William III (1304–37).

Perplexed by the wave of revolts that raged throughout the Low Countries at the turn of the fourteenth century, Stoke's contemporary Jan van Boendale zoomed in on urban uprisings in Malines (1301–3) and Brussels (1303–6). He failed to record, however, that sometime between 14 May and 5 June 1302 similar disturbances had also scourged Antwerp, the city in and for which he wrote.[85] It is most significant that the only reference to the Antwerp incidents appears in the context of rare criticism on ducal policy. Boendale reports that when Duke John II arrived before Malines, determined to chastise the insurgent craftsmen for their insolence, those who had remained inside refused him access to the city, afraid that '[t]he duke, in a state of anger, might judge rashly, as he had done before, in Antwerp, where people had been executed. That had better not happened at all'.[86] About 14 years later, when Boendale wrote a first version of his chronicle at the request of the influential Antwerp politician Willem Bornecolve, the memory of the uprising may still have been too uncomfortable or embarrassing to record. Moreover, it is plausible that, perhaps in second instance, the chronicle was intended as a gift to the duke's son and heir, the young John III, in order to reinforce the alliance between the Antwerp city magistrate and the ducal administration.[87] Specifically, in such a context, it would not have been opportune to commemorate the Antwerp revolt.

In his study of *Die alder excellenste cronyke van Brabant*, Jaap Tigelaar reproached the 'compiler' for being insensitive to the dire consequences of recent political events or inept to report them.[88] In view of the above, this evaluation of the compiler's political awareness deserves to be nuanced and it may be more plausible that the chronicler was intentionally concise about the communality's cruelty and their 'incomprehensible actions' (*sy stelden voerts wonderlijke dinghen*) after the deaths of Charles the Bold and his daughter Mary of Burgundy, because he was perfectly aware of the gravity of these disturbances.[89] That a precise and comprehensive report may have been controversial at the time of writing (cf. *supra*), may also shimmer through in the compiler's closing remarks. There, he predicted that some people would slander (*lasteren*) or openly question (*debatteren*) his representation of events because they were 'uncivilised' or 'insufficiently intelligent' (*eenighe onbescheydene*). These 'haters' might specifically reproach the compiler for omitting some of the tall tales that featured in a rivalling text 'called the short chronicle of Brabant' (*ghehieten die 'Corte cronike van Brabant'*). This chronicle was apparently widely read in Antwerp and other cities in Brabant, in spite of the fact that, from the compiler's perspective, it was packed with 'lies and idle gossip' (*loghenen ende ydele clappinghen*).[90] An obvious candidate, already suggested by Tigelaar, is the *Cronyke van Brabant int prose int corte*.[91] Unfortunately, the compiler is vague as to the reasons why people might object, which makes it hard to identify the part of his narrative that was most likely to raise protest. Tigelaar proposed that the colophon referred to the mythological prehistory of Brabant as presented in the *Cornyke int prose int corte* and particularly the legend of Brabo, the giant slayer. However, that the compiler listed partisanship (*partijelike menschen*) as one of the principal causes for criticism, suggests that the expected protest was politically charged. In one manuscript of the *Cornyke*, now kept in the Royal Library in Brussels, the historiographical narrative is continued up to 1478–9.[92] This continuation contains a competing account of the troubles that flared up in Flanders after the death of Charles the Bold, and particularly of the execution of chancellor Guillaume Hugonet and Guy de Brimeu, lord of Humbercourt, on Maundy Thursday (3 April) 1477. While according to the compiler Hugonet had been 'wise, just, and lenient' and Humbercourt had also been 'a wise lord',[93] the continuation in the Brussels manuscript presents them as frauds, who had raised and pocketed taxes without the knowledge of their prince and who, in the continuator's opinion, could even be held accountable for the duke's untimely death.

Michel van Gent noticed a similar aversion towards discussing local conflicts in the historiography of Holland. In spite of the fact that during the Burgundian–Habsburg period the factional wars between 'Hooks' (*Hoeken*) and 'Cods' (*Kabeljauwen*) had regularly flared up, these confrontations were rarely mentioned in local narrative sources.[94] This led Van Gent to believe that authors purposefully withheld information. The best examples of this are probably Jan Allertsz., Cornelis Jansz., and Jan van Naaldwijk. Allertsz., secretary of Rotterdam between c.1450 and 1489, is known as the author-compiler of a collection of historiographical notes in the *Oud memoriaal of schepenen* (Old Memorialbook of Aldermen) which were later continued by his son and successor Cornelis Jansz.[95] Between c.1514 and 1520, Van Naaldwijk compiled two regional chronicles of Holland. Significantly, the Rotterdam notes and Naaldwijk's chronicles combine an apparent disregard for local uproar with a fascination for foreign uprisings (cf. also *infra*). While Allertsz. commemorates the outbreaks of factional conflict in Holland in 1479 and in Leiden and Dordrecht in 1481, he is completely silent about the *Jonker Fransenoorlog* (War of Squire Francis) a revolt of the Hooks against Maximilian's regency in 1488–90. In November 1488, the rebels had taken over in Rotterdam and installed a council led by Hooks. The sudden change of government, which ultimately led to the secretary's execution on 20 January 1489 may explain why Allertsz. did not give an account of the tumultuous events of 1488. Quite possibly, he could not access his professional documentation during the rebellion. It is strange, however, that Allertsz.'s son, Cornelis Jansz. did not update his father's notes, when he succeeded him as secretary in October 1489. Instead, Jansz.'s notes start in 1494 and thus not only skip the War of Squire Francis, but also the Uprising of the Cheese and Bread people in 1492. Obviously, both Allertsz. and his son were well informed about contemporary politics. Did they prefer to play it safe by not describing or potentially commenting on issues from his direct surroundings that were politically sensitive, as was suggested by Michel van Gent?[96] Or is their silence rather an indication of their pro-Maximilian orientation? At any rate, Allertsz. proudly remembered the installation of Maximilian in Holland on 14 April 1478 where he, *Jannes die clerc*, had proclaimed (*staefde*) the duke's oath, standing on a table surrounded by the Rotterdam magistracy.[97] That Allertsz. emphasised and condemned uprisings against the Burgundian regime in Flanders and Liège, while similar troubles at home were (intentionally?) swept under the rug, paints a peaceful, but in some ways distorted, picture of the political situation in Holland at the end of the fifteenth century. Similarly, in his chronicles of Holland, Jan van Naaldwijk demonstrated a particular taste for foreign revolts, but glossed over these local protests against Maximilian's regime.[98] This is particularly remarkable in the second redaction of his chronicle. For this version, Naaldwijk had sourced the newly printed *Divisiekroniek* (Division chronicle) with detailed descriptions of the uprisings of 1488–90 and 1491–2. It is plausible that here, too, the lack of enthusiasm to report on recent troubles was inspired by the author's political orientation. The chronicler's partisanship is also suggested by the fact that whenever Naaldwijk cited the *Divisiekroniek* with relation to factional conflict, he consistently manipulated his source in favour of the Hook party.[99]

Finally, a short French prose chronicle of Holland and Hainault further suggests that some chroniclers indeed preferred to celebrate the (imaginary) era of international peace rung in by the accession of Philip the Good.[100] The text, a copy of which was kept in the Burgundian library, was translated from a Dutch original, probably shortly after 1456. It asserts that after the duke of Burgundy had taken over control in the region, there had been peace and unity (*pais et union*) for approximately 20 years, thus virtually characterising Philip's reign as a time of 'Pax Burgundica'. The chronicle deceptively emphasises the absence of international warfare (*aussi sans avoir aucune guerre à l'encontre d'aulcuns des pays ou seigneurs voisins ou aultres*) and intentionally glosses over a tumultuous period of domestic troubles.[101] Most significantly, the narrative skips over local outbreaks of party strife in 1444–5, which were the result of Stadtholder Guillaume de Lalaing's preferential treatment of the Hook faction over its political rivals, the Cods (cf. *supra*). The urgency of the matter was clear from the fact that Duchess Isabella of Portugal personally travelled to Holland to pacify her husband's most northern territories. Dordrecht, Haarlem, and Amsterdam were officially proclaimed rebel cities.[102] Stadtholder Lalaing was deposed. The narrative halts in 1455 with a cliff-hanger, only hinting at yet another pending conflict, this time between the duke of Burgundy and Gijsbrecht van Brederode, bishop-elect of Utrecht.[103] However, the chronicle also does not describe revolts elsewhere in the Burgundian conglomerate. The text omits, for instance, the protracted rebellion instigated by a Bruges militia in 1437 and the Second Ghent War. The cover up is probably related to the position held by the author of the Dutch original at the Burgundian court and, again, the political circumstances in which he wrote. This extended redaction of a pre-existing prose chronicle of Holland was probably authored by Hendrik van Heessel, herald in the service of Philip the Good and, as far as the extant evidence tells us, specialist in matters related to Holland. Although the Dutch version breaks off in 1415 in the only manuscript in which it is preserved, it is probable that the text in this armorial book now kept in Antwerp, like the French translation, originally ran up to 1455.[104] Wim van Anrooij has convincingly demonstrated that the Antwerp armorial was kept and updated by Van Heessel over a period of *c.* 20 years.[105] An obvious occasion for Van Heessel to have composed this continuation is the chapter of the Golden Fleece, held at The Hague on 2 May 1456. One of the points on the agenda was the conflict with the bishop-elect of Utrecht and – from a Burgundian perspective – the disloyal actions of Fleece knight Reinoud II van Brederode in support of his brother, Gijsbrecht. In this volatile context, the emphasis on Burgundian peace and the idyllic representation of Philip's reign may have served to stress that, after 20 peaceful years, the duke's opponents were prepared to plunge Holland and Utrecht into a period of violent conflict.[106]

Cross-border representations of revolt in the Low Countries

In the following, I will further explore why authors of regional chronicles incorporated transnational reports of revolt into their narratives. As will become clear, it was rarely the social impact of the revolts that dictated the inclusion of these foreign uprisings, but rather local connections and alliances in international warfare. After the Burgundian integration, chroniclers appear to have seized every opportunity to underline the differences between the supposedly peaceful home region and the rebellious territories.

Before Burgundy: international politics and badmouthing the neighbours

It is time now to return to Boendale's account of the war in Flanders. Although John II of Brabant did not partake in the hostilities at Courtrai, the local interest in the event is clear. A group of Brabantine noblemen led by the duke's uncle, Godfrey of Aarschot, had rallied to the aid of Philip the Fair. Many of these Francophile aristocrats would never return. Among them were Godfrey of Aarschot, his son, John of Vierson, and the lords of Wezemaal, Boutersem, and Waelem. There was also an obvious connection with Boendale's city of Antwerp. Laurent Volckaert, member of a line of prominent Antwerp aldermen, had also joined the pro-French faction and fell on the Flemish battlefield. In a list of casualties, the author evoked the hardship associated with the death of each of the Brabantine warriors, which suggests that Boendale's main purpose was to commemorate the Brabanters who had fallen at Courtrai. Nonetheless, his position towards the conflict was ambiguous. Boendale's hesitancy in picking sides was potentially related to the political context of the battle. In the Anglo-French conflict, John II of Brabant had supported his English father-in-law, Edward I. Moreover, the duke had fallen out with his uncle, Godfrey of Aarschot who had negotiated a peace with France. Potentially, while it was not in Boendale's nature openly to support insurgency (cf. *supra*), it was also not opportune to side completely with Philip the Fair. Still, it was probably the dynastic connection and the Antwerp involvement that instigated Boendale to report on the Battle of the Golden Spurs.

Additionally the 'Flemish' episode also provided additional narrative context for two events that followed later in the chronicle. The first was the aforementioned 'incomprehensible' wave of popular revolts that had raged 'through all lands' (*in allen lande*) at the beginning of the fourteenth century. A second event connected to the Flemish uprising equally flabbergasted Boendale. Six years after the battle at Courtrai, three knights who were thought to have perished, among them the aforementioned John of Vierson, had supposedly found their way back to Brabant. Given the Brabanters' enthusiasm at the noblemen's return, the pretenders' routine must have been extremely convincing: Vierson's wife was even fooled into sharing her bed with the fraudster posing for her husband! Finally exposed, the impostors were imprisoned and left to die in captivity.

Boendale's attention for another Flemish crisis that had started with the Ghent uprising of 1337 and still went on at the moment of writing, is also best explained by a dynastic connection. In 1347, John III's second daughter, Margaret of Brabant had married Louis of Male, count of Flanders. Not recognised by the people of Flanders as their lawful sovereign, Louis had taken refuge in France. In the light of history Boendale's final words on the topic sound prophetic: the Flemish insurgence 'would break down when least expected' and perhaps should be read as a concealed reference to preparations for an invasion of Flanders, staged from Brabant in September 1348. At any rate, Boendale probably wrote this portion of his chronicle sometime after the battle of Tourinnes-les-Chaussées (21 July 1347, cf. *infra*) and before the final capitulation of the Ghent weavers on 'Good Tuesday', 13 January 1349.[107]

That dynastic relations were an important reason for regional chroniclers to report on foreign revolts is also evidenced by Bavaria herald's chronicle of Holland.[108] In the closing paragraphs of his dynastic history of the county, the herald briefly describes an uprising in Liège. Again, the family bond between the bishop-elect and the count of Holland was probably the sole reason for him to include this report. When in 1408, bishop-elect John the Pitiless was forced to flee to Maastricht, his older brother, William IV 'the noble prince of Holland', had readily come to his aid, burning and raiding villages in the vicinity. In September, with the support of their brother-in-law, John the Fearless, duke of Burgundy, the Wittelsbach princes had finally managed to subdue the Liège insurgents in the bloody Battle of Othée (23 September 1408).[109]

In spite of the fact that Boendale and Melis Stoke were contemporaries, the latter's reasons for discussing the Battle of the Golden Spurs and more generally the wars in Flanders differed considerably from his colleague's. Stoke's account is probably best read against the background of the long-standing territorial conflict between Flanders and Holland over the control of the region 'Zeeland-bewester-Schelde' (currently Central Zeeland). The situation had derailed in 1290, when Count Florent V of Holland was captured by his father in-law, Guy of Dampierre, the count of Flanders. When after the death of Count John I in November 1299, John I of Hainault succeeded in Holland as John II, the county became even further entangled in the war of succession that raged between Holland's new dynasty and the Flemish Dampierres. When Stoke wrote his part of the *Rijmkroniek of Holland*, including the account of Flemish war against Philip the Fair and the battle of the Golden Spurs, hostilities between Flanders and Holland were still ongoing.[110] In this view, it is not at all surprising that he sided with the French king, deplored that the Zeeland aristocrat Wolfert van Borselen had advised the young count of Holland to support his Dampierre relatives, and stated that the Flemish were out of their minds for rising up against their lawful sovereign.[111] The uproar in Flanders, and especially the Bruges Matins massacre (18 May 1302), was scandalous (*scande*). With relation to the Battle of the Golden Spurs, like Boendale, Stoke commemorates his fellow countrymen who had fallen while defending the French cause. Next to a number of unnamed Hainaulters, he especially regrets the death of the count's oldest son and heir, John of Ostrevant, on the Courtrai battlefield.[112]

The examples above show that the interest of transnational revolts primarily lay in dynastic relations and participation in international warfare. In addition to this, Stoke's account of the Flemish war against France may have been inspired by the enduring enmity between Flanders and Holland. An altogether different motivation may have pushed Boendale to write a report of the Liège rebellion against the newly appointed bishop, Englebert III de la Marcke in 1345–7. The account of the *Brabantsche yeesten* is divided over two chapters, each centred on a pivotal battle. In these sections, Boendale does not treat the Liège rebels substantially different from their Brabantine counterparts. The Liège craftsmen are equally 'haughty' (*Soe wies hem soe hoghe dien moet*) and 'senseless' (*Als lieden die sonder sin waren*).[113] The chronicler makes a direct connection between the intention of the Liège insurgents to occupy the bishopric and the recent action of the communality in Flanders (*Ghelijk als dat ghemeine diet/In Vlaenren plach ende noch pliet*). They had chosen a miller as their captain, like the Flemish had chosen Jacob van Artevelde.[114] According to Boendale's report, the Brabanters had not been present at the Battle of Vottem (19 July 1346) where the Liège communality won the victory.[115] The next year during the Battle of Tourinnes-les-Chaussées and Les Waleffes (21 July 1347), after the duke of Guelders had been attacked at the break of dawn, the Brabanters had saved the day. The town of St-Trond had surrendered to Brabant and, if we should believe Boendale, Duke John III had single-handedly reinstalled Englebert de la Marcke as bishop of Liège.[116] Based on the information in the *Brabantsche yeesten* one would assume that the main purpose of this account was to add to the duke's reputation. However, the contemporaneous accounts of the native Liègeois Jean le Bel and the anonymous monk who authored the account of the battle in the chronicle of the abbey of Saint-Trond tell a different story altogether and present John III as a compulsive slacker. According to Jean le Bel, when the duke arrived at the battlefield, the fight had been over.[117] These reports suggest that slanderous(?) rumours coming in from the bishopric may have provided an additional motivation for Boendale to recount the events from his own, Brabantine point of view.

After Burgundy: united we stand?

The incorporation of Brabant and Holland into the Burgundian conglomerate also left its mark on the transnational representation of revolt. In spite of the fact that, with the disappearance of the regional courts, urban centres had become the most important suppliers of regional historiography, the main principle of organisation, the dynastic line, remained in place. Although this is probably the principal reason why attention was given to insurgencies in the adjacent Burgundian territories, the cross-border accounts could be superficially perceived as a sign of a nascent 'Burgundian' collective identity. However, and this may seem a bit contradictory, these transnational reports of revolt could also be read as expressions of regional particularism and the need to stand out from the neighbours. Even more than before, when each principality had had its own dynasty, urban centres had to compete for the sovereign's favour, which in the new composite state had to be divided over multiple regions. As it appears, narratives of revolt – or rather the absence thereof – may have been a way to catch the sovereign's ear or at least to advertise a programme of pacification that would carry away princely approval, and thus improve the relations between the duke and regional or urban pressure groups.

Brabant: the importance of being loyal

Significantly, 'revolt' and particularly its antonym 'loyalty' occupy a special place in the prologues of the *Cronyke van Brabant int prose int corte* and *Die alder excellenste cronyke van Brabant*. Both chronicles were composed in the second half of the fifteenth century, in or after periods of political turmoil. The last event described in the first (extant) redaction of the *Cronyke van Brabant int prose int corte* is the destruction of Liège in 1468. As mentioned above, *Die alder excellenste cronyke* ends in 1486, with Maximilian's election as king of the Romans. In the prologue to his short prose chronicle, the anonymous author of the *Cronyke van Brabant int prose* boasts that it is mentioned in 'no book or history' that 'the dukes of Brabant waged war on their country or the common land of Brabant [rose] against its lord'. In the mind of the chronicler, Brabant is to be compared to three diamonds: (1) Brabant never waged war against its sovereign, (2) the Brabanters never deserted their prince on the battlefield, and (3) they never exiled their lord. Therefore, or so tells us the anonymous, 'Brabant is more noble than other lands'. By 'other lands' we should probably understand the duchy's closest neighbours. All three properties were easily applied to Flanders. With relation to Holland, the so-called 'Gouda chronicle' tells us that the Slavs, the mythical ancestors of the Hollanders, were a fierce and cruel people, who for a long time had refused to accept foreign rule, not even that of King Arthur. Even more significantly, the chronicler reports that, after an initial period of peace, the Frisians and Hollanders had driven their first count, Dirk I, out of the county.[118]

Likewise, the elaborate etymology of *Brabancia* at the beginning of *Die alder excellenste cronyke van Brabant*, should be understood as a way for Brabant to stand out from the surrounding regions. Similar etymologies with slight variations in the meaning of the letters appear in Brabantine historiography as from the first decades of the fifteenth century, at a time when the grip of the Valois dukes of Burgundy on Brabant and its neighbours started to tighten.[119] In this particular instance it is striking that 'loyalty', or the absence of revolt, almost becomes some kind of meta-virtue, playing a role of some importance in the explanation of no less than four out of nine letters. The Brabanters' loyalty is specifically addressed in the ninth and final letter 'A' for *amabilis* (amiable). There, the inhabitants of Brabant are described as a peaceful people, who usually live together in unity and concord. Their gentleness has 'only occasionally been disturbed by malicious rulers and corrupt officials, who like demons spread argument and discord, because they were more concerned with staying in office, than with the reputation or common welfare of the region or its prince'. In this way, local and foreign agitators alike had 'tempted the poor, common people to partake in their party strife'. The anonymous compiler, possibly a Carthusian monk from Antwerp, concluded that, 'in line with scripture, these agitators surely should be damned for all eternity', and further adds that 'wherever they travel, Brabanters are appreciated above most other people, because of their sincerity and loyalty'. The Brabanter's exemplary loyalty features in the compiler's elaboration of three additional virtues. One of the main reasons for him to refer to Brabant as *Bona* ('good', the third letter) echoes the three 'diamonds' of the *Cronyke van Brabant int prose int corte*: throughout history, the Brabanters had proven to be a good and loyal people, who had never betrayed, surrendered, or abandoned their duke in battle. These same arguments were later repeated to illustrate the fifth (*Audax*, 'brave') and sixth (*Nobilis*, 'noble') letters. This near-proverbial loyalty should probably be read in a very specific and pragmatic context. In addition to the aforementioned virtues, the duchy boasted a royal lineage (the second letter: *Regalis*, 'royal') and a long history (the third letter, *Antiqua*, 'ancient'), predating that of all surrounding regions. In order to demonstrate that Brabant was *Antiqua*, the compiler asserted that sovereign lords had ruled the duchy long before any other territory in its vicinity. Charlemagne, an illustrious forebear of the Brabantine dynasty, had chosen the first forester in Flanders. His son, Louis the Pious, appointed the first count of Holland. With reference to similar statements of ancient descent, as for instance found in Merchtenen's chronicle, Sjoerd Bijker has shown that, on several occasions, Brabanters exploited their presumed 'antiquity' and regal descent to command preferential treatment.[120] This demonstrates that these discursive strategies, through which local historiographers constructed a framework of identification for their audience were 'all about claiming a higher status than the neighbours'. The emphasis on 'loyalty' in the prologues of these chronicles of Brabant further suggests that the presumed absence of revolt played a significant role in setting the region apart from the surrounding principalities.

'Othering' the neighbours, taking up collective culpability, or both?

From an elite point of view, the mixed strategy that combined covering up instances of domestic insurgency (cf. *supra*) with a focus on foreign uprisings, displaced a socially and politically undesirable behaviour to the adjacent regions. While neighbouring principalities were put in a negative light, the home region was associated with positive attributes, like in the Brabantine examples listed above. In a sense, one could say that representations of 'revolt' were used to 'other' the neighbours and direct a positive spotlight on to the motherland. In a short report of the Second Ghent War (1447–53), the author of the *Gouda chronicle* designated the Ghent rebellion as *een quaet fel oerloch* (a cruel and immoral war) and emphasised the dire consequences: many fell in battle, were hanged, decapitated, etc. and many villages were burnt and destroyed.[121] This description might serve as a forbidding example. However, it may also have been motivated by the author's political preferences. As was mentioned above, the anonymous author who wrote this part of the chronicle probably was a moderate supporter of the Hook faction. In 1453, Reinoud II van Brederode and his brother Gijsbrecht had financed a military mission to support Duke Philip the Good in the war against the Ghent insurgents. That the chronicler did not explicitly mention this may be explained by the tension that had risen between the Brederodes and their sovereign after Gijsbrecht's election as bishop of Utrecht in 1455. The author who continued the chronicle after 1455, emphasised that after Philip's death the populace of Ghent had rebelled against their new sovereign, Charles the Bold, and had coerced their prince into approving new priviliges.[122] In his account of the Liège uprising in 1467, he highlighted that after the battle of Brustem (28 October 1467), 300 men were knighted, among them five Hollanders: Jan van Cruninghe, Sweder van Montfoort, Albert van Schagen, and Jan and Willem Ruychrock.[123]

The Liège wars and frequent uprisings in Flanders are recurrent subjects in the regional chronicles that were written in Holland and Brabant during or shortly after the regency of Maximilian of Austria. This observation becomes all the more relevant in the light of the fact that many of these texts lack descriptions of similar (important) troubles in the region in which they were composed. On the one hand these cross-border representations of revolt can be explained by the same factors that dictated the inclusion of foreign uprisings before the Burgundian incorporation: dynastic alliances and regional involvement in international warfare. Jan Allertsz.'s attention for the War of the Roses also fits these categories. In 1468, Charles the Bold had married Margaret of York, the sister of the English king, Edward IV. In his historiographical notes, he refers to the wedding festivities in Flanders and mentions that on the occasion the wells were poisoned.[124] Perhaps more important is that when in October 1470, Edward IV fled across the English Channel, he was taken in by Louis of Bruges, lord of Gruuthuse, and at the time stadtholder of Holland. That the English king briefly stayed in The Hague, and reconquered his throne with the aid of a fleet that had been equipped by Louis of Bruges and the Zeeland nobleman Hendrik van Borselen was possibly the main reason why Allertsz. paid so much attention to the troubles in England.[125] The Rotterdam secretary recorded the events surrounding the issuing of the Great Privilege of 1477 and the rebellions in Ghent and Bruges.[126] With relation to Maximilian's regency, Allertsz. rejected the uprisings against Maximilian in Flanders (1485) and reported the pro-Maximilian march in Ghent led by Matthijs Pedaert.[127] Although the language of his chronicle usually is factual and concise, he referred to the rebel actions in Ghent as *quaetheit* (criminal acts) and *oirloge* (acts of war).[128] Maximilian's imprisonment in Bruges was portrayed as 'dishonourable'. His imprisoners were called 'shameful' and 'unworthy of even sweeping the ashes in his cell'.[129]

In spite of the particularistic tendencies in the prologues of the *Cronyke van Brabant int prose int corte* and *Die alder excellenste cronyke van Brabant*, in these texts the descriptions of the protests following the deaths of Charles the Bold (5 January 1477) and his daughter Mary of Burgundy (27 March 1482) are more inclusive. The compiler of *Die alder excellenste cronyke*, for instance, specifically referred to the atrocities that had occurred in Ghent on Maundy Thursday 1477. There, the 'weavers and other guilds' had violently decapitated the Burgundian chancellor Hugonet and Guy de Brimeu, lord of Humbercourt.[130] However, he also acknowledged that after the death of Charles the Bold there had been revolts in the cities of Brabant as well. The compiler recognised that uproar had ravaged the four main cities of Brabant and 'in some places those in charge were put to justice [by the rebels]'. The compiler paused at the troubles in Brussels (cf. *supra*); Louvain had long persisted in its errant ways.[131] When news reached the cities that the planned marriage between the emperor's son, Maximilian of Austria and Mary of Burgundy would finally take place, the turmoil subsided for a while.[132] However, the 'hard times, lasting long, long years' did not begin until after the death of Mary of Burgundy in 1482. Strange things happened throughout the Burgundian Low Countries, because of 'malevolent rule'. The princely domains of Brabant, Flanders, Holland, etc. were burdened to such an extent that it was still deplored at the time of writing.[133] These events were *wonderlijc*, which in this context should be understood as 'totally incomprehensible'. Ultimately, it seems that in spite of the above, the compiler could not bring himself to give Brabant its deserved place among the 'many wars and tribulations Maximilian had endured in these lands, sometimes in Flanders, sometimes in Holland and in the bishopric of Utrecht ... and other factional conflicts that had flared up because of regimes that were hard to understand'.[134] Although the narrative of the *Alder excellenste cronyke* halts in 1486, it is unclear if the chronicle was written shortly after, or a decade later, shortly before it was printed in 1498. Was this cut-off point intentional, in order to avoid discussion of further troubles in Brabant, for instance the violent confrontations in Brussels in 1486–7 and the city's defection to Maximilian's adversary, Louis XI of France? It seems plausible that the compiler's willingness to share the blame for the uprisings after the death of Charles the Bold, together with his aversion to detail further Brabant's role in more recent troubles may ultimately have served to promote a message of pacification.

Conclusion: integration, particularism, and revolt

Reading these regional chronicles of Brabant and Holland through the lens of popular revolts, further focalises the socio-political context in and for which they were written. The way in which authors positioned their narratives with relation to social unrest at home and abroad provides valuable information about their political orientation, the opinions held by their commissioning patrons, or those of their imagined audiences. Using discursive strategies such as 'othering', authors erected an ideological wall between the dominant elites and dissident social groups, who were represented as callous and incapable. At the same time, the negative representation of rebels, their actions, and objectives, construed or confirmed a positive collective identity for the social in-group(s) at which these narratives were aimed. The camouflaging of domestic revolt displaced this evidently undesirable behaviour to another place, for instance to adjacent cities such as Malines or Louvain and later also to different regions altogether.

Princely courts and urban administrations provided a natural habitat for many of these regional chronicles. In these contexts, their use was mainly pragmatic, they were important sources for precedents in negotiations, could support ideological views, or condone contemporary policy. Because of their politically sensitive charge, the descriptions of social unrest contained within these practical documents were easily affected by fluctuations in the political climate. Additionally, they were challenged by competing narratives spread by political opponents. In this respect, it is not surprising that scribes, when they produced a new copy, frequently intervened and refashioned (part of) the narrative to suit better the requirements of the context in which the new manuscript would be used.[135] When, during the late fourteenth and early fifteenth century, representatives of the guilds increasingly participated in branches of the urban administrations, (parts of) the ideological walls between patricians and non-patricians appear to have come down, which went hand in hand with a growing degree of nuance and understanding in the portrayal of insurgents and their aspirations. The reconfiguration of the dominant in-groups for which these historiographical discourses were produced, also changed the associated narratives about political agency and revolt.

The incorporation of the Low Countries into the Burgundian conglomerate constituted another benchmark in the development of representations of social revolt in the historiography of the Low Countries. However, instead of establishing a trans-regional Burgundian identity, as might be expected, the integration of previously independent principalities only added fuel to the fire of particularism, also in the field of historiography. All of a sudden, there were a lot more people, entire regions even, to 'other'. While before the incorporation into the Burgundian composite state, the only competition for the sovereign's favour had been other cities in the same region, urban administrations now had to compete with their equals in neighbouring territories.

The prologues of the *Alder excellenste cronyke* and the *Cronyke van Brabant int prose int corte* give evidence of the fact that 'othering' and 'selective representation' were henceforth applied on an international scale. According to these historiographers from Brabant, their fellow countrymen were no troublemakers; revolts happened elsewhere, in adjacent lands, like Liège or Flanders. In this respect, transnational representations of revolt were indeed 'reflections on analogous phenomena at home', but rather than transmitting ideas about domestic rebellion, the insistence on foreign uprisings obfuscated similar troubles at home. By indicating that the adjacent regions were at the heart of the problem ('othering'), while intramural conflicts in the home region were carefully concealed ('selective appropriation'), chroniclers could reaffirm the positive image of the motherland. Alternatively, as with the troubles after the death of Charles the Bold, protests against princely policy (the Great Tradition) were preferentially reframed as revolts against local governments (the Little Tradition). A combination of these strategies, allowed local elites to get rid of unbecoming stains on the blazon of the city or region, which could prove to be especially useful after a period of rocky relations with the prince.

Notes

1 R. Stein, 'Wanneer schreef Jan van Boendale zijn Brabantsche yeesten?', *Tijdschrift voor Nederlandse Taal- en Letterkunde*, 106, 1990, pp. 262–77; R. Sleiderink, *De stem van de meester: De hertogen van Brabant en hun rol in het literaire leven (1106–1430)*, Amsterdam: Prometheus, 2003, p. 118; Jan van Boendale, *Les gestes des ducs de Brabant: De Brabantsche Yeesten, of Rymkronyk van Braband, door Jan de Klerk, van Antwerpen*, eds J. F. Willems and H. Bormans, 3 vols, Brussels: M. Hayes, 1839–69.

2 Boendale, *Brabantsche yeesten*, ed. Willems and Bormans, Book V, vv. 219–22. On this battle, see J. F. Verbruggen and K. DeVries (eds), *The Battle of the Golden Spurs (Courtrai, 11 July 1302): A Contribution to the History of Flanders' War of Liberation, 1297–1305*, trans. D. R. Ferguson, Woodbridge: Boydell & Brewer, 2002.

3 Boendale, *Brabantsche yeesten*, ed. Willems and Bormans, Book V, vv. 271–2. For Boendale's full account of the conflict: ibid., vv. 188–272.
4 Boendale, *Brabantsche yeesten*, ed. Willems and Bormans, Book I, vv. 40–1, 50–1.
5 M. Griesse, 'Introduction: representing revolts across boundaries in pre-modern times', in *From Mutual Observation to Propaganda War: Premodern Revolts in their Transnational Representations*, Bielefeld: Transcript Verlag, 2014, pp. 7–33, at 13–14. See also the manifesto of the research group 'Revolts as communicative events' at the University of Konstanz: M. Griesse, 'Revolts as communicative events in early-modern Europe: circulation of knowledge and the development of political grammars', p. 2, www.exzellenzcluster.uni-konstanz.de/fileadmin/all/downloads/stellen-stipendien/Circulation-of-Knowledge-Early-Modern-Revolts.pdf.
6 H. Hinck and B. Bommersbach, 'Cross-border representations of revolt in the later Middle Ages: France and England during the Hundred Years' War (1337–1453)', in Griesse (ed.), *From Mutual Observation*, pp. 37–51, at 40–1.
7 N. Bulst, '"Jacquerie" und "Peasants' Revolt" in der fransözischen und englischen Chronistik', in H. Patze (ed.), *Geschichtsschreibung und Geschichtsbewußtsein im späten Mittelalter*, Sigmaringen: Thorbecke Verlag, 1987, pp. 791–819.
8 Hinck and Bommersbach, 'Cross-border representations', pp. 42–5.
9 On urban information networks in the Empire, see the chapter by Gisela Naegle in this volume.
10 Jan van Boendale, 'Boec vander wraken', in F. A. Snellaert (ed.), *Nederlandsche gedichten uit de veertiende eeuw van Jan van Boendale, Hein van Aken e.a.*, Brussels: M. Hayez, 1869, pp. 287–488, at 376–8 and 458–60. On this text, see also: W. van Anrooij, 'Boendales "Boec van der wraken": datering en ontstaansgeschiedenis', *Queeste*, 2, 1995, pp. 40–53. Boendale more specifically refers to the battles of Vottem (19 July 1346) and Tourinnes-les-Chaussées/Les Waleffes (21 July 1347), which he also discusses in his chronicle of Brabant, cf. *infra*.
11 A. G. Jongkees, 'III. Gentse oorlog', in E. O. van der Werff, C. A. A. Linssen, and B. Evels-Hoving (eds), *Burgundica et varia: Keuze uit verspreide opstellen van prof. dr. A. G. Jongkees*, Hilversum: Verloren, 1990, pp. 48–51.
12 On the integration process, see W. Prevenier and W. Blockmans, *The Promised Lands: The Low Countries under Burgundian Rule, 1369–1530*, trans. E. Fackelman, rev. edn, trans. E. Peters, Philadelphia: University of Pennsylvania Press, 1999. More recently: R. Stein, *De hertog en zijn staten: De eenwording van de Bourgondische Nederlanden, ca. 1380–ca. 1480*, Hilversum: Verloren, 2014.
13 Stein, *Hertog*, pp. 274–5.
14 W. Blockmans, 'Une cour, XVII principautés', in W. Paravicini (ed.), *La cour de Bourgogne et l'Europe: Le rayonnement et les limites d'un modèle culturel*, Ostfildern: Jan Thorbecke Verlag, 2013, pp. 785–96, at 788.
15 On revolts, collective identities and social memory, see J. Haemers, 'Social memory and rebellion in fifteenth-century Ghent', *Social History*, 36, 2011, pp. 443–63.
16 Anne-Laure Van Bruaene, *De Gentse memorieboeken als spiegel van stedelijk historisch bewustzijn (14de tot 16de eeuw)*, Ghent: Maatschappij voor Geschiedenis en Oudheidkunde te Gent, 1998, pp. 117–20, 130–62, esp. 161–2.
17 The French *Chronique rimée des troubles de Flandres* was written by a Dutch-speaking author, possibly a clerk in the chancery of Flanders, during or not long after the civil war and is dedicated to Philip the Bold. The third continuation of the *Rijmkroniek van Vlaanderen* (Verse chronicle of Flanders) detailing the events in the county as from 1380 was probably written c.1415 in Ghent by an eye-witness. *Chronique rimée des troubles de Flandre en 1379–1380*, ed. H. Pirenne, Ghent: J. Vuylsteke éditeur, 1902; the Dutch text is edited in *Het Comburgse handschrift: Hs. Stuttgart, Württembergische Landesbibliothek, Cod. Poet. Et phil. 2° 22*, eds H. Brinkman and J. Schenkel, 2 vols, Hilversum: Verloren, 1997, vol. 2, pp. 1229–491.
18 I thank Remco Sleiderink (KU Leuven, Campus Brussel) for allowing me to consult his introduction and edition which will be published in *Handelingen van de Koninklijke Commissie voor Geschiedenis*.
19 W. van Eeghem, 'Een onbekende bewerking van Hennen van Merchtenens "Cornicke van Brabant" (1415)', *Verslagen en Mededelingen van de Koninklijke Vlaamsche Academie voor Taal-en Letterkunde*, 1940, pp. 507–28 (with edition, I further refer to this edition as *Oude gesten seggen ons*). In spite of the fact that Wim van Anrooij has presented arguments in favour of dating *Oude gesten* in the fifteenth century, the precise relation between Van Merchtenen's *Cornicke* and the *Gesten* is still unclear. See W. van Anrooij, 'Zwaanridder en historiografie bij Hennen van Merchtenen', *Spiegel der Letteren*, 36, 1994, pp. 279–306. Hennen van Merchtenen's chronicle is edited in G. Gezelle, 'Hennen van Merchtenen's

Cornicke van Brabant (1414)', *Koninklijke Vlaamsche Academie voor Taal-en Letterkunde. Verslagen en Mededeelingen*, Serie III, 14, 1896, pp. 29–167. I further refer to this edition as *Cornicke*.
20 J. Pacquay, 'Kroniek der Luiksche Oorlogen uit de XVe eeuw', *Verslagen en Mededelingen van de Koninklijke Vlaamse Academie voor Taal- en Letterkunde*, 1928, pp. 203–46.
21 A number of these have been (partially) edited in C. Piot, *Chroniques de Brabant et de Flandre*, Brussels: F. Hayez, 1879.
22 B. Guenée, *Histoire et culture historique dans l'occident médiéval*, Paris: Aubier, 1980, pp. 203–11, esp. 207.
23 P. Hoppenbrouwers, 'Rebels with a cause: the peasant movements of northern Holland in the later Middle Ages', in W. Blockmans and A. Janse (eds), *Showing Status: Representations of Social Positions in the Late Middle Ages*, Turnhout: Brepols, 1999, pp. 446–82, at 459 and 482.
24 B. Ashcroft, G. Griffiths, and H. Tiffin, *Post-Colonial Studies: The Key Concepts*, 2nd edn, London and New York: Routledge, 2007, pp. 156–9; on the 'other': pp. 154–6. The concept was first coined by G. Spivak, 'The Rani of Simur', in F. Baker, P. Hulme, M. Iversen, and D. Loxley (eds), *Europe and its Others*, vol. 1, *Proceedings of the Essex Conference on the Sociology of Literature*, Colchester: University of Essex, 1985, pp. 128–51.
25 For the negative portrayal of rebels and their actions, including accusations of anthropophagy, see the essay by Vincent Challet in this volume.
26 On the continuation of Boendale's chronicle, see R. Stein, *Politiek en historiografie: Het ontstaansmilieu van Brabantse kronieken in de eerste helft van de vijftiende eeuw*, Leuven: Peeters, 1994 and A. Houthuys, *Middeleeuws kladwerk: De autograaf van de Brabantsche yeesten, boek VI (vijftiende eeuw)*, Hilversum: Verloren, 2009. The text was published by H. Bormans in the edition of the *Brabantsche yeesten*. Remco Sleiderink has proposed that the anonymous author of the continuation should be identified with chorister and chaplain Wein van Cotthem. Sleiderink, *Stem*, pp. 152–5; Houthuys, *Middeleeuws kladwerk*, pp. 43–50. More recently, Joris Reynaert has reopened the case for the authorship of the ducal officer Hennen van Merchtenen: J. Reynaert, 'Het "Spel van Olivier van Leefdale": Toneel en geschiedschrijving in de vijftiende eeuw', *Queeste*, 21, 2014, pp. 23–55, at 41–4.
27 Stein, *Politiek*, esp. pp. 297–304; Sleiderink, *Stem*, pp. 118–19.
28 Hoppenbrouwers, 'Rebels', p. 456.
29 Boendale, *Brabantsche yeesten*, ed. Willems and Bormans, Book V, vv. 379–8.
30 Ibid., v. 438.
31 Ibid., vv. 443–4.
32 Ibid., vv. 298, 498.
33 J. Dumolyn and J. Haemers, 'Patterns of urban rebellion in medieval Flanders', *JMH*, 31, 2005, pp. 369–93.
34 Boendale, *Brabantsche yeesten*, ed. Willems and Bormans, Book V, v. 4916.
35 Ibid., vv. 4946–7.
36 Cf. Stein, *Politiek*.
37 Boendale, *Brabantsche yeesten*, ed. Willems and Bormans, Book VI, vv. 4920–1.
38 Ibid., vv. 4972–3.
39 Ibid., vv. 4789–90.
40 Ibid., vv. 7135–226.
41 Ibid., v. 7168. In neutral contexts, the Middle Dutch word *gebuur*, rendered here as 'peasant', means 'neighbour' or 'fellow townsman'. With a negative connotation, it can be translated as 'enemy'. *Middelnederlands Woordenboek*, http://gtb.inl.nl/iWDB/search?actie=article&wdb=MNW&id=10576&lemma=gebuur.
42 Boendale, *Brabantsche yeesten*, ed. Willems and Bormans, Book VI, v. 7167.
43 Ibid., v. 7179.
44 Ibid., vv. 7228–30.
45 Ibid., Book V, vv. 516–18.
46 Ibid., vv. 4935–6.
47 Ibid., vv. 288–9.
48 Ibid., vv. 441–2.
49 *Rijmkroniek van Holland (366–1305) door een anoniem auteur en Melis Stoke*, ed. J. W. J. Burgers, The Hague: Instituut voor Nederlandse Geschiedenis, 2004.
50 Ibid., vv. 7166–74; Hoppenbrouwers, 'Rebels', p. 456.
51 Boendale, *Brabantsche yeesten*, ed. Willems and Bormans, Book VI, v. 4462.

52 *Die cronycke van Hollandt, Zeelandt ende Vrieslant, met die cronike der biscoppen van Uutrecht*, ed. A. de Hamer, http://resources.huygens.knaw.nl/divisiekroniek. I further refer to this edition as *Divisiekroniek*. The authorship of Cornelius Aurelius has been recently questioned by Sjoerd Levelt in his study of Jan van Naaldwijk's chronicles of Holland: S. Levelt, *Jan van Naaldwijk's Chronicles of Holland: Continuity and Transformation in the Historical Tradition of Holland during the Early Sixteenth Century*, Hilversum: Verloren, 2011, pp. 162–8.
53 *Divisiekroniek*, fols 290v–1r.
54 *Die cronike of die hystorie van hollant van zeelant ende vrieslant ende van den sticht van Utrecht*, Gouda: Gerard Leeu, 1478; The Hague: Koninklijke Bibliotheek, 169 G 95. I further refer to this edition as *Gouds Kroniekje*. At: fol. 95.
55 The Hague, Nationaal Archief, GRRek 146, fols 94r, 98v, 99r; R. W. G. Lombarts, L. J. Van Soest-Zuurdeeg, and H. W. Van Soest (eds), *Memoriale T uit de Almarie van Bourgonje 1445–1448 (1453)*, The Hague: Algemeen Rijksarchief, 1996, pp. 26–8; R. W. G. Lombarts, P. C. M. Schölvinck, J. Th. de Smidt, H. W. van Soest, and M. R. van den Toorn (eds), *Memorialen van het hof (den raad) van Holland, Zeeland en West Friesland van den secretaris Jan Rosa, IV–XIII*, Leiden: Brill/Universitaire Pers, 1982–8, pp. 11–13, 110–11.
56 Boendale, *Brabantsche yeesten*, ed. Willems and Bormans, Book V, vv. 415–25.
57 Ibid., vv. 4931–4.
58 Ibid., vv. 455–8.
59 Ibid., v. 4938.
60 Ibid., vv. 4941–2.
61 Ibid., vv. 4919–26.
62 *Cornicke*, vv. 2965–80.
63 *Oude gesten*, vv. 330–3.
64 Ibid., vv. 338–9.
65 Boendale, *Brabantsche yeesten*, ed. Willems and Bormans, Book VI, vv. 4407 and following chapters.
66 R. Van Uytven, C. Bruneel, H. Coppers, and B. Augustyn (eds), *De gewestelijke en lokale overheidsinstellingen in Brabant en Mechelen tot 1795*, Brussels: Algemeen Rijksarchief, 2014.
67 Part of *Oude gesten* was prosified and included in the manuscript of the sixteenth-century diary of Jan de Pottre, a merchant from Brussels and employed in the city council: Jan de Pottre, *Dagboek van Jan de Pottre, 1549–1602*, ed. B. de St. Genois, Ghent: C. Annoot-Braeckman, 1861; Van Eeghem, 'Bewerking', 525.
68 H. Lowagie, 'The political implications of urban archival documents in the late medieval Flemish cities: the example of the diary of Ghent', in M. Mostert (ed.), *Writing and the Administration of Medieval Towns: Medieval Urban Literacy*, Turnhout: Brepols, 2014, pp. 209–18, at 213.
69 Stein, *Politiek*, p. 302.
70 D. Hogenelst and F. van Oostrom, *Handgeschreven wereld: Nederlandse literatuur en cultuur in de middeleeuwen*, Vianen: Uitgeverij Aeropagus, 1995, pp. 266–7; Brussels, Koninklijke Bibliotheek/Bibliothèque royale, MS 19.607.
71 Lowagie, 'Political implications', pp. 213–17.
72 Sleiderink, *Stem*, p. 110.
73 The title of the two final chapters feature in the list of *tituli* at the start of Book V (fol. 90v.), but the actual text of these *capitula* was not copied (fol. 117r). I will return to this elsewhere.
74 Boendale, *Brabantsche yeesten*, ed. Willems and Bormans, Book VII, vv. 11079–12206.
75 Van Anrooij, 'Zwaanridder'.
76 Piot, *Chroniques*, p. 56.
77 On this chronicle, see J. Tigelaar, *Brabants historie ontvouwd: Die alder excellenste cronyke van Brabant en het Brabantse geschiedbeeld anno 1500*, Hilversum: Verloren, 2006. A transcription is an appendix on the accompanying CD-ROM. I further refer to this transcription as *Die alder excellenste cronyke van Brabant*.
78 *Die alder excellenste cronyke van Brabant*, [dd1v].
79 Ibid.
80 Van Uytven et al., *De gewestelijke en lokale overheidsinstellingen in Brabant en Mechelen*.
81 Dumolyn and Haemers, 'Patterns', p. 371; W. Blockmans, 'Alternatives to monarchical centralisation: the great tradition of revolt in Flanders and Brabant', in H. Koenigsberger (ed.), *Republiken und Republikanismus im Europa der frühen Neuzeit*, Munich: Oldenbourg Verlag, 1988, pp. 145–54; M. Boone and M. Prak, 'Patricians and burghers: the great and the little tradition of urban revolt in the

Low Countries', in K. Davids and J. Lucassen (eds), *A Miracle Mirrored: The Dutch Republic in European Perspective*, Cambridge: Cambridge University Press, 1995, pp. 99–134.
82 *Die alder excellenste cronyke van Brabant*, [dd2v].
83 Van Bruaene, *Memorieboeken*, pp. 144–7.
84 J. W. J. Burgers, *De rijmkroniek van Holland en zijn auteurs*, Hilversum: Verloren, 1999, p. 306. On the Kennemer uprising, see Hoppenbrouwers, 'Rebels', pp. 453, 458–9, 461.
85 On the Brussels uprising, see H. Vandecandelaere, 'Een opstand in zeven "aktes": Brussel 1303–1306', *Brusselse Cahiers Bruxellois*, 2008, pp. 4–67. On the disturbances in Antwerp, F. Prims, *Geschiedenis van Antwerpen: III. Onder Hertog Jan den Tweede (1294–1312)*, Brussel: N.V. Standaard Boekhandel, 1931, pp. 23–5.
86 Boendale, *Brabantsche yeesten*, ed. Willems and Bormans, Book V, vv. 303–11.
87 Sleiderink, *Stem*, pp. 118–19.
88 Tigelaar, *Brabants historie*, pp. 102–6.
89 *Die alder excellenste cronyke van Brabant*, [cc2ra]–[dd4rb], quote at [dd1vb].
90 Ibid., [dd4r]. See also Tigelaar, *Brabants historie*, pp. 142–9.
91 A transcription by J. Tigelaar and Willem Kuiper based on Ghent, Universiteitsbibliotheek, MS 908 is available online, http://cf.hum.uva.nl/dsp/scriptamanent/bml/Brabant/Brabant.html.
92 Brussels, Koninklijke Bibliotheek/Bibliothèque royale, MS 18001, fols 45v–8r.
93 *Die alder excellenste cronyke van Brabant*, [cc2r].
94 M. van Gent, *'Pertijelijke saken': Hoeken en Kabeljauwen in het Bourgondisch-Oostenrijkse tijdperk*, The Hague: Stichting Hollandse Historische Reeks, 1994, pp. 16–21.
95 The historical notes in the manuscript have been edited in H. ten Boom and J. van Herwaarden, 'Rotterdamse kroniek: Aantekeningen van Rotterdamse stadssecretarissen, 1315–1499 (1570)', in C. Dekker, J. G. Smit, J. Th. M. Bank, G. A. M. Beekelaar, A. E. Kersten, G. van Herwijnen, and O. Vries (eds), *Nederlandse historische bronnen 2*, The Hague: Martinus Nijhoff, 1980, pp. 1–102. I further refer to this edition as 'Rotterdamse kroniek'. Further information on Allertsz. and Jansz. in H. ten Boom, 'De eerste secretarissen van Rotterdam: Gegevens over ambt, werkzaamheden en personen tot circa 1530', *Rotterdams jaarboekje*, series 8, 7, 1979, pp. 151–74.
96 Van Gent, *Pertijelijke saken*, p. 18.
97 'Rotterdamse kroniek', p. 66.
98 On this chronicle, see Levelt, *Chronicles*. Transcriptions of both versions in the appendices on the accompanying CD-ROM.
99 Levelt, *Chronicles*, pp. 82, 92, 191–2, 195–200.
100 Edited in: De Reiffenberg, 'Chronique inédite de Hollande et de Hainaut publiée pour la première fois par le baron de Reiffenberg', *Bulletin de la Commission royale d'histoire*, XII, [1847].
101 *Chronique inédite de Hollande*, p. 23.
102 Van Gent, *Pertijelijke Saken*, pp. 58–61.
103 On this conflict, see A. Janse, 'Yolande van Lalaing (1422–1497)', in E. den Hartog and H. Wijsman (eds), *Yolande van Lalaing (1422–1497, kasteelvrouwe van Brederode*, Haarlem: Kastelenstichting Holland en Zeeland, 2010, pp. 7–36 at 20–4.
104 The last quire, originally a sexternion, is incomplete and only has 11 folios. It therefore seems that at least one page has been lost at the end of the codex. Since the catchword for the following gathering would have been on the verso side of this folio, it is not implausible that an additional number of leaves has gone missing.
105 On Hendrik van Heessel and his armorial see W. van Anrooij, 'Hendrik Van Heessel, héraut à la cour impériale et à la cour de Bourgogne', *Revue du Nord*, 366–7, 2006, pp. 709–26. The shelfmark of the armorial is Antwerp, Bibliotheek Hendrik Conscience, MS B.89420. An online facsimile is available, http://anet.be/submit.phtml?UDses=45169879%3A890680&UDstate=1&UDmode=&UDaccess=&UDrou=%25Start:bopwexe&UDopac=opacehc&UDextra=digital=ehc~oloi=o:lvd:1072220.
106 Interestingly, the *Gouda chronicle* also pauses at this point in the narrative. Possibly its author, probably a mild supporter of the Hooks, did not want to cause further disrepute to the Brederode family, who, at least in the minds of its partisans, were closely connected to the Hook party.
107 Boendale, *Brabantsche yeesten*, ed. Willems and Bormans, Book V, vv. 4950–4.
108 On this chronicle see J. Verbij-Schillings, *Beeldvorming in Holland: Heraut Beyeren en de historiografie omstreeks 1400*, Amsterdam: Prometheus, 1995.
109 Edited in S. Muller Fz., 'Die Hollantsche Cronike van den Heraut: Eene studie over de Hollandsche geschied-bronnen uit het Beijersche tijdperk', *Bijdragen voor Vaderlandsche Geschiedenis en Oudheidkunde*,

series 3, 2, 1885, pp. 1–124, at 119–22. A more elaborate version of the episode appears at the end of another short dynastic prose chronicle of Holland (The Hague, Rijksmuseum Meermanno-Westreenianum, MS 10 D 36) dated to after 1417. The relevant portion of the text was also edited by Muller, 'Hollantsche Cronike', pp. 122–4.

110 Burgers, *De rijmkroniek van Holland en zijn auteurs*, pp. 135–6.
111 Ibid., p. 279.
112 Ibid., p. 372.
113 Boendale, *Brabantsche yeesten*, ed. Willems and Bormans, Book V, vv. 4776, 4780.
114 Ibid., vv. 4785–94.
115 Ibid., vv. 4453–526.
116 Ibid., vv. 4837–900.
117 Jean le Bel, *Chronique de Jean le Bel*, ed. J. Viard and E. Déprez, 2 vols, Paris: Renouard, 1904, vol. 2, pp. 139–44; E. Lavigne, *Kroniek van de abdij van Sint-Truiden: Vertaling van de 'Gesta abbatum Trudonensium' met annotaties van prof. dr. W. Jappe Alberts en prof. dr. J. C. G. M. Jansen*, 3 vols, Leeuwarden/Maastricht: Eisma B.V., vol. 2, pp. 174–8.
118 *Gouds kroniekje*, fol. 18.
119 W. van Anrooij, 'Hennen van Merchtenen en de lof op Brabancia', *Spiegel der Letteren*, 35, 1993, pp. 153–7.
120 S. Bijker, 'The functions of the late medieval Brabantine legend of Brabon', in R. Stein and J. Pollmann (eds), *Networks, Regions and Nations: Shaping Identities in the Low Countries, 1300–1650*, Leiden: Brill, 2009, pp. 91–110.
121 *Gouds kroniekje*, fol. 95v.
122 Ibid., fol. 100r.
123 Ibid., fol. 100v.
124 'Rotterdamse kroniek', p. 39.
125 Ibid., pp. 44–50; Mario Damen, *De staat van dienst: De gewestelijke ambtenaren van Holland en Zeeland in de Bourgondische periode (1425–1482)*, Hilversum: Verloren, 2000, pp. 284–5.
126 'Rotterdamse kroniek', p. 62.
127 Ibid., pp. 75–9.
128 Ibid., p. 76.
129 Ibid., pp. 82–4.
130 *Die alderexcellentste cronyke van Brabant*, [cc2r].
131 Ibid., [dd1v].
132 Ibid., [dd2r].
133 Ibid., [dd3v].
134 Ibid., [dd4r].
135 See M. Fisher, *Scribal Authorship and the Writing of History in Medieval England*, Columbus: Ohio State University Press, 2012.

6

AN EXEMPLARY REVOLT OF THE CENTRAL MIDDLE AGES?

Echoes of the first Lombard League across the Christian world around the year 1200

Gianluca Raccagni

There is some consensus among historians on the fact that the central Middle Ages played a pivotal role in the growth of European administrative institutions and the development of principles of accountability, consultation, and public responsibility. This study engages with that scholarship by discussing some neglected viewpoints, that is, the degree of awareness and the perception across the Christian world of contemporary developments and local socio-political variations, which will be tackled by focusing on the momentous conflict between the Lombard League and the Holy Roman Emperor Frederick Barbarossa of 1167–83. There is no wide-ranging study of that awareness, but this analysis argues that the representation of the conflict between Barbarossa and the League across Christendom could represent a valuable paradigm, which, moreover, challenges some significant noteworthy preconceptions. Indeed, scholarly considerations of the broader European power dynamics in the central Middle Ages and their legacy have tended to sideline Communal Italy (as scholarship often calls the northern half of the peninsula, dominated as it was by numerous quasi-independent city communes), and to neglect the conflict between the League (an association that united most of the city communes of the Po Plain) and Barbarossa as well as its status of revolt by subjects against their ruler.[1]

Three main factors have traditionally led to that state of the research regarding the conflict between the League and Barbarossa, and they are the perceived exceptionalism of Communal Italy, its peculiar relationship with its emperor, and the challenge categorising the social features of that conflict. To start with, the Italian cities' contribution to central medieval political culture has been primarily considered in the intellectual spheres, rather than in more practical political terms.[2] That is largely due to the fact that the autonomy of the numerous Lombard city communes, and their degree of regional dominance were quite atypical in the European panorama of that time.[3] Indeed, the claims of the German emperor over Italy are considered as little more than notional, and his presence there sporadic at best. That has created the general perception that imperial authority was a foreign body in Communal Italy, which, in turn, has induced scholars to focus on the bilateral features of the conflicts between the Italian cities and the emperors, rather than hierarchical ones.[4] Finally, on one side, the predominant urban features of Communal Italy have meant that historians have not fully seen its conflicts with the emperors as aristocratic revolts. On the other, the often-prevailing interpretation of twelfth-century

Lombard urban governments as oligarchic/aristocratic in nature, together with the existence of pro-imperial factions, has precluded the classification of those conflicts as popular revolts (this will be discussed more in depth later).

This study challenges those views by arguing that, in the decades straddling the turn of the twelfth century, the conflict between the League and Barbarossa was one of the best known practical examples, if not the best known, across the Christian world, from England to Byzantium, of a successful rebellion by subjects against their ultimate ruler. Indeed, the way in which non-Italian sources described that conflict suggests that its distinctive urban communal features were not perceived as necessarily discordant with wider contemporary European and Mediterranean political culture. On the one hand, Barbarossa was far more present in Northern Italy than any of his predecessors and successors, and he wished to 'normalise' the region by enhancing his control and administration there to the detriment of the city communes. On the other, the varied and communal features of the opposition to him led to the League being generically portrayed as a rebellion by subjects as a whole against a despotic ruler or, in the case of German sources, as a reprehensible rebellion by unruly subjects against their legitimate ruler. In point of fact, the conflict between the League and Barbarossa reflected very well the above-mentioned developments that characterised European power dynamics in that period, representing a celebrated case in point of successful resistance against what was perceived as a tyrannical growth of royal government.

After outlining the history of the conflict between the League and Barbarossa, this study will chart the awareness and representation of it outside the lands of the empire, from England to Byzantium passing through France and Southern Italy, by mainly relying on historical works from the decades around the year 1200. That information will then be compared to representations of the League from within the empire, considering both Northern Italy and the vast area north of the Alps, from the border of Denmark to Bohemia. The findings will then be combined with a brief discussion of the socio-political features of the Lombard city communes and of the League through the lenses of non-Italian primary sources and of modern scholarship. Finally the impact of those features on the conflict against Barbarossa and on its portrayal by primary sources will be considered by focusing on some representative examples.

Historical background

By the time of Barbarossa's imperial coronation at Rome in 1154, the Kingdom of Italy/Lombardy (*Regnum Italie* or *Lombardorum* in the sources), which comprised the northern half of the peninsula, was a very loose commonwealth dominated by autonomous city communes under the distant authority of German Holy Roman Emperors/kings. That was especially the case in the Po Valley, then known as Lombardy (now that name applies to a fraction of that region), which throughout the Middle Ages featured probably the highest urban density in Europe. In the central Middle Ages the Lombard cities were growing fast, and that growth also took a political turn with the birth of autonomous communal governments between the end of the eleventh and the beginning of the twelfth century, which, half a century later, had already reached a respectable level of maturity. At the peak of its success in 1172, for example, the Lombard League, despite its relatively small geographical size, included more than 20 city communes (*civitates*), all of which were fairly large by European standards, and each of which claimed authority over the surrounding lands. There were some territorial lordships in the region too, but very few matched any of its *civitates* in size and resources, and most of them orbited around *civitates*. The League, in any case, was the regional association of a land dominated by cities, rather than a mere league of towns. Its full official name was *Societas civitatum*, *locorum et hominum Lombardie*, that is, the League of the cities, non-urban communities and men of Lombardy, with the term *homines* including territorial lords. Indeed, the League did not preclude membership to them: the Marquis Malaspina, for example, who was largely autonomous, consistently sided with the League after it was founded in 1167, and his standing within it was comparable to that of a *civitas*.[5]

The Lombard League, however, was a complete novelty in that region, which was expressly created in order to repel the radical attempt by Barbarossa to enhance imperial authority in Italy, because no analogous general regional association had previously existed there. During his long reign, Barbarossa, who could count on unusually stable support in Germany, spent far more time in Italy than any of his predecessors. In the first half of the 1160s he established an administrative structure in Lombardy whose pervasiveness was comparable to the most advanced central governments of the time, such as those of England and Sicily. He secured fortifications in key points and appointed officials (many of them Germans) to govern towns and districts, with special emphasis on the collection of imperial dues.[6] A highpoint in the development of Barbarossa's Italian ambitions was the famous Diet of Roncaglia in 1158, whose expansive definition of royal/imperial prerogatives (*iura regalia*) is commonly regarded as a milestone in the conceptualisation of public law in Western Europe.[7] In order to implement his claims, though, Barbarossa first had to defeat the leading power in the region, that is, the city of Milan and its network of allies. The emperor achieved that in 1162, partly thanks to the support of Milan's regional enemies, such as Cremona and Pavia, which led to the destruction of Milan that year. Indeed, Barbarossa's domination across the region reached its peak between 1162 and 1167, though it is important to recognise that it was uneven: he granted a degree of autonomy to his supporters, while his officials had almost free rein to rule over former enemies.[8]

Yet it is from former allies, like Cremona, where rebellion first stirred in 1164. The reasons for their revolt were multiple: they felt vexed by Barbarossa's domination and by the exploitative behaviour of his agents, but they were also bribed by his enemies, like Byzantium, and supported by Pope Alexander III, who had taken the upper hand in the papal schism that had started in 1159 (while Barbarossa was the principal backer of a series of anti-popes). By 1168, the rebellion against Barbarossa had enveloped the whole of Lombardy, leading to the reconstruction of Milan, the creation of the League, and the obliteration of Barbarossa's governing structure across the region. After the League's victory at the Battle of Legnano in 1176 and the Peace of Venice in 1177 between Barbarossa and Alexander III (which also entailed negotiations between the League, the king of Sicily, and Barbarossa), the League and the emperor reached a written settlement at the Peace of Constance in 1183.[9]

The Peace of Constance, however, was not a capitulation by Barbarossa but a compromise, which aimed to set the future balance of power in the region. On one side, it recognised a very extensive level of self-government for so many Lombard communes (not all of which were included in the settlement) that these freedoms practically became a general benchmark of autonomy for the entire region.[10] On the other, the Peace of Constance acknowledged imperial superiority over Lombardy. That superiority was embodied by a set of reserved prerogatives, such as appellate jurisdiction, the duty of city consuls to take an oath of fealty to the emperor and to seek investiture from him, as well as the duty to help the emperor in times of need and during his coronation journey to Rome, and imperial control over some districts.[11]

The Peace of Constance worked well until the death of Emperor Henry VI in 1197, when a long struggle for the succession ensued, lasting for over two decades and vastly eroding the remaining imperial prerogatives in Italy.[12] When Emperor Frederick II, having stabilised his rule in Germany and in Southern Italy (a maternal inheritance), turned his attention to Lombardy in 1226, a long conflict ensued with the renewed League that continued until his death in 1250 and beyond.[13] The fortunes of the empire in Italy then rapidly and lastingly declined, but Lombardy notionally remained under imperial sovereignty, emperors intermittently paying heed to it now and again, and the Peace of Constance continued to be considered and celebrated as the legal foundation of the autonomy of the Lombard cities until the end of the Middle Ages and beyond.[14]

Representations of the conflict outside the Empire (England, France, Southern Italy, and Byzantium)

In late 1167, John of Salisbury sent a letter to William Brito, sub-prior of Christ Church in Canterbury. In it, after outlining the collapse of Barbarossa's rule in Lombardy and his narrow escape to Germany, John asked:

> Why do I tell you what you know already? Everywhere news of this is being loudly proclaimed. Everyone, I think, knows it, save only those perhaps who live apart from the crisis of the age, exiles in their own home.[15]

John's statement is confirmed by the vast coverage of the conflict in historical works produced across Christendom from the last quarter of the twelfth century through the first quarter of the thirteenth. Substantial coverage of those events can be found, for example, in the work of the Byzantine John Kinnamos (d. *c*.1185, secretary and biographer of Emperor Manuel Komnenos) and of the Southern Italian Romuald Guarna (d. 1178, archbishop of Salerno and envoy for the king of Sicily, including at the Peace of Venice), but also in those of English authors such as William of Newburgh (d. *c*.1198, an Augustinian canon from the priory of Newburgh), Robert of Torigni (d. 1186, abbot of Mont Saint-Michel in Normandy), and Ralph of Diceto (d. *c*.1202, dean of Saint Paul's Cathedral in London, who visited Italy in the 1170s during a diplomatic mission for King Henry of England in the aftermath of the murder of the Archbishop of Canterbury Thomas Becket),[16] and in an anonymous French chronicle from Laon (completed around 1218). Passing references can be found in other works from those countries, and especially from France and England, including the chronicle of Ralph Niger (d. *c*.1217, theologian and cleric), that of Richard of Poitiers (d. 1174, a monk at Cluny), an anonymous English eyewitness account of the Peace of Venice, and the historical/political poetry of Bertran de Born (d. 1215, a lord from the Limousin).[17] This list does not claim to be exhaustive, but it is certainly representative of the spread of the fame of the revolt.

Despite coming from different corners of the Christian world, these sources are remarkably consistent in presenting the conflict as a struggle to preserve time-honoured rights against a tyrannical ruler intent on trampling them, with ethnic issues exacerbating tensions. Their terminology is also remarkably consistent across the board, key words among them being *libertas* (freedom) for the objective of the Lombards, and *insolentia* (want of moderation, arrogance, but also unusualness) for Barbarossa's actions. Scholarship has spent rivers of ink on medieval views on *libertas*, but the use of the term *insolentia*, which these sources portray as its nemesis, has largely passed unnoticed. Differently from many later medieval revolts, these appeals to *libertas* did not have a socially charged dimension.[18] Yet, as in some late medieval revolts, they took a truly communal nature. As will be further discussed later, that evidence suggest that the distinction between community rights defined by elites as opposed to those defined by commoners was far less clear than scholarship has often taken it to be.[19] Indeed, those sources ascribe the Lombard uprising to urban communities coalesced into a general regional association of the emperor's subjects, which is sometimes presented as capable of collective actions on its own terms. Overall, the *libertas* of these sources is a collection of traditional communal rights regarding self-rule, taxation, property holding, but it is also the very freedom from arbitrary rule that the term *insolentia* typified.

Starting in the Christian East, we see that Kinnamos explained Lombard disaffection towards Barbarossa, 'king of the Germans', with the fact that, out of lust for power and insatiable greed, he strove to undo effortlessly what had been long established by time and custom, especially by laying claim to money. This pushed various Lombard cities, of which Kinnamos named some, to seek help against him and eventually to go over to the Byzantine emperor.[20]

On the other side of Christendom, comparable arguments can be found in Anglo-Norman sources, which are particularly rich in references to the League.[21] Ralph Niger mentioned that the Lombards toppled the insolence and oppression (*insolentia* and *opressiones*) of Barbarossa and of his Germans.[22] On similar lines, William of Newburgh, who called Frederick the 'German and Italian emperor' (*Teutonicus atque Italicus imperator*), and explained the conflict with the fact that, after his destruction of the rebel (*rebellem*) city of Milan, he acted insolently (*insolentius ageret*) and that the Lombards could not tolerate the resulting 'German yoke' (*jugum Alemannicum*).[23] According to Ralph of Diceto, the Lombards were Barbarossa's subjects, but he invaded Italy in order to cast his name above those of all the other magnates of the Earth; he found his main obstacle in the city of Milan, which enjoyed immunity from extraordinary obligations, was conscious of its *libertas*, and thus refused to acknowledge to him more than the customary dues; eventually the people of Milan, Piacenza, Brescia, and Verona decided to defend the *libertas* of their homeland (*patria*) with their lives;[24] following his defeat at Legnano, judging that Italy was rebellious to him (*sibi rebellem intelligens*), and that he could not face the Lombards on the battlefield again without recovering his strength, he moved to Germany.[25] The anonymous English eyewitness of the Peace of Venice underlined that the emperor had introduced grievous and previously unheard of customs in Northern Italy (*importunas et antea inauditas consuetudines*) as the cause of Lombard opposition to him.[26]

The Southern Italian Romuald of Salerno wrote that Barbarossa, after his victory over Milan, had Lombardy at his will and turned it into his domain (which probably referred to Barbarossa's reclamations of what he perceived were usurped public estates and assets) by appointing officials in cities and castles, the result being that, by supporting the emperor against Milan, the Lombards had placed themselves in servitude to the Germans.[27] Then at the Peace of Venice (more on which later), the representatives of the Lombards assured that they recognised the emperor's ancient dues and were happy to comply with them, but they categorically refused to relinquish the *libertas* which they held by hereditary right from their ancestors, and which they were ready to defend with their lives, equating the alternative to servitude.[28]

Moving to France, the anonymous chronicler of Laon mentioned Barbarossa's growing power in the region and the destruction of Milan in 1162, but also that, weary of his *insolentia*, the Lombards decided to submit their kingdom to the Byzantine emperor and shortly after this entered into similar negotiations with King Henry II of England.[29] Indeed, according to this chronicle, 'as they say', Barbarossa later took the cross because he was filled with remorse for the injuries he had inflicted on the Lombards.[30]

Those authors clearly viewed the outcome of the struggle as favourable to the Lombards. Kinnamos's work ends in 1176, but he had lost interest in Northern Italy after stating that many of the main cities of the region had gone over from Barbarossa to his emperor (which came to nothing in the end).[31] According to Ralph Niger, the Lombards, having driven the oppression off, obtained 'greater liberty' (*maiorem libertatem*).[32] Ralph Diceto inserted in his work a letter sent by the Milanese to the Bolognese announcing the triumph of Legnano, and, although he did not mention the final outcome of the conflict, his work implies that a settlement had been reached, because it mentions the wedding of the future Emperor Henry VI with Constance of Sicily, together with the resulting coronation ceremony, that took place at Milan (by then the leading city of the League) in 1186.[33] For William of Newburgh, the Lombards eventually recovered their ancient liberty (*in libertatem se pristinam receperunt*), and he also implied that a settlement was reached when he mentioned how Frederick made his son Henry king of the Lombards.[34] Robert of Torigni ended his account of the conflict with the crushing victory of the League at Legnano.[35] Romuald of Salerno died before the Peace of Constance, but he also described the Lombard triumph at Legnano, and his work is one of the best sources on the negotiations between Barbarossa and the League during the Peace of Venice. The chronicle of Laon closes its account of the conflict with Barbarossa's calamitous failure at the siege of Alessandria of 1174–5.[36]

Indeed, the sympathy of these non-imperial sources is largely on the side of the Lombards, and criticism of the uprising is hard to come by, which is perhaps surprising, given how many of those sources came from countries with strong central governments, such as England, Southern Italy, and Byzantium. Some sources do highlight the urban nature of the Lombard society and its unusual degree of *libertas*, and some of them also consider Barbarossa's point of view, but none of them particularly emphasise those distinctive features. The best example of such comments probably comes from Romuald of Salerno, who noted that, before Barbarossa, the Lombards enjoyed an extraordinary degree of liberty when compared to other nations (*inter alias nationes libertatis singularitate gaudebant*), but he also later stated that in his 1170s campaigns, Barbarossa took action against the 'injury' (*iniuria*) he had received from the Lombards.[37] Similar, but perhaps more judgemental, views can be found in the work of William of Newburgh, who described as *immoderata* (which probably means excessive and extravagant here) the *libertas* which the Lombards enjoyed before Barbarossa, when they had largely freed themselves from the emperor; indeed, for William the Lombard people (*gens*) were restless and warlike (*inquieta, bellicose*), as well as *superba* for its number of cities and strength, an adjective which in a bad sense means arrogant and in a good one outstanding;[38] in any case, the Lombards do seem to have redeemed themselves in William's eyes when he notes that the Milanese, fighting against Barbarossa, converted 'the desire of dominion [over other Lombards] into an obstinate defense of liberty', and how they fought back against Barbarossa's *insolentia*.[39]

The French troubadour Bertran de Born approved of the covenant formed by the Lombards in one of his poems, in which he noticed how the Gascons had similarly coalesced against their king (Henry II of England or his son Henry the Young King) (*Li Gascon si son acordat/entr' elhs et ves lui revelat/quon aissilh de Lombardia . . . D'aitan lur trac guaranteia*).[40] Other poems by Bertran also approvingly alluded to the conflict between the League and Barbarossa, one portraying the situation in Limousin as the 'little Lombardy" (*Sa pauca Lombardia*) of Count Aimar of Limoges.[41]

The most sympathetic with the emperor among these authors seems to have been Robert of Torigni, but he has no particularly harsh comment for the Lombards, especially when compared to the causticity of the German sources discussed below. After mentioning that the emperor had subjected Lombardy to his will – a statement which might harbour negative overtones of arbitrary rule – Robert underlined how that had brought peace and security for natives and strangers as well as a restoration of royal revenues; perhaps surprise, hinting to some measure of criticism against the Lombards, can be detected in his prose when he notices how 'on the other hand' (*iterum*), the cities of the Veronese March rebelled in 1164 (a prologue to the Lombard League).[42]

Those sources generally portray the conflict between the League and Barbarossa as a collective struggle by a regional community, even a people, that is, the *Lombardi* whose constituent parts were urban communities. Some sources acknowledge that some Lombard cities sided with the emperor, but they usually point out they were a small minority, which justifies their consistent use of the collective ethnic name *Lombardi* to describe Barbarossa's opponents. William of Newburgh called those Lombards a *gens* and Romuald of Salerno a *natio*.[43] Robert of Torigni provided a sketch of the political and religious configuration of the region, stating that it was divided into three archdioceses (Milan, Ravenna, and Genoa) and 25 cities.[44] He subsequently remarked that all the 25 cities of Lombardy defected from the emperor apart from Pavia and Vercelli, and that the *Lombardi* won the Battle of Legnano.[45]

While Anglo-Norman and Byzantine sources did not enter into the details of the bond between the Lombard cities, French, German, and Southern Italian ones describe it as a *coniuratio* capable of major public collective actions. That reflected the structure of the League, which partially filled the power vacuum left by the conflict with its emperor and his papal excommunication, the result being that, to some extent, the League even usurped imperial prerogatives, such as judging appeals against the sentences of local judges and recognising urban status to the new centre of Alessandria.[46] *Coniuratio* literally means collective oath, or sworn alliance, but it often had the negative connotation of plot or conspiracy (from which the modern Italian *congiura* comes).[47] Yet, overall, the way in which the sources examined above explained the conflict, and their general lack of other negative comments on the Lombards (which, as we shall see, are abundant in German sources), suggest ruling out that negative connotation.

Romuald, for example, wrote that almost all of the Lombards made a *coniuratio* against the emperor.[48] Bertran de Born simply refers to it as a collective agreement among the Lombards (*si son acordat/entr' elhs*).[49] The chronicle of Laon describes the *Lombardi* as taking deliberations (*deliberaverunt*) on matters such as offering the Lombard kingdom to other rulers, although it also notices how the Lombards were divided into an anti-imperial group led by Milan and a smaller number of imperial supporters, describing the former as a Milanese confederacy (*confederatio mediolanice*), or 'the cities that had formed a *coniuratio* together with Milan' (*urbes que mediolano coniuraverant*).[50] This focus on Milanese leadership might have been influenced by developments after the Battle of Legnano, and particularly during the first quarter of the thirteenth century, when the chronicle of Laon was produced, because the Milanese influence over the League took time to build up after the city's reconstruction.[51] On similar lines, according to the *Chronica Regia Coloniensis*, which is more fully discussed below, a vast *coniuratio* covering the whole of Lombardy was made against the emperor, and in 1175 it declared a public war (*bellum publicum*) against him, gathering an extraordinary mass of people from all over the region.[52] Likewise, an addition to the chronicle of Richard of Poitiers reports that Barbarossa's plan to submit the whole of Italy to his rule was foiled by the fact that all the Italian cities (read here Northern Italy), apart from Pavia, formed a *coniuratio* against him with the approbation of Pope Alexander III.[53]

The interest and sympathy of non-Italian sources for the League was certainly connected to the conflict between Pope Alexander III and Barbarossa. Apart from Bertran de Born, all the authors mentioned above were, after all, clerics, as was the norm in that period outside Italy. Lombardy traditionally played a crucial geopolitical role in the relations between empire and papacy, whose conflicts, in turn, inevitably touched the whole of Christendom and were interlaced with myriad other local and regional issues across it. The conflict between Barbarossa and Alexander had started as a papal schism, but well before the creation of the League most of Christendom had already accepted Alexander, to whom the League became the principal ally, and who had excommunicated Barbarossa.[54] Allegiance to the series of anti-popes who opposed Alexander was restricted to Barbarossa's areas of control, especially Germany and central Italy.[55] It is probably not a coincidence that, as we shall see, German sources are also the only ones across Christendom that consistently criticised the League. In addition to the conflict between empire and papacy, there was the fact that the resources that Barbarossa was gathering by controlling an area as rich as Lombardy threatened to upset continental and Mediterranean balances of power, and thus greatly worried his neighbours (Kinnamos mentioned that explicitly in the account mentioned above). On the other hand, the sources examined above undoubtedly treat the uprising on its own terms and do not confuse it with the papal schism or with the conflict between pope and emperor.

Representations of the League within the Empire (Northern Italy and Germany)

The representation of the League outside the Empire was far closer to that by Italian sources than to German ones, whose attitude clearly stands out from the rest of the surviving sources.

Among Italian historical works, one of the most exhaustive explanations for the Lombard uprising comes from the chronicles of Lodi, a city which originally supported the emperor, but was forced to join the League in its early stages and then consistently sided with it for the rest of the conflict. One of their authors, the lay judge Acerbo Morena (an imperial supporter who died in the epidemic which forced Barbarossa to retreat from Rome in 1167) blamed the massive burdens (*enormiter gravatos*) that imperial representatives (*missi imperatoris*) imposed over the cities which gave birth to the Veronese League in 1164, but also the *pecunia Venetorum* (that is, the bribes mentioned above, Venice being the conduit of the financial incentives from Byzantium and Norman Sicily).[56] His anonymous continuator, who wrote after Lodi joined the League, stated that the Lombards were not used to the intrusive imperial presence introduced by Barbarossa: accustomed to living freely and comfortably, they suddenly found themselves victims of a plethora of uncustomary taxes and expropriations, which led to open opposition against the emperor and to the creation of the League by 1167–8.[57] On the same line was Cardinal Boso (supporter and biographer for Pope Alexander III), who pointed to arbitrary extortions, expropriations, and also sexual violence by imperial officers, and described how, during the negotiations between League and emperor of 1175, some mediators likened Frederick's deeds to a lord who has taken by force what belongs to his serfs by right.[58]

The most stirring Italian account, however, comes from a Milanese source eloquently known as 'the story of the oppression of Lombardy' (*Narratio de Longobardiae obpressione*), which describes the misfortunes of the Milanese in the years between the destruction of their city in 1162 and their return to it in 1167. During this time, they had been dispersed in settlements in the surrounding countryside and found themselves under the rule of imperial representatives who clearly treated them as defeated recidivist rebels, making them provide free labour, extorting money, and forcing expropriations in various unpleasant ways.[59] The comments on expropriations closely recall Romuald's passage according to which Barbarossa transformed most of Lombardy into his domain. Documentary evidence from Piacenza, which was in a similar position to Milan, would confirm that the claims of Lombard writers were not just rhetoric.[60]

Those accounts largely mirror the appeals, found in the documentary evidence of the creation of the League and of its negotiations with the emperor, to the by and large unwritten good customs (*salvis rationibus et bonis usibus*), which in the eyes of the Lombards justified their control of what Barbarossa perceived as public, read imperial, assets.[61] A letter sent to Archbishop Becket of Canterbury by his representatives at the papal curia in May 1164, on the eve of the uprising of the Veronese League, exemplifies how that information travelled outside Italy: it noticed how relations between the emperor and the Lombard cities had deteriorated so much that they were threatening to abandon him if he did not change his tyrannical attitude and adopt a more civilised one, so that they could regain the liberty they had enjoyed under his predecessors (*nisi deponat tirannidem et civiles induat mores, ut liberi esse possint, sicut in diebus aliorum imperatorum*).[62]

In works produced in the Italian schools of law and rhetoric the status quo as it existed before Barbarossa was also justified by pointing to the privileges (known as *Ius Italicum*) that Italy had enjoyed within the ancient Roman empire of which Barbarossa claimed to be the heir. Those privileges mainly featured exemption from tributes, but they implied far more than that, because they also had strong communal elements (the *Corpus Iuris Civilis* cites them in relation to grants to non-Italian cities). Indeed, they originally derived from the identification of the Italian peninsula with the Roman state itself, which meant that Italians were not mere subjects of the emperor (a position which applied to the inhabitants of the provinces of the empire, who were subjects by right of conquest), but Roman citizens of the highest rate, which secured personal property and protected from arbitrary jurisdiction.[63]

No explicit references to the ancient *Ius Italicum* can be found in chronicles and in the surviving records of the negotiations between the League and Barbarossa. Those references were rather part of a learned debate linked to the participation of jurists from the law schools of Bologna to Barbarossa's Diet of Roncaglia of 1158, where they had helped shaping imperial claims by connecting them to the Roman law of Justinian *Corpus Iuris Civilis*. That compilation was also the main source of information regarding the *Ius Italicum*, which other jurists and rhetoricians then used to criticise the findings of their colleagues at Roncaglia.[64] Indeed, a wider debate existed at that time on the relationship between unwritten customs, written laws, and new legislation.[65] Ultimately, however, the intentions of the upholders of the *Ius Italicum* were the same as those based on good custom, but they preferred to back them with Roman law.

At the same time, it should not been taken for granted that those learned arguments were necessarily confined to academic ivory towers. As jurists helped Barbarossa at Roncaglia, Lombard schools of law and rhetoric (which attracted students from all over Western Europe) often had a symbiotic relationship with Italian communal governments, and that was especially the case at Bologna, which became a consistent member of the League a decade after Roncaglia.[66] In fact, references to the Roman heritage and to ideas of citizenship in relation to the Lombard city communes can be found in some contemporary sources that will be examined shortly, and most notably those of the German Otto of Freising and of the Italian Boncompagno da Signa, the latter in a work which he publicly read to the township of Ancona.

Regarding the bond among the insurgents, Italian sources sometimes feature the term *coniuratio*, but more often *concordia* (agreement or harmony) or *societas civitatum* (league of cities), which are interchangeable but not totally synonymous. The term *concordia* had intrinsically positive connotations, and *societas* was quite neutral, but again, like in non-imperial sources, *coniuratio* did not necessarily entail negative implications. The work of the continuator of Morena, for example, states that by 1168 the cities which had already formed a *coniuratio* (*iam coniurate fuerant*) evolved into a corporate association (*atque insimul unum corpus omnes effecto sunt*), which coincided with the creation of the governing college of the rectors of the League and the appearance of its official name.[67] In that case *coniuratio* was probably simply meant to refer to a pre-incorporation stage, when the League was only a sworn multilateral agreement.[68]

The contrast between Italian and non-imperial sources on one side and those from the empire north of the Alps (from as far north as Schleswig-Holstein, on the border with Denmark, to as far east as Bohemia) could not be starker, because the latter unmistakably and consistently portrayed the League as the villain. Indeed, with the partial exception of Burchard von Ursperg (who also used the term *insolentia* referring to Barbarossa's agents), they feature no remarks concerning uncustomary rule and oppression by Barbarossa. Vincent of Prague (d. 1170, a notary and canon from Prague who took part in Barbarossa's Italian expeditions), whose work ends just before the formation of the League, remarked that, after the fall of Milan in 1162, Barbarossa exercised his authority over the whole of Italy, which trembled in his presence, and he appointed his governors (*potestates*) over the Italian cities, the result being that 'what he wished in Lombardy he did'.[69] The latter echoes some of the statements considered above, but it was clearly meant as praise for Barbarossa's might, because Vincent consistently sided with him throughout his work. The *Chronica Regia Coloniensis* (written around 1200 by an unidentified canon from Cologne) also remarks that, after the destruction of Milan, the whole of Lombardy bowed to Barbarossa's will.[70] Gottfried of Viterbo (d. 1202, a member of the imperial court) praised imperial rule in that period for bringing peace and suitable royal revenues.[71] Only Burchard of Ursperg (provost of the Swabian Premonstratensian monastery of Ursperg, who was writing around 1230) stated that, when the League was created, the Lombards expelled the governors (here called *iuduces*) whom Barbarossa had appointed throughout Lombardy because of the *insolentias* with which those Germans had behaved. Incidentally, Burchard's work features one of the most informative and balanced accounts of the Peace of Constance, mentioning that Barbarossa reached an agreement with the Lombards regarding what they owed him, and that since then they had been refusing to do more than what that written settlement prescribed.[72]

German authors also referred to the League more consistently as a rebellion, and they often described it as a *conspiratio*, a term (from which the English 'conspiracy' comes) far less ambiguously negative than *coniuratio*, as confirmed by frequent derogatory comments on the Lombards. The *Chronica Regia Coloniensis* calls the League a *coniuratio*, mentions the *perfidia* of the Milanese while reporting its reconstruction without the emperor's permission, and describes the new city of Alessandria (a member of the League) as a collection of petty thieves, robbers, and serfs freshly escaped from their lords, to which the League lent its support.[73] For Gottfried of Viterbo, the Lombards (here called with the more classical resounding name of Ligurians) conspired to form a sworn rebellion (*conspirant ligures ... rebellio iurata*), the League was the revival of the previous rebellion by Milan, a city which he had called barbarous, arrogant, untamed, and fully rebellious (*seva, superba, fera, tota rebellis*), but the Lombards as a whole were a bad rabble (*plebs mala*), their deeds crimes (*crimina*), and their arrogance repressed all royal rights and replaced them with self-rule.[74] The verb *rebellant* was used by Rahewin and the *Annales Magdeburgenses* (from the last quarter of the twelfth century), which called the Lombards 'a perfidious people deserving reproach/chastisement' (*gentem perfidam digna animadversione*).[75] The *Chronica Slavorum* of Helmold of Bosau (d. *c*.1177, priest at Bosau in Schleswig-Holstein) states that, with the destruction of Milan, fear for Barbarossa temporarily put an end to Lombard rebellions, who had so ill-treated his predecessors, but then the Lombards unanimously conspired (*conspiraverunt*) against the emperor.[76] Despite his relatively balanced explanation of the Lombard uprising, Burchard of Ursbergh also described the League as a *conspiratio*.[77]

The representation of the League by those German sources reflected closely that by the imperial court, from whose propaganda the inhabitants of the ultramontane empire obtained at least some of their information about it. The appendix to Rahewin's work, for example, states that in 1167 Barbarossa sent letters throughout the empire denouncing the 'rebellion of the Italians' (*rebellionem Italorum*).[78] This is probably a reference to the extant letter in which Barbarossa highlighted how the Lombards had rebelled against him as well as against the *Teutonicorum Imperio*, with no good reason or fault by the emperor (*sine causa* and *sine aliqua praecedenti culpa*), but because of the *malitia* and *perfidia* of the Italians. That is exactly how the German sources examined above described those events.[79]

The socio-political features of the Lombard city communes

The sources considered above do not explicitly discuss the situation within the Lombard city communes, and for that we must turn primarily to the German Otto of Freising (d. 1158, bishop of Freising and a close relative of Barbarossa himself), who, interestingly, explained it by adopting the dichotomy *libertas* versus *insolentia* as well. Otto died just before the beginning of the papal schism, which means that he did not see the formation of the League, but he did witness the early Italian campaigns of Barbarossa against Milan, and it was in order to explain them that he left what is probably the most compelling cross-sectional and panoramic view of twelfth-century Communal Italy.[80]

While Otto outlined the regional domination by cities and their relations with the emperor, he also discussed their form of government and their internal social stratification. Regarding politics, Otto noticed how, following their ancient Roman heritage, the Lombards loved *libertas* (*Denique libertatem tantopere affectant*) and rejected the insolence of power (*ut potestatis insolentiam fugiendo*), so that, rather than by masters, they preferred to be ruled by officers called consuls (*consulum potius quam imperantium regantur arbitrio*), who were drawn from different social groups and, lest they exceeded their bounds by lust for power, held short-term office.[81] On one side, Otto criticised the relative social mobility of the Lombard city communes, as when he mentioned how they offered 'knighthoods and grades of distinction to young men of inferior status or workers of the vile mechanical arts, whom other peoples barred like the pest'.[82] On the other, he obviously admired the overall results of that Lombard system, which, he stated, meant that the Lombards surpassed all other cities (or body politics) of the world in riches and power (*Ex quo factum est, ut caeteris orbis civitatibus divitiis et potentia praemineant*).[83] That, however had a dark side, because, while the Lombards claimed to adhere to the law (Otto most probably referred to Roman law there), they forgot their ancient nobility, and in reality disdained the law by disregarding their rightful ultimate ruler, that is, the emperor, to whom they should have displayed a voluntary deference of obedience. The result was that the Lombards did not behave like citizens – Otto used the term *civis*, which in this case seems to refer to the concept of the Roman citizen rather than a mere town dweller – but like an enemy (*adversarius*) who needed to be subjugated by force of arms, which seems to reflect the lawyers' distinction between Italians and conquered provincials in the Roman empire mentioned above. That excused the emperor for such actions in the sight of God. Barbarossa's predecessors had allowed that situation to worsen with their neglect, but he planned to put remedy to it.[84]

Otto's account can be coupled with passages from John of Salisbury's *Policraticus*, which was one of the most influential political works from the central Middle Ages. Scholarship seems to have utterly overlooked those passages, but they engage with themes that are similar to those of Otto's work by presenting non-German points of view on them. Indeed, they present the Lombard cities as epitomes of popular sovereignty, and, as many of the other works here considered, feature the dichotomy *libertas* versus *insolentia* too. John travelled to Italy on several occasions, and his *Policraticus* includes a conversation he had with an anonymous person who hosted him at Piacenza. In it this host argued that as long as the inhabitants of the Italian cities cherished peace and justice, they rejoiced in liberty (*libertas*) and peace; indeed, the merits of the people make princely regimes superfluous or cause them to be administered with the greatest mildness (*merita populi omnem evacuant principatum aut eum faciunt esse mitissimum*); conversely people's sins bring hypocrites to reign, Roman arrogance, and the German fury being examples of how God punished the Italians when they strayed away from the above-mentioned merits.[85] The term used for Roman arrogance, *fastus*, was a synonym of *insolentia*, and, together with the *furor Teutonicus*, in all probability referred to the emperor. As with Otto of Freising, John of Salisbury wrote the *Policraticus* in the late 1150s too, before the beginning of the papal schism, and roughly a decade before his letters commenting on Lombard affairs mentioned above.[86] Therefore those passages from the *Policraticus* probably commented on Barbarossa's early campaigns against Milan, of which Piacenza was the closest ally in the region.[87]

Although the other sources examined above do not explicitly discuss the internal features of the Lombard cities' communal governments, their representation of the Lombards' acts as undertaken collectively by a regional community constituted by urban ones suggests that they took for granted at least some of the features that Otto and John depicted. On the other hand, the *Annales Magdeburgenses* represented the League as a rebellion by 'Italian princes' (*Italici principes*).[88] What those annals actually meant by *principes* is open to interpretation. In the light of the minor role that territorial lords played in the League, one is left wondering whether *principes* simply meant the leading powers in the region by comparing the city communes to collective forms of lordship. Yet it is also perhaps possible that it referred to the local elite that largely controlled the Italian city communes.

Scholarship has largely ignored these passages from John of Salisbury and the *Annales Magdeburgenses*, but the seeming contrast between the *populus* of the former and the *principes* of the latter echoes the existence of opposite scholarly traditions regarding the social and institutional makeup of the Italian city communes. One school of thought portrays twelfth-century city communes as primordial models of representative institutions, and the other as oligarchies dominating urban masses.[89] It is now generally accepted that the city communes of that period acted as public entities; after all, they described themselves in terms such as *res publica*, *commune*, or *civitas* (republic, commune, city). On the other, in the second half of the twentieth century scholarship focused particular attention on the local aristocracies and elites called *milites* (usually translated as knights or consular aristocracy, as opposed to the *populus*, or *pedites* whose members fought on foot), who controlled and ran the communal governments. In some cases that scholarship portrayed the rise of the city communes as the conquest of cities by the rural nobility and its integration with urban mercantile, administrative, and financial elites. In this approach, the city communes are effectively understood as collective lordships based on the concord between aristocratic families, rather than on the concord of the *cives* as a whole. This view resonates with suggestions to replace the use of the term state with lordship for the Middle Ages, especially for this period.[90]

More recently, however, this focus on the urban aristocracy has been attacked as unjustifiably slighting the public and more inclusive features of twelfth century Italian communal governments.[91] This has led to renewed attention upon issues such as offices, judicial and fiscal administrations, assembly politics, and the expansion of rhetorical and legal education as the forgers of a distinctive communal political culture. After all, the *milites* themselves were a relatively fluid, porous, and diverse group at that time, whose composition and features varied from town to town, and who did not completely monopolise the running of the communes. Consuls did exchange oaths with the assembly of all the *cives*, who gathered for that and other important purposes in the main square of the cities. The relatively high cohesion of Lombard urban communities of that time, which was quite remarkable in comparison to previous and later periods, is suggestive: indeed, overall, their communal governments had been created out of broad compromise among the various components of local communities.[92] It was a few decades after the end of the conflict with Barbarossa, for example, that the Italian cities started to be lacerated by clashes between the *milites*, or magnates, and the *populus*.[93] Overall, this evidence implies that communal institutions were not as frail and diminutive in the twelfth century as has often been assumed. This does not deny the preponderance of the local elites, but integrates their dominance within a more complex communal setting. Indeed, in many ways that re-evaluation of twelfth-century communal institutions does some justice to the account by Otto of Freising, and suggest that those by John of Salisbury and the *Annales Magdeburgenses* did not necessarily represent contrasting images, but reflected the complexity of the Italian cities and the awareness of it outside Italy.

The League's approach to politics

The modern historiography on the League presents similar dichotomies to that of the city communes, but in its case they are less a product of opposing schools, than a reflection of changes in scholarship over time related to contemporary political experiences. While, at the beginning of the eighteenth century, the League could be portrayed as a precursor of the French Revolution, it took stronger and stronger nationalistic overtones during the Risorgimento (the movement that unified the Italian peninsula and expelled the Austrian empire). Then the topic started to go out of fashion after the creation of the Kingdom of Italy in 1861, to which the League bore little geographic or qualitative correspondence, and it never recovered its previous popularity. Although the Fascist regime named military units after the Battle of Legnano, it did not pay much attention to the League itself. Post-war scholarship has regularly mentioned the League, but mostly in passing and primarily to debunk what remained of its Risorgimento myth, which still lingers in popular perceptions. The political party of the Lega Nord/Lega Lombarda, for example, has adopted a warped version of that Risorgimento myth in the last decades of the twentieth century, switching, as opponent, the German emperor with the Italian central government and with Southern Italian influences, while, most recently, it has focused its attention on criticising the European Union.[94]

To some extent the shadow of the Risorgimento still lingers in academia as well, and it shoulders the responsibility for dictating the evaluation of the League in terms of nationhood and state formation, in which it has always been found wanting, or simply in terms of preservation of the Lombard city communes (viewed as they are as an early stage for the city-states of the Italian Renaissance).[95] On the other hand, the tacit corollary of the above-mentioned focus on urban aristocracies was that the League was represented as little more than a fleeting alliance of petty local oligarchic interests. The recent re-evaluation of twelfth-century communal governments has rather focused on how the experience of the League helped to consolidate them collectively by rejecting Barbarossa's threat and by improving political and institutional integration across the region.[96]

Those views have overshadowed how the League attracted attention as a case of rejection of a despotic princely government, as well as how it also stood for, and, as will be shown in a moment, put a spotlight on a certain approach to the exercise of power that reflected the experience of the city communes, as opposed to the top down style that Barbarossa's critics attributed to him. To be sure, the depiction, by the sources examined above, of the League as a *coniuratio* that was capable of complex collective actions is confirmed by documentary evidence regarding its structure and activity, which were infused with principles of consultation, accountability, and public responsibility. The League was built on a chain of collective oaths that were routinely confirmed: it was founded by agreements between city communes, which were then cemented by the oaths of their whole male population between the ages of 15 and 60. Clauses of allegiance to the League were also inserted in the oaths that city consuls took upon entering office, in which they swore not to contradict the terms of the League, but to act for the common utility of all the men of the association. In turn, a college of rectors governed the League, who held short-time office, took an oath in which they also swore to act for the common utility, and also to share any goods they received during their mandate, since cases of corruption and duress officially disqualified their actions. The college of the rectors had its own seal and they met in assemblies where they took decisions by majority vote. Each of them came from one of the *civitates* of the League, each of which therefore had, at least in principle, equal representation. Finally the League did not only deal with the war against the emperor, but coordinated the collaboration and relations between its members more generally, including the resolution of disputes. Yet in their activity the rectors relied entirely on the goodwill of the members, though they could ban members from the association.[97]

Boncompagno da Signa's *Liber de Obsidione Ancone* (Book of the Siege of Ancona) is well known among scholars of political thought as one of the most convincing displays of Italian communal ideology, but it has been often neglected by wider scholarship, and it has been virtually disregarded as the most compelling proof that the opposition against Barbarossa in Communal Italy came to be perceived as a particularly powerful example of resistance against bad princely government. Boncompagno was a teacher of rhetoric whom the Bolognese lawyer and knight Ugolinus Gosia commissioned the *Liber de Obsidione Ancone* to be publicly read in Ancona for the celebrations of his appointment as the city's *podestà* (the executive officer, usually a foreigner, who gradually replaced the college of consuls from the end of the twelfth century) in 1201. Yet Boncompagno's work recounted the heroic resistance against the imperial army that besieged Ancona during the reign of Barbarossa, in 1173, which was broken by in the intervention of the Lombard League.

A *podestà* celebrating his appointment by commemorating an act of defiance by the city that he was about to rule against its ultimate ruler is quite remarkable in and of itself. Indeed, Boncompagno's piece reviews the significance of Barbarossa's Italian wars by stating that kings naturally tend to imitate rulers such as Nebuchadnezzar (the quintessential biblical tyrant), that without memory humans would regress to the state of irrational animals, and nothing would be undertaken according to law, but the will of anyone who happens to be in power would be the law and the weak would only be able to submit. 'Therefore if any citizens [*cives*] are besieged by kings or princes, let them take the Anconitans as an example.'[98] By sponsoring this work, Ugolinus clearly made a political statement, which wished to underline the distinction between his office as temporary rector of the city, and his intended approach to it, as opposed to those of a notorious emperor. At the same time, Boncompagno's *Liber* does not reject imperial authority per se, and it actually introduces Ugolinus Gosia by noticing the close and traditional links between his family and the imperial court.[99]

Regarding communal ideology, Boncompagno built his depiction of the siege of 1173 around a series of speeches and vignettes, which portray the city's resistance as a truly communal endeavour. The settings of the speeches are not ceremonial assemblies but genuine debates: the central speech of the work is delivered by an old man (who claims to have been a consul in the 1130s, around 40 years before the siege) in the course of a very divided assembly attended by the council of consuls and notables which governed the city, whom, however, Boncompagno described by using terms designating quality and expertise rather than mere social stratification (*viri discreti et sapientes ... quorum consilio civitas regebantur*).[100] The old man succeeded in convincing the assembly not to surrender to the imperial army, but the continuation of the siege worsened the hardships for the Anconitans, which brought further assemblies involving this time the entire Anconitan *populus*.[101] It might be argued that a siege is an emergency situation and that those behaviours might not have reflected more mundane meetings. Yet when Boncompagno describes the Anconitan invitation to the Bolognese Ugolinus in 1201, the latter asks an assembly of his fellow citizens composed by the podestà, the *milites*, as well as the *populous*, permission to accept that invitation, which they grant him collectively.[102]

Boncompagno's vignettes of the siege equally cut across Anconitan society, and they are gender inclusive too. The first vignette concerns a commoner widow called Stamira, who surpasses in daring all the defenders by setting fire to the war machines of the besiegers with an axe and a torch.[103] Another vignette features a cathedral canon, who swims to the vessels that besieged the city by sea and causes havoc by cutting their anchors.[104] Then a noblewoman carrying a baby offers her breast milk to a starving crossbowman who has no strength left to recharge his weapon but feels so ashamed at this that he springs to action.[105] The expeditionary force sent by the League is led by a man and a woman: the man is formally in charge and the woman represents her minor son, but she is of far higher social ranking: he is an influential knight (*miles*) from the city of Ferrara, but she is the countess of Bertinoro, who is called here 'a model for female lords' (*speculum dominarum*), and they both deliver speeches to their troops, which comprised members both of the *milites* and of the *populus*.[106]

The communal features of the League then came to the fore in episodes of contacts with the emperor that attracted widespread attention outside the empire, including the decisive Battle of Legnano of 1176. Many sources here considered mention that battle, from the English Ralph of Diceto, Robert of Torigni, and Roger Howeden, to the Southern Italian Romuald of Salerno, for example. Most simply ascribe the victory to the *Lombardi*, but Romuald provided an overview of the dynamics of the battle. He recounted that it was decided by the foot-soldiers (who were usually commoners): the imperial cavalry (in this occasion the imperial army had no infantry) routed its Lombard counterpart (which was recruited from the local elite), but the Lombard's 'multitude of footsoldiers' (*pedestris multitudo*) stood its ground in defence of the Milanese *carroccio* (a totemic emblem of the city), and it repelled imperial assaults, which gave time for the Lombard cavalry to rally.[107]

Another prime and momentous episode of contact between the emperor and the League, which bore the imprint of Lombard political culture and touched the whole of Christendom, was the Peace of Venice of 1177, and once again the most valuable testimony comes from Romuald of Salerno, who eyewitnessed the core of that peace conference. Indeed, he was the chief negotiator of the king of Sicily, who, together with the League, on that occasion reached a truce with Barbarossa. The Peace of Venice was a truly international event, which lay and ecclesiastical authorities from across Western Christendom attended. As we have seen, for example, the account of an anonymous English eyewitness also survives, but it is far less detailed than that by Romuald. The *Historia Ducum Veneticorum* listed more than 8,000 participants, with some leading lay and ecclesiastical authorities being escorted by hundreds of people; they included a delegation jointly sent by the kings of England and France led by the Cistercian Abbot Hugh of Bonnevaux, who during the negotiations acted as mediator between the warring parties, and thus must have been acquainted with a suggestive incident to which I will now turn.[108]

Romuald recounted how, during the peace negotiations, at which the pope presided, the leading representative of the emperor, Archbishop Christian of Mainz, gave three options to the delegation of the Lombards (whose members, incidentally, Romuald described as extraordinarily knowledgeable in public speaking to the people: *ad concionandum populo mirabiliter eruditi*).[109] One of the options simply asked to do justice to imperial rights. The second was to enforce the verdict (*sententia*) that the Bolognese judges had issued against the Lombard cities at the Diet of Roncaglia of 1158, and the third was to take as a model the situation as it was under the reign of Emperor Henry IV (d. 1106).[110] To that the chief negotiator of the League, the Milanese judge and ex-consul Gerardo Cagapesto (who came from a well-to-do family, but whose name, which literally means 'crush-a-shit', betrays quite obvious non-aristocratic origins),[111] replied that they were ready to render the emperor his due as their lord, but, since Cagapesto represented a multitude of people and cities, he needed time to consult them.[112] Even so Cagapesto openly refused to recognise the proceedings of the Diet of Roncaglia as a *sententia*, stating that it was rather an imperial order (*imperatoriam iussionem*), and, in any case, many members of the League had not attended that diet, though not because they were contumacious, and a *sententia* issued *in absentia* had no value; finally Cagapesto reasoned that there was no living memory of the reign of Henry IV, which therefore could not be reconstructed in a suitably detailed manner.[113]

It was then Cagapesto's time to make counterproposals. Rather than the reign of Henry IV, he suggested considering more recent ones, from that of Henry V to that of Conrad III (which entirely mirrored the position of the League as testified by the documentary evidence since its inception); otherwise the assembly could rely upon the written settlements that the League and the emperor had reached a couple of years earlier through the mediation of Cremona, which had eventually come to nothing, leading to the Battle of Legnano; in the end it was this proposal that won the day, but that led to several days of discussions because the parties had different interpretations of that settlement, and although the Cremonesi (who had recently left the League for the emperor) were summoned to testify, no satisfactory conclusion could be reached. Pope Alexander III eventually suggested a six-year truce between the League of Barbarossa, and the parties kept it until the Peace of Constance of 1183.[114]

Of particular interest in Romuald's account of the Peace of Venice are its references to the Diet of Roncaglia of 1158. As mentioned above, scholarship commonly regards its expansive definition of royal/imperial prerogatives as a milestone in the conceptualisation of public law in Western Europe. On the other hand, historians have generally ignored the reconstruction of the events offered by Romuald's account, which, however, is fundamental in order to evaluate the Lombards' perception of that momentous event, because imperial supporters produced all the other surviving accounts of that diet.[115] Not to mention that, in Romuald's account, the Lombard perception of Roncaglia was delivered at such a Western Christendom-wide event as the Peace of Venice. Indeed, Romuald's account lends support to Bisson's recent remark that, in line with the common practices of the time, the Diet of Roncaglia was a convocation aimed at eliciting submission rather than a consultative assembly.[116] On the other hand, those features of the Diet of Roncaglia are precisely the reason that Cagapesto openly gave to reject its proceedings utterly, suggesting that, in order to be acceptable, that diet should have been a consultative assembly instead, or that it should have followed judicial procedures, which, in his view, Barbarossa had ignored.

Conclusion

Scholarship has generally perceived the conflict between the League and Barbarossa in terms of nationhood, state formation, rejection by the Lombard cities of an external threat, or, indeed, of defence of petty local interests. Yet the sources here examined show that, in the decades straddling the turn of the twelfth century, that conflict acquired widespread fame throughout Christendom as a prime case of a successful uprising against what was perceived as a tyrannical ruler who wished to introduce a pervasive, intrusive, and exploitative administration. Furthermore, with the exception of German sources, that uprising was generally portrayed in a favourable light, which is quite notable because many authors considered here were close to royal courts, which, in theory, should have shown sympathy for a fellow monarch. Given the lack of similar studies regarding other momentous central medieval revolts, it is impossible to evaluate accurately how exceptional was the fame of the League. It is very likely, however, that it was highly remarkable, possibly constituting the most widely known case of its kind at that time. Only further comparative research will be able to test that.

The widespread knowledge and approval for the actions of the League were probably related to its close connections with the parallel conflict between empire and papacy, which inevitably touched the whole of Christendom, and in which the papacy enjoyed the support of most rulers. Moreover, the geographical distance between the authors who covered the League outside the empire certainly made it less troublesome to approach it for them. The consistent criticism for the League found in German sources is a good opposite case in point, because it mirrored Barbarossa's strong support there, which he harnessed for his Italian campaigns.

The conflict between pope and emperor was not the only factor, though. The interest for the Lombard cities found in works such as those by Otto of Freising and John of Salisbury predated it. The other sources examined here did consider the conflict between League and emperor on its own terms, showing awareness of the fact that it was not fully coterminous with that between empire and papacy. In other words the role of the League in the conflict between Barbarossa and Alexander III served to multiply the audience for Barbarossa's conflict with the League rather than supply it.

Regarding the fame of the League, Bertran de Born's likening of it to occurrences which were directed not only against royal, but also against comital power, and which took place in regions of France that were not particularly similar to Lombardy, suggests that the Lombard challenge against Barbarossa had become somewhat archetypal. It is significant that even some pro-imperial sources from within the empire, such as Acerbo Morena in Italy and Burchard von Ursberg in Germany, recognised that Barbarossa's agents had behaved in an unacceptable way. That points to the existence of a contemporary sensitivity, shared across Christendom, regarding the boundaries of proper rulership and legitimate responses to their infringement. Indeed, the sources here examined show a notable terminological consistency in the way they portray the conflict and its causes, with key words being on one side *libertas* and on the other *insolentia*. The former represented traditional rights of self-rule, taxation, and property holding, but also the very freedom from the kind of arbitrary and top down rule embodying *insolentia*.

In effect, anyone across the Christian world of the central Middle Ages could relate to at least some of the themes touched upon by the League. Exploitative lordship, exacerbated by the growth of administrative institutions that was typical of that age, as well as cases of resistance to it taking the shape of *coniurationes*, abounded.[117] Just to give a couple of examples: under Emperor Henry IV Germany itself had experienced the Saxon Revolt against the emperor and his representatives, which had many parallels with the rebellion of the League. The rhetoric and motivations of the Saxons, whose protagonists were local nobles and free peasants, had equally featured complains of infringement of local customs and common rights, challenges to proprietary titles, cries of liberty, tyranny, and accusations of imposing servility.[118] On a very different scale, the Lombard case, and the way it was resolved, bore many affinities with the dispute that raged in the 1110s in the diocese of Autun, in Central France, regarding the new 'evil customs' that the duke of Burgundy had imposed over certain villages and persons, while the latter were supported by the bishop: eventually the parties drew up written statements regarding their positions, but the final settlement was reached by an assembly that featured representatives of each party, which judged against the duke on the basis of the available memory of his father's practices and then wrote that settlement down.[119] In turn, the constitutional role of the Peace of Constance recalls in many ways even the later case of the English Magna Carta.[120]

The sources here examined show awareness of the distinctive urban features of the Lombard setting, of the rather unusual autonomy that its cities had achieved, and, to some extent, of regional power dynamics within Lombardy, but they do not use them in order to set apart the League from the rest of Western Europe and discard it. On the contrary, they rather portray that of the League in generic terms as a conflict between subjects, indeed, a people, against their ultimate ruler. Once again, the poems of Bertran de Born epitomise the non-specific character of the perception of the League particularly well, by likening it to occurrences in French regions that were not particularly similar to Lombardy.

In actual fact, the Lombard communal setting probably greatly helped in evoking such a representation of the League as a collective endeavour. The German Otto of Freising used the very *libertas*–*insolentia* dichotomy to discuss the particular Lombard communal approach to politics, underlining its relatively inclusive attitude, social mobility, and implying that, with that system, the Lombard city communes had achieved local success in avoiding *insolentia*. The English John of Salisbury represented the Lombard cities as prime examples of how the merits of the people (*merita populi*) could stir princely regimes towards the greatest mildness or even make them superfluous. Those passages struck a chord with the latest scholarly debates among historians of the Italian city communes, who have sought to contextualise better the role of local elites in Lombard urban communal governance. After all, twelfth-century Lombard city communes did display a remarkable degree of social cohesion when compared to previous periods, but especially with later ones.

The conflict between Barbarossa and the Lombard League tested those features of Lombard politics dramatically, but the League itself embodied them, and its conflict with the emperor, together with its close connection to that between empire and papacy, put a spotlight on them that attracted the attention of the whole of Christendom. In that respect, the League provided what was probably the best known practical case in point addressing some of the most distinctive political developments of the central Middle Ages directly: in the eyes of contemporary sources from outside the empire the League successfully stood against what was perceived as a despotic and exploitative growth of administrative institutions and, as Romuald's portrayal of negotiations testifies, its arguments were based on principles of accountability, consultation, and public responsibility.

Notes

1 For most recent cases: T. N. Bisson, *The Crisis of the Twelfth Century: Power, Lordship and the Origins of European Government*, Princeton, NJ: Princeton University Press, 2009; R. I. Moore, *The First European Revolution*, Oxford: Blackwell, 2000. That trend has recently been also noted in M. C. Miller, 'Italy in the long twelfth century: ecclesiastical reform and the legitimation of a new political order, 1059–1183', in T. F. X. Noble and J. Van Engen (eds), *European Transformations: The Long Twelfth Century*, Notre Dame: University of Notre Dame Press, 2012, pp. 117–31; Communal Italy is more organically integrated in S. Reynolds, *Kingdoms and Communities in Western Europe, 900–1300*, 2nd edn, Oxford: Clarendon Press, 1997, which, however, does not particularly focus on Barbarossa and the League.
2 There is an immense bibliography on the influence of Communal Italy on history of political thought, but a very influential example is Q. Skinner, *The Foundation of Modern Political Thought. Volume 1: The Renaissance*, Cambridge: Cambridge University Press, 1978.
3 For a comparison with other urban environments in Western Christendom: D. Nicolas, *The Growth of the Medieval City: From Late Antiquity to the Early Fourteenth Century*, London: Longman, 1997.
4 D. Waley, *The Italian City Republics*, 3rd edn, London: Longman, 1988, which is probably the leading survey on the topic in English, examines the role of the empire in a chapter entitled 'External relations'.
5 For an overview of the political geography of the region: G. Raccagni, *The Lombard League 1167–1225*, Oxford: Oxford University Press, 2010.
6 A. Haverkamp. *Herrschaftsformen der Frühstaufer in Reichsitalien*, 2 vols, Stuttgart: Hiesermann, 1970–1.
7 On Roncaglia: K. Pennington, *The Prince and the Law, 1200–1600: Sovereignty and Rights in the Western Legal Tradition*, Berkeley: University of California Press, 1993, pp. 12–21; G. Dilcher and D. Quaglioni (eds), *Gli inizi del diritto pubblico: l'età di Federico Barbarossa: legislazione e scienza del diritto*, Bologna and Berlin: Il mulino and Duncker & Humblot, 2006.
8 Raccagni, *The Lombard League*, pp. 25–9.
9 Ibid.
10 G. Raccagni, 'Il diritto pubblico, la Pace di Costanza e i *libri iurium* dei comuni', in Dilcher and Quaglioni (eds), *Gli inizi del diritto pubblico*, pp. 309–39.
11 For the text of the *Friderici I Diplomata. 1181–1190*, in MGH, DD, F I. 4, ed. H. Appelt, Hanover: Hahn, 1990, no. 848.
12 Raccagni, *The Lombard League*, pp. 147–59.

13 G. Raccagni, 'The teaching of rhetoric and the Magna Carta of the Lombard cities: the Peace of Constance, the Empire and the Papacy in the works of Guido Faba and his leading contemporary colleagues', *JMH*, 39, 2013, pp. 61–79.
14 Ibid.
15 *The Letters of John of Salisbury*, 2 vols, ed. W. J. Millor and C. N. L. Brooke, Oxford: Clarendon Press, 1979, vol. 2, no. 242: *Sed quid nota recenseo? Hoc ubique locorum fama quasi praeconia voce concelebrat, nec aliquibus dubium puto, nisi forte lateat illos qui soli tempestate hac exulant domi suae.*
16 J. F. A. Mason, 'Diceto, Ralph de (*d.* 1199/1200)', *Oxford Dictionary of National Biography*, Oxford: Oxford University Press, www.oxforddnb.com/view/article/7591.
17 Biographical and bibliographical information on these works and authors can be found in G. Dunphy (ed.), *Encyclopedia of the Medieval Chronicle*, Leiden: Brill, 2010. I could not find references to the League in Spain, but its Latin historical sources for that period are far fewer, thin, and less interested in non-native affairs than those from north of the Pyrenees: R. M. A. de la Peña, 'Latin chronicles and histories', in F. A. Domínguez and G. Greenia (eds), *Dictionary of Literary Biography*, vol. 337, *Castilian Writers: 1200–1400*, Detroit: Thomson Gale, 2008, pp. 325–32.
18 S. K. Cohn, Jr., *Lust for Liberty: The Politics of Social Revolt in Medieval Europe, 1200–1425. Italy, France and Flanders*, Cambridge, MA, and London: Harvard University Press, 2006, pp. 228–44. Regarding the twelfth century: R. L. Benson, '*Libertas* in Italy (1152–1226)', in G. Makdisi, D. Sourdel, and J. Sourdel-Thomine (eds), *La notion de liberté au Moyen Âge: Islam, Byzance, Occident*, Paris: Belles Lettres, 1985, pp. 191–213.
19 A. Harding, 'Political liberty in the Middle Ages', *Speculum*, 55, 1980, pp. 423–42.
20 Ioannes Kinnamos, *Epitome Rerum ab Joanne et Alexio Comnenis Gestarum*, ed. A. Meineke, Bonn: Impensis ed. Weberi, 1836, pp. 230–1.
21 G. Raccagni, 'English views on Lombard city communes and their conflicts with Emperor Frederick I Barbarossa', *Quaderni storici*, 145, 2014, pp. 183–218.
22 *Radulfi Nigri Chronica universali*, ed. R. Pauli and F. Liebermann, MGH, SS, 27, Hanover: Hahn, 1885, p. 335: *Veruntamen insolentiam Theotonicorum non diu sustinuerunt Lumbardi; unde et apud eundem imperatorem, explosis opressionibus, maiorem libertatem evicerunt.*
23 William of Newburgh, *Historia rerum anglicarum*, in *Chronicles of the Reigns of Stephen, Henry II, and Richard I*, ed. R. Howlett, 4 vols, London: Longman 1884, vol. 1, pp. 115, 144: *Cum enim in Longobardos insolentius ageret, illi jugum Alemannicum non ferentes, in libertatem se pristinam receperunt.*
24 *The Historical Works of Ralph of Diceto*, ed. W. Stubbs, 2 vols, London: Longman 1876, vol. 1, pp. 427, 408–9.
25 Ibid., vol. 2, p. 39.
26 R. M. Thomson, 'An English eyewitness of the Peace of Venice, 1177', *Speculum*, 50, 1975, pp. 29–30.
27 Romualdo Guarna, *Chronicon*, ed. C. Bonetti, Cava de' Tirreni: Avagliano, 2001, pp. 184–5:

> *Qua victoria positus, imperator Lombardiam cepit pro sua voluntate disponere, ministros et baiulos in castellis et civitatibus ordinare, regalia et tributa exquirere et magnam partem Lombardie in demanio suo convertere. Sicque factum est, quod Lombardi, qui inter alias nationes libertatis singularitate gaudebant, pro Mediolani invidia cum Mediolano pariter corruerunt et se Teutonicorum servituti misere subdiderunt.*

28 Ibid., pp. 230–3.
29 *Ex chronico universali anonymi Laudunensis*, in MGH, SS, 26, Hanover: Hahn, 1882, pp. 444–6:

> *Lumbardi per insolentias imperatoris Frederici tedio et angore fatigati, Manueli Gregorum imperatori submittere eorum regnum deliberaverunt ... Currente adhuc anno Domini 1169 ... Henricus rex Anglorum, illectus promissione regni Lumbardorum, inter filios fecit regni sui et aliarum provinciarum suarum distribucionem.*

30 Ibid., p. 451: *Federicus, pro malis que Lumbardis intulerat, ut aiunt, compungtus, signum cruces ad subventionem Terre Sancte suscepit.*
31 Kinnamos, *Epitome*, pp. 230–1.
32 *Radulfi Nigri Chronica*, p. 335.
33 *The Historical Works of Ralph of Diceto*, 2: 39.
34 William of Newburgh, *Historia rerum anglicarum*, pp. 115, 144, 286.
35 *The Chronicle of Robert of Torigni*, in *Chronicles of the Reigns of Stephen, Henry II, and Richard I*, ed. Howlett, vol. 4, p. 270.
36 *Ex chronico universali anonymi Laudunensis*, p. 449.

37 Romualdo, *Chronicon*, pp. 184–5, 208–9.
38 William of Newburgh, *Historia rerum anglicarum*, p. 115.
39 Ibid., pp. 115, 144.
40 *The Poems of the Troubadour Bertran de Born*, ed. and trans. W. D. Paden, T. Sankowitch, and P. H. Stäblein, Berkeley: University of California Press, 1986, p. 209.
41 Ibid., pp. 117, 229.
42 *The Chronicle of Robert of Torigni*, p. 222: *Fredericus imperator cum ad libitum subdisset sibi Langobardiam ... et fiscum regium ad L. milia marcarum summam in eodem regno reparasset, et pacem ibidem tam indigenis quam peregrinis reformasset: iterum Verona et quedam alie civitates adversus eum rebellant.*
43 William of Newburgh, *Historia rerum anglicarum*, p. 115; Romualdo, *Chronicon*, pp. 184–5.
44 *The Chronicle of Robert of Torigni*, p. 222.
45 Ibid., p. 231.
46 Raccagni, *The Lombard League*, pp. 81–122.
47 Ibid., pp. 123–36.
48 Romualdo, *Chronicon*, pp. 208, 212.
49 *The Poems of the Troubadour Bertran de Born*, p. 209.
50 *Ex chronico universali anonymi Laudunensis*, pp. 444–6.
51 Raccagni, *Lombard League*, pp. 171–98.
52 *Chronica Regia Coloniensis*, p. 126: *Igitur ante pascalem sollempnitatem coniuratio grandis per omnem Longobardiam contra imperatorem et suos facta est. Coadunatis itaque viribus Mediolanenses, Veronenses, Novarienses, Brixienses aliarumque Italiae urbium populi incredibilem conduxere exercitum, indicto bello publico imperatori in campis Alexandriae.*
53 *Ex Richardi pictaviensis chronica*, in MGH, SS, 26, p. 83.
54 J. Laudage, *Alexander III und Friedrich Barbarossa*, Cologne: Böhlau, 1997.
55 J. Johrendt, 'The "empire and the schism"', in P. D. Clarke and A. J. Duggan (eds), *Pope Alexander III (1159–1181): The Arts of Survival*, Farnham: Ashgate, 2012, pp. 99–126.
56 *Ottonis Morenae eiusdenque continuatorum Libellus de rebus a Frederico imperatore gestis*, in *Italische Quellen über die Taten Kaiser Friedrichs I.*, ed. and trans. F. J. Schmale, Darmstadt: Wissenschaftliche Buchgesellschaft, 1986, p. 194.
57 Ibid., pp. 198–200.
58 *Liber Pontificalis*, ed. L. Duchesne, 2 vols, Paris: E. Thorin, 1886–92, 2: 411, 429:

> Que maior insania vel quod excellentius malum excogitari potest aut operari, quam ut dominus servum sive servi dominum iure suo privare omnino conentur et per violentiam possidere? Sit ergo unaqueque pars suo iure contenta, et tam gravibus malis iam cessantibus pax optata inter vos cooperante Domino reformetur.

59 *Civis Mediolanensis anonymi Narratio de Longobardiae obpressione*, in *Italische Quellen uber die Taten Kaiser Friedrichs I*, pp. 268–88.
60 F. Güterbock, 'Alla vigilia della Lega Lombarda: il dispotismo dei vicari imperiali a Piacenza', *Archivio storico italiano*, 95, 1937, pp. 199–201.
61 C. Vignati, *Storia diplomatica della Lega Lombarda*, Milan: Agnelli, 1866, pp. 105–7.
62 *The Correspondence of Thomas Becket*, ed. A. Duggan, 2 vols, Oxford: Oxford University Press, 2000, vol. 1, no. 29.
63 G. Raccagni, 'Reintroducing the emperor and repositioning the city republics in the "republican" thought of the rhetorician Boncompagno da Signa', *Historical Research*, 86, 2013, pp. 579–600.
64 Ibid.
65 Ibid.
66 R. Greci, 'Bologna nel duecento', in Ovidio Capitani (ed.), *Storia di Bologna*, II: *Bologna nel medioevo*, Bologna: Clueb, 2007, p. 533.
67 *Ottonis Morenae eiusdenque continuatorum Libellus*, p. 234.
68 On the conceptualisation of the League: Raccagni, *The Lombard League*, pp. 123–46.
69 *Vincentii Pragensis Annales*, ed. W. Wattenbach, in MGH, SS, 17, Hanover: Hahn, 1861, p. 681: *in tota italia imperialem exercebat potestatem, tota enim in conspectu eius tremebat ... et in urbibus Italie suis positis potestatibus*; ibid., p. 683: *et sic in Lonbardia quod volebat faciebat*. On Vincent's background: L. Wolverton, 'Vincent of Prague', in G. Dunphy (ed.), *Encyclopedia of the Medieval Chronicle*, http://referenceworks.brillonline.com/entries/encyclopedia-of-the-medieval-chronicle/vincent-of-prague-EMCSIM_02496.
70 *Chronica Regia Coloniensis*, p. 112: *et sic tota Lonbardia ac Tuscia et Romania ad nutum imperatoris fuit inclinata*, and p. 120.

71 *Gotifredi Viterbiensis Gesta Friderici I. et Heinrici VI. imperatorum metrice scripta*, ed. G. H. Pertz, in MGH, SS rer. Germ., 30, Hanover: Hahn, 1870, pp. 1, 4, 20, 29, 32. For Godfrey's background: K. Hering, 'Godfrey of Viterbo: historical writing and imperial legitimacy at the early Hohenstaufen court', in T. Foester (ed.), *Godfrey of Viterbo and His Readers: Imperial Tradition and Universal History in Late Medieval Europe*, Farnham: Ashgate, 2015, pp. 67–88.

72 *Burchardi praepositi urspergensis chonicon*, ed. O. Holder-Hegger and B. von Simon, in MGH, SS rer. Germ., 16, Hanover: Hahn, 1916, p. 52: *Quod factum est propter multiplices insolentias, quas Teutonici in partibus illis exercebant*; ibid., p. 57:

> Eo tempore iam bellis nimis fatigatus imperator Lombardis omnibus condixit curiam apud Constantiam, ubi principes et potestates eorum se representaverunt, et pacta quedam de faciendo servito imperatori de singulis civitatibus Lombardie ibidem statuta sunt, que adhuc dicunt se tenere in scriptis nec ad serviendum ultra hec compelli volunt.

73 *Chronica Regia Coloniensis*, p. 112: *et sic tota Lonbardia ac Tuscia et Romania ad nutum imperatoris fuit inclinata*, and pp. 120–6.

74 *Gotifredi Viterbiensis Gesta Friderici I. et Heinrici VI. imperatorum metrice scripta*, ed. G. H. Pertz, in MGH, SS rer. Germ., 30, Hanover: Hahn, 1870, pp. 1, 4, 20, 29, 32.

75 *Annales Magdeburgenses*, ed. G. H. Pertz, in MGH, SS, 16, Hanover: Hahn, 1859, p. 193.

76 *Helmoldi presbyteri chronica Slavorum*, ed. J. M. Lappenberg, in MGH, SS, 21, Hanover: Hahn, 1869, p. 95.

77 *Burchardi praepositi urspergensis chonicon*, ed. O. Holder-Hegger and B. von Simon, in MGH, SS rer. Germ., 16, p. 52: *Quod factum est propter multiplices insolentias, quas Teutonici in partibus illis exercebant*; ibid., p. 57:

> Eo tempore iam bellis nimis fatigatus imperator Lombardis omnibus condixit curiam apud Constantiam, ubi principes et potestates eorum se representaverunt, et pacta quedam de faciendo servito imperatori de singulis civitatibus Lombardie ibidem statuta sunt, que adhuc dicunt se tenere in scriptis nec ad serviendum ultra hec compelli volunt.

78 *Gesta Friderici I. imperatoris auctoribus Ottone et Ragewino praeposito Frisingensibus*, ed. G. H. Pertz, in MGH, SS, 20, Hanover: Hahn, p. 492.

79 MGH, Const., 1, ed. L. Weiland, Hanover: Hahn, 1893, no. 230.

80 M. Zabbia, 'Tra modelli letterari e autopsia: la città comunale nell'opera di Ottone di Frisinga e nella cultura storiografica del XII secolo', *Bullettino dell'istituto storico italiano*, 106, 2004, pp. 105–38.

81 *Gesta Friderici I.*, pp. 396–7.

82 Ibid.: *inferioris conditionis iuvenes vel quoslibet contemptibilium etiam mechanicarum atrium opifices, quos caeterae gentes ab honestioribus et liberioribus studiis tanquam pestem propellant, ut militiae cingulum vel dignitatum gradus assumere non dedignantur*.

83 Ibid.

84 Ibid., p. 349.

85 *Ioannis Saresberiensis Policraticus*, ed. K. S. B. Keats-Rohan, Turnhout: Brepols, 1993, p. 271:

> Adiciebat etiam quod merita populi omnem euacuant principatum aut eum faciunt esse mitissimum, cum e contrario certum sit quod propter peccata populi permittit Deus regnare hypocritam, et impossibile esse ut diu regno gaudeat qui in populi humiliatione et proprio fastigio superbe nimis exultat.

86 D. Luscombe, 'Salisbury, John of (late 1110s–1180)', in *Oxford Dictionary of National Biography*, Oxford: Oxford University Press, 2004, online edn, www.oxforddnb.com/view/article/14849.

87 Raccagni, *The Lombard League*, pp. 25–8.

88 *Annales Magdeburgenses*, p. 193.

89 For a recent discussion of these schools of thought: M. Vallerani, 'Comune e comuni: una dialettica non risolta', in M. C. De Matteis and B. Pio (eds), *Sperimentazioni di governo nell'Italia centro-settentrionale nel processo storico dal primo comune alla signoria*, Bologna: Bononia University Press, 2011, pp. 9–34; C. Wickham, *Sleepwalking into a New World: The Emergence of Italian City Communes in the Twelfth Century*, Princeton, NJ: Princeton University Press, 2015, pp. 1–20.

90 R. Davis, 'The medieval state: the tyranny of a concept?', *Journal of Historical Sociology*, 16, 2003, pp. 280–300; for a response to this article: S. Reynolds, 'There were states in medieval Europe: a response to Rees Davies', *Journal of Historical Sociology*, 16, 2003, pp. 550–5.

91 P. Grillo, 'La frattura inesistente', *Archivio storico italiano*, 167, 2009, pp. 673–700, who noted the relative lack of attention that the twelfth century has attracted when compared to the thirteenth.

The same applies to rhetorical education, which was much needed in assembly politics: S. Hartman, *Ars dictaminis. Briefsteller und verbale Kommunikation in den 11. bis 13. Jahrunderts*, Ostfildern: Jan Thorbecke, 2013.
92 Wickham, *Sleepwalking into a New World*, p. 9.
93 For a recent overview of the subsequent rise of conflicts between magnates and *popolo*: A. Poloni, *Potere al popolo: Conflitti sociali e lotte politiche nell'Italia comunale del duecento*, Milan, Mondadori, 2010.
94 E. Coleman, 'The Lombard League: history and myth', in J. Devlin and H. B. Clarke (eds), *European Encounters: Essays in Memory of Albert Lovett*, Dublin: University College Dublin Press, 2003, pp. 22–45.
95 For a good recent example, which briefly examines the League under the heading 'the missed federalist development': M. Ascheri, *Le città stato*, Bologna: Il mulino, 2006, pp. 72–7.
96 R. I. Bordone, 'I comuni italiani nella prima Lega Lombarda: confronto di modelli istituzionali in un'esperienza politico-diplomatica', in H. Maurer (ed.), *Kommunale Bündnisse Oberitaliens und Oberdeutschlands im Vergleich*, Sigmaringen: J. Thorbecke, 1987, pp. 45–62; M. Vallerai, *I rapporti intercittadini nella regione lombarda tra XII e XIII secolo*, in G. Rossetti (ed.), *Legislazione e prassi istituzionale nell'Europa medievale*, Naples: Liguori, 2001, pp. 221–90.
97 Raccagni, *The Lombard League*, pp. 55–80.
98 Boncopagno da Signa, *Liber de obsidione Ancone*, ed. G. Zimolo, Bologna: Zanichelli, 1936, section 8, http://scrineum.unipv.it/wight/index.htm. On Boncompagno's ideology: Raccagni, 'Reintroducing the emperor', pp. 582–6.
99 Boncopagno da Signa, *Liber de obsidione Ancone*, section 28.
100 Ibid., section 8.
101 Ibid., section 14.
102 Ibid., sections 28–30.
103 Ibid., section 4.
104 Ibid., section 5.
105 Ibid., section 13.
106 Ibid., sections 19–24.
107 Romualdo, *Chronicon*, pp. 216–17; for a recent analysis of the Battle, including its social features: P. Grillo, *Legnano 1176, una battaglia per la libertà*, Rome-Bari: Laterza, 2010, pp. 116–52.
108 For a list of participants: *Historia Ducum Veneticorum*, ed. H. Simonsfeld, in MGH, SS, 14, Hanover: Hahn, 1863, pp. 84–9.
109 Romualdo, *Chronicon*, p. 230.
110 Ibid., p. 236.
111 F. Menant, 'Une forme de distinction inattendue', in D. Boisseuil, P. Chastang, L. Feller, and J. Morsel (eds), *Écritures de l'espace social*, Paris: Publications de la Sorbonne, 2010, pp. 437–56.
112 Romualdo, *Chronicon*, pp. 236–8.
113 Ibid.
114 Ibid., pp. 236–41.
115 For an overview of the sources, excluding Romuald: B. Frenz, 'Barbarossa und der Hoftag von Roncaglia (1158) in der Historiographie des 12. und 13. Jahrhunderts', in Dilcher and Quaglioni (eds), *Gli inizi del diritto pubblico*, pp. 101–26.
116 Bisson, *The Crisis of the Twelfth Century*, p. 563.
117 See the bibliography in n. 1.
118 K. Leyser, 'The crisis of medieval Germany', *Proceedings of the British Academy*, 6, 1983, pp. 409–43.
119 J. Van Engen, 'The twelfth century: reading, reason, and revolt in a world of custom', in Noble and Van Engen (eds), *European Transformations*, p. 26.
120 J. C. Holt, *Magna Carta*, Cambridge, Cambridge University Press, 1992, pp. 25, 76, 87, 519.

PART II

Socio-political contexts
Identity, motivation, and mobilisation

7
LOOKING FORWARD
Peasant revolts in Europe, 600–1200

Chris Wickham

The standard belief that popular revolts were relatively rare in the early and central Middle Ages, became more common in the thirteenth century, and then increased substantially in number after the Black Death, appears to be true. Sam Cohn in his fundamental book on the subject noted how his less systematic work on the pre-1200 period turned up 'only a handful of examples'.[1] My own work, as systematic as possible for Western and Northern Europe up to *c*.1000, less so for 1000–1200 in my case too (although I have kept my eye out for popular revolts in later centuries for decades), fits that exactly. The imagery of revolt fits far fewer of the forms of non-elite political action in the medieval world before 1200 than it does later. Nor is this always simply a matter of sources; it is true that the early Middle Ages as a whole is notoriously source-poor, but for some parts of these six centuries (the high Carolingian period in the Frankish heartland; Northern France, England, and parts of Italy and Germany after 1050), narrative source material is relatively dense, without giving us more evidence of revolt to work with. My task is therefore, in a book focused on comparative studies of revolts, to try to analyse why this is so, through a survey of what sort of revolts we do find, and what they seem to have been about.

I worked on the history of early medieval popular revolt about a decade ago, and published the results; inevitably, some of that material will have to be reprised here, although in a different form.[2] But it has to be stressed at the outset that the historiographical framing for such work has changed in this last decade, in two basic respects. First, as is visible in the other chapters in this volume, as well as many of the other major works of recent years which they cite, there is much more attention now being paid to the discourse of revolt. It is not that we did not know a decade ago that revolts were systematically falsified by the literary tropes of chroniclers, who were simultaneously keen to de-legitimate them rhetorically and unwilling to understand that non-elites could have justifiable grievances at all, let alone what mental frame the latter might actually have – Rolf Köhn and Steven Justice are only two notable examples of people who put this at the centre of their discussions.[3] But there is now far more attention being paid to the language of sources, as also, where there is evidence (which is very rare in the period before 1200), to the language of the participants in revolt themselves. Myles Lavan's contribution to this volume is particularly useful here, for he is dealing with a period, the early Roman empire, which is as source-poor as the early Middle Ages, and he concludes that, given the systematic framing of his sources, 'The prospect of an adequate social history of revolt, particularly popular revolt, seems to me ever more illusory' – what he is left with is a 'discursive history' which analyses the way revolts were tamed rhetorically. That is not a small subject, as it turns out; Roman sources – generally even more uninterested in talking about non-elites than medieval ones are – seem to argue, perhaps as a result, that revolts were rarely threatening at all, and therefore could be discussed in terms of what local rulers (supposedly) actually had done wrong.[4] That is still a distorting mirror; but it is a different kind of distortion from that which we find in the Middle Ages, even the early Middle Ages.

The second change is simply discovery. Sam Cohn's book showed us, for the first time, not only how common revolt could be in the Middle Ages, but also how 'normal', even before the Black Death, never mind afterwards. (I put 'normal' in inverted commas because it is in a strict sense inaccurate: revolts, however they are defined, are abnormal almost automatically.) Certainly, this was more the case in towns than in the countryside; the great majority of Cohn's 1,000+ cases for Flanders, France, and Italy are urban revolts, a preponderance which is also reflected in the chapters in this volume. But even in the countryside, the possibility of contestation of a variety of kinds always existed; and, although it was always condemned by our elite sources, it was also, at least sometimes, discussed without surprise. One key thing follows from this: it is not the case that most such revolts were drowned in blood, as it was still standard to assume a decade ago. The more 'normal' revolts are, the more transactional they can become – the more, that is to say, they can be a part of negotiating between elites and non-elites, even if they are at the extreme end of such negotiations, just as killing lies at the extreme end of the negotiations between kin-groups in feuding situations. Recent work by a variety of people, not least those writing in this book, makes this point firmly for the later Middle Ages,[5] and it is true for at least some instances in the early period too. This in itself makes revolt less wholly risky, of course, and therefore potentially still less uncommon. All the same, it was never risk-free; peasants, tendentially risk-averse as they are, did not undertake it lightly, even when they were used to other forms of violence, as medieval males tended to be (I will come back to this). In this arena, the balance between transactionality and risk may well have been in people's minds in a systematic way in every medieval century. But that has to be hypothesis; our sources do not take us there. We can only look at decision-making from the outside; and that is above all the case for the centuries I shall be discussing.

For my six centuries, I shall focus on rural, not urban, revolts. It is certainly not that there were no urban revolts in the period, at least in the last two centuries of it: in Italy, Verona and Venice already in the 960s–70s, Pavia in 1024, Cremona in the 1030s and onwards from that, Milan in the 1040s–70s, Arezzo in 1110 and 1129, Rome in 1143–9; in Northern France and England, Le Mans in 1070, Laon in 1112, the Flemish towns in 1127–8, London in 1141 and 1196, a list, already matching in scale that for rural revolts, which is far from exhaustive. In part, I will not deal with these for simple lack of space; but it is also hard in these cases and other, less documented, ones, to be sure if we are dealing with elite or with popular revolts – in Italy, for example, only Milan (at times) and Rome fell into the latter category with certainty.[6] For most of Europe, too, towns were as yet too small to have a critical mass of popular protagonists, so a concentration on this category of revolt would unbalance the analysis geographically as well. For the entirety of the Middle Ages, the great majority – in the early Middle Ages, the huge majority – of the inhabitants of Europe were anyway peasants, which is a justification for a rural focus in itself.

Two initial points need to be made about the set of peasant revolts we do have. The first is that in the period discussed here revolts were mostly not against taxation or the pressure of the state, simply because before 1200 taxation was still at its beginnings (the mountains above Faenza and then the city itself in 1184, and London in 1196, are the earliest apparently anti-tax revolts I have found),[7] and public power was by the standards of earlier or later periods also relatively unintrusive at a local level (there are exceptions here, however, as we shall see). This contrasts early medieval Europe immediately with the later Roman empire and the early Arab caliphate, which both did tax, more heavily than most late medieval European states, and where tax revolts are indeed documented: the Bagaudae in Northern Gaul and Spain in the fifth century (I accept the view, not held by all, that this was a mostly popular revolt, although its target seems to have been wider than taxation on its own) and Egypt in the 720s–830s are the major examples here.[8] Most revolts in medieval Europe before 1200 were, rather, against landlords and the local usurpations of lords in general. Cohn found in his post-1200 dataset that only ten rural revolts, around 15 per cent of the total, were against landlords; that is to say, political and fiscal oppression was much more likely to cause peasants to react violently than were the simple quotidian bad relations between lords and tenants which class struggle mostly involved. Justine Firnhaber-Baker, too, has found that in the Jacquerie, certainly a revolt against (lay) lords, attacks by peasants on *their own* lords was less common than on the lords of others. It was, indeed, normally easier to negotiate with one's own lord without the comprehensive eversive violence which we tend to classify as 'revolt', as we shall see.[9] So it is less surprising that there were fewer revolts in periods when landlords were seen as the main oppressors of peasants; this has always been assumed to be the reason why there were fewer early medieval revolts, and I think this assumption is largely accurate. Setting aside ethnic-based revolts, such as those of the Baltic Slavs against German aggression in the late tenth and early eleventh centuries, I have identified 15 rural popular revolts before 1200 – six before 1000, nine after – in Western and Northern Europe. (I have not looked at the evidence for Eastern Europe, or al-Andalus.) The great majority of these were visibly against lords, but the total number is small by comparison with what would come later.

The second point, however, partially counters this. Before 1200, as indeed later, most of our evidence for tension between lords and peasants comes from formal pleas to outside bodies, court cases, and, after 1050 or so, collective agreements. The formal pleas, which tend to come from the periods when lords were establishing the private political lordships known as *seigneuries banales*, regularly cast peasants in the role of victims, simply suffering aristocratic brutality.[10] But they were not only the victims. The court cases show that it was possible for peasants to contest lords in public; and, given that some of the dispute documents we have show the lords as plaintiffs, we also have accounts of the 'violence' with which peasants pressed their claims. *Violentia* was a technical term for illegal activity of all sorts in this period, but forceful direct action (occupying fields, burning woodland or even houses) was also a genuine part of constructing a claim, for, if you were not resisted, you had a stronger legal case.[11] Sometimes, even early on, it is clear that peasants were engaging in tactical violence against lords in precisely this way, as when in 664–5 the abbot of St-Bénigne in Dijon raised a plea before King Chlotar III against the peasants of the *villa* of Larrey in Burgundy:

> the men living inside those bounds [of Larrey] ... refused to give the rents of the land to the church, and they devastated the woods in the territory, and invaded the [arable] land and meadows in many places, and planted vines, and cleared wasteland.

The peasants were in fact claiming that they were not the tenants of the monastery, and this targeted violence, which was a claim for autonomous activity in the disputed territory, formed part of their case.[12] When we find agreements between peasants and lords – most famously, in the *franchises* or *franchigie* which mark the twelfth century (and later) in much of France, Italy, and Spain – we may also wonder how often part of the means by which the peasants negotiated what were in some cases quite far-reaching charters of rights was by the use of similar forms of violence. The texts seldom say so, but the formats they use would hardly permit it (they say little about peasant pay-offs either, although we know that these were common), and anyway hints of trouble do indeed sometimes leak out.[13] The fact that peasants all had experience of 'ordinary' violence (as with the knife fights which seem to have been a standard feature of rural life, with often very forceful collective boundary disputes, which in some cases led to deaths, and indeed in some cases with more systematic feuding)[14] makes all of this less surprising. So also does a steady trickle of reports of the murders of lords by peasants, which start already in the 570s and continue through the centuries up to 1200 and beyond.[15]

I would not classify any of these activities as revolts, but they do show that force was a transactional part of negotiating of all types – as aristocratic brutality was in return, of course. There must always have been a wide grey area between this everyday violence and something sufficiently large scale that we, and they on occasion, could term *seditio*, *tumultus*, 'revolt'. This is generally recognised for the later Middle Ages, in both town and country; what counted as a revolt was indeed sufficiently part of narrative strategies that not only could chroniclers and lords write up a dispute of this ordinary kind as something much more threatening, for political purposes, but peasants and townsmen, too, could make the case that they had not engaged in a 'real' revolt, but only tactical forms of subversion.[16] It is important to remember that this sort of procedure was old, and that the restricted number of clearly characterised early medieval revolts are only the tip of an iceberg of threatening behaviours of all types.

As already noted, my database is small: only 15 revolts before 1200, some of them on the boundary between the sort of everyday violence just discussed and full-scale revolt. So, in order to increase my dataset, I followed rural revolts through to around 1260, adding another nine (partly overlapping with Sam Cohn's set but partly not, as my set covers all Western and Northern Europe); they show similar patterns, even though the frequency of revolts has by now increased.[17] The geographical distribution of the entire set up to the 1250s is three for Scandinavia, six for North Germany and Frisia, four for France, three for Northern Spain, and eight for Italy, a distribution which looks wide but which has some significant concentrations. Most of them are only discussed fragmentarily in our sources, but we can still say some things about them, as we shall see. Let us look at some of them in more detail; I shall discuss them more or less chronologically, and then make some general points at the end.

One example which is at least attested in an exactly contemporary letter is the first of all in chronological terms. It is a rural uprising (*seditio*) in the hinterland of Naples in 592, in which the *mancipia* (technically 'slaves', but it is most likely that these were unfree tenants) belonging to Clementina, a senatorial leader of that city, had persuaded the dependants of the papal administrator for Naples (and of other *domini*) to rise up and attack the latter. Our source is Gregory the Great, who had a track record of sympathy with peasants who were mistreated by lords; he envisaged severe punishments for the *mancipia*, asked if Clementina was involved, but also wondered if the rebels had a *iusta querella* (just complaint) against their lords. That is to say, this sort of violence could be seen, even by a pope, as part of a legitimate politics.[18]

A second example is also contemporary, in that the revolts (a sequence of them, from 779 to 873) are attested in eight documents drawn up by a monastery, S. Vincenzo al Volturno in the central Italian mountains, referring in all to nine court hearings concerning disputes with its claimed tenants, although in this case in much less neutral terms. Around 758, the Lombard King Desiderius had given a high mountain valley, the Valle Trita (it lies under the highest peaks of the Appennines, and is largely silvo-pastoral land), to S. Vincenzo; but its inhabitants also had independent rights, safeguarded, they said, by diplomas (*precepta*) of the dukes of Spoleto. S. Vincenzo established an estate there and regarded the (ex-)public dues owed by the inhabitants as rents; it soon claimed that most of the inhabitants were unfree too. In 779 the inhabitants were already refusing dues and services; further refusals occurred in 787, 822–4, 854, and 872–3. In 872–3, the monastery could only get the openly resisting peasants to court at all because the Emperor Louis II and his army were in the vicinity, and the peasants could not take to the hills because of winter; they were rounded up in January 873. In every case they lost, and S. Vincenzo sometimes managed to get them to recognise their unfree status; but it is easy to see that the situation on the ground was only intermittently under monastic control – Trita is 100 km from the monastery, across two mountain passes. The year 873 may only be the last case because S. Vincenzo was sacked by the Arabs in 881 and did not re-establish control over many of its estates for decades. These texts show how the collective action and the remoteness characteristic of peasants in marginal lands could hold off a powerful and determined monastery, even though the latter was backed up by all the state power that was available.[19]

A much larger-scale example of resistance – it was probably the largest-scale popular revolt in Europe before the great sequence of Flemish revolts which began in the 1290s – comes from Saxony in the 840s. Saxony had not been fully under aristocratic control at the time of Charlemagne's bloody conquest in the late eighth century, and its free and more dependent peasantry (*frilingi* and *lazzi*) seem to have sent representatives to an annual assembly, which was the only central body that Saxony had had. Under Charlemagne and Louis the Pious, however, native and Frankish lords, and newly established churches, rapidly increased their landowning; instead of autonomous peasantries, what we find in our early Saxon documents is estates with dependent tenants, and *lazzi* are increasingly described as unfree. When the Carolingian state dissolved into civil war at Louis's death in 840, the *frilingi* and *lazzi* quickly reacted, and set off the Stellinga revolt. Their main enemy, according to the contemporary chronicler Nithard's relatively detailed account, was the Saxon aristocracy, and more generally they are said to have sought the re-establishment of paganism (although this is the sort of thing hostile chroniclers always say in the early Middle Ages) and, above all, the re-establishment of 'the custom of the ancient Saxons', instead of the 'law', *lex*, of the Carolingians. Louis's son the emperor Lothar, keen to use them against his brother Louis the German, said he was prepared to grant them this. In the winter and spring of 841–2, the Stellinga had the run of Saxony, but in the following summer and autumn, after Lothar's defeat, Louis and the local aristocracy put the rising down with great violence. The Stellinga are doubtless not at all accurately depicted in our sources, but the imagery of the 'custom of the ancient Saxons' is important, for, although this will not have been Nithard's intent, it ascribes to the rebels a clear – even practical – programme. This was, simply, the reversal of the social changes of the last two generations, which must have been highly visible to the Saxon peasantry as a whole, and were evidently highly resented. The Stellinga, that is to say, show us that peasants were fully capable in our period of recognising, and opposing, global increases in aristocratic power, as indeed the historiography of the Stellinga correctly stresses; and also of choosing the right moment, the break in royal and aristocratic hegemony through civil war, to resist it.[20] It must be added that 842 by no means marked the end of Saxon peasant protagonism; a later peasant movement formed part of the Saxon revolt of 1073–5, which was also one of aristocrats, against Henry IV. Although this might make it seem to be a different sort of operation, it is clear from the chroniclers, notably Lampert of Hersfeld, that the peasants pursued different aims and were often acting autonomously; they also suffered rather more than their lords did when Henry, at least temporarily, won. The fact was that Saxony had remained a region in which peasants were not in all areas fully subjected to lords; here, unlike in 841–2, their target was the king, not local aristocrats, but the issue was still lordship, for they were reacting above all against Henry's assertions of his own domain rights.[21]

A parallel uprising – parallel more to 1073 than to 841 – was that of the *bœndr*, the free men, of Norway, against King Óláfr Haraldsson in 1030, which led to the latter's death at the battle of Stiklarstaðir. Their fighting force was called the *lið bónda* and other synonyms, the '*bóndi* army', in Snorri Sturluson's *Heimskringla*, this time by no means contemporary, for it dates to *c*.1230. It was led by *lendir menn*, major aristocrats, but was still associated with the *bændr*: both *ríkir* ('powerful') and *thorparar ok verkmenn* ('cottagers and labourers') – i.e. not just aristocrats but also the peasantry. Snorri Sturluson, a very aristocratic figure, saw *bændr* as leaderless unless aristocrats were available; but their political protagonism is not in doubt, and is rather more stressed by Snorri than peasant protagonism is in Lampert. There is, in particular, no hint that this was an inappropriate thing for *bændr* to be doing, both poor and rich ones, even though our authors wrote after Óláfr Haraldsson was recognised as a saint; it was the *lendir menn* who are criticised by Snorri for their selfishness, not the *bændr* they were allied with. Snorri had no real sympathy for *bóndi* protagonism, but it was still a normal part of his world in the thirteenth century.[22] This in itself is very unusual in medieval European narratives, which otherwise, as noted earlier, so exclude the possibility of peasant protagonism that it was sometimes incomprehensible to writers even when – as with fourteenth-century peasant revolts – it was impossible to deny.

The events of 1030 might on one level seem to be on the very fringes of 'popular' risings, given the claimed aristocratic leadership of the '*bóndi* army', and also the late date of most of our sources for it – many of our late sources elsewhere, as with Normandy and L'Aquila (see below), write up peasant protagonism for dramatic purposes. But Norway was a polity in which not only did aristocrats not have full control, but they never gained it: peasant landowning covered a third of the country even in the sixteenth century,[23] and peasants had a major voice in most of the deliberative assemblies which dominated local politics, which was a crucial arena in a country famous for mountains and poor communications. In this world a '*bóndi* army' would not automatically be under the control of its leaders, and indeed aristocratic leadership is likely, far from being written down, to have been written up by a very hierarchical-minded writer such as Snorri. This revolt was, in fact, against not landlords but, even more than in Saxony in 1073, aggressive and high-handed kingship; but peasants as well as lords reacted against it, and peasants as well as lords had enough agency to react, militarily and with success. Nor was this the only example of it in Norway; the peasant army of *birkibeinar*, 'birchlegs', which chose Sverre as their leader in 1177 and took him to the throne of Norway in 1184, gives us a similar example of popular protagonists.[24] In these cases, peasants were acting on the level of high politics, rather than opposing landlords; but here there were fewer landlords to fight.

The Norman rising of *c*.1000 takes us to the beginning of a different political world. William of Jumièges in the 1050s recounts that when Richard II (996–1026) was in his early years as duke, the *rustici* of (probably) the eastern edge of Normandy formed assemblies (*conventicula*) and sought to live 'according to their own wishes', especially with respect to rights in woodland and river traffic. They all sent delegates to a single *conventus*, but a ducal army broke this up and mutilated the peasant leaders, thus ending the rising. The violence here was evidently not initiated by the peasants, but the threat to the by-now standard rules of aristocratic power was not the less for that. (A later verse account, by Wace, makes that threat still more visible, but it has no independent value as a source for the years around 1000.) These peasants had an ambitious image of decision-making, which seems to have been modelled on the old traditions of the public *placitum*. That is to say, a bid for autonomy here invoked the same sort of assembly politics of the free which the Stellinga had been aiming at; but in the 840s such a politics was still a standard part of public practice across the Carolingian empire, whereas by 1000 it was no longer so in most of France, so, even though the violence involved on the peasant side here was far less than in Saxony, it may have seemed more radical. But what they were reacting to was not a threat to ownership and freedom, but rather menaces to wood-rights and commerce, and these were not only more restricted but probably newer: wood and transport tolls were characteristic of the establishment of the private dues of the *seigneurie banale*, which were just beginning in the France of the 990s. The privatisation of traditional public rights characteristically meant, among other things, that peasantries found that they had to pay for access to certain sorts of space that they had previously taken for granted. This, as we have seen, did not normally lead to revolt in Europe, even of this non-violent kind; why it did here is not easy to see, given our scarce sources, although it may well be that the accession of Duke Richard seemed to some to mark a break in the hegemonic power structure, and thus an opportunity for autonomous action.[25] But these changes would indeed be a terrain for the sort of cautious violence and negotiation which would culminate in the stabilisation of exactions in the *franchises* of the twelfth century.

Normandy in 1000 was, all the same, not unique; a partly parallel set of events is recorded for the countryside outside Sahagún in Castile in 1111. Here, a late fourteenth-century Castilian chronicle, apparently using earlier sources (and also not in these sections obviously rhetorical), relates how, in the context of a war between the town dwellers and the abbot of Sahagún which caused the devastation of the countryside, the peasants and workers and lesser people (*rrusticos e labradores e menuda gente*) made a sworn brotherhood (*hermandad*, a word with a long future in Spanish conflict, thus here maybe with fourteenth-century, not twelfth-century, resonance) against their lords: they refused to pay rents and seigneurial dues, or else only paid what they considered to be fair; they destroyed seigneurial buildings, killed rent-collectors and Jews, and nearly killed the abbot of Sahagún (the principal local lord), although he escaped. This ended up in a three-way war between peasants, townsmen, and lords, in which the peasants were the principal victims, but apparently only because they were always the principal victims of wars, not as specific reprisals for their autonomous activity. I take the emphasis on dues (*portalgos*) to mean that this uprising was as much framed by the seigneurial rights of local lords as by rent-collection, especially as the peasants were prepared to pay some rents, and also accepted at one point the lordship of a layman instead of the abbot. The break in local hegemony which the town–abbot conflict caused once again gives a clear context to this rising.[26] A further seigneurial example seems to come from Denmark, where the participants in the failed Skåne uprising of 1180-2 sought *libertas* (liberties) against the increasingly aggressive activities of their lord, Absalon archbishop of Lund: not obviously concerning rent-collection, but over demeaning labour-services in woods, a seigneurial-style due which could have been demanded from owner-cultivators too. Here there is no obvious break in the archbishop's hegemony, but, as with the Saxon and Norwegian risings, the peasants of Skåne were less far from the peasant autonomies of the past than in some of our other examples, and their protagonism was thus less unusual.[27]

Moving into the thirteenth century, and past the nominal end-point of this chapter, let us finally look at two more revolts, that of the Stedinger around 1230 and that of several villages in the central Appennines in the 1250s; not because they add so much to the broad typology which is visible in the examples just cited, but simply because of their intrinsic interest. The Stedinger lived north of Bremen on the banks of the Weser, on the edge of Frisia, which, like parts of Saxony and much of Scandinavia, was an area of very weak landlord rights – as is further shown by the inhabitants of Dithmarschen slightly to the north-east, who established their full autonomy against all neighbouring powers, both German and Danish, in the 1220s, an autonomy which they maintained, often by force, until the 1550s. The Stedinger therefore fit some of the northern revolts we have already seen, although they were also different, in that they had settled, apparently from Holland, only a century previously, with, for at least some of them, defined freehold rights and a charter of liberties from the archbishop of Bremen. They were thus more like the free settlers of the German *Ostsiedlung*, even if in this case on the edge of relatively independent peasant territories which may have provided models for action. The main narrative account of the revolt (again, problematically, it is from nearly a century later), stresses that they withheld tithes from the archbishop, plus *tributa*, which were probably the dues which the archbishop exacted as territorial lord even from freeholders; they again fought for *libertas*, which doubtless means, as Köhn stresses, freedom from specific dues, not a generic 'freedom'. The revolt appears to have been sparked off by a reaction by the Stedinger communities against the bad behaviour of *milites* in local castles at an unspecified date before the late 1220s, but to have spread to cover a rejection of all the obligations they owed to lords. This does not sound enormously dangerous in itself, but it rapidly became so when a punitive expedition led against them in 1229 by the archbishop's brother resulted in his death; the archbishop excommunicated them as a result, then, taking advantage of the heresy scares of Gregory IX's pontificate, got them declared heretics in 1231. This peasants' revolt thus, uniquely, resulted in full-blown crusades being called against it, one of which the Stedinger held off, in 1233, although they fell bloodily to the second, in 1234.[28]

I end with a revolt which seems to have ended with full success. It is one coming from a set of fortified villages in the high Appennines, a little to the west of the Valle Trita, shortly before 1254. It was written up in verse a century later by Buccio di Ranallo in romantic terms, but the core of the revolt is set out more telegraphically in the chronicle of Saba Malaspina, only some 20 years after the events. Malaspina stated that the *villani* of the area, a *congeries rusticorum* ('gathering of peasants', although clearly with the help of richer notables as well), founded the city of L'Aquila 'in hatred of the barons' (*in odium baronum*), and that King Conrad IV had supported their actions – we in fact have the royal diploma of support, which claims the construction of the city for the king, but nonetheless frees its inhabitants from dependence on their prior lords. We do not know what caused that 'hate', but the results are clear. One of Italy's major cities thus appears to have been founded as a result of a peasants' revolt, which was, furthermore, not forgotten, if Buccio still remembered it as such.[29]

This survey allows us to see some common themes and trends; in a concluding section, let us look at them more closely. The first point is, to repeat, that most of these revolts were against landlords: not often against single lords, but at least against lordly power. The major exceptions are the Norwegian examples, in which peasants were more ambitious protagonists, precisely because Norwegian political practice gave their public actions more legitimacy. There is a grey area here too, of course: since kings and emperors (and ruling dukes, bishops, and popes) got involved in many of these revolts before the peasants gave in, they could be figured as being in opposition to public power as well; but this was not usually the case, as far as we can tell, at the beginning of the revolt – public intervention and defiance of it came later, that is to say. The second point is that some of these revolts were successful – the Valle Trita in the end, the Norwegian ones, Dithmarschen, L'Aquila – and even when they were not, they were not always harshly punished – as with the Sahagún revolt, which fizzled out, or the Capuchins of the Velay in 1182–4 (not mentioned up to now), whose peace-movement-turned-vigilante-rising was for the most part punished by humiliation, not violence.[30]

These conclusions fit closely with the assumptions of the most recent literature. What is, however, more interesting, when we look at the geographical range of the revolts we are dealing with, is how often they focus on specific areas of Europe: a good half of them derive from areas of the continent with incomplete aristocratic dominance, and only a quarter from areas where aristocratic power had always been strong. The early Middle Ages was, as a period, one in which the map of Europe was far from covered uniformly by strong aristocratic landowning, of a type which we are used to in analyses of late medieval England or Northern France or the Rhineland or the Po Plain. Lords were thus not entirely hegemonic in many areas; it is not that aristocrats, and powerful landowners, did not exist, but they did not control the whole of the landscape, and sometimes not even the basic patterns of the economy. In some areas, they did already; the Frankish heartland is one very clear example, already by the seventh century. Elsewhere, though, peasantries were often used to considerable degrees of autonomy, and, as we have seen, in some cases to forms of political protagonism: in the whole of Scandinavia (even if less so in Denmark by 1100 or so), on the coast of Frisia, and in Saxony until Charlemagne's conquest – and, across the north of the Low Countries and Germany, they had a substantial degree of practical independence after that as well, at least in some areas. These are areas which furnish a high proportion of our revolts. Furthermore, in Spain we can see a similar de facto autonomy in much of the northern mountains, and even down into parts of the north Duero plain after its occupation by the kings of Asturias in the early tenth century.[31] The ill-documented Asturias revolt of 770 and the century-long defiance of outside lordship by the frontier settlement of Castrojeriz in the years around 1000 (also not mentioned in the foregoing), give a similar sense of peasantries which felt they had a right to protagonism because there was no deep local tradition of aristocratic hegemony; and it is at least plausible (although less certain, given the power of the monastery of Sahagún since the tenth century) that the peasants of the lands around the latter had a sense of similar rights as late as 1111.[32] The central Appennines in Italy were similar, hence the defiance of the Valle Trita in the ninth century; again, at L'Aquila four centuries later we might hesitate to say the same, given the steady developments of aristocratic power in the area from the mid-tenth century onwards, but the coincidence of geographical location is striking all the same.[33] Although our information as to these revolts is, as I have said, fragmentary, and we must always be highly suspicious of the detail of the claims of our often late sources about even simple elements in these revolts (including not small issues such as composition, causes, aims, and leadership), the geographical patterning I have characterised cannot easily be argued away, and the consistency of some of the descriptions we find across regions, languages, and genres is notable too.

What this means is that most peasant revolts in the period up to 1200/1250 were of a different type from those found thereafter. Although they were against lords, they were not so often, unlike later, reactions to lordship in an environment of effectively complete lordly control – so complete, indeed, that few late medieval revolts envisaged an actual end to rent-paying to landlords. Nor, in most cases (Sahagún is an exception), were they desperate reactions to the devastations of war. And, even in some places where lords were definitely at least locally strong, as with the Skåne revolt and that of the Stedinger, the exactions which are mentioned in our sources do not sound particularly extreme ones. Rather – again for the most part – they were defensive reactions to the growing power of lords in environments where that power was not yet taken for granted. That is even so for the Norwegian cases, for Óláfr Haraldsson undoubtedly represented a stronger kingship (and therefore a more oppressive one) than ordinary Norwegians were used to or appreciated, even if by continental standards this kingship would not have seemed to amount to much. Although I have excluded the Slav revolts against German encroachment, they show some similarities in this respect too.[34] In Western and Northern Europe, it is indeed the case that in nearly every area where, in the centuries after 700, we can see an erosion of peasant economic and/or political autonomy, we can see signs of resistance. Not all the time, but at least sometimes, and sometimes (in Saxony and Scandinavia) on quite a large scale. Even in Normandy in 1000, where aristocratic dominance was long-standing (unless, as remains uncertain and in my view unlikely, the Viking settlement had disrupted it), the traditions the Norman rebels drew on consisted of the local public assemblies of the Carolingian and Merovingian period which could still be remembered, presumably as markers of a (restricted) political autonomy which was still valued and worth invoking. This perhaps also – together, of course, with the constant presence of unfreedom as a state of dependence in early and central medieval Europe – contributed to the development of *libertas* imagery, which would have a substantial post-1200 history too; this initially translated better as 'liberties' than the abstract concept of 'liberty',[35] but such practical 'liberties' had once been quite wide-ranging, and were not always forgotten, as, among others, some of the demands of the English rebels in 1381 show. The major exception to these generalisations about resistance to the spread of aristocratic dominance is, conversely, also England, which moved from a world of weak aristocratic power to one of exceptionally strong dominance by great lords in little over two centuries, c.800 to c.1000, without any documented protest at all.[36] I single this out as an anomaly which needs to be explained, not as a norm of peasant quiescence.

Conversely, the spread after the tenth century in much of Europe of private political rights over peasants who were usually *already* dependent, which can be summed up in the French term *seigneurie banale* (in much of France, Western Germany, Italy, Northern Spain, with signs of parallel patterns more widely than that), and the often associated tendency for lords to ratchet up straightforward land rents when they could, was seldom met with as clear a response. In the examples of such resistance discussed here, Normandy, Sahagún, and Skåne, plus the more complex but parallel case of the Stedinger, there are likely or possible elements of memories of much greater earlier protagonism at their back; without such memories, dependent peasants reacted less violently. It may be that this process was normally too capillary, lordship by lordship, with peasant communities subdued one by one by gangs of *milites* who were different from those operating in the next-door village, for a consciousness of common interest to develop fast enough. It was only at a later stage that peasant communities reacted here, in the moves to get agreements by lords for local *franchises*: not violently on a large scale, as we have seen, and sometimes not violently at all, but quite consistently all the same. *Franchises* were in France, not insignificantly, assembled into families of texts, which were copied from place to place. This shows that by then villagers knew quite well that a template of rights did indeed exist elsewhere; once such agreements existed for one village, the model could be taken up by others.[37] This was therefore not only less violent a process than, but a different one from, a revolt which had at its back an experience or a memory of past autonomy; these were negotiations using contemporary parallels. The Capuchins fit this later stage too, in that they were a systematic reaction to lordly violence using relatively new images (the Peace of God), not ancient rights.

Which all means: peasant revolts were not the same across the Middle Ages. This is not simply an issue of frequency, the point I started with, with later revolts much more frequent than earlier ones, but also of imagery and legitimacy. I would counterpose, to a late medieval landscape of revolts which tended to be about taxation, political rights, and the public sphere, an early medieval landscape of revolts about real and long-standing, but now eroded, political/economic autonomies. Between these two broad periods, we can discern, if more inconsistently and unevenly, a landscape of struggle over rural rights which was less often violent, and more often focused on gaining written charters of liberties. These are generalisations at the very widest level, and consciously ignore exceptions; all the same, they set out a set of distinctions which seem to me useful, for when we try to understand the complexities of peasant reactions to the constraints put on them by others.

Notes

1 S. K. Cohn, Jr., *Lust for Liberty: The Politics of Social Revolt in Medieval Europe, 1200–1425*, Cambridge, MA: Harvard University Press, 2006, p. 14. Since 'revolt' is a discursive category in part, I do not attempt a definition here; the issue of definition is anyway fully discussed elsewhere in this volume. I am very grateful to Sam Cohn for a critique of this text, and to all the St Andrews conference participants for brainstorming and stimulus.

2 C. Wickham, 'Space and society in early medieval peasant conflicts', *Settimane di studio*, 50, 2003, pp. 551–87; C. Wickham, *Framing the Early Middle Ages*, Oxford: Oxford University Press, 2005, pp. 578–88.
3 R. Köhn, 'Freiheit als Forderung und Ziel bäuerlichen Widerstands (Mittel- und Westeuropa, 11.–13. Jahrhundert', *Vorträge und Forschungen*, 39, 1991, pp. 325–87; S. Justice, *Writing and Rebellion*, Berkeley: University of California Press, 1994.
4 M. Lavan, 'Writing revolt in the early Roman empire', in this volume; E. Auerbach, *Mimesis*, new edn, Princeton, NJ: Princeton University Press, 2003, pp. 50–3.
5 See among others Cohn, *Lust for Liberty*, e.g. pp. 105–7; J. Dumolyn and J. Haemers, 'Patterns of urban rebellion in medieval Flanders', *JMH*, 31, 2005, pp. 369–93; P. Lantschner, 'Revolts and the political order of cities in the late Middle Ages', *P&P*, 225, 2014, pp. 3–46.
6 See in general for Italy the bibliography in C. Wickham, *Sleepwalking into a New World*, Princeton, NJ: Princeton University Press, 2015; for Milan, Rome, Cremona, and Arezzo, pp. 23–5, 128–36, 174–6, 184–90. See J.-C. Maire Vigueur, *Cavaliers et citoyens*, Paris: Éditions EHESS, 2003, for a wide elite dominance of urban politics in Italy, including civic disturbance, in the twelfth and thirteenth centuries.
7 For Faenza, which Sam Cohn brought to my attention, see Tolosano, *Chronicon Faventinum*, ed. G. Rossini, RIS, 2nd edn, vol. 28.1–2, Bologna: Zanichelli, 1936, pp. 90–2; in the mountains the 'revolt' may simply have consisted of refusing to pay, with the violence all on the side of the city, but the urban revolt was more aggressive. For London, see esp. *Chronica magistri Rogeri de Hovedene*, 4 vols, ed. W. Stubbs, Rolls series, 51, London: Public Record Office, 1871, vol. 4, pp. 5–6; the most useful commentary is S. K. Cohn, Jr., *Popular Protest in Late Medieval English Towns*, Cambridge: Cambridge University Press, 2013, pp. 61–3.
8 Wickham, *Framing*, pp. 140–3, 529–33.
9 Cohn, *Lust for Liberty*, pp. 25–32; J. Firnhaber-Baker, 'The eponymous Jacquerie: making revolt mean some things', in this volume.
10 See for an Italian example *I brevi dei consoli del Comune di Pisa degli anni 1162 e 1164*, ed. O. Banti, Rome: Istituto storico italiano per il medioevo, 1997, pp. 108–10; for Catalonia, T. N. Bisson, *Tormented Voices*, Cambridge, MA: Harvard University Press, 1998.
11 For violence as a court strategy, C. Wickham, *Courts and Conflict in Twelfth-Century Tuscany*, Oxford: Oxford University Press, 2003, e.g. pp. 185–223. See further E. Hartrich, 'Rebellion and the law in fifteenth-century English towns', in this volume.
12 MGH, DD Mer., 1, ed. T. Kölzer, Hanover: Hahn, 2001, no. 103, with Wickham, *Framing*, pp. 579–80.
13 For the problems of the rhetoric of *franchises*, see M. Bourin and P. Martínez Sopena (eds), *Pour une anthropologie du prélèvement seigneurial dans les campagnes médiévales (XIe–XIVe siècles)*, 2 vols, Paris: Publications de la Sorbonne, 2004–7, esp. vol. 2, pp. 137–309, 503–5; for a survey, see e.g. C. Wickham, *Community and Clientele in Twelfth-Century Tuscany*, Oxford: Oxford University Press, 1998, pp. 192–231 (for violence, pp. 210, 224–7).
14 For violent boundary disputes, see e.g. *Documentación medieval de Leire*, ed. A. J. Martín Duque, Pamplona: Institución Príncipe de Viana, 1983, n. 3 (*c*.900); *Codex diplomaticus civitatis et ecclesiae Bergomatis*, ed. M. Lupo, 2 vols, Bergamo: Vincent Antoine, 1784–99, vol. 2, cols 775–6 (1092). For violent death in villages, which in late medieval England matched the scale of twentieth-century US cities, see T. R. Gurr, 'Historical trends in violent crime', *Crime and Justice*, 3, 1981, pp. 295–353. For feuds, against equals and on occasion lords, see the excellent discussion of late fifteenth-century Bavaria in C. Reinle, *Bauernfehden. Studien zur Fehdeführung Nichtadliger im spätmittelalterlichen römisch–deutschen Reich, besonders in den bayerischen Herzogtümern*, Stuttgart: Franz Steiner, 2003. Only the evidence for boundary disputes comes from the period before 1200, however.
15 *Vitas sanctorum patrum Emeritensium*, ed. A. Maya Sánchez, Turnhout: Brepols, 1992, III.11–15; *Passio Thrudperti martyris Brisgoviensis*, ed. B. Krusch, MGH, SS rer. Merov., 4, Hanover: Hahn, 1902, cc. 3–7; R. Jacob, 'Le meurtre du seigneur dans la société féodale', *Annales E.S.C.*, 45, 1990, pp. 247–63.
16 Cf. for 1381 in England, well-documented even if no one claimed that the Peasants' Revolt was simply tactical, H. Lacey, '"Grace for the rebels"', *JMH*, 34, 2008, pp. 36–63.
17 Those not otherwise mentioned here are *Edictus Rothari*, cc. 279–80 in *Leges Langobardorum 643–866*, ed. F. Beyerle, Witzenhausen: Deutschrechtlicher Instituts-Verlag, 1962; K. Göldner, 'Der Thüringer Bauernaufstand vom Jahre 1123', in *Aus der Vergangenheit der Stadt Erfurt*, vol. 1, Erfurt: Rat der Stadt Erfurt, 1955, pp. 78–81 (which I have not seen); and the set of revolts from the 1230s onwards in Cohn, *Lust for Liberty*, pp. 27ff.

18 Gregory the Great, *Registrum epistolarum*, ed. P. Ewald and L. M. Hartmann, MGH, Epp., 1–2, Berlin: Weidmann, 1891–9, III.1; for other examples of Gregory's interest in peasant welfare, see e.g. I.42, II.50, XIII.35. The text to this note, as also those to nn. 19, 20, 22, 24, are revised versions of paragraphs in three publications, 'Space and society', *Framing*, and 'Passages to feudalism in medieval Scandinavia', in L. da Graca and A. Zingarelli (eds), *Studies on Pre-capitalist Modes of Production*, Leiden: Brill, 2015, pp. 141–57.

19 C. Wickham, *Studi sulla società degli Appennini nell'alto medioevo*, Bologna: Clueb, 1982, pp. 18–28, 104–5; L. Feller, *Les Abruzzes médiévales*, Rome: École française de Rome, 1998, pp. 191–6, 540–6.

20 See above all E. Müller-Mertens, 'Der Stellingaaufstand', *Zeitschrift für Geschichtswissenschaft*, 20, 1972, pp. 818–42; W. Eggert, 'Rebelliones servorum', *Zeitschrift für Geschichtswissenschaft*, 23, 1975, pp. 1147–64, at pp. 1154–60; and E. Goldberg, 'Popular revolt, dynastic politics and aristocratic factionalism in the early Middle Ages: the Saxon *Stellinga* reconsidered', *Speculum*, 70, 1995, pp. 467–501, the best and most detailed.

21 Lampert of Hersfeld, *Annales*, in *Lamperti monachi Hersfeldensis Opera*, ed. O. Holder-Egger, MGH, SS rer. Germ., 38, Hanover: Hahn, 1894, pp. 179, 183–5, 216, 220–2, 228, 236–8; Eggert, 'Rebelliones servorum', pp. 1160–4; I. S. Robinson, *Henry IV of Germany, 1056–1106*, Cambridge: Cambridge University Press, 1999, pp. 97–102.

22 See in most detail *Óláfs saga ins Helga*, ed. Bjarni Aðalbjarnarson, *Heimskringla*, 2, Íslenzk fornrit, 27, Reykjavík: Hið Íslenzka fornritafélag, 1945, esp. cc. 215–35. For the *bóndi* army, e.g. c. 226; cf. for similar phrasing in one of the poems by Sighvatr *skáld*, contemporary with the battle, c. 235. For *thorparar ok verkmenn*, c. 216. For selfishness, c. 181, contrast c. 205.

23 For the percentages of peasant landowning, J. R. Myking and C. Porskrog Rasmussen, 'Scandinavia, 1000–1750', in B. van Bavel and R. Hoyle (eds), *Social Relations: Property and Power*, Turnhout: Brepols, 2010, pp. 290–1.

24 See for Snorri's rhetorical strategies S. Bagge, *Society and Politics in Snorri Sturluson's Heimskringla*, Berkeley: University of California Press, 1991. For the birchlegs, see *Sverris saga*, ed. Thorleifur Hauksson, Íslenzk fornrit, 30, Reykjavík: Hið Íslenzka fornritafélag, 2007, cc. 8, 11, and following; and *Kulturhistorisk leksikon for nordisk middelalder*, 22 vols, Copenhagen: Rosenkilde og Bagger, 1956–78, s.v. Birkebeiner, vol. 1, cols 600–10.

25 See *The Gesta Normannorum Ducum of William of Jumièges, Orderic Vitalis and Robert of Torigni*, vol. 2, ed. E. M. C. van Houts, Oxford: Oxford University Press, 1995, p. 8; the best commentary is now B. Gowers, '996 and all that', *Early Medieval Europe*, 21, 2013, pp. 71–98.

26 R. Pastor, *Resistencias y luchas campesinas en la época del crecimiento y consolidación de la formación feudal Castilla y León, siglos X–XIII*, Madrid: Siglo veintiuno, 1980, pp. 122–41; for the main events, J. Puyol y Alonso, 'Las Crónicas anónimas de Sahagún', *Boletín de la Real Academia de la Historia*, 76, 1920, pp. 7–26, 111–22, 242–57, 339–56, 395–419, 512–19, at pp. 245, 253, 340, 399–400.

27 See Saxo Grammaticus, *Gesta Danorum*, 2 vols, ed. K. Friis-Jensen, Oxford: Oxford University Press, 2015, XV.4.1–30; Köhn, 'Freiheit', pp. 354–60, who also stresses provincial separatism – a motive which seems to me less important.

28 For Dithmarschen, P. Freedman, *Images of the Medieval Peasant*, Stanford, CA: Stanford University Press, 1999, pp. 199–201 gives a good guide. For the Stedinger, Köhn, 'Freiheit', pp. 325–34, summing up his previous work; W. Zihn, *Die Stedinger*, Oldenburg: self-published, 1983 (which I have not seen); M. Cassidy-Welch, 'The Stedinger crusade', *Viator*, 44, 2013, pp. 159–74. There was a parallel not-quite-crusade against the rebellious peasants of Drenthe in Frisia in 1227–34: R. de Graaf, *Oorlog om Holland, 1000–1375*, Hilversum: Uitgeverij Verloren, 2004, pp. 265–71.

29 *Die Chronik des Saba Malaspina*, ed. W. Koller and A. Nitschke, MGH, SS, 35, Hanover: Hahn, 1999, 120 (the peasants also sought help from the pope to protect their *libertatis status*); see S. Carocci, *Signorie di Mezzogiorno*, Rome: Viella, 2014, pp. 525–7. Cohn, *Lust for Liberty*, p. 28, missed the Malaspina reference.

30 Capuchins/Caputiati in 1182–4: see Köhn, 'Freiheit', pp. 360–4; J. H. Arnold, 'Religion and popular rebellion, from the Capuciati to Niklashausen', *Cultural and Social History*, 6, 2009, pp. 149–69, at pp. 158–62; T. N. Bisson, *The Crisis of the Twelfth Century*, Princeton, NJ: Princeton University Press, 2009, pp. 475–82.

31 See for guides to recent work Wickham, *Framing*, pp. 551–78; S. Castellanos and I. Martín Viso, 'The local articulation of central power in the north of the Iberian peninsula (500–1000)', *Early Medieval Europe*, 13, 2005, pp. 1–42.

32 Asturias: *Crónicas asturianas*, ed. J. Gil Fernández, J. L. Moralejo, and J. I. Ruiz de la Peña, Oviedo: Universidad de Oviedo, 1985, pp. 136–7, 174. Castrojeriz: see Wickham, 'Space and society', n.23, for references. See in general Pastor, *Resistencias*, pp. 74–112.

33 Cohn, *Lust for Liberty*, pp. 28–30, makes a similar point for the Ligurian and Tuscan highlands.
34 Thietmar of Merseburg, *Chronicon*, ed. R. Holtzmann, MGH, SS rer. Germ., N. S., 9, Berlin: Weidmann, 1935, III.17–19, IV.13, VI.22–5, for the Liutizi revolts; for the parallel Polish revolts against Mieszko II and Kazimierz I in 1031–9, outside my area of study, see e.g. N. Berend, P. Urbańczyk, and P. Wiszewski, *Central Europe in the High Middle Ages*, Cambridge: Cambridge University Press, 2013, pp. 161–2.
35 See above all Köhn, 'Freiheit', for pre–1300; Cohn, *Lust for Liberty*, pp. 236–42, for how the meaning of *libertas* developed from 'liberties' to 'liberty', particularly after the Black Death.
36 See R. Faith, *The English Peasantry and the Growth of Lordship*, Leicester: Leicester University Press, 1997, for the process. English peasants did not, all the same, forget it: see R. Faith, 'The "Great Rumour" of 1377 and peasant ideology', in R. H. Hilton and T. H. Aston (eds), *The English Rising of 1381*, Cambridge: Cambridge University Press, 1984, pp. 43–73.
37 For an introduction to these families of texts with bibliography, see R. Fossier, *Enfance de l'Europe, Xe–XIIe siècles*, Paris: Presses universitaires de France, 1982, pp. 557–60.

8
INVOKING AND CONSTRUCTING LEGITIMACY
Rebels in the late medieval European and Islamic worlds

Patrick Lantschner

Introduction

Tyranny was a matter of concern to protesters and rebels in many urban societies around the late medieval Mediterranean world. To the minds of many city dwellers, it was not only expedient, but also right to oppose tyrants. This was as much true in late medieval Bologna, Northern Italy, as it was in the far-away city of Damascus, Syria.

In May 1459, a visit by Pope Pius II to Bologna, a subject city of the Papal State, took an unusual turn. In his oration to the pope, the city's official orator, Bornio da Sala, did not celebrate the city government, as was expected of him, but instead used this opportunity to denounce it. A famous jurist at Bologna's university, Bornio proclaimed, with an unmistakable allusion to the city's ruling elite, that it was more appropriate to say that Bologna was governed by a tyranny than to claim that it was free. The city government certainly got the message, and stripped Bornio of all his offices. The pope, whose relationship with Bologna was often fractious, was less displeased. He rewarded Bornio with a place on his delegation.[1]

Far away from Bologna, the inhabitants of al-Salihiyya, a suburb north of Damascus, held a banquet on 10 Jumada II 899/19 March 1494 to celebrate the dismissal of two particularly oppressive officials of the Mamluk regime, under whose rule Damascus had been since 658/1260. As the local chronicler informs us, inhabitants of this suburb had themselves only just killed an aide of 'tyrants' (*zalama,* sing. *zalim*) – quite possibly another official of the regime. They had been threatened with a heavy punishment by the city's Mamluk governor, but another cause for celebration at the banquet was that Ibn al-Furfur, one of the city's chief judges and a descendant of one of the most illustrious families of Damascus, had successfully intervened to prevent this penalty from being imposed.[2]

In both cases, city dwellers were not only concerned about tyranny, but they felt at liberty to act on their complaints. In Bologna, Bornio da Sala critiqued the regime headed by the Bentivoglio family who stood accused of ruling the city like tyrants and found themselves threatened by plots in 1449, 1488, and 1501. However, it took until 1506 for the Bentivoglio to be ousted in the wake of warfare and internal revolt.[3] In the final decades of Mamluk rule in Damascus, accusations of tyranny and oppression against numerous Mamluk officials led to murders, protests, and riots. In 903/1497, the urban population of Damascus was embroiled in a full-scale civil war over which Mamluk faction to support, and in 907/1501 three of the city's suburbs were involved in battles with the governor's troops over Mamluk fiscal policies.[4]

Situated in highly urbanised regions and of roughly equal size at the end of the fifteenth century, Bologna and Damascus are two interesting cities to compare because they saw an especially marked density of revolts and wars. In spite of the fact that they represented mostly unconnected historical realities, tyranny and the organisation of political activities against it constituted an important part of public life in both cities. Protesters and rebels frequently made claims and engaged in actions which suggested that they thought of their activities as legitimate. In both cities, such ideas were deeply embedded in the fragmentation of their respective political arenas. This fragmentation manifested itself on two levels: it concerned the organisational structures of urban life as much as the legal frameworks of cities. I have argued elsewhere that Bologna and Damascus were the sites of multiple units of political organisation around which continuous negotiations of political alliances took place.[5] In the context of this chapter, I will especially focus on the legal frameworks which crystallised around the fragmented organisational structures of urban life, and in whose context protesters and rebels were able to construct their own rationalities of political action.

The complexity of the legal frameworks of Bologna and Damascus is clearly apparent in these cities' structures of governance. Bologna, like other central and later medieval Italian cities, was governed by a communal government which was itself fragmented into different jurisdictional agencies. At the same time, guilds and guild-like organisations, neighbourhoods, ecclesiastical bodies, or even factions and parties were directly or indirectly involved in regulating, policing, and competing for control over different aspects of public life. Although the commune was progressively able to assert its power over the city and the *contado* (the hinterland under the city's jurisdictional control), communal governments rarely stood above political competition in the city: they often were the coveted prize for rival political coalitions that did not shy away from revolt to plot their way to power. External political players also played important jurisdictional roles. For most of the late Middle Ages, Bologna was subject to popes, their legates, and other instruments of papal rule, although the degree to which these interfered in urban governance varied considerably. For particular periods, Bologna slipped out of papal control and was instead ruled by independent communal governments, the lordships (*signorie*) of powerful families, or by the state of Milan and its governors.[6]

Mamluk Damascus, like other cities in the Near East, did not have an Italian-style urban government. However, a multiplicity of other political units were involved in the organisation of public life. The city's administration was headed by the Mamluk governor (*na'ib*) who belonged to the Turkoman-Circassian elite of slave origin that ruled the Mamluk state, whose capital was Cairo. In practice, there was a sprawling number of Mamluk jurisdictional agencies in Damascus, which were headed by rival Mamluk military commanders (*amirs*) and had varying judicial, fiscal, or military powers. Most prominent was the *muhtasib*, the state-appointed official in charge of public spaces, and the *wali*, the city's police chief. Other units of political organisation were more firmly grounded in the city's own structures. This could be said for the city's suburbs whose fighting bands were involved in negotiations with governors and military confrontations, or the city's religious scholars (*ulama*) who played an important role in judicial and legal administration. Many of the city's chief judges (singl. *qadi*) were drawn from major Damascene families and part of the patronage networks that developed around endowed religious institutions (*waqf*).[7]

The multiple centres of governance in Bologna and Damascus themselves existed in the context of plural systems of law, an issue of relevance to protesters and rebels who were eager to claim legitimacy for their actions. Both our cities were major centres for the systematic study of specific legal systems that were of critical importance in respectively Latin Europe and the Islamic world: Roman and canon law in Bologna, and Islamic law in Damascus.[8] At the same time, other forms of law existed alongside these highly systematised and scholarly legal systems. Bologna's pacts (*capitula*) with the Papal State enjoyed an important legal status, as did the statutes of the commune and the guilds. Moreover, canon law in Bologna regulated not only the Church and issues pertaining to the Church, but was also the law of the Papal State.[9] In Damascus, the equity-based jurisdiction (*siyasa*) of state agencies extended into a large area of social life that was not or only insufficiently covered by Islamic law, but was at the same time closely informed by it. Recent research into *siyasa* jurisdiction suggests that the absence of codification should not suggest that it was arbitrary and unsystematic.[10] Moreover, in both later medieval Europe and the Near East other legal sources, such as legal opinions or custom, could be said to enjoy a particular legal status and were also often recognised as such by official law.[11]

The fragmented political landscapes of Bologna and Damascus provided entirely the right substrate for rebels. As we know from recent studies of late medieval revolts in both European[12] and Near Eastern cities,[13] rebels were eager to develop a wide range of strategies to justify and legitimate their actions. This chapter considers how the fragmented legal frameworks of Bologna and Damascus allowed rebels to carve out their own rationalities of legitimation. Accusations against tyranny, and actions based on them, revealed precisely such a process. On the one hand, city dwellers drew on existing ideas about justice and the law which condemned tyrannical rule, but, on the other hand, city dwellers also developed their own rationales which could include notions of tyrannicide or rebellion in spite of the fact that much of the political theory of Latin Europe and the Islamic world rejected acts of political disobedience. This is a trend well known to scholars of legal anthropology. Earlier interpretative frameworks often viewed the law as a static force which existed autonomously from social processes, and which actors either aspired to or broke. Scholars now prefer to speak of how a variety of actors created their own 'legal cultures'. They acted on the basis of an amalgam of existing legal norms, practices, and institutions, but at the same time created their own rules and rationalities.[14] Such processes have often been seen as disjointed from how political and intellectual elites understood the law, but in the fragmented political frameworks of Bologna and Damascus no such rigid lines can be drawn.[15]

In this light, when protesters and rebels claimed legitimacy for their actions, they appropriated and transformed a mixture of explicit or implicit rules that were recognised as regulating public life and that thereby provided a framework for argumentation. Anthropologists and legal scholars disagree profoundly on whether to apply the epithet 'legal' to a vast variety of rules emanating from different sources, but it seems defensible to do so in the fragmented context of medieval European and Islamic cities where the boundaries between 'official' and other kinds of rules were fluid.[16] The case studies of Bologna and Damascus illustrate a variety of ways in which rebels invoked legitimacy for their actions within the complex legal frameworks of their cities: they showed an understanding of the current political and legal system, often acted in close cooperation with legal professionals, and adopted practices which were closely related to legal procedures. Their opponents could, of course, argue that such appropriations were illicit and amounted to acts of disobedience. Rebels, however, rarely admitted to or even viewed themselves as guilty of disobedience. It is in this respect that it becomes clear how rebels were constructing their own legal spheres. What is interesting is that there was a certain regularity and continuity to such constructions: the cases here chosen for both Bologna and Damascus show continuities that ran over more than 100 years, and suggest that it was possible to invoke and construct rationales of political action according to which protest and rebellion could be understood as legitimate. As will be seen, even jurists in both Europe and the Islamic world, perhaps in response to the political realities that surrounded them, developed various rationales to legitimate, or at least mitigate punishments for, rebellion.

Bologna

A concern with the law has always permeated the political culture of late medieval Bologna, as recent work by Giuliano Milani, Sarah Blanshei, Angela De Benedictis, and myself has suggested.[17] Much of this was, of course, a reflection of Bologna's status as a major centre for the study of law. In her study of Bologna's revolt of 1506, on which this chapter also draws, De Benedictis has shown in great detail how juristic theories of just war and licit resistance framed the argumentation of the major players.[18] Such conceived notions of legality did not only inform the activities of legal professionals. A comparison between the revolt of 1506 and another episode of intense political conflict 100 years earlier, in 1376, suggest that rebels from many different walks of life were keen on operating, or be seen as operating, within existing legal frameworks whose particular institutions, structures of obedience, and underlying legal traditions they did not want to disrupt.

On the night of 19–20 March 1376, amidst a disastrous war that affected the entire Papal State, a coalition of Bologna's guilds, its university, and its two main parties rebelled against papal overlordship. Many of the actions of the rebels suggested that they were themselves fighting a war: they carried a banner with the inscription *Libertà*, the troops of major families in the city's *contado* occupied strategic points in the city, and the papal legate, who had been deprived of his ring by one of the rebels, was effectively forced to flee the city. At the same time, the rebels were concerned to take actions which suggested continuity with known legal arrangements. First and foremost, they re-established the city's commune whose powers had been greatly reduced in the preceding period, but whose history reached back more than 200 years. Not only communal institutions benefited from the revolt. Guilds, which had been potent organisations in the thirteenth century, saw their powers boosted through the creation of a new governmental college for guild leaders and the redaction of new guild statutes.[19]

The rebels were also keen on stressing that their aim was not disobedience to their overlord. One month after the revolt, the urban government despatched a lawyer, Giacomo Preunti, to argue Bologna's case before a court that the papal legate had set up in neighbouring Ferrara. Preunti argued that, amidst the terrible war that was ravaging around Bologna, the Bolognese simply had to act in this way, in order to prevent the city from falling 'into the hands of tyrants' (*in manibus tirannorum*).[20] Rumours had, in fact, been circulating that the pope was willing to deliver Bologna to the marquis of Ferrara and it is presumably to him that Preunti was referring.[21] As so often, tyranny was presented as a legitimate cause for even as drastic a political act as the de facto overthrow of the papal regime in Bologna. The very concept of tyranny was itself closely bound up with ideas of law and justice. In the most famous medieval treatise on this subject, the contemporary jurist Bartolo da Sassoferrato (d. *c.*1357) had defined a tyrant, in a formulation borrowed from Pope Gregory the Great, as someone who 'does not rule by law' (*non iure principatur*).[22] On the basis of a long tradition of thought in which diverse strands of Roman and canon law, theology, and Aristotelian philosophy intersected, Bartolo distinguished between two types of tyrant: first, tyrants 'by defect of title' (*ex defectu tituli*) who had usurped their office and had no legal entitlement to it; second, tyrants 'by conduct' (*ex parte exercitii*) whose actions, instead of serving the common good, only benefit the tyrant himself. By acting unfairly, the tyrant kept the city in a state of permanent division and this, according to Bartolo, prevented him from delivering fair judgements, thus leading to a breach of the *Lex Iulia de vi publica*.[23] It is unlikely that the Bolognese only had the marquis of Ferrara in mind when they were concerned about tyranny. In the previous decade, Bologna had seen the heavy-handed rule of Cardinal-Legate Gil Albornoz who had streamlined papal rule in Central Italy. Many of the rebels, particularly the *contado*-based families that played such an important role in the revolt, bore grudges against the papal regime.[24] In fact, they also attacked one of the city's principal judicial officers, the *podestà* – not, as one of the chroniclers explained, because he was a man with a particularly evil disposition, but because governments that do not let their officers exercise justice bring about harm in the city.[25]

The rebel coalition, in any case, rapidly broke apart. By July 1377, a splinter group negotiated a peace treaty with Pope Gregory XI which, in return for the city's 'perpetual' subjection to papal rule, foresaw a wide-ranging administrative, fiscal, and judicial autonomy for the commune of Bologna.[26] This did not stop further revolts from happening over the coming decades.[27] Indeed, a more lasting settlement was only achieved in 1447 when Pope Nicholas V established shared rule by the papal legate and the *Sedici Riformatori della Libertà*, an exclusive college which existed largely outside the complex jurisdictional structures of communal government in Bologna and which was manned by members of Bologna's elite. This was a clever move, if one that showed less regard for legal traditions than many rebels did. The *Sedici Riformatori* had existed intermittently since 1393, ostensibly to protect Bologna's liberty, but in practice became a quasi-government in the city that undermined ancient communal institutions and political procedures that had been prescribed in the city's statutes. Since the college was increasingly the preserve of a faction around the Bentivoglio family, their behaviour was somewhat easier to predict and, perhaps, to control. Although at times rocky, it was the partnership between the pope and the Bentivoglio faction which somewhat calmed down the turbulent politics of Bologna for the following decades.[28]

However, this agreement, too, broke apart in 1506 – the second episode of revolt in Bologna that is discussed here.[29] This year saw two distinct moments of intense political conflict. The first was between Pope Julius II and the Bentivoglio faction, and lasted from summer to early November.[30] Himself formerly a bishop of Bologna, Julius had become concerned about the Bentivoglio family's overweening power. After a failed attempt at achieving a negotiated solution, Julius took the drastic step of putting Bologna under interdict and mobilised his troops to take over the city with the help of allied French troops. Bologna defied papal orders to deliver the Bentivoglio to the pope and also mobilised its own troops for war. Accusations of tyranny were, again, at the centre of this confrontation, and were made by both sides. According to Niccolò Machiavelli, then present at the papal court, Julius claimed that he wanted to free Bologna from the tyranny of the Bentivoglio, thereby echoing accusations which had again and again been made from within Bologna throughout the second half of the fifteenth century.[31] Bologna again mobilised one of its jurists against the pope. In a legal opinion, the Bolognese law lecturer Giovanni Crotto argued that it was Julius II who operated against the law: Julius acted against the settlement of 1447 and disturbed the city's order, he created fear and suspicion and damaged the Papal State as a whole, and he associated himself with men who wanted to destroy Bologna. In Crotto's view, all this justified Bologna's resistance to papal orders – indeed, he even argued that the Bolognese could legitimately appeal to a general church council about the pope's reprehensible conduct.[32] Such accusations were themselves linked to the Europe-wide unpopularity of Julius II who was famously ridiculed by Erasmus as 'a tyrant worse than worldly, an enemy of Christ, the bane of the Church'.[33]

The second conflict erupted after 2 November when, to everyone's surprise, the Bentivoglio fled the city with their closest associates.[34] In an even more surprising volteface, the *Sedici Riformatori*, manned by associates of the Bentivoglio, promptly declared their intention to submit to the pope and rumours circulated that they came to an agreement with the French troops which had besieged Bologna in the name of the pope. Between 3 and 4 November, the *popolo* of Bologna, apparently led by minor guildsmen, stormed the city's central square, forced the *Sedici* and all other communal office-holders to leave the governmental palace, appointed their own government, and coordinated attacks against the French troops. This clearly was a revolt which was aimed at the Bentivoglio faction, but the degree to which the rebels were in favour of or hostile to the pope is not fully clear. At any rate, they had little choice. As early as 6 November, they let the pope and his troops into his city against guarantees that promised the withdrawal of the French. It is unlikely, however, that the pope, who later confirmed the terms of the 1447 settlement, was held in particularly high regard. In the following years, two statues that had been erected in Julius's honour were destroyed, as was the citadel which Julius built in order to exercise better control over the city. As early as 1511 the Bentivoglio returned to Bologna, this time with the help of French troops.[35]

One of the ways in which rebels invoked and constructed their own ideas of legitimacy was their slogan for greater 'liberty' (*libertas, libertà*), something that was also characteristic of revolts in other European cities.[36] The insurgents of March 1376 proclaimed 'the state of the *popolo* and of liberty' (*stato popolare e di libertà*), and carried a banner with the inscription *Libertà* which had been handed to them by the famously independent city-state of Florence.[37] In the crisis of 1506, both sides claimed to act in the name of liberty. Christoph Scheurl, a German law student in Bologna and a supporter of the Bentivoglio, wrote to his uncle that the Bolognese wanted to preserve the 'sweetest liberty' (*libertatem dulcissimam*) which they had enjoyed for years under the Bentivoglio rather than succumb to 'the papal yoke' (*iugum pontificium*).[38] By contrast, in a meeting of the papal consistory on 17 August, Pope Julius II declared his intention to go to Bologna 'to reform or liberate the city and the *popolo* from the yoke of the Bentivoglio' (*pro reformatione, seu liberatione ipsius Civitatis et Populi a iugo Bentivolorum*).[39] 'Liberty' was, of course, a term with many meanings, but it was closely associated with the polycentric landscape of medieval cities like Bologna. Communes, guilds, and other jurisdictional institutions all possessed specific 'liberties' alongside other 'franchises' and 'privileges' which were enshrined in numerous medieval charters and characteristic of the legal language which rebels invoked. In both 1376 and 1506, rebels framed their demands in such ways as to increase or reduce the positive 'liberties' held by specific institutions, such as powers of the commune, the guilds, or external powers to pass statutes, elect officials, or fulfil particular judicial roles.[40]

Another meaning of liberty was much less important in the revolts of 1376 and 1506, and perhaps in many other urban revolts: the complete independence from a superior jurisdiction. In 1376, the rebels did throw out the papal legate and did also not seek papal permission for their re-establishment of the commune, but they were careful not to claim independence from the Papal State – nor was this even the primary aim of most rebels, as their willingness to return under papal overlordship only one year later demonstrates. When arguing before the legatine court, Giacomo Preunti even denied that the Bolognese had rebelled and argued that they had been constrained to form their own government in order to safeguard peace when the papal legate had left the city.[41] In 1506, not even Julius II's wildest accusations mentioned any ambitions for independence on the part of Bologna. In fact, the stated objective of the Bolognese, to have the settlement of 1447 reaffirmed, foresaw joint sovereignty between the papal legate and the *Sedici Riformatori di Libertà*. It was on the basis of this settlement that they justified their resistance. As Crotto argued in his legal opinion, the pope's disrespect for the settlement and his attempt wholly to appropriate power over the city entitled the Bolognese to resist his demands, even though the pope needed justly to be recognised as its ruler.[42]

Rebels in 1376 and 1506 were also concerned to follow procedures that were connected with the legal and jurisdictional framework of Bologna. At different moments in these revolts, rebels rang the commune's bells to assemble the *popolo* – a type of legal action identified by contemporary jurists as indicating corporate responsibility, whether this was through 'ordinary' councils or 'extraordinary' assemblies. This, too, was the invocation of an established political identity: a large part of Bologna's ruling elite in the fourteenth and fifteenth centuries had emerged from the *popolo*, a political force which had its origins in legal corporations composed of artisans and merchants and which had come to control the commune in the course of the thirteenth century.[43] Immediately after the revolt of March 1376, bells were rung to convene the commune and the *popolo* of the city of Bologna.[44] A famous lawyer, Riccardo da Saliceto, explained to this assembly in both Latin and Italian that, in the absence of a governor, the Bolognese needed to make their own provisions. Stating that the jurisdictional rights of other parties would not be infringed, the assembly charged Riccardo with the defence of the city and elected 16 officials to whom it delegated full legal authority, jointly to be held with other communal institutions created by them, for the months of March and April. In the following months, this led to thorough institutional reforms, such as an overhaul of the colleges and councils of the commune as well as the redaction of new statutes for the city.[45] Similarly, on 3 November 1506, rebels, led by the carpenter Salvestro, stormed the palace of the *podestà*, climbed its turret, and rang the bells. Within half an hour, the *popolo* assembled in arms on Bologna's square and forcibly entered the Palazzo dei Signori where the *Sedici Riformatori* had been meeting. In an act that was presumably designed to mock their opponents, but also to reaffirm Bologna's peculiar legal identity, they caused the current office-holders to mount horses, carry the banner of the Church and other banners, and shout 'Church, Church, *popolo, popolo*' (*Ghiexia, Ghiexia, populo, populo*). Their opponents were then ordered to confront the French enemy troops alongside the militias of the *popolo*.[46] On the following day, the rebels elected a provisional government of 20 men which was to hold full legal authority and replaced the *Sedici Riformatori*. The rebels respected the customary practice to divide up the new government's membership equally between Bologna's four large neighbourhood districts (*quartieri*).[47]

Of course, it was not just legal practices, but also violence that characterised the revolts of 1376 and 1506. Rebels were also concerned about the legal dimensions of such activities. Giacomo Preunti, speaking before the legatine court at Ferrara, was keen to point out that any abuses against the legate and his personnel during the revolt of March 1376 would be investigated by the commune.[48] As a matter of fact, there had been transgressions, such as lootings, but a popular assembly condemned such episodes already five days after the uprising, and the *podestà* investigated more than 20 individuals for robbery in the wake of the revolt.[49] There were also types of violence which it was possible to view as licit. Rebels often imitated official judicial procedures or appropriated the city's judicial apparatus to punish or execute opponents in ways that frequently exceeded levels of violence or death tolls in actual street fighting.[50] One type of violence that rebels fell back on with particular frequency was connected with practices reminiscent of warfare. As has been seen, the revolt of 1376 itself took place amidst external war and in subsequent developments the troops of major families in the Bolognese *contado* also played an important role. In 1506, the Bolognese swiftly reacted to the pope's threats by mobilising for war. They appointed a war committee (*Cinque Savij della Guerra*), mobilised the militia of the *popolo*, and made them swear oaths. By preparing for war, Bologna's city government also made claims concerning its own political status. Its militia were, in fact, organised on the basis of neighbourhood structures that were closely associated with communal self-government: the *quartieri* as well as another smaller neighbourhood unit, the *gonfaloni*, both of which had traditionally fulfilled important roles in the organisation of communal government, fiscal administration, and policing.[51]

According to the medieval legal theory of war, formulated most powerfully by the theologians Raymond of Peñafort (d. 1275) and Thomas Aquinas (d. 1274), wars were licit if they were fought for a just cause (*iusta causa*), righteous intention (*recta intentio*), and authority (*auctoritas*).[52] Ironically, it was Pope Julius II who was arguing in his bull of excommunication, on the basis of these very principles, that he was embarking on a just war against the Bolognese.[53] Many political theorists denied that subjects could legitimately embark on wars against their superiors, since such forms of violence should be seen as acts of rebellion, and not of just war. However, in one tradition of interpretation, formulated by the Bolognese canon lawyer Giovanni da Legnano (d. 1383) and relevant throughout the early modern period, it was possible to fight a defensive war against one's superior if he acted 'against the law' (*contra ius*). As a papal supporter, Giovanni himself opposed the revolt of 1376, but his ideas were again echoed by jurists in the 1506 conflict.[54] The rebels themselves drew on practices that were closely associated with just war, such as the unfurled banners of sovereign powers which signified the declaration of public war.[55] During a parade on 28 October 1506, the urban militia carried the banners of the *popolo* as well as of particular *quartieri* and *gonfaloni*. While shouting 'War, war' (*Guera, guera*), they were undoubtedly once again invoking Bologna's past as an independent commune. After the revolt of the *popolo*, as we have seen, they forced their enemies, not without some irony, to carry the banners of the Church in whose true interest the rebels could claim to be acting.[56] The banner with the inscription *Libertas*, which the Bolognese rebels of 1376 were waving, itself had a connection with external warfare. The banner had been handed to Bologna by the sovereign commune of Florence which was, at this point, fighting a year-long war against the papacy. In 1378, a similar banner was to be used in the Ciompi revolt in Florence itself.[57]

Rebels in Bologna could fall back on an ample repertoire of slogans and practices that they could deploy in innovative ways. Many of these were connected to wider ideas that belonged to an amalgam of medieval interpretations of Roman law, Christian theology, and Aristotelian philosophy – links that were often made explicit by the legal professionals who were themselves part of or at least cooperated with rebel coalitions. In complex ways, such ideas underlay the multi-jurisdictional environment which ultimately directly inspired many of the rebels' slogans and practices: their concern with enhancing or reducing the liberties of particular institutions, their interest in legal procedures that were enshrined in decades or centuries of urban political life, and their appropriation of a military vocabulary in the name of their fight against tyranny.

Damascus

Two episodes of political conflict in Damascus, in respectively 791/1389 and 907/1501, also suggest that complaints against tyranny and demands for greater justice were closely tied up with the political and legal arrangements which regulated public life in that city. The fact that rebels were not concerned with the powers held by a communal government represents a critical difference with patterns of conflict in Bologna, but should also not be exaggerated, since rebels in Bologna did not only focus on the commune. Rebels in Damascus were just as concerned about numerous political agencies that governed political life in the city. Often these were agencies associated with the Mamluk regime, but urban centres of power, such as neighbourhoods, were also at stake in situations of protest and revolt. The Islamic framework of justice and Islamic law played an important role in framing the actions of city dwellers, but their interest in various urban political units suggests that rebels also invoked and constructed rationales of legitimation that were embedded in customary legal arrangements or in *siyasa*.

Damascenes were concerned about who ruled them, as their involvement in the frequent episodes of warfare between rival Mamluk factions suggests. A well-documented case is the civil war between Sultan Barquq and the Mamluk amir Mintash, governor of Malatya, which affected urban politics in Damascus, as well as virtually the entire Mamluk state, between 791/1389 and 795/1393. Initially a war between Mamluk factions, Damascenes themselves got embroiled once Mintash conquered Damascus in Rabi' II 791/April 1389 and ruled the city until Rajab 792/June 1390. Mintash's attempt to regain Damascus in Rajab 793/June 1391 again led to the involvement of various urban groups.[58] As is all too often the case, chroniclers identified such city dwellers rather indiscriminately as 'inhabitants of Damascus' (*ahl Dimashq*) or 'the people' (*al-'amma*), but there is mention of particular factions, markets, and neighbourhoods.[59] Three outlying suburbs of Damascus in particular, Maydan al-Hasa, al-Shuwayka, and al-Salihiyya, were identified as supporters of Mintash.[60] The crowds that supported Mintash brought grievances of their own to this conflict. Upon his conquest of Damascus, they not only stormed and plundered the houses of the Mamluk governor Turuntay, but also of al-Haydabani and Ibn al-'Ala'i, two officials that were closely associated with the fiscal system of the Mamluk regime in Damascus. Grievances about fiscal exactions often directly turned against officials who were assigned the collection of specific taxes, confiscations, or the enforcement of forced purchases as part of their payment. Al-Haydabani was a high-ranking amir who stood accused of accumulating wealth through his fiscal oppression, and Ibn al-'Ala'i was one of the government's highest-ranking officials (*ustadar*).[61] As they left al-Haydabani's house, carrying clothing, money, and furnishings in their hands, the crowds were chanting: 'The house of the tyrant [*zalim*] is destroyed, albeit at the right time'.[62]

As in Bologna, legal experts took a keen interest in such conflicts. The most extensive contemporary chronicler of these events, Ibn Sasra, was himself a prominent member of the city's *ulama* and, therefore, almost certainly well-versed in Islamic law. Ibn Sasra left little doubt that just governance was at the heart of these conflicts. Initially, he welcomed Mintash's takeover, bemoaning the injustice reigning in Damascus and citing a barrage of passages in the Quran and Hadith, but also the Torah and the Bible, about the punishments awaiting tyrants.[63] Soon disappointed by the new regime, Ibn Sasra then came to denounce Mintash as a tyrant about whose fall the people rejoiced.[64] This, however, did not stop Ibn Sasra from applying the same epithet to Sudun Baq, the governor appointed by Barquq after Mintash's fall.[65] Drawing on a long tradition of Islamic political thought, Ibn Sasra repeatedly invoked the duty of rulers to provide justice. In one lengthy digression, in which he relied heavily on a political tract by the Andalusian-born scholar al-Turtushi (d. 520/1126 or 525/1131), Ibn Sasra warned:

> When the sultan acts justly, justice spreads out among his subjects ... But when the sultan is unjust, injustice spreads in the land and the people become weak; rights are suppressed; they become addicted to wrongdoing and they pervert weights and measures. Thereupon blessing is withheld and the heavens are prevented from giving rain; the seeds dry up and cattle perish, because of their withholding charity and because false oaths have spread among them. Cunning and stratagems increase in their midst and shame grows amongst them.[66]

Ibn Sasra was unwilling to condone rebellion in explicit terms and left it rather unclear how the collapse of unjustly governed politics would come about. However, he was clearly aware that resistance was one option. Rather approvingly, he cited the case of one 'Abbasid governor of Damascus, Salim ibn Hamid, whose injustice cost him his life in a rebellion of the city's inhabitants.[67]

Rebels and their supporters were highly concerned about how they were ruled. This became especially evident in another violent conflict in Jumada I 907/November 1501, when battles erupted between the Mamluk regime and city dwellers. The rebel coalition was mainly composed by the people (*ahl*) of the outlying suburbs al-Shaghur and Maydan al-Hasa – later to be joined by inhabitants of the suburb al-Qubaybat – who had agreed to proceed against the newly arrived governor, Qansuh al-Burj, and his entourage. In the words of the principal chronicler of these events, the religious scholar Ibn Tulun, their alliance was aimed at the 'tyranny' (*zulm*) of the regime.[68] Again, the rebels associated particular officials with bad rule. Initially at least, they rejected negotiating with Qansuh until he handed over the *ustadar* 'Abd al-'Aziz who was hated for the spiralling fiscal exactions that he had imposed on Maydan al-Hasa, one of the suburbs which played a leading role in the uprising. A similar demand was made concerning an official associated with the entourage of the *muhtasib*.[69] The grievances of the rebels were closely associated with their expectations of just government. The rebels especially hated a penalty tax which governors routinely imposed on neighbourhoods where a murder had been committed by an unknown killer. This tax had developed out of the payment of blood money (*diya*) which according to Islamic law was owed in such cases by the inhabitants of the quarter, the owner of the house, or the passenger and crew of the boat where a dead body was found. In late ninth- and early tenth-/late fifteenth- and early sixteenth-century Damascus, however, governors had drastically increased the frequency and remit of such penalties whose revenues seem to have disappeared in their coffers.[70] Sultan al-'Adil al-Tumanbay had actually banned such fines only one year before the outbreak of hostilities, as was confirmed across Damascus by inscriptions that survived into the twentieth century. It was, in fact, only Qansuh's promised abolition of this penalty which, at least temporarily, halted the hostilities in early Jumada II 907/December 1501.[71]

The penalties did, in fact, not only provoke such hostility because they violated the urban population's understanding of right, but because they touched on important structures of urban governance. The target of these fiscal exactions often were the major suburbs of Damascus which had their own forms of political organisation and which were threatened to be undermined by intrusive Mamluk officials. Most important among these forms of organisation were fighting bands known as *zu'r*, semi-permanent groups of youths whose activities ranged from enforcing local economic monopolies to conducting negotiations with, as well as organising violent attacks on, the Mamluk regime.[72] The murder fines were themselves a device of suppressing the violent activities of the *zu'r* who retaliated in the name of their neighbourhoods by killing the officials that were supposed to collect them.[73] It is not surprising that the *zu'r* also played a fundamental role in the bloody conflict of 907/1501. In their negotiations with the governor's representatives it was the *zu'r* who were identified as doing the fighting, and it was their leaders who put forward the rebels' demands which included the execution of tax collectors. True to their role as political players, it was also the *zu'r* leader of al-Shaghur, Ibn al-Tabbakh, who struck the deal with the governor, and it was the *zu'r* who invited one of the governor's officials to celebrate this agreement over a dinner.[74] The legitimacy of the *zu'r* was much contested, and many of their suburbs' inhabitants were deeply aggrieved by the violence which they unleashed.[75] Nevertheless, some city dwellers undoubtedly supported the *zu'r* and indeed benefited from their activities. Even the *ulama* were engaged in a debate on whether the violence of the *zu'r* could be justified as licit when they acted against the subordinates of tyrants.[76] The stance of the Mamluk regime itself remained ambiguous: although Qansuh and his troops brutally suppressed the *zu'r* half a year after the peace, Mamluk governors and amirs continued to hire *zu'r* as military forces in the years to come.[77]

Rebels' concerns about the political agencies of the Mamluk state or neighbourhoods showed that they were acutely aware of and concerned about the distribution of power in their city. Shifts in the structures of power also prompted shifts in the patterns of conflict: in the wake of political reforms during the Ottoman period, popular protest particularly targeted the chief *qadi* of the Hanafi school of Islamic law, who had become one of the Ottoman regime's most powerful figures in Damascus.[78] Their interest in the distribution of power between different organisational structures was, however, not the only way in which protesters and rebels showed a concern with legal arrangements, whether they were officially sanctioned or just recognised as legitimate by many of the city dwellers. An important role in their actions was also played by their understanding of practices that were closely associated with Islam and its provision of justice. One of Islam's fundamental tenets was that it prescribed a divine or revealed law (*shari'a*) which promised justice as much in this world as in the next. This law preceded all human political formations and it was the duty of every Muslim to obey it.[79] There was much debate among Islamic scholars, including legal circles of Damascus in the later Middle Ages, on who should enforce this law, and more specifically who should enforce the Quranic prescription to 'command right and forbid wrong' (Q. 3:104). Most, though not all, scholars agreed that the state should play the main role, but many also accorded this duty to legally competent ordinary believers. Indeed, the term *muhtasib* was not only used for the state official in charge of public order, but could also be used for anyone who exercised this duty.[80]

Two important caveats are necessary before describing the behaviour of rebels in this respect. In developing their arguments and practices, rebels were not only drawing upon an existing Islamic framework of justice, but also constructing what Islamic law meant to them. As recent scholarship, including scholarship on the Mamluk period, has pointed out, Islamic law was not a monolithic block, but subject to constant evolution, continuous disputes, and ongoing reinterpretation in the wake of its appropriation by numerous political actors. In invoking and constructing an Islamic framework of justice, rebels mirrored the behaviour of other powerful players, such as state agencies whose jurisdiction was often closely informed by and itself further developed the Islamic framework of justice. For instances, *muhtasibs*, as Karen Stilt has shown, were not only involved in the regulation of markets and the policing of the public order, but also the supervision of public devotional practices from the organisation of mandatory prayer lessons to the enforcement of fasting.[81] The other important caveat is that the rhetoric and practices associated with the Islamic framework of justice were, of course, not the only vocabulary of legitimation which protesters and rebels could draw on. Amina Elbendary, Konrad Hirschler, Boaz Shoshan, and James Grehan have studied a whole range of possible vocabularies, such as shutting shops or rioting out of a sense of 'moral economy' about the unfair distribution of food supplies, or using state courts to petition the sultan or other officials about their grievances in the context of the Mamluk state's own promise to deliver justice.[82] As far as the latter is concerned it is interesting that towards the end of the Mamluk period the availability of such courts also drastically increased, often precisely in order to respond to the growing numbers of petitions from disgruntled commoners about supposedly tyrannical officers. As Yossef Rapoport has recently suggested, such courts, although ostensibly based on the authority of *siyasa*, also took account of, invoked, and even the transformed the application of Islamic law.[83] The Islamic framework of justice was therefore not the only relevant framework, but it offered a crucial point of orientation. As far as the rebels of Damascus were concerned, this manifested itself in two ways: first, religious leaders could play an important role in conflict; second, protesters and rebels frequently invoked slogans and practices that were associated with Islam.

Protesters were often keen to associate themselves with or accept the intercession of *ulama* or other religious leaders, such as Sufi shaykhs. Religious scholars often disapproved of disobedience and rebellion, but their behaviour in actual situations of political conflict was complex. Amina Elbendary has argued that many *ulama* were often surprisingly ambiguous, also because many of them were more directly involved in conflicts than meets the eye.[84] An interesting example is Taqi al-Din Ibn Qadi 'Ajlun, a prominent scholar at several madrasas in late ninth-/fifteenth-century Damascus who for a while was also one of the city's chief *qadi*s. In the rebellion of 907/1501, it was Taqi al-Din who acted as a mediator between the Mamluk authorities and the protesters – a role which he had taken on again and again since the mid-880s/mid-1480s, when he helped broker agreements between protesters and the authorities over the exchange rate of silver and a forced sale of sugar. In 891/1486, when protest broke out over extraordinary taxes, the Mamluk governor asked Taqi al-Din to legitimate the tax and convey his opinion to the influential people of each neighbourhood. At the same time, Taqi al-Din also actively participated in collective action, such as when he was, directly or indirectly, involved in campaigns to seize and destroy alcohol.[85]

There were two areas of political conflict in which *ulama* and other religious leaders were involved with particular frequency. One of these was the policing of the public order in the name of Islam and their involvement in activities that came close to the responsibility of the *muhtasib*, such as in public campaigns against drinking.[86] Sometimes such actions were not necessarily hostile, but complementary to state power. In Dhu al-Hijja 885/February 1481, Taqi al-Din acted with the Mamluk grand chamberlain (*hajib al-hujjab*) Yashbak al-'Alay, although their target was a drinking place by the residence of another Mamluk amir. However, on other occasions, religious leaders did act against state authorities which they accused of tolerance and collusion. In Muharram 890/February 1485, Shaykh 'Abd al-Qadir was imprisoned and threatened with a fine because his followers had seized and burned hashish that they had found in the city. After an unsuccessful appeal to one of the chief *qadi*s, the protesters stormed the Umayyad Mosque before prayers, carrying banners, and chanting 'Allahu akbar'. They intimidated the governor so much that he chose to pray elsewhere and eventually gave in.[87]

Another area of conflict in which religious leaders became embroiled was the relatively frequent periods when the Mamluk regime broke down during factional warfare.[88] During a Mamluk civil war in 903/1497, the *muhaddith* (scholar of Prophetic traditions) Jamal al Din ibn al-Mabrad al-Salihi acted as a leader for the suburb of al-Salihiyya. Jamal al-Din apparently favoured neither side: in a statement reported by Ibn Tulun, he spoke badly of the rebels, but also added that the most treacherous men of all was one of the amirs on the sultan's side. Perhaps favouring a position in which al-Salihiyya would remain neutral, and enjoy greater autonomy, he persuaded the inhabitants to desist from directly fighting the rebel Mamluk faction. At the request of the suburb's inhabitants, he then authored a letter to turn down the cooperation offered to the suburb by one of the rebel leaders.[89] This was not the position of other *ulama*. When the Mamluk rebels made progress in capturing important sites in the town, Taqi al-Din and another shaykh, Shibab al-Din al-Mahwajab, actually met with the rebels, who told these representatives that they were not engaging in any act of rebellion at all.[90]

The support, or at least connivance, of the *ulama* and other religious leaders certainly went some way towards lending legitimacy to protests. Another way in which the Islamic framework of justice mattered was some of the slogans and practices which rebels adopted.[91] The slogan that they were most commonly reported to have shouted was 'Allahu akbar' (God is greatest), the so-called *takbir* – a pious exclamation constantly used in daily life, but one that unequivocally declared the shouter's affinity with Islam.[92] Protesters also had a predilection for Fridays, the day on which communal prayers took place.[93] Since masses of people met on this day, this was an obvious moment for rebels to organise, but it also was a highly symbolic one, since communal prayers had always been as much an occasion for the gathering of the Muslim community as it had been one in which political authority was displayed. Occasionally, rebels also disrupted the holding of communal prayers: they stopped muezzins from issuing the call to prayer, or they refused to attend such prayers outright.[94] Protest in Damascus did not only take place before the residences of Mamluk officials or in the neighbourhoods whose place in public life was at stake. The most frequent site of protest was the Umayyad Mosque whose minaret protesters sometimes also climbed to proclaim their aims. The Umayyad Mosque was not only the city's prominent Friday Mosque, but also an important gathering place for other public activities, such as reading sessions.[95] Mosques also sometimes played an important role in protest in other ways, such as when, in Muharram 897/November 1491, silk weavers from different neighbourhoods of Damascus protested against a tax on looms by waving the banners of their local mosques in front of the governor's residence.[96]

The interrelationship between Islamic and other practices of conflict is usefully illustrated in two days of protest in Jumada II 885/April 1490 which were described in great detail by Ibn Tulun and Ibn Tawq, a Damascene notary.[97] The regime viewed these events as so dangerous that it stopped their investigation only one month later out of a fear that this might provoke strife (*fitna*), a term which itself had strong Islamic connotations, as it referred to conflict within the Muslim community.[98] Protest erupted at the Umayyad Mosque after Friday prayer, while worshippers were delivering their individual supplications. A pious man from Maydan al-Hasa, Yusuf al-Bahlul, shouted: 'Woe to Islam! Where is the Islamic sense of honour [*al-ghayra al-islamiyya*] when this official from the entourage of the sultan [*al-khassaki*] oppresses the people through his confiscations?' Qarqamas,[99] the official in question, had arrived in Damascus to enforce confiscations and had attended Friday prayer with other Mamluk dignitaries. However, as he heard Yusuf's cry, he fled to his lodgings, while the other Mamluks took refuge inside the mosque. The crowds also began to shout the *takbir*, and Yusuf, crying out for succour, was helped to flee by a group around one Shaykh Faraj, perhaps a Sufi leader. In a turn of fortune, Faraj, who might have acted as a spokesperson for the protesters, found himself imprisoned and beaten by Mamluks. The fact that the protesters had used Islamic rhetoric against them was a matter of concern to the Mamluk dignitaries. One of them, the grand chamberlain, asked Faraj in the prison: 'Did you pronounce the *takbir* against me?' Faraj responded provocatively: 'I seek succour with Allah' (*a'udhu bi-Allah*).[100] A similar pattern was unfolding on the following day. This time, Shaykh Ibrahim al-Naji led a group of protesters from Maydan al-Hasa back to the city centre, where they staged further protests against Shaykh Faraj's imprisonment while shouting the *takbir* and waving banners. According to Ibn Tawq, this happened in the Umayyad Mosque, while Ibn Tulun suggests that Shaykh Ibrahim led the protesters to Qarqamas's lodgings. Quite clearly, the protest was coming dangerously close to escalating in ways that greatly worried the ruling elites of Damascus who saw themselves threatened by this sudden outburst of popular anger. In any case, the protesters only dispersed after the intercession of Mamluk dignitaries, the *qadi*, and the merchant 'Isa al-Qari, and with the promise that there would be no further mistreatment of the population.

The involvement of religious leaders, and the keenness of participants to employ a rhetoric and practices clearly associated with Islam, suggest that they were invoking the Islamic framework of justice to frame their actions – actions which, when viewed from a different angle, could be construed as amounting to disobedience and rebellion. Most of the protesters did not question the legality and authority of the Mamluk state or its particular agencies, but they constructed their own sense of where to draw the line between legitimate government and tyranny.

Conclusion

Patterns of conflict in other cities did not necessarily resemble the political cultures of Damascus or Bologna. In Cairo, the capital of the Mamluk state, protest took place much more frequently around the centres of Mamluk power, such as the space around the citadel which was not only the headquarters of the sultan and the Mamluk military, but also the site of the sultan's court of equity jurisdiction (*mazalim*). The killings of officials were somewhat rarer – instead, protest often took different forms: such as various modes of petitioning, perhaps stimulated by the profusion of Mamluk jurisdictional agencies in the city, or concealed forms of contestation, such as the mocking of Mamluk amirs during the annual feast of Nawruz, which was pre-Islamic in origin.[101] Florence, a famously factious city-state, was the site of Europe's most prominent revolt, the Ciompi uprising of July 1378 in which wool-workers, guilds, and a faction around the Medici took over the city's centres of authority in a quasi-military operation involving material, banners, and other symbols of war. However, outside that dramatic confrontation, conflict usually took different forms: it either centred on attempts of political factions to gain control over and subvert electoral procedures, communal councils, and the judicial apparatus through manipulation, or on concerted episodes of protest which could include the targeted assassination of opponents, but fell short of full-blown urban war.[102]

Because of the sheer variation between cities, it is not easy, and perhaps not even desirable, to make generalisations about the Near East and Italy as a whole. Indeed, some oft-repeated generalisations are not true. Rebels in Damascus were concerned about the balance and organisation of power in their city, even though their demands were not framed in terms of communes or corporations. Likewise, rebels in Bologna did not necessarily contest superior jurisdictions and were, in fact, often happy to find accommodation with external powers. It may be truer to say in that in Damascus rebels were ultimately more concerned about how power was *exercised* than how it was *distributed*: of course, it mattered which Mamluk faction was in power, or what role neighbourhoods were supposed to play in the urban arena, but such questions were arguably less central than the rebels' aspiration to principles that they derived from a complex framework of justice that was also, but not exclusively, influenced by Islam. Bolognese rebels were arguably much more directly obsessed with the precise jurisdictional and constitutional powers of external agencies, cities, and other institutions on which hinged the language of liberty, legal procedures, and military practices through which they expressed themselves in situations of protest and revolt.

It is striking that in Bologna no single legal framework played as central a role as that of Islam did in Damascus, even if we accept that the Islamic framework of justice was itself multidimensional and fraught with internal tensions. Indirectly, of course, Christian ideas of justice permeated theories of just war and city dwellers' expectations of just rule. However, for the most part, the protagonists of political conflicts in Bologna, a subject city of the Papal State, were often careful about dragging an *explicitly* religious dimension into their conflicts. There were, of course, exceptions. In 1506, the pope did put the city under interdict – a punishment which, among other sanctions, foresaw the suspension of most church services – while the pope's Bolognese enemies threatened to appeal against the pope to a general council of the church. On both sides, such a religious language of conflict was, however, generally avoided and there are remarkably few references to the direct invocation of Christian ideas and practices by rival political coalitions to justify their engagement in conflict.[103] The Christian religion was no less important to the city dwellers of Bologna than Islam was to the inhabitants of Damascus, and there were multiple ways in which the urban politics of Bologna and that of other Italian communes were deeply affected by the ideas, practices, and elites connected with their religious system.[104] A major difference with the Islamic world was, however, that in addition to being a framework of ideas and practices, Christianity also had its own well-defined institutional apparatus: the Church, which itself was an active political player in many different ways. The rebels of 1506 were, after all, invoking the pope not as their spiritual head, but as their overlord when they screamed 'Church, Church'.[105] Any mistaken application of such rhetoric could have terrible consequences. As was found by 'heretics' in many Italian cities, some of whom also had political ambitions, the invocation of Christian ideas and practices outside the parameters laid down by Church authorities could result in bitter repression. Rebels in the Islamic world could, of course, also face consequences for encroaching upon religious rhetoric, but in places like Bologna the Church apparatus added an additional dimension to the policing of religious rhetoric.[106]

In spite of such differences it is remarkable that, in both cities, city dwellers were able to construct particular rationales for the legitimation of protest and rebellion. It is tempting to speculate about possible links that might explain this convergence in the urban political cultures of two areas that were so distant from each other. Common to both Latin Europe and the Islamic world were ideas about the so-called circle of justice according to which the king at the top of society was dependent on the peasants at the bottom: they could only provide him with revenue if he was able to provide justice. Possibly originating in ancient Greek philosophy or with even earlier roots, the idea of the circle of justice circulated amply in both the Islamic world and Europe through texts such as the *Sirr al-asrar* or the *Secretum secretorum*, its Latin rendering.[107] More tangible than any direct ideological links was, however, the urban environment in which city dwellers operated. Bologna and Damascus were deeply fragmented into multiple units of political organisation and were characterised by a fragmented legal framework in ways that made cities of either region much more similar to each other than to the more monolithic and streamlined political entities of the modern Western world. Unlike the latter, the complex urban political arenas of Bologna and Damascus of the later Middle Ages offered a particular substrate on whose basis city dwellers were able to construct legal cultures that made it not only possible, but also potentially legitimate to fight tyranny.

In the fragmented urban arenas of Bologna and Damascus, the legitimacy of any particular action was, of course, itself controversial. As such, it is not surprising that in both Italy and the Near East jurists of this period developed legal doctrines that condemned any disobedience to rulers as acts of rebellion. At the same time, it may be no coincidence that jurists – most of whom lived in cities and were no doubt themselves exposed to political conflict – also hotly debated the question of legitimate resistance. In his above-mentioned defence of wars against superiors, Giovanni da Legnano drew on two passages of the Justinianic Code of Roman Law which jurists of the later Middle Ages and the early modern period continued to use in theories of legitimate resistance. In commenting on these passages, Bartolo da Sassoferrato, perhaps the most famous late medieval jurist, specifically allowed the rejection of governmental authority if an official carried out his duties against the interests of justice (*iniuste*), or if soldiers committed acts of injustice by, for instance, breaking agreements on billeting or by defiling property. Bartolo was as much concerned with legal theory as he was with political practice: he explained the circumstances under which friends and neighbours could be called for support, and even specified the words (*Succurrite, succurrite*) to shout in such a situation.[108] However, it should also be pointed out that in other writings, Bartolo was much less inclined to take such a position and instead extolled the importance of political obedience.[109] It must be wondered to what extent such apparent inconsistencies were related to the fact that such thinkers, particularly jurists, were themselves involved in political conflicts and developed their views accordingly.[110]

Islamic legal thinkers were somewhat less willing to justify resistance. However, they also developed a substantial body of laws, known as *ahkam al-bughat*, which mitigated punishments for rebellion if, among other conditions, the rebels' cause was based on the interpretation of recognised Islamic sources (*ijtihad*). Violence against rebels was only to be used as an absolute last resort, captured rebels were not to be killed, their property could not be confiscated, and all imprisoned rebels needed to be released as soon as the rebellion had ended.[111] In any case, the above-mentioned Islamic duty to command right and forbid wrong also provided legitimating rationales for the actions of protesters. Most Islamic lawyers agreed that legally competent Muslims could exercise it, although by our period few endorsed the exercise of this duty against the interests of state authorities. However, in practice, it may have been difficult to draw a line between acceptable and transgressive actions: state authority itself was often fractious, and rebels rarely saw themselves as such and openly questioned the authority of the state. Even chroniclers who were themselves trained in the religious sciences, as we have seen, often refrained from open criticism or even sympathised with protesters.[112]

Urban rebels were certainly aware of such debates, but their legal cultures existed and developed semi-autonomously from them. Theirs was, of course, not an understanding of 'legitimacy' that would necessarily have been recognisable even to those jurists who were sympathetic to them. However, the very difficulty of knowing where legitimacy lay in a web of intersecting normative rules, and of tying it to any of numerous political institutions, was the very stuff of urban politics and conflict. Ultimately, it was on the basis of this complex political and legal framework that rebels constructed their understanding of legitimacy and their particular legal spheres. It is remarkable that they were able to do so, over a sustained period of time, in two cities at opposite ends of the Mediterranean world.

Notes

1 This chapter follows a simplified version of the transliteration system used by the *International Journal of Middle East Studies*: diacritical markings have been omitted, and commonly used terms are given in their anglicised form. I gratefully acknowledge the assistance of Nikola Dukas Sardelis and Wahid Amin with certain of the Arabic texts cited in this chapter. Cherubino Ghirardacci, *Della historia di Bologna: Parte Terza*, ed. A. Sorbelli, RIS, new ser., 33/1, Città di Castello: Lapi, 1915–32, p. 170 (*chiamando più tosto tirannia, che libertà, che la città haveva*). See also Girolamo de' Borselli, *Cronica gestorum ac factorum memorabilium civitatis Bononie*, ed. A. Sorbelli, RIS, new ser., 23/2, Città di Castello: Lapi, 1912–29, pp. 94–5; Fileno Dalla Tuata, *Istoria di Bologna*, ed. B. Fortunato, 3 vols, Bologna: Costa, 2005, vol. 1, p. 321.

2 Ibn Tulun, *Mufakahat al-khillan fi hawadith al-zaman*, ed. M. Mustafa, 2 vols, Cairo: Wizara al-Thaqafa, 1962–4, vol. 1, p. 160.

3 Borselli, *Cronica*, pp. 89, 109–10; Ghirardacci, *Della historia*, pp. 130–7, 247–53, 303–6; Dalla Tuata, *Istoria*, vol. 1, p. 321; *Corpus chronicorum bononiensium*, ed. A. Sorbelli, 4 vols, RIS, 18/1, Città di Castello: Lapi, 1906–40, vol. 4, pp. 164–6, 173–5, 495–6, 505–8. For 1506, see below.

4 Ibn Tulun, *Mufakahat*, vol. 1, pp. 185–96, 199–200, 250–2; Ibn Tulun, *I'lam al-wara bi-man wulliya na'iban min al-atrak bi-Dimashq al-Sham al-kubra*, ed. M. A. Duhman, Damascus: Al-Matb'a wa-al-Jarida al-Rasmiyya, 1964, pp. 82–7, 141–5; Ibn Tawq, *Al-Ta'liq: yawmiyyat Shihab al-Din Ahmad ibn Tawq*, ed. J. al-Muhajir, 4 vols, Damascus: Institut français de Damas, 2000–7, vol. 4, pp. 1541–72.

5 P. Lantschner, 'Fragmented cities in the later Middle Ages: Italy and the Near East compared', *EHR*, 130, 2015, pp. 546–82.

6 For introductions to late medieval Bologna with extensive bibliographies, see R. Dondarini, *Bologna medievale nella storia della città*, Bologna: Pàtron, 2000; O. Capitani (ed.), *Bologna nel Medioevo*, Bologna: Bononia University Press, 2007. For an introduction to Italian cities and political formations in this period, see P. J. Jones, *The Italian City-State: From Commune to Signoria*, Oxford: Oxford University Press, 1997, pp. 521–83; A. Gamberini and I. Lazzarini (eds), *The Italian Renaissance State*, Cambridge: Cambridge University Press, 2012.

7 For introductions to Damascus and other Mamluk cities, see especially T. Miura, 'Urban society in Damascus as the Mamluk era was ending', *Mamluk Studies Review*, 10, 2006, pp. 157–93; I. Lapidus, *Muslim Cities in the Later Middle Ages*, Cambridge, MA: Harvard University Press, 1967; N. Luz, *The Mamluk City in the Middle East: History, Culture, and the Urban Landscape*, New York: Oxford University Press, 2014; K. Stilt, *Islamic Law in Action: Authority, Discretion, and Everyday Experiences in Mamluk Egypt*, Oxford: Oxford University Press, 2012.

8 For Bologna, A. Sorbelli, *Storia dell'Università di Bologna: il medioevo*, Bologna: Zanichelli, 1940; O. Capitani (ed.), *Cultura universitaria e pubblici poteri a Bologna dal XII al XV secolo*, Bologna: Istituto per la storia di Bologna, 1990. For Damascus, L. Pouzet, *Damas au VIIe/XIIIe siècle: Vie et structures religieuses dans une métropole islamique*, Beirut: Dar al-Machreq, 1991; M. Chamberlain, *Knowledge and Social Practice in Medieval Damascus*, Cambridge: Cambridge University Press, 1994; R. van Leeuwen, *Waqfs and Urban Structures: The Case of Ottoman Damascus*, Leiden: Brill, 1999.

9 A. De Benedictis, *Repubblica per contratto: Bologna: una città europea nello Stato della Chiesa*, Bologna: Il Mulino, 1995; the editors' introductions to *Gli statuti del comune di Bologna degli anni 1352, 1357, 1376 e 1389*, ed. V. Braidi, Bologna: Forni, 2002 and *Haec sunt statuta: le corporazioni medievali nelle miniature bolognesi*, ed. M. Medica, Modena: Panini, 1999. For the complex legal order in later medieval Europe and Italy, see P. Grossi, *L'ordine giuridico medievale*, Bari: Laterza, 1995; M. Sbriccoli, 'Legislation, justice and political power in Italian cities, 1200–1400', in A. Padoa Schioppa (ed.), *Legislation and Justice*, Oxford: Clarendon Press, 1997, pp. 37–55.

10 Y. Rapoport, 'Legal diversity in the age of Taqlid: the four chief qadis under the Mamluks', *Islamic Law and Society*, 10, 2003, pp. 210–28; Y. Rapoport, 'Royal justice and religious law: siyasah and shari'ah under the Mamluks', *Mamluk Studies Review*, 16, 2012, pp. 71–102; Stilt, *Islamic Law*. For a historical and conceptual introduction to Islamic law, see W. B. Hallaq, *Shari'a: Theory, Practice, Transformations*, Cambridge: Cambridge University Press, 2009.

11 For the Islamic world, see M. K. Masud, B. Messick, and D. S. Powers (eds), *Islamic Legal Interpretation: Muftis and their Fatwas*, Cambridge, MA: Harvard University Press, 1996; R. Shaham (ed.), *Law, Custom, and Statute in the Muslim World*, Leiden: Brill, 2007. For medieval Europe, see M. Sbriccoli, *L'interpretazione dello statuto: Contributo allo studio della funzione dei giuristi nell'età comunale*, Milan: Giuffrè, 1969; E. Cohen, *The Crossroads of Justice: Law and Culture in Later Medieval France*, Leiden: Brill, 1993, pp. 28–42.

12 See the contributions by Hartrich, Challet, Titone, among others, in this volume. See also the contributions in J. Dumolyn, J. Haemers, H. R. Oliva Herrer, and V. Challet (eds), *The Voices of the People in Late Medieval Europe*, Turnhout: Brepols, 2014; J. Dumolyn and J. Haemers, '"A bad chicken was brooding": subversive speech in late medieval Flanders', *P&P*, 214, 2012, pp. 45–86; C. Liddy and J. Haemers, 'Popular politics in the late medieval city: York and Bruges', *EHR*, 128, 2013, pp. 771–805; P. Lantschner, *The Logic of Political Conflict in Medieval Cities: Italy and the Southern Low Countries, 1370–1440*, Oxford: Oxford University Press, 2015, pp. 21–39.

13 A. Elbendary, *Crowds and Sultans: Urban Protest in Late Medieval Egypt and Syria*, Cairo and New York: The American University in Cairo Press, 2015; K. Hirschler, 'Riten der Gewalt: Protest und Aufruhr in Kairo und Damaskus', in S. Conermann and S. van Hees (eds), *Islamwissenschaft als Kulturwissenschaft*, Schenefeld: EB-Verlag, 2007, pp. 205–33; J. Grehan, 'Street violence and social imagination in late-Mamluk and Ottoman Damascus', *International Journal of Middle East Studies*, 35, 2003, pp. 215–36; D. Beaumont, 'Political violence and ideology in Mamluk society', *Mamluk Studies Review*, 8, 2004, pp. 201–25; B. Shoshan, 'Grain riots and the "moral economy": Cairo, 1350–1517', *Journal of Interdisciplinary History*, 10, 1980, pp. 459–78.

14 For the concept of legal culture, see L. M. Friedman, 'The place of legal culture in the sociology of law' and D. Nelken, 'Rethinking legal culture', in M. Freeman (ed.), *Law and Sociology*, Oxford: Oxford University Press, 2006, pp. 185–99, 200–24.

15 A similar point was made by L. Benton in her *Law and Colonial Cultures: Legal Regimes in World History*, Cambridge: Cambridge University Press, 2002, pp. 8–9.

16 See, for instance, Simon Roberts's argument for a distinction between government-backed 'law' and other kinds of rules: S. Roberts, 'After government: on representing law without the state', *Modern Law Review*, 68, 2005, pp. 1–24. For overviews on this debate, G. R. Woodman, 'Ideological combat and social observation: recent debate about legal pluralism', *Journal of Legal Pluralism and Unofficial Law*, 42, 1998, pp. 21–59; P. S. Berman, 'The new legal pluralism', *Annual Review of Law and Social Science*, 5, 2009, pp. 225–42. For interesting contributions to the subject of 'legalism' from both a historical and anthropological perspective, see P. Dresch and H. Skoda (eds), *Legalism: Anthropology and History*, Oxford: Oxford University Press, 2012; F. Pirie and J. Scheele (eds), *Legalism: Community and Justice*, Oxford: Oxford University Press, 2014.

17 G. Milani, *L'esclusione dal comune: Conflitti e bandi politici a Bologna e in altre città italiane tra XII e XIV secolo*, Rome: Istituto storico italiano per il Medio Evo, 2003; S. Blanshei, *Politics and Justice in Late Medieval Bologna*, Leiden: Brill, 2010; A. De Benedictis, 'Lo "stato popolare di libertà": pratica di governo e cultura di governo', in Capitani (ed.), *Bologna nel Medioevo*, pp. 899–950; De Benedictis, *Repubblica per contratto*; P. Lantschner, 'Justice contested and affirmed: jurisdiction and conflict in late medieval Italian cities', in Pirie and Scheele (eds), *Legalism*, pp. 77–96.

18 A. De Benedictis, *Una guerra d'Italia, una resistenza di Bologna: Bologna 1506*, Bologna: Il Mulino, 2004. For a similar argument concerning early modern Italy more broadly, see her recent *Tumulti: Moltitudini ribelli in età moderna*, Bologna: Il Mulino, 2013.

19 *Corpus chronicorum bononiensium*, vol. 3, pp. 309–18; Matteo Griffoni, *Memoriale historicum de rebus*

bononiensium, ed. L. Frati and A. Sorbelli, RIS, 18/1, Città di Castello: Forni, 1902, pp. 72–3. For this revolt, see O. Vancini, *La rivolta dei bolognesi al governo dei vicari della Chiesa*, Bologna: Zanichelli, 1906.
20 Published in Vancini, *La rivolta*, pp. 79–83.
21 *Corpus chronicorum bononiensium*, vol. 3, pp. 307–8.
22 Bartolo da Sassoferrato, 'Tractatus de Tyranno', in D. Quaglioni, *Politica e diritto nel Trecento italiano: Il 'De tyranno' di Bartolo da Sassoferrato*, Florence: Olschki, 1983, pp. 175–213, at 184.
23 Bartolo, 'Tractatus de tyranno', pp. 185–202.
24 Lantschner, *Logic of Conflict*, pp. 122–3; O. Vancini, 'Bologna della Chiesa', *Atti e memorie della R. Deputazione di storia patria per le provincie di Romagna*, 3rd ser., 24, 1906, pp. 239–320, 508–52; 25, 1907, pp. 16–108.
25 *Corpus chronicorum bononiensium*, vol. 3, p. 313.
26 *Codex diplomaticus dominii temporalis S. Sedis*, ed. A. Theiner, 3 vols, Rome: Imprimerie du Vatican, 1861–2, vol. 2, p. 599.
27 Lantschner, *The Logic of Political Conflict*, pp. 95–130.
28 On 1447, see De Benedictis, *Repubblica per contratto*, pp. 107–36. For the Bentivoglio regime, see also I. Robertson, *Tyranny under the Mantle of St Peter: Pope Paul II and Bologna*, Turnhout: Brepols, 2002; C. Ady, *The Bentivoglio of Bologna: A Study in Despotism*, Oxford: Oxford University Press, 1937.
29 In my analysis I have greatly learnt from and relied on Angela De Benedictis's study and interpretation of this revolt, *Una guerra d'Italia*, and followed her guidance on the principal sources.
30 Dalla Tuata, *Istoria*, vol. 2, pp. 470–81; Ghirardacci, *Della historia*, pp. 343–8.
31 Niccolò Machiavelli, *Opere*, ed. C. Vivanti, 3 vols, Turin: Einaudi, 1997–2005, vol. 2 (*Lettere: Legazioni e Commissarie*), pp. 1028–9, 1038–40.
32 Quoted and discussed in De Benedictis, *Una guerra*, pp. 116–22.
33 Erasmus, *The Julius Exclusus*, trans. P. Pascal, ed. J. Kelley Sowards, Bloomington: Indiana University Press, 1968, p. 83.
34 Dalla Tuata, *Istoria*, vol. 2, pp. 481–7; Ghirardacci, *Della historia*, pp. 348–53.
35 De Benedictis, *Una guerra*, pp. 158–60.
36 S. K. Cohn, Jr., *Lust for Liberty: The Politics of Social Revolt in Medieval Europe, 1200–1425*, Cambridge, MA: Harvard University Press, 2006, pp. 236–42; S. Ferente, 'Guelphs! Factions, liberty and sovereignty', *History of Political Thought*, 28, 2007, pp. 571–98; De Benedictis, 'Lo "stato popolare"'.
37 *Corpus chronicorum bononiensium*, vol. 3, p. 314.
38 *Christoph Scheurl's Briefbuch*, ed. F. von Soden and J. K. F. Knaake, Potsdam: Gropius'sche Bunchhandlung, 1867, p. 24. For Scheurl and an interpretation of this passage, see De Benedictis, *Una guerra*, pp. 26–9, 49–50.
39 *Le due spedizioni militari di Giulio II tratte dal Diario di Paride Grassi bolognese*, ed. L. Frati, Bologna: Tipografia Regia, 1886, p. 4.
40 Lantschner, *Logic of Political Conflict*, pp. 29–33.
41 Published in Vancini, *La rivolta*, pp. 81–2.
42 Machiavelli, *Opere*, vol. 2, p. 1039; for an analysis of Crotto's views on the settlement, De Benedictis, *Una guerra*, pp. 115–17.
43 W. Ullmann, 'The delictal responsibility of medieval corporations', *Law Quarterly Review*, 64, 1948, pp. 77–96. For the *popolo* movements, see A. Zorzi, 'The popolo', in J. M. Najemy (ed.), *Italy in the Age of the Renaissance*, Oxford: Oxford University Press, 2004, pp. 145–64.
44 Archivio di Stato, Bologna, Provvigioni in Capreto, 1, fols 1–3; published in *Gli statuti del comune di Bologna*, pp. lxxi–lxxviii.
45 *Gli statuti del comune di Bologna*, pp. lxxxix–cxxiv; G. Bosdari, 'Il comune di Bologna alla fine del secolo XIV', *Atti e memorie della R. Deputazione di storia patria per le provincie di Romagna*, 4th ser., 4, 1914, pp. 123–88.
46 Dalla Tuata, *Istoria*, vol. 2, pp. 483–4.
47 Ibid., vol. 2, pp. 484–5; Ghirardacci, *Della historia*, pp. 351–2.
48 Published in Vancini, *La rivolta*, p. 81.
49 Archivio di Stato Bologna, Curia del Podestà, Libri Inquisitionum et Testium, 224, no. 1, fols 1–3, 5–9r, 17–18r, 88–9r; Vancini, *La rivolta*, pp. 71–6.
50 H. Skoda, *Medieval Violence: Physical Brutality in Northern France 1270–1330*, Oxford: Oxford University Press, 2013, pp. 159–92; Lantschner, *The Logic of Political Conflict*, pp. 52–9.
51 Dalla Tuata, *Istoria*, vol. 2, pp. 475, 478; Ghirardacci, *Della historia*, p. 345. For the roots of these

topographical structures, see A. I. Pini, *Le ripartizioni territoriali urbane di Bologna medievale*, Bologna: Atesa, 1977; for *gonfaloni*, see *Gli statuti del comune di Bologna*, pp. 415–27.

52 Raymond of Peñafort, *Summa de poenitentia et matrimonio cum glossis I. de Friburgo*, Rome: Tallini, 1603, pp. 184–5; *S. Thomae Aquinatis doctoris angelici opera omnia iussu impensaque Leonis XIII. P. M. edita*, 50 vols, Rome: Typographia Polyglotta, 1882–, vol. 8, pp. 312–14 (*Summa theologiae*, 2a 2ae 40.1). See also M. Keen, *The Laws of War in the Late Middle Ages*, London: Routledge & Kegan Paul, 1965, pp. 63–81.

53 De Benedictis, *Una guerra*, pp. 101–11.

54 Giovanni da Legnano, *Tractatus de bello, de represaliis et de duello*, ed. T. E. Holland, trans. J. L. Brierly, Oxford: Oxford University Press, 1917, pp. 130, 140. For this tradition of interpretation, see n. 108 below; for 1506, see De Benedictis, *Una guerra*, pp. 121–2, 134.

55 Keen, *Laws of War*, pp. 106–8. For banners in the context of revolts, Cohn, *Lust for Liberty*, pp. 177–88.

56 Dalla Tuata, *Istoria*, vol. 2, pp. 480–1; Ghirardacci, *Della historia*, pp. 347–8.

57 *Corpus chronicorum bononiensium*, vol. 3, p. 314; R. C. Trexler, 'Follow the flag: the Ciompi Revolt seen from the streets', *Bibliothèque d'humanisme et Renaissance*, 46, 1984, pp. 357–92.

58 The principal source is Ibn Sasra, *al-Durra al-mudi'a fi al-dawla al-Zahiriyya/A Chronicle of Damascus, 1389–1397*, ed. and trans. W. Brinner, 2 vols, Berkeley: University of California Press, 1963, vol. 2, pp. 13–141. See also Bertrando de' Mignanelli, *Ascensus Barroch*, ed. W. Fischel, *Arabica*, 6, 1959, pp. 57–74, 152–72; *Ta'rikh Ibn Qadi Shuhba*, ed. A. Darwish, 4 vols, Damascus: Institut français de Damas, 1977–97, vol. 1, pp. 263–387.

59 Ibn Sasra, vol. 2, p. 82.

60 Ibid., vol. 2, pp. 33–5, 59–60, 78–9, 82–3.

61 Ibid., vol. 2, pp. 13–16. Also attacked was the house of Ibn al-Saradara, who could not be identified. See also J. L. Meloy, 'The privatization of protection: extortion and the state in the Circassian Mamluk period', *Journal of the Economic and Social History of the Orient*, 47, 2004, pp. 195–212.

62 Ibn Sasra, vol. 2, p. 13. This is also among the proverbs collected by Burckhardt in the nineteenth century: John Lewis Burckhardt, *Arabic Proverbs*, London: Murray, 1830, p. 82.

63 Ibn Sasra, vol. 2, pp. 14–15.

64 Ibid., vol. 2, pp. 59, 63.

65 Ibid., vol. 2, p. 99.

66 Ibid., vol. 2, pp. 142–4, at 143; trans. in vol. 1, pp. 191–2; Al-Turtushi, *Siraj al-muluk*, London: Riad El-Rayyes, 1990, pp. 146–7.

67 Ibn Sasra, vol. 2, p. 149. Like most other thinkers, Ibn Sasra also warned against warfare between Muslims: ibid., vol. 2, pp. 37–8.

68 Ibn Tulun, *Mufakahat*, vol. 1, pp. 250–2; Ibn Tulun, *I'lam*, pp. 141–5. I gratefully acknowledge the assistance of Nikola Dukas Sardelis and Wahid Amin with the texts of Ibn Tulun and Ibn Tawq.

69 The rebels also demanded the handover of one Ibn al-Fuqaha'i, but I was not able to identify him.

70 For such cases, see Miura, 'Urban society', pp. 171–3. On the position of Islamic law, see J. Schacht, *An Introduction to Islamic Law*, Oxford: Oxford University Press, 1964, pp. 184–5.

71 'Décrets mamelouks de Syrie', ed. J. Sauvaget, *Bulletin d'études orientales*, 2, 1932, pp. 1–52, at 44–6.

72 Lantschner, 'Fragmented cities', pp. 571–4. See also Lapidus, *Muslim Cities*, pp. 173–77; A. al-'Ulabi, *Dimashq bayna 'asr al-mamalik wa-al-'uthmaniyyin*, Damascus: Al-Sharika al-Muttahida, 1982, pp. 95–110; Miura, 'Urban society', pp. 177–88.

73 See, for instance, the case in Ibn Tulun, *Mufakahat*, vol. 1, pp. 279–80.

74 Ibn Tulun, *Mufakahat*, vol. 1, pp. 251–2; Ibn Tulun, *I'lam*, pp. 144–5.

75 Ibn Tulun, *Mufakahat*, vol. 1, pp. 185, 195; Ibn Tulun, *I'lam*, pp. 91, 178; Ibn Tawq, *Al-Ta'liq*, vol. 4, pp. 1555, 1566–7.

76 Ibn Tulun, *Mufakahat*, vol. 1, pp. 181–2 presents the negative view of the Hanbali jurist Ibn al-Mibrad. Miura has located the positive view in the National Asad Library of Syria, MS. 3243: Miura, 'Urban society', n. 156.

77 Ibn Tulun, *Mufakahat*, vol. 1, pp. 259–60; Ibn Tulun, *I'lam*, pp. 149–50. On the *zu'r* as Mamluk mercenaries, Ibn Tulun, *Mufakahat*, vol. 1, pp. 92, 269, 283, 295, 330; Ibn Tulun, *I'lam*, pp. 83, 118, 158.

78 Grehan, 'Street violence', pp. 224–8.

79 A. Lambton, *State and Government in Medieval Islam*, Oxford: Oxford University Press, 1981, p. xiv; P. Crone, *Medieval Islamic Political Thought*, Edinburgh: Edinburgh University Press, 2005, pp. 4–10; W. B. Hallaq, *Shari'a*, pp. 72–124.

80 M. Cook, *Commanding Right and Forbidding Wrong in Islamic Law*, Cambridge: Cambridge University Press, 2000, pp. 470–9, at 475, n. 33. For this debate in Damascus, see ibid., pp. 145–64.
81 Stilt, *Islamic Law*, pp. 24–34; Rapoport, 'Legal diversity'; Rapoport, 'Royal justice'.
82 Elbendary, *Crowds and Sultans*, pp. 121–55; Hirschler, 'Riten der Gewalt', pp. 210–15, 226–9; B. Shoshan, *Popular Culture in Medieval Cairo*, Cambridge: Cambridge University Press, 1993, pp. 40–66; Grehan, 'Street violence', pp. 221–4.
83 Rapoport, 'Royal justice'; A. Fuess, 'Zulm or mazalim? The political implications of the use of mazalim jurisdiction by the Mamluk sultans', *Mamluk Studies Review*, 13, 2009, pp. 121–47.
84 Elbendary, *Crowds and Sultans*, pp. 157-64, 176–89.
85 Ibn Tulun, *Mufakahat*, vol. 1, pp. 30, 41, 251; Ibn Tulun, *I'lam*, pp. 76–7, 143–4; Ibn Tawq, *Al-Ta'liq*, vol. 1, pp. 27, 62, 63, 66, 275, 431; vol. 2, p. 673. See T. Wollina, *Zwanzig Jahre Alltag. Lebens-, Welt- und Selbstbild im Journal des Ahmad Ibn Tawq*, Bonn: Bonn University Press, 2014, pp. 9, 46, 119, 128, 180; Elbendary, *Crowds and Sultans*, 127–9..
86 Wollina, *Zwanzig Jahre Alltag*, pp. 176–83; Lapidus, *Muslim Cities*, p. 106; Elbendary, *Crowds and Sultans*, pp. 161–3 (with a more exhaustive discussion of the two cases here described); Cook, *Commanding Right*, pp. 494–501.
87 Ibn Tulun, *Mufakahat*, vol. 1, pp. 32, 65; Ibn Tawq, *Al-Ta'liq*, vol. 1, pp. 36–7, 431–2.
88 Members of the *ulama* also played an important rule during the Mongol, Timurid, and Ottoman takeovers in 699/1299–1300, 803/1400, and 922/1516: Lapidus, *Muslim Cities*, pp. 131–4.
89 Ibn Tulun, *Mufakahat*, vol. 1, pp. 199–200.
90 Ibn Tulun, *Mufakahat*, vol. 1, p. 187; Ibn Tulun, *I'lam*, p. 96.
91 On this question, see also Hirschler, 'Riten der Gewalt', pp. 210–18; Elbendary, *Crowds and Sultans*, pp. 191–3.
92 Ibn Tulun, *Mufakahat*, vol. 1, pp. 65, 124–5, 146, 147; Ibn Tawq, *Al-Ta'liq*, vol. 1, pp. 431–2; vol. 2, pp. 951–2.
93 Ibn Tulun, *Mufakahat*, vol. 1, pp. 124–5, 250, 303; Ibn Tawq, *Al-Ta'liq*, vol. 1, pp. 26–7; vol. 2, pp. 951–2.
94 Ibn Tulun, *Mufakahat*, vol. 1, pp. 153–4, 251.
95 Ibn Tulun, *Mufakahat*, vol. 1, pp. 65, 124–5, 147, 153–4, 299; Ibn Tawq, *Al-Ta'liq*, vol. 1, pp. 431–2; vol. 2, pp. 951–2.
96 Ibn Tulun, *Mufakahat*, vol. 1, p. 146; Ibn Tawq, *Al-Ta'liq*, vol. 3, p. 1085.
97 Ibn Tulun, *Mufakahat*, vol. 1, pp. 124–5; Ibn Tawq, *Al-Ta'liq*, vol. 2, pp. 951–2. See Elbendary, *Crowds and Sultans*, pp.129–31 for an analysis of the underlying networks.
98 Ibn Tulun, *Mufakahat*, vol. 1, p. 132.
99 According to Ibn Tawq, the official in question was called Ghanam, but see the editor's remark: Ibn Tawq, *Al-Ta'liq*, vol. 2, p. 951, n. 1.
100 This episode is only reported by Ibn Tawq.
101 Hirschler, 'Riten der Gewalt', pp. 212–14, 226–9; Lapidus, *Muslim Cities*, pp. 143–53, 170–83; Shoshan, *Popular Culture*, pp. 40–51.
102 Lantschner, *Logic of Political Conflict*, pp. 131–68.
103 Dalla Tuata, *Istoria*, vol. 2, p. 477; De Benedictis, *Una guerra*, pp. 119–22.
104 For Bologna, see especially A. I. Pini, *Città, chiesa e culti civici in Bologna medievale*, Bologna: Clueb, 1999; N. Terpstra, *Lay Confraternities and Civic Religion in Renaissance Bologna*, Cambridge: Cambridge University Press, 1995. For the broader Italian picture, see A. Thompson, *Cities of God: The Religion of the Italian Communes*, University Park: Pennsylvania State University Press, 2005.
105 Dalla Tuata, *Istoria*, vol. 2, pp. 482, 484.
106 The historiography is vast, but a good starting point is C. Lansing, *Power and Purity: Cathar Heresy in Medieval Italy*, New York: Oxford University Press, 1998. For heresy in Bologna, see L. Paolini and R. Orioli (eds), *L'eresia a Bologna fra XIII e XVI secolo*, 2 vols, Rome: Istituto storico italiano per il Medio Evo, 1975.
107 L. Darling, *A History of Social Justice and Political Power in the Middle East*, New York: Routledge, 2013, pp. 3–8, 74–7.
108 A. De Benedictis, 'Rebellion – Widerstand. Politische Kommunikation als Normenkonflikt in der frühen Neuzeit', in A. De Benedictis, G. Corni, B. Mazohl-Wallnig, and L. Schorn-Schütte (eds), *Die Sprache des Politischen in actu*, Göttingen: V&R, 2009, pp. 113–38; Lantschner, *Logic of Political Conflict*, pp. 33–9.

109 D. Quaglioni, '"Rebellare idem est quam resistere": obéissance et résistance dans les glosses de Bartole à la constitution "Quoniam Nuper" d'Henri VII (1355)', in J.-C. Zancarini (ed.), *Le droit de résistance, XII–XXe siècle*, Fontenay-aux-Roses: Imprimerie ENS, 1999, pp. 39–46.
110 M. Ryan, 'Bartolus of Sassoferrato and free cities', *Transactions of the Royal Historical Society*, 6th ser., 10, 2000, pp. 65–89.
111 K. Abou El Fadl, *Rebellion and Violence in Islamic Law*, Cambridge: Cambridge University Press, 2001, pp. 234–94, 321–42.
112 Cook, *Commanding Right*, pp. 476–8, 582–4; see, for instance, the complex position of the famous fourteenth-century Damascene jurist Ibn Taymiyya (d. 728/1328): ibid., pp. 149–57; Y. Rapoport and S. Ahmed (eds), *Ibn Taymiyya and His Times*, Karachi: Oxford University Press, 2010. See also Elbendary, *Crowds and Sultans*, pp. 112-19, 157-64, 176–89.

9

REBELLION AND THE LAW IN FIFTEENTH-CENTURY ENGLISH TOWNS[1]

Eliza Hartrich

The records of the court of the King's Bench include a description of a session of the court of the Steward and Marshal of the King's Household held on 29 August 1422 at Warwick and presided over by Humphrey, duke of Gloucester. There, jurors claimed that on 5 August, 30 men from Coventry and 'other unknown malefactors and disturbers of the king's peace' had 'conspired and confederated in the manner of war ... to subvert the laws, ordinances, and statutes of the town of Coventry'. The offenders were said to have been armed with bows, arrows, swords, daggers, stakes, and other weapons when they assembled in a field called the Poddycroft to mount an insurrection. They 'made abominable cries', declaring that unless Mayor John Esterton released two prisoners from the town gaol, that the crowd of rebels would remove the prisoners by force. Esterton said that he would die before he would release the prisoners, but in the end Adam Deyster and Richard Joy agreed to serve as bail for the prisoners, who were permitted to leave the gaol peaceably. This did not stop the disorder in Coventry, however. Those assembled at the Poddycroft proceeded forcibly to break into a garden that the mayor and commonalty of Coventry had rented out to Giles Allesley. It was reported that the rebels carried swords, bows, and arrows, and that their actions were in 'disturbance of the peace of the lord King and against the laws, statutes, and ordinances of the City and against the peace of the said lord King'. On 8 August, the rebels struck again. This time, 'armed and arrayed in the manner of war with swords, bows, and arrows' they broke into enclosed gardens and pastures rented out by the town of Coventry to Richard Southam, and there

> made riots, rumours, and congregations ... in contempt of the said lord our King and in disturbance of the peace of the said king and his people and in breach of the peace and to the grave damage of the same Mayor and Commonalty of the aforesaid City of Coventry.[2]

The rebels in Coventry in 1422 were protesting the town council's decision in 1421 to enclose lands acquired by the town and lease them out to private individuals, rather than using them as pasture open to all citizens. It was but one of many similar types of protest occurring in the town at various points in the later Middle Ages.[3] The case is interesting, however, not only for its unique features and for its prominent place in Coventry's local history, but for what it reveals about how fifteenth-century English society defined and categorised urban rebellions. In accounts of urban revolts in later medieval England, such as that of the Coventry rebellion of 1422, the motivations and specific grievances of the rebels are rarely spelt out; what mattered to the English Crown, and what determined how the incidents were treated and prosecuted, was the format that such displays of defiance took. The features of the rebellion that drew the attention of the authorities were that property had been broken into or destroyed, that there was a large group of illicitly assembled persons, that many in the crowd were in possession of weapons, and that the offenders had committed or expressly threatened violent action. These were the attributes that turned an occasion on which municipal ordinances were flouted into a matter for royal concern – a rebellion, insurrection, or riot, which threatened the king's peace and thus came under his jurisdiction.[4]

Rebellion, then, was a legal category as much as a political activity. Actions taken by urban rebels undoubtedly had a great deal of symbolic or practical significance for the community concerned – breaking enclosures, for example, both demonstrated the community's resistance to the private usage of public lands and ensured citizens' access to pasture that was vital for their livelihood – but they also determined the legal channels through which the offenders would be prosecuted, and whether their demonstration would be deemed a breach of the king's peace.[5] Even if the king was not the object of protest, he had an interest in prosecuting any action that involved a collective, and potentially violent, threat to existing political authorities and to their persons and property. Contemporaries were well aware of the legal attributes of rebellion (and its close cousin, riot), and Andrew Prescott and Philippa Maddern have shown that both royal authorities and private litigants manipulated their accounts of disorderly incidents to ensure that they would be classified as rebellions or riots.[6] It is important to remember that those participating in demonstrations against urban authorities would also have known the legal significance of the particular actions in which they engaged, and may well have chosen to contest municipal elites in such a way so as to gain access to the legal institutions that typically investigated riots and rebellions. In other words, the legal profile of rebellion moulded not only how demonstrations were interpreted and depicted, but also very probably conditioned the actions taken by the demonstrators themselves.

This chapter will explore the legal attributes associated with rebellion, and the ways in which residents of fifteenth-century English towns used rebellion against municipal authorities to navigate a complex series of local and national jurisdictions. This interpretation of rebellion – as part of a functioning legal system rather than a symptom of crisis within it – draws from the revisionist historiography of rebellion appearing since the new millennium, much of it published by my fellow contributors. These works, by Samuel Cohn, Christian Liddy, Patrick Lantschner, Jelle Haemers, and Jan Dumolyn, among others, have demonstrated that rebellion in the later Middle Ages did not conform to the models proposed by Michel Mollat, Philippe Wolff, and Guy Fourquin in the 1970s, which presented rebellion as an unusual event, occurring only after a long build-up of tensions between haves and have-nots. Instead, the revisionists have shown, rebellion was not necessarily the desperate action of a poverty-stricken peasantry or proletariat whose options had run out, but more typically a strategic demonstration made by people fully integrated into the political life of the realm or city.[7] That rebellion was often a rational and well-informed choice is made even more apparent through the analysis of its role as a legal device. In late medieval English towns, citizens chose to rebel, in part, because they wished to take advantage of the legal mechanisms associated with the investigation of rebellions. When English legal administration and peacekeeping mechanisms changed, so, too, did the frequency with which English townspeople rebelled against their civic governments. Therefore, the meaning and utility of rebellions was not determined strictly by political needs, but was also framed by legal practice, as those with grievances tried to pursue the most effective means of seeking remedy.

Rebellion in English law

The act of rebellion itself – namely, public and collective resistance to governing authorities in which violence is committed or threatened – was well known in medieval England, as Samuel Cohn's survey of popular protest in medieval English towns between 1196 and 1450 demonstrates vividly.[8] From the late fourteenth century, however, rebellion became subject to specific legal procedures. These remained relatively vague in their particulars, but nevertheless shaped definitions of rebellion and accorded it a clearer place in the English jurisdictional landscape.[9] A 1391 act of parliament mandated that raids, riots, insurrections, and forcible entries into property should be dealt with by the justices of the peace (JPs) – a group of local notables appointed for each county by the Crown.[10] The significance of this act was twofold. First, it made explicit that acts of rebellion did not fall under the customary or common law jurisdiction held by civic governments themselves; rebellion, even against municipal governments, was always a breach of the king's peace. As I will discuss more fully later, this aspect of rebellion was eroded over time, as many towns received charters allowing their municipal officials to act as JPs or sheriffs and thus became equipped to investigate and punish rebellions on behalf of the Crown; nevertheless, the general principle remained intact that rebellion was an offence that pertained to the king and his officers.[11] Second, the act made no distinction between rebellions and other acts of collective violence or threatened violence, such as riots or forcible entries. Cohn distinguishes 'rebellion' from 'riot' and other collective demonstrations on the basis that rebellion had a clear political objective, while the other activities did not.[12] For the Crown in late medieval England, however, such distinctions were immaterial to the way in which rebellion was prosecuted; the point at issue was that a group of people had threatened violence, not why it had done so. Further legislation from the early fifteenth century continued to treat rebellion as an offence akin to riots and property break-ins, and amplified the involvement of royal officeholders and institutions in their punishment. The Riot Act of 1411 proclaimed that if the JPs, now also accompanied in their activities by the county sheriff, were unable to discover the truth regarding acts of riot, illegal assembly, or forced entry within one month of the event's occurrence, then they should send a certificate detailing the circumstances of the affair to the king and his council, who would then decide how the matter should be addressed.[13] A 1414 statute made royal interference in cases of rebellion even more probable, as it was instituted that individuals could sue for a royal commission of JPs and sheriffs to investigate riots and rebellions, and that the findings of this commission would be returnable to the royal Chancery.[14]

The officials and institutions made responsible for investigating rebellions in late fourteenth- and early fifteenth-century England – in the first instance, JPs and the county sheriff, and, in the second instance, the Chancery, the royal council, and any number of bodies that the royal council might request to hear the case, such as the court of King's Bench or a specially appointed arbitration panel – were not ones to which citizens of English towns typically had access. Most English municipal governments had long-standing civic ordinances, fortified by clauses in their royal charters, forbidding citizens from suing other citizens in any venue outside the town courts, provided that the town court possessed the jurisdictional authority to decide the suit. The penalties for flouting such ordinances were severe: the loss of the franchise in London, Southampton, Bristol, and Hull, a fine of 100s. or imprisonment in Coventry, and a fine of £4 in Sandwich for members of the civic governments and 40s. for ordinary freemen.[15] By the later Middle Ages, civic governments claimed jurisdiction over a wide array of urban activities: they held borough courts that decided cases of trespass, affray, and petty debts according to the system of royal common law; they presided over piepowder courts that decided disputes pertaining to markets and fairs; leading members of urban elites were also often officers of the staple courts responsible for determining disagreements between merchants according to law merchant; and, in addition, many mayors and aldermanic councils claimed the right to exercise equity jurisdiction – namely, to use their personal judgement to determine cases that had no clear solution according to either custom or common law.[16] There were, consequently, few matters that citizens could bring into royal courts without risking the wrath of their municipal governors. Moreover, several civic governments, such as Coventry and Beverley, also passed ordinances requiring that matters liable to be settled by arbitration be done through the aegis of the mayor and aldermen before any outside authorities were approached to serve as umpires.[17] These stringent regulations concerning the town's monopoly of justice were not simply enacted, but also enforced. Citizens in a number of towns lost their franchise, suffered imprisonment, or paid significant fines for suing writs at common law or through other jurisdictions.[18]

The laws of medieval England may have made rebellion a sort of informal method of judicial appeal – a legal loophole allowing citizens to present internal municipal grievances before an external audience without inevitably compromising their town's historic jurisdictional claims, since the right of the Crown and its officials to become involved in incidents that threatened public order was rarely contested. Those who had been removed from municipal power or had been punished by those holding it could bring their cases before officers of the Crown by claiming that their opponents had obtained power through rebellions. In a petition to the Chancellor, John Shapwyk of Totnes in Devon claimed that on 23 May 1435 John Shiplegh, Richard Hogge, Henry atte Beare, Walter Lygha, and others 'with force and armes in riottys wyse in maner of insurreccion ensembled with grete confederecy and alyaunce ayenst the pees and lawe of this lande' and forcibly removed Shapwyk from his position as mayor of the town. In alleging that he was deposed from the mayoralty by an armed confederacy 'ayens the Kynges Corone, his lawe, and his dignitee', Shapwyk was able to secure the Chancellor's attention to an internal power struggle in the Devon town that would otherwise not have come under Crown jurisdiction.[19] Similarly, a conflict within the borough of Liskeard in Cornwall was brought before the Chancellor probably because a statement by one of the burgesses, Richard John, ensured that the deposition of the mayor, John Clement, and his replacement by Richard Vage could be classified as a rebellion: Richard John declared that John Colis, John Attewylle, Robert May, Richard Knolle, and a crowd of others 'broke into the house of the Guildhall of the same town' to elect Vage.[20] It is unknown what the dispute concerned or how it was resolved, but it appears that Richard John's plea of rebellion did prompt the Crown to send a commission of local landowners to enquire into the matter.[21]

It is quite possible, too, that legislation pertaining to rebellions helped to determine not only how conflicts were depicted in contemporary written accounts, but also framed the actions of the rebels themselves. In rebelling against a civic government, dissenting citizens, even if they did not succeed in unseating their opponents from power or modifying their policies, could at least ensure that their grievances were heard by the royal officials before whom rebellions were tried. It is often difficult to tell exactly how external intervention in the aftermath of urban rebellions affected municipal politics – records from the sessions of the JPs are scanty, and those of Chancery and the King's Bench, the venues in which cases of rebellion were often presented after having been investigated by the JPs, typically preserve documents describing the alleged rebellion but not those detailing how the rebellion was punished or how the issues involved were resolved.[22] Nevertheless, cases such as the Coventry rebellion of 1422, with which this essay began, hint that sometimes the intervention of royal officials prompted by rebellion could work in the rebels' favour. The Coventry rebels were indicted both before sessions of the Court of the Steward and Marshal of the King's Household as well as before the Court of King's Bench, but there is no evidence that they were ever arrested or fined.[23] Indeed, the involvement of the Crown seems to have facilitated a compromise agreement between the civic government of Coventry and its opponents; a new survey of lands in Coventry made in February 1423 determined that, while some of the contested lands had, in fact, been lawfully enclosed by private individuals, others, such as the Poddycroft itself, were actually common pasture and would in future be treated as such.[24] In York in 1464 and 1473, the Crown's involvement in quieting election riots resulted in an out-and-out victory for the rebels: the king ordered that the role of craft guilds in electing the mayor be extended, which had apparently been the aim of the rebels all along.[25]

Historians of medieval English towns typically maintain that outside intervention in civic affairs was always unwanted and usually detrimental to the town's liberties.[26] Sometimes, undoubtedly, it was. Rioting in Norwich in 1436 and 1443 provoked the Crown to suspend the city's liberties, with authority over the city transferred from the mayor to a royally appointed warden, and, in the latter instance, to slap a 1,000-mark fine on the city.[27] This should not blind us to the fact, however, that situations like Norwich's suspension of liberties were unusual, or that, for some citizens, involvement of the Crown or other external parties in municipal politics may have been welcome and beneficial.[28] John Shapwyk of Totnes and Richard John of Liskeard actively sought assistance from the Crown in solving local disputes, and by categorising the actions of their local opponents as rebellions that they were able to do so without harming their town's ancient claims to jurisdictions. The rebellions of the citizens of Coventry and York may also have been designed to secure the hearing of their grievances by the Crown; certainly, in both cases, the involvement of royal officials facilitated the achievement of the rebels' political aims. It appears, then, that rebellion, and the involvement of the Crown in urban politics that it occasioned, was not always a threat to municipal independence but could be a savvy legal manoeuvre for disaffected residents of towns.[29]

Rebellions, lawsuits, and legal change: *c.*1440–60

Legal practice in later medieval England, however, was not a set of stationary structures, but evolved to meet the needs of litigants and the Crown. Such alterations in the legal make-up of medieval England also occasioned considerable changes in the frequency and usage of urban rebellion, suggesting that it was, indeed, an activity closely linked with the pursuit of grievances through legal means. Here, we will present a case study of the period 1440 to 1460 to show how changes in the enforcement and administration of the law could affect the manner in which English townspeople chose to resist their civic governments. This era was a time of notoriously weak kingship, encompassing the minority of Henry VI and his incompetent adult rule, and yet witnessed fewer documented revolts against urban authorities than are found for either the fourteenth and early fifteenth centuries or even the period of Yorkist and Tudor 'New Monarchy' in 1460–1525. Most striking is the fact that, while numerous rebellions are recorded against urban governments during and immediately before the Peasants' Revolt of 1381, the years surrounding the Jack Cade Revolt of 1450 did not see the same boom in collective violent resistance against municipal elites.[30] Coinciding with this lull in rebellions against civic governments was a number of high-profile lawsuits made by citizens outside the town courts.[31] These lawsuits were not weaker forms of resistance than rebellion, but constituted significant challenges to the power of the urban governments targeted. That aggrieved citizens chose to challenge civic officers through this means, and not through the rebellions they employed in the previous and succeeding periods, was intimately connected to changes in the operation of English law at both central and local levels. The widespread implementation of urban officers as JPs and sheriffs *ex officio* rendered rebellions less efficacious a means of appealing to external authorities, and the rise in legal petitions brought before the royal Chancellor made lawsuits against municipal officers a more serious political threat.

JPs and sheriffs

From the late fourteenth century, the English Crown increasingly let urban officials perform peacekeeping duties within their own towns. Before, sheriffs and JPs were appointed for each county, and would have jurisdiction over the towns within that county. Between 1373 and 1414, 11 English towns (Bristol, Southampton, York, Gloucester, Coventry, Hereford, Nottingham, Newcastle-upon-Tyne, Norwich, Lincoln, and Scarborough) received royal charters removing them from the remit of the county peace commission and allowing mayors, aldermen, recorders, and other municipal officers to become JPs for their towns *ex officio*; five of these towns (Bristol, York, Newcastle, Norwich, and Lincoln) were also incorporated into freestanding counties, with the town's elected bailiffs turned into sheriffs.[32]

As noted earlier, one of the defining characteristics of rebellion as a form of resistance was that it immediately entailed the intervention of outside officials in internal disputes through the deployment of JPs and sheriffs. When mayors, aldermen, bailiffs, and other urban officials became JPs and sheriffs themselves, they inherited the role of investigating and adjudicating rebellions in the town on behalf of the Crown, compromising one of the primary purposes of rebellions in the first place, which was to bypass the civic government and secure the involvement of neutral arbiters. Now, in many towns, municipal officers were, in effect, charged with investigating and punishing rebellions mounted against themselves. This effect was probably not merely a convenient byproduct of the grants of new powers, but part of the reason that civic governments sought such grants in the first place. The first charter to give JP and shrieval jurisdiction to urban authorities, that of Bristol in 1373, was explicit that the new grants should deposit power over rebellious burgesses solely in the hands of the mayor, sheriff, and their fellow civic officers; it even made special mention of the fact that they were to have jurisdiction over disturbances occurring at elections.[33] In Bristol, at least, the acquisition of new peacekeeping offices by the civic government seems to have been effective in quelling internal rebellions; the town had been the scene of uprisings against municipal elites in 1312–16, 1347, and 1363, but witnessed remarkably few thereafter.[34] Newcastle also remained relatively free from internal rebellions after its 1404 charter giving JP and shrieval powers to its civic officers.[35] Even York, often seen as the posterchild for medieval urban revolt, saw far fewer rebellions against its civic officers in the 50-odd years following the 1393 and 1396 charters that turned its civic officers into JPs and sheriffs than it had done in the fourteenth century (with major election riots in 1365 and 1380) and would do in the later fifteenth and early sixteenth centuries after the legal framework had changed once more (with rebellions in 1464, 1471, 1473, 1480, 1482, 1484, 1486, 1489, 1492, 1494, and 1504).[36] The disorder that plagued Norwich throughout the early fifteenth century seems to have been the exception, rather than the rule, when it came to the towns whose civic governments had received new peacekeeping powers in 1373–1414.[37]

This policy for delegation of JP and shrieval jurisdiction to civic officials reappeared, at an accelerated pace, in the mid-fifteenth century. In the 12 years between 1439 and 1451, a further 13 towns (Windsor, Plymouth, Hull, Winchester, London, Shrewsbury, Bridgnorth, Derby, Ipswich, Bath, Colchester, Canterbury, and Chichester) were granted the right to have their civic officers serve as JPs, and four towns (Hull, Southampton, Nottingham, and Coventry) became counties with their own elected sheriffs.[38] This cluster of grants gave a number of civic governments whose officers had previously had no permanent role in peacekeeping a position *ex officio* as prosecutors of internal rebellions. Furthermore, in London, where civic officers had already acted as sheriffs, they were now also made JPs, and in Southampton and Coventry, where civic officers were already JPs, they were now also sheriffs. In these three towns, therefore, the possibility of any external official being involved in the identification and punishment of revolt in the first instance became especially remote, since both the main types of offices typically involved in these procedures were now held by members of the municipal government.

Contemporaries were very much aware of these changes to the legal powers of their civic officers and of their potential significance. Indeed, one of the few urban rebellions to occur in the mid-fifteenth century, that of Ralph Holland and the London artisans against that city's government, was in protest against the imminent transformation by royal charter of London's mayor, aldermen, and recorder into JPs in 1444.[39] When looked at in this light, the Holland rebellion may be seen, in part, as a last-gasp attempt to use urban rebellion as a device for securing royal intervention, before its purpose as such disappeared with the bestowal of JP jurisdiction on London's leading civic officers. In Coventry, the acquisition of shrieval powers by the town's bailiffs was also a matter for public comment. The town's charter of 1451, which also transformed Coventry into a county and added a number of neighbouring hamlets to the town's jurisdiction, was noted in civic chronicles and municipal government records chiefly for the fact that it 'made the baylys of Coventre scherefs'.[40] Moreover, the new jurisdiction given to Coventry's officers was, as in 1373 in Bristol, associated with a decline in rebellion. Immediately after transforming Coventry's bailiffs into sheriffs during his 1451 visit to the town, Henry VI allegedly said, 'we charge you withe our pease among you to be kepte; and that ye suffer no Ryottes, Conventiculs ne congregasions of lewde pepull among you'.[41] Coventry was historically a hotbed for discontent, and witnessed rebellions against the civic government in 1351, 1378, 1384, 1390, and 1422, and again in 1469, 1481, 1489, 1494, and 1495.[42] It is probably no coincidence that the two lacuna in revolts against Coventry's civic government occurred in the years following the grant of JP jurisdiction to the town's officers in 1399 and in those following the grant of shrieval jurisdiction to the town's bailiffs in 1451. The one rebellion against Coventry's civic government that did occur in the years after 1399, the insurrection of 1422 with which this essay began, was notable for the fact that it appears to have been prosecuted in the first instance not by the mayor and councillors as JPs, but by the county sheriff: the judicial sessions in which the rebels were indicted took place not in Coventry, but in Warwick, the 'county town' for Warwickshire, and the presenting jurors were also not from Coventry.[43] Once the 1451 charter had divorced Coventry from the county of Warwickshire and its sheriff, the means by which the 1422 rebellion had reached the judgement of the king's courts were now closed off.

Chancery

The paucity of urban rebellions in 1440–60, however, was not due purely to the fact that rebellion was no longer capable of fulfilling some of its earlier functions. It was also because unauthorised lawsuits outside the town courts had become more potent and effective means of defying civic authority. As shown above, citizens were forbidden from entering lawsuits against other citizens in law courts apart from those run by civic government officials.[44] This monopoly over citizens' litigation was highly prized by municipal governments and closely guarded; it was, in part, to evade these restrictions that town residents turned to rebellion as a means of expressing their grievances to an outside authority. The expansion of the royal Chancery as a court of equity, however, was beginning to erode the control that civic governments exercised over lawsuits between citizens. Since the late fourteenth century or earlier, litigants who believed that their cases did not fit within the formulaic legal writs available through the English common law began to petition the Chancellor for legal redress. From the 1430s the business before the court of Chancery expanded considerably. Although, over time, the court of Chancery began to specialise in cases involving alien merchants or informal land transfers, in theory, its remit was limitless. Also, part of the role of Chancery was to supervise the dispensation of justice in other courts in the realm; those convicted in local courts or arrested by local authorities could sue Chancery for writs requiring that the defendant be released and the records of the case reviewed by the Chancellor.[45] The rise of Chancery as a court of equity and as a supervisory court therefore threatened the claims of town courts, presided over by the leading urban officers, to exercise a monopoly on litigation between citizens, and also subjected the decisions made by civic officers to scrutiny from above.

The increase in legal business before Chancery in the 1430s and 1440s not only brought more opportunities for citizens to sue outside the town courts and, in particular, to sue the mayors, aldermen, and officers of their municipality, but also heightened the dramatic impact that such suits would have. City governments, themselves expanding their jurisdictional powers in the mid-fifteenth century through the acquisition of JP and shrieval powers for their members and a number of other legal privileges, found the development of Chancery jurisdiction highly threatening, especially as it was in its early stages and there were as yet no clear institutionalised limits to its scope. Consequently, suits outside the town courts, and especially to Chancery, in the mid-fifteenth century were an extremely effective way of incensing municipal officers and challenging their power. That external lawsuits were a sensitive subject for civic governments can be seen from a spike in the number of urban ordinances passed in these years forbidding citizens from suing other citizens in outside courts: Coventry passed ordinances to this effect in 1455, 1456, and 1457; Dublin in 1452 and 1460; London in 1454; Sandwich in 1435; and Hull in the 1440s.[46] It is also perhaps no coincidence that many of these civic governments had also recently acquired JP and shrieval powers: Coventry's bailiffs had been made sheriffs in 1451, London's mayor and aldermen JPs in 1444, and Hull's bailiffs had become sheriffs and its mayor and aldermen JPs by a 1440 charter, while Dublin's mayor and councillors had served as JPs since 1420.[47] Marjorie McIntosh noted a similar correlation in the manor of Havering in Essex: writs of error sued by residents of the manor against their local officials increased with the rise of Chancery as a court of equity and in the aftermath of the manor's acquisition of the right to elect its own JPs in 1465.[48] That ordinances against external lawsuits followed fairly closely upon the augmentation of the municipal government's peacekeeping powers in Coventry, London, and Hull suggests that the two phenomena – an increase in suits to outside courts and the decreasing probability that rebellion would secure an outside audience – were, indeed, connected.

Such a suggestion is strengthened when we consider that the most serious conflict to occur among Ipswich's citizens in this period was occasioned by an unauthorised external lawsuit made by William Heede and William Ridout in 1455. On 8 September, they were summoned before the bailiffs of the town to 'shew cause whie they should not be disfranchised for suing John Caldwell, a free Burgess of this Towne, out of the liberty of this Towne, unjustly and contrary to the Charter of King John'.[49] This was the first of a number of very public quarrels between Heede and Ridout, on the one hand, and the Ipswich civic government, on the other, during 1455–6.[50] That Heede and Ridout's lawsuit was regarded as a significant threat to the corporation of Ipswich is apparent from the fact that the men were accused of contesting the liberties granted by King John's charter of 1200 to the town – one that has been lauded as the first in England to outline structures of communal urban government in any detail, and even described as an important step in the advance of democracy.[51] Also of particular interest is the fact that Ipswich had received a charter in 1446 turnings its civic officers into JPs, and the target of Heede and Ridout's suit, John Caldwell, was one of the town's bailiffs (the leading officers of Ipswich) in that year and acted as JP for the town in 1449–60.[52] In suing Caldwell, therefore, Heede and Ridout were able to direct grievances against a person who would have been difficult to target through rebellion, since he would have been among those acting as their judge in the first instance.

Resistance by lawsuit: some prominent examples

At first glance, lawsuits outside the town courts and rebellions seem to be actions with little in common. One was a formal legal process entered into by private individuals, citing specific grievances against other named individuals, and the latter an illicit assembly of people who threatened violence against formally constituted authorities. Even the revisionist historiography of rebellion, which has demonstrated that rebellion was an integrated component of medieval political life rather than a perversion of it, maintains that rebellion was still different from other means of positing grievances against civic governments: it was more threatening, more public, and more political. Lawsuits and other expressions of complaint were either preludes to rebellion, less combative or less dangerous alternatives to rebellion, or options to be pursued by people who did not have the institutional resources to undertake a full-scale rebellion.[53]

This distinction, however, does not appear to have been present in late medieval England. Patrick Lantschner writes that in Italian and Low Countries cities of the later Middle Ages, residents of cities featuring a large number of intermediate associational groups tended to pursue grievances against their civic government through rebellion, while those who lived in cities where guild and parish resources were less accessible tended to make complaints or express resistance through other means.[54] Citizens of individual English towns, however, used both rebellion and lawsuits to contest civic authority, as the situation dictated. Indeed, it was far from uncommon for one man to posit grievances against municipal government through several different means. William Chetill was fined 2s. for his participation in a 1423 election riot against the governors of Beverley, while in 1443 he fell foul of Beverley's civic government for entering a lawsuit against a fellow citizen in an external court, this time paying a fine of 6s. 8d. for his misdeed.[55] John Payn of Southampton, together with his son-in-law Thomas White, sued the leading members of Southampton's civic government outside the town courts on a number of occasions in the mid-fifteenth century and led a successful rebellion at the mayoral election of 1460.[56] There is little detail on what motivated Chetill's actions, but in the case of White and Payn, it does not appear that their aims had changed significantly between 1449 and 1460 – on both occasions, they sought to remove a faction from power in Southampton that accommodated the interests of Italian merchants trading within the town. In the 1440s and 1450s, it was simply more expedient, more effective, and more dramatic to channel grievances through lawsuits than through rebellion.

Two Chancery petitions from this period – the first brought by Henry May of Bristol and the second by John Payn and Thomas White of Southampton – will demonstrate, moreover, that unauthorised lawsuits made outside the borough courts, too, could be suitable vehicles for addressing issues of public interest. These were both long-running disputes – Henry May's concerning the higher fees charged for Anglo-Irishmen to become freemen of Bristol, and Payn and White's contesting the power of a faction in Southampton that looked kindly upon the presence of Italian merchants there.[57] In 1460, their resistance would take on more obviously 'rebellious' forms – May supported Henry VI when the Bristol civic government lent military aid to the Yorkists during the early dynastic battles of the Wars of the Roses, while Payn and White led a successful rebellion at the 1460 Southampton mayoral election.[58] But, in 1455–6 and 1448–9, respectively, these tensions were playing out in law courts. The legal battles that ensued, however, were not just petty private quarrels that would serve as preludes to more meaningful and more public rebellions, but were constitutionally significant struggles that represented the interests of substantial groups of citizens and challenged the very essence of urban authority.

In late 1455, May, incensed at the exorbitant sum that Bristol's civic government required that his brother pay for admission to the franchise, entered a petition in Chancery against the town's mayor and chamberlains. May's petition was clearly regarded as a serious threat to the civic government of Bristol, and prompted harsh reprisals. May and four men 'to hym well wyllyng' were removed from the freedom of the town.[59] Bristol's leading municipal officers also sought to implement an act of parliament legitimating the action they had taken against May and other Anglo-Irish residents of Bristol. The efforts of Bristol's civic officers in parliament were countered not through a collective demonstration, but through an – apparently successful – attempt by Anglo-Irish Bristolians to lobby parliament to defeat the proposed legislation. Moreover, May sued a further petition against Bristol's civic government in Chancery. It was, in form, a private lawsuit concerning the unjust removal of May and his colleagues from the franchise, but it was also the culmination of a larger campaign made by the Anglo-Irish residents of Bristol to contest their exclusion from the civic political arena. That this lawsuit was viewed as a substantial challenge to municipal authority is apparent from the impassioned replication to it submitted by the mayor and chamberlains, in which they asserted that the civic government had sole right to determine who and who was not a member of its franchise, without external interference. They also declared proudly that 'the towne of Bristowe ys and of the tyme that no mynde ys hath ben and be burgh Corporat', and then set out the full terms of the 1373 charter that had 'made the said towne a Counte and a shire by hit self and a sheryf to be of the same'.[60] This sally was but the first in a lengthy series of lawsuits, lasting until 1458, in which May and the civic government debated who had control over admissions to the town's franchise and what rules should govern its membership.[61]

May's Chancery suit was one of several made by Bristol citizens during the first half of the 1450s alleging gross misconduct by the town's officials. Agnes Knight claimed that John Joce, Bristol's common clerk, in retaliation for a lawsuit that her son had made against him in the king's courts, had seized £40-worth of goods from her home; Knight wrote that because Joce held a position in the Bristol civic government, he 'hath so grete rule and power there that he may overawe whom hym list in right and wronge'.[62] Thomas Broun also complained that he had been persecuted at law and physically threatened by Joce and Bristol councillors Richard Alberton and William Spencer.[63] Around the same time, Thomas Pratant petitioned that the sheriff of Bristol, Thomas Balle, had seized £360 from his home, and that when Pratant went to London to sue for a remedy, Balle ransacked Pratant's house and inspired such fear in Pratant's pregnant wife that she died. Pratant also claimed that Balle 'beyng Sheryf of the said Toune by divers fayned and untrue meanes vexed youre said beseecher' and had unlawfully imprisoned him.[64] What became of Balle remains a mystery, but in November 1455, coinciding nearly exactly with May's suit, Joce was dismissed from his office as town clerk and forbidden from pleading before the town courts; the litigants' private suits appear to have achieved a concrete political result.[65] Each of these Chancery suits, with the exception of May's, alleged purely personal grievances, but collectively they formed a significant offensive against Bristol's political elite in the early to mid-1450s. May's lawsuit was the culmination of a larger political movement against the Bristol civic government, pursued through a series of controversial lawsuits in Chancery rather than through the medium of rebellion.

The suit lodged by John Payn and Thomas White against the civic government of Southampton in the late 1440s certainly reinforces the impression that Chancery was the most dramatic venue for contesting urban power in this period. White had been stripped of his franchise on account of the many lawsuits he had brought against Southampton's civic officers in Chancery as well as the Courts of King's Bench and Common Pleas. In an attempt to overturn the civic government's decision, White submitted yet another suit in Chancery, in which he contended that his previous suits were necessary because John Fleming, former mayor and now recorder of Southampton, 'calleth himself a man lerned in the lawe where … he is none', and used his pretended expertise in the law to imprison and distrain those residing in Southampton until they obeyed his will. White also accused Fleming, when he was mayor of Southampton, of refusing to comply with any writs issued from Chancery and other royal law courts for the review of cases tried before the town's courts.[66] Fleming responded that White and his father-in-law, John Payn, had obtained their Chancery writs maliciously as a way of delaying the course of justice and intimidating the residents of Southampton.[67]

This debate over Chancery writs was far from technical, but struck at the heart of constitutional politics in Southampton. In White and Payn's response to Fleming's defence, White proclaimed that he had never 'offended ayens the Comune wele of the saide towne'.[68] This is one of the earliest uses of the term 'common weal' in vernacular English – a phrase that would become increasingly important in English national politics from 1459 onwards, as warring dynastic parties in the Wars of the Roses fought to prove that they, and not their opponents, represented the good of the realm.[69] That the term was found in an urban Chancery suit in the late 1440s, and not in complaints issued by rebels against a civic government, is indicative of the shift in patterns of resistance in municipal politics taking place in the mid-fifteenth century. It is also important to note that White and Payn cited not only their own personal grievances in their suit against Fleming, but also those of a wider group of citizens. They complained of miscarriages of justice committed against John Clement and John Meke, who were not parties to the suit. More broadly, White and Payn asserted that Fleming had 'enpresseth the king's people ... and enprisoneth meny and dyvers of the king's lieges and other straungers till thei make grement with hym after his entent'.[70] White and Payn concluded their second petition to the Chancery by requesting that the writs be sent to 'certeyne notable persones' to examine the people of Southampton not only regarding Fleming's conduct towards White and Payn, but also concerning 'all other Iniuries don by the saide fflemyng to eny persone aswele withyn the towne of Southampton as withoute'.[71]

They appear to have been successful in their aim: in 1448, the Crown appointed a commission of local country gentlemen – not citizens of Southampton – to enquire into 'extortions, oppressions, maintenances and other misdeeds committed by John Flemyng of Southampton'.[72] Such an outcome would have been unlikely had White and Payn organised a rebellion to pursue their grievances. Fleming and his fellow members of the Southampton civic government acted as JPs for the town, and, since a charter granted in 1447, the bailiffs of Southampton, Fleming's colleagues on the town council, acted as sheriffs.[73] Consequently, all but the most serious rebellions in the town would have been judged by Fleming's circle, and would not have elicited the intervention of outside parties to investigate Fleming's alleged misconduct.

The Chancery suits of May, White, and Payn were not second-rate acts of resistance; they were well calculated to enrage civic governments much occupied both with extending their own judicial powers and with fighting off the threats that expanded business before royal equity courts posed to their claims for exclusive jurisdiction within the town. Though they took the form of private grievances, they represented the interests of larger segments of the community who wished to curb abuses committed by municipal elites and strike a blow at their pretensions to hold absolute power within the town. These lawsuits possibly constitute only the tip of the iceberg of politically charged external lawsuits made in the mid-fifteenth century. The cases of May and of White and Payn are recorded in unusual detail, but other lawsuits from this period which have not left such an extensive paper trail, such as that of Heede and Ridout against the bailiff of Ipswich, inspired similar ire from the urban governments against which they were directed, suggesting that they, too, may have been collective and public challenges to municipal authority.[74]

Changes in the administration of royal and local law in the mid-fifteenth century had made lawsuits a potent means of contesting urban authority and reduced the efficacy of rebellion as a legal device. This shift, however, was not a permanent one. From 1460, recorded rebellions against civic governments would increase. It has already been shown that in the years following 1460 the citizens of York and Coventry resumed a tradition of rebellion against their civic governments that had been in abeyance in the 1430s–50s, and in this a number of other towns followed suit.[75] There are many factors that may have contributed to this change: the advent of dynastic civil war may have encouraged those dissatisfied with urban government to express their frustrations through violence rather than lawsuits; the stronger presence of the Crown in the provinces and the infiltration of royal servants into urban government may have increased the possibility of an external audience to urban revolt; or the gradual acceptance by urban governments of an institutionalised court of Chancery may have blunted the dramatic impact of an unauthorised external lawsuit.[76] One factor, though, was certainly the new legislation passed during the reign of Henry VII that limited the role of sheriffs and JPs in the prosecution of riots, thereby restoring rebellion as a useful device for ensuring that grievances would be presented before outside authorities even in towns in which municipal officers served as commissioners of the peace.[77] Groups and individuals who wished to pursue grievances against municipal governments in later medieval England took account of such changes to institutions, policies, and jurisdictions, and chose the method of attack that was likely to be most effective in the new legal environment within which they found themselves.

Conclusion

Rebellion was, undoubtedly, a menace to English municipal governments and a means well suited for the expression of collective political grievances. Crowds of people changed the course of civic elections by barging into guildhalls from which they had been barred, tore down hedges to protest the private use of public lands, and forcibly released prisoners from the town gaol. Its frequency in English towns, however, can also be explained by its usefulness as a legal device. The Bristol, Southampton, and Ipswich lawsuits of the 1450s demonstrate why, during certain periods of the fifteenth century, rebellion may have been an attractive option for English townspeople. The rebellions in Coventry, Totnes, and Liskeard mentioned earlier in this chapter were described in contemporary documents as subversions of the king's peace and as actions detrimental to the ordinances and customs of the towns concerned, but, unlike the lawsuits outside the town courts made by May, Heede, and Ridout, they were not described as fundamental violations of the jurisdictional privileges that had been granted to the town by royal charter.[78] The very factors that often make rebellions seem the most dangerous and most public form of urban protest – the presence of an illicit assembly that committed or threatened violence – were also those that allowed the grievances of townspeople to be presented before outside authorities in ways that did not threaten the corporation's historic legal claims. Therefore, when English townspeople rebelled against their municipal officers, it is not necessarily the case that their anger had reached its highest pitch or that other more 'peaceful' avenues for resolution had been exhausted; they may simply have wished to access the judicial venues through which rebellion was investigated and prosecuted.

This is not to say that rebellion performed these same functions throughout medieval Europe, or even throughout medieval England. What I have tried to show here is that rebellion was the product of the legal systems under which its perpetrators lived, and changed in format and purpose alongside changes in legislation and legal practice. As Patrick Lantschner has shown, different jurisdictional configurations in different societies produced different repertoires of resistance.[79] In the cases explored by Lantschner, the utility of rebellion was determined largely by the presence (or lack thereof) of smaller associational units within the city, but in England the situation was rather more complex, as the means through which discontented citizens protested the actions of civic governments was moulded not only by the jurisdictional balance-of-power within the town itself but also by the dictates of an ever-evolving central legal system operated by a powerful monarchy. The peculiar role that rebellion occupied in English towns for much of the fifteenth century, as a 'safer' means of securing an outside hearing for internal complaints, was born from the jurisdictional claims, sometimes competing and sometimes complementary, made by the authorities under which they lived – the municipal government and the Crown, further complicated in some instances by the presence of a noble or ecclesiastic as the immediate overlord of a town. Rebellion, in allowing urban disputes to appear before royal or other courts without inevitably compromising the rights of civic governments to exercise a monopoly over citizens' litigation, was a means for townspeople to navigate this complicated jurisdictional set-up.

Even elsewhere within England, rebellion probably took on a different meaning from that for townspeople, since those who did not live in towns were operating within different legal frameworks. For English aristocrats and gentry, for example, lawsuits and external arbitration were means of jockeying for power, but not really of resisting it.[80] Unhindered by municipal prohibitions on the use of outside jurisdictions, free people with a certain degree of financial wherewithal could use whichever legal mechanisms they liked, whether royal, ecclesiastical, or equitable, to assert their claims in local society. For rural landed society, the act of making a suit in court, was not in itself a defiance of another jurisdictional authority to which they were subject. Rebellion among the aristocratic classes, therefore, was less likely to be a purely legal manoeuvre, since they had access to a full range of legal venues already. Conversely, for the unfree peasant in medieval England, the lawsuit was perhaps the weapon of resistance par excellence. Serfs were not permitted to sue in courts outside their lord's jurisdiction without permission, and the act of doing so was essentially a declaration that the serf concerned was a free man not subject to his lord's control.[81] Indeed, for unfree peasants in fourteenth-century England, rebellion and external lawsuits often went hand-in-hand as twinned methods for contesting seigneurial authority.[82]

Because rebellion in later medieval Europe, therefore, was conditioned by and derived its meaning from jurisdictional relationships between larger polities and their constituent parts, it should not be taken for granted that 'rebellion' signified the same thing to residents of different societies, nor should it be assumed that the meaning of 'rebellion' remained stable over time in a particular location – especially considering the important changes in the relationship between locality and polity that took place in many different regions of Europe in the fifteenth century.[83] In some societies at some times, rebellion was a less potent threat to civic governments than other avenues for expressing grievance. By acknowledging that rebellion was not always the most dangerous or most public means for political complaint available to the medieval populace and that its meaning was tied to changing legal structures, it becomes necessary to re-evaluate the significance of time periods featuring infrequent rebellion; they indicate not necessarily that the people concerned were unable to rebel against their governors or were afraid of their retaliation, but perhaps that legal circumstances had conspired to make other forms of protest more appealing or more effective. After all, rebellion, like other modes of protest, rarely constituted an end in and of itself. It was, rather, a means for achieving goals or for presenting grievances before a particular audience, and its ability to perform these functions was tied closely to the legal systems within which it operated.

Notes

1 I would like to thank John Watts, Patrick Lantschner, Tom Johnson, and the editors for their helpful comments on earlier drafts of this chapter. Any errors that remain are my own.

Please note that quotations from Middle English have been provided in the original language, with slight modifications for clarity. The letter 'þ', or thorn, is represented in the text by 'th'. In some instances, the letters 'u' and 'v', and 'i' and 'j', have been exchanged to conform to modern spelling conventions.

Abbreviations used:
- CChR   *Calendar of the Charter Rolls*, 6 vols, London: Her Majesty's Stationery Office, 1903–27.
- CHC   Coventry, Coventry History Centre.
- ERALS   Beverley, East Riding Archives and Local Studies.
- KHLC   Maidstone, Kent History and Library Centre.
- LLB   R. R. Sharpe (ed.), *Calendar of Letter-Books Preserved among the Archives of the Corporation of the City of London at the Guildhall*, 11 vols (A–L), London: Corporation of London, 1899–1912.
- LMA   London, London Metropolitan Archives.
- PROME   C. Given-Wilson et al. (eds), *The Parliament Rolls of Medieval England, 1275–1504*, Leicester: Scholarly Digital Editions, 2005.

2 TNA, KB9/935, m. 19: *cum aliis malefactoribus incognitis et pacis dicti domini Regis perturbatoribus; modo guerriuo . . . conspirauerunt et confederauerunt leges ordinaciones et statute ville de Coventre predicte subuertere; abhominabiles clamores; in perturbacionem pacis dicti domini Regis ac legum, statutorum et ordinacionum Ciuitatis predicte ac contra pacem dicti domini Regis; gladiis, arcibus et sagittis modo guerriuo armati et arraiati; riottes, rumuroures [et] congregaciones adtunc et ibidem fecerunt in contemptum dicti domini Regis ac in perturbacionem pacis ipsius domini Regis et populi sui lesionem manifestam et ad graue dampnum ipsius Maioris ac Communitatis Ciuitatis predicte*. See also M. Jurkowski, 'Lollardy in Coventry and the revolt of 1431', in L. Clark (ed.), *The Fifteenth Century VI: Identity and Insurgency in the Late Middle Ages*, Woodbridge: Boydell, 2006, pp. 145–64, at 156–7.

3 Many of these are discussed in C. D. Liddy, 'Urban enclosure riots: risings of the commons in English towns, 1480–1525', *P&P*, 226, 2015, pp. 41–77, at 41–2, 46–7, 51, 57–8, 63, 67–9, 74.

4 See below, pp. 191, as well as P. C. Maddern, *Violence and Social Order: East Anglia 1422–1441*, Oxford: Clarendon Press, 1992. For the blurred distinction between individual interests and Crown interests in the law courts of medieval France, see J. Firnhaber-Baker, '*Jura in medio*: the settlement of seigneurial disputes in later medieval Languedoc', *French History*, 26, 2012, pp. 441–59, at 457.

5 For the political symbolism of rebellions in medieval England, see esp. Liddy, 'Urban enclosure riots', pp. 41–77, and S. Justice, *Writing and Rebellion: England in 1381*, Berkeley, CA: University of California Press, 1994.

6 A. Prescott, 'Writing about rebellion: using the records of the Peasants' Revolt of 1381', *History Workshop Journal*, 45, 1998, pp. 1–28, at 11–13; Maddern, *Violence and Social Order*.

7 S. K. Cohn, Jr., *Lust for Liberty: The Politics of Social Revolt in Medieval Europe, 1200–1425*, Cambridge, MA: Harvard University Press, 2006; S. K. Cohn, Jr., *Popular Protest in Late Medieval English Towns*, Cambridge: Cambridge University Press, 2013; P. Lantschner, 'Justice contested and affirmed: jurisdiction and conflict in late medieval Italian cities', in F. Pirie and J. Scheele (eds), *Legalism: Community and Justice*, Oxford: Oxford University Press, 2014, pp. 77–96, at 82, 93; P. Lantschner, 'Revolts and the political order of cities in the later Middle Ages', *P&P*, 225, 2014, pp. 3–46; P. Lantschner, *The Logic of Political Conflict in Medieval Cities: Italy and the Southern Low Countries, 1370–1440*, Oxford: Oxford University Press, 2015; C. D. Liddy, 'Urban enclosure riots', pp. 41–77; C. D. Liddy, '"Bee war of gyle in borugh": taxation and political discourse in late medieval English towns', in A. Gamberini, J.-P. Genet, and A. Zorzi (eds), *The Languages of Political Society: Western Europe, 14th–17th Centuries*, Rome: Viella, 2011, pp. 461–85; J. Dumolyn and J. Haemers, 'Patterns of urban rebellion in medieval Flanders', *Journal of Medieval History*, 31, 2005, pp. 369–93, at 385–6; H. Skoda, *Medieval Violence: Physical Brutality in Northern France, 1270–1330*, Oxford: Oxford University Press, 2013, pp. 162–92, 243; C. D. Liddy and J. Haemers, 'Popular politics in the late medieval city: York and Bruges', *EHR*, 128, 2013, pp. 771–805. For the earlier generation of rebellion scholarship, see M. Mollat and P. Wolff, *The Popular Revolutions of the Late Middle Ages*, trans. A. L. Lytton-Sells, London: George Allen & Unwin, 1973, and G. Fourquin, *The Anatomy of Popular Rebellion in the Middle Ages*, trans. A. Chesters, Amsterdam: Elsevier Science Ltd, 1978.

8 Cohn, *Popular Protest*.
9 For a general discussion of the legal procedures associated with riots, rebellions, and forcible entry, see J. G. Bellamy, *Criminal Law and Society in Late Medieval and Tudor England*, Gloucester: Alan Sutton, 1984, pp. 10–12, 15, 54–89.
10 *PROME*, November 1391 parliament, item 27; *The Statutes of the Realm*, 12 vols, London: Eyre and Strahan, 1810–28, 15 Richard II, c. 2; E. Powell, *Kingship, Law, and Society: Criminal Justice in the Reign of Henry V*, Oxford: Clarendon Press, 1989, p. 59. For the changing relationship between urban jurisdictions and commissions of the peace, see E. G. Kimball, 'Commissions of the peace for urban jurisdictions in England, 1327–1485', *Proceedings of the American Philosophical Society*, 121, 1977, pp. 448–74.
11 See below, pp. 194–5.
12 Cohn, *Popular Protest*, pp. 27–8.
13 *Statutes of the Realm*, 13 Henry IV, c. 7; Maddern, *Violence and Social Order*, p. 174.
14 *PROME*, April 1414 parliament, item 25; *Statutes of the Realm*, 2 Henry V, c. 8; Powell, *Kingship, Law, and Society*, pp. 171–2; N. Pronay, 'The Chancellor, the Chancery, and the Council at the end of the fifteenth century', in H. Hearder and H. R. Loyn (eds), *British Government and Administration: Studies Presented to S. B. Chrimes*, Cardiff: University of Wales Press, 1974, pp. 87–103, at 97–8.
15 For Bristol and Southampton, see below, p. 198. LMA, COL/CC/01/01/001, fol. 68; *LLB*, vol. K, pp. 363–4; Hull, Hull History Centre, C BRE/1/2, fol. 14; M. D. Harris (ed.), *The Coventry Leet Book, or Mayor's Register...*, 4 vols, Early English Text Society, Original Series, 134–46, London: Kegan Paul, Trench, Trübner & Co., 1907–13, pp. 194, 281; KHLC, Old Black Book of Sandwich, Sa/AC1, fol. 26v.
16 J. H. Baker, *The Oxford History of the Laws of England. Volume VI, 1483–1558*, Oxford: Oxford University Press, 2003, pp. 303–14, 318; E. E. Rich (ed.), *The Staple Court Books of Bristol*, Bristol Record Soc., 5, [Bristol]: Bristol Record Society, 1934, pp. 29–66, 78–88; P. Tucker, *Law Courts and Lawyers in the City of London 1300–1550*, Cambridge: Cambridge University Press, 2007; M. Bateson, *Borough Customs*, 2 vols, Selden Soc., 18, London: B. Quaritch, 1904–6, vol. 2, p. 59.
17 For example, Harris (ed.), *Coventry Leet Book*, pp. 302–3; A. F. Leach (ed.), *Beverley Town Documents*, Selden Soc., 14, London: B. Quaritch, 1900, p. 55. Urban guilds also passed ordinances requiring that arbitration be performed within the guild and not by external legal bodies: G. Rosser, *The Art of Solidarity in the Middle Ages: Guilds in England, 1250–1550*, Oxford: Oxford University Press, 2015, pp. 69, 206–7.
18 See below, pp. 197–8; Harris (ed.), *Coventry Leet Book*, p. 194; ERALS, BC/II/7/1, fols 64, 74, 77, 79v, 205; TNA, C1/16/20. See also, A. P. M. Wright, 'The relations between the king's government and the English cities and boroughs in the fifteenth century', PhD thesis, Oxford University, 1965, p. 142. A small but increasing number of Londoners, however, pursued suits against each other at the Court of Common Pleas without incident: M. F. Stevens, 'Londoners and the Court of Common Pleas in the fifteenth century', in M. Davies and J. A. Galloway (eds), *London and Beyond: Essays in Honour of Derek Keene*, London: London Institute of Historical Research, 2012, pp. 225–45, at 239–40.
19 TNA, C1/19/301.
20 TNA, C1/12/237: *le huse del Gyldehalle de mesme le Burgh debruserent*.
21 *CPR 1436–41*, p. 371.
22 J. B. Post, 'Crime in later medieval England: some historiographical limitations', *Continuity and Change*, 2, 1987, pp. 211–24, at 215–16; Maddern, *Violence and Social Order*, pp. 22–4, 47–8.
23 TNA, KB9/935, m. 19.
24 Harris (ed.), *Coventry Leet Book*, pp. 45–53; Jurkowski, 'Lollardy in Coventry', pp. 156–7.
25 *CPR 1461–7*, p. 366; T. Rymer (ed.), *Foedera, Conventiones, Literae...*, 17 vols, London: J. Tonson, 1727, vol. 11, pp. 529–31; J. I. Kermode, 'Obvious observations on the formation of oligarchies in late medieval English towns', in J. A. F. Thomson (ed.), *Towns and Townspeople in the Fifteenth Century*, Gloucester: Sutton, 1988, pp. 87–106, at 89; E. Miller, 'Medieval York: the later Middle Ages', in P. M. Tillott (ed.), *Victoria County History: A History of Yorkshire: The City of York*, Oxford: Oxford University Press, 1961, pp. 25–116, at 71; *CPR 1467–77*, p. 416; Liddy and Haemers, 'Popular politics', p. 792.
26 For example, A. S. Green, *Town Life in the Fifteenth Century*, 2 vols, London: Macmillan, 1894, vol. 2, pp. 387, 398; Liddy and Haemers, 'Popular politics', pp. 794–5; and C. M. Barron, *London in the Later Middle Ages: Government and People 1200–1500*, Oxford: Oxford University Press, 2004, pp. 9–42.
27 For the 1433–43 conflicts in Norwich, see Maddern, *Violence and Social Order*, pp. 175–205; R. L. Storey, *The End of the House of Lancaster*, London: Barrie & Rockliffe, 1966, Appendix III; B. R. McRee, 'Peacemaking and its limits in late medieval Norwich', *EHR*, 109, 1994, pp. 831–66, at 853–65; B. R. McRee, 'The mayor's body', in L. E. Mitchell, K. L. French, and D. L. Biggs (eds), *The*

Ties that Bind: Essays in Medieval British History in Honor of Barbara Hanawalt, Farnham: Ashgate, 2011, pp. 39–53, at 40, 45–52; L. Attreed, *The King's Towns: Identity and Survival in Late Medieval English Boroughs*, New York and Oxford: Lang, 2001, pp. 289–94; W. Hudson and J. C. Tingey (eds), *The Records of the City of Norwich*, 2 vols, Norwich: Jarrold, 1906–10, vol. 1, pp. 114–22, 281–3, 299, 324–56; vol. 2, pp. 68–71; and Norwich, Norfolk Record Office, Norwich City Records case 8a/10, doc. 1; case 9c/1,/6–9,/12–15; case 9d/5; case 16d/1, fols 5–10, 13v; case 17b, fols 67v–73.

28 See the comments in Wright, 'Government and cities', pp. iv–v, 60–7.

29 For similar observations regarding the involvement of French royal officials in settling seigneurial wars, see Firnhaber-Baker, '*Jura in medio*', pp. 441–2, 450–2, 455, 457, 459.

30 E. Hartrich, 'Town, crown, and urban system: the position of towns in the English polity, 1413–71', PhD thesis, Oxford University, 2014, pp. 90–101, 159–73, 182–201, 214–29, 245–8, 267–86, 290–309; Cohn, *Popular Protest*, pp. 99–111, 312–15; H. Hinck, 'The rising of 1381 in Winchester', *EHR*, 125, 2010, pp. 112–31; R. B. Dobson, 'The risings in York, Beverley and Scarborough, 1380–1381', in R. H. Hilton and T. H. Aston (eds), *The English Rising of 1381*, Cambridge: Cambridge University Press, 1984, pp. 112–42; A. F. Butcher, 'English urban society and the revolt of 1381', in Hilton and Aston (eds), *English Rising*, pp. 84–111; C. D. Liddy, 'Urban conflict in late fourteenth-century England: the case of York in 1380–1', *EHR*, 118, 2003, pp. 1–32; C. D. Liddy, 'Urban enclosure riots', pp. 41–77; Liddy and Haemers, 'Popular politics', pp. 771–805. Also, see below, pp. 194–5.

31 See below, pp. 196–9.

32 M. Weinbaum (ed.), *British Borough Charters, 1307–1660*, Cambridge: Cambridge University Press, 1943, pp. 38–9, 42, 48, 52, 72, 84, 89, 91, 116, 131, 132; *CChR*, vol. 5, pp. 336, 372, 380, 383, 398, 422–3, 473; N. D. Harding (ed.), *Bristol Charters 1155–1373*, Bristol Record Soc., 1, [Bristol]: Bristol Record Society, 1930, pp. 118–41; *Royal Charters Granted to the Burgesses of Nottingham A.D. 1155–1712*, London: Bernard Quaritch, 1890, pp. 44–5; W. de Gray Birch (ed.), *The Royal Charters of the City of Lincoln: Henry II to William III*, Cambridge: Cambridge University Press, 1911, pp. 80–1; Kimball, 'Commissions of the peace', pp. 465–6; C. D. Liddy, *War, Politics and Finance in Late Medieval English Towns: Bristol, York and the Crown, 1350–1400*, Woodbridge: Boydell, 2005, pp. 190–212.

33 Harding (ed.), *Bristol Charters 1155–1373*, pp. 136–9.

34 Cohn, *Popular Protest*, pp. 43, 116–17, 130–43, 187.

35 The recorded rebellions against municipal officials in Newcastle-upon-Tyne are in 1341 and 1364: Cohn, *Popular Protest*, pp. 190, 319.

36 Cohn, *Popular Protest*, p. 190; Liddy, 'Urban conflict', pp. 1–32; Dobson, 'Risings in York, Beverley and Scarborough', pp. 120–4; Liddy, 'Urban enclosure riots', pp. 41, 50–2, 71–2, 74; Liddy and Haemers, 'Popular politics', pp. 771, 777–9, 782–3, 785–8, 792; Kermode, 'Obvious observations', pp. 89–90, 100. There was a small disturbance in York in 1420: M. Sellers (ed.), *York Memorandum Book*, 2 vols, Surtees Society, 120, 125, Durham: Andrews & Co., 1912–15, vol. 1, pp. 90–2; Liddy, 'Bee war of gyle', pp. 44–5. The citizens of York took part in the 1405 rebellion against Henry IV, but it is unclear if they were also protesting the actions of civic leaders: C. D. Liddy, 'William Frost, the city of York and Scrope's rebellion of 1405', in P. J. P. Goldberg (ed.), *Richard Scrope: Archbishop, Rebel, Martyr*, Donington: Shaun Tyas, 2007, pp. 64–85.

37 For Norwich, see above, p. 193, as well as Hudson and Tingey (eds), *Records of the City of Norwich*, vol. 1, pp. 66–113; McRee, 'Mayor's body', pp. 40–3; McRee, 'Peacemaking and its limits', pp. 848–52; Maddern, *Violence and Social Order*, pp. 179–80; Attreed, *King's Towns*, pp. 40–2. It should be noted that a 1433 rebellion in Norwich reached royal attention, partially through Thomas Wetherby's crafty description of the events concerned to meet the legal requirements for a 'riot' or 'rebellion', only after failed attempts by the city's JPs to restore order.

38 *CChR*, vol. 6, pp. 6, 10–11, 41–3, 45, 54–5, 65, 71, 77, 84, 98, 116; *CPR 1441–6*, p. 84; *CPR 1446–52*, pp. 181–3, 523; Weinbaum (ed.), *British Borough Charters, 1307–1660*, pp. 6, 21, 25–6, 35, 49, 50, 56–7, 77–8, 91, 96, 99, 101, 109–10, 117, 128; J. R. Boyle (ed.), *Charters and Letters Patent Granted to Kingston upon Hull*, Hull: Corporation of Hull, 1905, pp. 34–45; W. H. Stevenson, W. T. Baker, E. L. Guilford, D. Gray, and V. W. Walker (eds), *Records of the Borough of Nottingham*, 9 vols, London: Quaritch, 1882–1956, vol. 2, pp. 188–209; H. W. Gidden (ed.), *The Charters of the Borough of Southampton*, 2 vols, Southampton: Cox & Sharland, 1909–10, vol. 1, pp. 70–81.

39 LMA, COL/CC/01/01/004, fols 4v, 7v, 8v, 9v–10; C. M. Barron, 'Ralph Holland and the London radicals, 1438–1444', in R. Holt and G. Rosser (eds), *The English Medieval Town: A Reader in English Urban History, 1200–1540*, London: Longman, 1990, pp. 160–83, at 173–82. The other major urban rebellion of the 1440s, that in Norwich, also addressed the role of municipal officials as JPs, although

in this case the issue was much less central to the rebels' grievances: R. H. Frost, 'The urban elite', in C. Rawcliffe and R. Wilson (eds), *Medieval Norwich*, London: Hambledon, 2004, pp. 235–53, at 249–50.

40 The charter is summarised in *CChR*, vol. 6, pp. 116–17. For the entry in the earliest Coventry chronicle (*c*.1461), see CHC, Aylesford Annal, PA 351, dorse, printed in P. Fleming, *Coventry and the Wars of the Roses*, Stratford-upon-Avon: Dugdale Society, 2011, p. 32. See also similar entries in later Coventry chronicles: CHC, PA 478/2, fol. 4; PA 535/1, fol. 7v; PA 958/1, fol. 9. For the Coventry chronicles as a genre, see R. W. Ingram (ed.), *Records of Early English Drama: Coventry*, Manchester: Manchester University Press, 1981, pp. xxxvii–xli. See also Harris (ed.), *Coventry Leet Book*, p. 265.

41 Harris (ed.), *Coventry Leet Book*, p. 265.

42 Cohn, *Popular Protest*, pp. 104, 122, 170, 187–8, 215–16; *CPR 1377–81*, pp. 303, 305–6; C. D. Liddy, 'Urban politics and material culture at the end of the Middle Ages: the Coventry tapestry in St Mary's Hall', *Urban History*, 39, 2012, pp. 203–24, at 220–3; Liddy, 'Urban enclosure riots', pp. 41–2, 46, 51, 57–8, 67, 74; CHC, PA 351, dorse, printed in Fleming, *Coventry and the Wars of the Roses*, pp. 30–1. For 1422, see above, pp. 189–90, 192–3. Some Coventry residents did participate in the 1431 'Jack Sharpe' rebellion, and the town was also under royal scrutiny in the 1420s and 1440s for the heretical and anti-ecclesiastical preaching of John Grace and John Bredon, but there are no recorded instances of rebellion against the town's civic government in these years apart from the 1422 enclosure riot: see Jurkowski, 'Lollardy in Coventry', pp. 145–64; *CPR 1422–9*, pp. 275–6; Harris (ed.), *Coventry Leet Book*, pp. 96–7; H. Nicolas (ed.), *Proceedings and Ordinances of the Privy Council*, 7 vols, London: Commission of Public Records, 1834–7, vol. 6, pp. 40–5. In 1441, there were apparently some riotous assemblies in Coventry provoked by Bredon asserting erroneously that Coventry's citizens had gained the right to use non-standard measures of corn, but the incident does not appear in any of the civic records and it is unclear exactly what occurred: *CPR 1436–41*, p. 545.

43 TNA, KB9/935, m. 19; Jurkowski, 'Lollardy in Coventry', p. 156.

44 See above, pp. 191–2.

45 There remains some debate about when, exactly, the greatest increase in legal business before Chancery occurred, but the 1430s–40s was, regardless, an important period of development. See e.g. M. E. Avery, 'The history of the equitable jurisdiction of Chancery before 1460', *BIHR*, 42, 1969, pp. 129–44; Pronay, 'Chancellor, Chancery, and Council', pp. 87–103; J. A. Guy, 'The development of equitable jurisdictions, 1450–1550', in E. W. Ives and A. H. Manchester (eds), *Law, Litigants and the Legal Profession*, London: Boydell & Brewer for Royal Historical Society, 1983, pp. 80–6; P. Tucker, 'The early history of the Court of Chancery: a comparative study', *EHR*, 115, 2000, pp. 791–811.

46 Harris (ed.), *Coventry Leet Book*, pp. 281, 294, 302–3; J. T. Gilbert (ed.), *Calendar of Ancient Records of Dublin, in Possession of the Municipal Corporation of that City*, 18 vols, Dublin: J. Dollard, 1889–1922, vol. 1, pp. 277, 303–4; *LLB*, vol. K, pp. 363–4; KHLC, Sa/AC1, fol. 26v; Hull History Centre, C BRE/1/2, fols 13v–14.

47 See above, pp. 194–5. For Dublin, see Gilbert (ed.), *Calendar of Ancient Records of Dublin*, vol. 1, pp. 28–9.

48 M. K. McIntosh, 'Central court supervision of the ancient demesne manor court of Havering, 1200–1625', in Ives and Manchester (eds), *Law, Litigants and the Legal Profession*, pp. 87–93, at 91–2.

49 N. Bacon, *The Annalls of Ipswche: The Lawes Customes and Government of the Same. Collected out of ye Records Bookes and Writings of that Towne*, ed. W. H. Richardson, Ipswich: S. H. Cowell, 1884, p. 113; N. Amor, *Late Medieval Ipswich: Trade and Industry*, Woodbridge: Boydell, 2011, pp. 13, 253, 260.

50 Bacon, *Annalls of Ipswche*, p. 114; Amor, *Late Medieval Ipswich*, pp. 145–6.

51 See e.g. Green, *Town Life*, vol. 1, pp. 223–4, and C. Platt, *The English Mediaeval Town*, London: Granada, 1976, pp. 117–9, 230.

52 Amor, *Late Medieval Ipswich*, p. 242.

53 Liddy and Haemers, 'Popular politics', pp. 784–8; Lantschner, *Logic of Political Conflict*, pp. 40–59, 89–199; J. Dumolyn and J. Haemers, ' "A bad chicken was brooding": subversive speech in late medieval Flanders', *P&P*, 214, 2012, pp. 45–86, at 86, although note 56, 84.

54 Lantschner, 'Revolts and the political order', pp. 3–46; P. Lantschner, 'Voices of the people in a city without revolts: Lille in the later Middle Ages', in J. Dumolyn, J. Haemers, H. R. Oliva Herrer, and V. Challet (eds), *The Voices of the People in Late Medieval Europe*, Turnhout: Brepols, 2014, pp. 73–88; Lantschner, 'Justice contested and affirmed', pp. 77–96; Lantschner, *Logic of Political Conflict*, pp. 89–199. See also Kermode, 'Obvious observations', pp. 87–106.

55 ERALS, BC/II/6/8; BC/II/7/1, fol. 64.

56 TNA, C1/16/352a–b, 353a–b; C. Platt, *Medieval Southampton*, London: Routledge & Kegan Paul, 1973, p. 175; A. A. Ruddock, *Italian Merchants and Shipping in Southampton 1270–1600*, Southampton: University College, 1951, pp. 176–7.
57 These disputes are chronicled in full in P. Fleming, 'Identity and belonging: Irish and Welsh in fifteenth-century Bristol', in L. Clark (ed.), *The Fifteenth Century VII: Conflict, Consequences and the Crown in the Late Middle Ages*, Woodbridge: Boydell, 2007, pp. 175–93, at 182–3; Wright, 'Government and cities', pp. 124–9; W. R. Childs, 'Irish merchants and seamen in late medieval England', *Irish Historical Studies*, 32, 2000, pp. 22–43, at 39–42; E. W. W. Veale (ed.), *The Great Red Book of Bristol*, 5 vols, Bristol Record Society, 2–18, [Bristol]: Bristol Record Society, vol. 1, pp. 136–8; P. Fleming, *Bristol and the Wars of the Roses, 1451–1471*, Bristol: Bristol Branch of the Historical Association, 113, 2005, pp. 8–9; P. Fleming, 'Politics and the provincial town: Bristol, 1451–1471', in K. Dockray and P. Fleming (eds), *People, Places and Perspectives: Essays on Later Medieval and Early Tudor England in Honour of R. A. Griffiths*, Stroud: Nonsuch, 2005, pp. 87–8; Ruddock, *Italian Merchants and Shipping*, pp. 160–92; A. A. Ruddock, 'John Payne's persecution of foreigners in the town court of Southampton in the fifteenth century: a study in municipal misrule', *Papers and Proceedings of the Hampshire Field Club and Archaeological Society*, 16, 1944, pp. 23–37; P. Nightingale, *A Medieval Mercantile Community: The Grocers' Company and the Politics and Trade of London, 1000–1485*, London and New Haven, CT: Yale University Press, 1995, pp. 449–50, 506–7, 531–2.
58 See above, nn. 56–7.
59 TNA, C1/17/213a.
60 TNA, C1/17/213c–d.
61 TNA, C1/17/213–15; C1/26/102–5. Also, see above, n. 56.
62 TNA, C1/18/3.
63 TNA, C1/19/252a.
64 TNA, C1/18/210.
65 Veale (ed.), *Great Red Book of Bristol*, vol. 1, p. 255.
66 TNA, C1/16/352a.
67 TNA, C1/16/352b.
68 TNA, C1/16/353a.
69 M. Knights *et al.*, 'Commonwealth: the social, cultural, and conceptual contexts of an early modern keyword', *Historical Journal*, 54, 2011, pp. 659–87, at 663–6; J. Watts, '"Common weal" and "commonwealth": England's monarchical republic in the making, *c*.1450–*c*.1530', in Gamberini *et al.* (eds), *Languages of Political Society*, pp. 147–63, at 147–53; D. Starkey, 'Which age of reform?', in C. Coleman and D. Starkey (eds), *Revolution Reassessed: Revisions in the History of Tudor Government and Administration*, Oxford: Clarendon Press, 1986, pp. 13–27, at 19–27.
70 TNA, C1/16/352a.
71 TNA, C1/16/353a.
72 *CPR 1446–52*, p. 189.
73 Gidden (ed.), *Charters of Southampton*, vol. 1, pp. 70–81.
74 See above, p. 196.
75 See above, pp. 193–5, as well as Hartrich, 'Town, crown, and urban system', pp. 267–77, 280, 283–6, 302–3, 306, and Liddy, 'Urban enclosure riots', pp. 41–77.
76 For changing relationships between royal and urban governments in the late fifteenth century, see especially, J. Lee, 'Urban recorders and the Crown in late medieval England', in L. Clark (ed.), *The Fifteenth Century III: Authority and Subversion*, Woodbridge: Boydell, 2003, pp. 163–77; S. Gunn, 'Henry VII in context: problems and possibilities', *History*, 92, 2007, pp. 301–17, at 316; and Wright, 'Government and cities', pp. 48–57, 68, 71–83, 394–5. Note also the attention paid by Edward IV to conflicts in Salisbury, contrasting with the minimal involvement of Henry VI's government in the city's internal disputes: Chippenham, Wiltshire and Swindon History Centre, G23/1/2, fols 13v, 18, 31, 32v, 76v–8, 79v–80, 85–7, 103, 104v–5.
77 Bellamy, *Criminal Law and Society*, pp. 75–7.
78 See above, pp. 189–90, 192–3, 196, 198.
79 Lantschner, *Logic of Political Conflict*; Lantschner, 'Justice contested and affirmed', pp. 77–96; Lantschner, 'Revolts and the political order', pp. 3–46; Lantschner, 'Voices of the people', pp. 73–88.
80 This has been illustrated by historical works in the McFarlanite tradition, which stress that aristocratic use of law, arbitration, and violence did not inherently challenge the stability and pretensions of the 'state'. See C. Carpenter, 'Law, justice and landowners in late medieval England', *Law and History*

Review, 1, 1983, pp. 205–37; C. Carpenter, *The Wars of the Roses: Politics and the Constitution in England, c.1437–1509*, Cambridge: Cambridge University Press, 1997, pp. 47–64; E. Powell, 'Arbitration and the law in England in the late middle ages', *TRHS*, 5th ser., 33, 1983, pp. 49–67; E. Powell, 'Settlement of disputes by arbitration in fifteenth-century England', *Law and History Review*, 2, 1984, pp. 21–43; Maddern, *Violence and Social Order*; and S. Payling, *Political Society in Lancastrian England: The Greater Gentry of Nottinghamshire*, Oxford: Clarendon Press, 1991, ch. 7. For similar comments regarding France, see J. Firnhaber-Baker, *Violence and the State in Languedoc, 1250–1400*, Cambridge: Cambridge University Press, 2014, and Firnhaber-Baker, '*Jura in Medio*', pp. 441–59.

81 C. Briggs, 'Seigniorial control of villagers' litigation beyond the manor in later medieval England', *Historical Research*, 81, 2008, pp. 405–21; R. H. Hilton, 'Peasant movements in England before 1381', *EcHR*, New Ser., 2, 1949, pp. 117–36, at 124–5.
82 Hilton, 'Peasant movements', pp. 124–30.
83 J. Watts, *The Making of Polities: Europe, 1300–1500*, Cambridge: Cambridge University Press, 2009, pp. 287–425.

10
WOMEN IN REVOLT IN MEDIEVAL AND EARLY MODERN EUROPE

Samuel Cohn, Jr.

The modern history of 'pre-modern' popular resistance must begin with George Rudé's classic works on crowds in history, which focused on the French Revolution. In reaction to scholars of the late nineteenth and early twentieth century, especially Gustave Le Bon and his psychological study of the crowd of the 'popular mind' (1895), Rudé disputed timeless generalisations on crowd psychology. As with so much else, the French Revolution demarcated here the start of modernity. With armed protests such as the Champs de Mars in July 1791, Rudé found a watershed. Before, he argued, riots and revolts bore a close relationship with the price of bread, matters of the hearth, the economics of subsistence. From this fact, Rudé and others following in his footsteps created and elaborated on models of popular insurrection in history, which divide by two vague temporal categories: modern and pre-modern types, forms, and 'repertoires' of revolt. For these, assumptions about women's roles in them have been pivotal. Because of the correlation of bread prices and the appearance of food riots early in the French Revolution, Rudé argued that women were often the mainstay of 'pre-modern' revolts as with the march on Versailles of 5 October 1789 that was spawned by the scarcity of bread. These matters of the hearth, according to Rudé, struck women and their children first and were principally the concerns of women. In the later stages of the French Revolution and thereafter, Rudé showed from his samples that riots became less sensitive to food prices and included fewer women. In their place, strikes arose as the characteristic form of 'modern' popular protest, which he argued were men's business.[1]

Over the past 50 years social scientists, most prominently, Charles Tilly, have buttressed this model of the 'pre-modern' riot with new emphases on ritual and performance, concepts, such as the 'repertoires of revolts'. In addition, the date of the transition from 'pre-modern' to 'modern' social movements and protest has moved steadily forward, from the French Revolution to as late as the mid-nineteenth century.[2] Some historians have gone further in generalising about women's revolutionary nature and their roles.[3] Yves-Marie Bercé saw grain scarcity as the usual precondition of pre-modern uprisings, and therefore women were the 'traditional' participants; protecting the hearth was in their 'biological' nature.[4] For Jean Delumeau, women's emotional and instinctive need to protect their offspring meant that their insurrectionary activities were even less sensitive to historical change. From the Middle Ages, he jumps to the 1970s (then, his present) to conclude that the same needs as in the past have led to the revolutionary initiative and the inspiration guiding contemporary women to join and lead movements such as Baader Meinhoff.[5]

Thus far, modernists more readily than medievalists have criticised the 'pre-modern'/modern model of popular revolt with particularly important implications for our understanding of women's participation. William Reddy argued that the late eighteenth-century bread riot was a sort of strike. John Bohstedt, Roger Manning, and others have shown that women were not the sole or even the principal rebels in early modern food riots.[6] Feminist historians such as Temma Kaplan and Eleanor Gordon have demonstrated that women had not retreated from organised collective action during the nineteenth and twentieth century; instead, their activities displayed a rich array of radical politics from street theatre to strike action.[7]

Women in medieval uprisings

In research for my book *Lust for Liberty* I found that women far from being the principal participants in late medieval popular protest were remarkable for their absence.[8] There were exceptions. The Florentine chronicler Giovanni Villani described women during the *Brugse Metten* (Matins of Bruges) of 1302, slicing up the hated French soldiers 'like tunny fish'. A Flemish chronicler placed them slightly further from the field of battle, but still they were involved. From sun roofs, they dumped the contents of chamber pots on to the French soldiers fighting in the streets below. At Douai in 1322, two 'foul-mouthed' women (*par leurs mauvaises lanwes et par leur mauvais parlers*) – one married, the other single – were arrested and tried for having cried out in the middle of the market place against the town's bourgeois and their grain dealers and for inciting other commoners to join the fray against the grain dealers. They were not, however, the only leaders or even the principal ones to incite the crowds; 16 men, including a Scot, a man from Arras, and another from Hennin, a porter of sacks at the Friars Minors, a smith, a sapper, and two weavers were also among the 'big talkers' (*gros parlers*), who threatened to rob and massacre the grain dealers of Douai, and to arouse other commoners. However, the women received the graver penalties: their tongues were cut out and they were banished from the city for life. The men, by contrast, received sentences of banishment from life to three years and three days and no mutilations.[9]

Women's involvement in popular protest could, moreover, be effective without a drastic end to their bodies. In Parma on 3 March 1331 'many men, women, the old, and the young' marched at night on Parma's cathedral square, chanting 'Vivat! vivat!' 'Long live the king' (Robert of Naples was then titular head of Parma), and afterwards 'Peace, peace', 'Down with the taxes and gabelles!', and 'Death to Riccardo' (*Moriantur dacia et gabelle et moriatur domnuis Ricardus*), the king's notary and governor of Parma, responsible for new taxes and 'much cruelty and wickedness'. Moreover, their march and chants came just after the decree of a new law prohibiting any chants beginning with 'Death to...' or the rallying cry, 'Vivat, vivat' (presumably even favouring the king). Shortly thereafter, these women, along with men and children, danced through city streets and into the countryside. Waving banners, chanting, singing, carrying twigs, branches, and garlands, they ultimately prevailed without shedding any blood: city taxes were lowered, peace negotiated with Lucca, and the dreaded Riccardo removed from office.[10]

Women, however, are more often seen in risky and subversive collective activities that lay on the margins of what is generally considered to be popular protest. First and foremost was their participation in heretical movements, such as with 60 heretics burnt at the stake in Padua on 21 July 1233;[11] or among the 'more than 3000' in 1315 who followed a man preaching he was an apostle of Christ through the countryside of Siena;[12] and, most famously, among Fra Dolcino's followers in the mountains around Novara in 1305–6, where his girlfriend, Margarita, appears as a leader.[13] Women also joined forces in villages and cities resisting occupation by foreign soldiers or billeting of their own sovereign's soldiers in their homes and against the general arrogance, abuses, and destruction that accompanied occupation and rule by foreign forces of cities and villages. Such was the case of Pavia's resistance to the rule from their overlords, Milan, and the indigenous noble families who supported them. From 1356 to 1360, women attended sermons by their insurrectionary leader, Friar Iacopo Bossolari, followed his commands, became part of his Roman-styled centurions, 'like ants' helped to dismantle a palace belonging to the city's ruling family, and participated in four city-wide revolts.[14] A decade later (September 1368 to November 1369) women of Trieste joined forces to battle against Venice's attempts to conquer their city. After daily attacks, they rebuilt and fortified their walls at night, and submitted to Venetian might only when faced with death by starvation.[15] Such defences against foreign invaders could be staffed by women alone as with Matteo Villani's story of Milan's threatened occupation of Florentine villages along the northern perimeter of the Florentine state in 1352. 'Screaming without stopping', 30 women chased 70 well-armed *condottieri* across the hilltops.[16]

Another story of women's popular struggle again involves bands of women only. In this case, peasant women were involved on both sides, but was it a case of 'popular protest'? According to the single source describing this *zuffa* or brawl, it looks more like a matter of internecine conflict, even if it concerned the collection of grain. In 1431 women from the village of Ambra in the Valdambra between Siena and Arezzo went to the neighbouring Cennina to collect grain. But Cennina's women greeted them with scythes and clubs. A 'big fight' ensued with Ambra's women winning, wounding many from Cennina, and leaving one woman dead, before they carried the harvest back to Ambra.[17] Medieval chronicles and administrative sources vividly describe further cases of women below the ranks of the nobility involved in collective action, concerning movements such as 'the Great Alleluia' of 1233, the post-Black Death flagellants of 1349, 'the Bianchi' in 1399–1400, and other flagellant and religious movements, which, as with 'the Great Alleluia' and 'the Bianchi', were in part peace movements.[18] The medieval sources were not blind to the public appearance of women as is sometimes asserted, but these movements were not matters of popular revolt demarcated by class antagonism.

On the other hand, women are hardly seen in the over 20 contemporary narrative accounts of the French Jacquerie of 1358, except as the victims of rape and pillaging. For this revolt, only the Carmelite chronicler Jean de Venette mentions an incident involving women as rebels and here only in passing. Moreover, these women were not those generally considered 'jacques' (or in this case 'jacquelines') from the countryside (*le plat pays*) but were townswomen. Somewhat similar to the women warriors at Bruges 56 years earlier, women rebels at Senlis in Picardy poured boiling water from their windows on the nobility invading from the streets below (*Posuerunt iterum mulieres ad fenestras, ut super eos aquas bullientes abundanter effunderent*).[19] But unlike in Bruges in 1302, where women appear on their own initiative emptying their chamber pots on the enemy, Senlis's male citizens (*cives Silvanectenses*) in 1358 were the tacticians who planned their city's defence against noblemen coming from their stunning victory at Meaux. Among other successful strategies such as 'strong men' rolling heavy carts through the narrow streets crippling the approaching cavalry, they placed the women at the windows.[20]

In addition, in the well-over-200 royal letters of remission issued to rebels and others concerning loss of life and destruction inflicted by the Jacquerie,[21] women rarely appear and, when they do, they remain in the background, as victims of rape, soliciting the pardons for their husbands who were on the run, or as liable for deceased husbands' obligations. Justine Firnhaber-Baker has combed through these archival documents and others, such as Parlement mandates, and has found two cases suggesting women's involvement as rebels. In 1365 a lord and his wife brought a suit against those who attacked their manors during 'the war against the nobles in 1358' by *homines et mulieres innobiles* (non-noble men and women). Thirteen of the alleged culprits were listed and one was a woman, Jeanne, wife of Nicolas Bonin. In a remission to 30 named rebels from the villages of Belleau and Givry,[22] one (but only one) of those listed was a woman, the widow Margot of Perrenet the short (*jadiz fame de feu Perrenet le brief*).[23]

More strikingly, no women appear as rebels in the Florentine chronicles of the Revolts of the Ciompi, 1378–82, and, in judicial lists from criminal inquisitions and sentences that I have collected, including over 1,000 rebels during Florentine riots and revolts comprised largely of commoners from Florence's earliest surviving criminal sentences in 1342 to the end of the century, only one woman appears, and she was hardly a popular rebel.[24] Born into the powerful Medici family, she was condemned in 1379 with many men, mostly possessing elite family names, for attempting to overthrow Florence's government of the 'Arti Minori' that was composed mostly of artisans. The closest I have found to a woman playing even a supporting role in these riots and revolts comes after the defeat of the radical wing of the Ciompi, 'the Eight of Santa Maria Novella', in September 1379. In August of the following year, when most of these insurgents had escaped to neighbouring cities or had been exiled, a certain Baldo had still kept illegally his flag of the Ciompi. He was then killed, and his unnamed girlfriend ran off with his illegal flag and was guarding it at her hometown of 'Vitorata' (possibly Vittorito, near L'Aquila).[25]

England appears exceptional for women's involvement in late medieval popular insurrection. With her husband, Joanna Ferrour was active in village risings in Kent in the early phases of the Peasants' Revolt of 1381. On 13 June she was involved in the burning of the Savoy Palace and the following day in the summary trials and executions of the archbishop, royal treasurer, and king's physician at the Tower of London. She was not alone among women named as participants or leaders in late medieval English revolts. The wife of Thomas Brembole and her daughter were charged with the burning of the Savoy and the hospital at Clerkenwell in 1381; Katharine Gamen blocked the escape of the Chief Justice of King's Bench, Sir John Cavendish, leading to his capture and ghoulish execution. At Petham hundred in Kent, seven were indicted for rebellion in 1381, three of whom were women. Other examples can be added from other late medieval English revolts.[26] Yet, despite these appearances, women rebels were certainly not typical even in England. From lists of thousands indicted, Andrew Prescott has found that they comprised no more than 1 per cent of rebels in 1381.[27]

The most remarkable example that I have discovered of a woman leading a revolt in late medieval Britain, at least from social levels beneath queens and their lovers, occurred in 1303 and appears in the Patent Rolls. As far as I can find no chronicler alludes to it. The first named, Isabella Borrey, led 20 men and unspecified others. They conspired 'by bonds and oaths', besieged the town of Shrewsbury, assaulted its three elected bailiffs, usurped the bailiff's peace, took over their functions and other matters pertaining to their office, stole their wands, and replaced these elected bailiffs with their own unelected ones. Further, they intimidated the men of the commonalty from trading in the town or outside it.[28] On first impression, this may have been an outside invasion but none of the named rebels is indicated from other places even by the common toponymic, 'atte'. Economic motives may have been a cause – competition between members of the ruling elite of traders or oppression by them.

Was this a factional or a class conflict? Although none of the indicted was identified by an occupation, except for a local parson, the first-named figure, Isabella, can be identified from other surviving documents. She had filed a complaint against 75 men, including four tailors, three pamenters (another type of tailor), a 'galey', a shearer ('scherer'), a barber, and a carpenter, just five days earlier, and this document gives us a better idea of the conflict that followed.

Isabella was not an outsider to Shrewsbury, impoverished, or from the labouring or artisan classes. Instead, her complaint against this mostly artisan group, probably then the backbone of the burgesses, later to be stripped of their elected officials by Isabella's 'revolt', had invaded her dwelling-place at Shrewsbury, broke her gates and houses, and beat and maimed her servants.[29]

What appears from the first document as a possible popular revolt and successful overthrowing of a government led by a firebrand woman against elected elites, emerges from the second as the opposite: the out-of-office wealthy led by a wealthy woman rose up and drove from office the legitimately elected officials, who were of the middling sort. Isabella's revolt was a *coup d'état* from above. Other documents in the British National Archives (TNA) highlight further her status. Twenty years later Edward II granted her special protection and privileges. She was then identified as 'the king's hostess' (*hospes Regis*), and guaranteed that 'nothing is to be taken of her corn at [her manor of] Caumpenden or elsewhere, and no bailiff or other minister of the king shall be lodged within her dwelling place at Shrewsbury'.[30] Further archival documents show her wealth extending beyond her manors. She acted regularly as a banker, making extensive loans to merchants, mercers, and knights throughout Shrewsbury's surrounding district and for as much as £100.[31] Thus, this wresting of power from elected officials was indeed a case of class conflict, but its direction was the opposite of what we may have expected from a reading of a single document. Like the Medici lady revolting against Florence's artisan government several generations later, lady Isabella was revolting against what she no doubt considered as the rabble. These cases bring to bear another topic yet to be studied for late medieval or early modern social history – the role of women as counter-revolutionaries.

Women in early modern uprisings

Although women may never have been the predominant force in revolutionary crowds in any period of history, certainly the sexual composition of insurrectionary crowds was changing dramatically in some regions of Europe by the sixteenth century or earlier. Roger Manning finds that 11 per cent of the participants in enclosure riots of Tudor and Stuart England were women, and several were mostly or entirely feminine protests as with one at Jowls in 1604 when 200 marched to destroy the duke of Suffolk's fences, ditches, and bridges to obtain rights of common pasture.[32] Unruly women in early modernity were not confined to the countryside. In Scotland, at St Giles' Cathedral, Edinburgh, in 1637, 'rascally serving women' resisted Charles I's imposition of the Book of Common Prayer by drowning out the Dean's reading; they then hurled prayer stools at the Bishop of Edinburgh. When evicted, they stoned the doors and windows of the church.[33] Women also emerged in leadership roles, as with grain riots at Maldon in 1629, when Ann Carter played a leading role not just in the rioting itself but in the planning, by first touring clothing townships to gain support and then sending letters in which she styled herself 'captain'. Unable to write, she employed a local baker as her secretary.[34]

Unlike in the later Middle Ages, early modern England does not appear exceptional relative to the rest of Europe. Revolts in seventeenth-century France produced equally colourful and significant cases of women's participation and leadership in major revolts. According to William Beik, the most compelling desire of seventeenth-century crowds was to punish the authorities, and often women led these revolts.[35] He also argued that one characteristic to distinguish popular rebellion from factional warfare in seventeenth-century French cities was the appearance of women as the participants in the former, but not in the latter.[36] Women started the tax revolt at Montpellier in 1645,[37] and a 'virago' named la Branlaire led it.[38] In a revolt at Dijon in 1668, women were enlisted to start the disorder.[39] The 1675 revolt of Bordeaux against royal taxation began with 'a fierce group of female peddlers wielding knives', who attacked and chased government agents from town, throwing rocks and calling them *gabeleurs*.[40] In the same year seditious women in Bergerac threw all the government's officially stamped paper into a stream.[41] Across early modern Europe, many other examples can be added, starting at least as early as the Hussite movement, in which women fought alongside men with the same weapons, participating not just as camp followers.[42] Women also became prevalent as rebels in regions east of the Elbe as in Stenka Razin's revolt against Moscow in 1670: not only did many women join the movement, several, as with Razin's mother, commanded rebel detachments.[43]

Early modern Britain and France thus far have been the two countries best explored for women in early modern popular protest. For early modern Italy, despite the thorough and excellent work of historians on women and religious movements, the family, property, literature, art, and work,[44] no Natalie Zemon Davis or William Beik has yet to emerge to explore them in popular revolt. From the shadows of the historiography, however, some signs of change in women's participation and importance to popular rebellion might be detectable at least in places by the late sixteenth or seventeenth century. During the famous Neapolitan revolt of 1647 – the one led by the crazed fisherman Masaniello – chronicles reported women marching under their own captains, armed with spits and shovels, and, according to some, with arquebuses and halberds. But historians have mostly ignored this evidence or, as in the case of Peter Burke, have deemed it untrustworthy. By his counter-intuitive reasoning, women appear in the accounts of the revolt because of Neapolitan 'machismo'![45]

Earlier examples can be culled, as with the description of a bread riot in the city of Florence in April 1497, after the Medici had been expelled and 'during the worst famine the city had known for decades'.[46] According to the diary of the druggist Luca Landucci, an uprising spread through Florence (*si levò un rumore per Firenze*) on 18 April that ended at the granary (Palazzo del Grano) and Florence's town hall (the Palazzo della Signoria). 'Certain poor women went to the gate of the Palace (probably del Grano), beseeched mercy and bread.' Then they began chanting, 'Push, Push' (*serra, serra*), trying to squeeze everyone inside (I presume inside the Palazzo del Grano), but they were stopped and 'the shop' closed. Reminiscent of grain riots at Siena, Rome, Florence, and Genoa during the decades of food shortages in the 1320s and 1330s, with the same cries of 'Misericordia e pane', little violence or threats to the state developed.[47] And the state now as with incidents in the early fourteenth century responded more with benevolence than with violence. The following day, the government lowered the price of grain. Landucci reports no violence at all, and later, the Florentine patrician Piero Parenti, remembered this famine (*carestia*) by how quickly the women became silent.[48] A letter in the Strozzi family archive, however, presents the women's gathering as slightly more threatening. Lionardo di Bartolomeo Nasi, in the city at the time of the women's 'noise' (*romore*) reported (among other things) the events to his friend Lord Lorenzo di Filippo Strozzi, then staying at his villa of Santuccio, south of the city. According to Nasi, it began with only 15 women, yelling 'bread, bread' (*pane, pane*) and running to the Palazzo della Signoria, but quickly it snowballed supposedly to 'more than 3,000 women', and some were shouting 'Pale, Pale', the pro-Medici chant (after the six balls of their family coats of arms). Despite such a political tinge and such numbers, the letter mentions only one incident of violence. An officer of the Florentine police and spy network, the Otto di Guardia (which had its own court of summary justice), wounded a young girl (*fanciulina*) in the head, and the girl's mother retaliated by 'throwing many rocks' at the cop, 'making a shameful spectacle of herself'. But as in Landucci's account, the crowd quickly dissipated because of government sympathy and assurances rather than repression. The Otto promised to supply 'good bread to every neighbourhood', and the women returned home.[49]

Does this event signal a change taking place in Renaissance Florence that might parallel trends in England and France? Perhaps with an increase in bread riots were women becoming more visible in popular protest? In fact, F. W. Kent has combed through various sources for Florence during the second half of the fifteenth and into the early sixteenth century and has found further examples of popular revolt, as with 'a tumult' in the Cathedral of Florence during the same 'terrible spring' of 1497, in which an officer of the Otto di Guardia was torn to pieces, and its chronicler remarked, 'Florence was about to be turned upside down'.[50] But from Kent's sample, nothing more is heard about any women participating in any of these events.

Another clue that such a profound transition may not yet have happened in parts of Italy comes from the work of Christine Shaw on organised popular resistance to the billeting of troops and the abuses of warfare imperilling villagers and commoners in towns during the Italian wars, particularly during the decade of the 1520s.[51] Based on chronicles and especially the voluminous Spanish correspondence between those on the scene in Northern Italy, where the wars were raging, and the rulers back home, Shaw depicts the surprisingly frequent and often successful defence of villages and cities as important as Milan by peasants and ordinary citizens. As she shows, these amounted not only to 'stabbing lone marauders', but to organised resistance with peasants attacking regiments of German or French pike infantry and driving them from their territories. These commoners were seasoned in handling the new weaponry of the sixteenth century and showed skills in military organisation: 'By the mid-1520s, French, German, Spanish, and Swiss troops had all suffered at the hands of vengeful Italian peasants.'[52] Yet, despite her substantial amassing of evidence for such actions by mountain peasants and 'people'[53] in Milan and Roveto,[54] women appear in her descriptions only once, and that case is telling. With German troops about to invade the remote mountain village of Breganze in the Vicentino, 'the women of the village with all the moveable property were sent to safety higher up the mountains'.[55] Although the absence of women in her cases does not arise from any blindness to women in the sources. The various letters exposing the resistance use gender-free language, such as inhabitants or 'pueblo',[56] others use terms such as 'citizens' which would imply only men,[57] or refer explicitly to men as with the insurrection against the German guards at Milan on 26 April 1526: the ones to initiate the insurrection were 'some young men of the city'.[58]

This absence of active resistance from women in sixteenth century Northern Italy is all the more surprising given that the one sort of popular insurgence in which women are most often seen during the late Middle Ages was community-wide resistance to invading or billeted soldiers. Could this possible change in the direction of women's insurgency have resulted from sixteenth-century advances in weaponry and tactics that would have sent women from the barricades to hiding in the hills as happened at Breganze in the 1520s?[59] Or was Italy a special case, different from France and England, when communities willingly enlisted women in their popular struggles and when women desired to become so engaged? To answer these questions comparative research is needed, but for Italy scholars must first dig through the sources to establish the early modern patterns of popular revolt and determine when, where, and in what sorts of conflicts women may have come to the fore. When did women-only bands of popular rebels emerge in Italy as can be seen in England as early as a tax revolt at Bristol in 1401 or the all-women's march on Parliament in 1427?[60] Were the Valdambra peasant women of 1431 a sign of new times?

Certainly, the evidence from the Neapolitan revolt of 1647 suggests that a transition from women's near absence to their increasing presence in popular protest, even possessing their own brigands, may have occurred, but when? I have taken two samples from sources rich in popular insurrections for early fifteenth-century Italy and which continue into the late fifteenth and sixteenth century – the *Diario della città di Roma di Stefano Infessura Scribasenato* and Bernardino

Corio's *Storia di Milano*. Popular riots of various sorts continue in these sources, such as a general strike against a tax on wine comprising 'all shopkeepers in Rome' in 1490, and a revolt of villagers against papal rule in the Marche in 1491 that resulted in papal officials being killed.[61] But none of these events yet mention any women insurgents.

Even jumping to the seventeenth century, was Naples an exception? Did the wave of revolts occurring at the same time in Salerno, Palermo, and through the countryside of Southern Italy from Sicily to the Abruzzi with many of the same characteristics and causes also see women marching under their own captains, with spits, shovels, and even arquebuses? Were similar movements on the rise in Central and Northern Italy as with one in Fermo in the Marche in 1648, where 'plebs' joined by patricians opposed their papal governor, ransacking his palace, storming the prison, and murdering him 'in cold blood'? Domenico Sella's description of it cites no women. Did the absence depend on the historian and the milieu in which he was writing? In his excellent survey of seventeenth-century Italy, he fails to mention women in any riots or revolts, including Masaniello's of 1647, for which the primary sources reveal their presence.

The problem in part for understanding women's role in popular insurrection in early modern Italy results from a lack of interest in popular insurrection in general that informed early modern social and political history in France and England from the late 1960s to the present – works of John Walter, Roger Manning, Andy Wood, Yves-Marie Bercé, René Pillorget, William Beik, Natalie Davis, and Charles Tilly to name a few. By contrast, works exposing popular protest for Italy have centred on specific regions or individual incidents such as Rosario Villari's study of Naples in the 1580s and on Masaniello in 1647,[62] H. G. Koenigsberger's pioneering work on Palermo in 1647,[63] Giuseppe Giarrizzo's work on the Kingdom of Two Sicilies,[64] Geoffrey Symcox's study of Amadeus II and the near-quarter century of resistance to his salt taxes in Savoy.[65]

A pan-peninsular work on popular revolt in early modern Italy, even for one aspect of it – the role of women insurgents – could, however, prove more difficult and time consuming than the study of popular insurrection across much of Western Europe. Not only do the administrative records for early modern states expand exponentially, for early modern Italy, no grand collections of chronicles and other narrative sources, such as Lodovico Muratori's *Rerum Italicarum Scriptores*, its modern editions of chronicles and other records, or the collections such as the *Fonti per la Storia d'Italia dall'Istituto Storico Italiano: Studi e Testi, Documenti di Storia*, etc. were assembled in the late Enlightenment or more recently. To be sure, other published sources such as series of diplomatic records, official letters, and ambassadorial reports in places such as Turin, Milan, Venice, and Rome are available. But the student of popular revolt for early modern Italy, even just for women's participation, would be forced to sample greater proportions of archival records and to devise more case studies than would be necessary for the late Middle Ages.[66]

Conclusion

Historians have thus far attempted to explain women's role in early modern popular revolt as though it were a near-timeless element of some amorphous and long 'pre-modern' past, that women were put on the front lines or initiated the rioting, because they were held less accountable for what they were doing than men, and, if caught, would be punished less harshly.[67] Natalie Zemon Davis added that sexual inversion also gave a more positive licence to unruly women.[68] But these explanations fail to address why women's remarkable participation and leadership in popular revolts was relatively recent in Europe, beginning sometime around the late fifteenth or sixteenth century, and thus cannot be attributed to deep structural aspects of some ambiguous 'pre-modern' past, or worse, explained trans-historically by women's 'biology'. New explanations need to be framed in contexts specific to early modernity. Perhaps, the role of women as insurgents in late medieval England may suggest a hypothesis: that the growth of stronger, more repressive states pressured men and families to rely more heavily on their kinswomen, who might be (or who were believed to be) treated more leniently than husbands or brothers. Yet, no one to my knowledge has compared punishments meted out to male and female popular rebels or how differences in their treatment may have changed from the late Middle Ages to the early modern period. Nor has anyone compared women's participation in riots during the early modern period between centralised, strong states and weaker and more fragmented ones. Moreover, as seen above with Douai's 'foul-mouthed' women of 1322, female insurgents could in fact be prosecuted more, and not less, severely than their male companions. Finally, historians have yet to consider seriously women's reasons for acting subversively against bosses or rulers, why they decided to risk their necks and become more frequently engaged in insurrectionary acts during the early modern period than they had done before during the Middle Ages.

An easy explanation might point to the greater frequency of periods of scarcity in early modern Europe compared with the later Middle Ages, especially after the Black Death to the end of the fifteenth century, and that these basic needs of the hearth bore more heavily on women and children than on men. Perhaps, Yves-Marie Bercé's and Jean Delumeau's biological determinacy should reappear in this more nuanced view of the 'pre-modern', that the new climatic and political conditions creating the new conditions of sixteenth- and seventeenth-century scarcity stimulated women's basic instincts to protect and preserve their offspring. Yet as seen above, the early modern riots organised by Ann Carter, la Branlaire, the ones at St Giles' Cathedral comprised 'rascally serving women', those at Jowl over rights in common, women's troops at Naples against Spanish absolutism, and many others staffed by women, did not centre on matters of famine or cries for bread but were organised actions against the nobility, matters of church doctrine, the abuses of ruling classes, and concerned overwhelmingly questions of rights similar to those revolts triggered during late medieval Europe. The question remains: why did women rebels become more prevalent in early modern Europe?

Notes

1 G. Rudé, *The Crowd in the French Revolution*, Oxford: Clarendon, 1959.
2 C. Tilly, 'How protest modernized in France, 1845–1855,' in W. Aydelotte, A. Bogue, and R. Fogel (eds), *The Dimensions of Quantitative Research in History*, Princeton, NJ: Princeton University Press, 1972, pp. 380–455; C. Tilly, 'Hauptformen kollektiver Aktion in Westeuropa, 1500–1975,' in R. Tilly (ed.), *Geschichte und Gesellschaft*, 1975: Heft 2: *Sozialer Protest*, Gottingen: Vandenhoeck and Ruprecht, 1977, pp. 154–63; C. Tilly, *European Revolutions, 1492–1992*, Oxford: Oxford University Press, 1993; and C. Tilly, *Contentious Performances*, Cambridge: University of Cambridge, 2008. Also, see S. Tarrow, *Power in Movements: Social Movements and Contentious Politics*, 3rd edn, Cambridge: Cambridge University Press, 2011, pp. 1–6, which relies heavily on Tilly. For J. Scott, *Weapons of the Weak: Everyday Forms of Peasant Resistance*, New Haven, CT: Yale University Press, 1985, the transition did not take place until the 1970s, but he was here concerned principally with Indonesia.
3 P. Crone, *Pre-industrial Societies*, Oxford: Oxford University Press, 1989. For a broader discussion of these sociological models of pre-industrial revolt and their application to the Middle Ages, see my *Lust for Liberty: The Politics of Social Revolt in Medieval Europe, 1200–1425*, Cambridge, MA: Harvard University Press, 2006, pp. 1–13, ch. 6; and my *Popular Protest in Late Medieval English Towns*, Cambridge: Cambridge University Press, 2012.
4 Y.-M. Bercé, *Revolt and Revolution in Early Modern Europe: An Essay on the History of Political Violence*, trans. J. Bergin, Manchester: Manchester University Press, 1987 [1980], p. 107; Y.-M. Bercé, *History of Peasant Revolts: The Social Origins of Rebellion in Early Modern France*, trans. A. Whitmore, Cambridge:

Cambridge University Press, 1990, pp. 174–5; Y.-M. Bercé, *Histoire des croquants: Étude des soulèvements populaires au XVIIe siècle dans le sud-ouest de la France*, 2 vols, Geneva: Droz, 1974, vol. 2, p. 543.
5 J. Delumeau, *La peur en Occident (XIVe–XVIIIe siècles): Une cité assiégée*, Paris: Fayard, 1978, pp. 181–2.
6 J. Bohstedt, 'The myth of the feminine food riot: women as proto-citizens in English community politics, 1790–1810,' in H. Applewhite and D. Levy (eds), *Women and Politics in the Age of the Democratic Revolution*, Ann Arbor: University of Michigan Press, 1990, pp. 21–60; R. Manning, *Village Revolts: Social Protest and Popular Disturbances in England, 1509–1640*, Oxford: Oxford University Press, 1988.
7 E. Gordon, 'Women, work, and collective action: Dundee jute workers 1870–1906', *Journal of Social History*, 21, 1987, pp. 27–47; T. Kaplan, *Red City, Blue Period: Social Movements in Picasso's Barcelona*, Berkeley: University of California Press, 1992.
8 Cohn, *Lust for Liberty*, ch. 6.
9 G. Espinas, *La vie urbaine de Douai au Moyen Âge*, 4 vols, Paris, A. Picard, 1913, vol. 2, pp. 663–5; vol. 4, doc. no. 1006.
10 Ibid., pp. 270–5.
11 Gerardi Maurisii, *Cronica Dominorum Ecelini et Alberici fratrum de Romano (AA. 1183–1237)*, ed. G. Soranzo, RIS, VIII/4, Città di Castello: S. Lapi, 1913–4, p. 33.
12 *Cronaca senese attribuita ad Agnolo di Tura del Grasso, detta La Cronaca maggiore*, in *Cronache senesi*, ed. A. Lisini and F. Iacometti, 15/6, Bologna: N. Zanichelli, 1931–9, p. 350.
13 See the various sources on Fra Dolcino's movement in *Historia Fratris Dulcini Heresiarche di Anonimo Sincrono*, ed. A. Segarizzi, RIS, IX/5, Città di Castello: S. Lapi, 1907.
14 Petri Azarii, *Liber gestorum in Lombardia*, ed. F. Cognasso, RIS, 16/4, Bologna: N. Zanichelli, 1925–39, p. 122; and Matteo Villani, *Cronica con la continuazione di Filippo Villani*, 2 vols, ed. G. Porta, Parma: Fondazione Pietro Bembo, 1995, vol. 1, pp. 751–2; vol. 2, pp. 139–41, 206, 364–6.
15 Marino Sanuto, *Vitæ Ducum Venetorum Italice Scriptae ab origine urbis sive ab anno 421 usque ad annum 1493*, RIS, XXII, ed. L. Muratori, Milan: ex typographia Societatis Palatinae, 1723, cols 669–71.
16 Matteo Villani, *Cronica*, ed. Porta, vol. 1, pp. 374–5.
17 *Cronaca senese conosciuta sotto il nome di Paolo di Tommaso Montauri*, in *Cronache senesi*, ed. Lisini and Iacometti, p. 834.
18 On these and other peace movements of the fourteenth and early fifteenth century, see Cohn, *Lust for Liberty*, pp. 4–6, 92–4, 105, 123, 132–3, 144, 158, 184, 202–3.
19 Jean de Venette, *Chronique dite de Jean de Venette*, ed. C. Beaune, Paris: Librarie Générale Française, 2011, p. 180. I wish to thank Justine Firnhaber-Baker for pointing me to these texts. It reflects, however, my reading of the passages.
20 Ibid., pp. 180–3.
21 On these letters, see S. Luce, *Histoire de la Jacquerie d'après des documents inédits*, 2nd edn, Paris: H. Champion, 1894, pp. 175–234; S. K. Cohn, Jr., *Popular Protest in Late Medieval Europe: Italy, France, and Flanders*, Manchester: Manchester University Press, 2004, ch. 3; and, most recently, D. Aiton, '"Shame on him who allows them to live": the Jacquerie of 1358', PhD thesis, Glasgow University, 2007.
22 For community-wide remissions of Jacquerie rebels, see examples in Cohn, *Popular Protest*, ch. 3.
23 Firnhaber-Baker has transcribed these documents (AN X2a 7, fol. 213r and JJ 86, no. 326, fol. 109v, respectively).
24 For these lists, see S. K. Cohn, Jr., *The Laboring Classes in Renaissance Florence*, New York: Academic Press, 1980, ch. 6; Cohn, *Lust for Liberty*; S. K. Cohn, Jr., 'Alliance in exile between the radical Ciompi and magnates...', in K. Jansen, J. Drell, and F. Andrews (eds), *Medieval Italy: Texts in Translation*, Philadelphia: University of Pennsylvania Press, 2009, no. 41, pp. 146–8.
25 Stefani, *Cronaca fiorentina di Marchionne di Coppo Stefani*, ed. N. Rodolico, RIS 30/1, Città di Castello: S. Lapi, 1903, p. 377. This part of the chronicle is badly damaged with several lacunae, including one about what the woman did after fleeing to 'Vitorata'.
26 For examples, see Cohn, *Popular Protest in Late Medieval English Towns*.
27 See S. Federico, 'The imaginary society: women in 1381', *Journal of British Studies*, 40, 2001, pp. 159–83; A. Réville, *Le soulèvement des travailleurs d'Angleterre en 1381*, Paris: A. Picard, 1898, Appendix II, documents no. 199 and 200; C. Petit-Dutaillis, 'Introduction historique', in ibid., lxxxvi–vii; Cohn, *Popular Protest in Late Medieval English Towns*, pp. 318–19; Oman, *The Great Revolt*, 2nd edn, Oxford: Oxford University Press, 1969, p. 107.
28 CPR, Edward I, vol. 4, p. 271, 1303.xi.30.
29 Ibid., p. 270, 1303.xi.25.

30 CPR, Edward II, vol. 4, p. 53, 1322.i.25.
31 In the online records from the National Archives, she appears 83 times, all in debtor–credit relations (TNA, C 241, Chancery: Certificates of Statute Merchant and Statute Staple), and in all but six of these transactions she was the creditor with loans ranged from 40s. to £100 made to merchants and mercers of Shrewsbury and knights and lords within the region.
32 Manning, *Village Revolts*, pp. 96, 99.
33 See N. Z. Davis, 'Women on top', in *Society and Culture in Early Modern France*, Stanford, CA: Stanford University Press, 1975, p. 146. Dr Laura Stewart has recently challenged this interpretation of the protest at St Giles', arguing that aristocratic men were behind the servant women's actions.
34 Davis, 'Women on top', pp. 124–51; J. Walter, *Crowds and Popular Politics in Early Modern England*, Manchester: Manchester University Press, 2006, ch. 2 especially pp. 49–58; K. Wrightson, *English Society 1580–1680*, London: Hutchison, 1982, pp. 177–8.
35 W. Beik, *Urban Protest in Seventeenth-Century France*, Cambridge: Cambridge University Press, 1997, p. 37.
36 Ibid., p. 196.
37 Ibid., p. 116; H. Kamen, *The Iron Century: Social Change in Europe 1550–1660*, London: Weidenfeld & Nicolson, 1971, p. 356; Davis, 'Women on top', p. 146; Bercé, *Histoire des Croquants*, vol. 1, p. 228.
38 Davis, 'Women on top', p. 146.
39 Beik, *Urban Protest*, p. 48.
40 Ibid., pp. 131, 147.
41 Ibid., p. 158.
42 S. Turnbull, *The Hussite Wars, 1419–36*, Oxford: Osprey, 2004, p. 18; T. Fudge, *The Magnificent Ride: The First Reformation in Hussite Bohemia*, Aldershot: Ashgate, 1998, pp. 171, 172, 255.
43 G. Parker, *Global Crisis: War, Climate Change & Catastrophe in the Seventeenth Century*, New Haven, CT: Yale University Press, 2013, p. 181.
44 See for instance, the many articles by G. Zarri and her *Le sante vive: Profezie di corte e devozione femminile tra '400 e '500*, Turin: Rosenberg & Sellier, 1990; S. Evangelisti, *Nuns: A History of Convent Life, 1450–1700*, Oxford: Oxford University Press, 2004; S. Matthews Grieco, *Ange ou diablesse: La représentation de la femme au XVIe siècle*, Paris: Flammarion, 1991; L. Scaraffia and G. Zarri (eds), *Donne e fede*, Bari: Laterza, 1994; D. Robin, *Publishing Women: Salons, the Presses, and the Counter-Reformation in Sixteenth-Century Italy*, Chicago, IL: University of Chicago Press, 2007; A. Groppi (ed.), *Il Lavoro delle donne*, Bari: Laterza, 1996, parts I and II; S. Cavaciocchi (ed.), *La donna nell'economia, secc. XIII–XVIII: atti della 'Ventunesima Settimana di studi', 10–15 aprile 1989*, Florence: Le Monnier, 1990; and many more.
45 Beik, *Urban Protest*, p. 146; A. Wood, *Riot, Rebellion and Popular Politics in Early Modern England*, Basingstoke: Palgrave, 2002, pp. 37, 48, 147, 158; Davis, 'Women on top', pp. 146, 147; P. Burke, 'The virgin of the Carmine and the Revolt of Masaniello', *P&P*, 99, 1983, p. 13. For a more recent and positive assessment of the role of women in this revolt, see F. Benigno, *Mirrors of Revolution: Conflict and Political Identity in Early Modern Europe*, Turnhout: Brepols, 2010, pp. 308–9.
46 F. Kent, '"Be rather loved than feared": class relations in Quattrocento Florence', in W. Connell (ed.), *Society and Individual in Renaissance Florence*, Berkeley: University of California Press, 2002, pp. 13–50, citation at pp. 24–5; on the economic crisis then afflicting the city more broadly, see J. Henderson, *Piety and Charity in Late Medieval Florence*, Oxford: Oxford University Press, 1994, pp. 201–6; also see the harrowing entries in Landucci's *Diario fiorentinio dal 1450 al 1516: continuato da un anonimo fino al 1542*, Florence: Sansoni, 1883, on 27 March 1497, p. 145, of men, women, and children fainting from starvation, some dying in the streets, 'many' in hospitals, and others while waiting for handouts at Florence's Palazzo del Grano on 4 April when the grain prices soared to their highest (p. 146).
47 On these grain riots, see Cohn, *Lust for Liberty*, pp. 70–5.
48 The reference to the Parenti diary is in C. Carnesecchi, 'Un tumulto di donne', in I. Del Badia (ed.), *Miscellanea Fiorentina di erudizione e storia*, 2 vols, Florence: Tip. dell'arte della stampa, 1886–1902, vol. 2, pp. 45–7.
49 The letter is transcribed in Carnesecchi, 'Un tumulto di donne', pp. 46–7.
50 Kent, '"Be rather loved than feared"' pp. 24–5.
51 C. Shaw, 'Popular resistance to military occupation during the Italian Wars', in S. K. Cohn, Jr. and F. Ricciardelli (eds), *The Culture of Violence in Renaissance Italy*, Florence: Le Lettere, 2012, pp. 257–71.
52 Ibid., p. 262.
53 Also, gender-neutral terms such as 'inhabitants' are used.

54 Ibid., pp. 263–6, 268. At Milan, it was against billeted German soldiers on 25 April 1526 and, at Roveto, against abuses committed by the Gascon infantry about the same time.
55 Ibid., p. 269; taken from *Una cronaca vicentina del Cinquecento*, ed. J. Gurin-Dalle Mese, Vicenza: Accademia Olimpica, 1983, p. 193.
56 *Calendar of Letters, Despatches and State Papers, Relating to Negotiations between England and Spain* ... III, part 1, ed. Pascual de Gayangos, London: Longman, 1873, pp. 661–2, describes Milanese rebels during a 'quistion' on St George's day with Germans soldiers posted at Milan's castle. 'People' is also used for village resistance in Piedmont at the same time, see p. 704.
57 See, again, the case of Milan, pp. 661–2.
58 Ibid., pp. 661–2.
59 Such an explanation would fly in the face with many resistance movements in contemporary history, when weaponry and tactics became still more sophisticated; yet women were among the rank and file and occasionally the leaders.
60 See Cohn, *Popular Protest in Late Medieval English Towns*, p. 320.
61 *Diario della città di Roma di Stefano Infessura Scribasenato*, new edn, ed. O. Tommasini, Fonti per la Storia d'Italia, Scrittori, Secolo XV, Rome: Forzani, 1890, pp. 260, 267.
62 See most recently, R. Villari, *Un sogno di libertà: Napoli nel declino di un impero, 1585–1648*, Milan: Mondadori, 2012.
63 H. Koenigsberger, 'The revolt of Palermo in 1647', *Cambridge Historical Journal*, 8, 1946, pp. 129–44.
64 G. Giarrizzo, 'La Sicilia dal Cinquecento all'Unità d'Italia', in V. D'Alessandro and G. Giarrizzo (eds), *La Sicilia dal Vespro all'unità d'Italia*, Turin: UTET, 1989, pp. 99–783.
65 G. Symcox, *Victor Amadeus II: Absolutism in the Savoyard State, 1675–1730*, Berkeley: University of California Press, 1983.
66 For the latter, see *Lust for Liberty* and its dependence on the grand collections of documents for the central and late Middle Ages.
67 This is Parker's argument in a section entitled 'Chicks Up Front', based largely on the trans-historical claims of Jean Nicolas that women's 'ritualized behaviour' in this regard 'transcended time' (*Global Crisis*, pp. 515–16).
68 Davis, 'Women on top'.

11
POPULAR MOVEMENTS AND ELITE LEADERSHIP
Exploring a late medieval conundrum in cities of the Low Countries and Germany[1]

Justine Smithuis

A historiographically controversial aspect of late medieval popular movements is the involvement of elites as leaders of, or coalition partners with, groups of common citizens and workers. For example in Utrecht, a relatively important episcopal city in the Northern Low Countries, craft guilds and other groups of artisans often worked together with factions within the ministerial (knightly) or bourgeois elite, a collaboration that became something of a tradition from the later fourteenth century. The rival parties in Utrecht, although of changing character and composition, became known by the names of the city's most important families: the *Gunterlingen* and the *Lichtenbergers*. In 1379–80, conflict arose over a range of issues of common interest, such as the election procedures for the city council, the role of the assembly of guild members (*morgensprake*) in local government, a contested milling excise, and other issues concerning public finances. During this civic crisis, the *Gunterlingen* were led by a certain Gerrit de Bole van Heemskerk, a knightly figure belonging to the Gunter family who had a castle in nearby Holland. He was later exiled with 27 men. In this struggle, Gerrit and other members of the faction of the *Gunterlingen* apparently stood on the side of those who, in vain, challenged the rule of the city council. While Gerrit's non-elite associates were not poor or marginal men – all of the banished participants were citizens and guild members – they were of much lower status than he and probably had very different interests at stake.[2]

Such partnerships as that between the aristocrat Gerrit and the guildsmen, whose objectives and interests appear fundamentally incompatible, might seem inexplicable. Drawing upon the recent work of Samuel Cohn, Jan Dumolyn, Jelle Haemers, and others, this contribution aims to explore such partnerships more fully and to offer the beginnings of an explanation by focusing on the conditions and circumstances for collective political action, particularly the organisation of violence. By exploring the conditions for successful political action, and developments therein, elite involvement and leadership can be understood more easily. As I will argue, elite involvement was partly a result of a culture of violence which permeated medieval urban politics as much as it did 'rural' politics. Elite leadership was further favoured by dramatic developments in the way that cities were governed in the course of the fourteenth and fifteenth centuries. In this contribution, I will mainly focus on cities in the Low Countries and Germany where craft guilds gained access to city councils and the political establishment. Many examples will be taken from Utrecht, which greatly resembled neighbouring Flemish and German cities in its political and social developments, but which is relatively unknown to modern researchers.[3]

Historiographical context

One of the central elements in the historiography on 'preindustrial revolts' that prevailed until very recently was the supposed spontaneity of protesting crowds.[4] These crowds seemed unable to organise themselves properly and were frequently led, or manipulated, by people who came from outside their ranks. These leaders were usually of (much) higher social standing than the protesters themselves, such as kings, nobles, mayors, or clerics. This picture of the typical 'pre-industrial revolt' was based predominantly on early modern cases, but the few medievalists who addressed medieval revolts from a synthetic point of view in the later twentieth century, notably Michel Mollat, Philippe Wolff, and Guy Fourquin, had come to similar conclusions about the leadership of revolts, though from other directions.[5] According to Fourquin, who was influenced by the economist Vilfredo Pareto and by anti-Marxism, political revolts in the (late) Middle Ages, especially in the growing cities, had typically been initiated and led by 'new' elites, while rebelling poor and common people, whether from rural or urban origin, tended to follow traditional elite figures.[6]

In the first new synthesis of late medieval revolt in Western Europe since the 1970s, Samuel Cohn showed that these ideas about medieval revolts needed revision. In the period between 1200 and 1425, he found that archival and narrative sources did not show that 'peasants, artisans, and workers failed to lead their own revolts and instead had to rely on the organizational skills, military expertise, eloquence, and charisma of class outsiders'.[7] Instead, to a much greater extent than had been assumed, commoners were capable of rational and strategic planning of collective political action; leadership 'from the inside' was not exceptional in medieval popular revolts.[8] In general, craft guilds – representing mostly artisans and shopkeepers from the middling groups – produced their own leaders. Even disenfranchised workers, such as the Florentine Ciompi (1378–82), Cohn found, were in some cases able to manage relatively successful collective actions by themselves.[9]

That commoners could and often did organise and lead their own movements is thus a well-accepted position. Nevertheless, elite participation is detectable in most revolts by artisans and workers in cities in the Low Countries, Germany, Italy, and elsewhere where craft guild revolutions took place. Elites appear in the sources as allies of guilds or other groups of commoners, as apparent leaders, or as those who represented the protest group to the outside world. Even during the heyday of urban craft guild revolutions, in the years and decades around 1300, coalitions between craft guilds and patrician factions, and probably shared leadership of the 'movement', were the rule rather than the exception.[10]

The presence of elites led earlier researchers to believe that political conflicts in these cities really originated with power struggles between elite families and that their leaders were able to assemble large followings from the local guild community to pursue their own private goals. Consciously or not, they thus downplayed the ability of the guilds and of commoners to pursue their own goals.[11] But this position, too, has been recently revised. In a joint effort of specialists on late medieval Flemish revolts and elites, Jonas Braekevelt, Frederik Buylaert, Jan Dumolyn, and Jelle Haemers turned the question on its head and looked at the leading role of patrician families and factions in Flemish cities in the context of fully fledged corporate politics.[12] They found that corporate groups supported one faction or another strategically, in order to profit politically from the divides within the elite. They also argued that the links between commoners and patrician leaders could be explained by ties of political clientelism, mostly in the periphery of the groups. Even then, though, they found it 'sometimes difficult to understand why corporate groups and common labourers supported factions led by patrician families'.[13]

It is not simply the presence of elites in 'popular' movements that demands better explanation, but also the periodisation of such cooperation. Most of the revolts by artisans and lower-class workers with leadership from their own ranks took place in the heyday of urban craft guild revolutions, in the decades before and around 1300 and in the fourteenth century.[14] At some point in the late Middle Ages, protesting groups of commoners began to rely more on leaders from the outside than before. Mollat and Wolff had explained this shift by linking what they supposed were revolts arising from poverty and misery to the social upheavals caused by the Black Death (1346–53).[15] Fourquin, for his part, argued that the (late) fourteenth and fifteenth century showed more revolts by poor people, and fewer revolts by middle-class citizens challenging ruling elites. This he explained by the growth of economic problems and social tensions as routes for social mobility were increasingly barred for lower-class people.[16] More recently, Samuel Cohn, refining his thesis from *Lust for Liberty* about the 'non-pre-modern' character of medieval revolts, suggested that the turning point for this transformation took place around 1400, or somewhat earlier or later, depending on the region and the circumstances.[17] From the fifteenth century onwards, in his view, popular revolts gradually developed into the 'classical' pre-industrial revolt which had been inspired in many ways by cases in the seventeenth and eighteenth centuries and which often had links to food shortage or subsistence problems, which involved more 'proletarian' protesters, and which were led by elites such as nobles, mayors, or clerics.

Cohn, while successfully challenging Mollat and Wolff's thesis about the Black Death, also tentatively linked the transformation to a 'growing gap between rulers and those they ruled' and 'an increasing imbalance in class power', leading in general to more repression of political dissent and more reliance, by protesters, on the military experience and leadership of prominent figures.[18] German and Flemish researchers of urban history have noted fundamental changes in the character and repression of urban revolts as well, which they assign roughly to the period from the later fourteenth and fifteenth century onwards. This is usually connected to processes of growing state power and of oligarchisation, in the cities as well as at a central level of government. Governments were on the whole more willing to repress protest actions by their poorer and/or unenfranchised subjects and had more means to do so.[19]

The question remains. Why did craft guilds and commoners, who knew their way around city politics and were capable of producing their own leaders, turn to patricians or other members of the ruling elite when their issues about local government turned to violent clashes? And, generally speaking, why did ordinary (middle-class or lower-class) people follow members of the social and political elites whose power they often sought to reduce? What explains the growth of elite involvement and leadership in popular revolts *after* the craft guilds had become established members of the community and political consciousness had developed among different layers of urban society? These changes cannot be connected simply to the abolition of the political craft guilds – the cradles of late medieval revolt – at the end of the Middle Ages. The development started earlier, in the late fourteenth or fifteenth century, only to speed up when the craft guilds lost their political rights in most cities in the course of the sixteenth century.

This contribution aims to explore the issue of leadership further and to examine developments in the conditions and circumstances for collective political action and revolt in cities, mainly in the Low Countries and Germany, from the late thirteenth until the sixteenth century. 'Leadership' will be understood in a very specific way. Here, I will use the term exclusively to refer to the practical leadership of a revolt in a political and military manner: leaders were those who commanded the protesters during their actions, who negotiated with the authorities or other parties, who decided on planning and strategies, whether or not assisted in this by others or delegated to do so by the group. Leaders were thus not necessarily those who roused the crowds and encouraged them to action in the first place.[20]

In what follows, I will suggest an explanation that, on the one hand, takes account of the relatively high level of political organisation and bottom-up initiatives within many late medieval cities. These were features that were particularly pronounced in cities where the craft guilds and middling groups gained access to local political institutions, as in many larger cities in the Low Countries and Germany.[21] On the other hand, it attempts to do justice to the sociopolitical developments that took place over the course of the fourteenth and fifteenth centuries in local government as well as within corporate organisations. It will incorporate some of the arguments already brought forward, such as the attractiveness of coalitions with groups from an already divided elite, and the importance of political clientelism. However, my argument hinges primarily on the organisation of violence.

The organisation of violence – as a threat or as actual (physical) violence – was a precondition for successful political action in the late Middle Ages (and arguably also before that time). As a result, the question of how to organise violence determined to a large degree how political action groups and coalitions came about and how they were structured and led. In order to be successful, this political violence, or the threat of it, needed to be managed in such a way that it was likely to lead to negotiation instead of sheer repression. If repression became inevitable, it had to be managed in such a way that the perpetrators could feel to some extent protected, and, if they lost, that they could reasonably hope to survive and return into their former positions in society again. How political dissent and violence was organised was strongly influenced by developments in urban governments and within the political craft guilds during the late Middle Ages. These developments particularly favoured the role of elite leadership in revolts, to the detriment of the craft guilds as the typical units of collective action.

Violence and political culture in late medieval cities

The state monopoly on violence, as well as modern norms and values concerning the use of violence in political conflicts, have made it possible to distinguish relatively sharply between peaceful forms of protest and negotiation, on the one hand, and violent conflict and revolts, on the other. Unwittingly, our modern political culture greatly influences the way we look at late medieval political conflict, too. But, confronted with overwhelming evidence, historians have increasingly acknowledged that violent encounters and armed protests in late medieval cities were an integral part of urban political culture in this period.[22] Marc Boone, who studied the role of violence in the major cities of Flanders, speaks of an almost uninterrupted flow of violent struggles in the city in which members of the craft guilds were involved, and concludes that violence, for the craft guilds, was a normal element of political action and an instrument of collective communication between the guilds and the city government.[23] Some might consider the medieval Flemish cities unique in their artisans' readiness to rebel, compared to other European cities, but the number of violent encounters in German cities, for example, does not seem to be much different.[24] Patrick Lantschner, who studied several cities in Italy, Flanders, and Northern France comparatively, summarised this view, stating that, generally speaking, 'revolts … formed a fundamental part of the political interactions in late medieval cities'.[25] Still, the sheer number of battles, small-size tumults, armed protest meetings, and other forms of violent political encounters, continues to amaze us.[26] The ease with which people seemed to take up weapons in urban political conflicts is often considered 'remarkable', or a 'paradox', particularly considering the availability, and popularity, of peaceful channels of negotiation, such as petitioning, pursuing lawsuits, and different forms of consultation.[27]

The occurrence of armed assemblies and (physically) violent protest in late medieval urban politics has been treated and analysed in a number of ways, but not usually as a precondition for successful political action. Often, it is analysed as part of repertoires or traditions of collective action, in the manner established by Charles Tilly, looking at the precise forms in which dissent was expressed, during one event or over a longer period of time, and the orchestrated or symbolic character of the violence used.[28] Violence is also viewed as a 'last resort' and therefore as a sign of the level of discontent or even desperation on the side of the protesters. Likewise, it is considered in the context of existing legal systems, norms, and values, paying attention to its legitimation in the face of repression.[29] These are all relevant ways of studying political violence. Nevertheless, integral to all of these approaches is the notion that the use of arms in political conflicts was extraordinary, and that it was, in short, an anomaly in the way urban politics functioned normally, or should have functioned. In this respect, modern historians seem influenced not only by modern circumstances, but also by the powerful late medieval discourse of peace and order which was advocated, amongst others, by the craft guilds themselves.

The popularity of viewing politics as bargaining is telling in this respect. In this view, bargaining and negotiating are supposed to be the rule, and violent encounters to be the opposite, the exception. It has been stated, for instance, that armed protests and revolts in late medieval Flemish cities were 'lapses' in the process of bargaining which needed to be solved so that the bargaining could resume.[30] There are many indications, however, that violence was considered an element of normal urban politics, and, moreover, that it was an essential part of the ongoing bargaining process within the city.[31] Jelle Haemers described the ritual of the *wapeninge*, or call to arms, in Flemish urban politics. In this political tradition, which has analogies in the German practice of *Bannerlauf* (literally, 'running with the banner') and similar practices in Italy, armed artisans marched up to the city hall under the banner of their craft guild when they felt their rights had been violated.[32] Standing armed on the central marketplace, they would threaten violence to support their demands, and would sometimes end up in fights with other guilds or with the city government.[33] Haemers has rightly characterised the *wapeninge* as 'a symbolic sign to start negotiations about the rights of the guilds'.[34] The often symbolic character of the violence was directed precisely at the goal of opening up negotiations, not of closing them down. It is also clear that violence was fundamental to craft guilds' acquisition of access to local governments in the first place. In the thirteenth and early fourteenth centuries, the ability of craft guilds to mobilise armed support and organise revolts of the citizenry, partly by taking over communal defence systems in their neighbourhoods, was arguably the most important factor in their political successes.[35]

The culture of violence in urban politics becomes less of a paradox if we compare it to the culture of feuding in the politics of the surrounding countryside. Feud remained an important practice in the late Middle Ages in the Low Countries and Germany, and, with some regional variation, in other parts of Europe as well (although there one might prefer to speak of warfare instead of feuding).[36] Central to feud was the defence of rights and the purposeful use of violence as a reaction to violations thereof, within the boundaries set by custom and law.[37] The violence itself was in many respects meant not only to redefine the status quo and take (back) what was considered 'right', but also to open up negotiations with the opposing party. It has been emphasised that feuds were usually conducted alongside, or as part of, legal procedures and diplomatic manoeuvres.[38]

Although much of the scholarship has concentrated on aristocratic feuds in the countryside, this feuding culture was undeniably also present in medieval cities. Feuds that were at least partly about the division of power were for a long time the most common means of political competition between knightly families and patrician factions. Communes, guilds, and city governments were also involved in feuding outside the city collectively. The intramural political conflicts which concern us here, between craft guilds, city governments, or other groups of city dwellers, were very similar to 'feuds' or 'wars', too. The comparison has been made within the context of German citizens' struggles (*Bürgerkämpfe*) ending in written peace settlements (*Friedebriefe*). In an analysis of the practice of *Friedebriefe*, Bernd Kannowski noted strong similarities between noble feuding and this type of inner-city conflict, although he did not equate the two because, as he argued, violent urban risings were usually grounded in the universally acknowledged right to rise against bad or illegal government (*Widerstandsrecht*) rather than in the right to feud (*Fehderecht*).[39] Patrick Lantschner, in turn, framed urban revolts within the general theory and practices of medieval warfare. I disagree with Lantschner, however, that rebels 'imitated' the practices of warfare of the surrounding countryside. Rather, they were fully engaged in these practices within the city.[40]

It seems safe to state, therefore, that inhabitants of cities and the countryside shared a similar culture of violence in politics, performed through feuding, revolts, or through other forms of violent political action.[41]

In medieval politics, this culture of violence was instrumental first of all in deterring the opposing party and threatening it into complying with one's demands. Showing off one's moral strength and willingness to use violence, as well as being able to mobilise armed supporters, was just as important – or even more important – than the actual use of violence. That feuding was about deterrence as much as about fighting has been pointed out by Hillay Zmora, amongst others. Focusing on feuds between German nobles and princes in the late Middle Ages, Zmora argued that to be successful in feuds – and, one might add, in politics in general – it was important not only that one win sufficient supporters and allies, but also that 'one was prepared to feud and, crucially, was believed to be so'.[42] Thus, being successful in feuding was closely related to one's moral reputation and one's ability to build and mobilise networks of friends and allies who would be prepared to support you with violence if needed. This was all the more important, because, as Zmora also noted, most feuds were conducted between parties who lived relatively close to each other and were largely dependent on the same social and political networks.

The same could be observed in the microcosms of late medieval cities. When we consider urban politics in this period in the light of a prevailing culture of violence, comparable to the mores and practices of feuding, the frequent occurrence of armed assemblies in the marketplace, the shouting of threatening cries, and, more in the background, the forging of alliances and coalitions in order to acquire more support, become more easily understandable. These phenomena were all signs to negotiate, or, in the case of groups outside the political establishment, they conveyed the message that they should be taken seriously as a negotiating partner. An important condition for political success – apart from actually having the means to challenge the existing balance of power – was that these symbolic performances needed to be in some way or another embedded in local customs, laws, and values concerning political violence. Thus, instead of starting from a contraposition between peaceful popular politics, on the one hand, and violent revolt, on the other, it may be more useful to allow for quite a large grey zone in late medieval urban politics (varying according to local and regional customs), in which the use and threat of violence co-existed with non-violent political practices and were considered perfectly normal forms of political action.

Forms of political action groups

Turning to the groups that initiated political action and revolt in the city, it becomes clear that these were also centred on the organisation of violence. This does not only apply to clear-cut military organisations, such as neighbourhood militias,[43] 'traditional' feuding groups based on strong mutual bonds of (quasi-) kinship, or their politically orientated counterparts: aristocratic factions with their armed and often liveried followings of relatives, helpers, and attendants which were long important to the political scene in medieval cities.[44] Organising violence was also central to the groups and coalitions that would challenge the rule of lords, aristocrats, and patricians in the city. These were the voluntary associations of the communes and the guilds, appearing from as early as the eleventh century onwards in both rural and urban contexts in Western Europe.[45]

The political cooperation in communes and guilds was based on an oath-bound association (*coniuratio*), creating horizontal bonds of brotherhood (*fraternitas*) between the members. The aim of the oath was to secure mutual protection and support (*mutuum auxilium, Schutz und Hilfe,* etc.).[46] The oath was not only meant to create a union of 'brothers', based on internal peace, consensus, and shared values and goals. It also had much to do with defining the group against the outside world and with providing military aid and physical protection to each other in case of resistance to the group's initiatives. The violent character of this form of political association was emphasised by Otto Oexle, an expert on the origins and development of the *coniuratio*. Oexle found that the organisation of violence was a fundamental element in the creation of oath-bound associations from the start. The peasants in Normandy who formed a *coniuratio* against some regional lords around the year 1000, did so with the explicit aim of organising armed resistance against aristocratic violence, and the fraternity of the *Capuciati*, a broad-based coalition of peasants, towns, and nobles in Southern France that aimed to restore peace in the region, crushed a mercenary army in 1183, based on the principle 'mutual aid against all' (*mutuum auxilium contra omnes*). The early communes in the eleventh and twelfth centuries were likewise set on pursuing their goals of peace and liberty violently, if needed. Of course, in the eyes of contemporary power holders – lords, nobles, and clerics – these initiatives were contradictory and bad: 'they pretended to bring peace, but in reality they exerted violence'.[47] These associations were characterised by the way in which the members worked and took decisions together. Based on the principle of equality, they would regularly hold assemblies and choose their leaders, who thus headed the group by means of delegation.

As Oexle argued, the appearance of the sworn association (*coniuratio*) constituted a foundation for the 'culture of [popular] rebellion' in the medieval West.[48] Indeed, this form of political collaboration typically started as an initiative outside the political establishment and within an often hostile world, though there are also cases in which communes managed to be integrated rather peacefully in the existing political structures through privileges from their overlords.[49] As we know, communes gradually became established government institutions in their own right, and guilds – originally merchant guilds, but later also craft guilds – partly too. Even so, the voluntary association of the *coniuratio* appears to have remained the basic form for political action and resistance in the city during the later Middle Ages, as Wilfried Ehbrecht and others have noted.[50] City records and other contemporary sources dating from the fourteenth and fifteenth centuries convey this by referring to political groups behind tumults or revolts in the city in terms indicating a voluntary association, such as *coniuratio, conspiratio/Verschwörung, eninge, confederacions, alliances*. Such initiatives within the city were in principle considered illegal by the local authorities because they implied an infringement on the internal peace and unity of the community. Alternatively, the formation of associations appears from terms referring to groups holding (illegal) meetings (*assemblé, vergaderinge*, etc.).[51] Similar associations seem to have formed the basis of very small groups of protesters as well. City council records in Utrecht from the 1360s, for instance, make note of trials of groups of artisans, consisting of a few men only, who had tried in vain to take up arms against local authorities. They were sentenced above all for making a 'unity' (*eninge*) among themselves, within their guilds, indicating probably the formation of an oath-bound association, for the purpose of mutual protection and support.[52]

In many cases, we lack explicit information about the way political protesters united precisely and what form(s) of collaboration and support was promised or understood between them before undertaking action. Usually, we have to rely on what authorities chose to say about them. In some instances, however, there is more information available. In the city of Regensburg in Germany, there is evidence about a *coniuratio* that formed the basis of political collaboration between an aristocratic family from the surrounding countryside, the Auer family, and 37 citizens of Regensburg in 1330. The *coniuratio* later grew to include about 200 citizens. In this association, they swore to provide each other protection and support (*Schutz und Hilf*) and also to uphold the alliance that they had concluded with several craft guilds in the city. The primary goal of the *coniuratio* was to hold the council accountable for their financial management. A violent tumult ensued, of which one of the results was to get craft guilds more involved in local government for the time being.[53] Another example is the classic *Bannerlauf* in Bremen, which took place in 1365. The protesters' group in this city was known as the Great Company (*Grande Cumpanie*), a clear indication of its military set-up; this was also an oath-bound association that was sworn in this case by a socially diverse group of citizens who united against policies of the city council.[54]

To summarise, there are many indications that political action groups in medieval cities were fundamentally constructed as associations capable of mobilising armed support, of providing physical protection, and of actually using violence if needed. The (threat of) violence that ensued from the formation of these groups, may be considered a normal part of the ongoing bargaining process in these cities. This urban political culture of violence formed part of a more general feuding culture, although the differences between noble feuding and urban political conflicts should not be ignored. At the same time, the political necessity to organise violence effectively put a heavy strain on the collective associations striving for political goals. The challenges for protesters to unite and organise themselves successfully in this way could only be solved in a limited number of cases. And these challenges became more demanding as time went by.

Urban developments in the later Middle Ages

The difficulties involved in organising violence and the increasing pressures put on late medieval urban protesters are well illustrated by a conflict that took place in Utrecht in 1346. In the autumn of 1346, the city of Utrecht was in a great uproar when first an armed protest against the city council and then a large-scale battle took place. It was the first time that Utrecht had experienced such political trouble within its community since the city's craft guilds had gained political recognition in 1304. The conflict, which could be characterised as a combination of elite faction struggle and popular movement, erupted between two alliances: on one side, the bishop of Utrecht with his troops, the city council, and at least one craft guild (the furriers) which appeared with its banner unfurled, and on the other, a large, diverse group of citizens from different guilds, amongst others butchers, tanners, and blacksmiths. When the two sides met in battle, on 22 November, the bishop's coalition won decisively. Some protesters were executed in the aftermath, while others were exiled for 100 years. The collective sentence of exile was pronounced publicly by the bishop, in close consultation with the city council.[55] The document named eight citizens and their 'collaborators' (*medewerkers*), who, in the words of the sentence, had been assisting those eight on the day of the battle and who fled the city with them afterwards. According to the text, they had not only left or 'cleared' (*ontrumet*) the city, but also 'cleared' their guilds.[56] In what followed, the names of the collaborators, nearly 100 men in total, were listed in the order of the guilds they had belonged to before they became involved in the action.

A further step was taken two weeks later: the bishop (as lord of the city), the city council, and the remaining guild community took a fundamental decision on the exact conditions for lawful violent resistance against the city government. These conditions were articulated negatively, so that anyone who resisted with violence against decisions of the city council was to be executed. However, there were a number of conditions: that the city council had been installed by the guilds and was sitting in the city hall at the time of the decision, that the case in question fell within the council's competence, and that their decision had been taken in the interest of the city.[57] The resolution continued by stating that, in case of such unlawful resistance, the city council could demand bystanders physically to 'protect the council and strengthen the law', and if any of the protesters got wounded or killed in the process, the council's helpers would not be punished harshly.[58]

This example from Utrecht in 1346 is indicative of a number of developments that were common to many late medieval cities, including those where craft guilds had not become part of the local government. There were three developments, in particular, which affected the conditions for political action and revolt. The first development was the swift expansion of law-making and judicial powers concentrated in the hands of local city councils and benches of aldermen, so that these were soon able to decide over the life and death of most of the city dwellers without much interference by other powers. This was a development that was shared by many cities in late medieval Europe, and certainly by the bigger ones in the Low Countries and Germany.[59] Part and parcel of this development was a more repressive attitude towards dissent and violence in general, which increasingly became matters of criminal justice and law enforcement. This negative attitude ensured that political dissent and protest were also framed more readily as rebellion and disobedience towards the authorities.[60] The 1346 resolution from Utrecht reflects this development in that it criminalised armed resistance against the city council, threatening offenders with no less than capital punishment, unless some general and probably highly debatable conditions about the lawfulness of the council's government had been met. Moreover, it provided the council with a licence to react immediately with violence itself. This obviously made the existing traditions concerning political protest more risky for action groups, and even for acknowledged corporations within the city, such as the guilds. The butchers' guild in Utrecht, which had gained access to the city government with the other craft guilds in 1304, was the first guild in Utrecht to be affected by the changed atmosphere regarding political protest and violence. Its members were put under stricter control by the city council, forbidding them to 'unite' without the council's approval and to meet outside the meat hall.[61] The guild was eventually abolished by the city council in 1433 on the grounds of the butchers' unceasing habit of meeting frequently in their guild hall and in the central marketplace, and of rushing out and starting fights, in performances that were probably similar to the *wapeninge* of craft guilds in Flemish cities.[62]

Second, the increasing level of law enforcement and intolerance was not only a matter of acquiring more effective means of government but also the result of a process of consensus building within the citizenry, especially within the ruling group. In cities with political guilds, in particular, this ruling group was not only involved in local government but often had great influence within the craft organisations, as well. A new ruling elite slowly emerged in these cities, which strove on the whole for consensus and the conservation of acquired rights in both corporate organisation and city government.[63] One result of this development was a growing social and political gap in many guilds between guild management and common guild members, as well as between politically successful guilds and 'minor' guilds.[64] Generally speaking, guild leaders who acted as members of government, and who possibly also belonged to the ruling elite, were less able or willing to serve as representatives for protest initiatives arising from their own guilds. These developments meant that political craft guilds typically became less apt to act as vehicles for political protest and dissent, unless the protest concerned the interests of the guild as a whole (as an institution). In fifteenth-century Flanders, for example, a new 'guild discourse' of middle-class (master) artisans, organized in the established craft guilds, was voiced in literary works by members of the chambers of rhetoric (*rederijkerskamers*). Instead of political action, these authors recommended that artisans and lower-class workers in the city practise silence, endurance, and obedience to authorities.[65]

At the same time, the grounds for political protest did not disappear as craft guilds and artisan interests became part of local political establishments. A third and final development was the evolution of new cleavages within the community which did not necessarily correspond to corporate divisions of interests. To the contrary, they were more likely to disrupt the guild community from within. This is illustrated by the fact that protesters in many late medieval urban revolts, such as in Utrecht in 1346, cannot easily be identified with one or a few guilds, but often came from a wider range of guilds and backgrounds.[66] For this reason, researchers of revolts in German cities have come to prefer to speak in more encompassing terms like *Bürgerkämpfe* (citizen conflicts) and *innerstädtische Auseinandersetzungen* (intramural clashes) as opposed to the *Zunftkämpfe* (guild conflicts) favoured by older historiography, which tended to ignore the complex divisions of interests and to reduce conflicts to a simple contraposition of craft guilds versus patrician government.[67] In Ghent, too, historians have found that cleavages that arose within the corporate community along socio-economic lines and divided (sub)elites from a 'proletarian basis', became increasingly important in the fifteenth century.[68] As a result of the developments mentioned above, political protest in the later Middle Ages was more likely due to other divisions of power and interest: between city government and ordinary citizens, between consensus and popular politics, between ruling elite and commoners, or between rich and poor.[69] And more often than not, the craft organisations were on the side of the status quo.

Conclusion: elite leadership of popular movements

What did these developments mean for the organisation of political action? Again, the case of Utrecht in the middle of the fourteenth century may serve as an example. According to the verdict after the battle in November 1346, those who had taken up arms against the city council had left their guilds and followed eight citizens in battle, and in exile.[70] In this case, leaving their guilds was probably not a voluntary act, but, in practice, it may have been the only choice they had. Small groups of guild members with dissenting views could have little hope of getting their guild leaders to defend their interests and march up to the city hall together with their guild brothers under the guild's banner. Or maybe they refused to march up with their guild to defend a cause that was not theirs, which could have been seen as a rebellious act in itself. In any case, they had to find other associations for cooperation, protection, and support. The actual arrangements and coalitions that resulted from this process may have been diverse and were often not successful. In general, however, the new challenges tended to encourage a leading role for elite figures – whether they were in- or outsiders to local government – who could attract a range of collectivities in the community ready for political action.

The advantages of elite leadership, or of close collaboration with elite leaders, were multiple. First of all, they were able to offer effective protection, support, and practical military leadership during a protest action, especially if they were knights versed in warfare. They could also provide arms and suitable clothing to those who did not have any (mainly lower class participants, as guild members and burghers usually had their own military equipment). In addition, with the help of their networks, they could continue to offer support and protection afterwards, in the event that the group lost and had to flee or was exiled. Elite members, especially if they were settled in the countryside, but also when they came from high-standing local families, were more likely to escape the city's justice. Moreover, they were in an excellent position to conduct or even command negotiations for the group as a whole. These negotiations could not only concern the political goals of the protesters, but also practical questions regarding their legal rights, their positions, properties, and families. Again, high connections within the regional nobility and at princely courts could help tip the power balance just enough in the advantage of the protesters, especially if the city had powerful enemies. In many cities, from Italy to Germany and the Low Countries, the fate of exiled rebels often became closely linked to regional and even international politics.[71] Of course, the risk remained that the elite participants would 'betray' the cause(s) of the rest of the group and attend their own concerns first.[72] However, this risk did probably not outweigh the perceived advantages of working together on the eve of revolt.

How should we define this type of collaboration? It was essentially a contractual relationship, pragmatic in nature. Nevertheless, it may also have created some form of subordination and dependence in the shorter or longer run. In the case of coalitions between relatively well-organised political groups (e.g. guilds) and elite factions, there was less dependency and rather a purely political and military, strategic collaboration. As in the case of the Auer revolt in Regensburg, the bond may have been that of an oath-bound association or a formal alliance.[73] In the case of small, relatively powerless urban groups seeking protection and mediation, however, the relationship may well have been one of clientelism from the start. In some studies, part of the networks of dependency around elite faction leaders have been unravelled through the prosopographic method.[74] The main point to be made here, is that the incentive to collaborate with elite leaders arose from the need to join or create action groups that were able to organise violence in such a way that it could be used effectively and with as few risks as possible for the participants. The relationship between (groups of) commoners and elite members did not, therefore, necessarily stem from pre-existing ties of social or economic dependence, although a combination of political and social motives to follow an elite leader was of course possible as well.

We may conclude that a focus on the practical conditions for political organisation in the late Middle Ages, and on the central role that violence played in political action in general, makes it much easier to account for elite leadership in late medieval urban revolts, even if it seems paradoxical at first. To collaborate with, or even submit to, leaders from outside their own groups and interests could be a perfectly reasonable choice for politically conscious groups of citizens and craft guild members. It was an option that was likely to become more popular as craft organisations and urban governments in cities with craft guild participation typically became less open to bottom-up initiatives and more repressive towards political dissent. In a schematic version of urban political development, three consecutive basic forms of political action and revolt could perhaps be discerned: first, the patrician feuding group or faction; second, the craft organisations; and third, diverse groups of craft guilds, artisans, and/or workers acting under shared or exclusive elite leadership. In reality, of course, these options overlapped and existed side by side, according to circumstances. What seems most remarkable, however, is that the leadership by elite members, even if it was a practical choice in the beginning, may in the end have had the opposite result of what the protest groups, struggling against consensus and oligarchy, stood for: the growth of ties of dependence and clientelism in the city.

Notes

1. I would like to thank the participants of the workshops 'Medieval Revolts in Comparative Perspective' at St Andrews for many inspiring and stimulating discussions, and Justine Firnhaber-Baker, Dirk Schoenaers, Samuel Cohn, and Jan Dumolyn for their very helpful comments on earlier drafts of this contribution. This research was financed by the Netherlands Organisation for Scientific Research (NWO).
2. S. Muller Fz. (ed.), *De middeleeuwse rechtsbronnen der stad Utrecht*, 4 vols, The Hague: Martinus Nijhoff, 1883–5, vol. 1, pp. 66–8; Het Utrechts Archief (hereafter HUA), Stadsarchief I, inv. 227, fols 80v–7; inv. 587 (1380/81), fol. 32v and *passim*; H. Bruch (ed.), *Croniken van den Stichte van Utrecht ende van Hollant*, The Hague: Martinus Nijhoff, 1982, p. 232; H. Bruch (ed.), *Chronographia Johannis de Beke*, The Hague: Martinus Nijhoff, 1973, pp. 343–4. In Holland, the family branch was known as Boel van Heemskerke. All banished participants in this crisis had citizen rights, implying that this was a revolt by those with political rights and guild membership at least, and not by impoverished people.
3. Utrecht was the largest city of the Northern Low Countries with about 13,000 inhabitants around 1400. Further reading on Utrecht: R. E. de Bruin, P. D. 't Hart, A. J. van den Hoven van Genderen, A. Pietersma and J. E. A. L. Struick (eds), *'Een paradijs vol weelde': Geschiedenis van de stad Utrecht*, Utrecht: Matrijs, 2000; J. M. van Winter, 'Verfassung und Verwaltung im spätmittelalterlichen Utrecht', in W. Ehbrecht (ed.), *Verwaltung und Politik in Städten Mitteleuropas. Beiträge zu Verfassungsnorm und Verfassungswirklichkeit in altständischer Zeit*, Cologne: Böhlau, 1994, pp. 47–54.
4. S. K. Cohn, Jr., *Lust for Liberty: The Politics of Social Revolt in Medieval Europe, 1200–1425: Italy, France, and Flanders*, Cambridge, MA: Harvard University Press, 2006; S. K. Cohn, Jr., 'Authority and popular resistance', in H. Scott (ed.), *The Oxford Handbook of Early Modern European History, 1350–1750*: Volume II: *Cultures and Power*, Oxford: Oxford University Press, 2015, pp. 418–39.
5. M. Mollat and Ph. Wolff, *Ongles bleus, Jacques et Ciompi: Les révolutions populaires en Europe aux XIVe et XVe siècles*, Paris: Calmann-Lévy, 1970; G. Fourquin, *Les soulèvements populaires au Moyen Age*, Paris: Presses universitaires de France, 1972.
6. Fourquin, *Les soulèvements populaires*, pp. 87–108, 143–209. Fourquin's discussion of the leadership of revolts, however, shows more nuance than Cohn's short remark in *Lust for Liberty*, p. 109, suggests.
7. Cohn, *Lust for Liberty*, p. 129.
8. See the discussion and examples in Cohn, *Lust for Liberty*, pp. 109–29.
9. Cohn, *Lust for Liberty*, pp. 119–29, see also the recent discussion by Patrick Lantschner in 'Revolts and the political order of cities in the late Middle Ages', *P&P*, 225, 2014, pp. 3–46.
10. J. Braekevelt, F. Buylaert, J. Dumolyn, and J. Haemers, 'The politics of factional conflict in late medieval Flanders', *Historical Research*, 85, 2012, pp. 13–31; J. Dumolyn and J. Haemers, 'Patterns of urban rebellion in medieval Flanders', *JMH*, 31, 2005, pp. 369–93; A. Haverkamp, '"Innerstädtische Auseinandersetzungen" und überlokale Zusammenhänge in deutschen Städten während der ersten Hälfte des 14. Jahrhunderts', in R. Elze and G. Fasoli (eds), *Stadtadel und Bürgertum in den italienischen und deutschen Städten des Spätmittelalters*, Berlin: Duncker & Humblot, 1991, pp. 89–126; E. Isenmann, *Die deutsche Stadt im Mittelalter, 1150–1550*, Cologne: Böhlau, 2012, p. 252; for Tournai in the early fifteenth century, see Lantschner, 'Revolts and the political order', pp. 12–17.
11. Most influential in this respect, amongst others on the historiography of the Northern Low Countries, was the (anti-Marxist) work by J. Heers, *Parties and Political Life in the Medieval West*, trans. D. Nicholas, Amsterdam: North Holland Publishing Company, 1977; compare also, for English historiography, C. Liddy and J. Haemers, 'Popular politics in the late medieval city: York and Bruges', *EHR*, 128, 2013, pp. 771–805, at 773–4.
12. Braekevelt *et al.*, 'The politics of factional conflict'.
13. Braekevelt *et al.*, 'The politics of factional conflict', p. 31.
14. Compare the non-exhaustive list in Cohn, 'Authority and popular resistance', pp. 422–3; Dumolyn and Haemers, 'Patterns of urban rebellion', pp. 374–8.
15. Mollat and Wolff, *Ongles bleus*. For criticism of the 'Black Death' theory, see Cohn, *Lust for Liberty*, pp. 205–27.
16. Fourquin, *Les soulèvements populaires*, pp. 193–209.
17. Cohn, 'Authority and popular resistance', pp. 426ff.
18. Cohn, 'Authority and popular resistance', p. 431.
19. See e.g. for Flanders Dumolyn and Haemers, 'Patterns of urban rebellion'; M. Boone, 'Het falen van de netwerken', in W. Prevenier (ed.), *Prinsen en poorters: Beelden van de laat-middeleeuwse samenleving in*

de Bourgondische Nederlanden, 1384–1530, Antwerpen: Mercatorfonds, 1998, pp. 344–54. For German cities, see Isenmann, *Die deutsche Stadt*, pp. 251–4, 412–14. Similar tendencies were at work elsewhere, compare J. Watts, *The Making of Polities: Europe, 1300–1500*, Cambridge: Cambridge University Press, 2009; J. M. Najemy, *A History of Florence, 1200–1575*, Malden, MA: Blackwell, 2006, pp. 156–87; K. Schreiner and U. Meier (eds), *Stadtregiment und Bürgerfreiheit. Handlungsspielräume in deutschen und italienischen Städten des Späten Mittelalters und der Frühen Neuzeit*, Göttingen: Vandenhoeck & Ruprecht, 1994.

20 Compare Cohn, *Lust for Liberty*, p. 109.
21 M. Prak, 'Corporate politics in the Low Countries: guilds as institutions, 14th to 18th centuries', in M. Prak, C. Lis, J. Lucassen, and H. Soly (eds), *Craft Guilds in the Early Modern Low Countries: Work, Power, and Representation*, Aldershot: Ashgate, 2006, pp. 74–106; Isenmann, *Die deutsche Stadt*, pp. 251–2.
22 Dumolyn and Haemers, 'Patterns of urban rebellion', p. 370, *passim*; M. Boone, '*Armes, coursses, assemblees et commocions*: les gens de métiers et l'usage de la violence dans la société urbaine flamande à la fin du Moyen Âge', *Revue du Nord*, 87, 2005, pp. 7–33; Lantschner, 'Revolts and the political order'. Compare also H. Schilling, 'Civic republicanism in late medieval and early modern German cities', in *Religion, Political Culture and the Emergence of Early Modern Society: Essays in German and Dutch History*, Leiden: Brill, 1992, pp. 3–59, at 6–30.
23 Boone, '*Armes, coursses, assemblees et commocions*', pp. 9, 13: *l'action des gens de métiers mêlés aux luttes intestines quasi ininterrompues*;

> *l'emploi de la violence par ces mêmes corps de métiers [doit nous inciter à considérer] non seulement comme un élément dans une lutte pour s'emparer du pouvoir dans la cité (ou pour le consolider), mais également comme un élément d'action politique. La violence et son utilisation étant un instrument de communication collective.*

24 Compare the large number of late medieval urban revolts and political unrest in German cities, estimated by Isenmann, *Die deutsche Stadt*, pp. 251, 413; and Haverkamp, '"Innerstädtische Auseinandersetzungen"', pp. 90–1. See also G. Naegle, 'Revolts and wars, corporations and leagues: remembering and communicating urban uprisings in the medieval Empire' in this volume.
25 Lantschner, 'Revolts and the political order', p. 4.
26 In addition, commoners could use all kinds of verbal forms of dissent and protest, e.g. by spreading rumours, or using mockery or insults towards rulers. Although these forms of dissent could have a large impact in the city, they will not concern us here as long as they were not the result of some organised form of political action. See for these forms of protest J. Dumolyn, J. Haemers, H. R. Oliva Herrer, and V. Challet (eds), *The Voices of the People in Late Medieval Europe: Communication and Popular Politics*, Turnhout: Brepols, 2014, esp. the editors' introduction, 'Medieval voices and popular politics', pp. 1–12; J. Dumolyn and J. Haemers, '"A bad chicken was brooding": subversive speech in late medieval Flanders', *P&P*, 214, 2012, pp. 45–86.
27 Dumolyn and Haemers, 'Patterns of urban rebellion'; Liddy and Haemers, 'Popular politics', p. 777, *passim*; M. Boone and M. Prak, 'Rulers, patricians and burghers: the great and the little traditions of urban revolt in the Low Countries', in K. Davids and J. Lucassen (eds), *A Miracle Mirrored: The Dutch Republic in European Perspective*, Cambridge: Cambridge University Press, 1995, pp. 99–134, at 102–3.
28 C. Tilly, *From Mobilization to Revolution*, Reading: Addison Wesley, 1978. Tilly has been most influential in Flemish historiography on late medieval revolts, see e.g. Dumolyn and Haemers, 'Patterns of urban rebellion'; R. Verbruggen, *Geweld in Vlaanderen: Macht en onderdrukking in de Vlaamse steden tijdens de veertiende eeuw*, Brugge: Van de Wiele, 2005; J. Haemers, *For the Common Good: State Power and Urban Revolts in the Reign of Mary of Burgundy (1477–1482)*, Turnhout: Brepols, 2009. See also M. P. Hanagan, L. P. Moch, and W. P. Te Brake (eds), *Challenging Authority: The Historical Study of Contentious Politics*, Minneapolis: University of Minnesota Press, 1998.
29 The legal aspects of revolt and violent political conflict have been a distinctive trait of German historiography. See e.g. R. Barth, *Argumentation und Selbstverständnis der Bürgeropposition in städtischen Auseinandersetzungen des Spätmittelalters*, Cologne: Böhlau, 1974; B. Kannowski, *Bürgerkämpfe und Friedebriefe. Rechtliche Streitbeilegung in spätmittelalterlichen Städten*, Cologne: Böhlau, 2001.
30 W. P. Blockmans, *De volksvertegenwoordiging in Vlaanderen in de overgang van Middeleeuwen naar Nieuwe Tijden (1384–1506)*, Brussels: Paleis der Academiën, 1978; J. Haemers, 'A victorious state and defeated rebels? Historians' views of violence and urban revolts in medieval Flanders', in D. Nicolas, B. S. Bachrach, and J. M. Murray (eds), *Comparative Perspectives on History and Historians: Essays in Memory of Bryce Lyon (1920–2007)*, Kalamazoo: Medieval Institute Publications, 2012, pp. 97–118, at 107–11.

31 Compare Lantschner, 'Revolts and the political order', p. 4, who stated in this context that revolts were 'intensifications of existing processes of negotiation'.
32 Compare the custom to carry guild banners or flags during urban revolts in Germany and Italy: W. Ehbrecht, 'Aufruhr', in *Lexikon des Mittelalters*, 10 vols, Stuttgart: Metzler, [1977]–1999, vol. 1, cols 1206–7, in *Brepolis Medieval Encyclopaedias: Lexikon des Mittelalters Online*; Cohn, *Lust for Liberty*, pp. 177–92.
33 J. Haemers, 'A moody community? Emotion and ritual in late medieval urban revolts', in E. Lecuppre-Desjardin and A.-L. van Bruaene (eds), *Emotions in the Heart of the City (14th–16th Century)*, Turnhout: Brepols, pp. 63–82; see also Verbruggen, *Geweld in Vlaanderen*, pp. 102–44.
34 Haemers, 'A moody community?', p. 75.
35 C. Wyffels, *De oorsprong der ambachten in Vlaanderen en Brabant*, Brussels: Koninklijke Vlaamse Academie voor Wetenschappen, Letteren en Schone Kunsten van België, 1951, ch. 5.
36 H. Kaminsky, 'The noble feud in the later Middle Ages', *P&P*, 177, 2002, pp. 55–83; J. B. Netterstrøm and B. Poulsen (eds), *Feud in Medieval and Early Modern Europe*, Aarhus: Aarhus University Press, 2007; P. C. M. Hoppenbrouwers, 'Bloedwraak en vete in de late middeleeuwen', *Tijdschrift voor Geschiedenis*, 123, 2010, pp. 158–77; J. Firnhaber-Baker, *'Jura in medio*: the settlement of seigneurial disputes in later medieval Languedoc', *French History*, 26, 2012, pp. 441–59, at 445–7.
37 Following the broad definition by C. Reinle, *Bauernfehden. Studien zur Fehdeführung Nichtadliger im spätmittelalterlichen römisch-deutschen Reich, besonders in den bayerischen Herzogtümern*, Wiesbaden: Franz Steiner, 2003, p. 61.
38 Netterstrøm and Poulsen (eds), *Feud*, esp. Netterstrøm's introduction, pp. 9–68; see also, for late medieval Southern France, Firnhaber-Baker, *'Jura in medio'*.
39 Kannowski, *Bürgerkämpfe und Friedebriefe*. I would like to thank Professor Christine Reinle for drawing my attention to this study. See also Reinle, *Bauernfehden*, p. 40.
40 Lantschner, 'Revolts and the political order', pp. 37–44.
41 Compare Reinle, *Bauernfehden*, p. 340: *Die Bereitschaft zum gewaltsamen Konfliktaustrag war ein Strukturmerkmal der spätmittelalterlichen wie der frühneuzeitlichen Gesellschaft. Sie war schichtenübergreifend gegeben und bildete die Grundlage für eine milieuübergreifende Akzeptanz von Fehdeführung*. See also Reinle's discussion of feuds by commoners: 'Peasants' feuds in medieval Bavaria (fourteenth-fifteenth century)', in Netterstrøm and Poulsen (eds), *Feud*, pp. 161–74.
42 H. Zmora, 'The morals of feuding in late medieval Germany', in Netterstrøm and Poulsen (eds), *Feud*, pp. 147–60, esp. 158. See also C. Garnier, 'Symbole der Konfliktführung im 14. Jahrhundert. Die Dortmunder Fehde von 1388/89', *Westfälische Zeitschrift*, 151/152, 2002, pp. 23–46.
43 For example, in fifteenth-century Brussels: R. van Uytven, 'Plutokratie in de "oude demokratieën der Nederlanden": cijfers en beschouwingen omtrent de korporatieve organisatie en de sociale struktuur der gemeenten in de late middeleeuwen', *Handelingen van de Koninklijke Zuidnederlandse Maatschappij voor taal- en letterkunde en geschiedenis*, 16, 1962, pp. 373–409, at 377–80; and in Tournai: Lantschner, 'Revolts and the political order', pp. 14–6, 26.
44 Their practices and culture of violence have been studied extensively, see e.g. for Ghent, F. Blockmans, *Het Gentsche stadspatriciaat tot omstreeks 1302*, Antwerpen: De Sikkel, 1938; for Florence, C. Lansing, *The Florentine Magnates: Lineage and Faction in a Medieval Commune*, Princeton, NJ: Princeton University Press, 1991.
45 O. G. Oexle, 'Die Kultur der Rebellion. Schwureinung und Verschwörung im früh- und hochmittelalterlichen Okzident', in M. T. Fögen (ed.), *Ordnung und Aufruhr im Mittelalter. Historische und juristische Studien zur Rebellion*, Frankfurt am Main: Vittorio Klostermann, 1995, pp. 119–37; O. G. Oexle, 'Gilde und Kommune. Über die Entstehung von "Einung" und "Gemeinde" als Grundformen des Zusammenlebens in Europa', in P. Blickle (ed.), *Theorien kommunaler Ordnung in Europa*, München: Oldenbourg, 1996, pp. 75–97; P. Blickle, *Kommunalismus. Skizzen einer gesellschaftlichen Organisationsform*, 2 vols, Munich: Oldenbourg, 2000; S. Reynolds, *Kingdoms and Communities in Western Europe, 900–1300*, Oxford: Clarendon Press, 1984.
46 The definition and following discussion based on Oexle, 'Die Kultur der Rebellion'.
47 According to a twelfth-century French chronicle, referred to by Oexle, 'Die Kultur der Rebellion', p. 135: *Sie geben vor, Frieden schaffen zu wollen, in Wahrheit aber üben sie Gewalt*.
48 Oexle, 'Die Kultur der Rebellion', p. 136.
49 Watts, *The Making of Polities*, pp. 98–109; J. Dumolyn and J. Haemers, 'Reclaiming the common sphere of the city: the revival of the Bruges commune in the late thirteenth century', in J.-P. Genet (ed.), *La légitimité implicite. Volume II: Le pouvoir symbolique en Occident (1300–1640)*, Paris: Publications de la Sorbonne, 2015, pp. 161–88, at 164–9.

50 Ehbrecht, 'Aufruhr'; see also Watts, *The Making of Polities*, p. 107, who speaks of 'a host of other associations modelled along similar lines' (as the commune, consulate or guild); and J. Dumolyn, 'The vengeance of the commune: sign systems of popular politics in medieval Bruges', in H. R. Oliva Herrer, V. Challet, J. Dumolyn, and M. A. Carmona Ruiz (eds), *La comunidad medieval como esfera pública*, Sevilla: Universidad de Sevilla, 2014, pp. 251–89.

51 Braekevelt *et al.*, 'The politics of factional conflict', p. 18; Isenmann, *Die deutsche Stadt*, p. 254; Dumolyn, 'The vengeance of the commune', pp. 251, 264. Compare, for Italian cities, J. K. Hyde, 'Contemporary views on faction and civil strife in the 13th and 14th centuries', in L. Martines (ed.), *Violence and Civil Disorder in Italian Cities, 1200–1500*, Berkeley: University of California Press, pp. 273–307.

52 HUA, Stadsarchief I, inv. 227, fols 23 and 27v; compare also Muller, *Rechtsbronnen*, vol. 1, p. 42, where members of the butchers' guild of Utrecht are forbidden to form 'unities' among themselves without the city council's consent.

53 K. Bosl, *Die Sozialstruktur der mittelalterlichen Residenz- und Fernhandelsstadt Regensburg. Die Entwicklung ihres Bürgertums vom 9.–14. Jahrhundert*, Munich: Verlag der bayerischen Akademie der Wissenschaft, 1966, pp. 86–7.

54 Ehbrecht, 'Aufruhr'; H. Schwarzwälder, '"Bannerlauf" und "Verrat" in Bremen, 1365–1366', *Bremisches Jahrbuch*, 53, 1975, pp. 43–90.

55 Muller, *Rechtsbronnen*, vol. 1, pp. 57–65, esp. 60–2 (sentence dated 4 December 1346); an extensive narration of the second confrontation, including a description of the executions (which have not been registered otherwise), is supplied by an anonymous editor of the well-known *Nederlandse Beke* chronicle, amongst others in The Hague, KB 71 F 30, fols 86v–7r; see also J. Smithuis, '1346: Bloedige burgertwisten in het centrum van Utrecht', *Oud-Utrecht. Tijdschrift voor de geschiedenis van stad en provincie Utrecht*, 88, 2015, pp. 136–9; J. E. A. L. Struick, *Utrecht door de eeuwen heen*, Utrecht: Spectrum, 1968, pp. 76–7.

56 Muller, *Rechtsbronnen*, vol. 1, pp. 60–1.

57 Muller, *Rechtsbronnen*, vol. 1, p. 64:

> oft gheviel dat die raet van Utrecht, die ware inder tijd ende opt huys zaten van der meenre ghilden weghen, enigherhande zaken overdroeghen om der stat orbaer, welke zaken den rade voerseyt gheboerden te berechten na der ghewoente der stat van Utrecht, so wi hem daer ieghens versette dat mit ghewelt te keren, dat soude men rechten aen sijn lijf.

58
> Ende waer oec yemant daer bi, die daer toe gheeyschet worde om den raet te bescermen ende om dat recht te starken, ende daer vechtende worde ende daer yemant quetsede of doet sloeghe van den ghenen die hem ieghens den raet versetten, daer en soude hi sijn lijf noch die stat van Utrecht nyet om verboren.

Compare the custom of German city councils to defend their position with armed helpers or 'friends', mirroring the political action by their opponents: Isenmann, *Die deutsche Stadt*, p. 254.

59 Watts, *The Making of Polities*, pp. 213–15; Isenmann, *Die deutsche Stadt*, pp. 327–9. For Utrecht, Muller, *Rechtsbronnen*, 3.

60 Compare the central notion of authority and obedience that was emphasised by German city governments from the fifteenth century onwards: Isenmann, *Die deutsche Stadt*, pp. 333–40; see also J. Watts, 'Public or plebs: the changing meaning of the commons, 1381–1549', in H. Pryce and J. Watts (eds), *Power and Identity in the Middle Ages: Essays in Memory of Rees Davies*, Oxford: Oxford University Press, 2007, pp. 242–60.

61 Muller, *Rechtsbronnen*, vol. 1, pp. 42–3 (undated resolution).

62 J. C. Overvoorde and J. G. C. Joosting (eds), *De gilden van Utrecht tot 1528*, 2 vols, The Hague: Martinus Nijhoff, 1897, vol. 1, pp. 89–92. In other cities, butchers and butchers' guilds were also relatively active in inner-city conflicts and revolts: see D. Nicholas, *The Later Medieval City, 1300–1500*, London: Longman, 1997, pp. 134, 139–40.

63 This process has been labelled in different regions as the advance of pacification politics, consociationalism, or consensus politics: see M. Boone, *Gent en de Bourgondische hertogen, ca. 1384–ca. 1453: Een sociaal-politieke studie van een staatsvormingsproces*, Brussels: Paleis der Academiën, 1990, pp. 158–60, *passim*; Boone and Prak, 'Rulers, patricians and burghers', p. 106; Najemy, *A History of Florence*, pp. 182–7; Schreiner and Meier, *Stadtregiment und Bürgerfreiheit*; compare Van Uytven, 'Plutokratie'; Dumolyn and Haemers, 'Patterns of urban rebellion', pp. 379–80; Isenmann, *Die deutsche Stadt*, pp. 769–72.

64 This mechanism is elucidated brilliantly in J. M. Najemy, *Corporatism and Consensus in Florentine Electoral Politics, 1280–1400*, Chapel Hill: University of North Carolina Press, 1982, pp. 9–14, *passim*.

65 J. Dumolyn and J. Haemers, '"Let each man carry on with his trade and remain silent": middle-class ideology in the urban literature of the late medieval Low Countries', *Cultural and Social History*, 10, 2013, pp. 169–89. The quotation in the title is derived from the title of an anonymous poem which survived in a sixteenth-century collection (*Elc doe sijn neringhe ende swijch al stille*).

66 See e.g. Lantschner, 'Revolts and the political order', pp. 10–11, *passim*, who, instead of speaking of 'guilds' or other established entities within the city, which often were not politically united, prefers to think in terms of an unorderly framework of 'units of varying degrees of consolidation' within an essentially 'polycentric political order' which would enter into ad hoc coalitions on the eve of revolt.

67 Following the influential arguments of K. Czok, see esp. K. Czok, 'Die Bürgerkämpfe in Süd- und Westdeutschland im 14. Jahrhundert', *Jahrbuch für Geschichte der oberdeutschen Reichsstädte*, 12/13, 1966/67, pp. 40–72; K. Czok, 'Zunftkämpfe, Zunftrevolution oder Bürgerkämpfe?', *Wissenschaftliche Zeitschrift der Karl-Marx-Universität Leipzig*, 8, 1958/59, pp. 129–43. See also Verbruggen, *Geweld in Vlaanderen*; Isenmann, *Die deutsche Stadt*, pp. 254–60.

68 Haemers, *De Gentse opstand (1449–1453): De strijd tussen rivaliserende netwerken om het stedelijke kapitaal*, Kortrijk-Heule: UGA, 2004, pp. 109–18.

69 Compare Isenmann, *Die deutsche Stadt*, pp. 412–14; Cohn, 'Authority and popular resistance'.

70 The order of events does not appear clearly from the source text: did the act of following the eight 'commanders' on the day of battle automatically mean that they left their guilds, in the eyes of the guilds and the city council? Or did the collaborators consciously leave their guilds behind in order to join the protest group?

71 C. Shaw, *The Politics of Exile in Renaissance Italy*, Cambridge: Cambridge University Press, 2000.

72 Braekevelt *et al.*, 'The politics of factional conflict', p. 28; Cohn, *Lust for Liberty*, pp. 127–8.

73 Bosl, *Die Sozialstruktur der mittelalterlichen Residenz- und Fernhandelsstadt Regensburg*, pp. 86–7.

74 For example, Haemers, *De Gentse opstand*; J. Haemers, 'Factionalism and state power in the Flemish revolt (1482–1492)', *Journal of Social History*, 42, 2009, pp. 1009–39; J. F. Padgett and C. K. Ansell, 'Robust action and the rise of the Medici, 1400–1434', *American Journal of Sociology*, 98, 1993, pp. 1259–1319; D. V. Kent, *The Rise of the Medici: Faction in Florence, 1426–1434*, Oxford: Oxford University Press, 1978.

12

REVOLTS AND WARS, CORPORATIONS AND LEAGUES

Remembering and communicating urban uprisings in the medieval Empire

Gisela Naegle

Uprisings and depositions of urban governments were rather frequent occurrences in the medieval Empire, but for the German-speaking parts of the Empire, they should not be overestimated. The evolution of the highly urbanised Low Countries – for which Marc Boone and Maarten Prak speak of a 'great' and a 'little' tradition of revolt,[1] but also of the impossibility of creating a network of city-states comparable to those of Northern Italy[2] – was different. It was a logical consequence, that, in the long run, the Low Countries and the future Swiss Confederation (which also had different constitutional structures and already presented strong elements of a real confederation) eventually left the Empire and became independent states. In general, in the German-speaking parts of the Empire, the political landscape was extremely fragmented, but it was not dominated by urban settlements. The decisive political factors were rival territorial principalities and dynasties. Many towns developed their own legal system, but, in the end, only economically successful 'big' free and imperial cities like Nuremberg, Ulm, Frankfurt, Hanseatic towns like Hamburg, Lübeck, or Bremen, or powerful seigneurial towns like Brunswick managed to defend themselves in an effective way against powerful threats to their autonomy. Hamburg and Bremen still survive as federal states (*Bundesländer*) today. In the Middle Ages, many towns were able to govern themselves, but most of them were too little to have real, decisive influence outside their walls. According to estimates, at the end of the Middle Ages, Cologne, the biggest German town, had around 40,000–45,000 inhabitants; another nine cities had more than 20,000, and 16 towns more than 10,000. A total of 94.5 per cent of settlements had a population fewer than 2000.[3] To defend their interests effectively, they had to unite their forces and to create coalitions.

The forms of urban rebellions or protest that imperial towns experienced reflected the fragmentary constitutional structures of the medieval Empire. In contrast with more centralised states like England or France, the Empire was a composite state with an electoral monarchy. This meant that in the Empire, urban protest movements against princes and conflicts took place on a double level in the form of two different patterns to express discontent: individual urban uprisings and forms of extended collective actions of coalitions of towns. Collective conflicts sometimes had Empire-wide or at least supra-regional effects and involved urban leagues and coalitions.[4] Such conflicts could even lead to war, as in the wars of the cities (*Städtekriege*),

1387–9 and 1449–50, when towns fought against territorial princes.[5] The towns understood their actions not as revolt or rebellion but as legitimate war. The outcome of these wars, which they lost, was crucial and definitely weakened the urban position. As in other European countries, there were also urban revolts on the 'individual' level of single towns. In some regions, particularly in the southern and south-western German-speaking parts of the Empire, on which this chapter will be mainly focused, craft guilds overthrew urban governments dominated by elites and patricians (*Geschlechter*). In many cases it was only a short-lived victory. In the Middle Ages, 'Germany' in a modern sense did not exist; one region was very different from another. So it is impossible – or would at least lead to undue simplification – to give a general description that applied to all of them.

This chapter looks at two levels of urban uprisings and collective protest/urban warfare in some parts of imperial German-speaking lands in the late Middle Ages. I will first outline some historical and constitutional factors that contributed to and affected urban revolts, before showing how the constitutional structure of the Empire itself favoured the development of specific forms of inter-urban protest movements. I then turn to look at intra-urban conflicts in a variety of constitutional contexts, comparing them to the situation in France, Spain, and Italian parts of the Empire. The second half of this essay is concerned with how people communicated about these events and the language in which they did so and about the way they were remembered and talked of by the people of the time and later historiography. Medieval revolts always passed through the filter of writers of their time who often supported one of the parties in conflict. When they belonged to town governments, they could be directly implicated in the events. Some of them wrote specifically commissioned 'official' urban chronicles. So we only know the 'real' events from their memories, or the image that they deliberately constructed. Sometimes authors deliberately chose to hide what had happened or even gave false information. It is important to scrutinise the terminology that they used. The patterns of revolt that we can observe in the medieval Empire were not simply ones of constitutional structure and social processes, but also reflected the communicative networks and semantic strategies available to contemporaries.

Background: the late Middle Ages and urban structures in the Empire

The late medieval Empire was buffeted by winds from many quarters, which deeply influenced the towns' evolution and which had serious repercussions for their internal and external peace. At the level of high politics, and especially during the Interregum (1250–73), when foreign candidates such as Richard of Cornwall (Plantagenet, 1257–72) and King Alphonso X of Castile (1257–75, d. 1284) vied for the throne,[6] but also in later periods, competition for the imperial office had important consequences for the political landscape of the towns and their room for manoeuvre. Such struggles took place repeatedly in the fourteenth century, first because of the dynastic rivalry of Habsburg and Wittelsbach (from 1314) and then due to the dynastic change from the Wittelsbachs to the Luxemburgs (1346/7).[7] The Hundred Years War (1337–1453), though waged between France and England, nevertheless had direct and serious implications for regions at the frontiers of France, as well as imperial fiefs in today's France like the Franche-Comté and for French-speaking free imperial cities like Metz, Toul, and Verdun. Swiss towns suffered from the military raids of 'Armagnacs' and the great companies,[8] and in the Burgundian Wars (1474–7), from the army of the duke of Burgundy. In the East, the danger of the Hussites and the war between the Teutonic Knights and the king of Poland (1453–67) had multiple effects. Such external events could incite to the formation of urban factions and sharpen existing conflicts or lead to their eruption into open revolt.[9]

Competition for the office of a bishop or archbishop could divide the population of cities under episcopal rule. This was especially the case when the candidates tried to influence the outcome by bribing the city with promises of privileges or by threatening it with ecclesiastical penalties like the interdict.[10] The fact that the three archbishops of Cologne, Trier, and Mainz numbered among the Electors (*Kurfürsten*) of the Holy Roman Empire and generally came from powerful princely families in their own right made this kind of struggle even more important, with knock-on effects for the whole Empire.

There were other, persistent dangers, as well. Securing peace and trying to prevent feuds was an important if not *the* paramount problem in medieval Germany. On the level of Imperial legislation, it could not be resolved before 1467/95. For a long time, all repeated efforts to criminalise or restrict feuds proved to be ineffective and met very strong resistance by noblemen.[11] Hillay Zmora emphasised that

> all differences and similarities are overshadowed by one predominant feature which all kinds of feuds had in common: they were ineluctably linked to larger political conflicts.... Feuds were a particularly effective instrument of political contestation, and this was taken advantage of both by the feuding parties themselves and those powers which were quick to become involved in them.[12]

The same observation can be applied for extended urban conflicts. Rivalries among regional barons or the competition of noble families for secular or ecclesiastical offices could very easily erupt into wars and feuds that affected a whole region,[13] such as in the *Thüringer Grafenfehde* (the comital feud of Thuringia) (1342–6), or the *Münsterische Stiftsfehde* (the feud in the *Hochstift* of Münster, 1450–7).[14] Conflicts like the *Markgrafenkrieg* (Margraves' war) in Northern Germany (1308–1317) which involved the Hanseatic towns of Rostock, Wismar, and Stralsund,[15] or the *Markgrafenkriege* (Margraves' wars)[16] of Nuremberg (1449–50 and 1552–5). A third form of collective protest was regional conflicts between towns and their prince that present more similarities with 'typical' urban uprisings in other European countries, such as the revolt of 1376 by 18 towns in Niederhessen against the *Landgraf* Hermann der Gelehrte.[17] Natural catastrophes, like bad harvests, also took a toll, as did man-made problems like new taxes, internal financial mismanagement,[18] and crises of succession.

In comparison to towns in other medieval kingdoms, the constitutional position of towns in the medieval Empire played an important role in the form of urban uprisings. There were powerful imperial towns that were directly subject to the king-emperor (*Reichsstädte*); free cities (*Freie Städte*) that had managed to win a large measure of autonomy from their lord, the bishop; regional capitals and residences of the emerging princely territories; and towns that belonged to nobles, etc. Free cities were even somewhat more independent than imperial cities because the Emperor could not use them as a pawn, but they could lose this status. Sometimes, as happened in Mainz in 1462, the archbishop re-established his power.[19] Later the two categories of imperial towns and of free towns merged and were described with a common term as *freie Reichsstädte* (free imperial towns).

Traditionally, German historiography refers to these 'ideal types' of towns as a classification tool.[20] But in reality, things were less clear, and the actual legal status of towns like Cologne or Hamburg was even subject to lawsuits.[21] The previously mentioned example of the conflicts of 1376 that opposed a regional group of towns and their lord, the *Landgraf* of Hessen, shows that uprisings were not exclusively limited to free and imperial towns in the south and south-west of Germany. They could even happen in less urbanised regions and in relatively small seigneurial towns. Small imperial towns were used by emperors like Charles IV to solve their financial problems. To get supplementary revenues, the emperors pawned them to princes (and sometimes never bought them back), a practice the towns disliked very much.[22] In contrast to France and other European countries, there was no 'central' capital like Paris or London; the situation was instead similar to Castile, where Valladolid, Burgos, and Toledo competed for this role.[23] In the Empire, Frankfurt was the site of royal/imperial elections, but Aachen the city of the royal coronation. Until the transfer to Vienna, Nuremberg kept the imperial insignia and was the theatre of the first diet of the new king. In contrast to the hereditary monarchs found in other European polities, the 'German' king, or more exactly, strictly speaking, the 'king of the Romans', because 'Germany' did not exist in the Middle Ages, claimed to be the direct successor of the Roman emperors. To get the title of emperor, he had to be crowned by the pope in Rome and to finance a costly and difficult journey that always required extensive negotiations. So he depended more strongly on consensus and support from princes and towns. The attitude and the measures of the emperors in case of urban uprisings or protest depended strongly upon the modalities of the political situation, their own position of strength or weakness, and that of the town in question. For example, in the late fourteenth century, King Wenzel tried to shore up his position by making important concessions to towns, concluding a temporary alliance with them in 1387, but he was deposed in 1400 nevertheless.[24]

In general, the king's own domains were rather small and, in case of troubles on a regional level outside his own hereditary territories, he could not rely on a permanent apparatus or network of his own officers. This aspect was decisive for the way that urban revolts were repressed: in general, in the case of seigneurial towns, repression came from the town's lord, or in the case of imperial towns, by urban elites. When there were widespread dangers of uprisings, the emperor-king had to seek assistance from princes or other towns. This is one of the reasons why, struggling against feuds or insecurity, the structure of the Empire as a mosaic of little principalities and lordships led to the formation of peace leagues (*Landfriedensbünde*).[25]

In addition to their manifold constitutional relationships to the emperor, the legal and constitutional structures within towns themselves showed considerable variation: there were towns governed by a small circle of *Geschlechter*, 'patrician'[26] elites (Nuremberg), others whose government was based on political corporations of craftsmen (for example Augsburg and Memmingen), or 'mixed' forms (Ulm). In 1548–52 Emperor Charles V abolished the constitutions of Augsburg and Ulm, as well as those of more than 20 other towns in the south and south-west of the Empire that were based on a preponderant role of political guilds. Their councils were thenceforth to follow the example of the oligarchic, 'patrician' type seen in Nuremberg.[27] The form of government and particularly the social groups that were allowed to participate in it were frequently discussed. Criticism of town government and of elites' financial mismanagement or discontent with the introduction of new taxes could lead to rebellions. The central argument of the rebels was the Common Good. Insurgent urban groups could justify themselves as defenders of the Empire's Common Good against selfish elites, an unworthy lord, or even the king or emperor.[28] Within urban coalitions, an individual member's disrespect for the general aims of a league or internal uprisings in a member town could also provoke exclusion, punishment, or military reactions from the league as a whole, or from some of its fellow members.

In many respects, the evolution of towns in the Empire was more similar to the situation in the Spanish kingdoms or in Northern Italy than in France.[29] Medieval writers were aware of this fact. The abbot Hermann of Niederaltaich, for example, compared the impressive but short-lived urban league of the Rhine region (1254–7) to the Lombard Leagues.[30] He thought that the league could have been an important instrument of peace and underlined that it was conceived with the participation of one of the most powerful local princes, the *Pfalzgraf* (Count Palatine of the Rhine) Louis, duke of Bavaria from the Wittelsbach family: *fedus societas laudabilis iniit cum civitatibus supradictis*.[31] Recent research also underlines the mixed composition of this league.[32] This case is a striking example for the complicated constitutional structure of the Empire. Not even the membership of a powerful potential protector from one of the great dynasties was enough. The league was torn apart by the rivalries that appeared in the difficult time of the Interregnum. Philippe de Beaumanoir (1283) presented the emperor's struggles against Italian towns as a negative example for the French king. He had the impression that the emperors were powerless against these mighty adversaries (*ne oncques puis ne trouverent empereeur qui cel fet venjast ne adreçast*)[33] and that the French king and the town lords should act vigorously against rebellions in their own country.[34]

For Philippe de Commynes (d. 1511), the fact that German towns employed soldiers and that they took such an active part in feuds was exotic. He emphasises the difference with France and the general insecurity in the Empire that led to armed self-defence of towns:

> To speak about Germany, in general, there are a lot of fortified places and many people who are inclined to evil doing and looting and robbery. They declare feud [*deffiances*] at minor occasions because a man who has nothing but himself and a servant defies a big city or a duke in order to rob them with the help of some little castle in the mountains ... where he has twenty or thirty riders ... This kind of person is not punished here by the princes of Germany because they are willing to use them if they need them; but the towns, when they get hold of them, punish them cruelly. And they have sometimes besieged and broken such castles and, in general, towns pay armed soldiers [*gens d'armes*].[35]

Collective movements in the Empire: urban leagues and wars of the cities (*Städtekriege*)

These events and constitutional structures meant that in the Empire movements of protest could become inter-urban affairs in which towns joined together to pursue their claims collectively. A characteristic feature of the German political landscape was large-scale coalitions of towns similar to the *hermandades* in the Spanish kingdoms.[36] In the German case, during the two urban wars (*Städtekriege*, 1387–9 and 1449–50), towns fought – ultimately unsuccessfully – against territorial princes.[37] In times when the king or emperor was not capable of securing peace effectively, the perception of leagues was ambiguous: like the Spanish *hermandades*, they could be an important tool for the preservation of peace. In the Holy Roman Empire, they could also take the form of 'Leagues of Peace' (*Landfriedensbünde*).[38] In this case, the emperor might encourage them. The emperor was sometimes even a member of a league, though his membership was qualified as one of a 'normal' territorial prince and the league tried to deny him stronger or special rights.[39] For instance, Emperor Sigismund even tried to found leagues under his direction and join them together with local societies of knights. The towns refused because they did not believe that the emperor could give them effective protection against possible repression from the princes. They preferred to search for alliances with powerful local princes and barons and not to endanger their existing ones.[40] At other times, the king-emperors were more hostile to urban leagues, and like the kings of France and of Castile,[41] they tried to prevent the formation of alliances and leagues without their approval. The Golden Bull promulgated by Sigismund's father, Emperor Charles IV (1356), one of the fundamental laws of the Empire, attempted to outlaw such leagues.[42]

In this respect, again, the importance of constitutional structures and large-scale political conflicts is underlined by the comparison with Castile. During the reign of Alphonso X (1252–84), who was also a claimant to the position of Emperor, the creation and division of the *hermandades* was influenced by the political attitude of towns who supported the *infante* Sancho in the conflict with his father (1282).[43] In this kingdom, during the conflicts of Henry IV and his half-sister Isabella, urban elites, the rising middle classes, and towns were also able to use the situation to their advantage[44] – a scenario which, like the theoretical concept of *pactismo*,[45] offers interesting parallels with the German situation. In both countries, the new, economically successful urban middle classes could provide useful resources for competing candidates to the throne.[46] As in France and Spain, German kings promulgated prohibitions of 'illegal' assemblies which were seen as dangerous threats to public peace. Nevertheless, as I mentioned, there are also examples of leagues that were tolerated or even joined by the king for the sake of peace. In the case of the Swabian League (*Schwäbischer Bund*), the league was used as an instrument of repression against rebellious common people in the Peasant's War (1524–6).[47] There are similarities between this war and the revolt of the Castilian *Comuneros*, that happened at the same time, in the 1520s. Both were directed against Emperor Charles V, in the Castilian case in his function as king of Castile. But there is also a difference: the *Comuneros* were a predominantly urban movement and in the German Peasants' War, the protest was much more rural.[48] Some towns were sympathetic with the peasants, but others like Nuremberg took an active part in the repression. In Castile, towns like Santander chose the party of Charles against their fellow towns and stressed their loyalty to the monarch, whereas others, like Toledo, supported the revolt.[49]

The *Chronicon Wormatiense* offers interesting examples of the particular opportunities of how an electoral monarchy with competing candidates could offer towns opportunities of enlarging their autonomy. But there was also a potentially high price: war and an outbreak of general violence. The importance of the distribution of political power in the Empire is evident in the events of 1257/8: Richard of Cornwall had been elected King of the Romans and, in May 1258, he was crowned in Aachen. Afterwards, as the anonymous chronicler says, he had attacked 'numerous cities', captured Bingen and then had come to Mainz, where he had been accepted as the Roman king, but:

> Worms and other cities did not wish to do the same unless they were compelled by force. The people of Worms and Speyer renewed their pact, namely that they would not be compelled to accept Richard by prayers, force or money. As a result, Richard caused many difficulties for them, because the bishop of Worms was in his party. Bishop Conrad of Cologne acted in a similar manner against the people of Cologne, stirring up trouble against them so that there was no peace on either land or water, but rather tribulation and discord everywhere [*propter quod nullibi pax neque in terra neque in aqua sed ubique discordia et tribulatio*].[50]

The situation got even more difficult, when King Alphonso of Spain was elected to the throne in opposition to Richard as counter-king (*Gegenkönig*). Now there were two different competing kings at the same time. The *Annales Wormatienses* state that, in 1257, King Richard was able to gain the support of Oppenheim, but this support came at a price for him: he promised that the destruction of the fortress in the city would never be held against them and that he would never rebuild it. The townspeople were freed from all service for three years, and most important: 'If a stronger king were named by the pope, and arrived in the meantime, they would no longer be bound to him in any way. They then swore loyalty to the king.'[51]

In the same region, in 1258, the cities of Speyer and Worms made a different choice: 'On 16 January 1258, the people of Speyer and Worms joined together in a confederation by unanimous consent' (*unanimi consensus confederati sunt*) in the following manner: if Lord Alphonso king elect of the Romans, wished to keep his promise, as he swore, to take control of the kingdom of the

Romans and to defend its citizens, then the cities would remain loyal to him. They would never ally themselves with another king 'except by their common consent' (*nisi unanimi consilio*). They also swore to be faithfully constant in this and 'never to separate from each other in this matter' (*nunquam se invicem in hac parte separando*).[52]

The relationship between the cities and the emperor was also important in terms of the resolution of such conflicts, which gave both parties room to manoeuvre. The emperor was useful as a mediator between towns or between factions within them. Before 1282, during the reign of Rudolf of Habsburg (1273–91), a collection of chancery formulae shows that there were already standardised models for royal conflict mediation. In order to put an end to hatred, divisions, and troubles in a town,[53] the king would send a mediator, a person (NN) who 'loved peace and concord' (*NN pacis et concordie zelatorem*).[54] Later, in the time of the Emperors Louis the Bavarian and Frederick III,[55] the monarch continued sometimes personally to play a role as a mediator, or he delegated mediation to people from other towns.

The direction of royal interventions could take different forms and the outcome was variable. Sometimes the conflicts ended with letters of peace (*Friedebriefe*) and the result also paid attention to the interests of the rebels.[56] In 1332, Louis the Bavarian acted carefully towards conflicts in the Alsatian town of Colmar where supporters of both urban factions the Blacks (who were loyal to the Emperor) and the Reds (who opposed him) had been expelled. Louis wanted to re-establish peace, and if the town agreed to readmit the Blacks, he promised to renounce punishment and to try to achieve a peaceful compromise (*so wolten wir schaffen, daz si mit einander verricht wurden lieplich, und daz furbaz dhein stozz zwischen in mer geschaehe*).[57] Charles IV frequently intervened in town constitutions.[58] In 1366, he abolished privileges of Frankfurt which he had previously granted and he ordered the seals of crafts guilds broken.[59] But in contrast to what he did in Nuremberg, where, due to his measures, political guilds vanished completely, he did not prohibit them entirely despite considerably restricting their rights.[60]

Towns also organised mediation and peace settlements by themselves. In 1334, the ambassadors of Frankfurt/Main, Oppenheim, and Worms recommended that the new Council of Speyer readmit persons from the families of ancient council members who had fled. In 1333, at Mainz, a conflict between the *Geschlechter* and their opponents (iron merchants, grocers, and craftsmen) was successfully settled after the intervention of envoys (*Städteboten*) from Worms, Speyer, and Frankfurt. In 1334, Mainz, Worms, Speyer, Freiburg, and Basel co-sealed the *Schwörbrief* of Strasbourg.[61]

Leagues tried sometimes to establish more formal procedures of mediation or intervention. In 1325, the League of the four imperial cities of the Wetterau (Frankfurt, Wetzlar, Friedberg, and Gelnhausen) decided to defend itself in common against all potential adversaries with the exception of the emperor. All litigations between the members were to be arbitrated by the others.[62] In 1340, they recommended that in case of internal troubles (*uffloufe, zweyunge*) in one of them, two of the others should mediate and pronounce a sentence of arbitration.[63] In a similar way, the German Hanse intervened in internal matters of its members when its interests were in danger.[64] There were times when the Hanse and the emperor intervened. After the *Große Schicht*, for instance, the Hanse had temporarily excluded Brunswick (1375–80)[65] but, in 1377, Charles IV urged the towns of the Hanse to readmit those merchants from Brunswick who were not guilty of participating in the *Große Schicht*.[66] Finally, Brunswick had to demand mercy for its deeds and the Hanse re-accepted it.[67]

The constitutional form of a town was not always decisive. Large, economically strong cities like Nuremberg or Ulm were even able to lead a kind of 'foreign policy' and had little satellite towns under their influence, but there were also strong seigneurial cities like Brunswick that were much more powerful than tiny imperial towns. The *Verbundbrief* of Cologne (1396), a fundamental text of that town's medieval constitution, stresses this important aspect of autonomous urban policy by saying that the city council had the right to decide about peace and war and could contract new alliances and other obligations with other towns and lords, but only after informing the community (*Gemeynde*) and with its approval.[68]

But the solidarity of urban leagues was limited. The cities' distance from one another limited members' willingness to contribute to common charges or to take part in active military measures.[69] The Augsburg chronicler Burkhard Zink (d. c.1474/5) observed that his town had not sufficiently helped Nuremberg in its war against the Margrave. But, in another part of his work, he complained also bitterly about a general lack of inter-urban solidarity. He wrote that in the past towns had chosen alliances with different lords (*herren*): Ulm and Nördlingen with Duke Louis of Bavaria; Augsburg with Duke Albrecht from Munich; Ravensburg and Schaffhausen with the Swiss Confederation. So their rivalry was so strong that they begrudged the others' wealth and honours and that they were not ready to give advice and help to each other. A fact that, according to him, was very harmful for the Empire which was torn to parts. The lucky bystanders of these disputes were the nobles.[70] Zink thought that this behaviour was extremely dangerous and would make the towns an easy prey for their enemies whom he compared to wolves: when four oxen stayed together, no one could harm them, but when they separated and followed the false wolf, they were eaten by the wolves.[71]

Intramural conflicts

As outside the cities, there was also conflict within them. Different authors arrive at different numbers of internal revolts due to different criteria – between 1301 and 1550, Erich Maschke counted at least 210 troubles in over 100 towns, while others have counted 250 conflicts in 150 for the years 1250–1550[72] – but it is clear that, as was the case elsewhere in Europe, uprisings were rather frequent and occurred with a certain concentration in time and space.[73] They appear to cluster around the years 1300, 1400, after 1480 and between 1510 and 1530. For example, Brunswick experienced the *Schicht der Gildemeister* of 1292–4, the *Große Schicht* of 1374–86, the *Pfaffenkrieg* of 1413–20, and the *Große Stadtfehde* of 1445–6, 1488–90, and 1492–4.[74] Similarly, Lübeck saw struggles in 1376, 1380, 1384, 1408–16, and 1523.[75] The concrete sequence of events and the repression of revolts often followed a rather schematic pattern. In Germany as in France, the rebels attacked predominantly symbolic places of urban power. They entered the town hall and the seat and assembly places of the council. It was also important to get control over the town keys, the treasury,[76] the chancery, the archives, and the seals. These places and objects, as well as chains, walls, and urban rights and privileges were particular targets of repression.[77]

Urban uprisings were precipitated by a variety of causes, most of them familiar from other European settings. Financial mismanagement and the pursuit of (what some perceived as) self-interest were typical accusations in urban uprisings. In some cities, members of the ruling oligarchy became too influential and powerful. Their fellow councillors were afraid that the balance of collective government could be in danger and that the relative stability of the system of a rather closed circle of leading families would be disturbed. In the fourteenth century, such patricians as Siboto Stolzhirsch in Augsburg (1303), the Auer family in Regensburg (1330–4), and Ulrich Kunzelmann in Ulm (1328–30) were not successful in monopolising power, though they tried.[78] Influential persons, who had served as mayors, or who had exercised high urban offices were sentenced to death in political procedures, such as happened to Ulrich Schwarz in Augsburg (1478), Hans Waldmann in Zürich (1489), and the patrician Niklas Muffel (1469) in Nuremberg.[79] Another example is that of Heinrich Rubenow, a jurist and mayor of Greifswald, who had played a decisive role in the foundation of the city's university in 1456. After troubles directed against him in the following year, he had to flee but was later able to return. In 1462, he was murdered.[80] A similar case was the suspicious death in the case of Heinrich Toppler of Rothenburg (1408), who died in prison in his hometown after being accused of several financial delicts, the exercise of undue seigneurial justice, and of trying to create a tyrannical regime in the town.[81] Imperial towns thus developed mechanisms to prevent 'revolts from above' and the domination of overly powerful urban family clans. The same phenomenon probably explains the relative rarity of armed inner-urban conflicts between patrician factions in imperial and free towns in the German-speaking parts of the Empire.

As was the case elsewhere in Europe, some professions, like butchers and weavers, seem to have been more likely to be involved in revolt. Butchers were involved in Germany in the *Knochenhauer* conspiracy in Lübeck as they were in the Cabochien revolt of 1413 in France.[82] Weavers played an active role in Cologne, Flemish towns, and other parts of the continent. Textile workers developed medieval forms of striking. The *Weverslaicht* (*Weberschlacht* or Battle of the Weavers), an anonymous rhymed text written between 1369 and 1396, possibly by the town clerk (*Stadtschreiber*) of Cologne, Heinrich von Lintorf, refers to the rebellion of 1369–71 as headed by the weavers.[83] According to the chronicler Burkhard Zink, in the 1466 struggles in Augsburg, weavers and bakers played a decisive role and, when it came to negotiations, they showed a particularly uncompromising and rigid attitude.[84] Although his own brother-in-law had been a weaver in the imperial town Memmingen, Zink's birthplace, he sharply reproved this behaviour. For Felix Fabri (d. 1502), a member of the Dominican order living in Ulm, who wrote a description of this city and its social stratification, the weavers were a dangerous craft, easily inclined to rebellion and presenting an elevated risk of disturbing and endangering the peaceful life of the entire urban community.[85] On the other hand, weavers who managed to expand their activity in form of the putting-out system (*Verlagssystem*) by becoming merchants-entrepreneurs who supplied other spinners and weavers with raw material, could also be economically successful: in 1367 the ancestor of the famous and rich Augsburg family of the Fugger came to the city as a simple weaver. Later, Jacob Fugger the Rich, who financed the election of Emperor Charles V, founded one of the world's first social housing complexes for poor craftsmen (1521). Headed by the Fugger family, who later became counts and princes, this foundation still exists today in Augsburg and serves its original function.[86]

Compared with Italy or Spain and towns in the Low Countries like Ghent,[87] armed struggles between internal, upper class urban factions that led to street battles were rather rare in the medieval Empire. Towns took an active part in feuds, but there was no culture of vendetta as in Italy. The struggle between the Zorn and the Müllenheim in Strasbourg is one of the rare examples of extended, open intramural fighting of family clan parties that resulted in deaths. In this respect there is a sharp difference from towns like Ghent and other regions of the Netherlands. Maybe the practices of eliminating people who got too powerful that I described above prevented this kind of struggle. In general, German urban elites ruled as an oligarchical group and were careful that no family or individual garnered too much influence. In a law suit of Memmingen of 1471–3, the patrician party complained about the fact that relatives were not allowed to be members of the council at the same time if their relationship was so close that it would constitute a legal obstacle to marriage. They said that Ulm and other towns did not have such regulations. The town government, mainly dominated by members of craft corporations, argued that such rules had been introduced by their forefathers to secure the equity of council decisions.[88]

The situation in Strasbourg in the fourteenth century was totally different. The dispute of rival family clans in Strasbourg dated to 1314, when against the backdrop of royal schism and double election between Duke Frederick of Austria and Louis the Bavarian, the two groups formed different parties. The Zorn were supporters of Frederick, the Müllenheim favoured Louis.[89] The rivalry erupted into open hostility at a feast celebrated by the Zorn which the Müllenheim attended on the evening of 20 May 1332, leading to violence, killings, and finally to the end of the exclusive rule of the *Geschlechter* in Strasbourg. Prior to these events, which became collectively known as the *Geschölle* of 1332, the council of Strasbourg consisted of 24 members who nominated their own successors once a year.[90] Following the *Geschölle*, this system was abolished and, in 1333, a new constitutional structure was instated: the council thenceforth was to consist of 25 representatives of the craft guilds, 14 *Burger*[91] with active and eight *Edle*[92] with passive right to vote. In addition, the number of *Stettmeister*[93] who presided over sessions of the council, was reduced from four to two, and the office of *Ammeister*[94] was newly introduced. The latter developed into the most powerful function of the town.[95] Still, although in this particular case the enmity of two leading families precipitated a change in the town's constitution, the change was not so radical as it seems. The old families continued to place their candidates in key posts and maintained effective network connections. So despite some change, the composition of the council also showed important elements of continuity.[96]

Indeed, it is important to note that there were many factors which tended to limit open conflict and constitutional change within cities. Illicit gatherings were forbidden by the Golden Bull's fifteenth article, which the craft guilds and the town government were sometimes accused of contravening.[97] Often, oligarchic urban governments themselves tried to prevent uncontrolled assemblies or exclude poor and unmarried people who had no real estate from the full rights of citizenship. Although the matter of who could decide upon urban policy and be elected in the council was often controversial, the obligation to assist regularly in its session was also a burden and, as elsewhere in Europe, towns had to fix sanctions for unauthorised absenteeism.[98] That is to say, many people were interested in obtaining an office but not in actually assuming its burdens or its negative side-effects.

Many towns had two systems of participation: a small restricted type of assembly, sometimes in the form of a 'small council' or 'inner council', that governed the city, and an extended one which was called together to ratify important decisions especially when they meant heavy financial burdens such as high taxes. There nearly are as many different types and names of assemblies and urban institutions as towns. Secret deliberations held in small, restricted assemblies were subject to mistrust and danger. They could be perceived as conspiracies,[99] a reproach that played an important role in the previously mentioned lawsuit from Memmingen (1471–3), which I will refer to again, below. In this suit, the patrician party and the imperial fiscal procurator accused the town government formed by members of the craft guilds of contravening the dispositions of the Golden Bull. The town government argued that secrecy was the essence of council sessions: therefore closed doors could be absolutely necessary:

> It may be that there are sometimes assemblies of the Council with closed doors, but this does not happen unnecessarily. The Council is called so because it is not meant to be public [*offenlich*] and because not everyone shall know what is treated there.[100]

A promise to keep deliberations secret was frequently part of oaths of urban councillors.

Another factor affecting the incidence of revolt was the constitution of and attitude towards social hierarchy in the towns. In contrast with Italian city-states, in the German-speaking parts of the medieval Empire there were no real city tyrants.[101] But sometimes, imperial towns could not manage to preserve their autonomy and were integrated in principalities. The Fugger from Augsburg financed the election of Emperor Charles V (1519) and, in the long run, were able to reach the rank of princes and counts, but the rise of such powerful urban families did not lead to the creation of new princely states as it did for the Medici or other great families in Italy.

In general, in Germany the high nobility did not live in towns in the same way as in Italy.[102] When urban patricians and members of elites became really successful, they often bought rural estates with seigneurial rights and tried to live like rural noblemen. They tried to marry into these strata of society, and according to Felix Fabri, an important social criterium was the right to take part in dances and tournaments. To improve the social acceptance of urban patrician elites by noblemen, he tried to prevent the 'intrusion' of outsiders from lower classes. Therefore, Fabri developed a detailed, casuistic model of hierarchy, quoting Roman law (Cod. 4.63.3) and the jurist Baldus: a merchant or craftsman could not be noble and a noble who exercises a lucrative activity lost his quality.[103] For instance, to keep the esteem of nobles, the good society of Ulm should never accept members of craft guilds at their dances. Only when the daughter of a craftsman married a patrician was she allowed to take part.[104] Fabri, who lived in Ulm, was born in Zürich and a nephew of its mayor, Rudolf Stüssi. He advocated a strict social closure of the town's elite and a firm segregation of the different orders. He developed a model of seven classes and wrote against the social ascension of rich craftsmen or lower class members of Ulm. In his text he admitted only the social ascent of rich social climbers from other towns, but not from Ulm. His argument is that otherwise this would create envy and social struggles within Ulm.[105] In Strasbourg, when persons from the craft corporations had been admitted to the distinguished patrician society of the *Constofler*[106] in the fifteenth century, some time later, this society tried to exclude them again.[107] Many ecclesiastical convents and functions were only open to members of the nobility. In this respect, the Basque country in Spain provides an interesting contrast because the inhabitants of this region developed the theory of a generalised noble status (*hidalguía general*).[108]

The lawsuit from Memmingen (1471–3) again offers another glimpse of the contemporary perception of social hierarchies. One of the arguments of the party of the craft guilds was that the *Geschlechter* (i.e. patricians, persons from the patrician lineages), which were organised in their own corporation, named the *Großzunft*,[109] could not be compared to 'real' noblemen. They were not of high birth as princes, counts, lords, or other nobles (*nit sonndre geborn person als fursten, grewen, herren oder edelleutte*), but rather simple merchants whose only social difference from the guildsmen themselves was that they did not earn their living as craftsmen.[110] According to the craft guilds they should not enjoy a particularly privileged legal status because their only real advantage was that sometimes princes took part in their dances and that, in times of carnival, they were allowed to dance at the town hall for three days and were accompanied by the town musicians.[111]

Examples from other cities show the importance of this kind of social regulation and segregation. In Nuremberg in 1506, for example, only six of the 450 couples married that year were allowed to celebrate their wedding dance in the town hall.[112] Many German towns promulgated sumptuary laws. They tried to limit the number of attendants at marriages, baptisms, or funerals, and the amount of money that was spent on them. The aim of these measures was manifold: social segregation and discipline, but also the exclusive reservation of the prestigious town hall for patrician representation. In towns like Strasbourg or Memmingen, patricians formed societies which combined elements of religious fraternities and more worldly aspects: solidarity, mutual assistance, religious prayers, and processions, but also a meeting point for political factions, common dances, drinking and amusement, and last but not least a potential marriage market for the offspring of members.[113] In Strasbourg, the fact that the *Trinkstube* (the meeting place of the patrician society of *Constoflers*, which also had a symbolic value as sign of their power and political influence) was built on *Allmende* (terrains of common use) was severely criticised, and after the *Geschölle* of 1332, it had to be demolished.[114] The conflicts of the Zorn and Müllenheim, discussed above, and the negative attitude to social climbers who sometimes got too powerful and adopted noble behaviour which was judged as inappropriate show the practical consequences of the hierarchical stratification of society. They had also a theoretical background.

Medieval German writers were aware of the differences in definitions of nobility in other parts of Europe and compared them unfavourably to the German emphasis on social hierarchy. Italian customs encountered the reprobation of Otto von Freising (d. 1158), the uncle of Emperor Frederick I. He wrote that to control fellow cities, the Lombards did not hesitate to raise young people and even craftsmen who exercised manual arts to the rank of knights, even those whom other people kept away from the most noble and the most honest activities as if they suffered from the plague.[115] Alexander of Roes (d. before 1300) went even farther when he said that Italy was ruled by the *populus*, Germany by the noblemen (*militia*), and France by the clerics (*clerus*).[116] Not even the emperor could fully change the social system of towns. He had the power to raise their citizens to nobility, but medieval urban contemporaries were not always ready to accept his measures. German urban elites and especially councils developed a terminology of honourability. Writers like Johannes Rothe and Felix Fabri mentioned legitimate birth as a necessary quality of the good councillor. Fabri wrote that in Italy, bastards could become the successors of their fathers in high offices, but that the Swabian people would never accept this. He believed that Ulm would rather dissolve its commune (*res publica*) than accept a bastard as mayor, even if he were the son of a prince.[117] In the long run, urban councils became and even presented themselves as authorities (*Obrigkeit*) that no longer governed their fellow citizens as had been intended by the original common oath (*coniuratio*). Instead they became rulers over subjects.[118] The language reflects this situation: sources from Frankfurt speak explicitly of subjects (*Untertanen*).[119]

Talking about revolt I: communication and networks

If the social and political factors particular to the Empire affected how and whether cities engaged in revolt, how people knew about uprisings, and how they spread is a problem related to the methods and networks of communication available. In some cases there were regional concentrations of revolt. For instance in 1374–5, insurrections took place in Brunswick, Hamburg, Lüneburg, Nordhausen, Danzig, Stade, and Anklam and the *Knochenhauer* conspiracy was discovered in Lübeck.[120] There are some indications in the sources of connections between revolts or of regional 'contagions', but it is difficult to get 'hard' proof of real connections.[121] In the case of revolt of Cologne (1512) Philippe de Vigneulles, a chronicler from the French-speaking free imperial city of Metz, clearly saw a direct influence on other incidents, and even spoke of the revolt of Liège and another small town in 1513 as following Cologne's example (*en ensuyvant les dit de Collongne*).[122] In 1468, when Liège was punished for its revolt and destroyed by Charles the Bold, the cities of Cologne, Nuremberg, and Frankfurt carefully observed the events and the presence and reactions of the French King Louis XI.[123] In 1513, Nuremberg confiscated a literary work about the guild uprising in Cologne that had been printed anonymously. One day after the publication, the council already knew where it had been printed and, shortly afterwards, imprisoned the printer for four days for ignoring the censure, because the council feared the work's 'poisonous opinions' (*giftige mainungen*), which might inspire trouble.[124]

The exchange of news about revolts was facilitated at the time by an extensive system of messengers and ambassadors sponsored by the big cities. These men sometimes made real careers for themselves as experts for certain regions or courts. Often, in the beginning, they were trained by more experienced persons, for example by executing common missions or by accompanying them to diets or on visits to princes or other towns.[125] Towns exchanged letters and information. Nuremberg was a major centre of communication whose chancery production was clearly linked to its political fortunes.[126] In the 1430s, its civic chancery wrote between 200 and 350 letters annually, but in the years 1448–50, during the crisis of the *Markgrafenkrieg* against Albrecht Achilles of Brandenburg-Ansbach, it sent over 1,000. Normally, the town had around 170 correspondents, but in these exceptional times, they numbered 300.[127] The city itself received 7,000 declarations of feud (*Absagebriefe*) from noble enemies.[128] The Swiss Confederation and cities like Strasbourg or Basel employed spies and supported huge communication networks.[129]

Cities were interested in the legal aspects of the constitution and administration of their peers and sometimes used this knowledge to improve their own legal system in times of political turmoil. So in its famous *enquête* (investigation) of 1476, Freiburg sent its town clerk (*Stadtschreiber*) on an investigative tour of 16 other towns, including Konstanz, Bolzano, Merano, Ravensburg, Augsburg, Nuremberg, Ulm, and Strasbourg.[130] During the anti-Jewish pogroms of 1349/50, Strasbourg, Würzburg, and Wesel inquired into the attitude of other towns. For instance, Strasbourg wrote to Chillon, Lausanne, Bern, Cologne, Colmar, Memmingen, Freiburg, and others, while Würzburg wrote to Obernai, Fulda, Frankfurt, Erfurt, Heilbronn, Strasbourg, and others.[131] After the uprising of 1368, before changing its constitution, Augsburg sent three ambassadors to consult the towns of Speyer, Worms, Mainz, Strasbourg, Konstanz, and Ulm, but not to Memmingen or Kaufbeuren (which had adopted the more radical solution of a government exclusively based on a political organisation of craft guilds, whereas others like Ulm had a 'mixed' constitution).[132]

Communication between towns could also have a more 'institutional' basis. In most cases, even if a city had its own territorial hinterlands (i.e. in some ways similar to the *contado* of an Italian or the territory of a Spanish city),[133] it was rather small. German cities did not found others or integrate neighbouring cities of similar importance to their own in their territory, though in some cases, they owned other small towns. For instance, in 1359, Lübeck bought Mölln.[134] Nevertheless many cities developed their own legal systems, which were sometimes even 'exported' to other cities. There were 'families of urban law' (*Stadtrechtsfamilien*), for example, like those based on the laws of Lübeck or Magdeburg.[135] The 'mother city' (*Mutterstadt*) gave legal advice to members of the same group or smaller cities came to ask for it at the *Oberhof*.[136] A similar phenomenon existed in Castile, where cities strived to defend and keep their own *fueros* (customs) against the introduction of the *fuero real* (royal custom) promoted by the kings. As in the German case,[137] legal historians speak of families of *fueros* (*familias de fueros*).[138]

Communication between towns was complemented by practices of memorialisation within them. Civic pride in Germany expressed itself, as it did in much of Italy, in the form of numerous urban chronicles and a wide variety of autobiographical documents. In Nuremberg, the city council collected and sometimes bought writings referring to the history of the town. Some authors tried to sell their work, but were not always successful. The humanist poet Conrad Celtis (d. 1508) complained about it and accused the city, in literary form, of ungratefulness.[139] After Nuremburg's successful battle at the *Pillenreuther Weiher* (1450) during the *Markgrafenkrieg*, 'political' literary works celebrated the victory, and the conflict strengthened civic interest in the town's past. Several texts about the war were transmitted in a collection attributed to Erhart Schürstab, which contains material about the events in which Schürstab himself had participated as a military leader of Nuremberg. The documents are known by 18 manuscripts and two different redactions from the fifteenth and sixteenth centuries. In one version, they were completed by law texts about war. Nuremberg had a special commission (the *Kriegsherren*, or 'Lords of the War') and a special office room for matters of war. Documents about military events were collected. Schürstab was one of the members of this urban commission.[140]

Talking about revolt II: terms

How the sources generated through these communicative practice spoke about revolt was varied. They speak of *Unwille, Upror, Zusammenrottung (samnung, stemperie), Auflauf/Uplop, Aufstand, Zweiung, Zwietracht, Schicht, Stöße, Spenn, Strauß, Widerpart*, etc.[141] All these words are synonyms for uproar, uprising, revolt, rebellion, division, quarrel, etc., but each of them has slightly different connotations or is used only on a regional basis. Most of them have disappeared today or have no exact 'modern' equivalents. In the case of feuds led by a city, the self-description and justification of its actions sometimes approximate the terminology of war, as was already shown for Nuremberg.[142] In many cases urban revolts were given a particular name, such as *Missehellung* (Worms, 1301–3), *Misshellung* (Rottweil, 1378–9),[143] *Geschölle/Geschelle* (Strasbourg, 1332, Sélestat, 1352–8),[144] *Große und kleine Schickung* (Cologne, 1481–2),[145] *Böse Fasnacht* ('Bad Carnival', Basel, 1376). In some cases, the events eventually became known under the name of one or more of the principal protagonists: *Stolzhirsch-Handel* (Augsburg, 1303, named after the patrician Siboto Stolzhirsch), *Auer-Aufstand* ('the Auer uprising', after the family of Auer, Regensburg, 1330–4), *Twingherrenstreit* (Bern, 1469–74), etc.[146]

The perception of confrontations was naturally different according to the respective position of the parties. For the towns, the *Städtekriege* were a legitimate war, for their princely opponents a rebellion. Both sides produced justifications but also 'propagandistic' sources like songs that justified and glorified their own actions as in the wars of Nuremberg against the Margrave of Brandenburg.[147] Some of the words used for internal revolts convey an implicit commentary and (negative) evaluation of the events. Terms like *Zweiung* or *Zwietracht* (both words mean 'division') refer to the internal divisions responsible for inciting the revolt. Words such as the German *murmern* (to murmur),[148] which were also used in Latin (*murmurare*), in French (*murmurer*), and in Dutch,[149] have an onomatopoeic aspect.[150] *Geschelle/Geschölle* reminds of noise, but also of division. In modern German 'schellen' still means 'to ring a bell'. Other words used for revolt, like *Auflauf* or *Uplop*, describe the crowds' actions, i.e. running or 'assemble together'. Like *Unwille* and *rumor*, they express discontent.

Often, especially in chronicles written by urban elites, such terminology also expressed elites' uncertainty about the identity of those protesting in what they perceived as an unsophisticated diffuse way, literally in the form of *rumours* and gossip. As has been emphasised in recent historiography, elite perceptions of disorganised, unintelligible protest should not be taken at face value or viewed through 'Weberian' criteria such as centralisation, territorialisation, and bureaucratisation.[151] We should be wary of adopting contemporary social categorisations of medieval rebels by authors intent on hiding certain aspects or silencing them altogether, especially in the case of 'political' urban law suits.[152] It is important to keep in mind that we will never know, what 'really' happened and to analyse carefully these kind of 'filters' and the original terminology of the sources. Modern language often has no equivalents for medieval words. Particularly translations into a foreign language are often misleading and make no sense. So it is crucial always to quote the original terminology. For the medieval Empire, instead of speaking of traditions of revolt or state building from below as such, which are convincing for the case of the Netherlands or the future Swiss Confederation – but which would not be an adequate description for most territories of the medieval Empire, because there, towns or rural communities were not the decisive political factor — it is more productive to think instead in terms of 'empowering interactions'. This concept describes

> a specific communicative situation emerging from diverse, but nevertheless reciprocal interests and demands from both the state's representatives and members of local societies. By appealing to state instances and by making use of them, groups or individuals also accepted them as sources of legitimate authority and power.[153]

In this model rising urban middle classes and rich craftsmen with some education and political ambition played a particular role, because they were very active 'users' of law courts.[154] University trained jurists often worked for towns and helped to develop their argumentation against threats to their autonomy.

Sometimes our sources' authors were directly implicated in town government and/or in the revolt and tried to justify their own actions. For example, both the *Hemelik Rekenscop* (Secret Justification), which was written by the former mayor of Brunswick Hermen von Vechelde (1406)[155] due to a decision of important town councillors (*Ratsälteste*), and the more private *Gedenkbuch* (Book of Memories) by Hans Porner give practical and financial advice for future councillors for the government of their city and, by acting so, for avoiding revolts. Von Vechelde's work, which describes the past history and the features of the constitution of 1368, was regularly updated and read to the city councillors.[156] The *Schichtbuch* of Hermann Bote (*c*.1510–14),[157] named for the word for urban uprisings, relates civic conflicts beginning in 1292. Bote connects the uprisings with the names of animals: oxen (1292–4), wild boars (*Säue*, 1374–86), dogs (1413–20), donkeys (1445–6), and wolves that endanger the flock of sheep (1488–90).[158] The *Nuwe Boich* (New Book) of Cologne, written by Gerlach vom Hawe, a civic chancery scribe, legitimised the change of power of 1396 and the new constitutional system that was introduced afterwards. It, too, was intended for the internal use of the council, though in 1399, its author was accused of secret relations with the overthrown patrician group named the *Greifen* and executed.[159]

The Latin vocabulary applied in the medieval Empire to describe revolts and leagues (*rumor, discordia, dissensio, seditio, conspiratio, tumultus, concursus, murmuracio, rebellio*) is similar to that of other countries[160] and often drew upon European-wide conventions. In contrast to this, German terminology often was regional and in many cases has no direct equivalents in other languages or modern German. Urban writers from different countries and times often attached paramount importance to internal consensus. The quotation from the Bible *omne regnum in se ipsum divisum desolabitur* (roughly, any kingdom divided against itself cannot stand) was frequently quoted. Sometimes authors like Johannes Rothe (*c*.1360–1434)[161] or Felix Fabri[162] also drew from authors such as Sallust or Isidore of Seville, who were part of a common reservoir used by medieval authors.[163]

These commonalities are partly due to the 'international' education of learned German writers, particularly those with a legal background. For a long time, there were few universities in the Empire, so German medieval jurists were trained in famous Italian or, less frequently, French universities.[164] Jurists imported Roman and canon law conceptions and definitions of revolt, including that of *lèse-majesté* (*crimen laesae majestatis*), but also the Italian jurists' idea of the *civitas sibi princeps* (the city as its own prince),[165] and the canon law maxim *quod omnes tangit* (what touches all [ought to be approved by all]).[166] Yet, the role of jurists in civic life was ambivalent. Towns like Nuremberg turned to universities and university-trained jurists for legal advice and counsel (*consilia*).[167] At the same time Nuremberg was suspicious of these jurists and tried to prevent them from gaining decisive political influence. They were not admitted to its town council.[168] We possess statements from the law suit in Memmingen (1471–3) before the supreme German royal court of the time, the *Königliches Kammergericht*, that suggest that members of the craft guilds had a strong distaste for professional jurists.[169]

The vocabulary of efforts to legitimise revolt emphasises the importance of the *Gemeinde* (different forms of 'communities' whose definition is subject to local variations)[170] and aspects of 'fraternity' with echoes elsewhere in Europe.[171] In 1383, in the times of the Rhenish League, the Council of Strasbourg wrote to 'our good special friends and allies' (*unsern sundern guten frunden unt eitgenoszen*) the mayors and Councils of Mainz, Frankfurt, Hagenau, Wissembourg, Wetzlar, Friedberg, Gelnhausen, and Pfeddersheim in order to make them take military measures against Worms and Speyer.[172] After the revolt (*Große Schicht*) of Brunswick 1379, the guilds addressed letters to their homologues from Lübeck, Lüneburg, and Hamburg as 'dear particular friends' (*leven sunderlichen frunde*) and 'brothers from the guilds' (*ghildenbrodere*), stressing equality and the horizontal aspect of their relationship.[173] The opposite party, for instance exiled or deposed members of patrician Councils or urban actors of repression after revolts, spoke differently about the events, stressing the social and hierarchical distance between themselves and the rebels. So according to a chronicler from Brunswick, the former mayor Hermen von Vechelde, common people and the guilds had brought great misfortune and misery upon the honourable part of the members of the council who had lost their lives in a miserable way despite the fact that they were innocent (*dar grod unghelucke unde jammer van quam, alzo dat der erbaren endeyls ut dem Rade jammerliken ane schult ore liff vorlōren*).[174]

Prohibitions against associations use a fairly standard set of pejorative terms such as *conjuratio, conspiratio, conventicula*, etc.[175] For example, the Golden Bull of 1356 repeated dispositions against leagues and illicit assemblies using terms like 'reprobate conspiracies', 'unlawful meetings', and 'illicit associations'.[176] But the vernacular German terminology of corporations, associations, alliances, unions, leagues, and brotherhoods shows a lot of variation[177] and includes regional words which often have no direct equivalent in Romance languages. When they refer to corporations of craftsmen, sources from Southern Germany often speak of *Zünfte* (corporations of craftsmen), in Cologne of *broderscap, fraternitas, confraternitas* (brotherhood), or, with a word specific to Cologne, of *Gaffel*. In other parts of the Empire similar institutions are called *Ämter* (i.e. offices),[178] *Innunge* (a regional word for corporations of craftsmen, for example, in Magdeburg and Kassel), *Gesellschaft* (society) in Frankfurt am Main, *Gilde* (guild) in Höxter, *Einung*[179] or in Latin *societas* (society, corporation) in Halle, and *consorcium* in Haguenau, Alsace, 1164.[180] A law promulgated in 1232 by Frederic II offers the interesting insight that the considerable regional diversity of vernacular terminology already existed in this time and that the emperor tried to find a formula that could cover all its possible forms. Prohibiting town assemblies and the creation of town councils or other civic offices without the lord of the town's permission,[181] it speaks of 'whatever sort of confraternities or societies of craftsmen, called by whatever name in the vernacular' (*cujuslibet artificii confraternitates seu societates, quocumque nomine vulgariter appellantur*).[182]

Such associations were particularly important in regions with strong traditions of urban autonomy. The cities of the Swiss confederation, for example, eventually developed their own constitutional pattern and left the Empire.[183] The memories of an original *coniuratio* or oath could play an important role in the formation of urban collective identity.[184] In cities like Ulm, the oath was repeated and transformed in a regular ritual that took place after the urban elections. The privileges of the towns were read in public once a year and the urban officials had to justify their administration. In recent times, some towns, such as Esslingen and Reutlingen (both ancient imperial cities located in today's Baden-Württemberg), have rediscovered this tradition and reintroduced the annual celebration of the 'day of the oath' (*Schwörtag*).

Conclusion

In the long run, peaceful means of political protest often proved more effective than revolt. This fact is illustrated by the successful mediation of envoys of other towns in urban conflicts, but also by the lawsuit won in the 1470s by the town government of Memmingen (whose government was dominated by craft guilds). In this case Emperor Frederick III and the imperial justice supported the position of the town against the patrician party and the imperial fiscal procurator. The constitution of the town and the preponderant role of the craft guilds were confirmed. On an individual level, towns did not have sufficient military and financial means at their disposal to lead successful wars against princes. The power and influence of imperial cities and free cities declined, even if some of them, like Hamburg or Bremen which are still *Bundesländer* (federal states) in their own right, were able to defend their autonomy until the twenty-first century. Because there were numerous differences, it is interesting to compare evolution of towns of different German-speaking parts of the Empire with other forms of constitutional organisation as the Swiss Confederation or the Netherlands which eventually completely left the medieval Empire.

It is important to avoid too much generalisation: in its urban structure, language, number of inhabitants, and integration in urban networks, for instance, Cologne was more similar to towns in the Low Countries than to a small imperial town in Franconia. For towns like Nuremberg or Augsburg the contact with Italy was crucial, whereas the trade network of Hanseatic towns as Lübeck from the North had a completely different orientation.

The analysis of vernacular and Latin terminology shows that in the Middle Ages each region had its specificities, its own terminology, and developed particular constitutional forms. In today's Germany some of them have survived. Some towns have *Bürgermeister* (mayors), others a *Stadtirektor* (director of the city), etc. Even the legal terminology of our own age still expresses constitutional differences from one *Bundesland* to another. The website of the German Federal Foreign Office (*Auswärtiges Amt*) proposes official English translations for the names of the Bundesländer: 'Free Hanseatic City of Bremen' and 'Free *and* Hanseatic city of Hamburg'.[185] The difficulties of translation learned jurists experienced, when they tried to make the Latin legal terminology fit together with their (vernacular) reality is apparent when we look at the different ways vernacular texts and Latin texts speak about revolt. The Latin terminology of different countries follows the same conventions, the vernacular does not. There were considerable differences between the North and the South, the East and the West. Medieval authors like Felix Fabri, Alexander von Roes, and Philippe de Commynes were already comparing different European countries. In the German-speaking parts of the Holy Roman Empire, there was a rich tradition of chronicles, autobiographical texts, and documents collected by urban chanceries. In contrast to France, there were no official royal chronicles, so the sources give us a rich, heterogeneous panorama from different viewpoints. Cities formed networks of communications, exchanged letters, information, and law texts.

Aware of their limited power, they tried to form alliances and coalitions and developed a rich culture of various forms of associations and leagues. In this respect there are parallels with the *hermandades* and the culture of *pactismo* in the Iberian kingdoms and with urban leagues in Northern Italy. But towns had to contend with powerful neighbours. In the medieval Empire, the emperor-king was often far away and much weaker than local princes and barons. He did not have a dense network of royal officials and there was no central system of taxes or of levying taxes. Especially in times of double elections or rivalries for the throne, the candidates had to search for allies and supplementary financial resources. These situations could be used by the towns to obtain new privileges and to expand their room for manoeuvre. There was a complex system of varying interactions with changing partners. It was important that they could offer effective aid and that they were not too far away. Cities refused commitments which implicated heavy charges and long distances. Collective urban action was important, but the decisive defeat at the end of the Wars of Cities was a heavy blow from which they never entirely recovered. It had shown their limits. Especially in areas of fragmented territorial structures, if they wanted to survive, towns had to seek arrangements with their princely and noble neighbours. As the Augsburg chronicler Burkhard Zink had feared, in many cases urban interests were divergent and prevented successful common actions and effective cooperation so that princes and the nobility were often really the lucky bystanders.

Notes

1 M. Boone, 'Rulers, patricians and burghers: the great and the little traditions of urban revolt in the Low Countries', in K. Davids and J. Lucassen (eds), *A Miracle Mirrored: The Dutch Republic in European Perspective*, Cambridge: Cambridge University Press, 1995, pp. 99–134; J. Dumolyn and J. Haemers, 'Patterns of urban rebellion in medieval Flanders', *JMH*, 31, 2005, pp. 369–93.

2 M. Boone, *À la recherche d'une modernité civique: La société urbaine des anciens Pays-Bas au bas Moyen Âge*, Brussels: Éditions de l'Université de Bruxelles, 2010, p. 72, pp. 68–73.

3 E. Isenmann, *Die deutsche Stadt im Spätmittelalter, 1150–1550*, Vienna and Cologne: Böhlau, 2014, pp. 60–2.

4 See for example: E. M. Distler, *Städtebünde im deutschen Spätmittelalter*, Frankfurt am Main: Klostermann, 2006.

5 A. Schubert, *Der Stadt Nutz oder Notdurft? Die Reichsstadt Nürnberg und der Städtekrieg von 1388/89*, Husum: Matthiesen, 2003; G. Zeilinger, *Lebensformen im Krieg. Eine Alltags- und Erfahrungsgeschichte des süddeutschen Städtekrieges 1449/50*, Stuttgart: Steiner, 2007.

6 M. Kaufhold, 'Die Könige des Interregnum. Konrad IV., Heinrich Raspe, Wilhelm, Alfons, Richard (1245–1273)', in B. Schneidmüller and S. Weinfurter (eds), *Die deutschen Herrscher des Mittelalters*, Munich: Beck, 2003, pp. 315–39.

7 This change saw a three-way rivalry between Emperor Louis IV the Bavarian (Wittelsbach, king 1314, emperor 1328, d. 1347), the future Charles IV (Luxembourg, king 1346–78, emperor 1355), and a third rival claimant, Günter von Schwarzburg (d. 1349) (see M. Menzel, 'Ludwig der Bayer (1314–1347) und Friedrich der Schöne (1314–1330)', and M. Kintzinger, 'Karl IV. (1346–1378). Mit Günther von Schwarzburg (1349)', in Schneidmüller and Weinfurter (eds), *Die deutschen Herrscher*, pp. 393–407, 408–32).

8 For instance, in his chronicle of Luzern, Melchior Russ complains about crimes and looting by the 'Englishmen' (*Engellschen*) under Enguerrand VII de Coucy in Alsatian and Swiss territories (1375). Melchior Russ, *Chronika*, ed. M. Vonarburg Züllig, Zurich: Chronos, 2009, p. 49 and nn. 65–7.

9 B.-U. Hergemöller, *Uplop-Seditio. Innerstädtische Unruhen des 14. und 15. Jahrhunderts im engeren Reichsgebiet*, Hamburg: Verlag Dr. Kovač, 2012, p. 12.

10 Hergemöller, *Uplop*, p. 12.

11 E. Isenmann, 'Weshalb wurde die Fehde im römisch-deutschen Reich seit 1467 reichsgesetzlich verboten? Der Diskurs über Fehde, Friede und Gewaltmonopol im 15. Jahrhundert', in J. Eulenstein, C. Reinle, and M. Rothmann (eds), *Fehde im spätmittelalterlichen Reich. Zwischen adeliger Handlungslogik und territorialer Verdichtung*, Affalterbach: Didymos, 2013, pp. 335–474.

12 H. Zmora, *State and Nobility in Early Modern Germany: The Knightly Feud in Franconia, 1440–1567*, Cambridge: Cambridge University Press, 1997, p. 34.

13 C. Reinle, 'Fehde', in A. Cordes and H. Lück (eds), *Handwörterbuch zur deutschen Rechtsgeschichte*, 2nd edn, 2 vols to date, Berlin: Schmidt, 2008–present, vol. 1, pp. 1515–25; Eulenstein *et al*. (eds), *Fehde im spätmittelalterlichen Reich*.

14 This feud started as a conflict over the office of bishop of Münster. The *Hochstift* of Münster was a huge territory ruled by this prince bishop (*Fürstbischof*). It was larger than his bishopric/diocese in an ecclesiastical sense. So the feud concerned the exercise of his secular rights as a ruler that were linked to his double functions.

15 It was thusly named because of the participation of the Markgrave of Brandenburg from the family of Askanier. The conflict had an exterior, 'international' dimension: it also concerned the relations with Denmark, several princes, and the Teutonic Knights.

16 The first war was named after the participation of Margrave Albrecht Achilles of Brandenburg-Ansbach from the family of Zollern, the future dynasty of Hohenzollern. Members of this family were margraves of Brandenburg and Electors (*Kurfürsten*) (from 1415/17), but still owned possessions in Franconia. The first *Markgrafenkrieg* evolved in the South-German war of the cities (*Städtekrieg*) that implicated 31 towns. Since *c*.1190/1, the Zollern family had exercised the office of *Burggraf* of Nuremberg. (In this case, but not necessarily in others, where it could also be a seigneurial or episcopal office, it was a royal office which, at its origins, was exercised from the castle in this town, but gradually fell out of use.) There were two lines of margraves from this dynasty: Brandenburg-Ansbach and Brandenburg-Kulmbach. For the explanation of the function and word *Burggraf*, see O. Spälter, 'Nürnberg, Burggrafschaft', in *Historisches Lexikon Bayerns*, www.historisches-lexikon-bayerns.de/Lexikon/Nürnberg, Burggrafschaft. The second war was named after the participation of Margrave Albrecht Alcibiades of Brandenburg-Kulmbach.

17 I. Baumgärtner, 'Niederhessen in der Krise? Städtischer Aufruhr im landgräflichen Kassel und im erzbischöflichen Hofgeismar', in I. Baumgärtner and W. Schich (eds), *Nordhessen im Mittelalter*, Marburg: Elwert, 2001, pp. 137–70.

18 Hergemöller, *Uplop*, p. 12.

19 P. Johanek, 'Imperial and free towns of the Holy Roman Empire: city-states in pre-modern Germany?', in M. H. Hansen (ed.), *A Comparative Study of Thirty City-State Cultures*, Copenhagen: Reitzel, 2000, pp. 295–319, reprinted in W. Freitag and M. Siekmann (eds), *Europäische Stadtgeschichte. Ausgewählte Beiträge von Peter Johanek*, Vienna and Cologne: Böhlau, 2012, pp. 252–88, at 256.

20 Isenmann, *Die deutsche Stadt*; P.-J. Heinig, *Reichsstädte, Freie Städte und Königtum, 1389–1450*, Wiesbaden: Steiner, 1983; P. Moraw, 'Reichsstadt, Reich und Königtum im späten Mittelalter', *Zeitschrift für Historische Forschung*, 6, 1979, pp. 385–424.

21 G. Naegle, '*Bonnes villes* et *güte stete*: quelques remarques sur le problème des *villes notables* en France et en Allemagne à la fin du Moyen Âge', *Francia*, 35, 2008, pp. 115–48, at 118.

22 G. Landwehr, *Die Verpfändung der deutschen Reichsstädte im Mittelalter*, Cologne and Graz: Böhlau, 1967.

23 E. Benito Ruano, *La prelación ciudadana: Las disputas por la precedencia entre las ciudades de la Corona de Castilla*, Toledo: Publicaciones del Centro Universitario de Toledo, 1972.

24 E. Schubert, *Königsabsetzung im deutschen Mittelalter*, Göttingen: Vandenhoeck & Ruprecht, 2005, pp. 362–403; F. Rexroth, 'Wie man einen König absetzte', in B. Jussen (ed.), *Die Macht des Königs. Herrschaft in Europa vom Frühmittelalter bis in die Neuzeit*, Munich: Beck, 2005, pp. 241–54. P.-J. Heinig, 'Städtekrieg, süddt.', in *Lexikon des Mittelalters*, 10 vols, Stuttgart and Weimar: Metzler, 1977–99, vol. 8, cols 18–19.

25 See for example, E. Wadle, 'Gottesfrieden und Landfrieden als Gegenstand der Forschung nach 1950', in K. Kroeschell and A. Cordes (eds), *Funktion und Form. Quellen- und Methodenprobleme der mittelalterlichen Rechtsgeschichte*, Berlin: Duncker & Humblot, 1996, pp. 63–91, reprinted in E. Wadle, *Landfrieden, Strafe, Recht. Zwölf Studien zum Mittelalter*, Berlin: Duncker & Humblot, 2001, pp. 11–39; A. Buschmann and E. Wadle (eds), *Landfrieden. Anspruch und Wirklichkeit*, Paderborn, Munich: Schöningh, 2002.

26 Though often used as an analytic category by modern historiography, the word 'patrician' is not contemporary. In German vernacular it is first used in the sixteenth century. An early example is the text about the constitution of Nuremberg of Christoph Scheurl (1516) (Isenmann, *Die deutsche Stadt*, p. 750). For Nuremberg, see also: P. Fleischmann, *Rat und Patriziat in Nürnberg. Die Herrschaft der Ratsgeschlechter vom 13. bis zum 18. Jahrhundert*, 3 vols, Nuremberg: Verein für Geschichte der Stadt Nürnberg, 2008. Edition: C. Hegel (ed.), 'Christoph Scheurl's Epistel über die Verfassung der Reichsstadt Nürnberg, 1516' in *Die Chroniken der fränkischen Städte. Nürnberg*, vol. 5/2, 2nd edn (= *Die Chroniken der deutschen Städte*, vol. 11), Leipzig: Hirzel, 1874, reprinted Göttingen: Vandenhoeck & Ruprecht, 1961, pp. 779–804 and, as contemporary German translation, *Christoph Scheurls Epistel vom Jahre 1516 über die Verfassung der Reichsstadt Nürnberg*, in A. Werminghoff, *Conrad Celtis und sein Buch über Nürnberg*, Freiburg im Breisgau: Boltze, 1921, pp. 212–27.

27 E. Naujoks, *Kaiser Karl V. und die Zunftverfassung. Ausgewählte Aktenstücke zu Verfassungsänderungen in den oberdeutschen Reichsstädten (1547–1556)*, Stuttgart: Kohlhammer, 1985, p. 12; E. Naujoks (ed.), *Obrigkeitsgedanke, Zunftverfassung und Reformation*, Stuttgart: Kohlhammer, 1958.

28 See É. Lecuppre-Desjardin and A.-L. Van Bruaene (eds), *De bono communi: The Discourse and Practice of the Common Good in the European City*, Turnhout: Brepols, 2010, esp. the essay by E. Isenmann, 'The notion of the common good, the concept of politics and practical politics in late medieval and early modern German cities', pp. 107–48.

29 For the comparison with France see G. Naegle, 'Omne regnum in se divisum desolabitur? Coopération urbaine en France et dans l'Empire médiéval', in L. Buchholzer and O. Richard (eds), *Ligues urbaines et espace à la fin du Moyen Âge/Städtebünde und Raum im Spätmittelalter*, Strasbourg: Presses universitaires de Strasbourg, 2012, pp. 53–69.

30 *Ista autem pax, more lombardicarum civitatum inchoata* (P. Jaffé (ed.), 'Hermanni Altahensis Annales', in MGH, SS, 17, Hanover: Hahn, 1871, pp. 381–416, at 397). In 1256, the league had more than 30 princely and more than 60 urban members, but was torn apart by rival claimants for the throne. See B. Kreutz, 'Rheinische Städtebünde (13./14. Jahrhundert)', in *Historisches Lexikon Bayerns*, www.historisches-lexikon-bayerns.de/Lexikon/Rheinische Städtebünde (13./14. Jahrhundert); B. Kreutz, *Städtebünde und Städtenetz am Mittelrhein im 13. und 14. Jahrhundert*, Trier: Kliomedia, 2005; G. Bönnen, 'Der Rheinische Bund von 1254/56. Voraussetzungen, Wirkungsweise, Nachleben', in F.-J. Felten (ed.), *Städtebünde. Städtetage im Wandel der Geschichte*, Stuttgart: Steiner, 2006, pp. 13–35.

31 'Hermanni Altahensis Annales', p. 397.

32 Kreutz, 'Rheinische Städtebünde'; G. Bönnen, 'Der Rheinische Bund', pp. 13–35.

33 Philippe de Beaumanoir, *Coutumes de Beauvaisis*, ed. A. Salmon, 2 vols, Paris: Picard, 1899–1900, vol. 1, p. 449, section 886.

34 Philippe de Beaumanoir, *Coutumes*, ed. Salmon, vol. 1, pp. 447–9, sections 885–6; for his ideas about the resolution of conflicts see G. Naegle, *Stadt, Recht und Krone. Französische Städte, Königtum und Parlement im späten Mittelalter*, 2 vols, Husum: Matthiesen, 2002, vol. 1, pp. 67–73. For the comparison with urban leagues see H. Maurer (ed.), *Kommunale Bündnisse Oberitaliens und Oberdeutschlands im Vergleich*, Sigmaringen: Thorbecke, 1987.

35 *Et pour parler d'Almaigne en general, a tant de fortes places qu'il y a et tant de gens enclins a mal faire et a piller et a rober et qui usent de ces deffiances pour petite occasion; car ung homme qui n'aura que luy et son varlet deffiera une grosse cité ou ung duc, . . . avecques le port de quelque petit chasteau rochier . . . , ou il y aura vingt ou trente hommes a cheval. . . . Ces gens icy ne sont gueres de foiz puniz des princes d'Almaigne, car ilz s'en veulent servir quant ilz en ont affaire; mais les villes, quant ilz les peuvent tenir, les punissent cruellement, et aulcunes foiz ont bien assiégé de telz chasteaulx et abatuz: et aussi tiennent lesdictes villes ordinairement des gens d'armes paiéz.*
(Philippe de Commynes, *Mémoires*, ed. J. Blanchard, 2 vols, Geneva: Droz, 2007, vol. 1, pp. 402–3, English translation: G. Naegle)

36 See G. Naegle, 'Einleitung', in *Frieden schaffen und sich verteidigen im Spätmittelalter/Faire la paix et se défendre à la fin du Moyen Âge*, Munich: Oldenbourg, 2012, pp. 9–48, at 16, 31–7; M. Diago Hernando, 'Die politische Rolle der Städtebünde im spätmittelalterlichen Kastilien (13.–16. Jh.). Selbstverteidigung, Herrschaftsstabilisierung und Friedenssicherung', in Naegle (ed.), *Frieden schaffen*, pp. 139–59.

37 Schubert, *Der Stadt Nutz*; Zeilinger, *Lebensformen*.

38 See e.g. E. Wadle, 'Gottesfrieden und Landfrieden als Gegenstand der Forschung nach 1950', in K. Kroeschell and A. Cordes (eds), *Funktion und Form. Quellen- und Methodenprobleme der mittelalterlichen Rechtsgeschichte*, Berlin: Duncker & Humblot, 1996, pp. 63–91, reprinted in E. Wadle, *Landfrieden, Strafe, Recht. Zwölf Studien zum Mittelalter*, Berlin: Duncker & Humblot, 2001, pp. 11–39; A. Buschmann and E. Wadle (eds), *Landfrieden. Anspruch und Wirklichkeit*, Paderborn, Munich: Schöningh, 2002.

39 H. Carl, *Der Schwäbische Bund 1488–1534*, Leinfelden-Echterdingen: DRW-Verlag, 2000, p. 57.

40 J. K. Hoensch, *Kaiser Sigismund. Ein Kaiser an der Schwelle zur Neuzeit 1368–1437*, Munich: Beck, 1996, pp. 262–3, see also S. Wefers, *Das politische System Kaiser Sigmunds*, Stuttgart: Steiner, 1989, pp. 117–18, 176.

41 Naegle, 'Omne regnum', in Buchholzer and Richard (eds), *Ligues urbaines*. See also J. Firnhaber-Baker, *'A son de cloche*: The interpretation of public order and legitimate authority in Northern France 1355–1358', in H. R. Oliva Herrer, V. Challet, J. Dumolyn, and M. A. Carmona Ruiz (eds), *La comunidad medieval como esfera pública*, Seville: Universidad de Sevilla, 2014, pp. 357–76, at 374–5.

42 G. Naegle and J. Á. Solórzano Telechea, 'Geschlechter und Zünfte, *principales* und *común*. Städtische Konflikte in Kastilien und dem spätmittelalterlichen Reich', *Zeitschrift für Historische Forschung*, 41, 2014, pp. 561–618, at 564–5.

43 M. González Jiménez, *Alfonso X el Sabio*, Barcelona: Ariel, 2004, pp. 353–61.

44 J. Á. Solórzano Telechea, 'The politics of the urban commons in northern Atlantic Spain in the later Middle Ages', *Urban History*, 44, 2014, pp. 183–203.
45 M. Asenjo González, 'Concordia, pactos y acuerdos en la sociedad política urbana de la Castilla medieval', in F. Foronda and A. I. Carrasco Manchado (eds), *El contrato político en la Corona de Castilla*, Madrid: Dykinson, 2008, pp. 125–57; E. Fuentes Ganzo, 'Pactismo, cortes y hermandades en León y Castilla: siglos XIII–XV', in ibid., pp. 415–52; L. Legaz y Lacambra, J. Sobrequés Callicó, J. B. Vallet de Goytisolo, J. Lalinde Abadía, A. García Gallo, and L. Sánchez Agesta (eds), *El pactismo en la historia de España*, Madrid: Instituto de España, 1980; T. de Montagut i Estragués, 'Pactisme o absolutisme a Catalunya: les grans institucions de govern (XV–XVI)', *Anuario de Estudios Medievales*, 19, 1989, pp. 669–79; F. Foronda and A. I. Carrasco Manchado (eds), *Du contrat d'alliance au contrat politique: Cultures et sociétés politiques dans la péninsule ibérique à la fin du Moyen Âge*, Toulouse: CNRS, Université Toulouse-Le Mirail, 2007.
46 Naegle and Solórzano Telechea, 'Geschlechter und Zünfte', pp. 563–5.
47 Carl, *Der Schwäbische Bund 1488–1534*.
48 L. Pelizaeus, *Dynamik der Macht. Städtischer Widerstand und Konfliktbewältigung im Reich Karls V.*, Münster: Aschendorff, 2007; F. Martínez Gil (ed.), *En torno a las comunidades de Castilla*, Cuenca: Ediciones de la Universidad de Castilla-La Mancha, 2000.
49 Naegle and Solórzano Telechea, 'Geschlechter und Zünfte', pp. 598–9.
50 *Chronicon Wormatiense*, ed. and trans. D. S. Bachrach, *The Histories of a Medieval German City, Worms c.1000–1300: Translation and Commentary*, Farnham: Ashgate, 2014, pp. 81–128, at 111; Latin original: H. Boos (ed.), *Quellen zur Geschichte der Stadt Worms*, vol. 3, Berlin: Weidmannsche Buchhandlung, 1893, no. V, pp. 162–99, 201–305, Latin quotation at 187.
51 *Annales Wormatienses*, in Bachrach, *The Histories*, pp. 129–59, at 146. Latin: *Annales Wormatienses (1226–1278)*, in Boos (ed.), *Quellen zur Geschichte*, vol. 3, no. IV, pp. 142–62, quotation at 155.
52 *Annales Wormatienses*, in Bachrach, *The Histories*, p. 147, Latin explanations: G.N.: quoted from Boos (ed.), *Quellen zur Geschichte*, vol. 3, p. 155.
53 *Germinantibus inter vos intestine discordie et civilium iurgiorum erroribus obviare et subortas simultates et odia extirpari* (no. 305, King Rudolf of Habsburg, before 1282, in B. Diestelkamp (ed.), *Urkundenregesten zur Tätigkeit des deutschen Königs- und Hofgerichts bis 1451*, 16 vols to date, Cologne and Vienna: Böhlau, 1986–present, vol. 3: B. Diestelkamp and U. Rödel (eds), *Die Zeit Rudolfs von Habsburg 1273–1291*, Cologne and Vienna: Böhlau, 1986, p. 223).
54 Ibid., no. 305 and, similar, no. 307, King Rudolf of Habsburg, before 1282, pp. 224–5.
55 R. Mitsch, 'Das Eingreifen Friedrichs III. in innerstädtische Konflikte', *Zeitschrift für Historische Forschung*, 25, 1998, pp. 1–54.
56 B. Diestelkamp, 'Bürgerunruhen vor dem spätmittelalterlichen deutschen Königsgericht', in A. Cordes, J. Rückert, and R. Schulze (eds), *Stadt – Gemeinde – Genossenschaft*, Berlin: Schmidt, 2003, pp. 67–101, at 79. For *Friedebriefe* (letters of peace) see B. Kannowski, *Bürgerkämpfe und Friedebriefe*, Cologne: Böhlau, 2001 (with numerous examples).
57 No. 121, Regensburg, 5 July 1331, in B. Diestelkamp (ed.), *Urkundenregesten zur Tätigkeit*, vol. 5: F. Battenberg (ed.), *Die Zeit Ludwigs des Bayern und Friedrichs des Schönen 1314–1347*, Cologne and Vienna: Böhlau, 1987, p. 74.
58 H. Lentze, *Der Kaiser und die Zunftverfassung in den Reichsstädten bis zum Tode Karls IV.*, Breslau: Marcus, 1933, reprinted Aalen: Scientia, 1964.
59 Naegle and Solórzano Telechea, 'Geschlechter und Zünfte', pp. 580–1.
60 S. von Heusinger, 'Von *Antwerk* bis *Zunft*. Methodische Überlegungen zu den Zünften im Mittelalter', *Zeitschrift für Historische Forschung*, 37, 2010, pp. 37–71, at 63; S. von Heusinger, *Die Zunft im Mittelalter. Zur Verflechtung von Politik, Wirtschaft und Gesellschaft in Straßburg*, Stuttgart: Steiner, 2009, pp. 297–315.
61 K. Czok, 'Die Bürgerkämpfe in Süd- und Westdeutschland im 14. Jahrhundert', *Jahrbuch für Geschichte der oberdeutschen Reichsstädte*, 12–13, 1966–67, pp. 40–72, esp. 60–63; O. Richard and B.-M. Tock, 'Des chartes ornées urbaines: les *Schwörbriefe* de Strasbourg', *Bibliothèque de l'École des chartes*, 169, 2011, pp. 109–28.
62 J. H. Lau (ed.), *Urkundenbuch der Reichsstadt Frankfurt*, vol. 2: 1314–40, Glashütten/Taunus: Auvermann, 1905, no. 284, 13 September 1325 (alliance for six years of Frankfurt, Friedberg, Wetzlar, and Gelnhausen), pp. 216–17, quotation at 216.
63 Ibid., no. 716, 12 October 1340, pp. 529–31, quotation at 530.

64 See e.g. *Hanserecesse von 1256–1430*, Leipzig: Duncker & Humblot, 1880, reprinted in Hildesheim, Olms, Section/Abteilung I, vol. 5, p. 975, no. 717:

> *Die Städte Lübeck, Rostock und Wismar urkunden über ein zwischen ihnen auf fünf Jahre geschlossenes Bündniss, in welchem Lübeck seine Streitigkeit mit dem alten Rath der Vermittelung der Städte Rostock und Wismar unterstellt und diese ihre Hilfe versprechen, wenn Jemand den alten Rath mit Gewalt in Lübeck wieder einführen wollte* [20 April 1410].

65 *Hanserecesse von 1256–1430*, subsection/Abteilung 1, vol. 2, Leipzig: Duncker & Humblot, 1872, *Hanserecesse*, I, vol. 2, p. 96.

66 M. Puhle, 'Die *Große Schicht* in Braunschweig', in J. Bracker, V. Henn, and R. Postel (eds), *Die Hanse, Lebenswirklichkeit und Mythos*, 4th edn, Lübeck: Schmidt-Römhild, 2006, pp. 812–22, at 819.

67 Assembly in Lübeck, 12 August 1380 in *Hanserecesse von 1256–1430*, subsection/Abteilung 1, vol. 2, Leipzig: Duncker & Humblot, 1872, *Hanserecesse*, I, vol. 2, pp. 261–2.

68 [G]*eyne hervart zo doin noch zu bestellen, geyne nuwe verbontenisse, brieve noch verdrach mit eyngen herren of steden anzogain off zo machen in eynger wijse* (M. Huiskes, 'Kölns Verfassung für 400 Jahre. Der Verbundbrief vom 14. September 1396', in Förderverein Geschichte in Köln (ed.), *Quellen zur Geschichte der Stadt Köln*, Cologne: Bachem, 1996–present, vol. 2, ed. J. Deeters, J. Helmrath, D. Rheker-Wunsch, and S. Wunsch, no. 1, pp. 6–7).

69 R. Schmid, '*Vorbehalt* und *Hilfskreis*. Grenzsetzungen in kommunalen Bündnissen des Spätmittelalters', in K. Hitzbleck and K. Hübner (eds), *Die Grenzen des Netzwerks 1200–1600*, Ostfildern: Thorbecke, 2014, pp. 175–95.

70 [I]*ede stat hat sich verpunden zu dem herrn, der ir gefallen hat. Also ist das reich alles zertrent und von ainander kommen und mugen ainander weder helfen noch ratten und gunnent ainander weder eren noch guets, das ist des adels gelächter* (Burkhard Zink, *Chronik*, in C. Hegel (ed.), *Die Chroniken der deutschen Städte*, vol. 5: *Augsburg*: vol. 2, Leipzig: Hirzel, 1866, reprinted Göttingen: Vandenhoeck & Ruprecht, Göttingen, 1966, p. 231); C. Meyer, *Die Stadt als Thema. Nürnbergs Entdeckung in Texten um 1500*, Ostfildern: Thorbecke, 2009, p. 365 (with further explanations).

71 Burkhard Zink, *Chronik*, p. 231.

72 Isenmann, *Die deutsche Stadt*, p. 251. See list of uprisings in Hergemöller, *Uplop*; critical commentary about such lists: A. Haverkamp, '"Innerstädtische Auseinandersetzungen" und überlokale Zusammenhänge in deutschen Städten während der ersten Hälfte des 14. Jahrhunderts', in R. Elze and G. Fasoli (eds), *Stadtadel und Bürgertum in den italienischen und deutschen Städten des Spätmittelalters*, Berlin: Duncker & Humblot, pp. 89–126.

73 M. Bourin, G. Cherubini, and G. Pinto (eds), *Rivolte urbane e rivolte contadine nell'Europa del Trecento: Un confronto*, Florence: Florence University Press, 2008; S. K. Cohn, Jr., *Lust for Liberty: The Politics of Social Revolt in Medieval Europe, 1200–1425: Italy, France, and Flanders*, Cambridge, MA: Harvard University Press, 2006; P. Blickle (ed.), *Resistance, Representation and Community*, Oxford: Clarendon Press, 1997; P. Blickle, *Unruhen in der ständischen Gesellschaft 1300–1800*, 2nd edn, Munich: Oldenbourg, 2010.

74 M. Puhle, 'Die Braunschweiger *Schichten* (Aufstände) des späten Mittelalters und ihre verfassungsrechtlichen Folgen', in M. R. W. Garzmann (ed.), *Rat und Verfassung im mittelalterlichen Braunschweig*, Brunswick: Stadtarchiv Braunschweig, 1986, pp. 235–51; M. Puhle, 'Die Braunschweiger *Schichten* des Mittelalters im Überblick und Vergleich', in B. Pollmann (ed.), *Schicht – Protest – Revolution in Braunschweig 1292–1947/48*, Brunswick: Stadtbibliothek, 1995, pp. 27–33; M. Puhle, 'Die *Große Schicht* in Braunschweig', in J. Bracker *et al.* (eds), *Die Hanse*, pp. 812–22.

75 Blickle, *Unruhen*, p. 10.

76 For example, below, n. 122: quotation from the chronicle of Philippe de Vigneulles.

77 P. Gilli and J.-P. Guilhembet (eds), *Le châtiment des villes dans les espaces méditerranéens (Antiquité, Moyen Âge, Époque moderne)*, Turnhout: Brepols, 2012.

78 P. Monnet, 'Les révoltes urbaines en Allemagne au XIVe siècle: un état de la question', in Bourin *et al.* (eds), *Rivolte*, pp. 105–52, at 115.

79 H. Boockmann, 'Spätmittelalterliche deutsche Stadt-Tyrannen', *Blätter für deutsche Landesgeschichte*, 119, 1983, pp. 73–91; Monnet, 'Les révoltes', pp. 115–16. About Waldmann, see M. Jucker, 'Der gestürzte Tyrann. Befriedung von Aufständen durch Gestik, Symbolik und Recht', in S. Rüther (ed.), *Integration und Konkurrenz. Symbolische Kommunikation in der spätmittelalterlichen Stadt*, Münster: Rhema, 2009, pp. 177–204. About Muffel, see Meyer, *Die Stadt*, pp. 424–7, 437, and G. Fouquet, 'Die Affäre Niklas Muffel. Die Hinrichtung eines Nürnberger Patriziers im Jahre 1469', *Vierteljahrschrift für Wirtschafts- und Sozialgeschichte*, 83, 1996, pp. 459–500.

80 W. Buchholz, 'Rubenow, Heinrich', in *Neue Deutsche Biographie*, 2005, 22, pp. 153–4, online version www.deutsche-biographie.de/pnd122863119.html.
81 L. Schnurrer, *Rothenburg im Mittelalter*, Rothenburg ob der Tauber: Verlag des Vereins Alt-Rothenburg, 1997, pp. 43–6.
82 A. Coville, *Les Cabochiens et l'ordonnance de 1413*, Paris: Hachette, 1888, reprinted Geneva: Slatkine-Mégariotis, 1974; B. Schnerb, 'Caboche et Capeluche: les insurrections parisiennes au début du XVe siècle', in F. Bluche and S. Rials (eds), *Les révolutions françaises*, Paris: Fayard, 1989, pp. 113–30; N. Bulst, 'Stände und Widerstand. Die Reformvorstellungen der Generalstände von 1413 und die *révolte cabochienne*', in P.-J. Heinig, S. Jahns, H.-J. Schmidt, R. C. Schwinges, and S. Wefers (eds), *Reich, Regionen und Europa in Mittelalter und Neuzeit, Festschrift für Peter Moraw*, Berlin: Duncker & Humblot, 2000, pp. 115–32.
83 Edition: C. Hegel (ed.), *Die Chroniken der niederrheinischen Städte, Cöln I* (= *Chroniken der deutschen Städte*, vol. 12), Leipzig: Hirzel, 1875, pp. 243–62; K. Militzer, *Ursachen und Folgen der innerstädtischen Auseinandersetzungen in Köln in der zweiten Hälfte des 14. Jahrhunderts*, Cologne: Wamper, 1980, pp. 151–82; K. Kuepper, 'Textform und Textabsicht der Kölner *weverslaicht* vom Ende des 14. Jahrhunderts', *Seminar: A Journal of Germanic Studies*, 28, 1992, pp. 222–32; G. Annas, 'Innerstädtische Auseinandersetzungen. "Weberaufstand" – "Weberherrschaft" – "Weberschlacht" (1370/71)', in W. Rosen and L. Wirtler (eds), *Quellen zur Geschichte der Stadt Köln*, 3 vols to date, Cologne: Bachem, 1996–present, vol. 1, pp. 264–83; C. Watson, 'Weverslaicht (the battle of the weavers)', in G. Dunphy (ed.), *Encyclopedia of the Medieval Chronicle*, 2 vols, Leiden and Boston: Brill, 2010, vol. 2, p. 1502.
84 Burkhard Zink, *Chronik*, p. 120.
85 Felix Fabri, O. P., *Tractatus de civitate Ulmensi*, ed. F. Reichert, Konstanz: Edition Isele, 2012, pp. 246–7: *Potens est hec zunfta turbare totam communitatem, dum in sedicionem vertitur, prout quondam factum fuit.*
86 M. Häberlein, *Die Fugger. Geschichte einer Augsburger Familie (1367–1650)*, Stuttgart: Kohlhammer, 2006, p. 17.
87 M. Diago Hernando, 'El papel de los linajes en las estructuras de gobierno urbano en Castilla y en el Imperio alemán durante los siglos bajomedievales', *En la España medieval*, 20, 1997, pp. 143–77; M. Diago Hernando, 'La participación de la nobleza en el gobierno de las ciudades europeas bajomedievales: análisis comparativo', *Anuario de estudios medievales*, 37, 2007, pp. 781–822; M. Á. Ladero Quesada, 'Lignages, *bandos* et partis dans la vie politique des villes castillanes (XIVe–XVe siècles)', in Département de recherches 'Pyrenaica', Université de Pau et des Pays de l'Adour (ed.), *Les sociétés urbaines en France méridionale et en péninsule Ibérique au Moyen Âge*, Paris: CNRS, 1991, pp. 105–30; M. I. del Val Valdivieso, 'Hiérarchie sociale et interventions royales dans les conflits urbains en Castille au XVe siècle', in N. Coulet, and O. Guyotjeannin (eds), *La ville au Moyen Âge*, 2 vols, Paris: CTHS, 1998, vol. 2, pp. 149–58.
88 Staatsarchiv Augsburg, Reichsstadt Memmingen, Urk. 394.
89 *Die Chronik des Jacob Twinger von Königshofen*, in C. Hegel (ed.), *Die Chroniken der oberrheinischen Städte. Straßburg*, 2 vols, Strasbourg, Leipzig: Hirzel, 1870–1, vol. 2, pp. 499–910, at 466.
90 Von Heusinger, *Die Zunft*, pp. 170–1.
91 In other contexts, the medieval word 'burger' would be equivalent to the modern German word *Bürger* and would mean 'citizen'. In Strasbourg this is *not* the case. Here, as in other medieval Southern German and Swiss sources, it refers to patrician families that were eligible for the Council. In some towns, as in Strasbourg, there are times when it only refers to non-noble patricians to distinguish them from noble patricians or, in other contexts, it marks the contrast to members of craft corporations. The use is variable. H.-J. Gilomen, 'Burger', in *Lexikon des Mittelalters*, vol. 2, col. 1006.
92 Literally 'Edle' would mean 'nobles'. In Strasbourg in the fourteenth century, it was used to describe noble patricians, P. Dollinger, 'Patriciat noble et patriciat bourgeois à Strasbourg au XIVe siècle', *Revue d'Alsace*, 90, 1951, pp. 52–82. Later the meaning changed.
93 Name of an office in Strasbourg. There is no modern German equivalent. Literally the word would mean 'master of the town', but this makes no sense. The word cannot be translated by 'mayor'.
94 The name of the most important office in Strasbourg. The word derives from *Amt* (office) and *Meister* (master). Literally the signification is 'master of the office' but, again, this makes no sense. There is no modern German equivalent. The word cannot be translated by 'mayor'.
95 Von Heusinger, *Die Zunft*, pp. 172–3; see also Y. Egawa, *Stadtherrschaft und Gemeinde in Straßburg vom Beginn des 13. Jahrhunderts bis zum Schwarzen Tod (1349)*, Trier: Kliomedia, 2007.

96 S. von Heusinger, *'Old Boys' Networks*. Die Verfassungswechsel in Straßburg im 14. Jahrhundert', in L. Buchholzer-Remy, S. von Heusinger, S. Hirbodian, O. Richard, and T. Zotz (eds), *Neue Forschungen zur elsässischen Geschichte im Mittelalter*, Freiburg: Karl Alber, 2012, pp. 153–75; S. von Heusinger 'Von *Antwerk* bis *Zunft*', pp. 37–71.

97 See the text of art. 15 below, n. 176.

98 For example, no. 75: 'Rathschlagen der Fünfzehner betreffend das Ausbleiben der Dreizehner aus den Sitzungen' (Strasbourg, 1465), in *Verfassungs- und Verwaltungsgeschichte der Stadt Strassburg*, vol. 1, pp. 223–4; no. 93: 'Rathschlagen der Fünfzehner und Erkenntnis des Rathes wegen Ausbleibens der Stadtmeister aus den Sitzungen' (Strasbourg, 1472), in ibid., pp. 246–7; other countries: Naegle, *Stadt*, vol. 1, p. 258 (Tours [1433], Poitiers [1420] and dispositions for this case in the *Établissements* of Rouen); A. Sousa Melo, 'Os mesteirais e o governo urbano do Porto nos séculos XIV e XV', in J. Á. Solórzano Telechea and B. Arízaga Bolumburu (eds), *La gobernanza de la ciudad europea en la Edad Media*, Logroño: Instituto de Estudios Riojanos, 2011, pp. 323–47, at 327, n. 9.

99 For the interdiction of 'illicit gatherings' in the Netherlands, see J. Dumolyn and J. Haemers, in this volume, pp. 44–9.

100 *So mochte auch sein, das sy czuzeiten mit beslossener Thûre Ratte hetten, das beschee nit unbillich, dann es hiesse darumb ein Rate, das es nit offennlich sein noch yederman wissen solt* (23 February 1473, Staatsarchiv Augsburg, Reichsstadt Memmingen, Urk. 405, not foliated, English Translation: G. Naegle).

101 P. Monnet, *Les villes d'Allemagne au Moyen Âge*, Paris: Picard, 2004, p. 161.

102 G. Chittolini and P. Johanek (eds), *Aspetti e componenti dell'identità urbana in Italia e in Germania (secoli XIV–XVI)*, Bologna: Il Mulino, 2003.

103 Felix Fabri, *Tractatus*, pp. 140–1.

104 Felix Fabri, *Tractatus*, pp. 138–9.

105 See a detailed presentation of his model in G. Naegle, 'Commun et communes, révoltes ou révolutions: participation politique et luttes de pouvoir dans les villes allemandes à la fin du Moyen Âge', in J. Á. Solórzano Telechea, B. Arízaga Bolumburu, and J. Haemers (eds), *Los grupos populares en la ciudad medieval europea*, Logroño: Instituto de Estudios Riojanos, 2014, pp. 413–39, at 428–36.

106 The word *Constofler* refers to a corporation of Strasbourg, whose members were no craftsmen and could not exercise a lucrative activity. The word does not exist in modern German, but similar names existed also in the Oberrhein/Swiss region. In this specific context of Strasbourg, it refers to the members of the patrician society who chose it as its name.

107 Naegle and Solórzano Telechea, 'Geschlechter und Zünfte', p. 584.

108 J. R. Díaz de Durana, *Anonymous Noblemen: The Generalization of Hidalgo Status in the Basque Country (1250–1525)*, Turnhout: Brepols, 2011; M. Asenjo González (ed.), *Urban Elites and Aristocratic Behaviour in the Spanish Kingdoms at the End of the Middle Ages*, Turnhout: Brepols, 2013.

109 *Großzunft* was a term specific to Memmingen. Literally meaning 'the Major Corporation', it implies that there were 'minor' ones.

110 Staatsarchiv Augsburg, Reichsstadt Memmingen, Urk. 394.

111 *So habe auch die groß zünffte nicht mer freiheit dann ain annder zunffte. Ausgenomen daz die groß zünffte die drey tage in der Vaßnacht auf dem ratthauss fur ander zunfften daselbs tanntzen und der statt pfeiffer darzu gebrauchen* (Staatsarchiv Augsburg, Reichsstadt Memmingen, Urk. 394).

112 Fleischmann, *Rat und Patriziat*, vol. 1, pp. 222.

113 G. Fouquet (ed.), *Geschlechtergesellschaften, Zunft-Trinkstuben und Bruderschaften in spätmittelalterlichen und frühneuzeitlichen Städten*, Ostfildern: Thorbecke, 2003.

114 *Fritsche (Friedrich) Closeners Chronik (1362)*, in Hegel (ed.), *Die Chroniken der oberrheinischen Städte. Straßburg*, vol. 1, pp. 79–151, at 125; *Die Chronik des Jacob Twinger von Königshofen*, in Hegel (ed.), *Die Chroniken der oberrheinischen Städte. Straßburg*, vol. 2, pp. 499–910, at 779–80.

115 *Ut etiam ad comprimendos vicinos materia non careant, inferioris conditionis iuvenes vel quoslibet contemptibilium etiam mechanicarum artium opifices, quos ceteres gentes ab honestioribus et liberioribus studiis tamquam pestem propellunt, ad militie cingulum vel dignitatum gradus assumere non dedignantur. Ex quo factum est, ut ceteris orbis civitatibus divitiis et potentia premineant.*
(F.-J. Schmale (ed.), *Ottonis Episcopi Frisingensis et Rahewini Gesta Friderici seu rectius Cronica*, Darmstadt: WBG, 1965, p. 308; G. Castelnuovo, *Être noble dans la cité: Les noblesses italiennes en quête d'identité (XIIIe–XVe siècle)*, Paris: Classiques Garnier, 2014, p. 34).

116 Alexander von Roes, 'Noticia Seculi', in *Alexander von Roes, Schriften*, ed. H. Grundmann and H. Heimpel, Stuttgart: Hiersemann, 1958, pp. 149–71, at 160–1; Castelnuovo, *Être noble*, p. 34.
117 Felix Fabri, *Tractatus*, pp. 112–13: *Credo enim, quod Ulmenses, antequam bastardum pro magistro civium acciperent, eciam cuiuscunque principus filium, quod pocius ipsi rem publicam propriam dissolverent.*
118 E. Isenmann, 'Obrigkeit und Stadtgemeinde in der frühen Neuzeit', in H. E. Specker (ed.), *Einwohner und Bürger auf dem Weg zur Demokratie*, Stuttgart: Kohlhammer, 1997, pp. 74–126.
119 In an oath of loyalty, citizens were requested to declare *dem riche und dem rade zu Frankinford undirtenyg zu syne* ('Richtung zwischen dem rath zu Frankfurt auf der einen und den hantwerken und der gemeinde auf der andern seite, verfasst durch Ulrich herrn zu Hanau', 11 November 1358, in J. F. Lau (ed.), *Urkundenbuch der Reichsstadt Frankfurt*, 2 vols, Frankfurt am Main: Baer, 1901–5, vol. 2, pp. 658–9).
120 G. Naegle, 'Commun et communes', pp. 413–39; Isenmann, *Die deutsche Stadt*, p. 251; C. Veltmann, *Knochenhauer in Lübeck am Ende des 14. Jahrhunderts*, Neumünster: Wachholtz, 1993.
121 For the problem of 'connections' in large-scale revolts and long-distance planning in the case of the Jacquerie, see J. Firnhaber-Baker in this volume, pp. 60–3.

122 *Item, tantost ung peu après, la commune de la cité de Liège, oyant les nouvelle des devant dit de Collongnie, se voullurent perreillement eslever et rebeller en l'encontre de leur recteur et gouverneurs. Et, ensuyvant les dit de Collongne, voulloient sçavoir le nombre de leur trésor, et voulloient avoir les comptes et receptes.*
 (C. Bruneau (ed.), *La chronique de Philippe de Vigneulles*, 4 vols, Metz: Société d'histoire et d'archéologie de la Lorraine: 1927–33, vol. 4, p. 145 and see vol. 4, p. 146: pareillement, en la dicte année, la commune de Nostre Damme d'Ays, en ensuyvant les dit de Collongne, se cuydairent mutiner).

123 M. Boone, 'Destructions des villes et menaces de destructions: éléments du discours princier aux Pays-Bas bourguignons', in M. Körner (ed.), *Stadtzerstörung und Wiederaufbau/Destruction et reconstruction des villes*, vol. 2: *Zerstörung durch die Stadtherrschaft, innere Unruhen und Kriege/Destruction par le pouvoir seigneurial, les troubles internes et les guerres*, Bern, Stuttgart: Haupt, 2000, pp. 97–111, at 107–8.
124 Meyer, *Die Stadt*, p. 399.
125 B. Walter, *Informationen, Wissen und Macht. Akteure und Techniken städtischer Außenpolitik: Bern, Straßburg und Basel im Kontext der Burgunderkriege (1468–1477)*, Stuttgart: Steiner, 2012, pp. 80–103, 148; C. Jörg and M. Jucker (eds), *Spezialisierung und Professionalisierung. Träger und Foren städtischer Außenpolitik während des späten Mittelalters und der frühen Neuzeit*, Wiesbaden: Reichert, 2010.
126 L. Buchholzer-Rémy, *Une ville en ses réseaux: Nuremberg à la fin du Moyen Âge*, Paris: Belin, 2006, pp. 177–97.
127 Buchholzer-Rémy, *Une ville*, pp. 186–7.
128 Meyer, *Die Stadt*, p. 358.
129 B. Walter, '*Bons amis* et *agents secrets*: les réseaux de communication informels entre alliés', in Buchholzer and Richard, *Ligues urbaines*, pp. 179–201; for examples underlining the role of town clerks, see B. Walter, 'Informelle Kontaktnetze in der Eidgenossenschaft und am Oberrhein (1468–1477)', in K. Hitzbleck and K. Hübner (eds), *Die Grenzen des Netzwerks 1200–1600*, Ostfildern: Thorbecke, 2014, pp. 137–55.
130 N. Bulst, *Recht, Raum und Politik. Von der spätmittelalterlichen Stadt zur Europäischen Union*, Düsseldorf: Wallstein, 2015, p. 30; T. Scott, *Die Freiburger Enquête von 1476*, Freiburg im Breisgau: Stadtarchiv, 1986.
131 N. Bulst, *Recht, Raum*, pp. 19–20; N. Bulst, 'Normative Texte als Quelle zur Kommunikationsstruktur zwischen städtischen und territorialen Obrigkeiten im späten Mittelalter und der frühen Neuzeit', in *Veröffentlichungen des Instituts für Realienkunde des Mittelalters und der frühen Neuzeit*, vol. 15: *Sitzungsberichte der österreichischen Akademie der Wissenschaften, philologisch-historische Klasse*, vol. 596, Vienna: Verlag der Österreichischen Akademie der Wissenschaften, 1992, pp. 127–44.
132 R. Kießling, 'Augsburg im Aufstand. Ein systematischer Vergleich von Unruhen des 14./16. mit denen des 17./18. Jahrhunderts', in A. Westermann and E. Westermann, with the collaboration of J. Pahl (ed.), *Streik im Revier. Unruhe, Protest und Ausstand vom 8. bis 20. Jahrhundert*, St. Katharinen: Scripta Mercaturae Verlag, 2007, pp. 153–75, at 160. About Augsburg, see also J. Rogge, *Für den gemeinen Nutzen. Politisches Handeln und Politikverständnis von Rat und Bürgerschaft in Augsburg im Spätmittelalter*, Tübingen: Niemeyer, 1996; D. Adrian, *Augsbourg à la fin du Moyen Âge*, Ostfildern: Thorbecke, 2013.

133 M. Diago Hernando, 'The territorial politics of the Spanish towns from the Middle Ages to the beginning of the nineteenth century', in M. Pauly and M. Scheutz (eds), *Cities and Their Spaces: Concepts of Their Use in Europe*, Cologne and Weimar: Böhlau, 2014, pp. 217–33, at 220.
134 P. Johanek, 'Imperial and free towns', pp. 252–88, particularly 263, 259.
135 H. Lück, M. Puhle, and A. Ranft (eds), *Grundlagen für ein neues Europa. Das Magdeburger und Lübecker Recht in Spätmittelalter und Früher Neuzeit*, Cologne and Weimar: Böhlau, 2009; for critical remarks about the concept of 'families' of urban law, see S. Dusil, *Die Soester Stadtrechtsfamilie*, Cologne, Weimar: Böhlau, 2007.
136 *Oberhöfe* were an institution of medieval German law. The word and the institution no longer exist, and it is only used in legal history. The word could describe a great variety of different forms and realities. The *Handwörterbuch zur deutschen Rechtsgeschichte* defines *Oberhof* as a typical institution of late medieval law, a

> legal term that refers to an institution that gives legal advice or information to other courts or sometimes to private persons in matters of law and procedure, particularly in the domain of substantive law [*materielles Recht*] and in the domain of proceedings of civil law [*Zivilprozeßrecht*].
> D. Werkmüller, 'Oberhof', in A. Erler and E. Kaufmann (eds), *Handwörterbuch zur deutschen Rechtsgeschichte*, 5 vols, Berlin: Schmidt, 1984–98, vol. 3, cols 1134–46, at 1134

The word is used to describe the relationship of towns belonging to the same 'family' of urban law, especially with their 'mother' town. There are partial similarities with the institution of 'chef de sens' in French-speaking Flanders, which was much more informal and less institutionalised.
137 Naegle, 'Einleitung', p. 17.
138 For the *familias de fueros*, see M. Á. Ladero Quesada, *Ciudades de la España medieval*, Madrid: Dykinson, 2010, pp. 85–6; A. M. Barrero García and M. L. Alonso Martín, *Textos de derecho local español en la Edad Media: Catálogo de fueros y costums municipales*, Madrid: CSIC, 1989, pp. 545–67.
139 Meyer, *Die Stadt*, pp. 466–8.
140 Meyer, *Die Stadt*, pp. 77–8, 356; K. Kellermann, *Abschied vom 'historischen Volkslied'*, Tübingen: Niemeyer, 2000, pp. 164–216. About the commemoration of battles, see K. Graf, 'Schlachtengedenken in der Stadt', in B. Kirchgässner and G. Scholz (eds), *Stadt und Krieg*, Sigmaringen: Thorbecke, 1989, pp. 83–104.
141 Isenmann, *Die deutsche Stadt*, pp. 254–63.
142 Monnet, 'Les révoltes', pp. 105–52, at 111; P. Monnet, 'La ville et la guerre dans quelques cités de l'Empire aux XIVe et XVe siècles: de l'urgence immédiate à la mémoire identitaire', in C. Raynaud (ed.), *Villes en guerre*, Aix-en-Provence: Publications de l'université de Provence, 2008, pp. 185–223, at 187; P. Lantschner, 'Revolts and the political order of cities in the late Middle Ages', *P&P*, 225, 2014, pp. 3–46, at 37–44, and J. Smithuis in this volume, pp. 224–7.
143 Medieval German: both words mean 'give different sounds', give 'dissonant bad sounds' = lat. *dissonare, absonare, dissonantia*; but 'misse-hëllen' can also mean 'not to be of the same opinion'.
144 Medieval word: this word has regional variants and apart from meaning 'uproar', 'tumult', it also expresses the idea of noise.
145 Medieval word: disposition, ordinance, order. Latin synonyms: *disposition, ordinatio, ordo* (M. Lexer, *Mittelhochdeutsches Handwörterbuch*, 3 vols, Leipzig: von Hirzel, 1873, reprinted Stuttgart: S. Hirzel, 1974, vol. 2, col. 721).
146 Lists e.g. in Hergemöller, *Uplop*, pp. 17–18.
147 K. Kellermann, *Abschied*, pp. 105–216.
148 For the year 1466, the Augsburg chronicler Burkhard Zink gives a description of troubles (*Strauß, Widerpart*) after the introduction of a new tax (*Ungelt*). Several corporations had refused to pay it and *murmered (murmerten sie)* (Burkhard Zink, *Chronik*, p. 118).
149 See J. Dumolyn and J. Haemers in this volume, p. 44.
150 Examples in medieval German (*Mittelhochdeutsch*): 'Murmeln, Murmelung', in H. Speer, R. Schröder, C. Kimmel, Preußische Akademie der Wissenschaften, Deutsche Akademie der Wissenschaften, and Heidelberger Akademie der Wissenschaften (eds), *Deutsches Rechtswörterbuch*, 13 vols to date, Weimar: Hermann Böhlaus Nachfolger, 1914–present, vol. 9, cols 1049–50; 'Murmer, murmel, murmerunge, murmelunge, murmelâtat', etc. in W. Müller and F. Zarncke (eds), *Mittelhochdeutsches Wörterbuch*, 3 vols, Leipzig: Hirzel, 1854–66, vol. 2, p. 1863, reprinted Hildesheim: Olms, 1963, vol. 2, pp. 276–7.
151 A. Holenstein, 'Introduction: empowering interactions; looking at statebuilding from below', in W. Blockmans, A. Holenstein, and J. Mathieu (eds), *Empowering Interactions: Political Cultures and the*

Emergence of the State in Europe 1300–1500, Farnham: Ashgate, 2009, pp. 1–31, quotation at 7; J. Dumolyn, J. Haemers, H. R. Oliva Herrer, and V. Challet (eds), *The Voices of the People in Late Medieval Europe*, Turnhout: Brepols, 2014; Oliva Herrer et al. (eds), *La comunidad*.

152 J. Rogge, 'Vom Schweigen der Chronisten', in J. Janota and W. Williams-Krapp (eds), *Literarisches Leben in Augsburg während des 15. Jahrhunderts*, Tübingen: Niemeyer, 1995, pp. 216–39.

153 Holenstein, 'Introduction', p. 26.

154 Naegle and Solórzano Telechea, 'Geschlechter und Zünfte', pp. 561–618 (with examples and supplementary literature).

155 *Heimliche Rechenschaft (1406)*, in *Die Chroniken der niedersächsischen Städte, Braunschweig*, vol. 1 (= *Die Chroniken der deutschen Städte*, vol. 6), Leipzig: Hirzel, 1868, pp. 121–207.

156 Isenmann, *Die Stadt*, pp. 442.

157 H. Blume and E. Rohse (eds), *Hermann Bote. Städtisch-hansischer Autor in Braunschweig 1488–1988*, Tübingen: Niemeyer, 1991.

158 W. Ehbrecht, 'Die Braunschweiger Schicht von 1488', in Blume and Rohse (eds), *Hermann Bote*, pp. 109–32, at 112.

159 Isenmann, *Die deutsche Stadt*, pp. 442–3.

160 Monnet, 'Les révoltes', p. 111; Naegle, 'Omne regnum', pp. 58–9.

161 Johannes Rothe wrote several chronicles and compiled the urban law of the town of Eisenach/Thuringia. He was also the author of poems about the duties of an urban council and good town government (*Ratsgedichte*). E. Isenmann, 'Ratsliteratur und städtische Ratsordnungen des späten Mittelalters und der frühen Neuzeit', in P. Monnet and O. G. Oexle (eds), *Stadt und Recht im Mittelalter*, Göttingen: Vandenhoeck & Ruprecht, 2003, pp. 215–479, at 251–91; H. Lähnemann and S. Linden (eds), *Dichtung und Didaxe*, Berlin: de Gruyter, 2009, section: 'Didaktischer Pluralismus. Johannes Rothe und seine Wirkung', pp. 413–79; S. Tebruck, 'Rothe, Johannes', *Neue Deutsche Biographie*, 25 vols to date, 2005, vol. 22, pp. 118–19, online version www.deutsche-biographie.de/pnd118603191.html.

162 *Dicitur eciam civitas, quia non saxa nec muri nec fossata, sed unitas civium civitatem facit (De rescriptis: Statutum; De sententia excommunicacionis: Si civitas). In Ulma autem est civium pulcra unitas.* (Felix Fabri, *Tractatus*, pp. 12–13, 377, n. 8; *De rescriptis: Statutum*, *Corpus Iuris Canonici*, ed. E. Friedberg and E. L. Richter, 2 vols, Leipzig: Tauchnitz, 1879–81, VI 1.3.11, 2: col. 941; *De sententia excommunicacionis*: (Si civitas, ibid., VI 5.11.17, 2: col. 1104)).

163 G. Naegle, 'Rothe, Johannes', in B. Méniel (ed.), *Écrivains juristes et juristes écrivains du Moyen Âge au siècle des Lumières*, Paris: Classiques Garnier, 2015, pp. 1097–103. *Civitas est hominum multitudo societatis vinculo adunata, dicta a civibus, id est ab ipsis incolis urbis [pro eo quod plurimorum consciscat et contineat vitas]. Nam urbs ipsa moenia sunt, civitas autem non saxa, sed habitatores vocantur* (*Isidori Hispalensis Episcopi Etymologiarum sive Originum Libri XX*, ed. W. M. Lindsay, 2 vols, Oxford: Clarendon, 1911, Liber XV, 2, 1).

164 The first university in the Empire, Prague was founded in 1348 and obtaining the degree of doctor in Bologna, Pavia, or another well-known university was considered helpful for a successful career. See H. de Ridder-Symoens, 'Mobilität', in W. Rüegg (ed.), *Geschichte der Universität in Europa*, 4 vols, Munich: Beck, 1993–2010, vol. 1, pp. 263–4; P. Moraw, 'Universitätsbesucher und Gelehrte im deutschen Reich', in *Gesammelte Beiträge zur deutschen und europäischen Universitätsgeschichte*, Leiden and Boston, MA: Brill, 2008, pp. 435–574; R. C. Schwinges, 'Repertorium Academicum Germanicum. Ein Who's Who der graduierten Gelehrten des Alten Reiches (1250–1550)', in Moraw (ed.), *Gesammelte Beiträge*, pp. 577–602; J. Schmutz, *Juristen für das Reich*, 2 vols, Basel: Schwabe, 2000.

165 *Sed tota civitas est una persona et unus homo artificialis et ymaginatus, ut ff. de iudiciis*, l. [D. 5.1.76] *proponebatur; et de fideijussoribus*, l. *mortua* [D. 46. 1. 22] (Bartolus da Sassoferrato, 'Tractatus de regimine civitatis', in D. Quaglioni (ed.), *Politica e diritto nel Trecento italiano*, Firenze: Olschki, 1983, pp. 154–5).

166 For this maxim, see J. Hauck, '*Quod omnes tangit debet ab omnibus approbari*. Eine Rechtsregel im Dialog der beiden Rechte', *Zeitschrift der Savigny-Stiftung für Rechtsgeschichte, Kanonistische Abteilung*, 99, 2014, pp. 398–417.

167 E. Isenmann, 'Funktionen und Leistungen gelehrter Juristen für deutsche Städte im Spätmittelalter', in J. Chiffoleau, C. Gauvard, and A. Zorzi (eds), *Pratiques sociales et politiques judiciaires dans les villes de l'Occident à la fin du Moyen Âge*, Rome: École française de Rome, 2007, pp. 243–322; E. Isenmann, 'Reichsrecht und Reichsverfassung in den Konsilien reichsstädtischer Juristen (15.–17. Jahrhundert)', in R. Schnur (ed.), *Die Rolle der Juristen bei der Entstehung des modernen Staates*, Berlin: Duncker & Humblot, 1986, pp. 545–628.

168 Isenmann, 'Reichsrecht', pp. 561–2.

169   *Dann solten die Stette all nach geschriben rechten regirt werden..., so musten albeg die burger* Doctores und gelert lewt sein, *das doch nit gesein noch stat haben mocht und wo die Stette in dem heiligen reich nach Ehingers* [the imperial *Fiskalprokurator*] *meynung regirt werden solten, wer ein gemeiner schad und verderben.*
      (Lawsuit of Memmingen, Staatsarchiv Augsburg, Reichsstadt Memmingen, Urk. 405, Naegle and Solórzano Telechea, 'Geschlechter und Zünfte', p. 585).

170   For the terminology of *Gemeinden* see Naegle and Solórzano Telechea, 'Geschlechter und Zünfte', particularly pp. 572–8; Naegle, 'Commun et communes', pp. 413–39.

171   Similar linguistic expressions of horizontal 'brotherhood' can be found in the Spanish terminology of *hermandades* and, like in the medieval Empire, urban leagues and alliances of nobles and towns were formed during royal power vacuums. See Naegle, 'Einleitung' and M. Diago Hernando, 'Die politische Rolle der Städtebünde im spätmittelalterlichen Kastilien (13.–16. Jh.). Selbstverteidigung, Herrschaftsstabilisierung und Friedenssicherung', in Naegle (ed.), *Frieden schaffen*, pp. 31–7, 139–59. For the parallels between the terminology of *hermandades* and of the *Tuchins*, see V. Challet, 'Pro deffensione rei publice et deffensione patrie: les paysans ont-ils une conscience politique?', in V. Challet, J.-Ph. Genet, H. R. Oliva Herrer, and J. Valdeón Baruque (eds), *La sociedad política a fines del siglo XV en los reinos ibéricos y en Europa* [Second = French title: *La société politique à la fin du XVe siècle dans les royaumes ibériques et en Europe*], Valladolid, Paris: Universidad de Valladolid, Publications de la Sorbonne, 2007, pp. 165–78, at 177–8.

172   J. Janssen (ed.), *Frankfurts Reichskorrespondenz nebst andem verwandten Aktenstücken von 1376–1519*, 2 vols, Freiburg im Breisgau: Herder'sche Verlagsbuchhandlung, 1863–66, vol. 1, p. 10, no. 30.

173   *Hanserecesse*, subsection/Abteilung 1, vol. 2, Leipzig: Duncker & Humblot, 1872, I, vol. 2, pp. 95–7, no. 84 [1374], quotation at 96.

174   *Heimliche Rechenschaft* (1406), pp. 137–8.

175   Naegle, 'Omne regnum', p. 59; Diago Hernando, 'Die politische Rolle', pp. 139–59; Maurer, *Kommunale Bündnisse*.

176   [D]*etestandas preterea et sacris legibus reprobatas conspirationes et conventiculas seu colligationes illicitas in civitatibus et extra vel intra civitatem et civitatem, inter personam et personam sive inter personam et civitatem pretextu parentele seu receptionis in cives vel alterius cuiuscumque coloris, coniurationes insuper et confederationes et pacta necnon et consuetudinem circa huiusmodi introductam.*
      (Die Goldene Bulle, art. 15, 10 January and 25 December 1356, in MGH, Const., 11, pp. 535–633, at 600. About this text see U. Hohensee, M. Lawo, M. Lindner, M. Menzel, and O. B. Rader (eds), Die Goldene Bulle, 2 vols, Berlin: Akademie Verlag, 2009).

177   R. Koselleck, 'Bund, Bündnis, Föderalismus, Bundesstaat', in O. Brunner, W. Conze, and R. Koselleck (eds), *Geschichtliche Grundbegriffe*, 4th edn, 8 vols in 9, Stuttgart: Klett-Cotta, 1972–92, vol. 1, pp. 582–671.

178   K. Fritze, 'Kompanien und Bruderschaften im spätmittelalterlichen Stralsund', in P. Johanek (ed.), *Einungen und Bruderschaften in der spätmittelalterlichen Stadt*, Cologne and Weimar: Böhlau, 1993, pp. 31–43, at 33. The idea of 'offices' behind that word resembles the Castilian terminology of *ofiçios* (Naegle and Solórzano Telechea, 'Geschlechter und Zünfte', p. 568).

179   Word that describes uniting into a group, an assembly, an association, a corporation, or an alliance, used in medieval texts and modern German historical scientific terminology, especially in constitutional history and by legal historians.

180   S. von Heusinger, *Die Zunft im Mittelalter. Zur Verflechtung von Politik, Wirtschaft und Gesellschaft in Straßburg*, Stuttgart: Steiner, 2009, p. 48; O. Von Gierke, *Das deutsche Genossenschaftsrecht*, 4 vols, Berlin: Weidmann, 1868–1913, vol. 1, pp. 359–60, n. 3.

181   *1. Hac nostra edictali sancione revocamus in irritum et cassamus in omni civitate vel oppido Alamannie communia, consilia, magistros civium seu rectores vel alios quoslibet officiales, qui ab universitate civium sine archiepiscoporum beneplacito statuuntur, quocumque per diversitatem locorum censeantur* (No. 147, April 1232, in C. Van de Kieft and J. F. Niermeijer (eds), *Elenchus fontium historiae urbanae*, 3 vols, Leiden: Brill, 1967–92, vol. 1, pp. 230–31, quote at 231).

182   Van de Kieft and Niermeijer, *Elenchus*, vol 1, no. 147, c. 2, p. 231; K. S. Bader and G. Dilcher, *Deutsche Rechtsgeschichte*, Berlin: Springer, 1999, p. 509; G. Dilcher, 'An den Ursprüngen der Normbildung. Verwandtschaft und Bruderschaft als Modelle gewillkürter Rechtsnormen', in G. Krieger (ed.), *Verwandtschaft – Freundschaft – Bruderschaft*, Berlin: Akademie Verlag, 2009, pp. 37–55.

183   T. A. Brady, *Turning Swiss: Cities and Empire 1450–1550*, Cambridge: Cambridge University Press, 1985.

184 W. Ebel, *Der Bürgereid als Geltungsgrund und Gestaltungsprinzip des mittelalterlichen deutschen Stadtrechts*, Weimar: Böhlau, 1958; P. Prodi, *Il sacramento del potere*, Bologna: Il Mulino, 1992, pp. 192–225; R. Jooß, 'Schwören und Schwörtage in süddeutschen Reichsstädten', in *Visualisierung städtischer Ordnung. Zeichen – Abzeichen – Hoheitszeichen*, Nuremberg: Maué, Hermann, 1993, pp. 153–68; L. Buchholzer-Rémy and O. Richard, 'Die städtischen Eidbücher im Elsaß', in L. Buchholzer-Remy et al. (eds), *Neue Forschungen*, pp. 177–96.

185 Website of the German Federal Foreign Office (*Auswärtiges Amt*), www.auswaertiges-amt.de/cae/servlet/contentblob/373608/publicationFile/3875/Englisch.pdf. The other *Bundesländer* are described as federal states with different denominations: *Land*, *Freistaat* (Free State of Bavaria, Thuringia, and Saxony), www.auswaertiges-amt.de/DE/Infoservice/Terminologie/BundeslaenderDownloads/Uebersicht_node.html.

PART III

Communication

Language, performance, and violence

13
A DOSSIER OF PEASANT AND SEIGNEURIAL VIOLENCE

Paul Freedman

In 2005 I published an article on atrocities described in medieval accounts of peasant rebellions and their suppression.[1] I began with a celebrated and elaborately awful example, the execution of the Hungarian peasant leader György Dózsa in July 1514 at Temesvár/Timişoara in Transylvania. Dózsa had been captured by John Zápolya, the governor and military commander (*voivod*) of Transylvania. He was placed naked on an iron 'throne' which was then heated in fire. A red-hot iron sceptre was placed in his hand and an iron circlet fitted around his head like a crown. This mock coronation alluded to Dózsa's supposed claim to rule as a 'peasant king'. After an hour or so of this torture, Dózsa was taken off the throne and his followers, soldiers of his entourage known as *heyduks*, were forced to eat pieces of his flesh (they had been starved for ten days previously). Refusal meant instant death. According to an account written just after the rebellion was suppressed, the heyduks were compelled to dance in a circle 'according to their custom' accompanied by music provided by fifes and viols, after which clerics sang the Te Deum as the execution unfolded.[2] Dózsa's remains were then decapitated and quartered. The pieces were sent for display in Buda, Pest, Belgrade, and Varad.[3]

In 2005 I wanted to show that uniquely horrific as this event was, its elements were anticipated in other times, places, and circumstances, and that seigneurial atrocities referred to real and imagined peasant violence. Though I think I succeeded in unearthing a number of instances of rustic and seigneurial violence involving red-hot implements, mock coronation, cannibalism, and ludic celebration, I wasn't concerned then about the typology of atrocity stories but preoccupied, rather, with showing how seigneurial and official violence mocked peasant pretences to rule and re-enacted real or imagined peasant atrocities vented on lords. Stories from the French Jacquerie of 1358 and the Tuchin revolt in 1384 involved iron crowns, roasting, and forced cannibalism which were appropriated by the authorities when they executed rebel leaders. Here I'd like to consider individual items in the dossier of theatrical horrors in order to discuss what these scenes evoked and communicated to their immediate and wider audiences.

A letter written by King Wladislas of Hungary to his representative before the Holy Roman Emperor Maximilian I matter-of-factly stated that as Dózsa had been in the habit of affectionately calling the heyduks his 'beasts', it was appropriate that he should be torn apart by their teeth – *vivus dentibus discerptus et devoratus est*.[4] The king had already granted Zápolya wide powers to put down the rebellion by beheading, flaying, burning, or inflicting other tortures.[5]

In its aftermath, Dózsa's execution was portrayed by King Wladislas as merciful, or at least efficient, because rebellious peasants immediately dispersed 'without [further] bloodshed'.

Some contemporaries were uneasy about the punishment, but decided it was more-or-less merited. Giovanni Vitale, an Italian living in Central Europe, described Dózsa's execution as *atrox*, but nevertheless justified by the circumstances of the rebellion. Ludovicus Tubero was more specific in his brief statement about the event in his chronicle of Hungarian history from 1490 to 1522. The punishment was atrocious and inhuman, representing a 'Scythian' level of cruelty, but the peasant rebels had also committed Scythian atrocities such as impaling nobles and raping women.[6] From early on, however, there was not only unease but a degree of outrage. The killing of Dózsa would become notorious, and the grisly event is well-known in Hungary and Western Romania (Transylvania; Banat) to this day. The torments meted out to reprobates and to innocent people are all too familiar in every era, including our own, so that while the late Middle Ages has its peculiar horrors, it does not stand alone as an age of mob or official violence.

Two woodcut illustrations depict Dózsa's torture. The more peaceful scene is the title page from a German pamphlet printed in Nuremberg in that same year, 1514, *Die auffrur so geschehen ist Im Ungerlandt mit den Creutzern, unnd auch darbey wie man den Creutzer Haubtman hat gefangen unnd getödt* (The Revolt that Occurred in Hungary with the Crusaders, and also, How the Leader of the Crusaders was Apprehended and Killed).[7] 'Crusaders' because what began as a licensed crusade against the Turks turned into a peasant revolt with the accusation that the nobility preferred to extort from their tenants than to fight the common enemy. Already in this publication the execution of Dózsa eclipses the actual insurrection. The pamphlet illustration has clear similarities to the iconography of Christ as the Man of Sorrows. Dózsa's crown, not visibly alight, resembles a crown of thorns. The figure's near-nakedness and tranquility also evoke Christ and show a degree of slippage in conceiving of the rebellion as irrational frenzy or the execution as appropriate.[8] The Man of Sorrows is usually represented in relation to Calvary, but in late medieval depictions Christ is often seated as the soldiers mock him before the crucifixion. In an article on anti-Jewish iconography at a pilgrimage church in Provence, Véronique Plesch showed examples of this seated representation from the work of the fifteenth-century painters Israhel van Meckenem and Giovanni Canavesio.[9] In the Nuremberg pamphlet the figure is seated on the throne and only one person is biting. The musical accompaniment, specific to this event, is prominent in this rather static and minimalist picture.

A second woodcut is from the frontispiece to the earliest edition (1519) of a mock-epic poetic account of the uprising entitled *Stauromachia*. Its author, the Moravian humanist Stephanus Stieröxel, Latinised his surname to 'Taurinus'. The title, 'battle of the cross', refers to the crusaders' cross, but the basic meaning of the Greek word *stauros*, a pole or stick, refers also to the grisly practice of impaling practised by both sides in this conflict.[10] As with the *Auffrur*, the execution of the rebel leader is depicted at the beginning of the book, but here as a far more crowded and emotional, not to say agonising scene. Dózsa is seated, nude from the waist up, clearly suffering. Flames leap from the crown which is being placed on his head with a tongs. One man is biting him, another may also be similarly engaged, or else he is performing a mock bow. Musicians are playing a trumpet, a bagpipe, and perhaps a viol. Three men are impaled on standing poles and another is in the foreground, already pierced but not yet lifted up.

Mock crowning

I begin with the crowning by means of a heated iron circlet because it conveys the clearest message. Insubordinate claims to rule are logically punished by derision involving attributes of

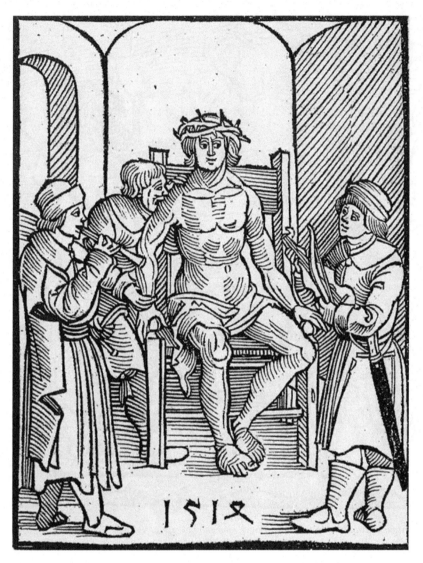

Figure 13.1 Frontispiece from *Die auffrur so geschehen ist im Ungerlandt* ... Nuremberg, 1514.

authority. The crown is easy to use in ceremonies of mockery because it is obvious in shape, the way in which it is worn and symbolic meaning. In Shakespeare's Henry VI, Part 3, Queen Margaret and Lord Clifford stand the captured duke of York on a molehill, place a paper crown on his head, and taunt him. Margaret specifically wants to humiliate the duke before he is killed and so stops her allies' plans to dispatch him immediately.

It is worth mentioning the fatal mock coronation in *A Game of Thrones* when Viserys Targaryen, the unpleasant claimant to the throne of Westeros, is promised a golden crown by Khal Drogo, the barbarian leader to whom Viserys has in effect sold his sister Daenerys. Having exhausted the patience of the Khal by his arrogance and presumption, Viserys receives his crown in the form of molten gold poured over his head, killing him. Although a murderous mock coronation, the incident is not about usurpation punished, but rather an example of a seemingly

Figure 13.2 Frontispiece from Johann Christian Engel, *monumenta Ungrica*, Vienna, 1809.

exalted promise literally kept, but you're dead anyway – the Lord of the Nazgûls (to shift fantasy oeuvres) cannot be killed by any *man*, but this doesn't prevent him from being extinguished by Éowyn, a female warrior; Macbeth can't be killed by any man born of a woman, but Macduff, 'ripped from the womb' by what would now be called Caesarean section, is exempt from the prophecy.

The archetype of inverted reverence in the (real) medieval world was the Crown of Thorns placed on Christ's head to mock the putative claim to be the King of the Jews. In Matthew, Mark, and John, after Pilate has consented to the crucifixion of Jesus and scourged Him, the soldiers strip Jesus and then clothe Him with either a red or purple robe. The crown of thorns is placed on His head and, according to Matthew, a reed is placed in His hand as a pseudo-sceptre. The soldiers hail Christ as King of the Jews, smite Him, and bow their knees to Him. The thorns are painful and, in many depictions, Christ's forehead is spattered with blood, a different image of mock coronation from the paper insubstantiality of Shakespeare's Wars of the Roses incident.

In the Middle Ages it might seem blasphemous to imitate a punishment meted out to Christ, but it was impossible to impose torture and exemplary, public capital punishment without reminding viewers of scenes of Christian martyrdom or Christ's painful sacrifice. The instruments of the Passion were those employed by the ordinary executioner. Far from being an uncomfortable resemblance for contemporaries, however, those inflicting torment or writing about it deliberately used the Passion of Christ to apply to secular castigation. Paul Lehmann identified an entire genre of parodic *passio*, where the crucifixion taken from the Gospels is applied to military conflicts, for example the English defeat of Robert the Bruce in 1306, or the Flemings' defeat of the French at Courtrai in 1302, or political struggles such as Edward I's punishment of a disloyal subordinate in 1289.[11]

The parodic passions use the tortures inflicted on Christ to rejoice at the humiliation of victims. A vividly disturbing example is an account of the massacre of the Jews of Prague in 1389 which took place after they were accused of desecrating the host being carried in a procession to a dying Christian. A contemporary screed against the Jews entitled *Passio Iudeorum Pragensium* celebrates the event through a parody of the Gospels.[12] Among other mayhem that it describes with jocular approval is that the tormentors of the Jews made crowns of wood and straw which they placed on the heads and bodies of Jews whom they then set on fire. 'And after they had mocked them, they stripped them of their clothing and clothed them in fire, and gave them flames to drink, mingled with smoke. And when they had tasted it, it was fitting for them to drink' (cf. Mt. 27, 29; 31, 34).

On the one hand this implies that far from being disturbed by the resemblance to the torments meted out to Christ, the murderers of Jews or the executioners of Dózsa were perfectly aware of and happy about the parodic aspects. As Lehmann remarked, 'anyone who takes offense at profanation of the Bible cannot understand the Middle Ages'.[13] At the same time, there is a way in which such cruel mockery communicated a sense of the injustice of the tortures, what Barbara Newman in her description of the Prague *passio* calls the textual unconscious.

An undertow of unease and reversal centres around the Man of Sorrows because of the central paradox of Christian belief- – that the constituted state authorities mocked, humiliated, and executed God – and its complementary inversion: that those whom He came to save were His tormentors. In a well-known 1983 article, Stephen Greenblatt showed that Albrecht Dürer's plan for a monument to the German Peasants' War of 1525 echoes the Man of Sorrows. While Dürer on one level may have meant the dejected and defeated peasant sitting slumped at the top of a column to be the object of mockery, the iconographical template itself undermines any unmediated presentation of the peasant as meriting suppression.[14]

Hagiographic literature provides images and precedents for dispatching by heated iron: St Lawrence's martyrdom on a red-hot gridiron is well-known. Less famous now is the heated iron helmet placed on St Christopher's head, frequently represented in late medieval Western Europe. In neither of these cases was the executioner attempting to communicate anything symbolically about secular rebellion, but stories of the execution of a number of saints included the imposition of a red-hot metal crown because religious defiance in the Roman Empire was a form of presumptuous political usurpation.[15]

The background to the treatment meted out to Christopher anticipates the iconography of Dózsa and the parallel logic that one side's exemplary punishment is another side's exemplary martyrdom. Christopher is best known for carrying the increasingly heavy Christ child across a river, hence his status as the protector of travellers until he was recently decommissioned by the Church. Often in the Eastern churches, less commonly in the West, he was also a dog-headed saint whose quasi-human nature exhibited the care of God for even the most distant and unpromising peoples. Christopher is one of those saints whose martyrdom was long and drawn out because tortures that would kill normal people left him untouched.[16]

An early text describing Christopher's passion is a fragment in the Anglo-Saxon manuscript, BL Cotton Vitellius A.xv which also contains the unique example of *Beowulf* and the collection of exotica known as *The Wonders of the East*. In this incomplete saint's life, Christopher is tortured over several days and dies on the third day by decapitation. The fragment in Cotton Vitellius begins with his torture, but in other early English accounts a more extensive biography describes a dog-headed semi-human miraculously transformed by his conversion and martyrdom. On the first day of his torture he is enthroned on an iron seat set over a fire and crowned with a burning helm, but this has no effect.[17] In the later and widely circulated *Golden Legend*, Christopher is crowned with an iron helmet and then placed in an iron chair above a raging fire fed by pitch, again to no avail.[18]

While artistic depictions of St Christopher usually show him carrying the Christ child, the details of his martyrdom were also occasionally presented. A Catalan Romanesque painted altar frontal from the twelfth-century shows Christopher's torture and death in panels surrounding a central representation of Christopher carrying Christ. In the lower left-hand section, he is half-lying on the ground, surrounded by flames as an iron cap is placed over his head at the order of the emperor while the hand of God protects him.[19] This is not necessarily a mock coronation because Christopher's attributed crime was not a claim to any sort of political authority. Nevertheless, his martyrdom imitated Christ's sacrificial humiliation, so association with the derisive crown of thorns was hardly illogical.

Turning to secular events, the metal crown was a punishment imposed by the Emperor Henry VI in 1197, when the leader of the Sicilian nobles' rebellion was executed by having a red-hot iron crown nailed to his head.[20] The *Anonimalle* chronicler claimed that the peasant leader of the Jacquerie of 1358 was executed by the King of Navarre by being placed naked on a heated piece of iron while being 'crowned' by a burning circlet. The iron bed was not exactly a throne, but the use of both an iron support and crown anticipates the execution of Dózsa.[21]

A post-Dózsa example is the death of Matja Gubec, the commander of a peasant rebellion in Croatia and Slovenia, in 1573.[22] Archbishop George Draskovic of Zagreb wrote to the Emperor Maximilian II, asking permission to impose a capital penalty by means of a burning iron crown. The archbishop refers to the rebel leader as 'Gubec Bey', the mock Ottoman honorific implying collaboration with the Turks. Draskovic states that Gubec had declared himself king, hence the appropriateness of the exceptional punishment, and the emperor agreed. A heated iron crown was placed on Gubec's head, then he was dragged by horses and torn by iron pincers. His body was quartered and sent to various towns, again following the Dózsa model.

The form of killing by means of a heated iron circle, deemed symbolically appropriate to inflict on rebels against the crown, had supposedly been perpetrated *by* peasants during the Tuchin uprisings in Languedoc during the early 1380s.[23] Allegedly the rebels stopped anyone they suspected of being of gentle birth. One of their victims, a Scotsman, whose hands showed he was unaccustomed to manual labour, was killed by having a burning metal tripod placed on his head. Not exactly a crown, but a similar idea showing the possibility of cruelty without immediately obvious iconographic significance.

Roasting and forced cannibalism

The burning crown was a cruel punishment imposed by the late medieval or early modern state on leaders of insurrections and there were at least rumours that peasants appropriated this form of killing in rebellions against their social superiors. Roasting and forced cannibalism are the reverse: conceived of first as peasant atrocities, but then adopted by rulers as part of a formal, memorable punishment. The Jacquerie features all manner of frightening stories, among them, according to the chronicles of Jean le Bel and Jean Froissart, the capture of a knight and his family by peasants who roasted the knight on a spit, according to Froissart, while forcing his family to watch. They made the wife eat her husband's flesh before raping and then killing her.[24] These bestial acts supplement accounts of generalised sexual assault. They demonstrate the uncontrollable ferocity of the peasants, but coerced cannibalism is understood as a gratuitous extreme, not the satisfaction of animal lust and rage, but something more unnatural and perverse than rape.

Examples of constituted authorities using cannibalism as an exemplary punishment all come from greater Hungary. The first was in the aftermath of the Belgrade Crusade of 1456 led against the Turks by the heroic commander John Hunyadi whose son would become the equally celebrated King Matthias Corvinus. An effort to betray the crusade army to the Turks was discovered, and the leader of the conspiracy was burned at the stake, after which his followers were made to eat his remains.[25]

In 1494, the remnants of a mercenary group known as the Black Army were dispersed near Belgrade by the Hungarian chancellor and military leader Pál Kinizsi. The mercenaries' ringleader, known as the Black Haugwitz, was accused of collaboration with the Turks and after his capture by Kinizsi, he was roasted alive, his followers being forced to eat pieces of his flesh.[26] There is no crown or mock coronation, but this event is the closest precedent in chronological and iconographic terms to the Dózsa execution. It is perhaps worth adding that according to folk tales, Kinizsi was accustomed to celebrate his victories by dancing with a Turkish corpse under each arm and a third held in his teeth.

Sexual violence

Far more than isolated cases of roasting and cannibalism, sexual violence was routinely associated with peasant revolts. The French Jacquerie set the vocabulary of rape and murder. The rage of the peasants was seen by chroniclers as a repressed natural force that exploded in the absence of vigilant preventive repression. This theme of barely suppressed peasant violence was taken up again during the Hungarian revolt of 1514. Four provincial governors signed a letter warning that the peasants' innate savagery had boiled over (*efferbuit*) and that if unchecked, they would murder all the nobles and rape and then kill their families.[27] At the height of the revolt, in a letter to Pope Leo X, King Wladislas describes the peasants as engaging in a kind of 'bacchant fury' that includes raping women in front of their husbands and flaying and impaling their aristocratic and clerical captives.[28]

No doubt rape was perpetrated by seigneurial armies against peasant captives and bystanders as well, but it does not appear in contemporary accounts. There is occasional mention of castration as part of executions, but these are not part of the suppression of peasant rebellions. What we do have from the Hungarian revolt is impaling, which among its many horrors is a form of sexual penetration. Impaling, in which the victim dies in agony slowly, sometimes taking days to do so, is attested for the Assyrian and Persian Achaemenid Empire (550–330 BCE) and mentioned in Cassius Dio's *Roman History* as an atrocity inflicted on Roman prisoners during Boudicca's uprising in Britain.[29]

Impaling does not seem to have been practised in medieval Europe, but appears again in the late fifteenth and early sixteenth centuries. It was promoted by the notorious Vlad the Impaler and taken up by the Turks who are first known to have used it to frighten the besieged at Constantinople in 1453. According to Western commentators, impaling was an emblem of Turkish barbarism used by the Ottomans for the purpose that all public executions are supposed to serve: to terrify and so discourage defiance by graphic example.[30] By the sixteenth century impalement was codified in Hungarian law as the appropriate punishment for murder, robbery, and brigandage.[31]

The letters and chronicles of the Hungarian insurrection of 1514 describe impaling as part of the repertoire of peasant atrocities. I have mentioned King Wladislas's letter to the pope which claims that peasants impaled and flayed noblemen and bishops as well as raping women before the eyes of their husbands. Stephanus Taurinus, writing in 1519, was assiduous in collecting stories of the misdeeds of the *rabidae plebes* whose leadership had, from the first, planned on using the crusade to kill off the nobles.[32] According to Giovanni Vitale, peasants impaled noblemen in the presence of their wives and children, or raped wives in front of their husbands. He also mentions the peasants' proclivity for impaling captured nobles. The bishop of Csanad, dressed in his pontifical robes, was murdered by impaling after the capture of the city by Dózsa's army. Interestingly enough, Miklós (Nicholas) Istvánffy, an historian writing in 1622, says this method of torture and killing was not only horrible but new at the time.[33] In turn Zápolya ordered that Dózsa's captured captains be impaled. The 1519 illustration shows impaling as simultaneous with the peasant leader's execution, but in fact it took place earlier and in another place.[34]

Music

Finally the musical and liturgical accompaniments to Dózsa execution: the Te Deum was performed by clerics while the musicians comically enacted both high court ceremony (trumpet fanfares) and low peasant festivities (bagpipes). Music was considered appropriate at executions. In early modern Nuremberg, chaplains might be joined by the jailors to sing hymns addressed to the person about to be executed, sometimes the condemned himself might sing.[35] The St Thomas School in Leipzig, where Johann Sebastian Bach trained choristers, provided an ensemble to sing hymns for the condemned criminals of the city and for the crowd. It is not known whether Bach was himself present in his official capacity at any executions. As late as 1843, school choirs sang hymns at German executions.[36]

In all these instances the music was serious and intended either to console the person about to die or to mark the execution's solemnity. Musical mockery at scenes of death was quite different and could take the form of rough music such as might accompany a charivari, wedding celebration, comical play, or masquerade.

There is something particularly ghastly about cheerful or celebratory music accompanying atrocities. Bands played at Auschwitz while the sorting out of those to be exterminated took place, and music was included in other terrible routines of the camps. Dózsa's is not the only late medieval/early modern execution in which the music is emphasised; the festive atmosphere of public executions by governments or at the behest of the Inquisition included ludic or solemn music, or both.

Here too, however, there is some possibility for contestation. Not only were classical orchestras painfully put together at Nazi camps such as Theriesenstadt, the result of brave efforts to demonstrate and preserve the humanity of the persecuted, but martyrdoms and self-sacrifice might involve music and chanting – the Jews of Prague in 1389 were reportedly singing as they killed themselves and their children rather than undergo forced conversion (an evocation of the children and the fiery furnace in the Book of Daniel).[37] Francis Poulenc's opera *Dialogues of the Carmelites* ends with the sisters of the Order singing the Salve Regina on their way to execution, their prayers interrupted by the sound of the guillotine as one by one the number of their voices diminishes.

Conclusion

The Dózsa execution included several violent attributes, none entirely without precedent. It is therefore unclear why this ceremony, however cruel it was, attained so much notoriety. Michel de Montaigne mentions the execution (although wrongly locating it in Poland) as a quintessential example of cruelty, this from an observer of the savage French religious wars. Why, by contrast, is there almost no historical memory of the roasting and enforced cannibalism of the mercenary leader of the Black Army in 1494? In Hungary itself, on the occasion of a peasant revolt in 1632, the aristocratic leader Nicolaus Esterházy favourably recalled the acts of the voivod John Zápolya. Once the peasant leader of the later uprising was captured, he was tortured and quartered. The Hungarian historian Istvánffy in the early seventeenth century described this execution as a recollection, at least to the elderly, of the treatment meted out to Dózsa.[38]

Dózsa would be remembered as a hero in modern Hungary. Soon after his death he was venerated as a saint and the place of his torment attracted pilgrims.[39] In the nineteenth century a monument was erected on the site of his death in the main square of Temesvár/Timişoara.[40]

Zápolya was said to have suffered for his cruelty, wracked with guilt and unable to see the elevated host at mass for two years according to some accounts, for his entire remaining life according to others. His mother and sister are supposed to have tried to atone for his deed with gifts to monasteries.[41] In fact, Zápolya had quite a long life and went on to become a claimant for the Hungarian Crown, or what remained of it, after the disastrous defeat at the hands of the Ottomans at Mohacs (1526), and then ruler of a quasi-independent Transylvania. The near extinction of the Christian Hungarian kingdom in the sixteenth century was linked to the sinful dispatching of Dózsa in the *Epistola de perdicione regni Hungarorum, 1484–1543*, written in the wake of the Turkish conquest. The author, George of Sirmium (Györgyi Szerémi), has Dózsa warn Zápolya that his execution will mean harm to the voivod and the entire Hungarian nobility. Dózsa's fortitude is likened to that of the martyr George of Macedonia, the St George of the dragon legends, a soldier tortured and executed under Diocletian.[42]

Hungary and Transylvania are among the European countries with peculiarly strong reputations for cruelty. The 'leyenda negra' of Spain, based primarily on the Inquisition, is paralleled by the image of Hungary as what one scholar in the grim year 1943 termed 'the bloody theatre of Europe'.[43] Transylvania has now surpassed other European regions in popular culture reputation for historical cruelty because of Dracula and his 'real' avatar Vlad the Impaler who has quite eclipsed such Hungarian luminaries as Countess Elizabeth Báthory who supposedly killed 650 people and bathed in human blood to preserve her complexion.[44] Whether based on Hungarians' own appropriation of fictitious Hun ancestors, or on the brutality of the Turkish frontier, or on specific characters and events, this part of Europe has a constantly re-invented reputation for ingenious savagery.

The fame or infamy of Dózsa's execution, as opposed to other atrocious incidents, is perhaps due to quick publicity via the printing of pamphlets just after the rebellion of 1514. It may also have to do with an iconography that lent itself both to exemplary lessons of the consequences of rebellion and the torments of the just, shifting between legal execution and martyrdom. It also seems to be reinforced by, as well as contributing to, the legend of exceptional Hungarian brutality.

One does not have to strain very hard to show that staged and ritualised atrocities are by no means limited to the medieval or early modern historical period. There is a difference in that public cruelty is not now supposed to take place under official auspices. The Nazis invented all sorts of ways of humiliating the Jewish population under their control, but efforts were made to keep the actual exterminations secret. Nevertheless, as Inga Clendinnen has emphasised, in the camps there was an irresistible desire on the part of the officials and guards to impose ritualised, theatrical torment on the victims, brought about through boredom among the perpetrators, dehumanisation of the victims, or something innate in the performance of atrocities.[45]

The American humiliation of Iraqi prisoners at Abu Ghraib was also a brutalised response to tedium as well as a gratuitous, flagrant violation of basic moral inhibitions. While the torture of prisoners at Abu Ghraib was also a secret, the damning photographs that publicised the incidents were part of the fun – the comical enacting, posing, and preservation of degrading treatment.[46] Lynchings of African-Americans in the South during the first part of the twentieth century were also open secrets. They might take place at night and the perpetrators sometimes wore masks or costumes to prevent identification, but the murder was often a public celebration with a picnic-like atmosphere. Memorabilia of the mob executions included photographic postcards.[47]

In the Dózsa execution, as in the many unfortunate later parallels, pity and terror intermingled with amusement and diversion. Public humiliation and horrific torment are lessons intended by the authorities for the benefit of cowed and awed bystanders, but far from being overwhelmed by the spectacle, those spectators may be busy chomping popcorn, chatting with neighbours, or gathering souvenirs.

Notes

1 P. Freedman, 'Atrocities and the executions of peasant rebel leaders in late medieval and early modern Europe', *Medievalia et humanistica*, new ser., 31, 2005, pp. 101–13.
2 All these elements are present in a Nuremberg *Flugschrift* of 1514, p. 321 in *Monumenta rusticorum in Hungaria rebellium anno MDXIV*, ed. A. Fekete Nagy, V. Kenéz, L. Solymosi, and G. Érszegi, Budapest: Akadémiai Kiadó, 1979. For information about the pamphlet, see below, n. 7.
3 Documents concerning the Hungarian uprising are collected in *Monumenta rusticorum*. Secondary literature on the rebellion includes S. Márki, *Dózsa György*, Budapest: Magyar Történelmi Társulat, 1913 (I thank Irina Denischenko for translating parts of this book for me); G. Barta, 'Der ungarische Bauernkrieg vom Jahre 1514', in G. Heckenast (ed.), *Aus der Geschichte der ostmitteleuropäische Bauernbewegungen im XVI–XVII Jahrhundert*, Budapest: Akadémiai Kiadó, 1977, pp. 63–9; P. Junst, 'Der ungarische Bauernaufstand von 1514', in P. Blickle (ed.), *Revolte und Revolution in Europa*, Munich: Oldenbourg, 1975, pp. 62–83; N. Housely, 'Crusading as social revolt: the Hungarian peasant uprising of 1514', *Journal of Ecclesiastical History*, 49, 1998, pp. 1–29; G. S. Pellathy, 'The Dózsa revolt: prelude and aftermath', *East European Quarterly*, 21, 1987, pp. 275–95; P. Freedman, 'The Hungarian peasant revolt of 1514', in *Grafenauerjev Zbornik*, Ljubljana: Znanstvenoraziaskovalni Center SAZU, 1996, pp. 431–46; G. Klaniczay, 'Images and designations for rebellious peasants in late medieval Hungary', in B. Nagy and M. Sebők (eds), *The Man of Many Devices, Who Wandered Full Many Ways...: Festschrift in Honor of János M. Bak*, Budapest: Central European University Press, 1999, pp. 115–27.
4 Letter of King Wladislas to Nikolai Székely de Kövend in *Monumenta rusticorum*, no. 142, pp. 175–6.
5 Márki, *Dózsa György*, p. 422.
6 Letter of Giovanni Vitale written late 1514 to a Roman friend, *Monumenta rusticorum*, no. 200, p. 245. A similar conclusion was reached by Gian Michele Bruto, an Italian chronicler of Hungary, in the late sixteenth century, Brutus János Mihály, *Magyar Históriája, 1440–1552*, ed. F. Toldy, Monumenta Hungariae Historia XII, vol. 1, Pest: Magyar Tudományos Akademia, 1963, pp. 372–6. Tubero's statement is in his *Commentarium de rebus suo tempore, nimirum ab A.C. MCCCCXC usque A. MDXXII in Pannonia et in finitimis regionibus gestis*, in Scriptores rerum Hungaricarum, vol. 2, Vienna: Typis Joannis Thomae nob. de Trattnern, 1746, pp. 333–4:

> Nec ab tam atrocem poenam, visus est Hungaris Ioannes, inhumana in Scytham usus crudelitate: eo quod rustici, ipsius Scythae instinctu nobilissimos Hungariae viros, fide interposita euocatos, crudeli ac foeda morte affecerant; quendam ex Chákia familia, Chauadiensium Episcopum, Georgiam Dócium, Petrum Reuosdien, Nicolam Torneum; ex quibus Chákium praesulem palo in viscera eius adacto truciderat, quamquam ferunt. Hunc antistitem, ob libidinis, et stupra feminis per vim illata, meritas dedisse poenas.

7 *Die auffrur so geschehen ist Im Ungerlandt mit den Creutzern, unnd auch darbey wie man den Creutzer Haubtman hat gefangen unnd getödt,* Nuremberg: Hieronymous Höltzel, 1514. Copies in Budapest, Magyar Tudományos Akadémia Könyvtára, RM IV 88; Wolfenbüttel, Herzog August Bibliothek 198. 13 Hist. (2). Its modern editors in *Monumenta rusticorum,* no. 227, pp. 313–23 demonstrate that although the description of Dózsa's torture and execution is unique to version D, six earlier versions described just the uprising with the title *Ein groß wundertzaychen*...
8 See M. Birnbaum, 'A mock Calvary in 1514? The Dózsa passion', in G. E. Szőnyi (ed.), *European Iconography East and West: Selected Papers of the Szeged International Conference, June 9–12, 1993,* Leiden: Brill, 1996, pp. 91–108.
9 V. Plesch, 'Not only against the Jews: antisemitic iconography and functions at La Brigue', *Studies in Iconography,* 23, 2002, pp. 137–81, esp. 144–7, 150.
10 S. Taurinus, *Stauromachia, id est cruciatorum servile bellum,* Vienna: Ioannes Singrenius, 1519. A copy of this first edition is in the Bayerische Staatsbibliothek and online through the Deutsche Forschungsgemeinschaft and Google Books. The original frontispiece is reproduced in *Monumenta Ungrica,* ed. J. C. Engel, Vienna: Antonius Doll, 1809 and the text of the *Stauromachia,* is on pp. 111–84. The 1944 edition *Stephanus Taurinus Olomucensis, Stauromachia,* Budapest: K. M. Egyetemi Nyomda, 1944, includes a useful introduction by Ladislaus Juhász. Taurinus, a Moravian humanist, wrote the *Stauromachia* under the influence of classical authors, especially Lucan, Cicero (*In Catalinam*), and Sallust. See L. Szörényi, 'L'influenza della Farsaglia di Lucano sull'epopea tardo-umanista latina in Ungheria: Stephanus Taurinus Stauromachia', *Neohelicon,* 37, 2000, pp. 97–111. Szörényi discusses the implications of *stauros* on pp. 100–1.
11 P. Lehmann, *Die Parodie im Mittelalter, mit 24 ausgewählten parodistischen Texten,* 2nd edn, Stuttgart: A. Hiersemann, 1963, pp. 199–211.
12 B. Newman, '*The Passion of the Jews of Prague:* the pogrom of 1389 and the lessons of a medieval parody', *Church History,* 81, 2012, pp. 1–26.
13 Lehmann, *Die Parodie,* p. 85, cited in Newman, '*The Passion of the Jews of Prague*', p. 9.
14 S. Greenblatt, 'Murdering peasants: status, genre, and the representation of rebellion', *Representations,* 1, 1983, pp. 1–29.
15 H. Delahaye, *Les passions des martyrs et les genres littérraires,* Brussels: Société des Bollandistes, 1921, pp. 282–7.
16 *Lexikon der Christlichen Ikonographie,* vol. 5, ed. W. Braunfels, Freiburg im Breisgau: Herder, 1994, p. 506; H.-F. Rosenfeld, 'Der Heilige Christophorus. Seine Verehrung und seine Legende', *Acta Academiae Aboensis, Humaniora,* 10, part 3, 1937, p. 358.
17 J. T. Lionarons, 'The Old English legend of Saint Christopher', in T. S. Jones and D. A. Sprunger (eds), *Marvels, Monsters and Miracles: Studies in the Medieval and Early Modern Imaginations,* Kalamazoo, MI: Medieval Institute, 2002, p. 180. See also the edition of an eighth-century passion of St Christopher from a Würzburg (Universitätsbibliothek) manuscript in Rosenfeld, 'Der Heilige Christophorus', p. 528, which also refers to an iron helmet (*cassidis*).
18 Jacobus de Voragine, *The Golden Legend,* trans. W. G. Ryan, vol. 2, Princeton, NJ: Princeton University Press, 1993, p. 14.
19 Barcelona, Museu Nacional d'Art de Catalunya, MNAC/MAC 4370, Taula de Sant Cristòfol. I am grateful to Montserrat Pages Paretas for this information.
20 D. Abulafia, *Frederick II, a Medieval Emperor,* London: Allen Lane, 1988, p. 85.
21 *The Anonimalle Chronicle,* ed. V. H. Galbraith, Manchester: Manchester University Press, 1927, p. 42.
22 His actual first name was Ambroz, but he is known to posterity as Matja Gubec. On his Turkish mock-honorific, F. Rački, 'Hrvatsko-Slovenska seljačka buna', *Starina,* 7, 1875, p. 212: *Quendam ex ipsis, Gubecz Begum vocatum et noviter regem nominatum, ferrea eaque candenti corona, si Maiestatis V.S. voluntas accesserit, in aliorum exemplum coronabimus.* I thank Oto Luthar of the Slovene Academy of Sciences for this reference and Jane Miles, formerly a graduate student at Yale, for translating portions of B. Grafenauer, *Boj za staro pravdo v 15. in 16 stoletju na Slovenskem* (The Struggle for the Old Right in Fifteenth and Sixteenth-Century Slovenia), Ljubljana: Država zal. Slovenije, 1974 and I. Voje, *Nemirno Balkan: zgodovinski pregled od 6 do 18. stoletja* (Balkan Unrest, An Historical Overview from the Sixth to Eighteenth Century), Ljubljana: D25, 1994, pp. 224–7.
23 *Chronique du religieux de Saint-Denys,* ed. L. Bellaguet, vol. 1, Paris: Crapelet, 1839, pp. 308–10. On the Tuchin Revolt, V. Challet, 'La révolte des Tuchins: banditisme social ou sociabilité villageoise?' *Médiévales,* 34, 1998, pp. 101–12.
24 M.-T. de Medeiros, *Jacques et chroniqueurs: Une étude comparée de récits contemporains relatant la Jacquerie de 1358,* Paris: H. Champion, 1979, pp. 186–9.

25 Birnbaum, 'A mock Calvary in 1514?', p. 95.
26 Pellathy, 'The Dózsa revolt', p. 280.
27 Letter of the counts of Nógrád, Hont, Pest, and Heves to the count of Abaúj, *Monumenta rusticorum*, no. 73, p. 116.
28 *Monumenta rusticorum*, no. 104, pp. 142–4.
29 B. Lincoln, *Religion, Empire and Torture: The Case of Achaemenian Persia with a Postscript on Abu Ghraib*, Chicago, IL: University of Chicago Press, 2007, p. 112; Cassius Dio, *Roman History* 62.7.1–2. I thank Dr Myles Lavan of the University of St Andrews for these references.
30 J. J. Reid, *The Crisis of the Ottoman Empire: Prelude to Collapse, 1839–1878*, Stuttgart: Franz Steiner, 2000, pp. 440–2.
31 P. Tóth, '"The bloody theatre of Europe": the culture of pain, cruelty and martyrdom in early modern Hungary', *Acta Ethnographica Hungarica*, 148, 2003, p. 391.
32 Taurinus, *Stauromachia*, fols XVIr–XVIIIv. Also the account of Tubero quoted above, n. 6.
33 Giovanni Vitale, letter in *Monumenta rusticorum*, no. 200, p. 244. Impaling is also emphasised by Taurinus in his *Stauromachia* as noted by Szörényi, 'L'influenza della Farsaglia', pp. 100–1. See also Pellathy, 'The Dózsa revolt', p. 287; Tóth, '"The bloody theatre of Europe"', pp. 388–9.
34 Birnbaum, 'A mock Calvary in 1514?', p. 93.
35 J. F. Harrington, *The Faithful Executioner*, New York, Farrar, Strauss & Giroux, 2013, pp. 77, 81, 85.
36 R. J. Evans, *Rituals of Retribution: Capital Punishment in Germany, 1600–1987*, Oxford: Oxford University Press, 1996, pp. 75–7.
37 Newman, '*The Passion of the Jews of Prague*', p. 21.
38 Cited by Gabriella Erdélyi, 'Tales of a peasant revolt: taboos and memories of 1514 in Hungary', in E. Kuijpers, J. Pollmann, J. Müller, and J. van der Steen (eds), *Memory Before Modernity: Practices of Memory in Early Modern Europe*, Leiden: Brill, 2013, p. 108.
39 Erdélyi, 'Tales of a peasant revolt', pp. 105, 108.
40 A statue of the Virgin Mary and a small chapel erected between 1864 and 1906 commemorate the execution, Márki, *Dózsa György*, pp. 395–7. For accounts of her appearance at the scene of execution, Birnbaum, 'A mock Calvary in 1514?', p. 104.
41 Pellathy, 'The Dózsa revolt', p. 288.
42 Györgyi Szerémi, *Epistola de perdicione regni Hungarorum, 1484–1543*, in Monumenta Hungariae Historica, Scriptores, vol. 1, ed. G. Wenzel, Pest: 1857, pp. 66–8: *Quod senisset Georgius perniciam suam per manus iniquorum, ait Georgius Siculus* (i.e. Dózsa): *Domine vaiuoda, noli me interficere; quia ad futurum tibi multa possum seruire, quam tota nobilitas Hungarorum, quia per istos bestialis multa passurus eris.* After the deed is nevertheless committed, the author of the *Epistola* observes: *Vt quasi secundus martir Georgius Macedonen. fuisset, et admirabantur, quod pacienter sufferauit.*
43 Tóth, '"The bloody theatre of Europe"', p. 388.
44 R. A. von Elsberg, *Elisabeth Báthory: (Die Blutgräfin). Ein Sitten- und Charakterbild*, Breslau: Schottlaender, 1904.
45 I. Clendinnen, *Reading the Holocaust*, Cambridge: Cambridge University Press, 1999, pp. 134–5.
46 See Lincoln, *Religion, Empire and Torture*.
47 J. Allen (ed.), *Without Sanctuary: Lynching Photography in America*, Santa Fe, NM: Twin Palms, 2000.

14
VIOLENCE AS A POLITICAL LANGUAGE
The uses and misuses of violence in late medieval French and English popular rebellions

Vincent Challet

Item, the next Monday, the 22nd day of August, some women were accused. They were killed and their bodies – without any clothing except for their shirts – were left on the pavement, and the executioner [a man named Capeluche] was happier to do this than any of the others. Among these women, he killed a pregnant woman, who was not guilty in this instance, on account of which it came to pass a few days later that he and two of his companions were arrested and put in the Châtelet prison, and three days later they had their heads cut off.[1]

This extract from the *Journal d'un bourgeois de Paris* written and composed between 1405 and 1449 by a member of the University of Paris who is still anonymous (though we do know that he was a member of the cathedral chapter of Notre Dame) is an excellent introduction to the complex question of the signification and acceptance of popular violence, especially in the context of rebellion. It depicts a very specific incident that occurred – or may have occurred, I will discuss this matter later – in Paris in August 1418 during the Cabochien uprising in the context of the French Civil War between the supporters of the deceased duke of Orléans, Louis, usually named 'Armagnacs' after the name of their leader, Bernard VII, count of Armagnac, and those of John the Fearless, duke of Burgundy. The two factions were engaged in a severe competition for controlling the person of the king, Charles VI, who was suffering from intermittent madness, and thus the access to royal power. John the Fearless was supported by most of the burgesses of Paris and, especially, by the powerful group of butchers which was able to mobilise armed men, particularly the skinners who took an active part in several riots which happened in Paris between 1413 and 1418. The main leader of the first popular movement against the Armagnacs which took place in 1413 was in fact a skinner, named Simon Caboche, while the most important figure of the 1418 uprising was Capeluche, the executioner of Paris.

These two episodes must be carefully distinguished as the movement seems to be much more 'radicalised' in 1418 than five years earlier, and it eventually lost the support of not only John the Fearless but even that of the butchers. Nevertheless, a kind of confusion has occurred between these two episodes which are conflated under the name the 'Cabochien movement'. The cover of this book perfectly reflects this state: the miniature was realised in 1484 – which means about 70 years after the events – for a manuscript of the *Vigiles de Charles VII* composed by Martial d'Auvergne and which is a mourning poem celebrating the deceased king.[2] The text includes a title, 'la turie de Paris' but refers only to the events that occurred in 1413 and to the bad enterprises of the 'butchers, killers, and skinners'[3] led by Simon Caboche and the lord Hélion de Jacqueville, including rapes, murders, and eventually beheadings but without any allusion to the executioner Capeluche. *A contrario*, the image represents the murdering of a pregnant woman, an episode which is generally linked to the events of 1418 and attributed to Capeluche as is shown in the initial extract from the *Journal d'un bourgeois de Paris*. It may be explained by the fact that the miniaturist chose intentionally to focus on the exactions committed by the rebels[4] but such a choice that summarises the entire Cabochien movement in the murder of a pregnant woman is highly significant of the transgressions implied by medieval rebellions.

The question of such transgressions is highly controversial because, for many years, scholars, strongly influenced by medieval and modern chronicles, tended to focus on the high level of irrational violence instigated by rebellious people. They often, for instance, invoked the idea of fury or madness (*furor*) to describe such events.[5] But more recently, many medievalists have begun to reconsider the role of violence; far from being senseless, violence is now increasingly understood as a fundamental component of medieval society, shaping and reshaping social and political relations, functioning much like a language of dominance and submission. This new historiography thus obliges us to recognise that violence was systemic to a society in which personal honour was of the utmost importance. Violence should not be considered antagonistic to the social order but, on the contrary, as an integrative force for communities, states, and power more generally.[6] Any reflexion on violence should also take into account recent studies focusing on 'war violence', especially in the context of the First World War, which defines it as a 'social fact'.[7] That we now consider 'war violence' as a specific type of violence with its own rules, rituals, and expressions, as a world in itself quite disconnected from the normal life – the contrast between the peaceful, early twentieth-century European societies and the outburst of violence in the battlefields of the First World War is particularly striking – should lead us to consider whether a specific 'rebellion violence' may have existed. As far as I know, 'rebellion violence' has never really been considered on its own, but rather has always been seen as a distorting mirror reflecting the general, pre-existing violence of medieval society. Obviously, the main sources for medieval rebellions, such as chronicles and judicial sources like royal pardons, are not always as informative as we might wish about this social grammar of 'rebellion violence'. Such texts generally consider rebellion only from the point of view of criminality, describing destruction, rapes or murders and naming rebels thieves and killers in order to be able to give to rebels the appropriate punishment for such acts.

The valences of violence: reconsidering the sources

If we turn back to the so-called *Bourgeois de Paris*, it is important to remember that his perspective is that of the canons and clerks of the University of Paris. Such men may have shared most of the ideas spread by Duke John the Fearless of Burgundy's propaganda and supported him against the Armagnacs during the French Civil War, but they did not number among the duke's fiercest supporters. They viewed with a certain mistrust and contempt the excesses of the butchers involved in the Cabochien movement in Paris of 1413 and then again during the summer of 1418. The '*Bourgeois*' is representative of the moderates who acted in favour of the duke of Burgundy but who strongly disapproved of the slaughters committed in Paris in 1418. His analysis of the acts of violence perpetrated by the people of Paris thus reflects not only his political opinions – which are, without any doubt, in favour of the duke of Burgundy – but also and, maybe mainly, the ideological point of view of the urban elites towards popular violence.

The initial extract of his *Journal* quoted above cannot only be considered on its own but should also be compared with other narrative sequences related to the riots that occurred in Paris around the same time. For instance, the *Bourgeois de Paris* tells us how, during the month of June 1418, Bernard VII, who was the Count of Armagnac and the Constable of France, was first arrested and then murdered by the people of Paris, along with many of the Armagnacs present in the city; he relates the mutilations of corpses[8] but in a kind of restrained manner. He omitted to mention that the nude corpse of the count was thrown in the streets, left without inhumation, and even mutilated, whereas he did note that the corpses of the victims killed on 29 May were left without any attention in the streets of Paris.[9] Such a difference cannot be explained by a difference of nature in the popular violence expressed in May and June. These two events are two sequences of a single movement: the difference between the massacres perpetrated in May 1418 and the killing of the Count of Armagnac only lies in the social status of the Constable of France which should have protected him, not from death – as a traitor, he could have been beheaded – but from such a dishonourable death. Both his qualities of count and his rank of one of the highest military royal officers should definitely have prevented him from perishing so miserably from the hands of commoners.

Later, relating the riots of August 1418 in Paris, the *Bourgeois de Paris* underlined several points that seem to be characteristic, in his eyes, of unacceptable popular violence, which finally leads to the execution of Capeluche. First of all, he noted the attacks on the royal jails – the Châtelet and the Petit Châtelet – where all the prisoners were killed without distinction or mercy.[10] Rebellions often included actions against prisons, either to deliver the prisoners or to murder them, depending on who the prisoners were. Indeed, the death of prisoners during a popular rebellion is fairly common. Among numerous examples, in February 1362 at Pont-Saint-Esprit commoners entered the prison and killed a few English pilgrims accused of spying for the benefit of the Gascon and English mercenaries, pillaging their belongings and sharing between them 2,000 golden pieces found on the pilgrims before throwing their corpses into the Rhône river.[11] In the context of popular riots, it also occurred in Montpellier in 1379 where the common people (*populares*) entered the royal jails and slaughtered the prisoners,[12] as well as in Paris during the Maillotins' movement in 1382. In this latter case, though, the insurgents invaded the Châtelet in order to free the prisoners, not to kill them.[13]

Whether to kill prisoners or to free them, invading royal – or seigniorial – jails thus seems quite common in rebellions and can even be seen as one of the most significant gestures of any revolt.[14] This seems particularly the case for the storming of the Châtelet of Paris, which was the seat of the *prévôté* (royal district) of Paris and a major symbol of the royal authority, and which had also been attacked during the Shepherds' Crusade of 1320.[15] The English Rising of 1381 offers a striking example of an attack against a prison: at St Albans, the rebels invaded the jails and freed all the prisoners, except one whom they considered deserving of execution. 'Making themselves judges and butchers', they beheaded him and put his head on the pillory of St Albans.[16] Nevertheless, during the events of 1418, the second attack against the Bastille Saint-Antoine (the same prison stormed on 14 July 1789) constituted a step towards unacceptable violence: the angry mob refused to calm down despite the duke of Burgundy's peaceful speech in defence of the prisoners' lives. Moreover, although John the Fearless made an agreement with the Parisian commoners, delivering the prisoners to them under the condition that their lives were preserved, they were killed anyway. The prince is thus portrayed as powerless to limit a kind of popular violence, which does not even respect the word of a royal prince and which constitutes, in the eyes of the *Journal*'s author, a real danger to the social order.

According not only to the chroniclers but also regarding to law, one of the most unacceptable forms of violence seems to be the murdering of women – even if, according to the *Bourgeois de Paris*, their corpses, left without dresses but still in shirts, were not completely naked (as if the narrator refused to face the nudity of female corpses)[17] – and, last but not least, the stabbing of a pregnant woman, which appears to be, in medieval society, the ultimate forbidden murder. As Claude Gauvard recalls, 'the pregnant woman is untouchable'[18] and any attempt on a pregnant woman was seen as a sacrilege: the judges of the Parlement de Paris clearly took the pregnancy of a victim in consideration and, already in the *Pactus Legus Salicae*, the *wergeld* that a murderer had to pay for killing a pregnant woman was the highest rate imposed in the Frankish law.[19] Significantly, there was even a specific word in ancient French to qualify the murdering of a pregnant woman – *encis*. The text of the *Établissements de Saint Louis* gives the following definition of the crime of *encis*: when someone strikes a pregnant woman and that she dies and the child with her.[20] In such a case, the penalty was always death and such a crime was always considered impossible to forgive.[21]

For my argument, it does not matter whether this stabbing really happened or if it was nothing more than a fictional *topos* employed to justify the execution of Capeluche. The important fact is that this narration draws a scale of what can be accepted or not in terms of popular violence in the ideological scheme of the urban elites. To stab a pregnant woman or to be accused of having stabbed a pregnant woman appears to be a political disaster as it leads to a break-up of the political process opened by the popular rebellion.[22] Nevertheless, such a crime appears to be a surprisingly common and regular *topos* in the sources. The Jacques, for example, were also accused by some chroniclers of having killed noble pregnant women, and even in one chronicle of tearing the foetuses from their mother's bellies, an accusation which is completely absent from the judicial documents and the pardon letters later issued to the Jacques.[23] The *Bourgeois de Paris* also made the same accusation against the bastard of Vaurus, an Armagnac knight who defended the town of Meaux against the troops of Henry V in 1422 and was then beheaded by order of the king of England; the bastard's corpse being exposed on a tree outside the town, after he surrendered. To justify his execution, which was contrary to the rules of war, the *Bourgeois* explains that he was the cruellest tyrant that ever existed and inserts a narration that possesses all the elements of a miserable fairy tale but without a happy ending. It ends with the death of a newly post-partum woman, left alone and naked in the forest during winter, eaten alive with her newborn baby by wolves (possibly a metaphor for the Armagnac troops). The inhumanity is here a narrative way to signal a political crime. The bastard of Vaurus was no crueller than hundreds of Armagnacs or Burgundian captains. His crime was only to be on the wrong side, according to the *Bourgeois*'s politics.[24]

Another forbidden act is clearly the anthropophagy of the corpses that the sources sometimes accuse rebels of committing.[25] Mutilation of corpses seems to be quite a common feature of rebellion. It echoes the legal mutilations imposed by the state's own justice – quartering the corpse of the traitors and beheading them in order to expose the five parts of the body in different areas of the town or on the gates.[26] But anthropophagy is a step beyond this. It transforms a banal mob murder into something unconceivable and changes the nature of the rebels themselves: they immediately ceased to be rebels, becoming instead complete strangers to Christendom. They thus lose any possibility of negotiation with royal power, since the king obviously, cannot grant his grace to subjects who divorced themselves from humankind.[27]

Or, at least, it should be that way. But, in fact, it does not really work like this. Accusations of anthropophagy are very unusual. Even Jean Froissart did not employ them directly against the Jacques. The famous scene in which the rebels killed a knight and then roasted him is not concluded by the Jacques' eating of their victim's flesh but rather by their unsuccessful attempt to force his wife and daughter to taste it.[28] The device is, here, somewhat different as Froissart shows us rebels at the threshold of inhumanity but refusing to cross it, as if the barrier was, even for the Jacques, too high to be jumped over. Instead, they try to transfer their forbidden drives to the widow of their victim. But, in another case in Montpellier in 1379, the accusation of anthropophagy actually appeared in the royal pardon letter. According to this document, the *populares* of the town were charged with high treason for having killed royal officers who came to collect taxes. They also stole their goods, burned some houses of the richest men, and threw the officers' corpses into wells after having eaten part of their flesh.[29] It is hard to believe – in one of France's biggest towns, the seat of its most ancient university, a cosmopolitan city governed by a powerful consulate dominated by merchants trading all over the Mediterranean[30] – that royal officers could really have been eaten! And we should not trust so easily such an accusation. However, after a spectacular ceremony of *amende honorable* (ritual submission), during which the university, the religious orders, the consuls, and the entire population, including women and children, begged Louis, duke of Anjou, who was acting as the king's lieutenant of Languedoc, for his pardon, no one was executed. The severe repression that the city might have expected was commuted to a huge fine, which was much more profitable to the king's lieutenant than the destruction of the town would have been.[31]

Violence as a system of communication

But, from this starting point, is it possible to understand, not only the way the sources present use and misuse of violence, but finally how rebels and their victims understood it? There is, obviously, a first methodological problem: we cannot be completely sure that the scale of violence is common to the entire society and that the *populares* share these degrees of violence drawn, not only in the *Journal*, but also in most medieval chronicles and royal sources, as well. This problem is readily apparent from reading the sorts of pardon letters that both the English and French royal chanceries granted to rebels. Nevertheless, while it is possible that peasants and *populares* did have a different perception of violence and its uses than elites, the essential question here is less the perception of violence by both parties than the fact that they shared a common sense of acceptable – or unacceptable – political violence. In other words, I would suggest that both the elites and the *populares* knew perfectly well which acts of violence were politically significant, which acts could be committed to open a public sphere of dialogue and discussion, and which ones should be avoided to remain in a rebellion context: in other words, 'the rites of violence are not the rights of violence in any *absolute* sense'.[32]

For instance, it seems clear that attacking royal jails and murdering – or freeing – the prisoners is an act of rebellion and of *lèse-majesté*. We could even say that it is an act that in and of itself meant rebellion, both for the rebels and for the king, because it challenged the power of death and life that the king possessed over his subjects. By seizing the prisoners and deciding by themselves who should be freed and live and who deserved to be executed, the rebels chose to exercise their own justice and took charge of the two-sided power of the king, based on the symbolic couple *ira* and *gratia* (anger and grace).[33] But such an act of rebellion, precisely because it belongs to the usual 'grammar of rebellion',[34] can be forgotten and forgiven by royal power as it was seen as political violence rather than as a criminal act.

Even murdering royal counsellors could be seen as a kind of political and, in a certain way, acceptable violence committed in the context of rebellion. Such murders seem to have been part of the normal repertoire of late medieval European rebellion. After all, the assassination in Paris in 1358, in the royal palace and in the Dauphin Charles's own private room, of his counsellors, Jean de Conflans and Robert de Clermont, did not put an end to the negotiations between the merchants' *prévôt*, Étienne Marcel, and the Crown. The murder took place so close to the Dauphin that one counsellor was actually killed on his bed and his blood was visible on the Dauphin's shirt.[35] But this did not prevent the Dauphin, who was then acting as the king's lieutenant, to deliver a pardon concerning these events a few days later. Likewise, on 15 June 1381, Richard II agreed to meet Wat Tyler at Smithfield, only two days after the execution of the archbishop Sudbury and of the treasurer Robert Hales who had become 'the predestined scapegoats of the year'.[36] Obviously, neither Charles nor Richard II had a real choice at these moments when their capitals were completely in rebel hands. But it does seem that the execution of royal counsellors was not viewed as a point of no return in the course of a rebellion, but rather an almost regular expression of popular violence. It may, too, have functioned as a system of protection for the monarchy: the rebels' anger being diverted to the body of the king's counsellors, rather than his own person. I would not go as far as saying that the Parisians were allowed to kill the marshals as long as they did not hurt the Dauphin himself, but almost!

Some scholars, including for example Claude Gauvard, have argued that there was a sort of inability for medieval society to use the concept of rebellion,[37] at least in political terms rather than juridical ones. (I mean in terms of *rebellion* and not a *rebellio* considered, according to the Roman law, as an act of disobedience.)[38] They point out the fact that medieval chronicles always described popular violence as a succession of murders, plunders, rapes, and so on, and that the rebels are portrayed as criminals, rather than rebels. Nevertheless, another reading of these chronicles is possible: our sources may intentionally hide the political side of popular violence, not really concealing it because they could not completely avoid mentioning this aspect, but revealing this political side through an accumulation of unacceptable violence.

In other words, I wonder if such an accumulation of horrible crimes – let us think for example on Froissart's insistence on the Jacques raping noble women or the striking episode when some Jacques roasted a knight and tried to force his wife and daughter to eat his flesh before raping and killing them – may in fact be a *topos* used by the chroniclers to denounce a political violence that they refused to reveal clearly to their readers. This fictional unacceptable violence would be thus a literary way to indicate to the readers that what was happening was in fact political violence, not crime, and that it should be understood in the frame of a medieval rebellion; it would act like a written, codified signal for the readers who were perfectly aware of what a rebellion was and who shared the same codes of representation as the chroniclers.

For instance, Froissart wrote that when a coalition of Parisian troops and Jacques besieged the Marché de Meaux in June 1358, where the wife of the Dauphin Charles had taken refuge, they intended to rape her and the noble women in her company and, eventually, to kill her.[39] Such an accusation is present in a letter sent by the Dauphin himself to the duke of Savoy at the end of the month of August 1358 relating the events that occurred in Paris under the government of Étienne Marcel. The Dauphin accused Étienne Marcel and his supporters of having 'gone with a great many armed men to attack the Marché of Meaux, where our companion the duchesse, our sisters, and many other ladies were, in order to take them prisoner and dishonour them' (*d'estre venu assaillir à grant quantité de gens d'armes, le marchié de Meaulx, où estoient la duchesse, notre compaigne, nos seurs et pluseurs autres dames, pour icelles emmener prisonnières et pour euls déshonorer*).[40] And, in a pardon letter delivered many years after the event, in December 1373, to Renaud d'Acy and other noblemen who were involved in the slaughter of the Jacques that followed the attack on the Marché de Meaux, the former Dauphin, now King Charles V, declared that 'our enemies and traitors, came to our town of Meaux with banners unfurled, to attack and take at will our said companion' (*noz ennemis et traytres, vindrent en notre dicte ville de Meauls à bannières despoliées, pour assaillir et prendre à leur volenté nostre dicte compaigne*), a fact that, if it had happened, would have been 'an irreparable scandal' (*un esclande irreparable*).[41] If it seems obvious that the attack of the Marché de Meaux was partly aimed at the presence of the Duchess of Normandy, it is nevertheless very unlikely that the commoners of Paris and their leaders had any real intention of raping the duchess and the Dauphin's sisters. The women would have been much more useful as hostages to keep the duke of Normandy under pressure. But, even 15 years after the siege of Meaux, both the chroniclers and the king himself go on writing as if the possibility of the rape of the duchess was not a phantasm, but a real threat on the royal house and its blood honour.

Rebels' diverting of symbolic and legal violence

If we move now from the field of representations to that of the actual rebellions, and from the perceptions of the elites to what we can recover of the *populares*' own views, it appears that the rebels used a sort of scale of violence ranging from simple threats to the most extreme physical violence, such as fires, murders, and even the mutilation of corpses. Outlining a scale of rebel violence on the rebels' own terms must encompass legal and symbolic violence, as well as physical attacks, in order to try to understand the different steps and the gradation in the violence used by the rebels.[42] Rebels took part in a wide range of action, including what we might term 'legal violence' against the authorities, suing them in front of various benches, even though they did not possess the juridical capacity to act as a collective group. This is what happened in Montpellier in the 1320s when the *populares* decided to gather themselves and to hire a lawyer and sue the consuls in order to obtain an audit of public expenses. However, the consuls considered this an infraction on the law since the *populares* did not have any right to constitute themselves as a group or as a separate part of the *universitas* (the legal and institutional entity which corresponded to but which was not identical with the community in its socio-political sense). Consequently, in the consuls' view, such an action should be considered as 'legal violence' against the *universitas* of Montpellier since the consuls claimed to be the unique custodians of legitimate public authority. This did not prevent the *populares* from gathering 1,000 supporters in the public square in front of the town hall, without arms, but 'shouting and screaming against the consuls that it would be better to die here than in Flanders' (*clamantes et vociferantes contra dictos consules melius esse quod moriamur hic quam in Flandria*),[43] meaning by this that they had no intention of participating in the military campaigns that the king of France was leading at this moment against the Flemish; neither with their blood, nor with their money.

Let us take another example: in 1357, in the little town of Lavaur, the *populares* protested against the domination of a local oligarchy, who were monopolising the town's consulate. This political movement was also a social one with clear fiscal implications. The *populares* claimed that these oligarchs were putting the town under pressure, imposing more taxes than were necessary for the common good of the *universitas*. They complained first to the seneschal of Toulouse, the region's highest-ranking royal officer, but they failed to obtain a modification of the election rules for the consulate. Then, one night at Pentecost, they gathered, took up arms, patrolled the streets, and stood in front of the houses of the wealthiest townsmen shouting: 'Where are those damn traitors and wreckers of this place?' (*Ubi sunt isti proditores et dampnificatores hujus loci*). The consuls, unable to re-establish public order, chose to remain in silence in their houses, fearing that they would be put to death and their houses burned down.[44] Perhaps surprisingly, such a demonstration actually effected a profound reorganisation of the consulate. The six consuls were thenceforth to be elected directly by a general assembly and strict oversight of public expenses was implemented.[45]

Sometimes, the *populares* did not even have to take arms to transform their protest into a success. The town of Alès was the theatre of a long conflict between 'common, poorer people' (*populares sive minus divites*) on one side and the 'great or rich people of this city' (*majors seu divitiores ejusdem ville*) on the other: in 1377, an initial agreement was concluded concerning the sharing out of taxes. This was an obvious victory for the *populares*, but the situation remained partly unfair as one-quarter of the taxes was still collected under the form of a capitation, meaning that each head of household (excepting the poorest) had to pay the same amount, with no consideration of his level of fortune.[46] Later, at Easter 1379, 300 men gathered, without arms, in the main square, and forced the consuls and the seigniorial officers to come with them. They also visited the houses of the former consuls who had held office between 1369 and 1379. They took the furniture, horses, wine, wheat, and, more generally, all the goods they could find and decided to sell them directly at auction – the money thus collected was donated to the town's public funds – because the *populares* believed that over the previous decade, the former consuls had imposed unfair taxes for their personal profit and not for the Common Good. Such a demonstration, even without arms, was considered as an act of rebellion and of *lèse-majesté* by the king's lieutenant in Languedoc, Duke Louis of Anjou, who nonetheless eventually delivered a pardon letter to the rebels.[47] But, in 1385, a new agreement was established between the *populares* and the *divites*, adopting the principle of a proportional tax and giving up the capitation. The *populares* thus emerged victorious from a struggle lasting over a decade.

Combining legal violence and the threat of physical violence thus seems to have been a common method employed by the *populares* to pursue their grievances: sufficient to require a response from the authorities but without risking bloody repression. Threats of violence function as the alphabet of this political language which was used by the rebels and clearly understood by the urban elites or royal power. But in many cases, of course, threats of violence by the commons were not effective, and this inefficiency led to an escalation of violence. The language of protest made abundant use of symbolic violence, but it is quite difficult to determine whether this form of violence was considered a moderate form of contestation, or, on the contrary, as the most violent one. Many actions might be considered under the rubric of symbolic violence, including destroying and lacerating charters or banners, burning or destroying seigniorial manors without plundering them, etc.[48] I would like to discuss here two very different forms of symbolic violence in order to show that the one that we might initially consider the most violent was not necessarily seen that way by contemporaries.

The first act of symbolic violence I will look at is the systematic destruction of seigniorial manors during Étienne Marcel's movement around Paris in 1358 and in London during the English Rising of 1381. In 1358, Étienne Marcel ordered the goldsmith Pierre des Barres and Peire Gilli, a spice merchant who originated from Saint-Guilhem-le-Désert in Southern France but set up in Paris for many years, to lead a military expedition to the north and east of the capital in order to destroy the manors owned by kings' counsellors and members of Paris parlement (the king's supreme judicial court) in the northern and eastern villages of Paris. For instance, the military troop went to Pomponne where Jean de Charny owned one of these manors and to Gonesse where Pierre d'Orgemont, first president of Paris parlement, also had one. Pierre des Barres and Peire Gilli ordered their fellows to perpetrate a systematic destruction of these manors, requiring for instance carpenters to take down the beams and roof tiles and forcing other villagers to participate in the destruction of the manors, before sharing the spoils and the cattle out to their men.[49] It was a very organised destruction, an act of symbolic violence, intended to erase the marks of domination of close royal counsellors. Similar destruction took place in England in 1381 at the houses of the knights of St John in London and at the Savoy palace, property of John of Gaunt, by rebels who deliberately decided not to plunder it but to destroy all the goods by burning them. They refused to take anything from the house in order to show that they were not robbers, in deep contrast with the fact that rebellions are normally portrayed by royal sources as a succession of criminal acts.[50] According to Thomas

Walsingham, the rebels even made a proclamation forbidding anyone to steal any object under pain of death, so that everybody should be aware that they were not thieves but, indeed, rebels.[51] In Paris, as well as in London, the rebels destroyed the properties of people who appeared to their eyes to be 'traitors', perhaps following the legal procedure known as the *abbatis de maison* (tearing down the house), and practising their own form of justice.[52]

The second type of symbolic violence that I would like to explore involves intimacy between a rebel leader and a prince. I know of three examples, each with a disastrous result for the rebel leader. In 1381, Wat Tyler is said to have acted as if he was a familiar of the young Richard II at Smithfield. According to the *Anonimalle Chronicle*, Wat Tyler took the king by the hand, shook his arm and called him 'brother', including him in a feeling of brotherhood which was common among the rebels, saying to the king that 'we shall be good companions'.[53] As we know, a few moments later, Wat Tyler was dead. In 1418, in Paris, the executioner Capeluche reportedly shook hands with John the Fearless, duke of Burgundy, and toasted the duke with a glass of wine. This was a common way to show friendship in medieval society, both for peasants and noblemen, but only between equals; a few days later, Capeluche was arrested and then executed, paying with his life the price of the familiarity he tried to create between an executioner and a prince of royal blood. To this list of rebel leaders who died for having crossed the red line of familiarity with a king or a prince, we may also add Guillaume Calle, captain of the Jacques, who agreed to meet in confidence with Charles, king of Navarre, just before the battle of Mello, without even taking the precaution of asking for hostages before the encounter. The simple fact that Guillaume Calle thought that the prince would be obliged to keep his word and that he could treat from equal to equal with a king, can be interpreted as a sign of familiarity. Of course, Charles of Navarre did not scruple to arrest him and then, after the defeat of the Jacques, to have him executed.

On the other hand, some other rebel leaders were not so confident: during the Tuchins' rebellion in Languedoc in 1382, one of the insurgents' captains, a former seigniorial officer, refused to drink from the same glass of wine as the major lord of the region, Guillaume Beaufort.[54] This surprising gesture is not much commented upon by the witnesses who reported it during a trial: they just mentioned it, saying that it could be seen as a sign of mistrust towards the lord. But, there is maybe more to it than this: the denial of a false friendship with the lord may reflect the Tuchins' captain's wish to act with caution, his refusal to cross this apparently tiny border which in reality was a point of no return for rebel leaders.

Entering into familiarity with a prince or seeming to enjoy this familiarity by acting as a familiar seems to have constituted a major taboo in medieval society because it abolished the social distance between the king and his subjects: if friendship – *amicitia* – was an essential value in political relationships, it could only be established between princes themselves. The king could not be the friend, or the fellow of a rebel leader. Efforts at creating such intimacy were understood as more unacceptable than attacking royal jails or murdering a prince's counsellors, or many actions that belonged to the usual repertoire of rebellion. And this familiarity, which was an offence to the majesty of the king, was even considered more violent than a critical speech directly addressed to the king. According to Christine de Pizan, after Étienne Marcel's death, when the Dauphin Charles entered Paris, a young commoner shouted at him, saying that he would never have allowed the Dauphin into the city.[55] The Count of Tancarville, a knight of the royal company, wanted to kill this boy for his insolence but Charles prevented the knight from doing so. Maybe Charles showed mercy because of his very generous spirit – this was Christine de Pizan's interpretation – or because he did not want to risk another rebellion. But Charles may well have just thought that even a public and direct speech against his authority was not very important after the other events of 1358.

It is, of course, difficult to know whether the temptation to establish familiarity with the king was real or was another fictional *topos* the chroniclers used to indicate that a boundary had been crossed and to justify the rebel leaders' executions. However, the main point is that to use – or not to use – violence is always a choice – a rational choice – made by the *populares* in a particular context. This means that when they used violence, they understood it as an unwritten message sent to the dominants and that the dominants were able to read and decrypt it, for violence was not only a code, but also a link between the rebels and the elites/government. Political violence was not a way of breaking a dialogue but, on the contrary, of opening it up by forcing the elites to hear and read these acts of violence that were completely determined by the rebellion's aims.

Conclusion: violence as a political language

Let us conclude with a final example to show how rebels could use violent actions to convey their own intentions. During the English Rising in 1381, rebels destroyed most of the charters they could find, whereas the Tuchins of Languedoc did not act this way. Instead, they agreed to give Guillaume Beaufort, viscount of Alès, the charters that belonged to him and proved his seigniorial rights over his lands, but they destroyed the documents relative to the payment of the salt taxes.[56] On both occasions, the message was perfectly clear, clear enough to be heard by the royal or seigniorial power targeted by the rebels. It does not mean that, if the 'grammar of rebellion' was common, if not all over medieval Europe, at least in France and England, reflecting a common political culture,[57] the vocabulary was strictly identical: violence may differ even in the same kingdom from one place to another. If we think of it as a language, it was perhaps less like Latin – used throughout Europe, at least by clerics – and more like vernaculars, specific to particular regions. Each violent act in a rebellious context must consequently be contextualised in a more local, as well as global, system of communication, which was only efficient because it was understood by both the rebels and their targets. In any case, violence was always meaning something. It opened a gap that had to be filled by negotiations and an elite/governmental response adapted to the claims that the violence expressed. Of all rebellious acts attested in late medieval England and France, familiarity with the prince appears to have been the most 'violent' in the eyes of contemporary observers, because it constituted a rupture of the social order. On the other hand, physical violence of the sort that might seem more objectionable to us – like murder, arson, or even post-mortem mutilation – was perceived as a regular way of speaking, not only for rebels, but also for the elites and government. This may be because these violent actions were, in fact, imitations of judicial procedures: cutting royal officers' bodies into pieces was nothing more than the execution of 'traitors'; seizing and auctioning off goods was the legal procedure observed for the payment of debts; systematic destruction of nobles' manors by taking off the doors and the roof tiles was a legal action against people who did not pay their taxes,[58] burning castles was not so far from the legal *abattis de maison* which is attested in the urban statutes, and so on. All these considerations help to explain why the rebels used such violent actions and how elites accepted and understood them as politically significant: they belong, after all, to the wide range of means used by the royal or seigniorial justice. But, to use or not to use violence, that is the question!

Notes

1   *Item, le lundi ensuivant, 22e jour d'août, furent accusées aucunes femmes, lesquelles furent tuées et mises sur les carreaux sans robe que leur chemise, et à ce faire était plus enclin le bourreau que nul des autres; entre lesquelles femmes il tua une femme grosse, qui en ce cas n'avait aucune coulpe, dont il advint un peu de jours après qu'il en fut pris et mis au Châtelet, lui troisième de ses complices, et au bout de trois jours après eurent les têtes coupées.*

      (*Journal d'un bourgeois de Paris de 1405 à 1449*, ed. C. Beaune, Paris, L.G.F., 1990, pp. 128–9)

2 BN, ms. fr. 5054. The miniature is present on fol. 8v.
3 Ibid.: *En l'an mil quatre cens et treize/Bouchiers, tueurs et escorcheurs/Par une entreprise mauvaise/A Paris firent les seigneurs.*
4 C. Raynaud, *La violence au Moyen-Âge XIIIe–XVe siècle*, Paris: Le léopard d'or, 1990, p. 27.
5 See for instance R. Mousnier, *Fureurs paysannes*, Paris: Calmann-Lévy, 1967. But the expression is also used in G. Fourquin, *Les soulèvements populaires au Moyen-Âge*, Paris: Presses Universitaires de France, 1972. At this point, Michel Mollat and Philippe Wolff could write that revolt remained 'a violent reaction and, for most of the participants, of a primary character'; M. Mollat and Ph. Wolff, *Ongles bleus, Jacques et Ciompi: Les révolutions populaires en Europe aux XIVe et XVe siècles*, Paris: Calmann-Lévy, 1970, p. 292.
6 Amongst many references, we may quote C. Gauvard, *Violence et ordre public au Moyen Âge*, Paris: Picard, 2005 and D. Nirenberg, *Communities of Violence: Persecution of Minorities in the Middle Ages*, Princeton, NJ: Princeton University Press, 1996. Both of them developed an acute reflection on violence used by medieval rebels.
7 As, for instance, Stéphane Audouin-Rouzeau who speaks of 'war violence' as

> *un fait social,... dans ses formes, dans les marques qu'elle laisse sur les corps, dans les représentations qu'elle fait émerger, dans ce qu'elle nous permet de comprendre sur les intentions de l'ennemi, la pratique de violence comme une confrontation des interprétations parmi les belligérants.*
> (S. Audouin-Rouzeau, *Combattre: Une anthropologie historique de la guerre moderne, XIXe–XXIe siècle*, Paris: Seuil, 2008, p. 22)

8 *Journal d'un bourgeois de Paris*, ed. Beaune, p. 116: concerning the corpses of the Armagnacs, he writes that they had *tant de coups de taille et d'estoc au visage, qu'on n'y pouvait homme connaître quel qu'il fût, ce ne fut le connétable et le chancelier qui furent connus au lit où tués étaient.*
9 Ibid., p. 112: *depuis que morts étaient, ne leur demeurait que leurs brayes, et étaient en tas comme porcs ou milieu de la boue.*
10 Ibid., pp. 125–8.
11 AN JJ 93, no. 44, fol. 19v; published in C. Devic and J. Vaissette, *Histoire générale de Languedoc*, new edn, 16 vols, Toulouse: Privat, 1872–1904, vol. 10, preuves [proofs], cols 1294–5.
12 A. Germain, *Histoire de la commune de Montpellier*, 3 vols, Montpellier: J. Martel aîné, 1851, vol. 3, p. 390: *atque captos in carceribus regiis, ubi securi esse debebant, occiderunt.* This sentence figures in the pardon letters delivered by Louis, duke of Anjou and king's lieutenant, to the town of Montpellier after the rebellion. On this rebellion, see V. Challet, 'Montpellier 1379: une communauté au miroir de sa révolte', in H. R. Oliva Herrer, V. Challet, J. Dumolyn, and M. A. Carmona Ruiz (eds), *La comunidad medieval como esfera publica*, Seville: Universidad de Sevilla, 2014, pp. 377–97.
13 L. Mirot, *Les insurrections urbaines au début du règne de Charles VI (1380–1383): Leurs causes, leurs conséquences*, Paris: Librairie des Écoles françaises d'Athènes et de Rome, 1905, pp. 120–40.
14 C. Gauvard, 'Les révoltes du règne de Charles VI: tentative pour expliquer un échec', in F. Gambrelle and M. Trebitsch (eds), *Révolte et société: Actes du IVe colloque d'histoire au présent*, 2 vols, Paris: Publications de la Sorbonne, 1989, vol. 1, pp. 53–61.
15 M. Barber, 'The Pastoureaux of 1320', *Journal of Ecclesiastical History*, 32, 1981, pp. 143–66.
16 T. Walsingham, *Historia anglicana*, ed. H. T. Riley, 2 vols, London: Longman, Roberts, and Green, 1863–4, vol. 1, pp. 467–73.
17 *Journal d'un bourgeois de Paris*, ed. Beaune, p. 128, excerpted at the beginning of this chapter.
18 C. Gauvard, *'De grace especial': Crime, état et société en France à la fin du Moyen Âge*, 2 vols, Paris: Publications de la Sorbonne, 1991, vol. 2, p. 824.
19 Quoted by N. Gradowicz-Pancer, 'Honneur féminin et pureté sexuelle; équation ou paradoxe?', in M. Rouche (ed.), *Mariage et sexualité au Moyen-Âge: Accord ou crise?*, Paris, Presses de l'Université de Paris-Sorbonne, 2000, pp. 37–52.
20 *Si est feme enceinte, quant l'en la fiert et elle muert de l'enfant*; see http://ducange.enc.sorbonne.fr/, at the word *Encisium*.
21 For a more complete discussion on this topic, see S. Cassagnes-Brouquet, 'L'intervention du genre dans l'événement: les massacres parisiens de 1418 et le meurtre d'une femme', in M. Bergère and L. Capdevilla (eds), *Genre et événement: Du masculin et du féminin en histoire des crises et des conflits*, Rennes: Presses Universitaires de Rennes, 2006, pp. 53–67.
22 On rebellion as a political process and a political language, see V. Challet and I. Forrest, 'The Masses', in C. Fletcher, J.-P. Genet, and J. Watts (eds), *Government and Political Life in England and France, c.1300–c.1500*, Cambridge: Cambridge University Press, 2015, pp. 279–316.

23 See J. Firnhaber-Baker, in this volume. The accusation of having killed pregnant women is reported by Jean le Bel (*puis tuerent la dame enchainte; les avoient tué mesmement, elles enchaintes*) and, after him, by Jean Froissart (*puis tuèrent la dame, qui estoit enchainte*) who was greatly inspired by Jean le Bel. But both chroniclers just mentioned this accusation without really developing it. In fact, the most complete accusation – but which seems so exaggerated that it is very difficult to see any truth in it – figures in an English text, that it is to say *The Anonimalle Chronicle*: *Et ledit Jak Bonehomme en plousors lieus arascia enfauntz de les ventres de lour meres et de le sanke de les ditz enfauntz pur soi refreschere enuncta soun corps*. All these texts quoted by M.-T. de Medeiros, *Jacques et chroniqueurs: Une étude comparée de récits contemporains relatant la Jacquerie de 1358*, Paris: H. Champion, 1979, pp. 185–6, 188, 204.
24 Concerning this episode, see B. Bove, 'Violence extrême, rumeur et crise de l'ordre public: la tyrannie du bâtard de Vaurus', in F. Foronda, C. Barralis, and B. Sère (eds), *Violences souveraines au Moyen Âge*, Paris: Presses universitaires de France, 2010, pp. 123–32.
25 For a few examples of mutilations of corpses that may be interpreted as ritual anthropophagy, mainly from Italian chronicles, see A. Zorzi, 'Dérision des corps et corps souffrants dans les exécutions en Italie à la fin du Moyen-Âge', in E. Crouzet-Pavan and J. Verger (eds), *La dérision au Moyen-Âge: De la pratique sociale au rituel politique*, Paris, Publications de l'Université Paris-Sorbonne, 2007, pp. 225–40.
26 See, for instance, N. Gonthier, *Le châtiment du crime au Moyen Âge*, Rennes: Presses Universitaires de Rennes, 1998.
27 See, for instance, the accusations of anthropophagy against the Tafurs during the first crusade in N. Cohn, *The Pursuit of the Millennium: Revolutionary Millenarians and Mystical Anarchists of the Middle Ages*, 2nd edn, Oxford, Oxford University Press, 1970. The question has been recently renewed by V. Vandenberg, *De chair et de sang: Images et pratiques du cannibalisme de l'Antiquité au Moyen-Âge*, Rennes, Presses Universitaires de Rennes, 2014.
28 On this scene and, more generally, on the positions of Froissart towards the Jacquerie, see de Medeiros, *Jacques et chroniqueurs*. This specific episode was borrowed by Jean Froissart from the *Chronique de Jean le Bel*, ed. J. Viard and E. Déprez, 2 vols, Paris: H. Laurens, 1904–5, vol. 1, p. 258; it figures in Jean Froissart, *Chroniques de Jean Froissart*, ed. S. Luce, G. Raynaud, L. Mirot, and A. Mirot, 15 vols, Paris: Mme. Ve. Jules Renouard and others, 1869–1919, vol. 5, p. 100.
29 AN, JJ 119, no. 185, fols 121v–3; published by Germain, *Histoire de la commune de Montpellier*, vol. 2, pp. 388–401, at 389 for the quotation: *Imo, quod maxime exemplo grave est, et abominabile in natura, et alias inauditum, interfectorum corpora aperiebant mucrone, et baptizatas carnes, ut ferae bestiae comedebant*.
30 K. L. Reyerson, *Society, Law, and Trade in Medieval Montpellier*, Aldershot: Ashgate, 1995.
31 On this ceremony, which is very close to the one observed at Calais in 1347 for the town's submission to the king of England, Edward III, see V. Challet, 'Émouvoir le prince: révoltes populaires et recours au roi en Languedoc vers 1380', *Hypothèses*, 5, 2002, pp. 325–33 and J.-M. Moeglin, *Les bourgeois de Calais: Essai sur un mythe historique*, Paris: Albin Michel, 2002.
32 N. Z. Davis, 'The rites of violence: religious riots in sixteenth-century France', *P&P*, 59, 1973, pp. 51–91, quotation at 91. On the possible use of the Habermas' concept of 'public sphere' for the Middle Ages, see P. Boucheron and N. Offenstadt, *L'espace public au Moyen Âge: Débats autour de Jürgen Habermas*, Paris: Presses universitaires de France, 2011.
33 On this two-sided royal power, see Gauvard, *'De grace especial'*.
34 Concerning this concept, see Challet and Forrest, 'The Masses', pp. 300–5.
35 J. d'Avout, *Le meurtre d'Étienne Marcel*, Paris: Gallimard, 1960, pp. 148–53.
36 R. B. Dobson, *The Peasants' Revolt of 1381*, London: Macmillan, 1970, p. 23. See also S. Justice, *Writing and Rebellion: England in 1381*, Berkeley: University of California Press, 1996.
37 Gauvard, 'Les révoltes du règne de Charles VI'.
38 On the equivalence between the concept of *rebellio* and disobedience, see the numerous works of Jacques Chiffoleau on this topic, especially J. Chiffoleau, 'Le crime de majesté, la politique et l'extraordinaire: note sur les collections érudites de procès de lèse-majesté du XVIIIe siècle français et sur leurs exemples médiévaux', in Y.-M. Bercé (ed.), *Les procès politiques (XIVe–XVIIe siècle)*, Rome: École Française de Rome, 2007, pp. 577–662.
39 d'Avout, *Le meurtre d'Étienne Marcel*, pp. 207–9.
40 M. F. Combes, *Lettre inédite du dauphin Charles sur la conjuration d'Étienne Marcel et du roi de Navarre adressée aux comtes de Savoie (31 août 1358)*, Paris: Imprimerie Impériale 1889, also published in *Oeuvres de Froissart*, ed. Kervyn de Lettenhove, 25 vols, Brussels: Victor Devaux, 1867–77, vol. 6, p. 477.
41 AN JJ 105, no. 91, fols 57–8r; published by S. Luce, *Histoire de la Jacquerie*, new edn, Paris: H. Champion, 1894, pp. 240–2.

42 On this idea of escalation of violence in the context of peasants' rebellions, see H. Neveux, *Les révoltes paysannes en Europe XIVe–XVIIe siècle*, Paris: Hachette, 1997, pp. 170–90.
43 On these events and the conflict of the *populares*, see J. Combes, 'Finances municipales et oppositions sociales à Montpellier au commencement du XIVe siècle', in *Vivarais et Languedoc*, Montpellier: Université Paul Valéry, 1972, pp. 99–120; J. Rogozinski, *Power, Caste, and Law: Social Conflict in Fourteenth-Century Montpellier*, Cambridge, MA: Medieval Academy of America, 1982 and, more recently, P. Chastang, *La ville, le gouvernement et l'écrit à Montpellier: Essai d'histoire sociale*, Paris: Publications de la Sorbonne, 2013.
44 AN JJ 89, no. 241, fol. 107v.
45 AN, JJ 89, no. 240, fol. 107; published by L. Secousse, *Ordonnances des rois de France de la troisième race*, 21 vols, Paris: Imprimerie Nationale, 1723–1849, vol. 3, p. 190.
46 This sentence, included in another one dating from 1385, is published by A. Bardon, *Histoire de la ville d'Alais*, Nîmes: Chastanier, 1896, pp. LIX–LXV.
47 AN JJ 118, no. 326; published De Vic and Vaissette, *Histoire générale de Languedoc*, vol. 10, col. 1630.
48 For a complete panorama of the different types of violence perpetrated by the insurgents, see S. K. Cohn, Jr., *Lust for Liberty: The Politics of Social Revolt in Medieval Europe, 1200–1425*, Cambridge, MA: Harvard University Press, 2006.
49 The systematic destruction of the house in Gonesse is quite well documented, thanks to a lawsuit initiated by its owner, Pierre d'Orgemont, against several persons involved in this action; AN X1a 14, fols 476–7; published by Luce, *Histoire de la Jacquerie*, pp. 313–20.
50 See, for instance, the description of the fire the rebels lit at the Savoy in the *Anonimalle Chronicle* published and translated by Dobson, *The Peasants' Revolt of 1381*, p. 157. The chronicler underlines the fact that insurgents chose to burn all the clothes and even a very valuable headboard, which was said to be worth 1,000 marks.
51 *Historia Anglicana*, p. 457.
52 See A. Delcourt, *La vengeance de la commune: L'arsin et l'abattis de maison en Flandre et en Hainaut*, Lille: É. Raoust, 1930 and discussion in J. Dumolyn, 'The vengeance of the commune: sign systems of popular politics in medieval Bruges', in Oliva Herrer *et al.* (eds), *La comunidad*, pp. 251–89.
53 Quoted and translated by Dobson, *The Peasants' Revolt of 1381*, p. 164.
54 V. Challet, 'Au miroir du Tuchinat: relations sociales et réseaux de solidarité dans les communautés languedociennes à la fin du XIVe siècle', *Cahiers de Recherches Médiévales (XIIIe–XVe siècles)*, 10, 2003, pp. 71–87.
55 Christine de Pizan, *Le livre des faits et bonnes mœurs du roi Charles V le Sage*, trans. E. Hicks and T. Moreau, Paris: Stock, 1997, pp. 82–3.
56 Challet, 'Au miroir du Tuchinat'.
57 J. Watts, *The Making of Polities (Europe, 1300–1500)*, Cambridge, Cambridge University Press, 2009.
58 This was a quite common procedure in French medieval towns; see for instance R. Grand, 'Justice criminelle, procédures et peines dans les villes aux XIIIe et XIVe siècles', *Bibliothèque de l'École des chartes*, 102, 1941, pp. 51–108.

15
DEVELOPING STRATEGIES OF PROTEST IN LATE MEDIEVAL SICILY[1]

Fabrizio Titone

Introduction

In late medieval Sicily acts of protest could vary markedly. Even if protests did not lack elements of spontaneity, they were often the outcome of a slow process of identifying rights that had been denied, the most effective forms of response, and the appropriate political context in which to act. The main periods in which strategies of protest were elaborated were the assumption of control over the island by the heads of the main magnate houses (the Vicars, 1377–92) and then the royal restoration effected by Martin I, king of Sicily (1392–1409).[2] If in the early fourteenth century, with the election of Frederick III as king of Sicily (1296–1337), there had been encouraging signs that the *universitates* (meaning legally recognised communities, urban or rural) were achieving a stronger identity,[3] under the Vicars the consolidation of the communities' rights was interrupted.[4] The Vicars' government represented a period of significant reduction both in the spaces of political participation and in the redistribution of resources at the local level. Conversely, the defeat of the Vicars by Martin I and his readiness to arrive at a political accommodation with the *universitates* greatly extended their room for manoeuvre and enhanced their prospects, in contrast with an earlier period in which their margins of autonomy were significantly limited. The suppression of local political aspirations under the Vicars and the political openness of Martin I allowed the *universitates* to identify more clearly the margins of autonomy that, if violated, justified revolt, as well as the modalities of response.

The present essay analyses different instances of protest which entailed different strategies or modalities, ranging from violent revolts to peaceful dissent expressed through institutional channels, as well as protests in which both violent and peaceful reactions may be identified. In Sicily, as in the other territories of the Crown of Aragon, the relationship between the king and his subjects is commonly defined as one of 'pactism'.[5] This term refers to a contractual relationship, the principal feature of which is traditionally held to be parliamentary activity. Parliament was, however, not the only site to feature such procedures, since similar arrangements assumed different forms in a range of other settings, chiefly on the basis of negotiations in the guise of petitions (*capitula*) entered into by the community with the king or his representatives.[6] While protests often involved negotiations of this kind, recourse to *capitula* could structure and contain dissent but did not necessarily do so. Recourse to petitions represented a possible alternative to various types of confrontation chosen on the basis of the dissenting protagonists' social and political context, but it was also a mechanism that could form part of a violent protest.

Among the cases to be examined here, the *tumulti* of Palermo and of Polizzi were due to such a heightened state of social tension that the socio-professional groups resorted to violence, whereas in Catania, Piazza, and Patti, there were open expressions of dissent without actual outbreaks of large-scale conflict.[7] With reference to non-violent protests, especially in Catania, I will discuss dissent in terms of the adoption of a conservative strategy, described here as one of 'disciplined dissent'. By 'disciplined dissent' I mean that those who were the target of policies of marginalisation and/or individuals with a less prominent socio-political role gradually adopted the rulers' political language, strategies and values.[8] The analysis of forms of disciplined dissent makes it possible to identify acts of protest involving the use of existing institutions and the framework of ideas shared by those who held political power. This conservative strategy enabled groups or individuals to expand their socio-political role. I should emphasise, however, that even in assimilating the rulers' strategies and values, those who were not in a position of authority nevertheless did so in the light of their own needs and expectations. Disciplined dissent also makes it possible to identify acts of protest which were often not overt but camouflaged.

Analysis of protest in Sicily allows me to nuance and expand two recent historiographic discussions. First, Patrick Lantschner has proposed a correlation between the absence of major revolts and the lack of pluralism of existing political structures which, when present, provided the rebels with the resources to mount a revolt.[9] This is an interpretation that may be generalised, being applicable for example (as I will indicate below) to the tumult in Palermo, but it is not exclusive. In my opinion the existence of a pluralism of political structures may also explain the *absence* of revolts, by offering an alternative to the outbreak of a major conflict. It was the political context that determined the decision to instigate a revolt or else to seek out an alternative, employing the institutional and cultural means available.

Second, explaining the widespread desire for liberty to which the protests gave voice as a reaction to social and political injustices, as Samuel Cohn has argued for the phase after 1355 and up to and including the early fifteenth century, serves to bring out only one possible cause of the protests.[10] In fact, protests could also develop in a period when enhanced rights and privileges, and more inclusive governments, encouraged high expectations. Consequently even a brief interruption in access to political and economic resources could be perceived in a dramatic way and trigger firm responses.

In this view, it is noteworthy that the highest concentration of revolts is recorded during the reign of Alfonso V (1416–58), that is, under a royal government that tended not to promote an invasive state but rather to extend to a significant degree the spaces of autonomy. In medieval Sicily the reign of Alfonso V was possibly the most favourable phase for the cities' freedom. Two different causes may account for the higher concentration of protests in this phase. The first is linked to the extension of local autonomy, which generally led to conflicts between socio-professional groups. The second factor refers to possible interventions by the king designed to limit liberty, at odds with a royal policy that generally served to promote local privileges. These interventions prompted a decisive response to those actions of the royal court or of the feudal *dominus* (lord) that evoked (albeit in a decidedly milder form) the preceding phase of the Vicars' government and its curbing of the liberties of the communities.

Under Alfonso V, royal financial pressure increased significantly, but the king managed to intensify his economic demands while avoiding open opposition from the subjects he taxed by significantly involving local administrations in the choices to be made regarding taxation.[11] Consequently there were frequent political clashes between the socio-professional groups, who were determined to obtain some representation in the government and to be accorded the right to decide how taxes were to be allocated. This phase witnessed a significant rise in the attempts made by groups (*parcialitates*) to obtain the exclusion from government of opposing groups, a stance that the royal court generally opposed. In this context, I believe it is possible to discern in the revolts a call for decisive royal intervention enabling coordination and the redistribution of resources, and by the same token a rejection of the policies of exclusion pursued by the most powerful socio-professional alignments.[12] The absence of any a priori royal opposition to protest movements may be explained in terms of the pursuit of a political equilibrium, in which the *universitates* had a central role in maintaining the 'peaceful state' frequently evoked in the royal chancery's acts under Martin I and particularly Alfonso V and favoured by the royal court.[13]

The cases considered here reflect the fact that the protests often delivered significant benefits to the community through a redistribution of resources and a more inclusive rebalancing of access to government. The royal response did not consist solely of repression, since it often, prudently and undemonstratively, granted the most pressing requests. In the historiography on Sicilian revolts, Henri Bresc first identified such cases, although he mainly associated them with a critical economic and political phase.[14] Stephan Epstein, for his part, identified the political role of the *universitates* and the significant social stratification around which the protests on economic and political grounds took shape.[15] My own previous work has highlighted the prominent role of the artisans and *populares* in the protests, along with the phenomenon both of a convergence of interests between distinct groups and of emulation between the communities.[16] In the present text, I will first consider Frederick III's royal policy of openness towards the *universitates* and the alteration in the balances that brought about its demise, and then discuss the curtailment of urban liberties under the Vicars, before turning to the very different policy adopted by Martin I. Following this contextualisation, I will look at protests during the reign of Alfonso V in Catania, Patti, and Piazza, where disciplined dissent was central, concluding my analysis with the more radical revolts under the same ruler in Palermo and in Polizzi.

From the first half of the fourteenth century until the reign of Alfonso V

From the advent of the Aragonese dynasty in 1282 the *universitates* gradually pushed to extend their role, an initiative that the royal government of Frederick III received favourably.[17] Frederick III's accession as king of Sicily gave the island autonomy from the crown of Aragon.[18] A gradual consolidation of the spaces of political participation enhanced the communities' expectations of royal policy, but also created a potential source of tension between individuals and/or urban groups. These features are identifiable in Palermo, an expanding political arena beset by mounting tension between *partes* with distinct interests. We have compelling evidence of this tension in the form of a royal ban, in 1321, which prohibited 26 *milites* (knights) found guilty of *zizaniae et dissensiones* (antagonisms and dissensions), from participating in governmental activity in Palermo.[19] Such concerns were also evident in measures to discipline funeral rites in order to neutralise and/or to contain potential excesses linked to emotional involvement in the processions. Frederick III issued edicts to this effect, sometimes affecting the whole of the kingdom and sometimes applied to Palermo alone.[20] In 1322 the sovereign issued an edict regarding the city of Palermo.[21] Linking potential revolts and the homage paid to the deceased, he requested priests and monks to accompany the bier and to calm any rioting that might erupt.

In the aftermath of the death of Frederick III there is record of a protest with features that would recur. In 1339, corruption on the part of officials, and speculative ventures by distributors of wheat, and the institution of a *posada* (a tax levied to pay for the reception of the king and his retinue), amongst other things, sparked an insurrection. Illuminato Peri has revealed the widespread discontent occasioned by rampant speculation relating to the sale of wheat.[22] The house of Roberto de Pando was in fact ransacked on account of his prominent role in the grain trade,

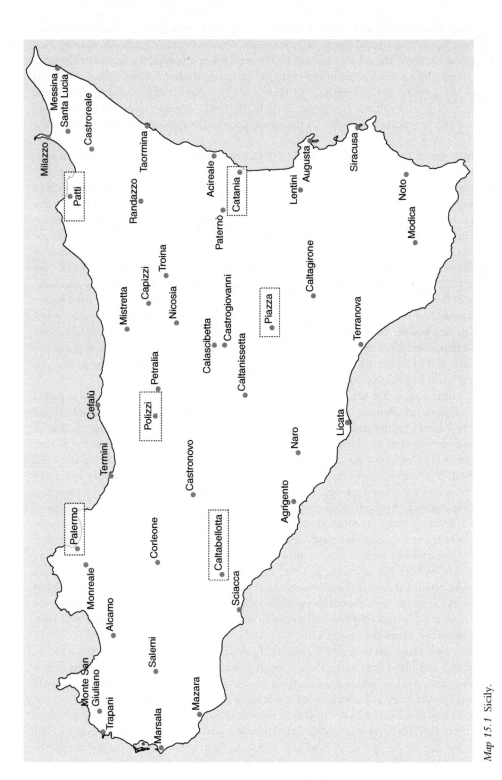

Map 15.1 Sicily.

Note
The communities enclosed in a rectangle are the ones discussed in the text.

his holding of local offices, and his part in setting indirect local taxes (*gabelle*). The first phase saw the *populus* assembling around the royal banner used when approaching officials, thereby intimating their loyalty to the royal house and by the same token affirming the legitimist character of the protest. In a second phase lower-group people (*plebs videlicet homines infimae conditionis*) shut the city gates on the sovereign. That there were two distinct reactions suggests that the universe of those in revolt was composite. Peter II (1337–42), despite having firmly suppressed the revolt and imprisoned some 200 of the rebels, granted the *universitas* exemption from the *posada*.

In my opinion, Frederick III's death in 1337 had caused grave disquiet and alarm that relations between the king and country would alter. His accession in 1296, in defiance of the policy favouring the Angevins espoused by his brother, James II, king of Aragon, had done much to foster expectations in the kingdom of Sicily of a royal policy of coordination between the various political subjects, and those expectations had generally been met. Although the information relating to the events of 1339 is fragmentary, it shows how the loss of a key figure might throw the governmental context into crisis. But it also demonstrates that the same phenomenon of rebellion could feature contrasting responses on the part of different protagonists. In 1339, the harsh reaction to Roberto de Pando was not directed against the royal house. To my mind, the shutting of the city gates against the king should not be considered as an act against royal power (*potestas regia*). Nor is it probable that it was an act for which the *plebs* (a highly derogatory term) was solely responsible. More plausibly, it represented a political signal to Peter II, involving several different sectors of the community and designed to persuade him to implement a policy in line with that of his predecessor. The exemption from the economic tribute (the *posada*) was a political signal in this same sense.

Let us turn now to the second half of the fourteenth century, when royal power passed through a phase of dramatic weakness and that of the seigneurial dynasties loomed ever larger. As I noted, at the death of Frederick IV members of the most eminent families in Sicily seized control of the kingdom as Vicars. Valuable information regarding the Vicars' government (1377–92) is contained in the petitions presented to Martin I during the royal restoration. In communities under royal control, the captain, an official ordinarily appointed by the king, and the court over which he presided, were responsible for criminal jurisdiction of the first instance. Analysis of the petitions presented in the kingdom during the reign of Martin I reveals a deep preoccupation with curtailing the captain's prerogatives, so as to check his overweening encroachments upon the civil court or upon other elected officials.[23] A further reduction of local autonomy under the *Vicarii* is particularly evident in the sphere of economic policy. For instance, in 1398, the *universitas* of Alcamo requested that levies imposed by tyrannical barons (*baruni tiranni*) be abolished, and, more specifically, that it be at liberty to decide what sums should be raised by local levies.[24] The 'tyrannical' violence of the barons served as a pretext for the bid to obtain a reinstatement of the corpus of privileges curbed when the *Vicarii* held sway.[25]

In the aftermath of the Vicars' rule, tyrannical government in Sicily was identified with the feudal lords. The island thus witnessed a political scenario resembling to some degree that of fifteenth-century Galicia, where the imperious demeanour of the feudal lords, combined with weak royal power, triggered a widespread revolt known as the *revuelta irmandiña* (1467–9), directed against seigneurial violence.[26] In Galicia the protagonists of the revolt identified the abuse they suffered with the lords who controlled extensive tracts of territory from their castles. The victory over the lords – not short lived and with long-term consequences on account of the number of fortresses destroyed – was symbolically evoked by the protagonists (according to a witness) in terms of a role reversal: the sparrows, that is, the vassals, harried the hawks, that is, the lords (*los gorriones abían de correr tras los falcones*).[27] Although there are important differences with Sicily, it is worth noting that in Galicia the king backed the revolt. In Sicily the repression of baronial power by Martin I likewise proceeded in tandem with support for the royal restoration from the communities suffering under feudal control. The traumatic years 1377–92 led the *universitates* to emphasise the boundaries of power between king and *universitates*: they maintained that the role of captain should be clearly counterbalanced by that of the elected officials, and that the general system of taxation should reflect negotiations with the king and internal debates. These features would characterise relations between rulers and ruled and cases of protest in subsequent years.

The reabsorption of Sicily into the Crown of Aragon at the death of Martin, king of Sicily, and the island's gradual shift from kingdom to vice-kingdom, through a process that began with the election of Ferdinand I in 1412, did not curtail its liberties. Systems of rights and privileges in urban milieux were indeed further enhanced during the reign of Alfonso V. This political context presented a number of specific features, namely, a marked extension of the spaces of local autonomy regarding taxation, albeit with significant growth in royal economic demands. Regarding the reduction of royal control, I will simply note the town councils' increasing involvement in deciding what form taxation should take. Allowing the communities to decide on the system of taxation led to socio-professional groups endeavouring to obtain a more formalised organisation, thereby ensuring that they had their own representatives in public life. In what appears to be a cascade effect, such a reinforcement of the internal organisation was reflected not only in the emergence of identifiable representatives in the public sphere but also in the actual management of the workplace activities of the socio-professional groups.

This process is particularly evident in Catania, a community for which significant revolts are not recorded in the late Middle Ages, although a culture of conflict had nonetheless tended to prevail.[28] As already mentioned, Patrick Lantschner has proposed a correlation between the absence of major revolts and the lack of 'pluralism of existing political structures – such as guilds, ecclesiastical bodies or other political organisations', which when present provided rebels with the ideological and financial resources to mount a revolt.[29] Verona's lack of artisan guilds with an independent role, and likewise of parties, would account for the absence of conflicts there, in contrast with Florence or Tournai.[30] In my opinion, the opposite interpretation is equally valid. The existence of a pluralism of political structures may also explain the absence of revolts, by offering an alternative – channelling dissent and organising forms of negotiation through institutional channels – to the outbreak of violent conflict. In advanced political contexts, reactions in the guise of disciplined dissent reveal the capacity of groups, who had been subjected to a policy of exclusion, to develop negotiating skills and to deploy the rhetoric of the elite on behalf of the common good, defusing these exclusionary policies and advancing themselves as guarantors of the community's peace.

Catania was a city with artisan guilds wielding sufficient influence to be emulated by nearby centres such as Randazzo in 1466,[31] but also a place beset by tensions between distinct parties, even if in the late Middle Ages no violent revolts are recorded there. In 1435 the Catanian artisans (*ministrali et artisti*) drafted a text of regulations relating to the organisation of the guilds and to their political representation, the first rules they had ever devised, as they themselves noted. The principal request concerned the right of each guild to meet every year to elect two consuls and two councillors; the consuls would then take part in the general council.[32] In addition they drafted a series of regulations relating to the supervision of their labour as artisans, and specified the legal prerogatives of the consuls so far as any abuses committed by artisans were concerned, paying particular attention to possible abuses to the detriment of labourers dependent upon the artisans. At the same time they emphasised their devotion to Saint Agatha – whose cult was reinvigorated in Catania during the twelfth century – and whom they called *madonna sancta Agata*. Every artisan was expected to take part in the ritual celebrations in honour of Saint Agatha.[33] In other words, their call for a measure of representation within the government was reinforced by a religious sentiment with deep roots in the community. Alfonso V accepted the requests, and with them in mind allowed the election of the consuls and councillors to proceed.[34]

In 1444 the artisans obtained from the King formal recognition of their control over the elective office responsible for overseeing the night watch: only artisans and citizens of Catania – who had rendered 'great usefulness to the state' (*grandi utilitate a la repuplica*) – would be elected to this office.[35] A prosopographic study of those elected confirms that the artisans did control the office.[36] In 1444 the artisans (and later also the *gentilhomini*), in evoking the spaces of autonomy of the *res publica*, affirmed the disciplined character of their government to be to the benefit of the community.[37] This foreshadowed an aspect of political confrontation that would become more apparent in subsequent years. It is not a coincidence that this process – the identification of who had the right and the authority to govern – unfolded during the phase of maximal expansion of urban autonomy and internal confrontations.

In April 1446, the Catanian *gentilhomini*, a citizen elite consisting of wealthy landowners and merchants, launched a fierce political assault, the aim of which was to exclude the artisans from government.[38] They presented a text containing petitions, the most significant feature of which concerned the fact that the artisans' representatives claimed as many votes as there were consuls in the council. But this, it was objected, would have served to marginalise the *gentilhomini*, who were numerically in the minority. They asked for the consular offices in the council to be abolished or for their power to be drastically curbed, leaving them no more than one or two votes (*voces*).[39] The Viceroy Lope Ximen de Urrea decreed that the consuls could voice two votes.[40] On 31 October 1446, a further denunciation of the consuls was issued, in this case presented to Alfonso V: they were said to be guilty of abusing their powers and of non-compliance with the privileges that they had obtained. The denunciation reiterated the call for the guilds to be abolished, but to no avail. Alfonso V did however stipulate that there should be two consuls for all the guilds on the general council.[41] The goal of the *gentilhomini* was the definitive exclusion of the artisans from the council, and with this in mind they asked the sovereign to 'destroy and annihilate' the consuls and their prerogatives (*distrugiri et anichilari li consuli predicti et loru potestati*).[42] The most radical claim in the primary source recording the protest against the artisans was that by favouring their interests and not the community and by resorting to factional policies in the guise of illicit assemblies (*usandu multi conventiculi et congregacioni*) that threatened the community's peace, they were endeavouring to control the city government.

Employing a very pointed phrase – designed to drive a wedge between the king and the artisans and between the artisans and the rest of the community – this same source declared that the artisans were jeopardising the well-being of the republic of the city of Catania (*beneficiu di la repuplica di la dicta chitati di Catania*).[43] The good of the *repuplica* was identified with respect for royal privileges, social peace, devotion to Saint Agatha, and with representing all of the community in the government.[44] The *gentilhomini* were deeply fearful of any consolidation of the artisans' group consciousness and of the influence that they might come to wield. The influence so feared by the *gentilhomini* would clearly be realised years later, in 1450, with the involvement of the *populares* alongside the artisans of Catania in negotiations with the royal court.[45] This development echoes that found in other contexts, for example, in Flanders, where the guilds gave a voice to groups ordinarily excluded from government.[46]

The response of the *ministrali et artisti*, appellations that probably indicated distinctions within the world of the artisans,[47] was both immediate and fierce. We are concerned here with an expression of disciplined dissent that reveals a capacity to utilise (while also modifying) the same ideological and institutional instruments as the elite – namely, the defence of the common good, participation in the council, negotiations with the court – in an attempt to counter the process of exclusion. The choice to eschew violent protest reflects a measure of political realism. The influence of the *gentilhomini* at the royal court, and the accusation levelled at the artisans that they were promoting factional policies, could be countered both with the claim that they were citizens concerned with the common good and by promoting a policy of negotiation with the royal court. Once again, on 31 October 1446, the artisans in fact appealed directly to the sovereign with the request that they be permitted to intervene in the general council not with two consuls for *all* the guilds, but with two consuls for *each* guild. Alfonso V therefore confirmed the right of intervention of two consuls for all the guilds.[48] This was a decision that was not contested by the artisans, who maintained some representation (albeit a numerically limited one), and, as I shall shortly indicate, obtained a significant recognition of their right to assemble, even independently of the general council. The more important city officials bitterly contested the artisans' right of representation, even when it was a question of a general council, an assembly in which the artisans were entitled to take part. It was therefore necessary to specify in the negotiations with the king that the general council, in contrast to the ordinary council, met to make decisions as regards taxation and in general extraordinary measures concerning both individual cases and the community as a whole (*causi extraordinari comu esti tractari novi imposicioni et ultri simuli ... quando occurranu negoci exordinarii li quali toccanu comodu et in comodo singulari et universali*).[49]

The confrontation hinged upon the right to representation with a view to deciding economic policy, the system of taxation, and the supervision of accounts. In general the common good (which the artisans only referred to indirectly) was at issue, as two facts confirm. First, there was a denunciation of the inappropriate running of the hospital, which had involved unsatisfactory management of the rents, with the poor suffering dire neglect.[50] This denunciation linked the artisan guilds and *caritas*, for if the founding of a hospital was principally an act of charity,[51] the running of a hospital was also an act of charity. It also repudiated the factional interests of which they had been accused. While the *gentilhomini* counted upon the exclusion of one party, the artisans responded by promoting a policy favouring the common good. The second fact concerns their evident piety, manifested in the construction of a crucifix worth the impressive value of 100 *onze* and the building of two organs in honour of the *madonna sancta Agata*.[52] Proposals of an eminently practical nature and the assertion of the right to assemble served to refute the accusation that they did so in order to foment disorder (*munapoliu*): they assembled in support of the royal cause and for the public good of the city.[53] The sovereign's concession of the right of the consuls to assemble without any restriction upon the discussion of legitimate and honest concerns (*ad tractandum licitam at honestam*)[54] was an unequivocal recognition of their political role. The negotiating skills of the artisans and their economic importance to the royal court guaranteed them a role in government. In the following years, the *gentilhomini* seemed to prevail politically, although in 1460 political recognition was restored to the guilds' consuls.[55]

Yet more light can be shed on the practice of disciplined dissent by considering other communities. Alfonso V's economic policy promoted local autonomy, with a greater involvement of the city council in taxation. However, the royal court's growing financial requirements, reflected in the sale of offices (that of the captain) or even the sale of entire communities, also represented a potential threat to autonomy. The captaincy, which the king frequently granted for a longer period than one year (the standard term of office), is an excellent example. The interests at stake in that office increased because the captain risked losing his impartial role and becoming the mouthpiece of a particular faction. In 1431, a protest was mounted by the main elected officials, the *Iurati* and the *universitas* of Patti, a community in North-eastern Sicily.[56] The king referred to this protest as a 'clamour made to us' about the management of the office by the captain, who had caused such grave offence that the *Iurati* (among the main elected officials) could no longer remain silent.[57] The mismanagement in question was linked to the royal concession to Manuele Giuxeres of the captaincy for the years 1425–6, 1427–8, 1429–30 and 1431–2 (however following the protests he was stripped of the captaincy at the beginning of his mandate for the year 1431–2).[58] The denunciation regarded acts of violence perpetrated by the captain and others of his entourage (*convichinii*). In the community's perception the threat Giuxeres posed was very far-reaching and reveals a deep fear, probably stemming from the feudal control of the cities in the fourteenth century under the Vicars. In short, there was an apprehension that Giuxeres would impose himself as lord of the community.

The community thus protested through institutional channels against an exercise of power which had institutionalised abuse and violence. It did so for three reasons. First, the king himself had appointed the official. A physical assault against Giuxeres would therefore have been interpreted as an attack against the royal will. Second, it helped to ensure that there was negotiation with the king. Third, those who had issued the denunciation were thereby able to differentiate themselves from the violent politics of the captain and his entourage. The insurrection against the captain in the guise of negotiation with the royal court had a positive outcome: Alfonso authorised the Viceroy to depose the captain, to investigate the case, and to pursue justice.[59]

The modalities of dissent voiced in response to royal officials' abuse of power could vary. They might, for example, follow a reduction in economic and political benefits in a general phase of political growth that had raised the expectations of profiting from that growth. This is what transpired in the community of Piazza in the mid-fifteenth century, where numerous socio-professional groups, who had seen their right of representation in the government of the city denied, issued a denunciation against the captains.[60] As at Patti, so too in the *universitas* of Piazza, the sale of the captaincy led to the proliferation of forms of patronage, often an exercise of partial power. This was the case with Ruggero Crapanzano and Bartolomeo Amuri, captains in Piazza from the year 1444–5 to May 1448. A network of relatives and friends (*parenti et amici et affini*) was headed by the two captains who had purchased the office.[61] This patronage network of people linked by dependence and reciprocity controlled the main elected offices and made it impossible for the town council to function. A government that was clientelist in nature and that trampled upon the rights of the town council had a cohesive effect on the protest of different socio-political groups, who chose not to act in a violent fashion, thereby emphasising their civic conscience in contrast to those who were denouncing them. They proposed and obtained from the king the right to summon the council on their own initiative when the officials acted without summoning the council.[62]

In fact, normative changes went further than this demand. The text of the petitions presented to the king, all accepted by him, actually ranged widely. One of the most significant points, concerning those appointed to the captaincy, granted that any royal measures not in conformity with the petitions should be declared null and void.[63] Alfonso V's decision to accept the petitions served to endorse three facts, namely, the economic and political roles played by the majority of those in the community of Piazza, the importance of negotiation in the political relationship between king and community, and the existence of a royal politics prepared to stint on its own spaces of intervention and thus to avoid the consolidation of an invasive state.

The significant political readiness of Alfonso V to countenance spaces of urban autonomy did not exclude the possibility of sporadic royal interventions of an opposite nature, as the petition mounted by Piazza (among others) indicates. I have in mind here in particular those cases in which Alfonso V decided upon the temporary sale of a community.[64] This was, however, a policy that ensured significant compensation for the communities in question, since they obtained important privileges favouring the autonomy of the community and to the detriment of the feudal lords, once their redemption had been effected. In reality it was the feudal protagonists whose expectations and room for manoeuvre were most drastically curtailed under Alfonso's reign. Hence the revolt in 1421 against Alfonso's attempt to raise a *colletta* (hearth tax) to promote his war on Naples. This resistance was led by a woman, the Countess of Caltabellotta, whose action was supported by towns both of the demesne and under feudal lordship.[65] This was, however, an isolated instance of open defiance of the king. In subsequent years Piazza, like the demesne communities that had made reference to a right of resistance,[66] did not oppose the *potestas regia*, articulating their opposition through negotiations with the king himself.

Revolts and processes of emulation

Of course, not every protest unfolded in this manner. There was, for example, a major tumult recorded at Palermo in 1450, where the most remarkable feature was the active role played by the *populus*. As I have shown elsewhere, the term *populus* had a polysemic value, and in Palermo itself the group included, possibly along with others, building-site workers and retail traders in the markets.[67] One of the causes of the rioting was the capture in 1448 of the office of *Acatapanus* (a magistracy responsible for overseeing the city markets) by those merchants and wealthy landowners who defined themselves as notable citizens and of great authority and opulence (*notabili chitatini gravi et de grandi auctoritate et opulenti*).[68] Prior to this intervention, political access to the government had had a markedly inclusive character. These 'notable citizens' obtained the exclusion of artisans and petty merchants from the magistracy, identifying them as low and common men lacking in adequate knowledge of the regulations (*homini comuni et ignoranti*). Further signs of a policy designed to exclude members of certain socio-professional groups from government appeared a few months later when the officials of 1448–9 decided to buy a significant quantity of grain without the approval of the town council.[69] Ordinarily, the town council made such decisions, so this development jeopardised the right of those who were less wealthy and who had no representation among the officials. The officials' decision the following year to proceed with a second purchase, this time with the involvement of the city council, proved highly unpopular. The purchase and the related taxation occurred when the existing stockpiles had not yet been sold, and – to make matters worse – it was evident that much of the grain from the previous purchase had been damaged but was, nevertheless, to be distributed in the city.[70] The perception in various sectors of society was of a persisting abuse, first with a purchase of grain through the sole intervention of officers incapable of managing it properly, and so much so that they ended up ruining it, and then with a second purchase resulting in further economic damage for the community. This occurred when Palermo was suffering a phase of economic depression.[71]

In April 1450, a revolt of the *populus* erupted, when they vented their rage upon the officials' houses, which were symbols of a power deemed to be corrupt and indifferent to their needs. They destroyed the wheat, along with other foodstuffs seized from the houses of the merchants who were guarding them. In other words, their rage was directed at those regarded as speculators. During this uprising, it should be stressed, the *populus* invoked the name of the king and displayed the royal emblems.[72] By evoking the king, a highly symbolic act, they bore witness to their right to protest against the perpetration of injustices. Even in so dramatic a context it is possible to discern a search for normalisation and a concern to keep channels of negotiation open: at his second attempt the Viceroy Lope Ximen de Urrea was allowed to enter the city.[73]

If violence did characterise the very first phase of the revolt, immediately afterwards the *populares* engaged in peaceful negotiations. They presented a number of petitions to the Viceroy, including a trenchant denunciation of the *Acatapani*, in marked contrast to what had transpired in 1448. The decision to begin by opposing the Viceroy (who had implemented the petitions of 1448 and had intervened in relation to the distribution of the spoiled grain) was therefore reversed immediately afterwards with the formulation of petitions of a wholly legitimist nature. The Viceroy managed very skilfully to distance himself from the request to accept the petitions: because no procedural shortcoming could be attributed to the formulation of the petitions, they had to be voted upon by the appropriate institution, namely, the town council.[74]

At the subsequent council sessions, the *populares* in fact put the petitions to the vote, while at the same time sending a delegation to the sovereign in order to submit the petitions which they had already presented to the Viceroy.[75] The *populares* thus succeeded in passing from a state of insurrection to abiding by the law, and urged the town council to vote on a series of requests. The precise wording of the *populares*' petitions is known to us only indirectly through the subsequent debates. The requests under scrutiny are: (on 29 April) the erection of defensive works against the Venetians and the question of who would be taxed to pay for them; the ban on the sale in public places of milk and of tuna fish that had gone off; the scrapping of the special privileges of the *Acatapani*;[76] (on 6 May) the question of who could bear weapons; relations with the Jews.[77] The most important petition, regarding the abolition of unspecified privileges enjoyed by the *Acatapani*, reveals the distance between the *populus* and these officials; the distance, in other words between these latter and those who no longer felt themselves to be represented by the *notabili chitatini* (notable citizens). When it was put to the vote, a large majority of the councillors spoke in favour of the first two requests; where the *Acatapani* were concerned, it was generally agreed that the point should be referred to the king. As for the session of 6 May, the petition of the *populares* calling for everyone to have the right to bear arms is clear, while what exactly they proposed in relation to the Jews is less certain. These latter had complained about abuses on the part of the *populus*, which had, I would stress, occurred close to Holy Week, when elements of the Jewish community had left the city.[78] The petition may therefore have called for confirmation of their removal. The majority voted against bearing arms and voted in favour of the return of the Jews, yet the political pre-eminence of the *populares*, which would soon be eclipsed, made it possible for the vote on the bearing of arms to be annulled. Given that the *populares* turned out not to be at all opposed to the vote in favour of a return of the Jews it seems plausible to posit a readiness on their part to accept an outcome favouring the Jews.

In those days the council reflected the rift within the body of citizens, there being a conflict between a *popularis* majority and those ranged against them, a delicate balance in which it is not really possible to speak of the isolation of the *populares* but rather of a tendency towards isolation.[79] These were the last phases in which the *populus* had a prominent role; the delegation sent to King Alfonso was arrested[80] and the subsequent phase of repression was to the detriment of the *populares*.[81] Afterwards, the sovereign decided upon a punishment for the insult or tumult (*insultum seu tumultum*) consisting of a monetary settlement of 10,000 *ducati*.[82] In order to see to the payment, the town council, being responsible for the financial negotiations, then met.[83]

It is worth highlighting the fact that the royal court salvaged a portion of the *populares*' requests. In other words, it opted not to oppose a mode of political representation that could safeguard its own interests. Thus, as early as July 1451, a council called to vote the purchase of stockpiles of grain, included councillors who had been present at the session in April, among them Henrico lu Munti and Antonio de Aprili,[84] who had been persecuted not long before.[85] Furthermore, in the aftermath of the rioting, the royal concessions of the magistracy of *Acatapanus* (elective offices could sometimes be decided by the sovereign), which were carried out along the lines indicated by local protagonists in contact with the royal court (*familiares et domestici*), no longer involved *notabili chitatini*, or at any rate not in the majority of cases.[86] The intercession of these *familiares et domestici* on behalf of representatives close to the world of those who had been in open revolt demonstrates that the opposed groupings did not reflect clear-cut differences between social classes; there were also convergent interests between people from different milieux. In fact the tumult of 1450 led to the office of *Acatapanus* being open to all once again, while the town council for its part once again became of central importance to economic policy, with those purportedly involved in the insurrection liable to inclusion rather than ostracism.

The protest likewise resulted in the capacity of the *populares* of Palermo to forge an alliance with the artisans with a view to them both claiming a right of representation. There are some analogies between the political conflict at Palermo and a contemporary but longer-lasting clash at Barcelona between the urban patriciate, composed of big capitalists and the wealthier merchants, joined together in the *Biga* party, and merchants, artisans, and even lowly artisans without any experience of government, identified with the *Busca* party, which was strongly backed by the common people. Where the *Busca* party was concerned, however, the leadership of the movement and the elaboration of a programme were from the outset in the hands of merchants and artisans, and it was certainly of more political weight than that of the Palermitan *populares*. The most telling analogy between Palermo and Barcelona lies in the fact that the *Busca* party too had decided to confront the patriciate over an unbalanced representation in government that was overwhelmingly to the advantage of the urban patriciate.[87]

The world of the *universitates* was a highly integrated one. There was, for example, a great deal of communication and sharing of experiences, sometimes in a spirit of emulation, regarding the systems of privileges of the metropolitan centres.[88] The emulation in question did not concern only the systems of privileges but also the forms of insurrection, as events recorded in the noteworthy case of the community of Polizzi, in the aftermath of the tumult in Palermo, serve to confirm. In June 1451, the Viceroy Lope Ximen de Urrea gave the *legum doctor* (law expert), Giovanni Aprea, full powers to investigate a violent protest intended to annihilate the Denti family in Polizzi. The accusations lodged by Andrea Denti and his father Francesco were against the priest (*presbiter*), Gandolfo de Aurifice; one of the principal elected officials (*iuratus*), Berengario Aiuto, in office at that date and as far back as 1444–5; the captain, Giovanni Amato, as well as other residents.[89] They had apparently stirred up the *populus*, declared that they sought an uprising such as occurred in Palermo, and incited the 'people' (*plebem*) to kill the Denti family and to seize the indirect taxes (*gabelle*) in their possession. In addition, they allegedly tried to exhume and burn the mortal remains of Francesco Denti's father.[90] These diverse actions taken with a view to overturning the power of the Dentis may be ascribed to people from distinct social segments, both elite and otherwise.

The rift between the Denti family and numerous segments of the community resulted from tensions arising from the family's significant control of Polizzi's resources and from abuses of power respecting the *gabelle* that they controlled. These tensions worsened following the intervention by the *Magna Regia Curia* (the highest court in the kingdom). Two court orders established compensation for the expenses sustained by Francesco and Andrea Denti as members of Polizzi's diplomatic corps in October 1442, during the time that the city was recovering its right to be part of the royal jurisdiction (*demanio*) rather than continue to be in the possession of Raimondo Cabrera,[91] who had acquired the city from the king, Alfonso V.

The *Magna Regia Curia* specifically stipulated that the *universitas* had to pay a surtax (*maldenaru*) on an unspecified *gabelle*.[92] Recourse to surtaxes was generally undertaken with great reluctance, and the *Magna Regia Curia*'s intervention reveals that it was a strain to persuade the *universitas* to pay out what was owed. It would not be until November 1448 that the final ruling was issued.[93] This period was one of hardship for the Polizzi community, particularly due to wheat shortages that strongly affected the poor (*poviri et miserabili*).[94] The seriousness of the rift between the Denti family and the rest of the community emerged in March 1451 when the Denti once again requested not only their due but also compensation for wheat that the community had seized from them.[95]

Probably because of the Aprea investigation, the king intervened in October 1454 against the two Dentis, who were guilty of having collected more than the allotted amount on the taxes granted to them. The *gabelle* had produced more than the 45 onze due to them per year, and they had appropriated the surplus from the first year (1448). Alfonso V therefore decreed that they should return their ill-gotten gains.[96] The enquiry therefore had an entirely unanticipated outcome, since members of the Denti family, having originally been plaintiffs, were now found guilty of a crime. The deeply violent reaction against the Denti family had, in my opinion, two precipitating causes. The first is the link between the abuses perpetrated by the Dentis, a concentration of power in their favour, and the oppression that the community of Polizzi had probably suffered under the rule of Raimondo Cabrera. The second cause has to do with emulation of the rioting recorded in a metropolitan centre like Palermo. The significant privileges from which the Dentis benefited and the relationships of the Dentis with the royal court from as early as the reign of Martin I[97] had gradually exacerbated the conflicts with those who had seen their own roles diminished. In other words, although the prestige and authority of the Dentis did not constitute an urban *signoria*, it did resemble one in certain respects: if the revolt in Polizzi was in emulation of the one in Palermo, the rule of the Dentis was by the same token in emulation of that of Cabrera. The community's liberation from the power of Raimondo Cabrera was a factor in the gradual consolidation of a refusal of the Dentis' authority, and the decision to bring them down, thus avenging itself upon both the Dentis and Cabrera.[98] The Dentis' role was thus dramatically scaled down: they turned out not to have been elected again to the government for almost 15 years.[99]

Conclusion

Protests could vary in the forms they took and in their outcomes. In the cases reviewed above it was mainly political representation, but also access to economic resources, that was at stake, and royal involvement might assume markedly different forms. In the phase of most serious crisis for local liberties – when Sicily was under the control of the four main feudal families – it is possible to trace the genesis of forms of defence of the autonomy of the *universitas*. Repression triggered resistance, which, however, became visible only after the government of the *Vicarii*. The case of Polizzi, for example, represents a very violent reaction against the Dentis and indirectly against Cabrera, which the community had not been able to oppose militarily during its period of domination. In Patti and in Piazza the sale of the office of captain represented a breach with the usual mechanisms of rotation of those appointed to offices, and was reminiscent of the role of captain under the government of the Vicars, when it impinged upon the other officers' prerogatives.

Paradoxically, most of the forms of dissent arose during a phase in which rights and liberties underwent considerable expansion. During the reign of Alfonso V the significant growth in local liberties (allowing, among other things, the communities to decide upon forms of taxation) caused tensions between the various groups. The temporary curtailment of freedom, in the main the consequence of conflicts between opposed groups – with regard to a reduction in the role of the city council, in abusive forms of power wielded by officers, and in policies of exclusion working to the detriment of specific groups – coincided with unprecedentedly high expectations and led to political reactions. Protesters aimed for achievable changes, alongside a search for consensus and for alliances, as in the case of the *populares* in Palermo and of the *magistri* in

Catania. The king did not pursue radical repression; a realistic strategy, one which turned out to be successful, prevailed in the confrontation.

Finally, the analysis of forms of disciplined dissent has made it possible to bring out the importance of protests of a conservative and inclusive nature. The cases discussed show how violent protests could cause a modification in the political balances, just as the rebels requested, but it is also true that protests involving forms of disciplined dissent could have a political impact. We are concerned here with a strategy regarded as the most appropriate for maintaining and/or expanding a role in government when challenged by the opposing alignment,[100] a scenario that was more readily achieved where there was a peaceful relationship with the sovereign. The artisans of Catania, like the numerous socio-professional groups in Patti and in Piazza, succeeded in avoiding forms of persecution on the part of the royal court, and in promoting an inclusive policy benefiting the community at large. They were the interpreters of the calm and peaceful state that Martin I and Alfonso V had asked for.

Notes

1 The present study is part of a research project funded by Universidad del País Vasco (EHUA/1301), Gobierno Vasco (IT 600–13; MV_2014_1_19), and Ministerio de Economía y Competitividad de España (HAR2013-44088-P). I would like to thank Martin Thom for the text's translation and Justine Firnhaber-Baker and Dirk Schoenaers for a further revision.

    The following abbreviations are used: ACP: Archivio Comunale of Palermo, *Atti del Senato*. CC: Archivio Comunale of Palermo, *Consigli civici*. ACA: Archivo de la Corona de Aragón of Barcelona, Cancillería, Registros. PR: Archivio di Stato of Palermo, Protonotaro del Regno. RC: Archivio di Stato of Palermo, Real Cancelleria. GG: S. Giambruno and L. Genuardi, *Capitoli inediti delle città demaniali di Sicilia*, Palermo: Boccone del Povero, 1918. *Consuetudines*: *Consuetudines terre Platee*, Biblioteca Comunale di Piazza Armerina.

2 The Crown of Aragon included various different territories, among them, at any rate from 1282, Sicily. In 1295, James II, king of Aragon, fostered an agreement with the papacy that was to return Sicily to the Angevins. Frederick, in opposition to the policy of his brother, James II, was elected *rex Siciliae/rex Trinacriae* by the Parliament of Catania in 1296. Sicily thus obtained full autonomy from Barcelona. The king's son, Peter, was associated with the throne from 1321–37, and having succeeded his father would rule until 1342. From the 1350s, royal authority was significantly weakened, especially during the reigns of Louis (1342–55) and of Frederick IV (1355–77). The Vicars were in control of the island from 1377–92. Martin I, king of Sicily from 1392 to 1409, put an end to the government of the Vicars. In 1409, Sicily lost its autonomy from Barcelona: the Sicilian throne passed to Martin of Aragon. Martin of Aragon died in 1410, and in 1412 Ferdinand I of the Castilian house of Trastámara was elected as king of Aragon, and Sicily was confirmed as an integral part of the Crown of Aragon. The election of Ferdinand resulted in a gradual institutional transformation of Sicily from kingdom to vice-kingdom. Ferdinand was succeeded by Alfonso V (1416–58).

3 Cf. the use of commons/community in England; J. Watts, 'Public or plebs: the changing meaning of "the commons", 1381–1549', in H. Pryce and J. Watts (eds), *Power and Identity in the Middle Ages*, Oxford: Oxford University Press, 2007, esp. pp. 243–54. The terms commons/community however take on different meanings over time, pp. 254–8.

4 From a methodological point of view, it is vital to take into account a gradual process on the basis of those factors that characterise a specific phase. N. Zemon Davis recently compared various positions in the historiographical debate over periodisation, in 'Early modern as category of analysis', at the conference *Rethinking Early Modernity: Methodological and Critical Innovation Since the Ritual Turn*, Centre of Reformation and Renaissance Studies, University of Toronto, 26 June 2014.

5 The pactist political system has stimulated contrasting interpretations. For an interpretation according to which pactism limited royal power, see J. Vallet de Goytisolo, 'Valor jurídico de las leyes paccionadas en el principato de Cataluña', in *El pactismo en la historia de España*, Simposio del 24–26 aprile 1978, Madrid: Istituto de España, 1980, pp. 75–110; J. Sobrequés Callicó, *El pactisme a Catalunya: Una praxi política en la història del país*, Barcelona: Edicions 62, 1982. For a contrasting interpretation, according to which there was no limitation whatsoever of royal power, see A. Iglesia Ferreirós, *La*

creación del derecho: Una historia de la formación de un derecho estatal español, 2 vols, Madrid: Marcial Pons, 1996, vol. 2, pp. 67–130.

6 See S. R. Epstein, 'Governo centrale e comunità del demanio nel governo della Sicilia tardomedievale: le fonti capitolari', in *XIV Congresso di storia della Corona d'Aragona, Sassari-Alghero, 19–24 maggio 1990*, 5 vols, Sassari: Carlo Delfino, 1996, vol. 3, pp. 383–415. On the different medieval practices of negotiation see M. T. Ferrer i Mallol, J.-M. Moeglin, S. Péquignot, and M. Sánchez Martínez (eds), 'Negociar en la edad media: négocier au Moyen Âge', in *Actas del Coloquio celebrado en Barcelona 14–16 octubre 2004: Actes du Colloque tenu à Barcelona 14–16 October 2004*, Barcelona: Consejo Superior de Investigaciones Científicas, 2005.

7 With regard to demographic values in the late 1430s, according to Bresc and Epstein (both posit an average of four to five persons per hearth) Palermo had 3,000 hearths and Catania 1,500. For Epstein, Polizzi had 1,200 hearths (Bresc does not provide any data for Polizzi), Piazza 1,500 hearths (Bresc reckons 1,100), Patti 375 hearths (Bresc estimates 250). In my analysis I will refer also to Palermo in 1339 but for this phase no demographic data is available; the community must have had a large population given that in the late fourteenth century it had 11,225 hearths (Bresc) or even 22,014 (Epstein). See H. Bresc, *Un monde méditerranéen: Économie et société en Sicile 1300–1450*, 2 vols, Rome-Palermo: École Française de Rome: Rome, 1986, vol. 1, pp. 61–5; S. R. Epstein, *An Island for Itself: Economic Development and Social Change in Late Medieval Sicily*, Cambridge: Cambridge University Press, 1992, pp. 33–72.

8 I am the principal investigator for a research group on forms of disciplined dissent and am editing a volume dedicated to this topic, *Disciplined Dissent: Strategies of Non-Confrontational Protest in Europe from the Twelfth to the Early Sixteenth Century*, Rome: Viella, 2016. I refer the reader to the Introduction to this volume – F. Titone, 'Introduction. The concept of disciplined dissent and its deployment: a methodology', pp. 7–22 – for a more detailed analysis of this topic. In the course of developing the concept of disciplined dissent, the studies I have used include J. Watts, *The Making of Polities: Europe, 1300–1500*, Cambridge: Cambridge University Press, 2009. W. W. Blockmans, A. Holenstein, and J. Mathieu (eds) in collaboration with D. Schläppi, *Empowering Interactions: Political Cultures and the Emergence of the State in Europe 1300–1900*, Farnham and Burlington, VT: Ashgate, 2009. Also G. Alessi, 'Discipline: i nuovi orizzonti del disciplinamento sociale', *Storica*, 2, 1996, pp. 7–37. P. Prodi (ed.) in collaboration with C. Penuti, *Disciplina dell'anima, disciplina del corpo e disciplina della società tra medioevo ed età moderna*, Bologna: Il Mulino, 1994.

9 P. Lantschner, 'Voices of the people in a city without revolts: Lille in the later Middle Ages', in J. Dumolyn, J. Haemers, H. R. Oliva Herrer, and V. Challet (eds), *The Voices of the People in Late Medieval Europe: Communication and Popular Politics*, Turnhout: Brepols, 2014, p. 77; P. Lantschner, 'Revolts and political order of cities in the late Middle Ages', *P&P*, 225, 2014, esp. pp. 25–8.

10 S. K. Cohn, Jr., *Lust for Liberty: The Politics of Social Revolt in Medieval Europe, 1200–1425*, Cambridge, MA: Harvard University Press, 2006, pp. 228–42, esp. 236–42.

11 Epstein, *An Island*, pp. 355–7; F. Titone, *Governments of the* Universitates: *Urban Communities of Sicily in the Fourteenth and Fifteenth Centuries*, Turnhout: Brepols, 2009, pp. 131–47.

12 Compare C. Gauvard, *Violence et ordre public au Moyen Âge*, Paris: Picard, 2005, pp. 206–13, where it is argued that the protests promoted a role for a more centralised state.

13 For some examples see RC, vol. 22, fols 62v–3r, [1393] (Polizzi) a decree signed by the father of Martin I; PR, vol. 45, fol. 96, [1453], Nicosia. PR, vol. 49, fols 212v–13r, 1457 (Sciacca). As regards the role of the *universitates* in the kingdom, and their relations with royal authority, see, for Campania, the texts by G. Vitolo collected in *L'Italia delle altre città: Un'immagine del Mezzogiorno Medievale*, Naples: Liguori, 2014, pp. 45–147.

14 Bresc, *Un monde*, pp. 737–41.

15 Epstein, *An Island*, pp. 357–74.

16 F. Titone, 'Citizens and freedom in medieval Sicily', in A. Nef (ed.), *A Companion to Medieval Palermo: The History of a Mediterranean City from 600 to 1500*, Leiden: Brill, 2013, pp. 504–23. F. Titone, 'Presentation and practice of violence in late medieval Sicily in Piazza, Polizzi and Randazzo', in S. K. Cohn, Jr., S. and F. Ricciardelli (eds), *The Culture of Violence in Late Medieval and Early Modern Italy*, Florence: Le Lettere, 2012, pp. 145–66. F. Titone, 'Il tumulto popularis del 1450: conflitto politico e società urbana a Palermo', *Archivio Storico Italiano*, 163, 2005, pp. 43–86.

17 I. Peri, *La Sicilia dopo il Vespro: Uomini, città e campagne. 1282/1376*, Rome and Bari: Laterza, 1990. Titone, *Governments*, pp. 17–40. A. Baviera Albanese, 'Studio introduttivo', in L. Citarda (ed.), *Acta Curie Felicis Urbis Panormi*, vol. III, Palermo: Municipio di Palermo, 1984, pp. XV–LXVIII.

18 See n. 2, above.

19 M. De Vio (ed.), *Felicis et fidelissimae Urbis Panormitanae selecta aliquot privilegia*, Palermo: Dominicum Cortese, 1706, pp. 80–1.
20 The whole kingdom: Francesco M. Testa, *Capitula regni Siciliae*, 2 vols, Palermo: Angelus Felicella, 1741, vol. 1, pp. 89–95 (1308–9 or 1323–4). The same Palermitan city council promulgated in 1330 the decree issued for the kingdom as a whole, De Vio (ed.), *Felicis*, p. 107. For the decree relating solely to Palermo see Salvatore S. Marino, *Le reputatrici in Sicilia nell'età di mezzo e moderna. Ricerche storiche*, Palermo: Giannone e Lamantia Editori, 1886, p. 15.
21 Marino, *Le reputatrici*, p. 15.
22 Peri, *La Sicilia dopo il Vespro*, pp. 147–50. Regarding the aforementioned events there are references in the chronicle 'Anonymi chronicon siculum ab anno DCCCXX usque ad MCCCXXVIII … et ad annum usque MCCCXLIII', in R. Gregorio, *Bibliotheca scriptorum qui res in Sicilia gestas sub Aragonum imperio retulere*, vol. II, Palermo: ex Regio typographeo, 1791–2, p. 257. There is an edition of the chronicle edited by P. Colletta, *Storia, cultura e propaganda nel regno di Sicilia nella prima metà del XIV secolo: La cronica Sicilie*, Rome: Istituto Italiano Storico per il Medioevo, 2011, which expresses some doubts about the naming of the chronicle and the chronology employed by Gregorio, pp. 11, 26–8.
23 Requests to ensure that the captain had no role in civil jurisdiction: RC, vol. 33, fols 120v–5, 1399 (Trapani) and GG, p. 248, 1401 (Agrigento).
24 V. Di Giovanni (ed.), *Capitoli gabelle e privilegi della città di Alcamo*, Palermo: Società siciliana per la storia patria, 1876, pp. 44–5.
25 For example GG, p. 351, 1392, (Licata); p. 29, 1396–7, a case in which the reference is to another feudal protagonist (Calascibetta). Subsequently, in Malta, in 1453, the previous government of tyrannical barons was evoked, GG, p. 418. The community of Caltagirone is an exception, since it did not resent the rule of the *Vicarii* but indeed relished being a part of the royal jurisdiction, and asked if it might in future not be given to any feudal lord, GG, pp. 41–2, 1392.
26 See C. Barros, 'Revuelta de los irmandiños: los gorriones corren tras los halcones', in R. Villares (ed.), *Historia de Galicia*, Vigo: Faro de Vigo, 1991, pp. 441–60, the passage cited is at p. 450; C. Barros, *Mentalidad justiciera de los irmandiños, siglo XV*, Madrid: Siglo XXI, 1990, stresses the thirst for justice and the anti-seigneurial stance of those taking part in the revolt. For an overview of the debate on the Galician revolt see C. Devia, *La violencia en la Edad Media: La rebelión irmandiña*, Vigo: Academia del Hispanismo, 2009.
27 Barros, 'Revuelta de los irmandiños'.
28 There has been a growing interest in forms of dissent that do not necessarily involve violent protests, such as those seen in Catania. J. Dumolyn and J. Haemers, '"A bad chicken was brooding": subversive speech in late medieval Flanders', *P&P*, 214, 2012, pp. 45–86. Lantschner, 'Voices of the people', pp. 73–88.
29 Lantschner, 'Voices of the people', p. 77. Lantschner, 'Revolts and the political order', esp. pp. 25–8.
30 Lantschner, 'Revolts and the political order', p. 33.
31 V. La Mantia, *Consuetudini di Randazzo*, Palermo: Giannitrapani, 1903, p. 2.
32 GG, pp. 150–1, 154.
33 GG, pp. 151–3. On the cult of Saint Agatha see P. Oldfield, 'The medieval cult of St Agatha of Catania and the consolidation of Christian Sicily', *Journal of Ecclesiastical History*, 62, 2011, pp. 439–56.
34 GG, p. 154.
35 GG, p. 170, 173.
36 In very rare instances one of those elected to the office (which involved four officials) might not be an artisan but the others elected invariably were, F. Titone, *I magistrati cittadini: Gli ufficiali scrutinati in Sicilia da Martino V ad Alfonso V*, Caltanissetta-Roma: Sciascia, 2008, pp. 179–89.
37 GG, pp. 172–3. Cf. I. E. Mineo, 'La repubblica come categoria storica', *Storica*, 43/45, 2009, esp. pp. 146–8, 163–7, with reference to the communes.
38 In 1436 the *gentilhomini* cited in the city council debates (see the summaries by Matteo Gaudioso, *Atti dei Giurati di Catania*, Archivio Storico Comunale of Catania, vol. 4, 1435–1436–1437, fol. 15), turn out to have belonged to families of landowners of ancient origin (Ansalono, Castelli, Gioeni, Traversa), to knightly families (Rizzari), and to 'bourgeois' families of more recent date (Paternò); see Bresc, *Un monde*, p. 726.
39 GG, pp. 181–2.
40 Ibid., p. 182.

41 Ibid., pp. 184–5.
42 Ibid., p. 185.
43 Ibid. For a comparison of the use of the notions of *res publica* and of *utilitas publica* and of the possible variations in meaning and purpose, see V. Challet, 'Political topos or community principle? Res publica as a source of legitimacy in the French peasants' revolts of the late Middle Ages', in Blockmans *et al.* (eds), *Empowering Interactions*, pp. 205–18.
44 The notion of the good of the *repuplica* and its association (more or less explicit) with justice, according to medieval legal texts, was probably familiar to the Catanian rulers on account of the numerous *legum doctores* active in Catania who had trained in Bologna or at other universities. On the basis of my prosopographic study of the officials elected in 16 communities during the reigns of Martin I and Alfonso V, out of a total of 7,323 officials, in Catania there were 21 *legum doctores* elected to the city government 32 times (an election covered the indictional year of 1 September to 31 August) between 1412 and 1458. Titone, *I magistrati*, pp. 179–89.
45 GG, pp. 200–6.
46 J. Dumolyn, 'Guild politics and political guilds in fourteenth-century Flanders', in Dumolyn *et al.* (eds), *The Voices of the People*, esp. pp. 29–48.
47 Compare the case of Barcelona, C. Batlle Gallart, *La crisis social y económica de Barcelona a mediados del siglo XV*, 2 vols, Barcelona: Consejo Superior de Investigaciones Científicas, 1973, vol. 1, pp. 55, 98–9, 146.
48 GG, pp. 190–1.
49 Ibid., 191–2.
50 Ibid., p. 193. For an analysis of the common good considered from a number of different perspectives see *Il bene comune: Forme di governo e gerarchie sociali nel basso Medioevo*, Atti del XLVIII convegno storico internazionale Todi, 9–12 October 2001, Centro Italiano di studi sull'alto Medioevo: Spoleto, 2012.
51 A. Rigaudière, 'Donner pour le bien commun et contribuer pour les biens communs dans les villes du midi Français du XIIIe au XVe siècle', in E. Lecupre-Desjardin and A. L. Van Bruaene (eds), *De bono communi: The Discourse and Practice of the Common Good in the European City (13th–16th c.)*, Turnhout: Brepols, 2010, pp. 32–4, which among other things brings to light the variety of expressions used to render the term 'the common good', pp. 13–27.
52 GG, pp. 195–6.
53 Ibid., pp. 196–7.
54 Ibid., p. 197. The king merely requested that the artisans give the officers due notice of their intention to meet.
55 Testa, *Capitula*, vol. I, p. 367, 1451. See Epstein, *An Island*, p. 359, footnote 182.
56 ACA, vol. 2817, fol. 189r, 20 September 1431.
57 For a comparison between the different usages of clamour, murmur, and noise in petitions, see W. M. Ormrod, 'Murmur, clamor and noise: voicing complaint and remedy in petitions to the English crown, *c*.1300–*c*.1460', in W. M. Ormrod, G. Dodd, and A. Musson (eds), *Medieval Petitions: Grace and Grievance*, Woodbridge: York Medieval Press, 2009, pp. 135–55.
58 PR, vol. 24, fol. 248v; ibid., vol. 27, fol. 85v; ibid., vol. 30, fols 136v–7r; ibid., vol. 31, fol. 157v. Generally the captain remained in office for the indictional year that began on 1 September and ended on 30 August. So far as the year 1429–30 (which corresponds to the eighth indiction) is concerned, there turns out to have been two royal concessions of the office of captain, to Manuele Giuxeres and to Antonio Bavera respectively. For Giuxeres the royal privilege is dated from 9 June third indiction 1425, and the application by the Viceroy from the September of the eighth indiction is dated 12 July seventh indiction 1429 (the reader will note a discrepancy: the Viceroy, in evoking the royal privilege, indicated that it had been decreed on 6 May 1421); ibid., vol. 24, fol. 248v and ibid., vol. 30, fols 136v–7r. Where Antonio Bavera was concerned, the royal privilege is dated 16 March 1426 and the application of the privilege by the Viceroy from September of the eighth indiction is dated 8 May fourth indiction; ibid., vol. 27, fol. 86r. Although we cannot rule out the possibility of there being two captains at one and the same time, it seems to me more probable that the royal privilege in favour of Bavera lapsed on account of the existence of an earlier one in favour of Giuxeres.
59 ACA, vol. 2817, fol. 189r. Cf. certain communities in Castile and León in which the *pecheros* (peasants) presented themselves politically as defenders of the public good, in opposition to the elite of *caballeros* (knights) and without having recourse to violence in their denunciation of these latter, who had been accused of guaranteeing private interests, J. M. Monsalvo Antón, 'Ideario sociopolítico y valores estamentales de los pecheros abulenses y salmantinos (ss. XIII–XV)', *Hispania*, 238, 2011,

pp. 325–62. Monsalvo Antón stresses the elaboration of a political message systematically at odds with the elite.
60 *Consuetudines*, fols 82–94. The numbering of the folios of the manuscript *Consuetudines* used here refers to what is indicated in the manuscript, which doesn't differentiate between *recto* and *verso*. I used a distinction between *recto* and *verso* with respect to the folios cited in F. Titone, 'Le "Consuetudines terre Plateæ": un esempio di cultura dello scritto', in I. Lazzarini (ed.), 'Scrittura e potere: pratiche documentarie e forme di governo nell'Italia tardomedievale, Reti Medievali-Rivista', IX, 2008, pp. 1–18.
61 As regards the links between opposing groups and governmental activities, compare G. Vitolo, *L'Italia delle altre città*, pp. 107–47.
62 *Consuetudines*, fols 91–4. For a comparison see A. Zorzi (ed.), *Conflitti, pace e vendette nell'Italia comunale*, Florence: Florence University Press, 2009, about conflicts and the competition for power in the Communes.
63 *Consuetudines*, fols 90–1.
64 Titone, *Governments*, pp. 162–8.
65 Epstein, *An island*, p. 380.
66 Titone, *Governments*, pp. 123–6. F. Titone, 'Sistema normativo e partecipazione politica: i *Libri* delle comunità siciliane nel tardo Medioevo', in F. Foronda and J.-P. Genet (eds), *Des chartes aux constitutions: Autour de l'idèe constitutionnelle en Europe (XIIe–XIIIe). De los fueros a las constituciones. En torno a la idea constitucional en Europa (siglos XII–XVII)*, Paris: Publications de la Sorbonne, forthcoming.
67 Titone, 'Il tumulto', p. 78. The different meanings of *populus* depend on context, as is the case with a variety of recurring terms such as *plebs* or *popolo minuto*, etc. which have been examined in other contexts. See e.g. C. Gauvard, 'Le petit peuple au Moyen Âge', in P. Boglioni, R. Delort, and C. Gauvard (eds), *Le petit peuple dans l'Occident médiéval: Terminologies, perceptions, réalités*, Paris: Publications de la Sorbonne, 2002, pp. 707–22 and Cohn, *Lust for Liberty*, pp. 9–13. The common people in the Cantabrian towns has recently been shown to consist of a heterogeneous set of urban groups, see J. R. Diaz de Durana, 'The political action of the common people in the towns of the Cantabrian coast at the end of the Middle Ages', in *Circulación y consumo de discursos políticos entre la gente común a fines de la Edad Media*, Seville, forthcoming.
68 Archivio Comunale di Palermo, Pergamena n. 37, 12 December 1448.
69 Titone, 'Il tumulto', pp. 65–6.
70 Ibid., pp. 66–8.
71 CC, vol. 61-1, fol. 17, 11 May 1449; CC, vol. 61-1, fols 96–7r, 1 February 1450. C. Trasselli, *Note per la storia dei banchi in Sicilia nel XV secolo: Parte II, I banchieri e i loro affari*, Palermo: Banco di Sicilia, 1968, pp. 215–17.
72 A chronicle of those events is in ACP, cassetta XXXIV, fols 100v–1.
73 Ibid., fols 100v–1r.
74 Ibid., fols 100v–1.
75 CC, vol. 61-1, fols 133–6r, 29 April 1450; fols 137r–8v, 6 May 1450.
76 Ibid., fols 133–6r.
77 Ibid., fols 137r–8v.
78 Ibid., fol. 138v, see the motions of Bernardo Pinos and of Giovanni Miraballi. Miraballi affirmed that 'the Jews who complained about the *populu* should provide proof of their accusations' (*quilli Iudei ki si lamentanu di lu populu lu digianu provari*).
79 By way of comparison, consider the growing isolation suffered by the Florentine 'popolo minuto' in the fifteenth century, S. K. Cohn, Jr., *The Laboring Classes in Renaissance Florence*, Academic Press: New York, 1980, p. 127.
80 Bresc, *Un monde*, cit., p. 740.
81 T. Fazello, *Della storia di Sicilia deche due*, 3 vols, Palermo: Tipografia Giuseppe Assenzio, 1817, vol. 3, p. 496. In October the *algozirius* Giovanni di Santo Clemente was still seeking out those reckoned to be guilty of rioting, RC, vol. 84, fol. 66.
82 ACP cass. XXXIV, fols 74–5r, 21 February 1451.
83 CC, vol. 61-1, fol. 179, 1 April 1451; a payment carried out using the credit of the Pisan bankers Antonio da Settimo, Filippo Aglata, Giovanni da Vivaia; A. Giuffrida, '"Lu quarteri de lu Cassaru" note sul quartiere del Cassaro a Palermo nella prima metà del secolo XV', *Melanges de l'École française de Rome temps modernes*, 83, 1971–2, p. 455.
84 CC, vol. 61-1, fols 188–90r, 13 July 1451.

85 RC, vol. 84, fols 106v–7r. On the effects of popular political actions liable to influence governmental balances compare José Ramón Diaz de Durana, 'The political action'.
86 Titone, 'Il tumulto', n. 127.
87 The most important consequence of the victory of the Busca party was an economic reform of a protectionist kind and the reform in 1455 of the organ of government with an executive power (*conselleria*), thereby guaranteeing the representation even of lower socio-professional groups. For a still valid study of the socio-economic context in Barcelona and of the conflict between the Busca party and the Biga see Batlle Gallart, *La crisis*, with the reference to artisans with no experience of government at p. 190. See also C. Batlle, 'El govern municipal a la baixa edat mitjana', in I. Rodà (ed.), *El govern de les ciutats catalanes*, Barcelona: La Magrana, 1985, pp. 74–9.
88 See F. Titone, 'Aragonese Sicily as a model of late medieval state building', *Viator*, 44, 2013, pp. 217–49.
89 See Titone, 'Presentation', pp. 151–8. On the elections of Berengario Aiuto, see Titone, *I magistrati*, pp. 270–1. On the appointment of Giovanni Amato, see RC, vol. 84, fol. 39.
90 RC, vol. 84, fol. 325.
91 ACA, vol. 2822, fol. 21r, 1442. See also RC, vol. 80, fols 273v–5, on the size of the payment as well as Cabrera's reluctance to relinquish the city.
92 The reference to the *maldenaru* is in ACA, vol. 2875, fols 89v–90r.
93 PR, vol. 40, fols 221v–30.
94 Ibid., vol. 41, fol. 22r.
95 RC, vol. 84, fols 244v–5; see also PR, vol. 43, fol. 199.
96 ACA, vol. 2875, fols 89v–90r.
97 RC, vol. 22, fol. 62v.
98 With reference to revenge, P. R. Hyams, 'Was there really such a thing as feud in the High Middle Ages?', in S. A. Throop and P. R. Hyams (eds), *Vengeance in the Middle Ages: Emotion, Religion and Feud*, Farnham and Burlington, VT: Ashgate, 2010, pp. 151–75, pp. 170–5 in particular, maintained that the vendetta and violence were integral aspects of society in the High Middle Ages. A different opinion is expressed in T. Dean, 'Violence, vendetta, and peacemaking in late medieval Bologna', *Criminal Justice History*, 17, 2002, pp. 1–17, who argues that there may have been a culture of vengeance but that this did not exclude legislative interventions which controlled and defused vengeance. See also M. Asenjo González, 'La venganza en el ámbito de las ciudades castellanas y su transformación en la baja edad media', in C. Gauvard and A. Zorzi (eds), *La vengeance en Europe XIIe–XVIIIe siècle*, Paris: Publications de la Sorbonne, 2015, pp. 227–47.
99 During the reign of Alfonso V, the Dentis had an important role in the government of the city up until 1451–2; Titone, *I magistrati*, pp. 272–4. As far as the phase following the reign of Alfonso V is concerned, they would be elected in the years 1466–7, 1468–9, 1470–1; PR, vol. 64, fol. 264r; ibid., vol. 67, fol. 2r; ibid., vol. 69, fol. 33v. Regarding the captains, my prosopographic investigation, which stops at 1459, did not uncover any members of the Denti family. As regards the elected officials, my prosopographic investigations stop at 1479.
100 Titone, *Governments*, pp. 169–214 and appendix.

16
CULTURES OF SURVEILLANCE IN LATE MEDIEVAL ENGLISH TOWNS

The monitoring of speech and the fear of revolt[1]

Christian D. Liddy

The sheriffs, wrote John Carpenter in his 1419 book of the customs of London, 'are called "the eyes of the mayor"'. They are 'the eyes of the mayor, watchful and supportive of the responsibilities which the said mayor, as one person, is not able to bear on his own' (*Sunt quoque Vicecomites Majoris oculi, conspicientes et supportantes partem sollicitudinis quae dicti Majoris personae singularitas portare non sufficit*).[2] At first glance, Carpenter's metaphor does not seem at all surprising: the inhabitants of late medieval English towns were accustomed to think of their communities as urban bodies. The organological metaphor was so familiar that it could serve multiple and, sometimes, conflicting functions. It informed contemporary attitudes towards public health and animated far-reaching social, moral, and environmental policies.[3] Politically, organic imagery could appeal for a state of reciprocity between the limbs of the urban body politic. More contentiously, it could demand the subordination of the various members of the body to the chief magistrate, the 'head'. Carpenter's appropriation of the metaphor was unusual because of his interest not only in the 'head', but also in the 'eyes'. If the 'head' represented intellect and reason, and was the source of wisdom, the 'eyes' were the senses. The burden of office in London was too great for any one man, Carpenter suggested. The mayor could not do everything; he needed help to discharge his official duties. The sheriffs were there to share the heavy weight of public responsibility. They were the mayor's 'eyes'; they could see what he could not.

Carpenter was not the first writer to approach the practice of government as a sensory experience. In Book 5 of the *Policraticus*, John of Salisbury deployed his classical learning to imagine the twelfth-century kingdom of England as a human body, in which the king was the head, and the judges and sheriffs – 'provincial governors' in the language of the Roman Empire – were the eyes, the ears, and the tongue. These three organs endowed the prince's judicial officers with the faculties of sight, hearing, and taste. Exercised by others on his behalf, these senses joined body and mind, increased the prince's cognitive powers, and enabled him to administer justice through greater knowledge and understanding.[4] Carpenter's description of the London sheriffs differs in three respects. First, where Salisbury is concerned with princely virtue and with the positive role of the prince, Carpenter's tone is less confident and more apprehensive.

311

Second, where Salisbury's framework is multi-sensory, Carpenter's attention is exclusively to the eyes. And, third, Carpenter's conception of the sheriffs' vision is much more literal. The nineteenth-century editor of the London custumal translated the participle *conspicientes* as 'ever on the watch'.[5] Against what were the sheriffs to be vigilant? Whom were they to watch? Upon which areas of the city were they to concentrate?

The short passage from Carpenter's *Liber albus* helpfully introduces the theme of this essay: the relationship between surveillance and urban disorder. Carpenter's choice of the noun *sollicitudo*, which could be translated not only as 'duty', but also as 'anxiety', conveyed the general uneasiness that surrounded the mayoral office in early fifteenth-century London. The memory of the 1380s – of confrontations on the streets of the capital between the supporters of rival claimants to the London mayoralty, John of Northampton and Nicholas Brembre – had not dimmed by the late 1410s, when Carpenter completed his book.[6] But in prioritising the eyes over the ears, Carpenter's dread was large-scale, open revolt. The argument here is that surveillance arose from a complex connection between rebellion and speech.

The *word* 'surveillance' is a nineteenth-century coinage; and in the wake of Michel Foucault's work on the invention of the prison during the Enlightenment, the *practice* of surveillance has tended to be examined in relation to one, or both, of two metanarratives: the onset of modernity and the emergence of the disciplining power of the state.[7] The origins of modernity are, of course, a matter of debate. Medievalists, interested in questions of power and social control, have explored concepts and mechanisms of surveillance in earlier periods and practised by a variety of institutions. R. I. Moore's now classic story of the Western church's use of techniques of religious and moral surveillance to ensure doctrinal orthodoxy, and to maintain authority between the twelfth and thirteenth centuries, continues to be a touchstone for scholarship on the classification, stigmatisation, and extirpation of 'dissent' in the Middle Ages.[8]

Surveillance has also been subsumed into the paradigm of 'early' modernity. To write about surveillance in the early modern period has been to reconstruct the processes by which states were centralised, extended, and consolidated. The dynamics of state growth were not homogeneous. To historians of continental Europe, Jacob Burckhardt's cultural history of the 'Renaissance', which the nineteenth-century historian saw not as a transition from but as a rupture with the medieval past, has cast a long shadow. According to Burckhardt, the Renaissance was not so much a rebirth as a new beginning, characterised by a modern kind of politics, which was brutal, calculating, and atomising, and by a new sense of individuality. Governments investigated, recorded, and counted their citizens, for reasons of state.[9] The Venetian city-state, Elisabeth Crouzet-Pavan has argued, was built on the collection and control of information. Between the late fifteenth and early sixteenth centuries, surveillance of the spoken and written word became an everyday political activity for a regime that aspired to omniscience. It was, Crouzet-Pavan concluded, an important stage in the movement towards 'modernity'.[10] Over the last 20 years, historians of early modern England have presented a cooperative and composite model of state development, in which the encroachment of the monarchical state upon the lives of ordinary subjects depended, simultaneously, upon their active participation in government. The governing culture of early modern England, where the multi-layered apparatus of the state was embedded in the structures of local society, was one of information gathering: names were listed, people counted, land surveys commissioned, and economic resources tabulated.[11] However we wish to consider the 'state', and however we define 'modernity', these concepts have dominated accounts of surveillance.[12]

This essay is about neither the dynamics of state formation nor the route to modernity. It makes three points. First, late medieval English towns were surveillance societies, in which townspeople habitually watched each other and reported their activities for the benefit of government. Second, there was a qualitative and quantitative expansion of surveillance, and changes in modes of data collection and record-keeping, from the last quarter of the fifteenth century. There was a specific, and sustained, focus upon the monitoring of speech. And third, the need for surveillance became more urgent in this period because of the fear of revolt. Ultimately, in linking surveillance to revolt, the intention of this essay is to reconceptualise 'revolt': to see it less as a single, extraordinary event than as a state of resistance, which could be verbal as well as physical. Rulers were not killed, and property was not destroyed, but speech was an act that struck at the social roots of political power.

Mutual surveillance

Following a meeting of the court of mayor and aldermen on 10 December 1478, a London draper named William Capell entered Newgate prison, where he was to remain until further notice. His wrongdoing was recorded by the clerk of the court. Capell had exclaimed publicly that he wanted to thrust his knife into Robert Drope, alderman and late mayor of the city, and that, 'if he were imprisoned on that account', he would break out straight away with 20 prisoners.[13] Capell's crime was not the completion of a violent assault, but the anticipatory longing to inflict bodily harm upon Robert Drope, to which he had given voice. His proud boast that the city gaol would not contain him was equally provocative. He was detained for the uttering of words, which were dangerous because of their publicity, their vivid imagining of the death of an alderman, and their brazen contempt towards an institution of law enforcement.

The cause of the dispute is unknown, although its origins may well have lain in a commercial quarrel. Both the perpetrator and the object of this verbal threat belonged to the drapers' craft, one of London's mercantile companies, from whose ranks the fifteenth-century mayors and aldermen were mostly drawn.[14] It was no doubt because of Capell's high status within London society that the king learned of his detention; and Edward IV sent a writ of *habeas corpus cum causa* to the mayor, aldermen, and sheriffs summoning Capell before his justices.[15] In response, London's magistrates summarised the circumstances of the case, about which they had been informed both at the personal complaint of the victim and on the more general report of 'many trustworthy witnesses, citizens of the city', who had heard Capell talking in an arrogant manner (*imperime*) and proclaiming 'various bold and opprobrious words on several occasions and in several locations, in the presence of many people'. In accounting for Capell's arrest and imprisonment, the mayor, aldermen, and sheriffs were eager to justify London's autonomy. In order to observe the 'good, politic and sound rule' of London, Capell's crime 'ought' to be punished and corrected by the mayor and aldermen, according to their discretion, 'just as other similar offences are, and have accustomed to be, punished and corrected, from time out of mind'. The efforts of London's mayor and aldermen to retain their judicial independence and to deal with Capell as they desired, free from crown intervention, were successful. The tone and content of their reply to the king's writ communicated a grudging reluctance to hand over the prisoner to an external court of law. On 22 December, less than two weeks after his arrival in royal custody, Capell was released back to the mayor and aldermen, who were now to decide his fate.

The case illustrates two aspects to the accumulation and verification of information in English towns. First, London's mayor and aldermen were given the news of Capell's speech acts by other citizens. Surveillance was not an instrument of social control, wielded by an all-powerful elite; it involved citizens informing the city council about the rebellious words of one of their own.[16] To understand how and why this happened, it is significant that the basic structure of urban policing – frankpledge – was communal and self-regulatory. Adult, male residents – householders and servants – each of whom had to swear an oath to keep the peace, were organised into groups of ten people. These tithings were headed by a capital pledge, whose role it was to bring to light the misconduct of his fellow pledges to the juries of the courts of the ward or leet, into which the town was divided.[17] Although they had no punitive power and could not prosecute the accused, these juries presided over local neighbourhood watch schemes that scrutinised the moral and social conduct of neighbours and household members. The household was not a private space; male householders were answerable, publicly, for all who lived under their roof. A patriarchal household of bourgeois respectability was the bedrock of a well-ordered city.[18] The imperative was practical as much as it was ideological. Towns were fluid and unstable societies, in which the regular arrival of incomers for the pursuit of trade and other opportunities created conditions of 'flux and mobility' that was not conducive to the preservation of urban peace.[19] While townspeople had to be enrolled in a tithing, the same principles of incorporation and regulation applied to foreign migrants who had newly arrived to trade. They were allowed to stay in the town only for a short period of time and were subject to a hosting system that, like frankpledge, was compulsory. The alien merchant was housed in the property of a civic householder, usually a citizen, who was to account for his behaviour before the town government. Hosting operated locally, in several major English towns and cities such as London and Norwich, before being rolled out nationally in the 1439–40 parliament.[20] Towns were not naturally face-to-face societies, in which everyone knew each other's affairs, but by the fifteenth century anonymity was made more difficult by the presence of deeply engrained structures of inclusion, supervision, and regulation centred upon the urban household. Surveillance was routine.

The second point of interest in the case of William Capell is that townspeople denounced the draper for what he had said and for what he hoped to do. Citizens had seen Capell, but they had also heard him speaking. Although fifteenth-century monarchs were able to adapt the 1352 treason statute and to incorporate the utterance of words within the act of plotting the king's death, it was not until the religious changes of the 1530s that the crown took the decisive legislative step of determining that words alone, without the necessity of an overt action, were enough to secure an indictment for treasonous desire.[21] Expressed grammatically almost entirely in the subjunctive mood – 'if he were imprisoned … if he were to go to prison' – William Capell's speech in 1478 was wishful, hypothetical, and contrary to fact. The sense of unreality was conveyed syntactically in Capell's alleged words, which transferred the human inclination to slay the London alderman, Robert Drope, to the murder weapon itself, the knife. Capell is supposed to have 'declared publicly to have wished his knife to have stabbed and cut open the body of Robert Drope'.[22] Already in London, before the redefinition of treason in 1534 that made fantastical yearnings towards immediate members of the royal family a treasonable offence, the city's rulers were policing the porous boundary between language, thought, and action. What made London's mayor and aldermen so anxious was the possibility that Capell's words might embolden others to follow his example of dissident speech.[23]

Civic elites were sensitive to any kind of verbal slight, whether it was personally abusive or endangering, or more widely critical of their policies. Confidence was brittle because the basis of their authority was inherently contestable. The townsmen who occupied the senior positions in civic government were known collectively as the *probi homines* ('worthy men'), their 'worthiness' a group attribute that was closely associated with 'wisdom' and that, therefore, validated their political leadership.[24] Reputations could easily be dented by a few contemptuous words, and civic officers, who were also citizens, were prone to verbal attacks from fellow citizens keen to remind them of this shared identity. Office was transitory.[25]

Their power was equally open to question. In contrast to the gentry and nobility in the countryside, their ability to reinforce orders through coercion was uncertain; they did not have the manpower derived from the ownership of land.[26] Mayors and sheriffs had official households, including macebearers and swordbearers, and mayors and aldermen wore a distinctive livery to denote their official status, but otherwise urban retinues were likely to provoke censure. Town clerks diligently copied royal missives against 'livery and maintenance' into their civic registers, and they issued their own laws against the practice.[27] In 1479 a Bristol burgess, who was charged locally with breaking parliamentary statutes on retaining, defended his activities on the grounds that he was a royal customs collector in the port of Bristol and that he was impotent to prevent merchants from bringing their goods to the quayside at night, when they might arrive under cover of darkness to avoid the payment of customs duties. He had searchers to assist him, but these 'pore' royal officers could not apprehend smugglers 'withoute supportacion of strong pouer at theire nede'. They had authority – they represented the crown – but they did not possess the brute strength that was sometimes needed and that could be supplied only by those prepared to risk life and limb in pursuit of justice.[28] The burgess's explanation may have been disingenuous, but he thought that it might carry weight with the king, whom he believed would recognise that what was applicable in the counties of late medieval England, where effective government demanded the exercise of patronage and the exploitation of private power to uphold public authority, would hold true in towns and cities.[29] But personal retinues were regarded as a source of division and a cause of conflict within urban communities.

In the event of serious unrest, civic magistrates could call upon the resources of the crown, but they were hesitant, for to invite intervention from outside was to weaken the tradition of self-government that townspeople swore to protect. In any case, royal officials tended to be of the opinion that, when push came to shove, there were others who had more power than elected mayors and aldermen. In 1517 Bishop Fox of Winchester wrote to Cardinal Wolsey to commend him for his handling of an enclosure riot in Southampton, which was 'better' than that of 'the governours of hampton' because Wolsey had entrusted one Master Sandes with the responsibility for its resolution. Among the population of Southampton, Sandes was 'ther mayre balif and all the holl [i.e. whole] Ruyller of the town', who enjoyed the king's favour and who garnered 'the love and credite' of 'the people'. When he was in Southampton, Sandes commanded their attention, and 'may more doo with theym then may doo the mayre and all officeres' of both the town and the port.[30] Sir William Sandes was not only a royal courtier, but a member of the Hampshire gentry, a soldier, and a constable of Southampton castle, who had troops at his disposal.[31]

How do the few govern the many, and how, especially, do they ensure compliance with their decisions? These are questions that can be asked of any government, in any period of history;[32] but if urban elites were not unusual in being vastly outnumbered by the people whom they ruled, these questions were more pressing and yet harder to answer in late medieval English towns because the sources of authority and the forms of power found outside the town walls were not so readily available. Surveillance worked as a means of integration by empowering householders and by giving them a stake – and a voice – in their community. Urban householders, who observed and reported the behaviour and speech of those permanent and temporary residents with whom they had contact, were complicit in their own governance. With mutual surveillance, the few did not govern the many; the many governed the many.

The monitoring of speech

In the last quarter of the fifteenth century the processes of monitoring and identification were directed, more insistently, from above, and the surveillance of speech acquired greater – and particular – significance. In April 1473 the mayor and aldermen of London sent out new guidelines to the juries of the city's wards. Unlike previous instructions, from the 1370s and the 1410s, the 1473 articles contained a provision about the spoken word: juries were to elicit 'the names of all persones dwellyng commyng or repairyng vnto your said wardes which fynde conterfet forge or tell any fals or feyned tales or tydynges or sowe any sedicious langage'.[33] Juries were expected to glean this information from the informal, social networks of local knowledge, which leave little or no trace in the civic records, but whose existence is suggested by the deponents who were ordered before the town council and who were enjoined, under oath, to reveal what they knew: people such as Elizabeth Worthowe, who in 1512 told the court of mayor and aldermen in Norwich that, whilst in the home of John Barne, a trader in second-hand goods, one William Herberd, a hatmaker, remarked that many a scoundrel had aspired to be a sheriff to cause hurt to others, but that they would inflict no harm upon him.[34] Witness statements were prone to inaccuracy, and though Worthowe attested that the hatmaker's boast had been made before a widow and a priest, returning from mass, neither claimed in court to have heard the words attributed to Herberd. The truth was secondary, however, to the rigours of examination.

Well before the Tudor treason and sedition laws of the 1530s, 1550s, 1570s, and 1580s enabled the early modern state to investigate treasonous and seditious words against the policies and personnel of the national government,[35] town governors were holding inquiries into speech crimes, whose prosecution depended upon the policing of space, the deposition of witnesses, and the interrogation of the accused. In 1480 a York butcher and parishioner of St Peter the Little, came into the council chamber, where he was quizzed about what he had 'herd' the parish priest 'say' about the city's mayor.[36] The appearance of a York merchant before the town council in 1498 can have been occasioned only by a fellow parishioner, who had seen the citizen approach one of the city's tax collectors during mass at the church of Holy Trinity, Micklegate, and had heard him expressing his surprise that he had been assessed at so high a rate for the recent parliamentary subsidy.[37] Like the parish church, the workshop was both a venue of social interaction and a political space. It was not that artisans *suddenly* started talking about politics; the difference is that the civic authorities were much more interested to discover what their citizens were saying, both while they worked and while they were at their leisure. When a cook who worked for the cathedral priory of Norwich walked into the shop of a local fletcher in 1506 and conversation turned to the mayoral election, the city's mayor and aldermen quickly knew what had been said and by whom.[38] The cook did not think highly of the choice of mayor, for he was no friend of the priory, but he assured the fletcher that he would speak to him again within six months, when he would 'come and tell the a newe Tale'. The balance of power between cathedral and city would soon alter, the cook avowed, when the citizens lost the support of the local lords and gentry,[39] after which 'the monkes truste to haue more priuilage in the Cite than they haue had be fore tyme'. Relations between the city and the cathedral priory had been antagonistic periodically from the thirteenth century, and in 1272 and 1443 the citizens had besieged the cathedral precinct.[40] In the early sixteenth century there were renewed strains in their relationship, the nature of which was a topic of public discourse on the streets of Norwich.

Townspeople drank and spoke about politics in the tavern and alehouse, as they always had. These drinking establishments had long been the repeated target of civic ordinances. Temporally and spatially, they were liminal places. In the eyes of London's mayor and aldermen, they encouraged Londoners to be out on the streets past the hour of curfew; as places of unlicensed social gathering, they were thought to be populated by a sub-culture of prostitutes, criminals, and the indolent, whose presence was a moral temptation and a physical threat to respectable citizens.[41] One of the charges put to the juries of London's ward courts in the late 1370s was to inquire whether any innkeeper, taverner, or brewer 'holdith his dore open after the houre lymyt bi the maire'.[42] Drinking houses were potential sites of violent crime and immorality. Behaviour, not speech, was the principal concern. Observation was visual. But 100 years later, it was emphatically auditory. The York tavern of the citizen and vintner, Richard Gascoigne, was under suspicion in the 1480s.[43] The city council learned, presumably through an informer, of the 'unsittyng language' – a phrase indicative of verbal abuse – employed 'enenst [i.e. against] the maire and shireffes' in 1480 by a tailor, who was in Gascoigne's tavern. Four years later, Gascoigne was found guilty of speaking offensive words against the then mayor and removed from the freedom of the city for not obeying a mayoral summons. Just as the later treason and sedition legislation of a succession of monarchs in early modern England produced a febrile climate of accusation and counter-accusation, in which 'suspects fell over one another to deny or modify their purported words',[44] so Gascoigne subsequently repudiated upon oath 'the langage reportid upon hym'. In February 1483 York's council had to sift through and mediate the conflicting accounts of a group of artisans, whose heated exchanges about the mayoral candidates in the forthcoming election, while they were 'sittyn at ale', first came to the attention of the city fathers through the contested testimony of another craftsman, a cooper by the name of William Welles.[45] In 1511, 'when he was settyng at the ayle house', a York miller lambasted one of the aldermen for having lost some of the city's common lands during his time as mayor, a treacherous exploit for which he would never again be elected to the mayoralty. The miller was obliged to deliver guarantees that he would 'never more ... comon [i.e. talk]' of the alderman or of any of the town council, when he was in either alehouse or tavern.[46] The Middle English verse, 'Ewyre say wylle, or hold the styll', dating from around 1480, recommended an attitude of studied caution towards those with whom one kept company ('who syttys the by'), at church, in the marketplace, or in the alehouse, lest 'he wylle repport thi talle'.[47] Like the York miller, he could never be sure who might be listening and who might denounce him.

This imposed culture of surveillance was accompanied by the intensification and invention of forms of identification. Historians have written extensively about contemporary understanding of the problem of poverty, the public perception of which 'increased, with a high point of concern around 1500', even though there were considerably fewer poor people in England in 1500 than, say, in 1300.[48] Anxieties focused on the phantom of 'vagabonds' and 'beggars', two related categories of able-bodied poor, supposedly disinclined to work and of no fixed abode, with a propensity to enter towns, to wander the streets in search of aid, and to commit crime.[49] But the bureaucratic energies of civic leaders were devoted less to the labelling of undesirable individuals among the lower orders and more to the registration of their own citizens: the enfranchised members of the urban community, also known as the freemen.

On the one hand, there was a vigorous campaign in London to make non-resident citizens assume permanent residence. The ambiguous status of this type of freeman had always been a grievance because of the feeling that those who lived outside the town were able to assert their entitlement to enjoy the privileges of citizenship, without having to bear its costs.[50] The temperature of this rhetoric rose dramatically. In 1472 the London court of mayor and aldermen discussed the proposition that all freemen dwelling outside the capital should return to the city with their household or else lose their liberty.[51] In 1476 a civic ordinance was proclaimed that citizens within 20 miles of London had six months to take up residency; people further afield had nine months.[52] When the alderman of one London ward continued to maintain his home beyond the capital, perhaps thinking that he was above the law, the mayor and aldermen threatened him with a financial penalty of £500.[53] In 1500 the time limit for the repatriation of non-residents within a radius of 20 miles was reduced to three months, but, more importantly, the acceptance of future entrants to the civic franchise was to be standardised and uniform: they were to live permanently in the city within six months of their admission as a citizen; and the wardens of the crafts (which controlled access to the freedom of London) were assigned to submit the names of each and every member of their craft who currently were, or who in future might be, absent to the mayor and aldermen.[54] Disquiet was not just one of inequity, but of uncertainty: who were these citizens? The answer to this question would provide the means of discrimination and exclusion.

On the other hand, there were stricter rules and new archival mechanisms for the enrolment of certificates of apprenticeship, one of the main routes to citizenship. In London it was customary for the master craftsman to present his apprentice in the Guildhall, where, before an audience of the mayor and aldermen, the indenture of service was examined and copied into a special register. This reproduction was to be made within one year of the sealing of the contract between master and apprentice.[55] The system was of financial value to the town government, which charged a small fee for the clerical work, but its chief importance was legal: in the event of breach of contract, the terms of the indenture could be enforced in the city's courts, an oversight that might be to the advantage of both the master and the apprentice.[56] From 1415 there were the same arrangements in Norwich, where citizens had to record the details of their new apprentices within 'twelmonth and oon day befor y[e] Meir' in the Guildhall.[57] Towards the end of the century, one year was too long. The process was debated in the city's common assembly in 1485, and in 1512 the assembly decided that the period between sealing and enrolment before the mayor would be shortened to three months.[58] The motives behind registration were neither financial nor legal. The impulse was bureaucratic. There was a desire for faster, more efficient, and more comprehensive methods of record-keeping.

In York and Coventry bespoke civic books of apprenticeship indentures were compiled for the first time. In York crafts such as the weavers had kept their own registers of apprentices, but in 1515 it was announced that in future a citizen should bring his apprentice, within one month of the making of an indenture, into the council chamber, 'and ther his indentier to be inrolled'.[59] In Coventry, where there was not yet a civic apprentice book, the city's legislative body – the leet court – issued a new ordinance in 1494 that henceforth made it mandatory for apprentices to swear an oath before a representative of the city government and for their names to be written into 'a Registre'.[60] Civic registration of the name of the apprentice was also to take place *before* the master even sealed the indenture with his apprentice. The reciprocal conditions of the agreement between master and apprentice were of little interest to Coventry's rulers: the name of the apprentice, his geographical origin, his master's name and occupation, plus the length of service, these were the bare – but essential – facts.[61] Unlike the convention in other towns, apprentices in Coventry were also to take the freeman's oath at the beginning, rather than at the end of the apprenticeship.[62] The other novelty was the wording of the oath. Where these oaths had previously spoken of mutuality, even if this was in the sense of the performance of civic duties, such as the responsibility to pay taxes and to hold office, to which everyone within the community of citizens was liable, the Coventry oath said nothing about mutual aid. To be sure, he was to defend the city's corporate liberties, but the oath was couched exclusively in a legalistic discourse, which emphasised hierarchy rather than fraternity: he was to be 'goode and true' to the king, the mayor, and sheriffs; he was not to commit or be party to any felony or treason, and he was to warn the 'kyng or his officers' if he knew that such a crime might be perpetrated; and he was 'duely' to 'obbey, observe kepe & perfourme' the city's laws.[63] This was the template for the law-abiding citizen, who was to be faithful and obedient not to his community and to his neighbours, but to his lords and masters.

From the late fifteenth century the monitoring of both the people and places that constituted the urban space entailed the making of new laws, the adoption of new archival practices and the writing of government registers, the listing of individuals, and a redefinition of citizenship, both in theory and in practice. What was distinctive about this period that explains these changes?

The fear of revolt

To read the royal charters and other written instruments from the late fifteenth century that remodelled town constitutions and that created closed, self-selecting structures of urban government, one might be inclined to believe that the position of the politically dominant in English towns – the so-called *probi homines* – was more hegemonic than ever.[64] To read the minutes of town council meetings, royal correspondence to towns, and craft ordinances from the late fifteenth and early sixteenth centuries is to detect a completely different atmosphere, politically fraught and socially fractious. The 'close corporation' existed in theory, but not in practice. Town government was not an entity in and of itself. There were pressures on civic rulers from above and from below, from without and from within the town walls. In these circumstances, surveillance, especially of the spoken word – and its regulation and documentation through the written word – was a necessity.

The charters that English towns had acquired from the crown in the communal movement of the twelfth and thirteenth centuries did not free them from royal overlordship.[65] They enshrined and propagated the seemingly paradoxical principle of self-government at the king's command and made urban governors aware that their authority – their legitimacy, their right to be obeyed – was derivative: it was the consequence of their role as the king's representatives. In the late fifteenth century the symbiotic relationship between royal and civic authority became a stick with which to beat town rulers should they not comply with the king's demands. A letter sent by Henry VII to Northampton in the later 1480s encapsulates the king's general mood towards towns. Belittling and abrasive in its overall style and content, the preamble treated the mayor to a lecture about the results of good and bad government in towns and cities. Peace, love, prosperity, justice, and the common good sprang from the former; conflict, poverty, and misery would ensue from the latter. All this was by way of telling the mayor, lest he forget, that it was the 'duete' of local officials to enforce law and order; that to rule effectively, they had to punish those who destroyed the king's peace; and that their failure to do so would amount to disobedience. Most of all, the mayor and his colleagues were admonished to be alert to those spreading seditious words, starting rumours, and fabricating news about the king or others of high rank, all of which led innocent subjects astray and persuaded them to rebel ('falle into rebellion and disobeissaunce'). They were to imprison indefinitely both those guilty and those suspected of such speech crimes and to send their names, along with the details of their offence, to the king.[66] Information would afforce the king's security.

So too would the maintenance of the law. When Henry VII summoned the mayor and aldermen of York to Greenwich in 1495, he recalled how their 'wyse and polytik ordre and rewle' in the past had been the source of York's 'prosperite and welth' and declared that he would not see the city go to ruin for the lack of good governance. There was no other city in the kingdom where the mayor could 'more boldly rewle or governe', 'for within your fraunches and libertiez ye may rewle accordyng to my lawez as and I were ther my nawn [i.e. own] person'. These were not words to comfort and to reassure but to intimidate. If the mayor and aldermen did not rule as the king required, they would be replaced: 'I most and woll put in other rewlers that woll rewle and govern the Citie accordyng to my lawez'.[67] A year later, the king wrote to the mayor and aldermen of Coventry, and lamented 'the disordering of our said citie and subuersion of such politik rules as hertofor haue been vsed'. Coventry, according to the king, had flourished hitherto under the wise governance of the city's magistrates, and they were commanded again 'duely' to 'execute' 'thauncient and laudable custumes of our said citie'. The city's economic health was imperilled.[68] Law, preceded by the definite article, was tangible, rather than abstract; the benefits of its rigorous administration particular, calculable, and enumerative.[69] The crown's insistence on the application of a body of rules, customs, and laws, not simply the obligation to render justice, did not so much empower as unsettle civic officeholders, who were under surveillance.

Royal government reiterated this language of law because of its fear of popular uprising. In the civil war of the middle decades of the fifteenth century successive kings were so worried about the power of public opinion and popular activism to resist royal authority that they employed spies.[70] Speech was toxic because of its dynamic and incremental potential to fuel rumour and gossip, inspire conspiracy, and provoke insurrection. In April 1485 Richard III wrote to a number of English towns, such as York and Southampton, to warn them of the destructive actions of 'diverse sedicious and evil disposed personnes', who had been active in London and in other unnamed locations within the kingdom. Some had written bills, some had sent 'furth of false and abhominable langage and lyes', and some had uttered 'bold and presumptuos speech'. Civic officials were to arrest not only individuals speaking ill of the king or of 'any othre lord', but those 'telling tales and tidinges wherby the people might be stird to commocions and unlaufull assembles', and to track down the original instigator of the story.[71] In 1487 Henry VII issued a mandate to the mayors and bailiffs of English towns, including the capital, that they should 'sette' such people 'vppon the pillorie' for as long as they thought appropriate.[72] Twenty years later, Edmund Dudley, the early Tudor social theorist, implored the common people to beware the temptation of rumour, which might 'induce you to grudge or disdain to be in suche obediens or subiection to your superiors or betters'.[73] Subversive speech was an infection to the body politic that could travel quickly. It was 'seditious' because it could incite commotion. The natural condition of the lower orders was one of quietude and conformity.

Civic officials had little choice but to cooperate with central government in the investigation of speech that was in contempt of the king.[74] On taking possession of Henry VII's writ in 1487, London's mayor and aldermen convened the common council, the masters and wardens of the crafts, and the constables of the city, with a view to its general dissemination.[75] In late fifteenth- and early sixteenth-century Norwich, prophetic talk of the return of royal contenders for the throne and predictions of an imminent tax revolt pricked the ears of the mayor and aldermen, who learned of conversations involving a draper at a window of a bookbinder in the cathedral close, and between two apprentice cordwainers in their master's workshop.[76] In 1515 the mayor and aldermen tried to establish not only the content, but the meaning of certain words attributed to a tax collector, appointed to assess and levy the subsidy granted that year in parliament.[77] The tax collector was reported to have said to the royal commissioners, on receiving his charge, that if he and 20,000 like-minded men, 'more such as I am hadde be in the parlement house', then 'we shuld [have] amended' the subsidy. Was this a call to arms? Another citizen, a painter by trade, who was present at the verbal altercation, confirmed the statement and added that the tax collector had gone on to say that his intention was 'not to make insurreccion', but that 'he and they' – the 20,000 – 'wold haue made peticion for the mater to the kyng'. Petitioning was an alternative to rebellion. But Norwich's mayor and aldermen were sceptical, and held further inquiries: a parish clerk gave testimony under oath, as did several fishermen, a dyer, and a worsted-weaver. These witnesses were from the same, artisanal stratum as the tax collector, who was a freeman and a pointmaker.[78] Perhaps he should have known better than to contend that the tax would be 'harde for the pore comouns to paie', that it was a pity that 'pore men aren thus pollid [i.e. fleeced]', and that the aim of his petition was tax relief for the 'pore comouns'.

The line between petitioning and violent collective action was blurred: a petition to the king at parliament was, of course, the normal method of obtaining redress, but what was the status of a petition if it was accompanied by the latent promise of coercive force?[79] Petitions were part of the traditional pattern of revolt. In the large-scale uprisings of 1381, 1450, 1497, 1536–7, and 1549, English rebels conceived themselves as petitioners of the king.[80] In the Peasants' Revolt of 1381 the rebels had assumed the name the 'true commons' to claim that they, and not the MPs who sat in the House of Commons, represented the wishes of the kingdom.[81] The connection in 1515 between popular mobilisation, petitioning, and parliament raised the spectre of armed resistance, which Norwich's aldermanic class could not ignore.

The apprehension was not entirely a figment of the collective imagination. While their authority was tested by the crown, the power of civic rulers was opposed and undermined by their own citizens. There were 'enclosure riots' in many English towns between the 1480s and 1520s, which were, in fact, neither of these things: the uprooting and levelling of hedges was not spontaneous and chaotic, but planned and disciplined; and they were *about* a much larger set of grievances than the enclosure of fields. They were, as I have argued elsewhere, 'risings of the commons',[82] and they had multiple causes: they arose from a conjunction of enduring, unresolved constitutional and political questions – about the relationship between ordinary citizens and the *probi homines* and about the concept of citizenship – and short-term, economic decline, the financial manifestation of which was visible in the balance sheets of civic income and expenditure. These risings were reason enough for urban elites to listen out for deviant speech. Speech could intensify and mutate, in an ever-widening circle of publicity, from murmur to rumour and from individual words of complaint, whispered secretively in an alehouse, to collective discussions in a craft's guildhall, and, ultimately, to open, collective action, with violent deeds as well as sharp words.[83]

Surveillance, along with the development and use of other means of personal identification, however, was the product of broader and deeper elite anxieties about the structure and composition of urban society. These cohered around the fear, not of a siege of the town hall or of any of the other actions upon the government of the town that historians have seen as characteristic of urban revolt, but of something less obviously confrontational, but far more routine, insidious, and fundamental: the uttering of words that challenged and subverted the social hierarchy.

How might social relations in England's larger towns around 1500 be understood? The subject awaits detailed study.[84] On the one hand, the work of social historians of early modern England, which has done so much to transform our knowledge of the structural inequalities and solidarities of Tudor and early Stuart society, has tended to start after the middle of the sixteenth century.[85] On the other hand, there is still little agreement about the economic fortunes of late medieval English towns. We know much about the 'great depression' of the mid-fifteenth century, which saw a severe bullion shortage and the precipitous collapse of overseas trade, particularly the export of cloth, upon which major English towns were dependent.[86] The symptoms of economic contraction – the 'flight' from civic office, appeals to the crown for tax reductions, the fall in rental values of urban property – have been endlessly debated, without a clear conclusion. What, precisely, do they demonstrate: the politics of urban poverty, or genuine decay? The evidence of accelerated population decline in many provincial towns seems irrefutable.[87] Yet with one or two exceptions, far too little attention has been paid to the results of these changes upon urban society.[88] London was different: its population was on an upward trajectory.[89] Population growth, as early modern social historians have underlined, brought its own problems. By contrast, studies of late medieval London have no more than hinted at rising social tensions in the capital arising from the lack of work, which can be discerned in the prickly conflicts over social precedence between the crafts, the amalgamation of several manufacturing crafts, and the large number of crafts that petitioned the mayor and aldermen for the enrolment of their ordinances from the later fifteenth century.[90] The overriding impression is of London's political stability and social cohesion at the end of the Middle Ages.[91]

Whether urban economies were undergoing recession or restructuring, or even expansion, townspeople were conscious of a changed constellation of power within their communities. And whether urban social relations were more unstable and fluid than in the period after the Black Death, upon which the research of medievalists has focused, is beside the point; crucially, urban inhabitants thought that they were. From the moment that they appeared in the written record as corporate bodies, their powers of self-government authorised by the crown, English towns were divided societies and townspeople were accustomed to think of the urban world in binary terms: between *probi homines* and commoners; between citizens and non-citizens. In later fifteenth-century London the petitions to the mayor and aldermen, from the 'good men' of many crafts about the economic activities of non-freemen, indicate that few believed that the linguistic categories of social differentiation matched the complexity of social place and the reality of work.[92] In York the expression of anti-alien sentiment was louder and had a harder, more insistent, calculating edge: foreigners were listed and their place of residence within the city ascertained.[93] The lines of social demarcation were redrawn and restated. The effect was to create 'sharper social distancing' between rulers and ruled, rich and poor, insiders and outsiders.[94]

Craft ordinances, scrutinised and endorsed by the civic authorities and enrolled in civic registers, reveal a fixation with the verbal language of social distinction, where interest among the crafts in social deference – as opposed to, say, the quality of workmanship or the conditions of work – had previously been sporadic.[95] In London these ordinances, which fill the pages of *Letter-Book L*, imagined a hostile relationship between the ordinary freemen and the craft officialdom, and almost all contained an edict about abusive speech directed to the wardens.[96] Upon their unification in 1479, the Bristol bowyers and fletchers settled upon a new governing structure of two wardens, whose position they endeavoured to shore up with a statute against the speaking of contemptuous words towards them. In 1483 the Bristol shearmen made it a crime verbally to rebuke or disobey their two chief officers with disorderly ('dessordinat') language.[97] The obsession with speech was the consequence of both a steeply polarised model of social relations and the dread of its rejection.

What was unacceptable was not so much the slanderous assault upon the good name of the individual guild official, but its disruption of the internal organisation of the fellowship, where the social gulf between the governing elite and the rank and file was symbolised, in the capital at least, by the wearing of a livery.[98] Bad language was not merely – not even – antisocial language. To speak offensively was to resist authority. To put it more strongly, rebellion was conceived increasingly as a speech act. When confronted by the 'mysrule & disobedience of certeyn persones' of the same craft in 1477, the leading men of the London girdlers drew up new corporate rules. The first ordinance warned liverymen that they should neither 'revile nor Rebuke' a member of the livery and admonished those outside the livery that they should not speak ill of a liveryman. To do so was to perpetrate 'wordes of violence', an illuminating phrase, communicative of the injurious act of speaking rather than of the use of excessive physical strength.[99] It was a perceived threat from 'self willed persones enfraunchesed' of the butchers, who spoke in an unruly fashion ('vnmanerly langage') to each other and who refused to do as they were told, that mobilised the 'wardens and oþer honest men' of the craft in 1484. In their preamble to the 1499 ordinances of the London stringers, the 'mayster wardeyns and gode Folkes' explained that the 'grete disobedience Rancour and malys' displayed by 'the Inferior persones to the superiors' of the craft was the reason for their remedial action. The first article targeted those craftsmen who were of low status, whether 'workeman', 'seruaunt', or 'apprentice', who might 'disobey rebuke or Revile' their betters, the wardens of the craft.[100] What, then, was considered appropriate speech and behaviour?

The *probi homines* of city and craft worked together, ever more closely, to monitor speech, and shared information about incidents of verbal dissent. Craft officials were 'the eyes and ears' of the civic magistracy,[101] but the relationship was also one of co-dependency. When the wiredrawers and cardmakers of Bristol merged in 1469–70, they decided that two wardens were to be chosen each year and that any craftsman who did not exhibit to the wardens the 'Reverence and Worschipp' due to them by virtue of their office, 'in worde and deede', should be handed over to the mayor and sheriff for punishment.[102] Those guilty of illicit speech generally had to apologise to the victim for their offence. Scripts were prepared by the civic government, so that the wrongdoer knew exactly what to say to make amends, and how. In 1517 a London haberdasher who had repeatedly 'disobeyed & mysbehaued' against the wardens of his craft, breached its rules, and spoken 'sedicious & unsyttyng wordes' to one of the wardens, was ordered by the mayor and aldermen to come to the haberdashers' hall, where he was to acknowledge, on bended knee, before a party of aldermen and the officers of the craft, the full extent of his rebelliousness. In this submissive pose, he placed himself at the mercy of his 'masters'.[103] The whole ritual was akin to an act of homage. Defiance was assuaged by deference.[104] Official scripts could be copied and their words repeated; their aim was to produce, and reproduce, a hierarchical social order and the normative social values of verbal self-control, respect for one's superiors, and compliance with the law.[105] These values constituted the fifteenth-century notion of 'governance': not only the 'ability' of the individual 'to master his or her own appetites', but 'obedience to the rule of those to whom the individual was subject'.[106]

The surveillance of words was, however, deeply problematic. It disclosed the social friction, and sometimes generated the contempt of social gradation and recalcitrance towards authority, that was feared. Scripts were an unreliable guide to the messy reality of social relations. When the case of a London dyer came before the mayor and aldermen in 1518, they learned that the dyer had not only used abusive words about the mayor, but had 'called' his wardens 'pollers & pyllers of pour men' and spoken 'many other Sedicious & obprobrious wordes'. In branding his wardens plunderers and thieves who oppressed the poor, the dyer thought little of his superiors; he dismissed their authority as tyrannical and unlawful. The mayor and aldermen ruled that the dyer should go 'Immediately' to the dyers' hall, where he was to appear before 'his seyd wardens & others good & Substanciall persones of the seyd ffelyship'. There he was to 'Submytte' to his wardens, from whom he was to ask pardon and forgiveness. To rebel was to sin. But the dyer did not follow the script. As the wardens later reported to the mayor and aldermen, the dyer came to the hall, where he was unwilling to perform the penitential part that was assigned to him. His demeanour obstinate and insolent, he pronounced publicly in the dyers' hall that he would sooner put a rope around his neck than yield to the wardens. Worse, he stood his ground and 'Justifyed' his opposition, stating that 'he knewe no cause' why he should apologise.[107] Here, in this one small scene played out in the dyers' hall, was an attempt to enact a magisterial concept of urban social order: one that was divinely ordained and hierarchical, in which the line between governors and governed was clear for all to see. As a craftsman but also a citizen, the dyer was much less certain of his social inferiority; he asserted his freedom to speak out publicly; and he was able to defend himself and to defy those in authority whom he deemed his equals. If the purpose of surveillance was, in the end, to limit what citizens could say and do, here was proof of its failure.

Conclusion

The fear of revolt was the principal motivation for increasing surveillance in English towns between the late fifteenth and early sixteenth centuries. This essay has not addressed the topics that a reader might expect to find in a discussion of 'revolt': the patterns of collective action; the ideology and goals of violence; the social profile of rebels. Indeed, there has been no analysis of an actual revolt – approached as a single event – at all. There has been very little physical violence, against person or property, not much group conflict, and nothing about rebel demands, such as the acquisition of power.

The concern of royal government was the external consequences of speech: the anxiety that dissident words would lead inexorably to rebellious actions; that rumour would explode in armed conflict. Civic rulers had their own agenda about the issue of speech. They made inquiries, assembled and inspected case material, and heard witness statements. They were attentive to the exchange of news and to the expression of political opinions that were critical of civic and royal authority, in a proliferation of settings, public and semi-public. But they were vexed, above all, by the speech act itself. They were troubled by speech that was not only offensive, but unruly; that lacked verbal control, but that was also disobedient in its inversion of the verbal cues and body language of social hierarchy. To urban elites, who more than ever saw their power as dependent upon a 'sense of differentiation and distance',[108] speech crimes advanced an opposing claim about its distribution. Behind this preoccupation with speech was profound unease about the social structure of English towns, which was translated also into new practices of civic writing, registration, and identification. Everyone had to know his or her place. The fluidity and fragility of urban social relations, it was believed, could be stabilised by being inscribed, and fixed, on parchment. Through the writing of scripts, elites hoped to transform social antagonism into social harmony and order. Life would mirror art.

In exploring how urban disorder was conceptualised as a problem of speech, and how verbal misconduct was defined as rebellion, perhaps it is not helpful to draw too neatly the boundaries between different categories of rebellious behaviour. Revolt, which might be a concrete action, visible, and collective, might also – as suggested here – be verbal, audible, and personal.

Notes

1 The following abbreviations are used:

    CLB M. D. Harris (ed.), *The Coventry Leet Book*, 4 vols, Early English Text Society, Original Series, 134–46, London: Kegan Paul, Trench, Trübner & Co., 1907–13.
    CRO Coventry Record Office.
    GRB E. W. W. Veale (ed.), *The Great Red Book of Bristol*, 5 vols, Bristol Record Society, 2–18, [Bristol: printed for the society], 1931–52.
    LMA London Metropolitan Archives
    NRO Norfolk Record Office
    YCR A. Raine (ed.), *York Civic Records*, 8 vols, Yorkshire Archaeological Society, Record Series, 98–119, [Wakefield: printed for the society], 1938–52.
    YHB L. C. Attreed (ed.), *York House Books, 1461–1490*, 2 vols, Stroud: Alan Sutton, 1991.

I would like to thank Caroline Barron for the photographs of Trinity College, Cambridge, MS. 0.3.11, and Emma Hamlett for her comments on a draft of the essay.

2 H. T. Riley (ed.), *Munimenta Gildhallae Londoniensis: Liber Albus, Liber Custumarum, et Liber Horn*, 3 vols in 4, Rolls Series, 1859–62, vol. 1, pp. 9, 42.

3 C. Rawcliffe, *Urban Bodies: Communal Health in Late Medieval English Towns and Cities*, Woodbridge: Boydell Press, 2013.

4 John of Salisbury, *Policraticus: Of the Frivolities of Courtiers and the Footprints of Philosophers*, ed. and trans. C. J. Nederman, Cambridge: Cambridge University Press, 1990, pp. 91–5.
5 *Liber Albus: The White Book of the City of London*, ed. and trans. H. T. Riley, London: Richard Griffin, 1861, p. 37.
6 There are several studies of the causes of this factional struggle, but on its consequences, see C. M. Barron, 'Richard II and London', in A. Goodman and J. Gillespie (eds), *Richard II: The Art of Kingship*, Oxford: Clarendon Press, 1999, pp. 129–54. For the link between the *Liber Albus* and the earlier disturbances, see H. Carrel, 'Food, drink and public order in the London *Liber Albus*', *Urban History*, 33, 2006, pp. 176–94.
7 F. Nevola, 'Surveillance and control of the street in Renaissance Italy', *I Tatti: Studies in the Italian Renaissance*, 16, 2013, pp. 85–106, at 93–4. The key text is M. Foucault, *Discipline and Punish: The Birth of the Prison*, London: Allen Lane, 1977. For its influence on studies of contemporary society, see D. Lyon, *The Electronic Eye: The Rise of Surveillance Society*, Cambridge: Polity Press, 1994, and W. G. Staples, *The Culture of Surveillance: Discipline and Social Control in the United States*, New York: St Martin's Press, 1997. For a more nuanced account, see E. Higgs, *The Information State in England: The Central Collection of Information on Citizens since 1500*, Basingstoke: Palgrave Macmillan, 2004.
8 R. I. Moore, *The Formation of a Persecuting Society: Power and Deviance in Western Europe, 950–1250*, Oxford: Basil Blackwell, 1987.
9 J. Burckhardt, *The Civilization of the Renaissance in Italy*, trans. S. G. C. Middlemore, London: Penguin Books, 1990, pp. 50, 59, 63–4. Valentin Groebner's book, *Who are You? Identification, Deception, and Surveillance in Early Modern Europe*, New York: Zone Books, 2007, argues instead for continuities between the Middle Ages and the early modern period.
10 E. Crouzet-Pavan, 'Les mots de Venise: sur le contrôle du langage dans une cité-état italienne', in M. Balard (ed.), *La circulation des nouvelles au Moyen Âge*, Rome: École Française de Rome, 1994, pp. 215–18.
11 P. Slack, 'Government and information in seventeenth-century England', *P&P*, 184, 2004, pp. 33–68. For analysis that emphasises local, urban initiative, see P. Griffiths, 'Local arithmetic: information cultures in early modern England', in S. Hindle, A. Shepard, and J. Walter (eds), *Remaking English Society: Social Relations and Social Change in Early Modern England*, Woodbridge: Boydell Press, 2013, pp. 113–34.
12 A point noted also in J. R. Brown, 'Drinking houses and the politics of surveillance in pre-industrial Southampton', in B. Kümin (ed.), *Political Space in Pre-industrial Europe*, Farnham: Ashgate, 2009, pp. 62–3.
13 LMA, COL/CC/01/01/008, fol. 189v: *pro eo quod dixit publice se voluisse cultellum suum penetrasse et perforasse corpus Roberti drope aldermanni nuper maioris huius Ciuitatis et si esset imprisonatum propter illam causam si iret ad prisonam cum vna exiret ab eadem cum xx personis.*
14 S. L. Thrupp, *The Merchant Class of Medieval London [1300–1500]*, Chicago, IL: University of Chicago Press, 1948, pp. 328, 337–8.
15 For this and what follows, see LMA, COL/CC/01/01/008, fol. 191r.
16 For historical doubts about the sociological model of 'social control', see G. Stedman Jones, 'Class expression versus social control? A critique of recent trends in the social history of "leisure"', *History Workshop Journal*, 4, 1977, pp. 162–70.
17 S. Rees Jones, 'Household, work and the problem of mobile labour: the regulation of labour in medieval English towns', in J. S. Bothwell, P. J. P. Goldberg, and W. M. Ormrod (eds), *The Problem of Labour in Fourteenth-Century England*, Woodbridge: York Medieval Press, 2000, pp. 133–53; C. M. Barron, 'Lay solidarities: the wards of medieval London', in P. Stafford, J. L. Nelson, and J. Martindale (eds), *Law, Laity and Solidarities: Essays in Honour of Susan Reynolds*, Manchester: Manchester University Press, 2001, pp. 218–33.
18 P. Maddern, 'Order and disorder', in C. Rawcliffe and R. Wilson (eds), *Medieval Norwich*, London: Hambledon & London, 2004, pp. 189–212; S. McSheffrey, *Marriage, Sex, and Civic Culture in Late Medieval London*, Philadelphia: University of Pennsylvania Press, 2006, ch. 6.
19 J. Barry, 'Bourgeois collectivism? Urban association and the middling sort', in J. Barry and C. Brooks (eds), *The Middling Sort of People: Culture, Society and Politics in England, 1550–1800*, Basingstoke: Macmillan, 1994, pp. 90–2.
20 *Liber Albus*, p. 287; W. Hudson and J. C. Tingey (eds), *The Records of the City of Norwich*, 2 vols, Norwich: Jarrold and Sons, 1906–10, vol. 2, pp. 188–9; A. A. Ruddock, 'Alien hosting in Southampton in the fifteenth century', *EcHR*, 16, 1946, pp. 30–7.

21 J. G. Bellamy, *The Law of Treason in England in the Later Middle Ages*, Cambridge: Cambridge University Press, 1970, pp. 107, 116–23; G. R. Elton, *Policy and Police: The Enforcement of the Reformation in the Age of Thomas Cromwell*, Cambridge: Cambridge University Press, 1972, pp. 286–9; S. J. Gunn, *Early Tudor Government, 1485–1558*, Basingstoke: Macmillan, 1995, pp. 181–2; C. R. Duggan, 'The advent of political thought-control in England: seditious and treasonable speech, 1485–1547', PhD thesis, Northwestern University, Chicago, 1993, chs 2, 5.

22 See above, n. 13.

23 LMA, COL/CC/01/01/008, fol. 191r.

24 R. Hilton, 'Status and class in the medieval town', in T. R. Slater and G. Rosser (eds), *The Church in the Medieval Town*, Aldershot: Ashgate, 1998, pp. 12–13.

25 C. D. Liddy, '"Sir ye be not kyng": citizenship and speech in late medieval and early modern England', *Historical Journal*, forthcoming.

26 P. Fleming, 'Telling tales of oligarchy in the late medieval town', in M. Hicks (ed.), *Revolution and Consumption in Late Medieval England*, Woodbridge: Boydell Press, 2004, p. 178. Cf. C. Carpenter, *Locality and Polity: A Study of Warwickshire Landed Society, 1401–1499*, Cambridge: Cambridge University Press, 1992, pp. 47–8, 283–4.

27 *CLB*, pp. 319–20, 373–5; M. Sellers (ed.), *York Memorandum Book*, 2 vols, Surtees Society, 120, 125, Durham: Andrews & co., 1912–14, vol. 2, pp. 200–2; *YCR*, vol. 2, p. 181.

28 *GRB*, vol. 5, pp. 62–7, 71–2, 88–91, esp. 90–1.

29 E. Powell, 'After "After McFarlane": the poverty of patronage and the case for constitutional history', in D. J. Clayton, R. G. Davies, and P. McNiven (eds), *Trade, Devotion and Governance: Papers in Later Medieval History*, Stroud: Sutton, 1994, pp. 11–13; J. Watts, *Henry VI and the Politics of Kingship*, Cambridge: Cambridge University Press, 1996, pp. 91–101.

30 TNA, SP 1/232, fol. 33.

31 R. H. Fritze, 'Sandys, William, first Baron Sandys (c.1470–1540)', *Oxford Dictionary of National Biography*, Oxford: Oxford University Press, 2004, www.oxforddnb.com/view/article/24653.

32 See e.g. P. Wormald, 'Germanic power structures: the early English experience', in L. Scales and O. Zimmer (eds), *Power and the Nation in European History*, Cambridge: Cambridge University Press, 2005, pp. 105–24.

33 LMA, COL/CC/01/01/008, fol. 49r. Cf. Trinity College, Cambridge, MS. 0.3.11, fols 144v–6, and *Liber Albus*, pp. 287–92.

34 NRO, NCR, 16a/2, p. 9.

35 This judicial material has been a rich mine for historians of early modern popular politics: A. Fox, 'Rumour, news and popular political opinion in Elizabethan and early Stuart England', *Historical Journal*, 40, 1997, pp. 597–620.

36 *YHB*, vol. 1, pp. 207–8.

37 *YCR*, vol. 2, p. 136: 'sayng he marveled that he was set so myche to the aiede'.

38 For what follows, see NRO, NCR, 17d/7, fol. 53r.

39 '[A]t yt tyme the Cyte wold nat be rewlyd nor uowert be lorde ne gentylmen in the Countre'. See *Middle English Dictionary*, *sub* 'vouen' (1c): 'to uphold, support'.

40 N. Tanner, 'The cathedral and the city', in I. Atherton, E. Fernie, C. Harper-Bill, and H. Smith (eds), *Norwich Cathedral: Church, City and Diocese, 1096–1996*, London: Hambledon Press, 1996, pp. 255–69.

41 H. T. Riley (ed.), *Memorials of London and London Life in the XIIIth, XIVth, and XVth Centuries*, London: Longmans, Green, and Co., 1868, pp. 193, 272–3, 534–5; F. Rexroth, *Deviance and Power in Late Medieval London*, Cambridge: Cambridge University Press, 2007.

42 Trinity College, Cambridge, MS. 0.3.11, fol. 145r.

43 For what follows, see *YHB*, vol. 1, pp. 223–4, 301–2, 421.

44 A. Wood, '"Poore men woll speke one daye": plebeian languages of deference and defiance in England, c.1520–1640', in T. Harris (ed.), *The Politics of the Excluded, c.1500–1850*, Basingstoke: Palgrave, 2001, p. 85.

45 *YHB*, vol. 2, p. 707.

46 *YCR*, vol. 3, p. 36.

47 J. O. Halliwell, *Early English Miscellanies, of Prose and Verse*, London, 1855, p. 63.

48 The quotation is from C. Dyer, 'Poverty and its relief in late medieval England', *P&P*, 216, 2012, p. 42. For the figures, and the methodology underpinning them, see ibid., pp. 42–3.

49 M. K. McIntosh, *Poor Relief in England, 1350–1600*, Cambridge: Cambridge University Press, 2012, is the most recent study of poverty, its definition and relief, across the late medieval–early modern divide.

50 See e.g. R. R. Sharpe (ed.), *Calendar of the Letter-Books of the City of London*, 11 vols, London: John Edward Francis, 1899–1912, *Letter-Book H*, p. 146, and *Letter-Book K*, pp. 161–3.
51 LMA, COL/CC/01/01/008, fol. 33v.
52 Ibid., fol. 127v.
53 LMA, COL/CC/01/01/009, fol. 46v.
54 LMA, COL/CC/01/01/010, fols 179v–80r.
55 E. Ralph and N. M. Hardwick (eds), *Calendar of the Bristol Apprentice Book 1532–1565, Part II: 1542–52*, Bristol Record Society, 33, [Bristol: printed for the society], 1980, p. ix; Robert Ricart, *The Maire of Bristowe is Kalendar*, ed. L. T. Smith, Camden New Series 5, [London: printed for the society], 1872, p. 102.
56 S. R. Hovland, 'Apprenticeship in later medieval London (c.1300–c.1530)', PhD thesis, University of London, 2006, pp. 15–16.
57 Hudson and Tingey (eds), *Records of the City of Norwich*, vol. 1, p. 106.
58 NRO, NCR, 16d/1, fol. 128v, and 16d/2, fol. 92v. Bundles of apprenticeship indentures are extant in the civic archives from 1515, and there are enrolments from 1510: NRO, NCR, 10a, and 1/22. My PhD student, Dana Durkee, kindly supplied these references.
59 For the weavers' register of apprentices, 1461–1502, see York City Archives, D11. The 1515 ordinance is in *YCR*, vol. 3, p. 46.
60 *CLB*, pp. 553–4, 558–9, 560. The claim that the ordinance was merely a confirmation of an older by-law was untrue. The *Leet Book* contains no such act.
61 *CLB*, pp. 560–3. Cf. N. R. Amor, 'Apprenticeship in late medieval Ipswich', *Proceedings of the Suffolk Institute for Archaeology and History*, 42, 2012, pp. 411–15.
62 C. M. Barron, *London in the Later Middle Ages: Government and People 1200–1500*, Oxford: Oxford University Press, 2004, p. 179.
63 *CLB*, p. 560. Cf. the oath of the Norwich freeman, in Hudson and Tingey (eds), *Records of the City of Norwich*, vol. 1, p. 129.
64 C. W. Colby, 'The growth of oligarchy in English towns', *EHR*, 5, 1890, pp. 633–53; J. Lee, 'Urban policy and urban political culture: Henry VII and his towns', *Historical Research*, 82, 2009, pp. 493–510.
65 D. M. Palliser, 'Towns and the English state, 1066–1500', in J. R. Maddicott and D. M. Palliser (eds), *The Medieval State: Essays presented to James Campbell*, London: Hambledon, 2000, pp. 127–45.
66 C. A. Markham and J. C. Cox (eds), *The Records of the Borough of Northampton*, 2 vols, London: Elliot Stock, 1898, vol. 1, pp. 203–4.
67 *YCR*, vol. 2, pp. 115–16.
68 CRO, BA/H/17/A79/19.
69 For the new emphasis on the 'rule of law', evident in Fortescue's *De Laudibus Legum Anglie* (written 1468–71) and in the texts and speeches of early Tudor statesmen, see J. L. Watts, '"A Newe Ffundacion of is Crowne": monarchy in the age of Henry VII', in B. Thompson (ed.), *The Reign of Henry VII*, Stamford: Paul Watkins, 1995, pp. 31–53, and J. L. Watts, '"Common weal" and "commonwealth": England's monarchical republic in the making, c.1450–c.1530', in A. Gamberini, J.-P. Genet, and A. Zorzi (eds), *The Languages of Political Society: Western Europe, 14th–17th Centuries*, Rome: Viella, 2011, pp. 147–63.
70 I. M. W. Harvey, 'Was there popular politics in fifteenth-century England?', in R. H. Britnell and A. J. Pollard (eds), *The McFarlane Legacy: Studies in Late Medieval Politics and Society*, Stroud: Alan Sutton, 1995, pp. 160–2; I. Arthurson, 'Espionage and intelligence from the Wars of the Roses to the Reformation', *Nottingham Medieval Studies*, 35, 1991, pp. 134–54.
71 *YHB*, vol. 1, pp. 359–60; 'The corporation of Southampton: letters and loose memoranda', in *Historical Manuscripts Commission, Eleventh Report, Appendix, Part III: The Manuscripts of the Corporations of Southampton and King's Lynn*, London: HMSO, 1887, pp. 106–7.
72 LMA, COL/CC/01/01/009, fol. 117.
73 Edmund Dudley, *The Tree of Commonwealth*, ed. D. M. Brodie, Cambridge: Cambridge University Press, 1948, p. 87.
74 NRO, NCR, 16a/2, p. 9; *YHB*, vol. 1, p. 402, and vol. 2, pp. 460, 627; LMA, COL/CC/01/01/010, fol. 250r.
75 LMA, COL/CC/01/01/009, fol. 117.
76 NRO, NCR, 17d/7, fols 12, 78v–9r.
77 For what follows, see NRO, NCR, 16a/2, pp. 16–19.

78 The taxer, William Holston, had entered the freedom of the city six years earlier: J. L'Estrange and W. Rye (eds), *Calendar of the Freemen of Norwich from 1307 to 1603*, London: Elliot Stock, 1888, p. 75.
79 See e.g. C. D. Liddy and J. Haemers, 'Popular politics in the late medieval city: York and Bruges', *EHR*, 128, 2013, pp. 771–805, at 785–9.
80 A. Wood, *The 1549 Rebellions and the Making of Early Modern England*, Cambridge: Cambridge University Press, 2007, pp. 151–64.
81 J. Watts, 'Public or plebs: the changing meaning of "the commons", 1381–1549', in H. Pryce and J. Watts (eds), *Power and Identity in the Middle Ages: Essays in Memory of Rees Davies*, Oxford: Oxford University Press, 2007, pp. 249–50.
82 C. D. Liddy, 'Urban enclosure riots: risings of the commons in English towns, 1480–1525', *P&P*, 226, 2015, pp. 41–77.
83 As argued in J. Dumolyn and J. Haemers, '"A bad chicken was brooding": subversive speech in late medieval Flanders', *P&P*, 214, 2012, pp. 45–86.
84 The important work of Marjorie McIntosh, beginning with her research into the Essex manor of Havering, has concentrated on villages and smaller market towns.
85 I would like to thank my colleague, Andy Wood, for this point. His new research project, funded by the Leverhulme Trust, begins in 1500: 'Social Relations and Everyday Life in England, 1500–1640', www.dur.ac.uk/history/research/research_projects/everydaylife/.
86 See e.g. J. Hatcher, 'The great slump of the mid-fifteenth century', in R. Britnell and J. Hatcher (eds), *Progress and Problems in Medieval England: Essays in Honour of Edward Miller*, Cambridge: Cambridge University Press, 1996, pp. 237–72.
87 S. H. Rigby, 'Urban population in late medieval England: the evidence of the lay subsidies', *EcHR*, 63, 2010, pp. 393–417.
88 See e.g. C. Phythian-Adams, *Desolation of a City: Coventry and the Urban Crisis of the Late Middle Ages*, Cambridge: Cambridge University Press, 1979. P. J. P. Goldberg, 'Coventry's "Lollard" programme of 1492 and the making of utopia', in R. Horrox and S. Rees Jones (eds), *Pragmatic Utopias: Ideals and Communities, 1200–1630*, Cambridge: Cambridge University Press, 2001, pp. 97–116, looks at issues of gender and religious belief.
89 R. H. Britnell, 'The English economy and the government, 1450–1550', in J. L. Watts (ed.), *The End of the Middle Ages? England in the Fifteenth and Sixteenth Centuries*, Stroud: Sutton, 1998, p. 95.
90 Barron, *London*, pp. 211, 229. See also M. Davies, 'Artisans, guilds and government in London', in R. H. Britnell (ed.), *Daily Life in the Late Middle Ages*, Stroud: Sutton, 1998, pp. 125–6, 143.
91 Barron, *London*, pp. 302–7.
92 S. Rees Jones, 'Thomas More's "Utopia" and medieval London', in Horrox and Rees Jones (eds), *Pragmatic Utopias*, p. 127; *Letter-Book L*, pp. 118–20, 154, 203, 259, 291, 295, 302, 308.
93 *YHB*, vol. 1, pp. 309–10. For the context, see ibid., vol. 1, pp. 214–15, 224–5, 229–31.
94 For the term, see P. Griffiths, 'Secrecy and authority in late sixteenth- and seventeenth-century London', *Historical Journal*, 40, 1997, p. 947.
95 For example, Sellers (ed.), *York Memorandum Book*, vol. 1, p. 248; F. B. Bickley (ed.), *The Little Red Book of Bristol*, 2 vols, Bristol: W. Crofton Hemmons, 1900, vol. 2, p. 162; CRO, PA 34/1, fol. 3r.
96 For example, LMA, COL/AD/01/011, fols 122r (bakers), 131v–2r (girdlers), 149v (turners), 151v (paviors), 159r (tilers), 167r (masons), 168r (wiremongers), 171v (leathersellers), 177v (dyers), 196v (fletchers), 202r (butchers), 230v (carpenters), 251r (coopers), 253v (plumbers), 254v (pouchmakers), 255 (waxchandlers), 257v (netmakers).
97 *GRB*, vol. 2, pp. 150–1, 160–1.
98 For this hierarchy in London, see Barron, *London*, pp. 214–16, 226; Davies, 'Artisans', pp. 126–32. For elsewhere, see the Coventry weavers, where there was an inner group of 12: CRO, PA 34/1, fols 4r, 5v.
99 LMA, COL/CC/01/01/008, fol. 165.
100 LMA, COL/CC/01/01/010, fol. 150v.
101 B. Scribner, 'Mündliche Kommunikation und Strategien der Macht in Deutschland im 16. Jahrhundert', in H. Kühnel (ed.), *Kommunikation und Alltag in Spätmittelalter und Früher Neuzeit*, Vienna: Verlag der Österreichischen Akademie der Wissenschaften, 1992, p. 191.
102 *GRB*, vol. 4, pp. 84, 87.
103 For this script, see LMA, COL/CA/01/01/003, fol. 155v, where a marginal entry reads: 'Memorandum that atkynson hathe a Copy'. John Atkynson was the name of the haberdasher.

104 For the friction between these two impulses, see A. Wood, 'Fear, hatred and the hidden injuries of class in early modern England', *Journal of Social History*, 39, 2006, pp. 803–26.
105 For such a reproduction, see LMA, COL/CA/01/01/003, fols 261–2r, 275r.
106 McSheffrey, *Marriage, Sex, and Civic Culture*, p. 137. See also B. Hanawalt, '"Good governance" in the medieval and early modern context', *Journal of British Studies*, 37, 1998, pp. 246–57.
107 LMA, COL/CA/01/01/003, fols 242v, 244r.
108 Griffiths, 'Secrecy', p. 928.

17
INTERPRETING LARGE-SCALE REVOLTS
Some evidence from the War of the Communities of Castile

Hipólito Rafael Oliva Herrer

My intention is to analyse some of the key aspects of the War of the Communities of Castile, which can be considered an example of a large-scale revolt. I shall concentrate particularly on questions relating to ideology, although I shall first briefly set it in context.[1]

One of the most important aspects of the movement, and the one that has attracted most attention from liberal historiography, is that it set out to establish a new model for defining the relationship between king and kingdom. This was reflected in legislation drawn up by a council of delegates from the cities, known as the *Junta comunera*. The *comunero* movement did not question the figure of the king, but it did plan to reduce his powers drastically, with the kingdom being granted a leading role, especially through the institution of the *Cortes*, which was given a prominent role in matters of government. There was therefore a strong element of opposition to the deployment of state centralism and a vindication of the autonomy and greater weight of the confederated cities in representing the kingdom as a whole.

A second aspect, which has received less emphasis, is that important transformations took place in the local political systems that had not been anticipated in the project for governing the kingdom. So, in some cities, the organs of local government were suppressed and replaced by a model based on assemblies that was organised around neighbourhoods or local parishes.

Third, the fact that a widespread anti-seigniorial revolt took place in large areas of northern Castile should also be taken into account. Those involved challenged their dependent status and manifested their desire to form part of the royal domain. Such uprisings were regarded coolly at first and even rejected by the *Junta comunera*, although it would eventually support them.

With respect to the social origins of the participants, it should be pointed out that a wide range of social groups were involved, namely, a large part of the common people, but also members of local elites who held important positions in both the administrative and the military systems of the movement, lawyers who collaborated in the drafting of the legislative project, some second-rank nobles, and even the odd member of the upper nobility who played a major role in the army of the *comuneros*.

Another aspect that I should like to mention briefly is its status as a unique event; the Crown of Castile had not known a large-scale uprising of these characteristics before. In truth, there had been a certain amount of strife in the decades leading up to the revolt of the *comuneros*, although only exceptionally did it lead to open confrontations. Just three years earlier, the cities had attempted to establish agreements that would enable them to oppose some of the measures taken by central government that they considered prejudicial to their interests; in other words, there was an obvious line of opposition led by the elites in quite a few cities, which did not however culminate in open conflict.[2]

Another line of confrontation in the preceding decades can be observed within the cities themselves. There was, in particular, a tradition of struggle for representation by the urban commons, although in most cases this had been channelled into peaceful forms of resistance, specifically by appealing to the monarchy to make a stand against the positions of the local authorities.[3] It is important to point out that the cities that joined the movement were precisely those in which the political activity of the commons had been greatest, although the role of the commons during the movement was initially a subordinate one.[4]

Social memory, especially of the civil war in Castile in the middle of the fifteenth century, also played a prominent role. Particularly in the sectors of the common people, there was a deep-rooted awareness of a political past, in which they represented themselves as defenders of the monarchy, in contrast to the openly hostile behaviour of the aristocracy, which they accused of subjugating the king, to the detriment of the kingdom.[5]

All these elements were undoubtedly at the root of the revolt of the *comuneros*, although this should be read, not so much as the culmination of a series of traditions of revolt, but as the crystallisation, at a moment of acute political crisis, of a type of political identity that brought together and inscribed traditions of political struggle that were in fact quite dissimilar.

The intensity of communication helps explain the spread of the conflict. There had already been abundant correspondence between the various cities involved before the *Junta comunera* was constituted; the *Junta* acted by taking on the functions of government and continued to do so afterwards. In fact, an intense propaganda campaign had developed protesting against the convening of the *Cortes* of la Coruña in 1520, where a new tax – which was what finally triggered the revolt – was going to be approved.[6] We should not underestimate the role of a central organ like the *Junta comunera* as a reference point and a coordinator; it was endowed with a powerful communicative apparatus, capable of conveying its messages to all the cities that were in sympathy with it, and it also developed a whole series of rituals of re-signification of space agreeing with the cause.[7] At the same time, though, its leading role in the spread of the movement should not be overestimated. We know that the political positions of the *Junta* were kept in a constant state of tension with local ones, and we know that all kinds of messages circulated via informal networks, not all of which coincided with those issued from the *Junta comunera*.[8]

Before proceeding further, a brief account of the major events is called for. From the time Charles I arrived in Castile in 1517, several cities had demonstrated their rejection of his policy with regard to taxation, as well as the implications for the kingdom of Castile of his acceptance of the imperial throne.[9] On 12 February, Charles I summoned the *Cortes* with the aim of demanding an extraordinary tax, before leaving Castile. During the month of February of that year, some cities drew up a programme of petitions, which included the refusal to pay a new tax. On 31 March 1520, the meeting of the *Cortes* began with the absence of the representatives of one of the most important cities in the kingdom, Toledo, which up to that point had led the opposition to the tax being approved. Charles I tried to replace the aldermen who had headed the city's opposition, which provoked a popular revolt in their defence.[10]

The tax was finally passed in the *Cortes* on 18 May 1520, after the majority of the citizen representatives resigned themselves to it. The return of these representatives to their cities of origin can be considered the beginning of the War of the Communities, in so far as a series of popular revolts broke out in cities like Segovia, Burgos, and Zamora, which culminated in some of the representatives being executed. These episodes, which scrupulously followed the ritual of execution reserved for traitors, can be interpreted strictly as acts of popular justice.[11] These mobilisations marked the moment from which the pressure exerted from below by the urban commons materialised as a notable factor in the conflict, which does not mean, however, that from that very moment there was a change in the traditional control of the local institutions by the elites in all the cities.[12]

In this state of upheaval, the city of Toledo called upon the cities with representation in the *Cortes* to send their delegates to the city of Avila on 1 August, with a programme that urged the abolition of the tax, among other things, and for Castilians to accept responsibility for government in the absence of the king. Five cities, Toledo, Segovia, Salamanca, Toro, and Zamora sent their representatives to the meeting, which can be regarded as the embryonic *Junta comunera*.

Nonetheless, the factor that ended up precipitating events was the march of the royal army on the city of Medina del Campo with the intent of picking up the royal artillery, in order to punish the city of Segovia; however, it met resistance from the inhabitants of the city. The result, on 21 August, was the burning and destruction of Medina del Campo, the most important financial and commercial centre in Castile. The news had an enormous impact. Several more cities then sent their representatives to the *Junta*.

At the beginning of September, the *Junta*, now with representatives from 13 of the 18 cities with votes in the *Cortes*, moved to the city of Tordesillas, which was where Juana, the Queen Mother, was being held captive, and kept away from power by her son Charles. From that point on, in order to give its positions legitimacy, the *Junta comunera* proclaimed that it was not only acting in the name of the king – a claim that it consistently reiterated during the revolt – but also in the name of Queen Juana, who, despite being kept away from power, had not in fact been deposed. The *Junta* assumed the functions of government when it proclaimed that its mission was to remedy the ills of the kingdom. During the month of October, the Junta drew up its project for political reform, on the basis of the petitions from the different cities, the Chapters of Tordesillas, or the *Ley perpetua* (Perpetual Law), which would be sent to the king for him to endorse. Its content included a limitation on royal power and the strengthening of the political role of the kingdom, particularly by reinforcing the institution of the *Cortes*.[13]

At the beginning of September, a wave of anti-seigniorial revolts broke out across a large part of the north and south of Castile. Initially, the *Junta* kept its distance from them.[14] During the month of October, the royal army was raised, with the support of most of the Grandees, who had also not been involved up to that point, fearful of the uprisings spreading through their lordly estates. That same month, some of the cities, among them Burgos, Cuenca, and Soria, started to distance themselves from the political positions defended by the *Junta*, either because they were wary of the *Junta*'s draft proposals for transforming the political structures, or because the elites of those cities feared that their position of control over the local institutions of government was being challenged in the course of the revolt, which was exactly what was happening.[15]

I shall not dwell at length on an account of the events, except to point out that the capture of Tordesillas by the royalist army on 5 December 1520 forced the *Junta comunera* to move to the nearby city of Valladolid, which became the capital of the movement from then on. After that, there was a succession of attempts at negotiation and military clashes, until the *comunero* army was finally defeated at Villalar on 23 April 1521.

Map 17.1 The scope of the War of the Communities.

The historiography of the War of the Communities of Castile: a critical review

There is an immense historiography on the War of the Communities of Castile, or the Revolt of the *Comuneros*, so I shall concentrate here on what I consider to be the central issues.[16] Readings of the movement began not long after it ended. Most descriptions of it in the chronicles were dismissive in tone, although, in a few of them, there was a veiled and diluted sense of sympathy for some of the demands made by the *comuneros*. Finally, a third group of chronicles presented the conflict as a plebeian revolt and characterised it as a populist, anti-seigniorial movement.[17]

For a long time, there were, in general terms, two major interpretations of the conflict. The first, which was whiggish in style and had a certain patriotic element, presented the *comuneros* as pioneers in the fight for freedom from royal absolutism. The second type of interpretation, which regarded the movement as conservative and somewhat xenophobic, focused on defending medieval privileges and was, therefore, opposed to the ideal of modernity that Imperial Spain and the progress of the state embodied.[18]

Mesocratic interpretations

With the more conservative interpretation of the movement in full force, Manuel Azaña, who later became President of the Second Republic, introduced the idea that it was the middle classes who led the *comunero* movement.[19] Some time later, Tierno Galván identified the conflict with echoes of a late Aristotelian strand of republican thought emanating from the University of Salamanca, and acclaimed the movement as being essentially middle class and learned in nature.[20]

In 1963, José Antonio Maravall took up these ideas again and amplified them in the first study of the *War of the Communities* that can be regarded as a classic. He interpreted it as a revolutionary type of movement and highlighted the representative nature of the *Junta comunera* of the whole of the political community of the kingdom and its preparation of a plan for a constitution, known as the *Ley perpetua* (Perpetual Law). According to Maravall, this was a set of provisions intended to correct the king's march towards absolutism and to set up a new institutional framework that would express a new type of relationship between king and kingdom in which the latter would possess the capacity for political control. In this way, Maravall presented the conflict as the first of the modern-style revolutions, the forerunner of the French and American ones.[21]

Maravall defined the political subject of that conflict as the citizen estate, which he associated with the term *comunidad* (community); to this end, he combined the various senses of the polysemic word 'community', which had different implications depending on the context in which it was uttered, but they were no less precise for all that. He concluded that the term came to represent that citizen estate imbued with democratic values, the result of the trickle down effect of learned political theories, republican in spirit, that were expressed as their own ideology and articulated around notions of freedom and the common good.

Maravall amplified his reasoning by noting that the political character of the movement ended up becoming a questioning of the social order, although here, his interpretation becomes vague. He detects the importance of the participation of the lower orders in the conflict and credits them with having a radicalising effect, but also attributes an irrational, messianic character to them, before concluding that the true agent of change was a set of intermediate groups whose capacity for upward social mobility had been blocked.[22] He had recourse, therefore, to a series of notions, such as the changes inherent in the way of life in the towns and cities and the affluent, middle-class nature of the movement.

From the perspective of the present, there is a great temptation to criticise Maravall's interpretation, because little was known at that time of either the urban political dynamics or the political language itself.[23] Hence, the most interesting part of his interpretation was the political implications of the *Junta*'s proposals, even though we now know that the dynamic of conflict between king and kingdom that derived from them was not as novel as Maravall claimed.

Nevertheless, Maravall's interpretation set the terms of the debate for a considerable period, so that even very recent studies more or less explicitly agree with his claims. José Joaquín Jerez, for example, maintained that the 'citizen estate' played the leading role in the revolt and that the conflict arose from the dissemination of new developments in political theory that made an impact in the cities and were expressed most clearly in the chapters proposed by the *Junta* of Tordesillas.[24]

Needless to say, we know that legal counsel was important to the *Junta* in the production of their texts and in their attempts to legitimise the revolt. We also know that some of the ideas taken from that late strand of political Aristotelianism did circulate during the conflict, although not even in the most fully developed of the texts produced by the *Junta comunera* was this connection made explicit. In reality, they resorted to much less controversial arguments to justify their positions, such as the *Siete Partidas de Alfonso X* (The Seven-Part Code of Alfonso X). However, this type of interpretation tends to present the reasoning as if the dissemination of learned doctrines about the right to resist was what drove the rebellion. In short, there is a merging of practices and scholastic thinking, an issue that Pierre Bourdieu drew our attention to in his day.[25]

Along similar lines to Maravall is the work of Antonio Suárez Varela, who went into greater detail about the political language of the *comuneros* and concluded that what was specific about the movement was the emergence of a discourse of the common good.[26] We now know that what the author presents as constituting original thought was, actually, merely the use of a more general repertoire of political language. In Castile, and in many other places, the notion of the *common good* was a standard expression of reference in governance.[27] It was a set of public concepts used by different actors – including those that opposed the *comuneros* – to construct their discursive strategies. Its specific content was not predetermined but was the object of discursive confrontation.[28] In this case, the pertinent question would be to ask to what extent the *comuneros* reproduced, re-elaborated, or injected new significance into that political language.

In general terms, one might argue that the problem with such interpretations stems from their initial assumption: conceiving the *comunero* movement as an expression of unified political thought, embodied in a single essential protagonist of the revolt. This was the position during the 1960s and 1970s, when the revolutionary agent par excellence was being sought in the middle classes, and there was an insistence on making very sharp distinctions between first-class revolutions endowed with a transformational political programme, and mere revolts.[29]

We owe the second major interpretation of mesocratic inspiration to Joseph Pérez, whose analysis of the conflict remains, even today, the standard work of reference. Thanks to his exhaustive analysis of a good many of the preserved documents, we know in great detail how events unfolded, as well as the geography of the *comunero* uprising. According to Pérez, the *comunero* programme corresponds to a modern type of political reorganisation, characterised as limiting the arbitrary power of the Crown, and which was triggered in the context of a crisis that had two dimensions. The first was the political crisis that originated with the death of the Catholic monarchs and did not conclude even when Charles I came to the throne, while the second was an economic crisis, marked by two cycles of high prices, which heightened awareness of excessive fiscal exploitation. Given this background and influenced by a series of protests and disturbances caused by the tax situation, the accession of Charles I to the title of emperor served as the trigger. The aspirations of Charles to the imperial throne and the sacrificing of Castilian interests lay behind the attempt to articulate the relationship between king and kingdom in a different way.[30] Pérez's interpretation, nonetheless, follows the line laid down by Maravall, albeit with some nuances, in as much as he attributes the failure of the movement to the immaturity of the middle class. This was revealed in the fact that they were unable both to coordinate and to integrate the economic interests of the textile producers and the merchants, who ended up opposing each other.

Stephen Haliczer's contribution to the debate turned the urban patriciate into the equivalent of those middle classes and consequently into the principal agent of the conflict.[31] He conceived the movement as a revolution that was different in substance from the series of fifteenth-century conflicts, adducing two basic reasons: first, because of its geographical spread and, second, because, in the course of it, a complex political programme was expressed. Strongly influenced by Talcott Parsons, he understood that the conflict that started in 1520 was not the result of the specific political events linked to the accession of Charles I as king, but of a series of long-term structural changes that gave rise to a pre-revolutionary society characterised by the growth of the middle classes, which Haliczer identified essentially with the urban patriciate. The escalating taxes and the very disenchantment of the same urban elites towards the monarchy, in whom they had hoped to find an ally with regard to the pressure applied by the aristocracy on the cities, eventually lit the revolutionary fuse.

Even if the principal role of those local elites during the *comunero* conflict seems obvious at certain times and in certain places, it is difficult to see them as the agent of change that Haliczer claims they were. Specific studies of this social group in the different towns and cities of Castile have revealed that, however much it comprised people from the world of commerce, there was a strong aristocratising tendency in this social group, which was expressed in the adoption of noble models as a reference and in the fact that many of its members belonged to clientelist networks that linked them to the most important lineages of the Castilian aristocracy.[32] Their fundamental concerns turned out to be participation in the state bureaucracy, together with the political control that they exercised over the cities themselves.[33] There was certainly a sense that the local elites rejected the processes of royal interventionism in the cities, although that rejection might have been shared by other urban social groups and there is no reason for it to be considered exclusive to the local elites.

He dwelt, correctly, on the behaviour of the aristocracy during the previous period, characterised by constant attempts to increase its income and lordships at the expense of the royal patrimony and the cities themselves. This behaviour, though, far from being exceptional, followed a pattern that can be observed during a large number of the political crises of the fifteenth century. Indeed, it provoked responses that clearly resembled the *comunero* conflict itself, which links the movement to earlier processes, such as the phenomenon of the *Hermandades*, or Brotherhoods, particularly those of the mid-fifteenth century.

Critiques of the mesocratic model, the ideal of modernity, and the inclusion of new agents

A few years after publishing his work on social conflicts in the late Middle Ages, Julio Valdeón took issue with interpretations that placed the *comunero* movement at the start of the essentially modern struggle for emancipation. Arguing against the artificial nature of academic chronological distinctions, he defined the conflict as the *last medieval revolt*. He asserted that the movement could not be understood without its immediate antecedents, recalling that it combined a whole series of troublesome issues that originated precisely in the final centuries of the Middle Ages: the strengthening of the aristocracy, the internal tensions and disputes within the cities, the antiseigniorial uprisings, even the leading political role taken by the confederations of cities, known as Brotherhoods. In short, for Valdeón, the *comunero* movement was the consequence of the formation of a heterogeneous coalition of actors with contradictory interests, which drifted eventually into a confrontation between the commons and the powerful, the main narrative thread running through the conflict, as some of the sixteenth-century chronicles indicated.[34]

It was precisely through his analysis of the mid-fifteenth century Brotherhoods that José Luis Bermejo presented a very forceful critique of Maravall's claims.[35] According to Bermejo, far from springing up as an original movement, the *Junta comunera* had not only organised itself as a Brotherhood, but had also absorbed many of the political proposals of the general Brotherhood movement of the mid-fifteenth century. Bermejo was certainly wide of the mark when he played down the political character of the two movements, as he stressed that their aim was the restoration, rather than the transformation, of the political order, and also highlighted the logic of service to the king, which appears in the documents of the *Juntas* of the Brotherhood as well as of the *Junta comunera* itself. Nonetheless, behind the political rhetoric of service lay a concealed practice in which royal competences were being taken over, starting with the capacity to legislate and exercise justice and concluding with the construction of their own separate institutional structure.[36] In short, the legitimisation of service to the king by the Brotherhoods was a front that masked the development of their own political programme, one that most certainly anticipated a good many of the questions that the *Junta comunera* would raise later, however much the political language it used occasionally differed. Apart from this, as Benjamín González Alonso highlighted, it confirmed that the history of troubled relations between the king and the political community already went back a long way, and that the cities' rejection of the process of the centralisation of the monarchy and their ambition to represent the kingdom as a whole had emerged previously in other contexts of general political crisis.[37]

We owe one of the most interesting contributions to the debate, without a doubt, to Pablo Sánchez León, who set aside the study of the political discourse of the *Junta* in order to inquire about the conditions that made revolt in the cities possible. Sánchez León carried out a critique of the middle-class type interpretations of the movement and attributed the difficulties of finding the social subject of the collective action to insufficiently detailed sociological analyses.[38]

Conscious of the multiple actors involved, he argued that this subject was the result of intra-class cooperation in a movement that was led by the urban elites and which the lower classes joined, spurred on by the increase in fiscal pressure. Strongly influenced by historical sociology, Sánchez León placed the roots of the revolt in long-term structural changes, in particular, the two sets of problems that were associated with incorporating the local elites into the state reorganisation of the political system, namely, their institutional integration and their participation in a centralised mechanism for distributing surpluses. The revolt, therefore, would be an antiabsolutist, conservative kind of movement, linked to the structural crisis in the minor urban nobility, which amounted to its difficulty in gaining access to the resources that would enable it to perpetuate itself.

Some years later, Sánchez León would partially reformulate his interpretation with a shift towards the cultural turn, by invoking the notion of identity. So, the *comunero* revolt would be the consequence of the genesis of a shared identity. Sánchez León invoked the notion of identity, however, in the strong, communitarian sense, in which there was no place for tensions or fissures. Furthermore, he considered that this identity was expressed in a political language unequivocal and distinct which took him closer to those interpretations that understood the conflict as the expression of unified thought.[39]

From another point of view, María Isabel del Val Valdivieso argued in favour of the leading role played by the urban commons when she pointed out the continuity between the conflicts that arose in the towns and cities during the revolt and confrontations for political representation in earlier decades that involved the urban commons.[40] In her opinion, it was one aspect to take into account in a more complex conflict. Finally, she stressed the major role played in those conflicts by a 'commons elite' – regarded as a class that was still being formed – and its desire to see itself represented.

Members of those wealthy elites certainly played a leading role during the movement, but not all of the *comunero* leaders were rich merchants or well-educated individuals. In fact, we know that, encouraged by the movement, new leaders emerged who were of obviously humble origin. Without going into the problematic relationship between class position and political subjectivity that the interpretation poses, the model presents other difficulties by not taking sufficient account of the politicisation of the rest of the urban commons, with the result that it tends to swing towards traditional mesocratic-type interpretations.[41]

The study of the unfolding of the revolt in the rural world was chronologically earlier, but has not enjoyed as much continuity. In 1973, Juan Ignacio Gutiérrez Nieto alerted us to the fact that the *comunero* movement had a strong impact in the countryside, where it took the form of a large-scale anti-seigniorial uprising.[42] In the majority of accounts about the War of the Communities, Gutiérrez Nieto's revelations were included as a circumstantial element, albeit acknowledging that it was a factor that ended up affecting alignments by triggering the hostility of the aristocracy towards the revolt. In order to present the anti-seigniorial explosion as something tangential to the main core of the revolt, it was pointed out that even some of the members of the *Junta comunera*, who supposedly viewed these movements from afar, held lordships.[43] But what may have been true at the level of the *Junta*, is less so if we consider the *comunero* movement as a complex revolt on a grand scale, and this is where the link shows up most clearly. We know that those uprisings were fuelled by a series of more widely shared ideological currents, which were kept alive by a deep-seated memory of political events in the kingdom; to such an extent that those who took part in the rural uprisings not only showed that the revolt affected them directly, but that they sought to inscribe their own political action as a necessary consequence of it.[44]

Otherwise, the treatment of the anti-seigniorial uprisings may be read as an example of historiography's difficulties in interpreting the *comunero* conflict as anything more than a movement exclusively made up of elites.[45] This is reflected in the historiographical treatment of the popular urban sectors in the conflict. Despite the fact that they were important participants in the movement, historiography has mostly assumed, with very few exceptions, that they had no political agenda.[46] One of the most widespread interpretations used to explain their activity was the influence of millenarian strands of thought, about which, however, there is scant evidence, apart from the erroneous interpretation of a few chronicles.[47]

The revolt and transformations in local government institutions

I should now like to consider the changes effected in the urban institutions, since, in my opinion, they show quite clearly some of the underlying assumptions of the most widely held interpretations of the conflict. This is a relatively neglected aspect of historiography, although one recently addressed by Máximo Diago Hernando and by myself. These studies emphasise the fact that the institutions underwent major changes that were linked to political struggles within the towns and cities. Furthermore, the extent to which the cities supported the revolt fluctuated according to the outcome of those confrontations; hence the cities in which the urban commons gained access to quotas of political power were the ones that ended up being the basic support of the *Junta comunera*.[48]

In spite of this, instead of reading the evolution of the cities as the result of the way power was distributed between different actors with different political projects, emphasis has been placed on the *comunero* revolt as involving the appearance of new ways of politically integrating the 'citizen estate', in the shape of a new institution, the *Comunidad*.[49] What was observed in some cities, however, was rather different: the controversial replacement of traditional forms of representation with a model of assemblies and representatives elected by *cuadrillas* (neighbourhoods), which occurred only in some cities. The institutions that emerged at the dawn of the conflict conformed rather to the traditional mechanism of incorporating members of the urban commons in subordinate positions. In other words, it was a way of expanding local political society that was not new, since it had been documented earlier in the cities of Castile in contexts of political crisis.[50]

Many of these interpretations rested, in fact, on erroneous readings of the political language. The concept of *comunidad* (community) was neither a novelty introduced during the *comunero* conflict, nor can a new institutional framework necessarily be inferred from it. The notion of *community* is problematic because its meaning varies depending on the context of utterance and because it is often opaque, so that it is not always possible to deduce a specific political dynamic from its use.[51]

In the first of its meanings, the concept of community was equivalent to 'sedition' or 'insurrection', and this is the sense that ended up colouring the definition of the movement, which was defined by the royal authority as 'the community'. The term *community*, however, appears with other meanings in the documents generated before and during the conflict. In political language about governance, it was known to function in the sense of *populus* to describe the whole of the urban body politic. It also had a standard use equivalent to 'the commons' or 'the common people', with the sense of *plebs*, that is, the unprivileged sector of the urban population that did not have access to local political power. Finally, there was also a sense with a certain egalitarian content, concerning the suppression of internal hierarchies in the local political community.[52]

Tellingly, the term *community* started to reflect institutional content in those cities where the urban commons managed to attain positions of power. It was not used in the sense of an integrative movement, but as a reversal of traditional forms of political representation, the fruit of a confrontation that was both political and, as we shall see, discursive, between actors who had different aims and aspirations.[53]

What is more, if we carefully examine the instructions sent by the different cities to the *Junta*, and even the government plan produced by the *Junta* itself, it can be observed that they did not envisage substantial transformations of the local political order, which corresponds to a phase of the movement when the political elites still controlled the large cities. This is an indication that transformations in the local political order were not the result of the dissemination from above of a unifying ideology that incorporated new forms of representation of the political community, but rather the result of pressures from below.

How to interpret a large-scale movement

Research into the conflict has not ceased in recent years, although a certain tendency to fragmentation can be detected. Together with a series of local studies that enable us to learn about the events in more detail, there is a perceptible dynamic of fragmentation.[54] This operates in two main ways. First, there is an emphasis on local particularities, accompanied by a certain refusal to offer overall interpretations and, second, attention is paid to partial aspects of the conflict and no attempt is made to question the classic interpretations.[55]

In short, historiography has revealed the complexity of the conflict and the plurality of the actors involved, even though it has generally tended to seek out a privileged agent, an essential protagonist of the revolt, often assuming that there was an explicit correspondence between political subjectivity and class position.

In my opinion, a valid interpretation of the movement as a whole should respect both the complex way in which the actors marked out their political positions and the diversity of experiences of actors who were involved in the movement and exhibited aspirations of different kinds.

Without doubt, one of the most significant aspects for explaining the spread of the conflict was that a type of discourse was produced on which a pre-existing set of demands of different kinds could be inscribed, and which also enabled the various groups that became involved in the movement – and whose ultimate aspirations were in many cases contradictory – to be incorporated into it. It was a discourse that created an unstable political identity in which tensions, ideological clashes, and shifts appeared.

I shall now try to analyse the main ideological currents by means of a series of key political concepts, beginning with the discourse that the *Junta comunera* addressed to the kingdom as a whole. The discourse issued by the *Junta comunera* can be reconstructed from the manifestos promulgated during its constitution and the many letters it sent justifying itself, to the cities in particular, but also to the monarch.

The letters contain a series of key notions: the first, that the kingdom was being tyrannised and destroyed, and the second, that the *comunero* cause was a movement in defence of the common good and the freedom of the kingdom. The letter sent to Emperor Charles V enables us to make a few observations. In this letter, the royal entourage was blamed for the bad government of the kingdom, while the monarch was exonerated. It was the greed of those who surrounded the king that caused the destruction of the royal patrimony, forcing him to crush the people with excessive taxes.[56] This statement should be understood in the context of a tradition of protests about giving away the royal patrimony.[57] The accusation, however, does not seem to be confined to the small circle of government councillors; the Grandees, in other words, the aristocracy, were also accused of having advised the king in the creation of the new tax and of facilitating its adoption, together with some representatives from the cities.[58]

In any event, by mentioning the aristocracy directly, the *Junta comunera* seems to be taking part in a more generalised ideological context of criticism of the Grandees. The political sermons delivered by Franciscan preachers in Valladolid some years before allow us partially to reconstruct it. The argument used is that the Grandees are not concerned with the common good, only with their own individual interests and benefiting themselves.[59] The idea that the nobles were destroying the royal patrimony was in fact present from the very moment that the new king arrived, as collected conversations that show fear of a king being manipulated by the higher nobility demonstrate.[60] In this respect, social memory was important, since we witness the reactivation of a kind of political discourse that had been expressed openly during the civil war in the mid-fifteenth century.[61]

This kind of discourse, which the *Junta comunera* adopted with a certain amount of caution, was expressed more crudely and using different language by the common people in cities such as Valladolid. According to the chronicler Anghiera, they called the Grandees 'usurpers of the Crown and wolves in the royal flock',[62] proclaiming that 'they have to finish off all the Grandees who possess something of the Royal Crown and that they have to increase its wealth'.[63] Only when the *Junta comunera* saw that it was heading for a confrontation with most of the aristocracy – which formed the core of the army against the *comuneros* – did it make this opposition explicit by stating that, unless action was taken against them: 'We would remain in *perpetual serfdom to these Grandees ... their purpose ... is to take the lordships for themselves, to our detriment, and to subject us for their own particular interests, and turn us from free* people *into slaves.*'[64]

One of the key questions is the use of the term *libertad* (freedom) in the *Junta*'s discourse. The various actors who took part in the movement all clearly coincide with the notion that what is being aired is the *freedom of the kingdom*. All those who acted in the name of the movement had to swear to commit themselves to the struggle for the freedom of the kingdom.[65]

The term *freedom* is in fact used with different meanings in different contexts. On occasions it is used in the plural, *libertades y franquezas* (liberties and exemptions),[66] which directs us to the notion of privileges. In *comunero* discourse, however, *libertad* takes on another meaning. It is used as the opposite of oppression, a term that is collocated with the concepts of *sujeción* (subjection), *servidumbre* (serfdom), and even *esclavitud* (slavery).

There is obviously a fiscal connotation to the word *freedom*, in the sense that it is the new tax that is threatening the freedom of the kingdom, although it does not refer strictly to the new tax. According to the way the term is used, imposing taxes is simply the consequence of being subject to the interests and will of others. In short, the absence of freedom is assimilated to the ideas of being dependent on others and of domination, which is more comprehensive in meaning and can be summed up in the notions of *tiranía* (tyranny) and *tiranizar* (tyrannising).[67] In a letter sent to Segovia, the city is called upon to: 'Follow the just purpose and freedom of the kingdom ... until the kingdoms are completely free, for then, their majesties will be better served than under the tyranny of the past.'[68]

So, it is claimed that the intention of the opponents is to return them to serfdom and once that had been achieved, impose more taxes on them and cause further grievances.[69] What is being denounced, therefore, rather than the imposition of taxes, is the situation of subjection that makes it possible. This is reflected in one of the most emphatic indictments: 'The enemies of the kingdom join together willing to destroy these kingdoms and through their individual desires to draw them into perpetual serfdom, for them to be treated worse than slaves.'[70]

The use of *freedom* with this meaning takes us back to a particular medieval legal tradition, which defines both the notion of serfdom and slavery in similar terms: to live subject to the control of another. It is essentially the same type of reasoning, also based on the Digest,[71] as that formulated some 200 years later against Charles I in the English parliament, as Quentin Skinner pointed out.[72]

According to this definition, which coincides with the reasoning used by the *Junta comunera*, slavery consists of being subject to the control of another. Obviously, the Digest was widely disseminated in legal circles and known to the lawyers that advised the *Junta*. This conceptual framework is reproduced in the main statutory code of Castile, *Las Siete Partidas* (Seven-Part Code), which translates almost literally the categories used in the Digest, with one exception: the Latin term *servitus* was translated not as slavery, but serfdom.[73]

This also explains why, in the *Junta's* discourse, *serfdom* and *slavery* were formulated interchangeably with similar meanings, as being opposites of the idea of freedom. What they are referring to is the notion of freedom in Roman law as the absence of dependence/domination.[74] This legal formulation was well known to the circle of experts that the *Junta* consulted for advice. However it is interesting to note that it was not just a set of theoretical categories; the argument had also been used previously in contexts of political opposition. So, for example, in the city of León, the commons had protested against the authorities, denouncing the fact that the latter were acting as if the city belonged to them and that they (the commons) were their dependents.[75] In the final analysis, freedom and serfdom were also common-sense terms to use, and when the *Junta* invoked them, it was using a language that was understood by the majority of the population. In fact, we know that, even before the meeting of the *Cortes* in 1520 that approved the tax, rumours had circulated employing arguments of this sort, stating that they were being treated worse than slaves.[76]

The central argument of the political discourse of the *Junta* was the defence of the freedom of the kingdom, strongly linked to the idea of being subjected to the will of others. It was proclaimed that a return to a pre-revolt status would be a return to 'subjection, imprisonment and serfdom'.[77] This accusation of oppression was initially directed at 'those who were against freedom',[78] that is, those who were held responsible for the kingdom's grievances, which were typically though not exclusively summed up in the granting of the new tax. It ultimately acquired a marked anti-aristocratic meaning, in as much as the *Junta* repeated an ideological line that was quite widespread, and the *comunero* project confronted the Grandees of the kingdom, the mainstay of the anti-*comunero* party.

In any event, apart from representing an idea of freedom from something that was considered oppressive, it is somewhat more complicated to assign the term particular political implications. In fact, defining its meaning was the object of political and discursive confrontation. The freedom of the kingdom was a concept that allowed them to synthesise the set of grievances they had suffered and consequently to accommodate a set of aspirations of various kinds. This explains why the readings that made use of the term were also different. To obtain the freedom of the kingdom was useful for calling for a greater share for the cities in the distribution of political power, so benefiting their elites by discrediting the governance of bureaucrats and Grandees, which was what some cities wanted.

However, it also served to accommodate a global project for the political transformation of the kingdom, which was what the *Junta comunera* wanted.[79] It was also a concept that served to justify the anti-seigniorial uprisings that occurred, since many of these revolts claimed to be a movement for returning the royal patrimony that had been stripped by the nobles. It could even have gone beyond any idea of political transformation, in order to turn into a sort of anti-aristocratic social war, which was what finally happened.

We know the extent of these debates about how far they should go in invoking the freedom of the kingdom; and not only between various cities, but also within many of them. At any rate, the dissemination of a structured discourse around this idea is one of the factors that help explain the significant degree to which the revolt of the *comuneros* spread. In other words, it inscribed a series of different aspirations on to a – at least in principle – common horizon, which was to secure the freedom of the kingdom.

Nevertheless, the first time that the concept of freedom was uttered during the *comunero* conflict was even earlier, and its meaning only partly overlaps. This occurred during the popular revolts that took place, with mixed results, against the procurators at *Cortes* when they returned to the cities after having accepted the new tax.

Here, the appeal to freedom is associated with public proclamations such as 'Death to the traitors and freedom!' or 'Long live the Community and freedom!',[80] which are linked to a very specific political subject: *community* in the sense of 'commons'.[81] The concept here has a twofold connotation: on the one hand, with respect to the arbitrary nature of the approval of the tax, and more broadly, in a sense very similar to what we have just seen, as being opposed to political domination by those who had collaborated in approving it. This is obviously considered also as a sacrifice of the general interests of the urban commons by part or all of the local elite, as the wife of one of the *comunero* leaders in Aranda de Duero publicly proclaimed: 'Never in the world would they return the offices to the aldermen, because they were traitors who robbed the world, and as long as there was a world, they would not give them back to them.'[82]

This was all in tune with the tradition of the continuous political struggle for representation on the part of the urban commons, so that the cry of 'community' and 'freedom' acquires a twofold connotation: as a demand for non-interference, but also for effective control of a life in common, following Charles Taylor's conception of the term.[83]

What such proclamations at local level show is the delegitimisation of the local authorities. Each one of the cities in which the *comunero* movement triumphed had a previous history of confrontations about local political power and of criticism of the actions of local government. The notion of *parcialidad* (partiality) and of serving individual interests rather than the good of the community is a recurrent theme in such conflicts. One element that strengthened this delegitimisation was precisely the clientelist links between members of the local governments and the aristocracy of the kingdom, so putting them in the spotlight.[84]

This argument emerged with some force in a few cities on the eve of the *comunero* conflict. So, for example, in 1518, the procurator of the commons in Aranda denounced the fact that all the aldermen in the town 'live with the Count of Miranda and seek to serve him'.[85] Similarly, in 1519, the procurator of the commons of Valladolid denounced the fact that the aldermen 'all ... or mostly all, live with the Lord Count of Benavente',[86] adding about one of them that 'he is driven solely by self interest'.[87]

Right in the middle of the *comunero* conflict, this turned into a wholesale condemnation of the urban elites, overlapping with a clash of discourses over who constituted the true community. This can be seen, for example, in Ciudad Rodrigo, where the people denounced the organ of local government, which supported the *Junta*, claiming that it could not form a legitimate part of the movement: 'They were not *community*, but *partiality*, because gentlemen who entered it followed their own desires and did not seek the universal good.'[88]

In other cities though, it can be seen that a different language is used in public conversations: 'they make distinctions between the community of people of low birth and the other community of gentlemen and people who are upright citizens'.[89]

This was an attempt to redefine the scope of the *comunero* movement. Those who defended outside interests and sacrificed those of most of the inhabitants of the community could not form a legitimate part of it. This placed a large part of the elites in the opposing camp. In addition, this same confrontation ran parallel to an attempt to transform the traditional system of governing the city, for which the concept of 'freedom of the commons' was invoked.

It is important to observe that, at a certain moment, identifying local elites with the notion of partiality as opposed to the defence of the common good, with reference to local political society, also starts to colour the writings of the *Junta comunera* itself. It can be discerned in the correspondence that the cities of Valladolid and Burgos maintained from October 1520 onwards, at precisely the moment when the two cities were trying to distance themselves from the *Junta*'s positions.[90] So, in a letter addressed to Valladolid, the *Junta* contests the decisions taken by the local government and calls upon the participation of the whole of the political community:

> Provision must be made in each city *with the agreement and opinion of the community generally and not of individuals, even if they hold a position that represents the general community ... individual desires can be pointed to* that give cause for disturbance or commotion and [also that] *freedom of the commons* is suppressed, since in what has happened up to now, *it is to these* [the commons] *that the Kingdom principally owes the preservation of its freedom.*[91]

Some days later, on 30 October, the *Junta* addressed Burgos – specifically the organ of local government – in similar terms, stating that their political positions were illegitimate:

> We believe that *particular individuals* among you who have ordered this will realize the error that they have committed and *we hold it for certain that your community will join us* and with *the common good* because *they do not have the individual desires and passions that you have.*[92]

The essence of the message in both letters is clear: the governing elites are partial, not neutral, and do not defend the common good. In consequence, the representation of the political community is being overturned and is swinging towards a definition that is egalitarian and inclusive, because it includes the whole of the urban community, even though it was exclusive with respect to the traditional model of representation, in as much as government was based on the idea of the 'freedom of the commons'. This was a novel theoretical formulation, since the concept of freedom functioned within frameworks that sanctioned political inequality,[93] but one that simply described what the mechanism of government would be in practice in some *comunero* cities, strongly based on assembly discussion.[94]

The *Junta comunera*'s appeal meant recognising the participation of the commons in the *comunero* movement and the legitimisation of its political aspirations. The freedom of the kingdom required the freedom of the commons because it was the only way to continue advancing along that path. Of course, this position was also new in the *Junta*'s political proposals, whose aspirations did not initially include the transformation of the order of government in the cities. However, the need to garner support at important moments and the pressure from below forced this abrupt about-turn that picked up the aspirations of the urban commons.

Every revolt has something special about it, even more so if it involves, like this one, a large-scale movement. However, I would like to present some arguments for discussion. Given that I have concentrated on ideological questions, it seems obvious to highlight the importance of the spread of a type of discourse that picked up on the generalised discontent, able to connect with a series of pre-existing demands that were quite different in nature and project them on to a new horizon. The existence of a unified political language was another factor that helps explain the amplitude of the conflict, in as much as it allowed a series of equivalences to be drawn up between a set of previous conflicts that had developed at a local level.

At the same time, another conclusion that we can draw is that pre-existing political ideas are not easy to dissolve and that the effectiveness of the new discourse depended on its ability to connect with them. In specific terms, part of the urban commons possessed a very distinctive political identity and that identity was also expanded and extended during the conflict itself. This contributed, in short, to giving it its final tone, that of a movement with a broad popular base, which led to an open confrontation with the aristocracy of the kingdom and a large part of the local elites and ended up accommodating a wave of anti-seigniorial revolts.

Notes

1 This chapter is the result of the research project ¿*El poder de la comunidad?: Lenguaje y prácticas políticas populares a fines de la Edad Media* (HAR 2011–30035), funded by the Ministerio de Economía y Competitividad of Spanish Government.
2 M. Asenjo González, 'Las ciudades castellanas al inicio del reinado de Carlos V', *Studia Historica. Historia Medieval*, 21, 1999, pp. 49–115.
3 M. Diago Hernández, 'El común castellano en la vida de las ciudades castellanas en visperas de la revuelta comunera (1504–1520)', in J. A. Solórzano Telechea, B. Arízaga Bolumburu, and J. Haemers (eds), *Los grupos populares en la ciudad Medieval europea*, Logroño: Instituto de Estudios Riojanos, 2014, pp. 271–99; B. Majo Tomé, 'Sociedad y conflictos en Valladolid en el tránsito de la Edad media a la Moderna: contexto y desarrollo de la revolución comunera', PhD thesis, University of Valladolid, 2015.
4 H. R. Oliva Herrer, '¡Viva el rey y la Comunidad!: arqueología del discurso político de las Comunidades', in H. R. Oliva Herrer, V. Challet, J. Dumolyn, and M. A. Carmona Ruiz (eds), *La comunidad Medieval como esfera pública*, Seville, Universidad de Sevilla, 2014, pp. 315–55; H. R. Oliva Herrer, '¿Qué es la comunidad?: Reflexiones acerca de un concepto político y sus implicaciones en Castilla a fines de la Edad Media', *Medievalismo: Boletín de la Sociedad Española de Estudios Medievales*, 24, 2014, pp. 281–306.
5 For social memory see H. R Oliva Herrer, 'Popular voices and revolt: exploring anti-noble uprisings on the eve of the War of the Communities of Castile', in J. Dumolyn, J. Haemers, H. R. Oliva Herrer, and V. Challet (eds), *The Voices of the People in Late Medieval Europe: Communication and Popular Politics*, Brepols, Turnhout, 2014, pp. 49–62; H. R Oliva Herrer, '¿Qué tiene de común el "común"? La construcción de una identidad política en Castilla a fines de la Edad Media', in Solórzano Telechea *et al.* (eds), *Los grupos populares*, pp. 241–70; H. R Oliva Herrer, *Justicia contra señores: El mundo rural y la política en tiempos de los Reyes Católicos*, Valladolid: Universidad de Valladolid, 2004.
6 J. Pérez, *La revolución de las Comunidades de Castilla (1520–1521)*, Madrid: Siglo XXI, 1977, p. 141.
7 Archivo General de Simancas. Patronato Real. Leg. 4, fol. 76. See M. C. Carmona Ruiz, 'The perception of popular discourse in late medieval chronicles: the case of the "Relación de las Comunidades de Castilla"', in J. Dumolyn *et al.* (eds), *The Voices of the People*, pp. 63–72.

8 On revolts and communication see S. K Cohn, 'Enigmas of communication: Jacques, Ciompi, and the English', in Oliva Herrer et al. (eds) *La comunidad Medieval*, pp. 227–47.
9 For a detailed account of events, see J. Pérez, *La revolución de las Comunidades*.
10 For events in Toledo, see F. Martínez Gil, *La ciudad inquieta: Toledo comunera, 1520–1522*, Toledo: Diputación provincial de Toledo, 1993.
11 A. Mackay and G. McKendrick, 'La semiología y los ritos de violencia: sociedad y poder en la Corona de Castilla', *En la España medieval*, 11, 1988, pp. 153–4. For the forms of execution reserved for traitors, see I. Bazán, 'La pena de muerte en Castilla en la Edad Media', *Clio & Crimen*, 4, 2007, pp. 306–52. For the performative dimension of acts of popular violence, see H. Skoda, *Medieval Violence: Physical Brutality in Northern France, 1270–1330*, Oxford: Oxford University Press, 2013. For the notion of popular justice, see M. Foucault, 'Sur la justice populaire: débat avec les maos', *Dits et écrits*, 2 vols, Paris: Gallimard, 2001, vol. 1, pp. 1208–25.
12 Oliva Herrer, '¿Qué es la comunidad?'.
13 For the *Ley perpetua* bill, see Pérez, *La revolución*, pp. 532–65; J. J. Jerez, *Pensamiento político y reforma institucional durante la Guerra de las Comunidades de Castilla*, Madrid: Marcial Pons, 2007, pp. 325–593.
14 H. R. Oliva Herrer, 'Popular voices and revolt: exploring anti-noble uprisings on the eve of the War of the Communities of Castile', in J. Dumolyn et al. (eds), *The Voices of the People*, pp. 49–62; J. I. Gutiérrez Nieto, *Las comunidades como movimiento antiseñorial: La formación del bando realista en la guerra civil castellana de 1520–1521*, Barcelona: Planeta, 1973.
15 On this question, see M. Diago Hernando, 'Transformaciones de las instituciones de gobierno local en las ciudades castellanas durante la revuelta comunera', *Hispania. Revista Española de Historia*, 214, 2003, pp. 623–56.
16 For an attempt to classify the bibliography, see F. Pérez Pérez, *Ensayo bibliográfico de los comuneros y Villalar*, Valladolid: Fundación Villalar, 2012.
17 Gutiérrez Nieto, *Las comunidades*, pp. 35–44.
18 Ibid., pp. 49–99; J. Pérez 'Pour une nouvelle interprétation des "Comunidades" de Castille', *Bulletin Hispanique*, 65, 1963, pp. 238–83.
19 M. Azaña, *Plumas y palabras*, Madrid: Ciap, 1930.
20 E. Tierno Galván, 'De las Comunidades, o la Historia como proceso', *Boletín Informativo del Seminario de Derecho Político*, 1957, pp. 127–49.
21 J. A. Maravall, *Las comunidades de Castilla*, Madrid: Alianza Editorial, 1981 (1st edn 1963).
22 Ibid., pp. 28, 183.
23 On the cities, M. I. Val Valdivieso, 'Oligarquía versus común: consecuencias sociopolíticas del triunfo del regimiento en las ciudades castellanas', *Medievalismo*, 4, 1994, pp. 41–58.
24 Jerez, *Pensamiento político*, pp. 98–108.
25 P. Bourdieu, *Méditations pascaliennes*, Paris: Le Seuil, 1997.
26 A. Suárez Varela, 'Celotismo communal: la máxima política del procomún en la revuelta comunera', *Tiempos Modernos. Revista electrónica de Historia Moderna*, 15 (2007), www.tiemposmodernos.org/tm3/index.php/tm/issue/view/18; A. Suárez Varela, 'La conjuración comunera: de la antigua germanitas a la confederación de Tordesillas', *Historia, Instituciones, Documentos*, 34, 2007, pp. 247–77.
27 See E. I. Mineo, 'Cose in comune e bene commune: l'ideologia della communità in Italia nel tardo medioevo', in A. Gamberini, J.-P. Genet, and A. Zorzi (eds), *The Languages of Political Society*, Roma: Viella, 2013, pp. 39–67; E. Lecuppre Desjardin and A.-L. Van Bruane (eds), *De Bono Communi: The Discourse and Practice of the Common God in the European City (13th–16th c.)*, Turnhout: Brepols, 2010; J. M. Nieto Soria, *Fundamentos ideológicos del poder regio en Castilla*, Madrid: Eudemau, 1988.
28 V. Challet, 'Le bien commun à l'épreuve de la pratique: discours monarchique et réinterprétation consulaire en Languedoc à la fin du Moyen Âge', *Revue française d'histoire des idées politiques*, 32, 2010, pp. 311–24; J. Dumolyn and E. Lecuppre-Desjardin, 'Le bien commun en Flandre médiévale: une lutte discursive entre prince et sujets', in Lecuppre-Desjardin and Van Bruaene (eds), *De Bono Communi*, pp. 253–68.
29 Interesting reflections on this in P. Freedman, 'La resistencia campesina y la historiografía en la Europa medieval', *Edad Media. Revista de Historia*, 3, 2000, pp. 17–38.
30 J. Pérez, *La révolution des 'Comunidades' de Castille*, Bordeaux: Université de Bordeaux, 1979; J. Pérez, 'Rey y reino: de los Reyes Católicos a la revolución de las Comunidades', I. Szászdi León-Borja and M. J. Galende Ruiz (eds), *Monarquía y revolución: En torno a las Comunidades de Castilla*, Valladolid: Fundación Villalar, 2010, pp. 17–28.
31 S. Haliczer, *Los comuneros de Castilla: La forja de una revolución (1474–1521)*, Valladolid: Junta de Castilla y León, 1987.

32 See M. Asenjo Gozález (ed.), *Urban Elites and Aristocratic Behaviour in the Spanish Kingdoms at the End of the Middle Ages*, Turnhout: Brepols, 2014; J. M. Monsalvo Antón, 'En torno a la cultura contractual de las élites urbanas: pactos y compromisos políticos (linajes y bandos de Salamanca, Ciudad Rodrigo y Alba de Tormes)', in F. Foronda and A. I. Carrasco Manchado (eds), *El contrato político en la Corona de Castilla: Cultura y sociedad política entre los siglos X al XVI*, Madrid: Dyckinson, 2008, pp. 189–94; M. Diago Hernando, 'El poder de la nobleza en los ámbitos regionales de la Corona de Castilla a fines del medievo: las estrategias políticas de los grandes linajes en la Rioja hasta la revuelta comunera', *Hispania*, 223, 2006, pp. 501–46; M. Diago Hernando, 'La proyección de las casas de la alta nobleza en las sociedades políticas regionales: el caso soriano a fines de la Edad Media', *Anuario de Estudios Medievales*, 39, 2009, pp. 843–76.
33 M. Asenjo González, 'La aportación del sistema urbano a la gobernabilidad del reino de Castilla durante la época de los Reyes Católicos (1464–1504)', *Anuario de Estudios Medievales*, 39, 2009, pp. 307–28.
34 J. Valdeón Baruque, '¿La última revuelta medieval?', *Historia 16*, 24, 1976, pp. 66–76.
35 J. L. Bermejo Cabrero, 'Hermandades y Comunidades de Castilla', *Anuario de Historia del Derecho Español*, 58, 1988, pp. 277–412. See also M. Asenjo González, 'Ciudades y Hermandades en la Corona de Castilla: aproximación sociopolítica', *Anuario de Estudios Medievales*, 27, 1997, pp. 103–46.
36 For these questions, see Oliva Herrer, '¡Viva el rey'.
37 B. González Alonso, 'Rey y reino en los siglos bajomedievales', in J. I de la Iglesia Duarte (ed.), *Conflictos sociales, políticos e intelectuales en la España de los siglos XIV y XV*, Logroño: IER, 2004, pp. 147–64.
38 P. Sánchez León, *Absolutismo y comunidad: los orígenes sociales de la guerra de los comuneros de Castilla*, Madrid: Siglo XXI, 1998.
39 P. Sánchez León, 'La constitución histórica del sujeto comunero: orden absolutista y lucha por la incorporación estamental en las ciudades de Castilla: 1350–1520', in F. Martínez Gil (ed.), *En torno a las Comunidades de Castilla: Actas del Congreso internacional 'Poder, conflicto y revuelta en la España de Carlos V'*, Cuenca: Universidad de Castilla-La Mancha, 2002, pp. 159–208.
40 M. I. Val Valdivieso, 'Ascenso social y lucha por el poder en las ciudades castellanas del siglo XV', *En la España Medieval*, 17, 1994, pp. 157–84; M. I. Val Valdivieso, 'La revolución comunera como punto de llegada de las luchas por el poder en las ciudades castellanas del siglo XV', *Scripta: Estudios en homenaje a Élida García García*, 2 vols, Oviedo: Universidad de Oviedo, 1998, vol. 2, pp. 617–33 and 'Elites populares urbanas en la época de Isabel I de Castilla', in V. Challet, J. P. Genet, H. R. Oliva Herrer, and J. Valdeón (eds), *La société politique à la fin du XVe siècle dans les royaumes ibériques et en Europe: Élites, peuple, sujets?*, Paris/Valladolid: Publications de la Sorbonne/Universidad de Valladolid, 2007, pp. 33–49; Diago Hernández, 'El común castellano en la vida de las ciudades castellanas'.
41 See Diago Hernando, 'Transformaciones'.
42 Gutiérrez Nieto, *Las comunidades*. Subsequently, M. F. Gómez Vozmediano, 'Menudos y revolvedores: el campesinado manchego, andaluz y murciano durante la revuelta comunera', in I. Szásdi León-Borja and M. J. Gallende Ruiz (eds), *Imperio y tiranía: La dimensión europea de las Comunidades de Castilla*, Valladolid: Universidad de Valladolid, 2013, pp. 111–42.
43 M. Diago Hernando, 'La representación ciudadana en las asambleas estamentales castellanas: Cortes y Santa Junta Comunera. Análisis comparativo del perfil sociopolítico de los procuradores', *Anuario de Estudios medievales*, 34, 2004, p. 636.
44 Oliva Herrer, 'Popular voices'.
45 A recent example of the insistence on interpreting the conflict only in terms of élites in D. Alonso García, 'Las Comunidades de Castilla en el siglo XXI', *Tiempos Modernos. Revista electrónica de Historia Moderna*, 19, 2009, www.tiemposmodernos.org/tm3/index.php/tm/article/view/183/240.
46 A striking exception to this is F. Martínez Gil, 'Furia popular: la participación de las multitudes urbanas en las Comunidades de Castilla', in Martínez Gil (ed.), *En torno*, pp. 309–20.
47 R. Alba, *Acerca de algunas particularidades de las Comunidades de Castilla tal vez relacionadas con el supuesto acaecer terreno del Milenio Igualitario*, Madrid: Editora Nacional, 1975 (following N. Cohn, *The Pursuit of the Millennium: Revolutionary Millenarians and Mystical Anarchists of the Middle Ages*, Oxford: Oxford University Press, 1970). More recently, J. Contreras, 'Profetismo y apocalipsismo: conflicto ideológico y tensión social en las Comunidades de Castilla', in Martínez Gil (ed.), *En torno*, pp. 517–27. I refer specifically to manuscript 1779 in the Biblioteca Nacional, which I am currently preparing for publication. The problem with this text is that it became an essential source for other chroniclers of the movement, who spread the erroneous idea of the link with prophecy. See also M. Diago Hernando, 'El factor

religioso en el conflicto de las Comunidades de Castilla (1520–1521): el papel del Clero', *Hispania Sacra*, 119, 2007, pp. 85–140.
48 M. Diago Hernando, 'Transformaciones'. Oliva Herrer, '¿Qué es la comunidad?'.
49 Pérez, 'Rey y reino', p. 28. Diago Hernando, 'Transformaciones', p. 651.
50 Specifically, between 1465 and 1468 during the civil war in Castile, in cities such as Burgos, Valladolid, and Cuenca, and also in 1517, in Valladolid itself. J. A. Pardos, 'Comunidad y tradición municipal: burgos a mediados del siglo XVI', *Mélanges de la Casa de Velázquez*, 22, 1986, pp. 131–56; A. Rucquoi, 'Del concejo a la comunidad', in *Valladolid: La villa del Esgueva*, Valladolid: Ayuntamiento de Valladolid, 1986, pp. 75–101; J. Jara Fuente, 'Sobre el concejo cerrado: asamblearismo y participación política en las ciudades castellanas', *Studia Histórica. Historia Medieval*, 17, 1999, p. 128. For Valladolid in 1517, Majo Tomé, 'Sociedad'.
51 As indicated by J. Watts, although in a slightly different context, '"Common weal" and "commonwealth": England's monarchical republic in the making, *c*.1450–*c*.1530', in A. Gamberini, J. P. Genet, and Andrea Zorzi (eds), *The Languages of Political Society*, Roma: Viella, 2013, pp. 147–66 and 'The commons in Medieval England', J. P. Genet (ed.), *La légitimité implicite*, Paris: Publications de la Sorbonne/École française de Rome, 2015, vol. II, pp. 207–31.
52 For a more detailed account, see Oliva Herrer, '¿Qué es la comunidad?'.
53 Ibid.
54 See the studies for the region of La Mancha in M. F. Gómez Vozmediano (ed.), *Castilla en Llamas: La mancha comunera*, Ciudad Real: Almud, 2008; the monographic work on Toledo by Martínez Gil, *La ciudad inquieta*. M. Diago Hernando, 'Las ciudades Castellanas contra Carlos I: Soria durante la Guerra de las Comunidades', *Celtiberia*, 94, 2001, pp. 125–84; M. Diago Hernando, 'El conflicto de las Comunidades en Cuenca', *Crónica Nova*, 29, 2002, pp. 27–62; M. Diago Hernando, 'Cambios políticos e institucionales en Aranda de Duero desde el acceso al trono de los Reyes Católicos hasta la revuelta comunera', *Edad Media. Revista de Historia*, 9, 2008, pp. 299–342; Majo Tomé, 'Sociedad'.
55 See Szássdi León-Borja and Gallende Ruiz (eds), *Monarquía y revolución*, Szássdi León-Borja and Gallende Ruiz (eds), *Imperio y tiranía*, and Szássdi León-Borja and Gallende Ruiz (eds), *Estudios en homenaje al profesor doctor Joseph Pérez*, Valladolid: Fundación Villalar, 2015.
56 Biblioteca Nacional Española, MS 1779, fol. 109r.
57 J. Valdeón Baruque, *Los conflictos sociales en el reino de Castilla en los siglos XIV y XV*, Madrid: Siglo XXI, 1975.
58 Biblioteca Nacional Española, MS 1779, fol. 109r.
59 Archivo General de Simancas, Cámara de Castilla, Memoriales, leg. 127, fol. 106. The document was discussed, with some errors, by J. Pérez, 'Moines frondeurs et sermons subversifs en Castille pendant le premier séjour de Charles-Quint en Espagne', *Bulletin hispanique*, 67, 1965, pp. 5–24.
60 Archivo General de Simancas, Consejo Real de Castilla, Comunidades des Castilla, leg. 6, 1, fol. 3v.
61 F. del Pulgar, *Crónica de los Reyes Católicos*, ed. J. M. Carriazo, 2 vols, Madrid: Espasa Calpe, 1943, vol. 1, p. 143.
62 *Cartas de Pedro Martir sobre las Comunidades*, trans. P. J. de la Canal, published by el Conde de Altares, El Escorial: Imprenta del Escorial, 1945, p. 46.
63 Ibid.
64 M. Dánvila y Collado, *Historia crítica y documentada las Comunidades de Castilla*, 6 vols, Madrid: Real Academia de la Historia, vol. 2, p. 525.
65 S. Rodríguez Salcedo, 'Historia de las Comunidades palentinas', *Publicaciones de la Institución Tello Téllez de Meneses*, 10, 1953, p. 153.
66 As for example in the deed of confederation of the cities in Tordesillas, with an explicit reference to the preservation of liberties, good uses, customs, and privileges. Archivo General de Simancas, Patronato Real, leg. 4, fol. 76.
67 Dánvila y Collado, *Historia*, vol. 2, p. 82.
68 Ibid., p. 28.
69 Biblioteca Nacional Española, MS 1779, fol. 176v.
70 Archivo General de Simancas, Registro General del Sello, leg. 2, fol. 42.
71 Digest. 1.4.5, http://droitromain.upmf-grenoble.fr/.
72 Q. Skinner, *Visions of Politics: Renaissance Virtues*, Cambridge: Cambridge University Press, 2002, pp. 287–307.
73 Part four, heading XXI, first law. *Las Siete Partidas de Alfonso el Sabio cotejadas por varios códices antiguos por la Real Academia de la Historia*, Madrid: Imprenta Real, 1807.

74 Q. Skinner, 'A third concept of liberty', *Proceedings of the British Academy*, 117, 2001, pp. 237–68.
75 R. González González, 'La otra identidad urbana: miedo, fragilidad y derrota en los discursos populares sobre la ciudad', *Medievalia*, 18, 2015, p. 43.
76 *Cartas de Pedro Martir*, trans. de la Canal, p. 28.
77 Biblioteca Nacional Española, MS 1779, fol. 175r.
78 Dánvila y Collado, *Historia*, vol. 2, p. 378.
79 Ibid., p. 368.
80 Ibid., vol. 5, p. 26; M. C. Baquero, *El proceso contra Juan Gaitán*, Toledo: Plaza de las cuatro calles, 2001, p. 444.
81 For this, see Oliva Herrer, '¿Qué es la comunidad?'.
82 Archivo General de Simancas, Consejo Real, leg. 49, fol. 15.
83 C. Taylor, 'What's wrong with negative liberty', *Philosophy and the Human Sciences. Philosophical Papers*, 2, 1985, pp. 211–29.
84 Monsalvo Antón, 'En torno'; Diago Hernando, 'El poder'; Diago Hernando, 'La proyección'.
85 J. Peribáñez Otero, 'Territorio, sociedad y conflictos en el tránsito hacia la modernidad: la Ribera del Duero burgalesa a finales de la Edad Media', PhD thesis, University of Valladolid, 2013.
86 M. A. Martín Romera, 'Las redes sociales de la oligarquía de la villa de Valladolid, (1450–1520)', PhD thesis, University of Madrid, 2013, p. 632, http://eprints.ucm.es/20400/.
87 Ibid.
88 Archivo General de Simancas, Patronato Real, leg. 1, fol. 73.
89 Archivo General de Simancas, Patronato Real, leg. 5, fol. 133.
90 Pérez, *La revolución*, pp. 203–10.
91 Dánvila y Collado, *Historia*, vol. 2, p. 137.
92 Ibid., p. 638.
93 E. I. Mineo, 'La repubblica come categoria storica', *Storica*, 43–44–45, 2009, pp. 125–67.
94 O. López Gómez, 'Representación política y rebelión urbana a fines del medievo: las asambleas del común toledano', *Anuario de Estudios Medievales*, 42, 2012, pp. 727–53. For Valladolid see, Archivo General de Simancas, Patronato Real, leg. 4, fol. 53.

18
PROPHETIC REBELLIONS
Radical urban theopolitics in the era of the Reformations

Phillip Haberkern

Introduction

Throughout the fifteenth and sixteenth centuries in Europe, cities served as the seedbeds of radical religious and political movements that sought to reorder urban life according to prophetic mandates. Most (in)famously in Savonarola's Florence (1494–8) and Anabaptist Münster (1534–5), these movements achieved their ends, which resulted in the creation of regimes that came to serve after the fact as cautionary tales about the potential excesses that could result from experiments in visionary theocracy.[1] Although these two regimes garnered reputations among contemporaries as extreme examples of medieval revivalism and Reformation *Schwärmerei*, respectively, neither Florence nor Münster was entirely unique. Rather, they were only the best known cases of a type of intertwined religious and political movement that arose in a potentially surprising number of cities during the era of the European reformations, including Hussite Prague in the 1410s, Breslau under the influence of St Giovanni da Capistrano in 1452–3, Reformed Zürich in the 1520s, Catholic York during the 1536 Pilgrimage of Grace, Lutheran Magdeburg after the Schmalkaldic War in 1547, Huguenot La Rochelle in 1572–3, and Paris under the Catholic League at the end of the sixteenth century.

Even this list is not exhaustive, but it does demonstrate that radical urban religious movements took root across the theological, national, and linguistic spectrum of late medieval and early modern Europe. Despite these cities' diversity, there were also a number features that united them. Their leaders referenced, for instance, a remarkably consistent body of biblical texts and political precedents to justify their innovations, and they also enlisted their cities' populations in a shared repertoire of ritual actions to instantiate their movements. Further, all of these urban reform movements came to power under the threat of war, and their apologists consequently employed parallel rhetorical strategies, if different media, to broadcast their intentions to the world at large. In short, all of these cities produced theopolitical rebellions that emerged out of religious conflicts between the traditional Church and the representatives of new forms of religious practice, as well as political struggles between cities with traditions of political autonomy and external actors who sought to encroach on or eliminate the urban communes' traditional prerogatives.[2]

One of the most prominent features that characterised these urban revolts was the role played by prophetic preachers in sparking them. In all of these cities, preachers claiming the authority of both their sacred office and more direct revelation from God catalysed theopolitical movements, using their pulpits as the launching pad for revolt. Given preachers' centrality in articulating a discourse of justified rebellion and orchestrating many of the collective actions that mobilised their cities' populations, both the rhetoric of their sermons and those sermons' textual afterlives illuminate the key ideological tenets of radical urban reform. An examination of these texts therefore reveals how the conjunction of political conflict and the introduction of novel theological ideas within a city could transpose a preacher's moral authority and celebrity into a more activist key, thus turning figures who might be expected to lead moral crusades or peace movements in other moments into the bearers of a more potent charismatic and political authority.[3]

This essay will analyse three cities in which preachers instigated urban rebellions as a window into the development of radical urban theopolitics, using Prague in 1419 as a point of comparison to Savonarola's career in Florence and the succession of prophets who attempted to reconstruct the Davidic monarchy in Münster in the mid-1530s. These selections enable a more sustained comparison within the confines of an essay, while highlighting the fact that religious rebellion was not the domain of any one confessional tradition. Further, the inclusion of Prague allows an exploration of how charismatic preachers could effectively serve as the focal point of urban rebellions in an era before print, and how the diffusion of that technology made it possible for such religious leaders to promote their prophetic status across a significantly wider spectrum of early modern society than their predecessors could. Certainly the development of mass media around the turn of the sixteenth century enabled urban prophets to establish their 'charisma in print', but the incorporation of Hussite Prague into this examination suggests that the advent of print marked more of a quantitative than qualitative shift in how prophetic preachers established and maintained their pre-eminence within their cities.[4]

Finally, by using preachers' exercise of power within these three cities as a lens through which the development of radical urban theopolitics can be discerned, it becomes possible to expand on the arguments and insights of two complementary bodies of recent research that have contextualised revolt within the repertoire of urban political action and emphasised how the manipulation and mastery of publicity underwrote that action. With regards to the former historiography, a comparative examination of prophetic rebellions extends the insights of scholars like Patrick Lantschner, Jan Dumolyn, and Jelle Haemers on revolt as an essential, if spectacular, element in urban political systems characterised by incessant conflicts between interest groups and corporate bodies by incorporating overtly religious rhetoric into their catalogue of political and economic motivations for rebellion.[5] Similarly, an analysis of radical urban theopolitics in this period clarifies how cities could function as 'resonating boxes' in which their prophets' messages echoed across oral and print media and came to dominate the shared consciousness of the urban community.[6] Indeed, it was the densely interconnected, polycentric, but circumscribed nature of cities' public spheres (to use a fraught term) that allowed the voices of prophetic figures to reverberate and amplify until their calls to religious and political action became nearly inescapable, thus enabling them to marshal the collective resources of the city and fuel rebellion.[7] In sum, by taking a comparative look at urban rebellions instigated by charismatic preachers, it becomes possible both to expand our understanding of the range of different rhetorical strategies used to instigate urban revolts and to integrate prophets into the spectrum of actors that scholars have recognised as key players within the medieval and early modern urban political tradition.

The case for comparison

The spectacular rise and fall of Girolamo Savonarola as the prophet of a renewed Florentine republic is, in many ways, paradigmatic for any analysis of preachers' roles in urban religious and political rebellion. Savonarola was a brilliant orator, a genius for self-promotion, and capable of creating fervent followers and bitter enemies in equal measure. His rise to prominence in Florence began in 1490, when he took over the pulpit of the convent of San Marco in Florence. The Dominican from Ferrara had occupied this space before; he had been lector to the convent during the previous decade and had undertaken a notoriously ineffective preaching campaign throughout the city. The figure who appeared in 1490, however, possessed a new confidence and articulated an uncompromising apocalyptic message. He preached on the Book of Revelation, and his sermons were filled with predictions of imminent tribulation and the subsequent renovation of the Church. He likened himself to Elijah and Amos, come to castigate the powerful and exhort the Christian people to repent.[8] Even a rival preacher, Giovanni Caroli, who resented the success of this 'foreigner', was forced to concede that Savonarola's 'sermons inflamed everyone's mind. It seemed as if it was not he who was talking, nor was it organized in the usual way. It was as if the Spirit was talking through his mout'.[9]

In the ensuing years, Savonarola's prophetic guidance became increasingly essential, as Lorenzo de Medici's death in 1492 and the ascension of his son, Piero 'the Unfortunate', threatened the economic pre-eminence and political standing of Florence within the Italian peninsula.[10] This crisis came to a head in the fall of 1494, when the French king Charles VIII led an army through Italy on his way south to press a claim to the throne of the Kingdom of the Two Sicilies. Piero's efforts to protect Florentine interests in the face of French aggression were disastrous, and his bungled diplomacy provoked an uprising that removed him from power on 9 November.[11] In the vacuum left by Piero's consequent exile from Florence, the prophet Savonarola came to the fore, both negotiating Florence's survival with the French king and helping to re-establish a republican form of government within the city. Savonarola himself described how he accomplished the former by convincing Charles that he bore the 'likeness of Cyrus' and would scourge an unrepentant Italy, but leave Florence in peace.[12] Savonarola's account of this matter must be taken with a grain (or shaker) of salt; it was in his interest to establish his influence on Charles in this matter. Still, the fact that Charles did spare Florence would indicate that Savonarola had made some impression and perhaps even convinced the king that he had been cast to play a leading role in an incipient, apocalyptic drama.

Savonarola also proved effective in recruiting Florence's larger populace to be actors in this cosmic play. With the Medici exiled, Florence set up a political regime that incorporated elements from the earlier practices of both the Florentine republic and the Venetian system of limited, elective government.[13] Savonarola was consistently engaged in this political process; he cajoled, admonished, and excoriated the emergent leaders of the republic and its citizens, guiding them towards the creation of a new Jerusalem in Florence. He often dangled a carrot in addressing his adopted city, promising that 'Florence would become richer and more powerful than she has ever been, and her empire would expand into many places' if she adopted the reforms espoused by her prophet.[14] Savonarola did not hesitate, however, to apply the stick in his prophetic discourse; he repeatedly invoked the threat posed by Charles, 'the sword of the Lord' that God had unsheathed in the midst of Italy, to emphasise the necessity of Florence submitting to his reformist agenda.[15] Taken together, then, Savonarola's alternating enticements and threats served as essential spurs to the development of the renewed Florentine republic in 1494 and after.

Many of the events that took place in Florence during Savonarola's initial rise to prominence had parallels in Prague during the tumultuous years of 1419–20. The Bohemian capital had witnessed the growth of a local reform movement over the previous decades that emphasised eucharistic piety, popular preaching, and moral regeneration based on the expectation of an imminent eschaton.[16] Beginning in 1403, the movement had as its champion Jan Hus, a preacher and university professor who dominated the city's religious life from his pulpit in the Bethlehem Chapel. Hus's sermons were sharply critical of the ecclesiastical hierarchy, and he was excommunicated and then exiled from Prague in 1412 for his refusal to accede to ecclesiastical authorities' demands that he stop preaching.[17] During his exile, Hus was invited under a safe conduct issued by the Hungarian King Sigismund to the Council of Constance to explain himself; upon arriving in the city, though, he was arrested, tried for heresy, and burned at the stake on 6 July 1415. In the wake of his death, Hus's friends and followers rejected the Church's judgement and authority, creating a national religious movement with the nobility's support that was distinguished by its administration of communion to the laity in both kinds and veneration of Hus as a saint.[18] In Prague, the leaders of this nascent church mobilised the city's population in acts of rebellion against traditional authorities. Catholic priests were ejected from their churches, 'Hussite' preachers were installed in their place, and the Czech king, Wenceslas IV, initially proved unable to stop it.

When Wenceslas did attempt to roll back Hussite gains in 1419 under pressure from Pope Martin V and King Sigismund, who was Wenceslas's brother and heir, the citizens of Prague rose up against him. Their protests crystallised in the first defenestration of Prague on 30 July 1419, when a mob killed a group of anti-Hussite city counsellors that had been installed by the king on the fourth anniversary of Hus's martyrdom.[19] Two weeks after this uprising, King Wenceslas died from an apoplectic fit, and King Sigismund and the pope subsequently mobilised a crusade against the Bohemian heretics. This crusade culminated in a siege of Prague in July 1420, which was easily repulsed by the Hussites. This seemingly divine validation of their reform emboldened the Bohemians in their break from the Church, which resulted in the prosecution of four more crusades (all spectacularly unsuccessful) against the Bohemians over the next decade and a 15-year interregnum in the kingdom.[20]

As the Hussite Revolution erupted in 1419–20, preachers played a crucial role in inciting the Czech people as a whole, and the population of Prague in particular, to collective action against the king and crusaders. Without a doubt, the most important of these religious leaders was the apostate monk Jan Želivský, whose incendiary anti-monarchical rhetoric and equation of Prague with Zion provided his audience with an eschatological language of revolution that equated salvation to the rejection of ecclesiastical and royal authority.[21] His sermon outlines from 1419 survive, and these, along with contemporary chronicles, enable us to trace his ascent to a leading position in Prague and to see how he transformed his religious authority into a mandate to lead political and military action. Even this brief sketch suggests several clear circumstantial parallels between Hussite Prague and Savonarolan Florence, including the collapse of local political authority, the threat of occupation by a foreign ruler, and the presence of a charismatic prophet who substantially filled the power vacuum in the city. There were also clear ideological overlaps, as both Želivský and Savonarola drew on a coherent repertoire of Christian prophetic and eschatological tropes to incite action among audiences that were conditioned by the liturgical and homiletic tradition of the medieval Church to recognise the preachers' legitimacy.

The Anabaptist theocracy that arose in the Westphalian city of Münster in the years 1534–5 also exhibited many of these characteristics, although it was also marked by notable differences.[22] Most obviously, Münster's Anabaptists sought to erect their kingdom in the context of the German reformation, when the rejection of traditional ecclesiastical authority and resistance to territorial overlords had become significantly more common. In fact, Münster had initiated a fairly typical local reformation that sought to finalise the city's independence from its prince-bishop during the 1520s, as burghers and evangelical preachers combined traditions of urban communalism with anti-clerical sentiments and the demand for a biblically based religion in which the laity could play an active role.[23] Münster began to diverge from the pattern established in other cities, though, with the arrival of Bernhard Rothmann, an evangelical preacher who came to be influenced by Anabaptist sacramental theology, in the city. Rothmann began preaching in Münster in 1530, and in the following years he established himself as a leading critic of the Church and advocate of religious reform.[24] Rothmann came into conflict with the city's bishop and cathedral canons, but the support he enjoyed among Münster's politically active burghers protected him from any efforts to suppress his preaching. The bishop, Franz von Waldeck, fearful of imperial intervention in the city and the loss of his realm's independence, fought back against Rothmann and the political party that coalesced around him, but their conflicts resulted in a deadlock by the end of 1533.[25]

This was the moment when Münster's reformation truly swerved. Dutch Anabaptists inspired by the eschatological prophecies of Melchior Hofmann, a furrier turned preacher who was imprisoned in Strasbourg, came to Münster in order to re-baptise adults in the city and spread their belief that the city would serve as a refuge during Antichrist's reign in the impending eschaton.[26] Led by an ecstatic visionary named Jan Matthys and his prophetic deputy Jan van Leiden, the Dutch Melchiorites spurred a dramatic evolution within Münster's evangelical party. Namely, they caused the local reformers to begin reimagining their local political and religious struggle in apocalyptic terms, a perception that was only strengthened by their bishop's preparations for war against the city.[27] Those preparations, as well as the rapid growth of the Anabaptist party within the city, led many citizens to flee. This exodus allowed the Anabaptists to dominate civic elections in 1534, and their political takeover provided the Anabaptists with a powerful argument in the conflict that was brewing. Now, armed resistance against the bishop could be construed as both a legal defence of Münster's political privileges and a godly act of defiance against the agents of Antichrist.[28]

In the following months, as the bishop besieged the city and Jan Matthys was killed during an ill-advised sortie, the city's leaders undertook a number of radical changes to the city's political order and religious life. In particular, Jan van Leiden stepped to the forefront of the city's government, first establishing the rule of 12 elders in the city before setting himself up as king of a restored Davidic monarchy by divine mandate.[29] Van Leiden also instituted community of goods and polygamy, both of which made some practical sense during a siege in which women outnumbered men nearly three-to-one.[30] Such innovations convinced the city's enemies of the Anabaptist's moral depravity, even as propaganda issued by the regime and carried forth by apostolic messengers asserted Jan van Leiden's sovereignty over the whole world and enjoined other Anabaptists to come join his kingdom.[31] Nearly all of the emissaries were captured and killed, while one of the few survivors turned traitor and helped the bishop successfully storm Münster on 25 June 1535. After the fall of the city, Jan van Leiden, his chief queen, and the leading political figures of the city were interrogated and executed (although Rothmann disappeared). The restored Davidic monarchy of the Anabaptists' new Jerusalem thus came to a messy and abrupt end.

Anabaptist Münster exhibited a number of similarities to Hussite Prague and Savonarolan Florence, most notably in its leaders' deployment of biblical models and apocalyptic rhetoric to justify its radical political and social experiments. Münster's differences, however, in terms of its confessional make-up, rise during the German reformation, and expansive employment of print media to justify its innovations, are just as important for this study, because they begin to delineate the breadth of confessional, linguistic, and media contexts that could give rise to radical urban theopolitics. Most essentially, this diversity suggests that the development of prophetic rebellions depended on key variables that were effectively supra-confessional, most notably: the introduction of novel religious practices and beliefs into urban communities which undermined the existing relationships between regional elites, local religious institutions, and the population at large; the intensification of conflicts over the city's traditional political autonomy in the face of pressure from external powers seeking to exercise authority over the urban commune; and, most tellingly, the activity of charismatic religious leaders who constructed their authority on a common foundation of biblical and historical precedents to justify political rebellion and religious transformation. Still, there was a central irony in the preachers' role in these processes, in that the successful invocation of divine authority for their theopolitical missions allowed them to assume power in unprecedented ways, thus temporarily short-circuiting the processes and forms of urban political life in order to preserve the autonomy that fundamentally underwrote them.[32]

Preaching and the prophetic feedback loop: the case of Florence

In writing about the political culture of early modern cities, Rudolf Schlögl has suggested that it was characterised by an interpersonal style in which face-to-face interactions and the presence (if not active participation) of the populace shaped political life and determined the contours of public discourse.[33] As such, preaching lent itself particularly well to constructing the authority of a rebellion's potential leader(s), because it allowed him to disseminate his message personally to a broad swathe of his city's population from an authoritative position. The advent of popular print only expanded the reach of such preachers. Sermons could be collected, published, and commented upon, so that print media thereby 'stretched the place and time of oral communication' and reached a broader audience with a more systematically developed message.[34] Oral speech and performance still remained essential, though, as both the basis for print elaborations and as the key sites where a prophet's charisma and insight were put on display.[35] For Savonarola, there is ample evidence that he employed multiple media to construct and reinforce his prophetic authority. Indeed, his printed *Compendium of Revelations* (1495) and *Dialogue Concerning Prophetic Truth* (1497) both outlined the process by which he revealed his prophetic gifts to the people of Florence, and thus constituted meta-prophetic commentaries on the sermons that served as the foundation for Savonarola's claims to authority.[36] What emerges most clearly from reading these sources together is Savonarola's understanding that the process of establishing a credible prophetic voice was gradual and methodical. He distinguished clearly between prophecy as a product of applied biblical exegesis and rational arguments, on the one hand, and of the prophet's visionary experiences, on the other. And Savonarola was quite clear that the former methods had to precede the latter, as only compelling biblical interpretation could prepare an audience to accept, as Savonarola wrote, 'that I possessed knowledge of future affairs by another light than the understanding of Scripture alone'.[37]

Consider, for instance, Savonarola's extended sermon series on Genesis, which he delivered during Lent and Advent from 1491 until 1494. In 1494, Savonarola's sermons focused on the construction of Noah's Ark, and he broke off his sermons in Lent at a seemingly innocuous point, Genesis 6:16, 'Make it with lower, second and third decks.' He then picked up the series, however, in September, with the following verse as his text: 'For behold, I will bring a flood of waters upon the earth, to destroy all flesh in which is the breath of life from under heaven; everything that is on the earth shall die.' As Savonarola would triumphantly point out, this reading perfectly described the arrival of Charles VIII in France, which had occurred in August, so that 'many were stunned and confessed that this passage of Genesis had been prepared little by little by God's hidden inspiration'.[38]

Beyond the impact on his audience that Savonarola attributed to this sermon, it also offered him a potent symbolic language for rehearsing two of his favourite themes. The first of these involved the imminent punishment of Italy by God, which would be accomplished by the French 'flood'. Savonarola later wrote that his preaching on Genesis had predisposed his audience towards recognising his prophetic insights, which allowed him to elucidate an earlier vision that he had hesitated to reveal. This particular vision centred on a sword hovering point down over Italy and 'angels coming who had a red cross in one hand and many white stoles in the other'. As Savonarola explained in the so-called 'Renovation Sermon' of 13 January 1495, the sword was Charles, the angels were 'preachers who announce this scourge to you', and the red cross symbolised the suffering of the martyrs, which would encourage believers 'to endure the scourging which has to occur during the renewal of the Church'.[39] Here, the successful application of scriptural interpretation to current events bolstered Savonarola's authority, which he expanded upon through his sharing of a visionary experience. It is crucial that his vision valorised the role that preachers and their words would play in preparing God's people for the coming tribulations; the vision closed a hermeneutical circle – or, alternately, created a positive prophetic feedback loop – by authorising the preaching that had initially underwritten the authenticity of Savonarola's prophetic vision.

The text of Genesis 6 also allowed Savonarola to explore a second, related theme concerning Florence's specific role in the unfolding of his predicted scourging of Italy and the Church. For the prophet, if the French were the flood, then Florence itself became the ark: a closed vessel that sheltered God's elect from the storms raging around them.[40] In his preaching, Savonarola repeatedly emphasised Florence's status as a chosen city, but he also made its election conditional. His sermons thus juxtaposed promises of protection with warnings about how God's wrath would descend on the city if it responded to divine mercy with ingratitude or failed to become the godly city that the prophet had foreseen: 'O citizens ... devote yourselves to simplicity; otherwise, God will be angry with you, should you be ungrateful and not acknowledge the favour which God has done for you.'[41] For Savonarola, God's preservation of Florence was only the first stage of a larger plan for the renewal of all Italy. As Savonarola put it in his *Compendium of Revelations*, Florence was the beating heart that would circulate God's prophetic plan for the reform of society throughout the larger body of Italy.[42] Savonarola's emphasis on the priority of Florence among her urban peers constituted an intrinsic part of his message's appeal. In a time of political uprising and foreign invasion, his identification of the city's primacy would have resonated among an audience who had been raised with the image of an autonomous, republican, and ascendant Florence and who longed to restore it through any means necessary.[43]

It is finally worth making the somewhat obvious point that every ark must have its designer and captain, the visionary who made preparations despite everyone mocking his plans. It is therefore not surprising that Savonarola self-identified with Noah in the context of the French invasion and Florence's 'miraculous' survival, or that he continued to liken his predictions and admonitions explicitly to the divinely authorised speech of biblical prophets.[44] In December 1494, for instance, Savonarola chose the texts for his sermons from Haggai, the prophet who had led the Israelites in their rebuilding of the Temple after the Babylonian exile. Likewise, Savonarola would lead the Florentines in the erection of God's dwelling in their midst, so that the city 'might soon become that celestial Jerusalem'.[45] At other times he likened his mission to that of Elijah and Daniel, but the specifics of Savonarola's prophetic name-checking were less significant than what its ubiquity suggested: that a crucial element of Savonarola's success in Florence was his ability to claim that he spoke with the same voice as the biblical prophets, whose authority lent additional weight to the preacher's call to reshape the political and religious fabric of the city.

When Savonarola and the post-Medicean leaders of Florence sought to restore the city's republic in 1494/5, they mixed conservative features, such as limiting participation in civic government to previous office holders, with a more radical elevation of these men's actual influence in the state through the vehicle of the Great Council.[46] In creating these hybrid structures, the leadership of the November coup sought to blend Florence's republican tradition with the need to keep the peace between the city's new leaders, past associates of the Medici, and Charles VIII, an effort that Savonarola assisted by overlaying the renewed republic's constitution with a religious ideology that prized the 'holy liberty' of the city and its maintenance through fraternal love, charity, and ethical improvement.[47] This sort of religious rhetoric imbued political changes with moral significance, but it also suggested a more generalisable rule of urban theopolitics. Essentially, Savonarola's preaching showed overlaying a city's political process with prophetic rhetoric did not invalidate traditional practices or institutions, but selectively invested them with an aura of sanctity that enabled revolutionary change while preserving the underlying dynamics of the city's power structures.[48]

Savonarola clearly seems to have understood that gaining the authority to guide this process would require that he establish his prophetic credibility, first by the application of scriptural interpretation to current events, and only subsequently by revealing visionary experiences that supplemented and confirmed his authoritative exegesis. Those visions, in turn, recast the contemporary conflicts in which his audience was embroiled in biblical terms, with Florence re-imagined as a New Jerusalem. Finally, Savonarola himself could emerge as a divinely inspired leader who made his authority over Zion manifest through his preaching and visions. This was the positive feedback loop that established and sustained the prophet's authority, as homiletic discourse, visionary experience, and printed commentary mutually reinforced each other's affirmation of his status and made the prophet's words nearly omnipresent throughout his city.

In Savonarola's case, establishing and closing this feedback loop was made easier because he emerged in an urban milieu that had been saturated by print in the previous decades. Florence's first press began production in 1471, and in the subsequent decades the city's printing houses produced over 1,000 editions of various texts.[49] Within this corpus, religious literature constituted a plurality of the overall publications. With the rise of Savonarola, though, the religious slant steepened, as over 100 editions of his works (or works directly about him) were published prior to 1500.[50] Even a conservative estimate of 500 copies per edition means that well over 50,000 Savonarolan texts were available by the end of the decade, many of them affordable to the majority of urban workers; Stefano Dall'Aglio has also emphasised that Savonarola's works appeared predominantly in the vernacular, another feature that made his writings widely available to the public within Florence and its surrounding territories.[51]

This number also tells only part of the story, as Savonarola's works prompted sharp rejoinders disputing his prophetic mission from authors such as the Dominican Giovanni Caroli and the Franciscan Samuele Cascini, whose critiques led Savonarola's supporters to respond in kind. Caroli first opposed Savonarola publicly in a disputation held on 18 January 1495, an event witnessed by many of the city's ecclesiastical and lay elites. After their face-to-face debate, Caroli published an open letter denying Savonarola's prophetic status and attributing his visionary claims to mere ambition. This attack spawned a number of heated responses, both attacking and defending Savonarola, which instigated a pamphlet war that lasted over three years.[52] Caroli's considerable reputation within Florence for learning and eloquence enabled his attacks on Savonarola to undermine the prophet's status in certain Florentine circles, but their circulation throughout the city also had a potentially unintended consequence. Namely, the open debate over the legitimacy of Savonarola's prophetic claims effectively kept them at the forefront of the city's consciousness. This extended literary jousting thus represented the final plank in a multi-media platform that enabled Savonarola's message to saturate the city of Florence in the 1490s, as citizens who had witnessed sermons and disputations, read the words of Savonarola and/or his opponents, or merely heard of his predictions collectively created a critical mass of potential actors who recognised his prophetic authority and stood ready to act on his injunctions. By tapping into the emergent print culture of Florence and tying it to his prophetic speech, Savonarola's words resonated throughout his adopted city during the period of his ascendancy and keyed his audience to undertake collective action, both religious and political, on his behalf.

Parallel prophetic processes

But did the Savonarolan 'model' apply to other cities? This is the crux of the interpretive matter, and for the cities of Prague and Münster the answer is yes. In both of these communes charismatic preachers achieved a status similar to that of Savonarola, and they gained the authority to lead rebellions through similar sets of processes and during comparable times of political and military crisis. In doing so, they also synthesised radical religious rhetoric and practice with more traditional political formulations, thereby enlisting figures and institutions imbued with authority within their movements. The results in both cities also closely paralleled those in Florence, in the sense that both cities' religious and political landscapes were radically reshaped under the guidance of their prophets. Take the case of Prague, where the radical preacher Jan Želivský assumed political authority among much of the city's population in 1419. We know less about his early career than we do about Savonarola's. All that can be said for sure is that he had started to preach in Prague by 1418 at the church of St Stephen's in Prague's New Town, but lost his place early in 1419, when King Wenceslas IV removed Hussite preachers who were administering communion in both kinds in their churches.[53] These priests were removed because most had obtained their churches without proper authorisation and had performed services in them while Prague was officially under interdict.[54] After his ejection, Želivský took up preaching in the monastery church of Our Lady of Snows, where his audience was primarily composed of the urban poor and Hussite sympathisers whose parishes had been closed to them by the king's decree.[55]

Želivský's preaching at the monastery was radical, to say the least; he repeatedly emphasised the king's failings as a ruler, the ecclesiastical hierarchy's immorality, and the complicity of many clerics in the suppression of the Gospel. In making these claims, Želivský was building on, but intensifying, the tradition of reform preaching in Prague that had begun during the previous century and culminated in the sermons of the martyr Jan Hus.[56] Whereas Hus's censure had largely been reserved for sinful priests, Želivský used his pulpit to agitate against the king and his appointed magistrates, who had sought to suppress divine truth and the 'law of God'.[57] Želivský thereby tapped into a vein of eschatological angst that had been opened up in the wake of Hus's execution; both university masters and popular preachers asserted that Hus's death was the work of Antichrist and his minions, who had subverted the ecclesiastical hierarchy in order to suppress divine truth.[58] What differentiated Želivský from his contemporaries, however, was the degree to which he identified himself as Hus's successor, a prophet whose authority derived from visions first given, but violently suppressed, in the previous generation. It is also necessary to remember that Prague's media culture was necessarily dominated by oral and performative forms of communication at this time. Some texts circulated, but the nascent Hussite revolution relied on frequent sermons and the liturgy to disseminate its doctrines, the performance of vernacular songs to galvanise popular opinion against the Roman church, and the citizen body's participation in riotous processions and street performances to incorporate them into the movement.[59] Želivský was ideally suited for this communicative milieu, as his mastery of homiletic discourse and claims to prophetic descent from Jan Hus enabled him to tap into an extant set of expectations within Prague for how religious dissent could and should be expressed, even as he channelled familiar forms of popular participation into new modes of collective action.

Želivský's prophetic claims constituted a major theme in his sermons at this time, whose most striking feature is their dependence on biblical texts as ciphers for understanding contemporary events. Like Savonarola, Želivský established his authority through applied biblical exegesis, and his sermon notes essentially comprise chains of linked scriptural citations with contemporary commentary that interpreted the biblical texts via events unfolding in Prague (and vice versa). Želivský also gave an eschatological spin to these texts, so that current events were read as end-time reiterations of conflicts that had first played out in the Old and New Testaments. Within this framework, Želivský himself became a new Elisha, who had inherited his prophetic mantle and 'a double measure of the Spirit' from Jan Hus (read: Elijah) and continued his predecessor's work.[60] This identification also functioned as an allusion to the two witnesses of Revelation 11, which embedded Želivský and his audience within an apocalyptic framework and marked Želivský himself as the heir to the biblical prophets, much as Savonarola would do nearly 80 years later.[61]

Želivský's prophetic self-identification was evident in another sermon from the spring of 1419 on Luke 14:17, 'And he sent his servant':

> Therefore the Lord, that we might live, sent his servant for preaching the gospel to all creatures and for calling the faithful to this great feast, just as he sent Moses in Exodus 24: 'Moses came and told the people all the words of the LORD and all his ordinances; and all the people answered with one voice, and said, "All the words which the LORD has spoken we will do".' Behold Moses, the faithful servant of God, did not dare to teach the people of God anything other than the Word of God, lest the people accede to something else, besides the Word of the Lord. May the city of Prague do the same![62]

This reference simultaneously affirmed the purely biblical nature of Želivský's preaching as the foundation and seal of his authority and identified his audience as the heirs of biblical Israel.[63] In the same sermon, he equated the Czech nation with the apostolic church, thus appropriating the holy people of both Testaments as models for the persecuted Hussite party. Želivský also routinely used biblical images of the earthly and celestial Jerusalem to describe the *communitas Pragensis*, referring to his city as Zion and a city on a hill, and most pointedly to his audience as 'citizens of Jerusalem, who receive Christ with honour on the day of the Lord'.[64] With such language, Želivský helped to foster a sense of divine election among his listeners, a theme which permeated Hussite discourse at this time and led to the development of what Rudolf Urbánek called a sense of 'national messianism' among the Bohemians.[65]

This rhetoric was to serve as the foundation for rebellion when, on 30 July 1419, Želivský preached a sermon on Mt. 7:15 – 'Beware of false prophets, which come to you in sheep's clothing, but are inwardly ravening wolves.'[66] The main argument of this sermon was that these wolves were the wicked priests and tyrannical magistrates who persecuted 'the faithful community' of Hussites. This persecution had been, according to Želivský, characteristic of the entire history of God's people on Earth. Just as Cain had slain Abel, Esau had attacked Jacob, and the Jews had tried to eradicate the early Christian community, so too had 'canons, common priests, monks, and nuns(!)' persecuted first Jan Hus, and subsequently his followers.[67] This sort of historical comparison between the Bohemians' suffering and that of the biblical patriarchs and apostolic martyrs was typical of early Hussite preaching, and Želivský made frequent use of such rhetoric. What was unusual about this sermon, however, was that many of those who heard it had come to church that morning with weapons, and that Želivský – bearing a monstrance containing a consecrated host – would lead these people on a sort of armed pilgrimage across the New Town to his old parish of St Stephen's. It was also unexpected that Želivský would subsequently have his followers break down the door to the church, eject the priest officiating at Mass, and then celebrate communion in both kinds at the high altar. Further, no one would have imagined that Želivský would then lead this crowd to the New Town Hall, where they would demand the release of Hussites who had been imprisoned there for their defence of Hussite sacramental practices. Or, that when this demand was not immediately met, the Hussites would storm the building and throw several of King Wenceslas's town counsellors out of a window and on to the weapons of those gathered below.[68] In short, very few people might have predicted that Želivský would orchestrate Prague's first defenestration in order to overturn King Wenceslas's efforts to suppress the Hussite movement.

This popular uprising had an immediate political impact. On the day of the defenestration, Hussite burghers selected new members of the town council that King Wenceslas ultimately recognised. King Wenceslas also died several weeks later from an apoplectic fit, an event that effectively ensured military conflict with King Sigismund of Hungary, who was Wenceslas's heir but had overseen Hus's execution. In this context, Želivský's sermons took on a more pronounced visionary cast; he predicted that the apocalyptic red dragon of Revelation 11 (i.e. Sigismund) would rise against the Bohemians, but that the godly Czechs would defeat this diabolical figure.[69] This prediction apparently came true the following July, when Sigismund and his crusading army were defeated at Prague by a coalition of Hussite forces. These events confirmed that Želivský spoke with the prophet's voice, and Hussite propaganda from that period both echoed Želivský's apocalyptic identification of Sigismund and amplified his claim that the Czechs had become a new Israel. This rhetoric animated satirical texts and manifestos that the Hussites dispatched across Europe, which rendered the prophetic framework espoused by Želivský normative for the Hussite understanding of the first crusade and established the prophet as one of the leading political and religious figures in Hussite Prague.[70] These texts also served as the kind of commentaries that inscribed a prophet's visions within popular consciousness and ingrained his predictions within the mythology that the Hussites were crafting for their movement. Thus, while Želivský could not benefit from the post facto diffusion of his visions afforded to later prophets by print, his sermons did initiate the same kind of feedback loop that enabled Savonarola's ascent in Florence by inspiring texts that encoded his predictions and apocalyptic rhetoric within the core political and religious ideology of the Hussite revolution.

A comparison such as this allows us to start sketching out a set of common ideas and actions that guided late medieval and early modern religious reformers in their attempts to marry traditions of political autonomy and resistance with the demand for religious transformation within their cities. In both Želivský's Prague and Savonarola's Florence, these reformers came to be seen as legitimate prophets by their audiences and were able to articulate a theopolitical discourse that helped inaugurate political movements that actualised that discourse. Not that the two cases were identical. Savonarola's rise, for instance, benefited enormously from the pamphlet war that ensued in the wake of his first predictions, as printed media disseminated his viewpoints – often refracted through the positive or negative assessments of others – throughout Florence. In effect, all of these voices confirmed Savonarola's primacy in the city, even if they doubted the legitimacy of his prophetic mission. Conversely, a crucial component of Želivský's success was his ability to conform to prophetic models established in Prague by earlier preachers, most notably Jan Hus. By claiming to be Hus's true successor and playing off eschatological tropes and themes that had become common in Prague, Želivský was able to generate public support and the recognition of his calling during a moment of crisis that necessitated a new type of religious leadership. Granted, Želivský's prophetic status was confirmed by later events and the production of texts that incorporated his visions into the Hussites' interpretation of the first crusade called against them, but this affirmation was secondary to Želivský's initial success in claiming a 'double portion' of authority from his prophetic forebears and using that authority to instigate an uprising in Prague that borrowed from the symbolic language of ritual processions.

The final case study offered here for a comparative assessment of early modern urban theopolitics splits the difference between Florence and Prague. In Anabaptist Münster, both claims to prophetic succession and widespread textual dissemination and debate played a vital role in establishing the legitimacy of the regime founded by Jan Matthys and climaxing under Jan van Leiden. This kingdom, like the renewed Florentine republic and the Hussite government of Prague, was based on the application of biblical models to sixteenth-century urban society, and in truth the chief difficulty in interpreting the role of prophetic preaching in its rise is sorting through the cacophony that resulted from the emergence of many prophets in the city within a short time. Indeed, if Savonarola saw prophecy as a process, and Želivský treated it as a carefully curated legacy, then the Münsterites considered prophecy to be a constant, a continuous source of guidance for sustaining the city throughout the end times. Münster's first prophetic figure was Bernard Rothmann, whose preaching and leadership had led to the establishment of an evangelical party in the city and helped prepare that party's acceptance of Anabaptist theology and practice at the beginning of 1534.[71] Rothmann ceded his primacy, though, with the arrival of Matthys and van Leiden to the city, and he evolved into the chief spokesman and apologist for the kingdom that the two Dutch prophets established. He remained vitally important in this role, as the texts he published during the siege clearly articulated biblical and visionary justifications for Münster's most notable social and political experiments.[72] But his textual activity was subsidiary within the city itself to the innovations that Matthys and van Leiden instituted under the influence of their own visions, as well as those of secondary prophetic figures (such as the urban patrician Bernd Knipperdollink and the crippled goldsmith Johann Dusentschur) who emerged at specific moments during the siege to offer visionary validation for the restored Davidic monarchy. The acknowledgement of these men's visions as legitimate by van Leiden and Rothmann both widened the scope of revelation in Münster and opened up the city's leaders to challenges from a divine voice that they did not exclusively control.[73]

The elevation of Jan van Leiden to the kingship of Münster is illustrative of these complicated dynamics. At the end of August 1534, the forces besieging Münster attempted to storm the city. Their assault was repelled, and in the wake of the battle a heightened sense of expectation regarding the imminent return of Christ gripped the Anabaptists. At this moment, Dusentschur began to predict that a leader would be raised up from God's people, and, according to his later trial records, van Leiden recognised that God was calling on him to become king. Van Leiden therefore began to search the Bible for confirmation of his calling, and he came upon Jeremiah 30:8–9 – 'They shall serve the Lord their God and David their king, whom I will raise up for them' – as a justification for the renewal of the Davidic monarchy, which would confer universal dominion upon the ruler of Münster.[74] After becoming convinced that his kingship was foreordained, van Leiden assembled the population of the city to await a sign endorsing this political transformation. Dusentschur obligingly proclaimed that van Leiden should be made king, and van Leiden took immediate steps to reconstitute the city as his royal seat. He dissolved the council of 12 elders that had been ruling the city (also based on the model of the biblical Israelites), created a royal court around himself, bestowed new titles and responsibilities upon the leaders of this royal government, and instituted a round of festivals, banquets, and tournaments that turned the city under siege into a 'theatre state'.[75] Van Leiden also had two crowns made for himself, created a seal and signet ring that borrowed from imperial iconography, and struck coins that declared: 'The Word was made flesh and dwells in us' and 'One just king over all, one God, one faith'.[76] These acts were again justified by recourse to Jeremiah 30, where God promised to rebuild Jerusalem so that 'the palace will stand in its proper place', a vow that was juxtaposed to the threat that 'the storm of the Lord will burst out in wrath, a driving wind swirling down on the heads of the wicked'.[77]

Although sources do not exist that relay the precise words used by van Leiden and other prophets to justify this remaking of the city, an eye-witness account to life in Anabaptist Münster reported that van Leiden would set up 'David's throne' amidst his royal court in the main city square and speak, after which sympathetic preachers would preach serially about van Leiden's sovereignty, identifying him as the new David and the Münsterites as true Israelites and the apostolic church reborn. Van Leiden also apparently asserted that the citizens' faithfulness would preserve Münster from the wrath of the unrighteous and make the city 'an example before the whole world' after God's imminent victory over the wicked.[78] The Anabaptist king also tried to use ritual and public space to strengthen these identifications, as he renamed the square in front of the cathedral 'Mount Zion' and christened the city's main thoroughfare the 'Street of Gold', a reference to Revelation 21:21. Van Leiden also celebrated enormous communion banquets in that square, during which he and his queen, who was the widow of Jan Matthys, would serve the elements and then make pronouncements regarding the military and political affairs of the city to the population.[79]

Even if our sources allow only indirect glimpses of the rhetoric that van Leiden and his fellow prophets used initially to justify the erection of the Davidic monarchy in Münster, a pair of writings issued by Bernard Rothmann around the beginning of 1535 provide a much more articulate sense of the city's theopolitics. Entitled *An Entirely Consoling Message on Vengeance* and *On the Hiddenness of Scripture*, these two tracts expanded upon the prophetic foundation that van Leiden had claimed for his kingdom and voiced a justification for apocalyptic violence that saw the warlike reign of David as a necessary precursor to the rule of a peaceful Solomon, i.e. Christ.[80] *On Vengeance* appeared first and can serve as a hermeneutic key to the longer *On the Hiddenness of Scripture*; in the earlier tract, Rothmann essentially set out to prove that the current moment would witness the final restitution of Christian life on the Earth, as the true church's 1,400 years of captivity under the power of the Antichrist would come to an end through purificatory violence undertaken by the renewed Davidic kingdom in Münster.[81] With divine aid, the godly Münsterites would raze the world around them and create space for the erection of Solomon's temple. The construction of this dwelling, which was a metaphor for Christ's millennial reign on Earth, therefore depended on the intervention of the Anabaptists in Münster to eradicate the godless. In elaborating on this central claim, Rothmann invoked the examples of Elijah and Haggai as prophets who had foreseen the necessity of violent resistance to diabolical powers and who had sought to rebuild – figuratively and literally – a haven for God's chosen people.[82] He also included an extended exegesis of Jeremiah 30 in this treatise, thus systematically expounding on the text that had first authorised van Leiden's assumption of the throne in Münster in order to assert that God 'had raised up his beleaguered David and equipped him and his people for vengeance and retribution against Babylon'.[83]

On the Hiddenness of Scripture provided a more exhaustive explanation for a theology of history that underlay these claims. This theology was based on an assertion that all of human history was reaching its culmination in Anabaptist Münster, and that the Münsterites alone understood this because their purity had enabled them to interpret clues about the eschatological timeline contained in the Bible.[84] According to this text, Münster had been prefigured by both Noah's Ark and Solomon's temple; the city also, however, had a more visionary parallel in the city of Zion seen by Ezra (in the deuteron-canonical 2 Esdras, chs 2–7), whose citizens were being punished in Babylon but would be imminently redeemed through God's direct intervention and destruction of the wicked.[85] For Rothmann, the only way that Münster could fulfil its destiny as the new Zion was first to erect the throne of David, whose occupant would defeat the earthly princes and other servants of the Antichrist who oppressed God's people. Then, and only then, 'will the true Solomon come in his wisdom, peace, and all his glory to rule over his kingdom, so that all will occur and be fulfilled, which the prophets have proclaimed to the world'.[86]

Obviously, neither Jan van Leiden's predictions nor Rothmann's elaborate calculations about the coming end of time proved to be true, although the two men's theopolitical vision for Münster held sway in the city and attracted the sympathy of outsiders up until the city's fall in June 1535. The Anabaptist regime, and Rothmann's apologetics for it, also provoked a remarkable outpouring of rebuttals in media spanning from official communiques and outraged sermons to pamphlets and broadsheets that, as in the case of Savonarola and the dispute his teaching generated, disseminated the content of the Anabaptists' prophetic politics and allowed it to survive the fall of the regime itself.[87] But what else can the case of Anabaptist Münster and its ruler's attempts to restore the Davidic monarchy tell us about religious rebellion and prophetic politics? Primarily, Münster sketches out the limits of early modern urban theopolitics, but mainly in the sense of showing how elastic those limits could be. In Münster, charismatic religious leaders refashioned the urban commune according to a brand of biblical literalism that must have stretched the credulity of their audience, but the combination of charismatic preaching, elaborate ritual, military success (albeit temporary), and a looming external threat proved to be stronger than the citizens' potential scepticism about the social and political innovations undertaken by van Leiden in the name of God. The persistence of Münsterite theopolitics in the face of such tensions demonstrates, in short, the potential strength of prophetic ideology to sustain a city during periods of intense conflict, even if the regime shaped by such an ideology did not survive it.

Conclusion

In many ways, Jan van Leiden's image of a revived Davidic monarchy coming to power in Münster was quite different from Savonarola's vision of a republican New Jerusalem in Florence, and both of these differed in turn from Želivský's desire for a Hussite Prague living under the law of God. And yet, underneath the disparities in how God's kingdom on Earth might be constructed and which set of religious practices would help structure it lay a very similar logic, one characterised by each religious leader's awareness of his prophetic mission and certainty that his respective city was engaged in actions laden with ultimate, apocalyptic significance. This logic was also marked by the way it elided the distance between contemporary events and their biblical templates, or between present actors and the ancient prophets they sought to emulate. What this essay has argued is that despite the different political ends and theological positions articulated by the various prophets of early modern cities, the authority that they established for themselves and the processes which they instigated ushered their cities towards very similar goals. At their root, all of these radical urban religious movements sought to imbue traditions of urban political autonomy with a divine aura through the medium of prophetic revelation, and this revelation sparked rebellions and guided them in turn through periods of internal conflict and war.

The urban prophets discussed here disseminated and amplified their visions through a variety of media that together constituted a positive feedback loop of prophetic discourse that proved essential to their success in inaugurating and sustaining religious and political change. Each of the prophets came to occupy a central space in their respective communities, but their use of oral and printed media allowed their message to extend throughout (and even beyond) them and permeate their respective public spheres. Churches, marketplaces, city streets, and council chambers: these were the places where the prophets' ideas were debated and repeated. Processions, liturgical ceremonies, disputations, and battles: these were the moments when the voices of charismatic religious leaders transformed discussion into action. The fact that cities from across the geographical and confessional spectrum of early modern Europe listened to these prophets' revolutionary voices and embraced the logic of urban theopolitics suggests that further comparisons – in terms of the development of apologetic strategies, the use of ritual in constructing cities' collective identity, the role of law in regulating new regimes, and the justification of military action, for example – could bear rich fruit, just as paying attention to the seemingly disparate agendas and actions of religious leaders like Savonarola, Želivský, Rothmann, and van Leiden makes it possible to perceive the chalk outlines of a fascinating body of early modern theopolitical thought that drove radical urban reform in the fifteenth and sixteenth centuries.

Notes

1 On Savonarola's reputation after his death and his role in sixteenth-century polemics, see T. Herzig, *Savonarola's Women: Visions and Reform in Renaissance Italy*, Chicago, IL: University of Chicago Press, 2008; and, with a more international focus, S. Dall'Aglio, *Savonarola in Francia: circolazione di un'eredita politico-religiosa nell'Europa del cinquecento*, Savigliano: N. Aragno, 2006. For detailed analyses of contemporary writings against Münster, see E. Laubach, 'Das Täuferreich zu Münster in seiner Wirkung auf die Nachwelt. Zur Entstehung und Tradierung eines Geschischtsbildes', *Westfälische Zeitschrift*, 141, 1991, pp. 123–50; and S. Haude, *'In the Shadow of Savage Wolves': Anabapstist Münster and the German Reformation During the 1530s*, Boston, MA: Brill, 2000.
2 I am here adapting Francis Oakley's terminology. For his conceptualisation of the Christian theopolitical tradition, see *Empty Bottles of Gentilism: Kingship and the Divine in Late Antiquity and the Early Middle Ages (to 1050)*, New Haven, CT: Yale University Press, 2010, esp. pp. 83–98. Cf. Nathan Rein's concept of 'urban theology and the siegeworks', which he develops in reference to Magdeburg in the wake of the Schmalkaldic War, see *The Chancery of God: Protestant Print, Polemic and Propaganda against the Empire, Magdeburg 1546–1551*, Aldershot: Ashgate, 2008, esp. ch. 4.
3 One might fruitfully compare Savonarola to St Bernardino of Siena with regards to the ways in which their preaching was politicised. On Bernardino, see C. Polecritti, *Preaching Peace in Renaissance Italy: Bernardino of Siena and his Audience*, Washington, DC: CUA Press, 2000. See also the more general conclusions on contemporary preaching in G. Dickson, 'Encounters in medieval revivalism: monks, friars, and popular enthusiasts', *Church History*, 68, 1999, pp. 265–93.
4 On this concept, see especially the introduction in L. Jardine, *Erasmus, Man of Letters: The Construction of Charisma in Print*, Princeton, NJ: Princeton University Press, 1993.
5 For these scholars' arguments rejecting the interpretation of rebellion as a fundamental break in urban political thought and practice, see J. Dumolyn and J. Haemers, 'Patterns of urban rebellion in medieval Flanders', *JMH*, 31, 2005, pp. 369–93; P. Lantschner, 'Revolts and the political order of cities in the late Middle Ages', *P&P*, 225, 2014, pp. 3–46. For a welcome intervention into the role of popular religion in medieval rebellions, both urban and rural, see J. Arnold, 'Religion and popular rebellion, from the Capuciati to Niklashausen', *Cultural and Social History*, 6, 2009, pp. 149–69.
6 On the role of print and publicity in rebellions, see D. Bellingradt, 'The early modern city as a resonating box: media, public opinion, and the urban space of the Holy Roman Empire, Cologne, and Hamburg ca. 1700', *Journal of Early Modern History*, 16, 2012, pp. 201–40; A. Würgler, 'Revolts in print: media and communication in early modern urban conflicts', in R. Schlögl (ed.), *Urban Elections and Decision Making in Early Modern Europe*, Newcastle: Cambridge Scholars, 2009, pp. 257–75.
7 Although referring to fifteenth- and sixteenth-century cities as having public spheres strains the temporal framework for this concept that Jürgen Habermas first established, current scholarship on urban history has largely adopted this terminology. On its use in the early modern context, see E. Körber, 'Vormoderne Öffentlichkeiten. Versuch einer Begriffs- und Strukturgeschichte', *Jahrbuch für Kommunikationsgeschichte*, 10, 2008, pp. 3–25; G. Schwerhoff's introductory essay, 'Stadt und Öffentlichkeit in der Frühen Neuzeit. Perspektiven der Forschung', in G. Schwerhoff (ed.), *Stadt und Öffentlichkeit in der Frühen Neuzeit*, Cologne: Böhlau Verlag, 2011, pp. 1–28. Cf. the essays and introduction in H. R. Oliva Herrer, V. Challet, J. Dumolyn, and M. A. Carmona Ruiz (eds), *La comunidad medieval como esfera pública*, Seville: Universidad de Sevilla, 2014.

8 A. Verde, 'Girolamo Savonarola: ideologo e profeta Il Quaresimale del 1491', in G. C. Garfagnini (ed.), *Savonarola: Democrazia tirannide profezia*, Florence: SISMEL edizioni del Galluzzo, 1998, pp. 127–47.

9 For this evaluation of Savonarola, see D. Weinstein, *Savonarola: The Rise and Fall of a Renaissance Prophet*, New Haven, CT: Yale University Press, 2011, p. 78. See also L. Polizzotto, 'The anti-Savonarolan polemic of fra Giovanni Caroli: an evaluation', *Vivens Homo*, 9, 1998, pp. 371–91.

10 For an overview of the political crises in Florence during this time, see N. Rubinstein, 'Politics and constitution in Florence at the end of the fifteenth century', in E. Jacob (ed.), *Italian Renaissance Studies*, London: Faber & Faber, 1960, pp. 148–83; and D. Weinstein, *Savonarola and Florence: Prophecy and Patriotism in the Renaissance*, Princeton, NJ: Princeton University Press, 1970, esp. ch. 2.

11 On Piero's brief reign in Florence, see the epilogue to N. Rubinstein, *The Government of Florence Under the Medici (1434–94)*, Oxford: Clarendon, 1966; A. Brown, 'The revolution of 1494 in Florence and its aftermath: a reassessment', in J. Everson and D. Zancani (eds), *Italy in Crisis, 1494*, Oxford: European Humanities Research Centre, 2000, pp. 13–40.

12 G. Savonarola, 'Compendio di Rivelazioni', in A. Crucitti (ed.), *Compendio di rivelazioni testo volgare e Latino e dialogus de veritate prophetica*, Rome: Belardetti, 1974, pp. 3–245, at 14–15. This reference to the Persian King Cyrus, who freed the Israelites from the Babylonian Captivity, is drawn from Isaiah 45:13: 'I will raise up Cyrus in my righteousness: I will make all his ways straight. He will rebuild my city, and set my exiles free.'

13 On Savonarola's role in Florence's constitutional reforms, see L. Polizzotto, *The Elect Nation: The Savonarolan Movement in Florence, 1494–1545*, Oxford: Clarendon, 1994, esp. ch. 1; P. Viti, 'Savonarola e la tradizione repubblicana fiorentina', in Garfagnini (ed.), *Savonarola: Democrazia tirannide profezia*, pp. 55–66.

14 G. Savonarola, 'Predica XIII: Fatta la terza Dominica Dell'Avvento', (1494) in L. Firpo (ed.), *Prediche sopra Aggeo*, Rome: Belardetti, 1965, pp. 209–28, at 213.

15 Savonarola, 'Compendio', p. 11. Cf. Isaiah 1:20 and Jeremiah 46:10 on the image of a devouring sword sent by God.

16 For a comprehensive and insightful analysis of the early development of the Prague reform movement as a whole, see O. Marin, *L'archevêque, le maître et le dévot: Genèses du mouvement réformateur pragois, Années 1360–1419*, Paris: Honoré Champion Éditeur, 2005. See also H. Kaminsky, *A History of the Hussite Revolution*, Berkeley and Los Angeles: University of California Press, 1967, esp. ch. 1.

17 On Hus's charismatic leadership of the Prague reform, see P. Rychterová, 'Jan Hus. Der Führer, Märtyrer und Prophet', in P. Rychterová, S. Seit, and R. Veit (eds), *Das Charisma. Funktionen und symbolische Repräsentationen*, Berlin: Akademie Verlag, 2008, pp. 423–45; T. Fudge, *Jan Hus: Religious Reform and Social Revolution in Bohemia*, New York: IB Tauris, 2010, chs 4–6. For detailed analyses of Hus's legal battle with the Church, see J. Kejř, *Husův Proces*, Prague: Historica, 2000; T. Fudge, *The Trial of Jan Hus: Medieval Heresy and Criminal Procedure*, New York: Oxford University Press, 2013.

18 On the development of the Hussite movement and its core ideological tenets, see the overviews in Kaminsky, *A History*; F. Šmahel, *Die Hussitische Revolution*, ed. and trans. A. Patchovsky and T. Krzenck, 3 vols, Hannover: Hahnsche Buchhandlung, 2002.

19 For an analysis of these events, see H. Kaminsky, 'The Prague insurrection of 30 July 1419', *Medievalia et Humanistica*, 17, 1966, pp. 106–26. Cf. A. Molnár, 'Želivský, prédicateur de la révolution', *Communio Viatorum*, 2, 1959, pp. 324–34.

20 On these crusades, see F. Heymann, 'The crusades against the Hussites', in H. Hazard (ed.), *A History of the Crusades, vol. III: The Fourteenth and Fifteenth Centuries*, Madison: University of Wisconsin Press, 1975, pp. 586–646; N. Housley, *Religious Warfare in Europe, 1400–1536*, New York: Oxford University Press, 2002, esp. ch. 2; and the exhaustive review of relevant literature in: Šmahel, *Die Hussitische Revolution*, chs 6 and 7.

21 On Želivský's leading role in the rise of revolutionary Hussitism in Prague, see Molnár, 'Želivský, prédicateur de la révolution'; and B. Kopičková, *Jan Želivský*, Prague: Melantrich, 1990.

22 The Anabaptist kingdom in Münster has been the subject of a substantial body of scholarship, although much of it is marred by confessional politics that either denigrate the Anabaptists as a whole or seek to marginalise the Münsterites within the larger development of early Anabaptist communities. For an overview of this earlier scholarship and a more even-handed consideration of the social, political, and religious lives of the Münster Anabaptists, see K. Kirchhoff, *Die Täufer in Münster 1534/35. Untersuchung zum Umfang und zur Sozialstruktur der Bewegung*, Münster: Aschendorff, 1973; R. Klötzer, *Die Täuferherrschaft von Münster. Stadtreformation und Welterneuerung*, Münster: Aschendorff, 1992.

23 For a classic formulation of the development of the German reformation among imperial cities, see B. Moeller, *Reichstadt und Reformation*, Gütersloh: G. Mohn, 1962. Cf. Steven Ozment, *The Reformation in the Cities: The Appeal of Protestantism to Sixteenth-Century Germany and Switzerland*, New Haven, CT: Yale University Press, 1975. On the rise of Anabaptist Münster as an unusual (but not totally unexpected) variation on this type of reform movement, see H. Schilling, 'Aufstandsbewegung in der stadtbürgerlichen Gesellschaft des Alten Reiches. Die Vorgeschichte des Münsteraner Täuferreichs', in H. Wehler (ed.), *Der deutsche Bauernkrieg, 1524–1526*, Göttingen: Vandenhoeck und Ruprecht, 1975, pp. 193–238.

24 On Rothmann, see Willem de Bakker, Michael Driedger, and James Stayer, *Bernhard Rothmann and the Reformation in Münster, 1530–1535*, Kitchener, ON: Pandora Press, 2009.

25 On the deadlock, see R. Klötzer, 'The Melchiorites and Münster', in J. Roth and J. Stayer (eds), *A Companion to Anabaptism and Spiritualism, 1521–1700*, Boston, MA: Brill, 2007, pp. 217–56, at 226–30; and de Bakker et al., *Bernhard Rothmann*, ch. 6.

26 On Hoffman and his impact on Dutch and Münsterite Anabaptism, see K. Depperman, *Melchior Hoffman: Social Unrest and Apocalyptic Visions in the Age of Reformation*, trans. M. Wren, Edinburgh: T&T Clark, 1987. On the Melchiorites' impact in Münster, see T. Kuratsuka, 'Gesamtgilde und Täufer. Der Radikalisierungsprozess in der Reformation Münsters. Von der reformatorischen Bewegung zum Täuferreich 1533/34', *Archiv für Reformationsgeschichte*, 76, 1985, pp. 231–70.

27 On this shift, see K. Kirchhoff, 'Was there a peaceful Anabaptist congregation in Münster in 1534?', *Mennonite Quarterly Review*, 44, 1970, pp. 357–70; K. Kirchhoff, 'Die Endzeitwartung der Täufergemeinde zu Münster 1534/35', *Jahrbuch für westfälische Kirchengeschichte*, 78, 1985, pp. 19–42.

28 Rothmann made this legal argument strongly in two texts written during the siege, *The Statement of the Congregation* and *Restitution*, which were published in Münster and circulated throughout the region in the summer and autumn of 1534. On Rothmann's arguments for the legality of the city's self-defence, see de Bakker et al., *Bernard Rothmann*, pp. 183–5, 191–2.

29 On these efforts to recreate biblical Israel's political structure within Münster, see C. Bernet, 'The concept of the New Jerusalem among the early Anabaptists in Münster 1534/35: an interpretation of political, social and religious rule', *Archiv für Reformationsgeschichte*, 102, 2011, pp. 175–94.

30 The majority of scholars tends to argue that the institution of polygamy was an effort to integrate and subordinate women into the social structure of paternal households, rather than allowing them to remain independent. The abolition of private property has also been seen as an economic necessity to manage food supplies during the siege. On community of goods in this light, see R. Scribner, 'Practical utopias: pre-modern communism and the Reformation', *Comparative Studies in Society and History*, 36, 1994, pp. 743–74. On polygamy, see J. Stayer, 'Vielweiberei als "innerweltliche Askese". Neue Eheauffassungen in der Reformationszeit', *Mennonitische Geschichtsblätter*, 32, 1980, pp. 24–41; L. Roper, 'Sexual utopianism in the German Reformation', *Journal of Ecclesiastical History*, 42, 1991, pp. 394–418.

31 On the polemics levelled against the city for its sexual innovations and political claims, see Haude, *'In the Shadow of Savage Wolves'*, pp. 17–38.

32 Both Samuel Cohn and Yves-Marie Bercé point to the defence of civic and religious freedoms vis-à-vis the tyrant as operative in many late medieval and early modern rebellions. See Cohn, *Lust for Liberty: The Politics of Social Revolt in Medieval Europe, 1200–1425: Italy, France, and Flanders*, Cambridge, MA: Harvard University Press, 2006, pp. 79ff.; Bercé, *Revolt and Revolution in Early Modern Europe: An Essay on the History of Political Violence*, trans. J. Bergin, Manchester: Manchester University Press, 1987, pp. 34ff. See also G. Raccagni, in this volume. With specific reference to Münster, Christopher Friedrichs notes the potentially subversive political potential of radical religion. In his view, however, Münster was unique. See Friedrichs, *Urban Politics in Early Modern Europe*, London: Routledge, 2000, pp. 60–1.

33 For a programmatic summary of Schlögl's position on the nature of early modern urban politics, see 'Vergesellschaftung unter Anwesenden in der frühneuzeitlichen Stadt und ihre (politische) Öffentlichkeit', in Schwerhoff (ed.), *Stadt und Öffentlichkeit*, pp. 29–37. See also his 'Vergesellschaftung unter Anwesenden. Zur kommunikativen Form des Politischen in der vormoderne Stadt', in R. Schlögl (ed.), *Interaktion und Herrschaft. Die Politik der frühneuzeitlichen Stadt*, Constance: UVK Verlagsgesellschaft, 2004, pp. 9–60.

34 The language of stretching is taken from R. Schlögl, 'Power and politics in the early modern city: elections and decision-making', in *Urban Elections and Decision-Making*, pp. 2–28, at 23. On the relationship between oral sermons and their textual embodiments in the medieval context, see particularly A.

Thompson, 'From texts to preaching: retrieving the medieval sermon as an event', in C. Muessig (ed.), *Preacher, Sermon, and Audience in the Middle Ages*, Boston, MA: Brill, 2002, pp. 13–37. On the early modern diffusion of sermons in print, see P. Matheson, *The Rhetoric of the Reformation*, Edinburgh: T&T Clark, 1998, ch. 2; J. Frymire, *The Primacy of the Postils: Catholics, Protestants, and the Dissemination of Ideas in Early Modern Germany*, Boston, MA: Brill, 2010.

35 Both Schlögl and Würgler argue that print media created a certain 'elasticity' in political events; they could be witnessed remotely, via print, and thus people could participate in them after the fact or coordinate responses to them that created chains of action. Still, it would seem that these chains were essentially local, and depended on the common experience of what Schlögl calls an 'integrative' public sphere to gain meaning and inspire action. On the limits of print in terms of transforming the public life of early modern cities, see Schlögl, 'Politik Beobachten: Öffentlichkeit und Medien in der Frühen Neuzeit', *Zeitschrift für Historische Forschung*, 25, 2008, pp. 581–616, at 615; Würgler, 'Revolts in print', pp. 267–9.

36 For an overview of the publication of Savonarola's sermons, see R. Rusconi, 'Le prediche di fra Girolamo da Ferrara: dai manoscritti al pulpito alle stampe', in G. C. Garfagnini (ed.), *Una città e il suo profeta: Firenze di fronte al Savonarola*, Florence: SISMEL edizioni del Galluzzo, 2001, pp. 201–34. See also the discussion of these sermons' relationship to Savonarola's more systematic considerations of his prophecy in S. Dall'Aglio, *Savonarola and Savonarolism*, trans. J. Gagné, Toronto: Centre for Reformation and Renaissance Studies, 2010, esp. pp. 24–7.

37 Savonarola, 'Compendio', p. 11. Cf. Savonarola, 'De Veritate Prophetica Dialogus', in Crucitti (ed.), *Compendio*, pp. 247–346, at 320ff.

38 Savonarola, 'Compendio', p. 11. See also the discussion of this imagery in Weinstein, *Savonarola and Florence*, pp. 138–43.

39 G. Savonarola, 'Fatta a' Di XIII di Gennaio 1494[/5] el Di della Ottava della Epifania', in V. Romano (ed.), *Prediche sopra I Psalmi*, vol. 1, Rome: Belardetti, 1969, pp. 37–62, at 52.

40 This is the image with which Savonarola opened his sermon of 28 November 1494. See G. Savonarola, 'Fatta la prima Dominica dell'Avvento sopra del Salmo "Dilexi Quoniam"', in L. Firpo (ed.), *Prediche sopra Aggeo*, pp. 105–22, at 106–7.

41 Ibid., p. 119.

42 Savonarola, 'Compendio', p. 8.

43 The Renaissance myth of this idealised Florence has generated a vast secondary literature. For an overview and critique of that myth, see the introduction and essays in J. Hankins (ed.), *Renaissance Civic Humanism: Reappraisals and Reflections*, New York: Cambridge University Press, 2000. See also D. Weinstein, 'The myth of Florence', in N. Rubinstein (ed.), *Florentine Studies: Politics and Society in Renaissance Florence*, London: Faber, 1968, pp. 15–44.

44 *El nostro Noè, che è quello che guida l'arca, ha chiamato tutti quelli che sono nell'arca e dice e grida che noi abbiama cura di non incorrere nel vizio della ingratitudine*. See Savonarola, 'Fatta la prima Dominica', pp. 106–7.

45 This quotation is from 15 December 1494: Savonarola, 'Fatta sopra el Salmo "Beatus Vir"', in L. Firpo (ed.), *Prediche sopra Aggeo*, pp. 143–53, at 151. On the ubiquity of this language in Savonarola's preaching, see Weinstein, *Savonarola and Florence*, ch. 4.

46 For an assessment of the elitist tendencies in the new Florentine republic, see the prosopographical work in R. P. Cooper, 'The Florentine ruling group under the "governo popolare", 1494–1512', *Studies in Medieval and Renaissance History*, 7, 1984–5, pp. 71–181; L. Polizzotto, 'Savonarola and the Florentine oligarchy', in S. Fletcher and C. Shaw (eds), *The World of Savonarola: Italian Elites and the Perception of Crisis*, Burlington, VT: Ashgate, 2000, pp. 55–64. On the new regime's radicalism, see G. Cadoni, *Lotte politiche e riforme instituzionali a Firene tra il 1494 e il 1502*, Rome: Nella sede dell'Istituto Palazzo Borromini, Piazza dell' Orologio, 1999, esp. pp. 7–19. See also the synthesis of these positions in A. Brown, 'Offices of honour and profit: the crisis of republicanism in Florence', and 'Ideology and faction in Savonarolan Florence', both in A. Brown, *Medicean and Savonarolan Florence: The Interplay of Politics, Humanism, and Religion*, Turnhout: Brepols, 2011, pp. 139–76, 201–22.

47 Polizzotto, *The Elect Nation*, p. 24.

48 The use of religious rhetoric to sacralise the notion of urban freedom here extends the 'logic' of political conflict and rebellion described in the introduction and first chapter of P. Lantschner, *The Logic of Political Conflict in Medieval Cities: Italy and the Southern Low Countries, 1370–1440*, Oxford: Oxford University Press, 2015.

49 On the relatively slow growth of the publishing industry in Florence, see S. Noakes, 'The development of the book market in late quattrocento Italy: printers' failures and the role of the middleman', *Journal*

of Medieval and Renaissance Studies, 11, 1981, pp. 23–55. Cf. the conclusions on the character of this emergent book market in M. Meserve, 'News from Negroponte: politics, popular opinion, and information exchange in the first decade of the Italian press', *Renaissance Quarterly*, 59, 2006, pp. 440–80.

50 According to Andrew Pettegree, over 100 (out of 264) editions published in Florence during the years of Savonarola's ascendancy comprised Savonarola's preaching. See *The Book in the Renaissance*, New Haven, CT: Yale University Press, 2010, p. 53, n. 15.

51 I. Gewirtz, 'Savonarola and the fifteenth-century Florentine press', in V. Hotchkiss and D. Weinstein (eds), *Girolamo Savonarola: Piety, Prophecy, and Politics in Renaissance Florence*, Dallas, TX: Bridwell Library, 1994, pp. 65–73; Dall'Aglio, *Savonarola and Savonarolism*, pp. 24–5.

52 The media campaign between Savonarola, Caroli, and their followers is detailed in Polizzotto, *The Elect Nation*, pp. 54–81; Weinstein, *Savonarola and Florence*, pp. 227–46.

53 On the beginning of Želivský's tenure in the city, see F. Bartoš, 'Počatky Jana Želivského v Praze', *Theologická Příloha: Křesťanské Revue*, 33, 1966, pp. 44–7. See also Kopičková, *Jan Želivský*, pp. 35ff.

54 The city had been put under the ban for harbouring the heretic Jan of Jesenice, who had been Jan Hus's lawyer. On Wenceslas's actions and their outcomes in Prague, see Šmahel, *Hussitische Revolution*, pp. 972–92. Cf. the contemporary account of these events published as an appendix to the chronicle of Lawrence of Březova, a Hussite resident of Prague: *Výtah z Kroniky Vavřince z Březové*, in J. Emler (ed.), *Fontes Rerum Bohemicarum*, vol. 5, Prague: Naklad. NF Palackého, 1893, pp. 537–43, at 538.

55 In the king's decree removing Hussite preachers from their churches, he allowed communion in both kinds to be administered in three Prague churches; Our Lady of Snows was one of these. On Želivský's audience and rhetoric at this church, see Šmahel, *Hussitische Revolution*, pp. 625–35.

56 On this tradition and Hus, see F. Šmahel, 'Literacy and heresy in Hussite Bohemia', in P. Biller and A. Hudson (eds), *Heresy and Literacy, 1000–1530*, New York: Cambridge University Press, 1994, pp. 237–54, at 243. See also Marin, *L'archevêque*, p. 227.

57 T. Fudge, 'Želivský's head: memory and new martyrs among the Hussites', *Bohemian Reformation and Religious Practice*, 6, 2007, pp. 111–32.

58 For an overview of preaching from these years and the surviving manuscripts of sermons, see F. Bartoš, 'Sborník husitského kazatele asi z r. 1415', *Vestník České Akademie Ved a Umení*, 57, 1948, pp. 15–33; F. Bartoš, 'Dvě studie o husitských postilách', *Rozpravy Československé Akademie Věd*, 65, 1955, pp. 1–56; P. Soukup, 'The masters and the end of the world: exegesis in the polemics with chiliasm', *Bohemian Reformation and Religious Practice*, 7, 2009, pp. 91–114.

59 On the role of these media in the development of the Hussite movement, see T. Fudge, *The Magnificent Ride: The First Reformation in Hussite Bohemia*, Aldershot: Ashgate, 1998, esp. ch. 4; B. Zilynská, 'From learned disputation to the happening: the propagation of faith through word and image', in M. Bartlová and M. Šroněk (eds), *Public Communication in European Reformation: Artistic and Other Media in Central Europe, 1380–1620*, Prague: Artefactum, 2007, pp. 55–67; M. Perett, 'Vernacular songs as "oral pamphlets": the Hussites and their propaganda campaign', *Viator*, 42, 2011, pp. 371–91.

60 J. Želivský, 'Octava Pasche', in A. Molnár (ed.), *Dochovaná Kázání z roku 1419*, pt 1, Prague: CSAV, 1953, pp. 48–59, at 57. The reference here was to 2 Kings 2:9, where Elijah offers his successor the same thing.

61 On the origins and persistence of this theme in the Hussite movement, see A. Molnár, 'Poslední věci v pohledu Jakoubka ze Stříbra', *Theologická Příloha: Křesťanské Revue*, 22, 1955, pp. 38–42. Cf. the introduction to R. Petersen, *Preaching in the Last Days: The Theme of 'Two Witnesses' in the Sixteenth and Seventeenth Centuries*, New York: Oxford University Press, 1993.

62 J. Želivský, 'Dominica Secunda post Trinitatem', in Molnár (ed.), *Dochovaná Kázání*, pp. 204–16, at 211.

63 Speaking of the Czechs as a new Israel was common during the Bohemian reformation, and among early modern reform movements more broadly. On this identification, see R. Urbánek, 'český mesianismus ve své době hrdinské', in *Z Husitského Věku: Výbor vistorických úvah a studii*, Prague: CSAV, 1957, pp. 7–28; P. Gorski, 'The Mosaic moment: an early modernist critique of modernist theories of nationalism', *American Journal of Sociology*, 105, 2000, pp. 1428–68.

64 See e.g. Želivský's sermons: 'Octava Pasche', p. 54; 'Vigilia Ascensionis', in Molnár (ed.), *Dochovaná Kázání*, pp. 115–17, at 116; 'Dominica Pentecostes', in Molnár (ed.), *Dochovaná Kázání*, pp. 149–56, at 154.

65 For this formulation, see Urbánek, 'český mesianismus', *passim*. See also F. Šmahel, 'The idea of the "nation" in Hussite Bohemia', trans. R. Samsour, *Historica*, 16, 1969, pp. 143–247, and 17, 1970, pp. 93–197.

66 This manuscript is held in the Czech National Library as MS Národní Knihovna Praha (hereafter, NKP) V G 3. This sermon is contained on folios 33–42. The sermon preached on this day has been the subject of scholarly debate, but Kaminsky persuasively argues that Želivský preached on Mt. 7 (which was to be the pericope for 6 August, not 30 July) in order to fire his audience up for the planned insurrection. In this, and in the reconstruction of events from that day, I follow Kaminsky's account in: 'The Prague insurrection', pp. 121–6.
67 MS NKP V G 3, 39r.
68 Several chronicle sources document the defenestration, and while they vary in many details, they are unanimous in presenting Želivský's active orchestration of the attack on the town hall and his encouragement of the mob in explicitly religious terms. For an analysis of the sources and their depiction of Želivský's leadership, see Kaminsky, 'The Prague insurrection', pp. 111–14.
69 The identification came from Želivský's sermon from 19 November on Mt. 22:15, 'Then the Pharisees went out and laid plans to trap him in his words'. This sermon is contained in MS NKP V G 3, folios 209–20, at 209v. On Želivský's preaching from that autumn more generally, see Kaminsky, *A History*, pp. 301–9.
70 For an overview of these texts and their relationship to the first crusade against the Hussites, see R. Urbánek, 'Vavřinec z Březové a jeho satirická skladby v rukopise Budyšínském', in *Z Husitského Věku*, pp. 29–35; J. Klassen, 'Images of anti-majesty in Hussite literature', *Bohemia*, 33, 1992, pp. 267–81; K. Hruza, 'Die hussitischen Manifeste vom April 1420', *Deutsches Archiv für Erforschung des Mittelalters*, 53, 1997, pp. 119–77; K. Hruza, '"Audite, celi!" Ein satirischer hussitischer Propagandatext gegen König Sigismund', in K. Hruza (ed.), *Propaganda, Kommunikation und Öffentlichkeit (11.–16. Jahrhundert)*, Vienna: Verlag der Österreichischen Akademie der Wissenschaften, 2002, pp. 129–52.
71 The most extensive source detailing Rothmann's role in Münster prior to the Anabaptist kingdom is unfortunately a hostile, often unreliable account by Hermann Kerssenbrock, who served as rector of the city's cathedral school from 1564–73. As a rule, von Kerssenbrock's conclusion are not to be taken at face value, but his narrative does contain many letters and pronouncements from Münster's episcopal archives that reveal the brewing conflict from 1532 to 1534. On Rothmann's ascent as a charismatic preacher in this text, see the modern edition published as H. von Kerssenbrock, *Narrative of the Anabaptist Madness: The Overthrow of Münster, the Famous Metropolis of Westphalia*, ed. and trans. C. Mackay, 2 vols, Boston, MA: Brill, 2007, esp. pp. 242–5, 434–7.
72 All told, Rothmann produced five major apologetic texts during the siege of Münster: *The Statement of the Faith and Life of the Christian Congregation in Münster*, *Restitution*, *A Consoling Message of Vengeance*, *The Hidden Meaning of Scripture*, and *Of Earth and Temporal Power*. Rothmann published the first in June 1534, while the last appeared in May 1535. For an analysis of these tracts' rhetoric and apocalyptic theology of history, see de Bakker *et al.*, *Bernhard Rothmann*, ch. 8.
73 For example, Knipperdollink experienced an ecstatic trance in the winter of 1534, during which he blessed the people of Münster and claimed the right reign over the city. He was imprisoned by van Leiden until this outburst ended. On this incident, see R. Klötzer, 'Herrschaft und Kommunikation. Propheten, König, und Stadtgemeinde im täuferischen Münster 1534/35', in M. Driedger, A. Schubert, and A. von Schlachta (eds), *Grenzen des Taufertums*, Heidelberg: Gütersloher Verlagshaus, 2009, pp. 326–45.
74 Van Leiden's elevation to the kingship is described in both a contemporary eye-witness account by Heinrich Gresbeck and the transcripts of van Leiden's trial after the fall of Münster. Gresbeck's account has been published in a modern, critical edition as *Summarisch Ertzelungk und Bericht der Wiederdope und wat sich binnen der Stat Monster in Westphalen sugetragen im Iair MDXXXV*, in C. A. Cornelius (ed.), *Berichte der Augenzeugen über das münsterische Wiedertauferrieich. Die Geschichtsquellen des Bisthums Münster*, vol. 2, Münster: Theissing, 1853, pp. 3–214, at 95–8. A critical edition of van Leiden's trial record has been published in R. Klötzer, 'Die Verhöre der Täuferführer von Münster vom 25. Juli auf Haus Dölmen', *Westfälische Zeitschrift*, 105, 2005, pp. 51–92, at 67–8.
75 This term derives from the work of Clifford Geertz, whose book *Negara: The Theatre State in Nineteenth-Century Bali*, Princeton, NJ: Princeton University Press, 1980, offered a sustained analysis of how political theatrics could constitute power, rather than merely representing it. For the application of Geertz's ideas to late medieval Europe, especially Burgundy, see D. Nicholas, 'In the pit of the Burgundian theater state: urban traditions and princely ambitions in Ghent, 1360–1420', in B. Hanawalt and K. Reyerson (eds), *City and Spectacle in Medieval Europe*, Minneapolis: University of Minnesota Press, 1994, pp. 271–95; and the introduction to P. Andrade, *Realms of Ritual: Burgundian Ceremony and Civic Life in Late Medieval Ghent*, Ithaca, NY: Cornell University Press, 1996.

76 On the creation of the royal retinue and regalia, see von Kerssenbrock, *Narrative*, pp. 592–600.
77 Gresbeck, *Bericht*, pp. 111–13.
78 On this preaching, see Gresbeck, *Bericht*, pp. 91–2.
79 The renaming of public space in the city and van Leiden's communion feasts are described in Gresbeck, *Bericht*, pp. 103–11. See also the analysis of efforts to build new Jerusalems in early modern Europe, with specific reference to Münster, in C. Bernet, *Gebaute Apokalypse. Die Utopie des himmlischen Jerusalem in der frühen Neuzeit*, Mainz: Verlag Philipp von Zabern, 2007, pp. 102–10.
80 The first of these texts was published in December as *Eyn gantz troestlick Bericht van der Wrake*, Münster: n.p., 1534. Contemporary reports state that 1,000 copies were distributed in the Netherlands, and the text engendered responses from the reformers Urbanus Rhegius and Nikolaus von Amsdorf in the following two years. The second text appeared as *Von der Verborgenheit der Schrift des Reiches Christi*, Münster: Twyfel, 1535. Three editions of this text appeared in 1535, and the Münsterites sent the text as an apology to the Landgrave Philip of Hesse. Modern critical editions of both texts have appeared in Robert Stupperich (ed.), *Die Schriften Bernhard Rothmanns*, Münster: Aschendorff, 1970, pp. 284–97, 298–372.
81 Rothmann, *Bericht von der Wrake*, pp. 294–5.
82 Ibid., pp. 290–2.
83 Ibid., p. 297.
84 For an overview of this theology of history and its relation to proper biblical interpretation, see de Bakker *et al.*, *Bernhard Rothmann*, pp. 196–201.
85 On Noah and Solomon, see Rothmann, *Von Verborgenheit der Schrift*, pp. 334–6. On Zion and Esdras, see ibid., pp. 359–60.
86 Ibid., p. 364.
87 On the literature written against the Münsterites after the fall of the city, see G. Vogler, 'Das Täuferreich zu Münster im Spiegel der Flugschriften', in H. J. Köhler (ed.), *Flugschriften als Massenmedium der Reformationszeit*, Stuttgart: Klett-Cotta, 1981, pp. 31–48.

CONCLUSION

John Watts

The understanding of later medieval popular revolts has taken a political turn.[1] For the majority of historians writing in the second half of the twentieth century, the convulsions of what Mollat and Wolff called 'the age *par excellence* of "popular revolutions"' arose primarily from social change – the supposedly widening gap between rich and poor in Europe's towns, the stirrings of transition from feudalism to capitalism, the dislocations of agrarian society produced by the Black Death, or, more simply, from crises of subsistence or production, in which misery provoked reaction.[2] To be sure, rising states were not absent from these accounts: the growing burden of taxation, and the disruption of seigneurial power by new juridical and military institutions intensified the pressure on the common people and helped to explain their novel tendency to address the centres of royal or civic authority.[3] But, in general, political history was too narrowly focused on the military, diplomatic, and factional activities of kings, lords, and patricians to offer much to scholars interested in mass movements, and the dominant frameworks for understanding social action were those of Marxian political economy, social anthropology, and *Annaliste* readings of culture.

As these essays show, we are now in a very different place. The political scene is everywhere in this book, providing the setting and the target for revolts, shaping their causation, digesting their implications. Popular rebels are seen as political actors, engaging with the authorities, and doing so in a partly civil manner, through institutions, practices, and rhetorics that were shared, to a greater or lesser extent, with the rest of political society. They acted to realise political goals – changes to the structure of government, reform of institutions, correction of leading individuals, defence of the realm, or of the city, or of the common good. It is not, of course, that this collection is blind to the social, economic, and cultural conditions in which politics were conducted, but that the sphere of the political has become a valid lens for the analysis of collective action by ordinary people. In these concluding remarks, I want first to consider how this change has come about and what it implies for the study of popular revolts. Then I want to take up a thread running throughout the essays in this volume, the ambivalent relationship between popular activism, on the one hand, and the norms and structures of later medieval states, on the other. Just how, and how smoothly, did 'revolts', as we have agreed to call them, fit into the politics of these highly unequal, but avowedly communitarian, polities? And what does the image of an 'age of revolts' imply – for our sense of the later Middle Ages, for our understanding of popular revolt, and more generally for our notions of politics?

Conclusion

The political history of the later Middle Ages has changed quite markedly over the last few decades. Instead of an emphasis on decline, crisis, and meaningless conflict, the growth of states and the consolidation of larger political communities have become the central themes.[4] Each of these developments is treated in more complex ways than was once the case. The historic focus on kingdoms has been widened to include many different kinds of states – from the international church to city-states, leagues, princely condominiums, and even peasant republics.[5] State-growth, in the sense of the multiplication and elaboration of governing institutions, has emerged as a universal phenomenon, as almost every kind of power-holder developed and extended juridical, fiscal, military, and representative competences. And the politics that attended these developments, as expanding and overlapping powers generated tensions and confrontations, has been more thoroughly examined: it has become plain that the forging, and deepening, of regional political communities – 'territorial states', 'regnal polities' – was a fraught and lengthy process, and that the notorious turbulence of medieval politics was both a response to, and a modifier of, the growth of government and the advance of political solidarities. State-growth did not produce orderly political communities: it produced copious conflict, out of which – via a long and aleatory process – more sizeable and coherent polities were eventually formed.[6]

Politics itself is conceived much more broadly. First of all, the centres of power are taken to be multiple – every cluster of resource and manpower had political potential in this period, and the capacity of rulers to organise politically was increasingly matched by similar capacities on the part of subjects. Drawing on their own resources – communes, guilds, lordships, local alliances – but also exploiting the facilities made available by growing states, whether frameworks of justice, fiscality, military recruitment, office, representation, or indeed ideology, subject groups (or groups adopting the role of subjects) exercised political agency, contesting demands, reforming regimes, re-shaping the governmental environment.[7] But it is not just in the recognition of multiple centres that accounts of politics have become more complex: as political historians have absorbed the perspectives of social and cultural history, the variety of routes through which power was transmitted and contested has come to be acknowledged – not just institutions, whether formal or informal; not just armed force; but also ideas and discourses, repertoires of presentation and performance, distinctions of age and gender, patterns of emotion and sensibility.[8] Later medieval politics is now regarded as a form of 'communication' just as readily as a transaction of power and interest; indeed, more attention is now given to its communicative dimensions than its structural means.[9] Many of these developments in the political history of later medieval Europe are shared with the political history of other periods, but they have particular significance for the understanding of fourteenth- and fifteenth-century polities, in which governments were increasingly able to intervene and gather resources across sizeable territories, but where jurisdiction was almost always shared or disputed, notions of authority were much debated, and regimes were highly vulnerable to division and disintegration.

The study of later medieval popular revolt has not been immune from these trends. We have come to understand that it was not an occasional phenomenon, but a near-continual feature of political life, especially in larger towns.[10] We have begun to pay more attention to the political aspirations expressed by popular rebels, and to consider how these were connected to political struggles occurring at other levels of polities that we have come to see as multi-layered and polycentric.[11] Without denying the inevitable tensions between lords and tenants, owners and workers, oligarchs and ordinary citizens, we now give much more weight to the 'cross-class coalitions' that are so consistently apparent in urban uprisings, and much more present than we once appreciated in those of the countryside.[12] These fusions of 'popular' and 'elite' politics are present in almost all of the essays in this volume: in the dialectic between the vices of rulers and native revolts in Myles Lavan's discussion of Roman attitudes; in the interplay of local and sectional disputes with national ones in the Jacquerie of 1358, the English rising of 1381, and the revolt of the *comuneros* in 1520–1; in Justine Smithuis's suggestive treatment of the routes by which local nobles came to lead the risings of urban artisans; or in the explorations of calculated violence on the part of authorities and dissenters, in the essays of Paul Freedman and Vincent Challet, respectively. These and other examples will be discussed further below, but there can now be no question that popular revolts were part and parcel of the political life of later medieval kingdoms, cities, and provinces, and that neither can be properly understood without attention to the other.

Perhaps equally striking, if scarcely unexpected, is the sharing of methods and approaches between the study of revolts and the study of other forms of politics. These essays are profoundly concerned with ideology and discourse, with representation and communication. The linkages between Gianluca Raccagni's second Lombard League and the wider struggles of *populares* across Northern Italy are ideological as well as inter-personal. 'Legal cultures' and shared legitimations enabled popular action in both Bologna and Damascus, as Patrick Lantschner demonstrates; something similar was happening in Christian Liddy's Norwich and London, where ideals of citizenship, community, equality, and openness clashed with those of secrecy and hierarchy, and motifs of kingship or carnival provided frames for action on the part of rulers and rebels alike. Eliza Hartrich examines the differing, and changing, valuations of well-established 'repertoires of resistance' in later medieval English towns; while Jan Dumolyn and Jelle Haemers uncover the meanings and contests encoded in the choice of names for episodes of popular political expression. If later medieval polities were complex, multiple, full of adventitious alliances and divisions, made amid partly shared and partly contested schemes of values, so too were the revolts that contributed to these volatile conditions.

But this prompts a question. If revolts were a familiar – one might almost say normal – part of political life in the later Middle Ages, and if the words and practices of rebels echoed, or mapped on to, those of the authorities, why are we able to identify these episodes as 'revolts', and what justification do we have for treating them as a particular branch of political activity? Historians of popular politics have long been at pains to insist on the continuities between rebel behaviour and the norms of social and political life among peasants, artisans, and workers; as we have seen, historians of high politics are now keen to emphasise the discourses and procedures shared by popular leaders and other politicians.[13] So what, we might ask, distinguishes popular uprisings from other forms of contention in the sprawling political communities of the period? How normal were they?

This is a question approached from various different angles in the chapters above, and I want to keep that breadth of perspective in play over the next few pages. But let us begin with the subtle matter of political norms. On the one hand, later medieval polities were full of conflict and frequently in disarray; few regimes were beyond challenge, whether we are talking about kingdoms, principalities, or self-governing cities (and all cities possessed some means of self-government). Kings and princes may have been appointed by God, or established by election, but this did not rescue them from contests in which alternative claimants were promoted, elections revoked, deposition demanded, or prerogatives circumscribed by demands for charters, councils, laws, or other concessions. The situation of urban regimes was still more precarious, resting on a mixture of historic usurpations and present-day coalitions of economic and political interests, coalitions that could easily be configured differently. Contests, then, were a normal feature of political life, and, by the later Middle Ages, they typically involved a broad social range, since ordinary subjects were enlisted as soldiers, mobs, witnesses, and petitioners by critics of the government. On the other hand, later medieval governments presented images of order, hierarchy, and social peace as normative; they channelled representative energies into more licit routes – councils, assemblies, petitions, in which protests, conveyed by elites, were transmuted into advice; they upheld rules about unlawful assembly, the carrying of arms, the display of banners, and so on, in order to deny legitimacy to unauthorised public activity; and they punished defeated opponents with theatrical severity. From this perspective, popular demonstrations were highly abnormal and wrong – against the canons of order, and led from the wrong place in the social and political hierarchy.

The essays in this volume show how demonstrators confronted this difficulty. First of all, they characteristically rose in circumstances when the government was not only failing, or acting oppressively, but lacking in credibility. In none of the revolts discussed above was it really clear where authority lay – in 1358, John II of France was in prison; in 1381, Richard II of England was a child, in thrall to an uncle who might be trying to seize the throne; in 1520, Charles I of Spain had left for Germany, and it was not clear why Castilians should accept the rule of a cardinal from the Low Countries in his stead. Equally, most of the urban uprisings discussed in the volume occurred at times when internal or external regimes were under stress, newly installed, or otherwise without secure foundation. In all of these cases, the weakness of authority helped to provoke mass action, as well as providing a cover for it and weakening the claims of governments against it: insecure regimes were less able to balance interests, wield the normal tools of power, or provide expected political services.[14] Rebels thus had a double justification for their actions – not only were governments failing in their duties, but it was not clear who should rule. While this in itself strengthened the common claim of rebels to be acting loyally, they typically reinforced their claims by drawing on established institutions and principles. The 'Jacques' of 1358 and the 'peasants' of 1381 formed up under captains, adopting conventional mechanisms of troop-raising and waving banners of the fleur-de-lys or the cross of St George, respectively; they posed as helping the king in the defence of the realm against traitors and foreign enemies. The people of Norwich rose up as a community of citizens against the uncustomary extension of ecclesiastical jurisdiction, while those of London invoked the charter of 1319 – their 'Magna Carta', in effect. The rebels in the papal city of Bologna upheld the Guelf traditions of commune, *popolo*, and *libertà* against 'foreign tyrants', and claimed to be defending papal assets; those in Damascus played on factional disputes among the Mamluk elites, invoked the shari'a principle of 'commanding right and forbidding wrong', and exploited the prestige and networks of local mosques to advance their claims. In every case, popular rebels invoked established principles against weak regimes; their strategy was designed to demonstrate that it was they, and not their opponents, who acted with rightful authority.

These attempts to associate themselves with political norms extended to other features of popular activism. The key figures in popular revolts, as far as we can tell, were the 'middling sort' or 'officer class' of reeves, constables, and captains, guild 'searchers' and *dekens* of the crafts, typically responsible for governing lesser men under the authority of kings, lords, and patricians.[15] To some extent, then, rebel hosts reflected the social make-up of normal and legitimate mass action; indeed, more than this, they also typically included dissident members of the elite – pretenders, saints, would-be kings, great lords, or knights, who claimed that their role in the proceedings was to appease the people and to represent their concerns. If revolts included few women, this was perhaps – as Sam Cohn implies – because they were anxious to reflect the norms of public action (and the corresponding prominence of women in demonstrations with a spiritual dimension, or against the sexual depravities of leading men, suggests the same dynamic). By adopting accepted regimes of counsel and petition, trumpeting accepted values of loyalty, truth, justice, and community, and ensuring – as far as possible – an acceptable social profile, popular rebels attempted to represent society and normalise their actions. As several contributors have pointed out, while the content of rebel protests was frequently endorsed by commentators, and sometimes even by the authorities, what they found remarkable, or regrettable, or wrong, was the presentation of these protests by huge numbers of ordinary people.[16] But even in this respect rebellions could enjoy a measure of legitimacy: on the one hand, it was good and right for those entrusted with public responsibility to hear the testimony of the 'commons' or community; on the other, there was something apocalyptic, something divine, about the vengeance of *vox populi* – the rising of the mass of the people was a salutary response to the vices of the powerful.[17]

Revolts were thus a response to the ambivalences in later medieval power-structures, to the inability of governments to deliver the social and political peace that could justify their increasingly numerous and heavy impositions, and to the partly conflicting principles – equality and hierarchy; community and sovereignty; carnival, violence, and order – proclaimed by rulers, poets, and preachers. But it is important to realise that they were also a deliberate and challenging response to these things; that rebels highlighted the gaps between expectations and realities, and pressed the rights and powers of subjects to the very limits. Much as they sought to legitimise their actions, popular activists were explicit about attacking those who claimed to possess authority. As Challet points out, they used calculated displays of violence, to demonstrate their anger and force negotiations. In Flemish and Dutch towns, they took up arms in *wapeninghen*, and if these ritualised assemblies had the sanction of custom, they were nonetheless a clear and provocative signal of intent. Other urban insurgents gathered on feast-days, swamped elections and local courts, rang bells, took part in 'runs' and rough music, banged drums, posted bills, and made processions – any of these could be acceptable activities, but they could also provide the launch-pads for riot and rebellion.[18] Popular captains carried swords and maces, ate porpoises, and issued orders as if they were kings or mayors, but of course they were not kings and mayors, and their actions were thus explicitly usurpatory.[19] They might carry loyal flags and banners, but they might also deface them, just as they might destroy aristocratic property.[20] Meanwhile, rebels' use of violent or insulting words, muttering, or shouting, marked them out from the humble petitioners they claimed to be.[21] So it was that activists combined licit moves with others that were clearly defiant.[22] How should we explain this mixture?

In part, it can be seen as a strategy – a form of forceful counsel – but if it is wrong to regard medieval rebels as incontinent hot-heads, it would also be wrong to overstate their capacity for calculation. The rules of the political game were unwritten and partly unclear – only in specific circumstances were the limits of acceptable behaviour revealed. As David Nirenberg and Hannah Skoda have pointed out, the boundaries between appropriate and inappropriate violence (to take one highly pertinent area of social regulation) were variable, adventitious, subjectively determined.[23] Leaders of revolts were short of reliable information, and they often had to make decisions quickly. Their willingness to triangulate with the authorities – to play the petitioner or loyalist – can rarely have been more than pragmatic, and it was surely circumscribed by the way those authorities behaved, and also by the attitudes of other members of the rebel host. Popular risings were difficult to control; they could evolve in unexpected ways – particularly when they encountered resistance – and individuals and groups within the rebel host may have wanted different things; as Justine Firnhaber-Baker says of the Jacquerie, the meanings and dynamics of revolts were 'multiple and mutable'. It was not hard for calculated violence to tip over into uncalculated violence, for acts of justice to become lynchings, for the recovery of the fisc to become looting. By acting assertively, and by assembling large numbers with more tenuous means to manage them than those at the disposal of a fully authoritative government, popular activists ran high risks, and it is not surprising that so many revolts turned into routs. But, of course, the same could be said of most forms of 'contentious politics' in the later Middle Ages, whether wars, or coups, or disputes at court or in public assemblies; the political manoeuvres of elites were equally

Conclusion

likely to deteriorate into squalid and violent conflict. Taken as a whole, therefore, popular revolts were not necessarily any more controversial than other forms of 'claim-making' behaviour.[24] They were normal enough in an era when shaky but interventionist governments bore down increasingly heavily on the mass of the population, but, while they embraced and reflected some of the prevailing principles of later medieval polities, they challenged others. Because of the numbers involved, and the sense that the inspiration for action came from the mass of the people and not from social elites, they made a distinctive impression on contemporaries, and – as a number of the essays in the collection indicate – they generated distinctive contests over their definition and representation. Let us now turn to these.

Revolts were events – *événements*, in the terminology of 1968 – but what events were they? Dumolyn and Haemers remind us that the term 'revolt' is a modern one, that older terms like 'rebellion' were rarely used of popular uprisings, and that the participants frequently denied that they were 'risers'.[25] Rebels posed as 'the commons' or 'the people', or invoked other terms denoting the political community; they emphasised their unity and made references to their 'gathering' or 'assembly'; they said they had come to uphold rights and customs, to defend the realm or the city, or to petition the authorities for redress. Observers and opponents often echoed these terms, writing neutrally of assemblies, alliances, or oath-swearings, or more colourfully of 'troubles', rumours, uproar, commotions, tumults, and terror; references to conspiracy, mutiny, and sedition were also common, but to rebellion and *lèse-majesté* rather rarer. There is an indication here of the partial legitimacy that attached to popular uprisings: like the torments of Hell, such episodes were unwelcome and horrifying, but they could serve a number of moral purposes, reminding the authorities of their responsibilities, while demonstrating to subjects that dissenting behaviour – however justifiable – would lead inexorably to anarchy and self-destruction. The emphasis on vocality and movement is striking – most later medieval polities were noisy and mobile places, full of persuasion, debate, and contention – but, in keeping with the classical tradition discussed by Lavan, the authorities figured them as 'still' and 'quiet'. Popular activists took an ambivalent line with that stillness, as we have seen. It is clear that they were highly sensitive to the question of how their actions would be perceived, and that they took steps to manage their own presentation, writing manifestoes declaring their aims, stressing their loyalty, attempting to keep order and to channel violence in appropriately punitive and acceptable directions. Their aim was to legitimise their acts of assertion without neutralising them, but as Dumolyn and Haemers and Firnhaber-Baker, among others, point out, only the balance of power and the course of events could determine the meaning of those contestatory ventures that we blithely call 'revolts'. Among those events were the responses of the authorities, which show that they too were quite as concerned as rebels with the politics of presentation. Typically, they punished ringleaders with exemplary severity, while pardoning the majority (partly with the pragmatic aim of getting them to disperse), and tacitly responding to the criticisms that had generated action in the first place.[26] Freedman and Challet draw attention to the contest of representations and inversions between rebels and the authorities: where insurgents used acceptable forms of violence, their opponents accused them of unacceptable forms; where insurgents aped the authorities, vengeful rulers satirised their pretensions. But the victors could also miscalculate: as Freedman shows, the hideous punishment of György Dósza in 1514 turned him into a Christ-like martyr, and came to seem the harbinger of the destruction of the medieval kingdom of Hungary at Mohács 12 years later.[27] In all, the memorialisation of revolts, which gave them their identity and meaning, reflected the kinds of ambivalence we have seen in other contexts: uprisings were awful, but they did correct some wrongs. They also, as Cohn points out, stayed alive in upper-class memories: popular rebels took action not only for their times, perhaps, but with an eye on posterity.[28]

There is much in these essays on rebel strategy: however complex and protean, revolts were partly or substantially organised, and leading activists presented their claims with a consciousness of what would be likely to attract support and persuade the authorities.[29] As political historians begin to pay more attention to the role of emotion in history – both the acknowledged repertoires of emotional behaviour, and the actual force of feeling as a factor in events – we might ask whether this approach to rebellion assumes too much rationality on the part of social actors.[30] The essays in this volume are surprisingly disengaged from questions of emotion and motivation. In part, of course, this is a continuing reaction to an older approach to revolt that regarded uprisings as incoherent expressions of pent-up feeling, an approach that reflected a common trope in the chronicle literature – of fury, frenzy, incontinence – and one that overlooked the impossibility of reaching the inner sensations of popular activists through the patchy and challenging evidence. Legal records (including pardons), manifestoes, and narratives patently reflect language games, played for purposes that were partly or totally distinct from the actual motives and feelings of the majority of rebels. But the utterances of clerks and chroniclers do make reference to the names, words, and actions of rebel hosts – the language game is not altogether closed, and reading for shifts and fissures, as Firnhaber-Baker has done for the Jacquerie, or chasing etymologies, with Dumolyn and Haemers, or noting consonances of action and pursuing prosopographies, as Andrew Prescott has done for 1381, may be expected to throw some light on the real circumstances of these revolts. We might recall too that emotional behaviour is still structured behaviour, and that it forms a certain continuity with the recognised rules and principles of public life. The injustices that rebels cited as the rationales for their actions are likely to have been felt as well as thought, even if they were accompanied by other feelings that were disguised or left unvoiced in rebel propaganda. Fabrizio Titone's notion of 'disciplined dissent' is helpful here. For one thing, it evokes the channelling of feeling and action down paths that were likely to be productive. For another, it reminds us that ordinary people were not completely without agency in the shaping of the rules of political and social life. Rather as Lantschner argues in respect of 'legal culture', or as John Arnold has proposed in relation to 'popular religion', the public realm inhabited by the participants in revolts was partly shaped by them – by traditions of assembly and merry-making, by communal organisations of various kinds, by schemes of values established in dialogue with preachers, confessors, and government officers; it was not simply handed down by social and political elites.[31] This insight may help to close the gap between emotive and strategic behaviour: even in the midst of a big public confrontation, there were always going to be some connections between what felt natural, what felt right, and what other people would recognise as right; equally, it was only at times that feelings ran so high that they overwhelmed instincts for prudence and compromise.

One final strand in the collection, which also bears on the question of how revolts fit into the rest of the political jigsaw, is the question of setting, and specifically whether urban, rural, and 'national' (or regnal, or many-centred) risings should be considered differently. It has become clear that popular revolts, including strikes and demonstrations, were a familiar and semi-ritualised feature of political life in larger towns, and that urban elites conducted their affairs accordingly, seeking to constrain or comply with popular initiatives quite as readily and routinely as they would work with oligarchical factions, external lords, and neighbouring municipalities.[32] Under these circumstances, urban popular activists had a known, and partly acceptable, repertoire of institutions and practices continually at their disposal. It has been suggested above that this marked them out from their counterparts in the countryside: peasant movements and ventures that sought to raise all the commons of a given region or country faced the difficult task of having to construct their own routines and legitimations *ab initio*, and this, in turn, might be one reason for the messiness of the Jacquerie, or the 'peasants' revolt' in England. While it seems undeniable that the urban environment was distinctive – nowhere outside the largest towns possessed quite the same concentrations of capital, population, built resource, political self-consciousness, governmental bricolage, and what Philip Haberkern neatly calls 'theopolitics' – it is possible that this difference could be pushed too far. The countryside, of course, was not a silent space dominated by lords: it was criss-crossed with routes of communication; it was a patchwork of jurisdictions; it was perforated by agencies of central government, so it felt the frustrations that gave rise to common action; and it provided plentiful means of raising men, from the hue and cry and the customs of manors to the royal and seigneurial networks that exercised justice, extracted tax, and raised troops.[33] While it is true that the 'Jacques', like the Flemish rebels of the 1320s and the English rebels of 1381, had to create their own programmes, they had analogous models, ideals, and practices to draw upon – those of neighbouring towns, for example, or of representative institutions – and their actions built on precedents that we could probably do more to unearth (William TeBrake makes numerous connections between the Flemish revolt, and the wars and urban uprisings in the region in the 1280s and around 1300; English historians are becoming more alert to popular participation in the Barons' War of the 1250s and 1960s, and in the troubles of Edward II's reign; the French Leagues of 1314–15 would also merit further research – can they really have been a movement restricted to the nobility when the pressures of Philip IV's wars and the economic difficulties of the 1310s were felt across society?).[34] Moreover, there were parts of Europe – admittedly highly urbanised – where large-scale, coordinated political action involving common people went back a long way: the Languedoc, for example, where the Albigensian crusades featured a struggle between inquisitors, churches, towns, and rural lordships in which local populations must have been politicised, or Castile in the decades around 1300, when large *hermandades* connected networks of towns to factions at the royal court.[35] The legacy of these thirteenth-century episodes is surely borne out in the activities of the Tuchins, the anti-Jewish (but also anti-state) uprisings of 1391, and, of course, in the revolt of the *comuneros* discussed by Rafael Oliva Herrer.[36] Certainly, there was something new about the big fourteenth-century demonstrations in Flanders, England, and the Paris Basin – that much is clear from the contemporary reaction – but there was a hinterland to these revolts, and they also, of course, laid down new conventions for the future. It was not only Flanders that enjoyed a 'great and little tradition' of popular uprising: British historians have noted the way in which 1381 inaugurated a tradition of commons revolts that shaped and punctuated English political history up to the middle of the sixteenth century.[37] Similar stories could be told of other countries.[38]

The aim of this book has not been to offer a single, global explanation of later medieval popular revolts, but to open up avenues for new research. Even so, in focusing on the political dimension of revolts, this conclusion captures certain convergences among the chapters. Almost all of them show popular activism to have been an embedded feature of later medieval political life: much as commentators often protested its outrageousness or incomprehensibility, and much as rebels often signalled their departures from normal obedience, corrective action from subjects was common enough to carry a certain kind of legitimacy, and to present itself as an available strategy in circumstances of oppressive or incompetent government. Equally, it is hard to deny that the prominence of revolt in the later Middle Ages owes a great deal to the prevailing political conditions of the period – the existence of strengthening states, the presence of communitarian values and institutions, a lively public culture in which appeals could be entertained, multiple centres of power, and the fragility or temporariness of regimes at every level. Seeing the two centuries between 1250 and 1450 as an 'age of revolts' offers more to historians of the period than both its previous reputation for decline and crisis and its newer one as an era of state growth. It draws attention to the organised contestation of authority, which was apparent at every level of political society, and reflects the growth and spread of political consciousness, sophistication, and technique. It opens the way for renewed attention to these 'cinderella centuries' as an ideal setting for the new political history.

Notes

1 I am most grateful to Justine Firnhaber-Baker, Jan Dumolyn, and Patrick Lantschner for their comments on an earlier draft of these conclusions.
2 M. Mollat and P. Wolff, *The Popular Revolutions of the Late Middle Ages*, trans. A. L. Lytton-Sells, London: George Allen & Unwin, 1973, p. 11. See also G. Fourquin, *The Anatomy of Popular Rebellion in the Middle Ages*, trans. A. Chesters, Amsterdam: North-Holland, 1978, esp. pp. 129–30, 161–2; V. Rutenburg, *Popolo e movimenti popolari nell'Italia de '300 e '400*, trans. G. Borghini, Bologna: Il Mulino, 1971; A. Leguai, 'Les révoltes rurales dans le royaume de France du milieu du XIVe siècle à la fin du XVe', *Le Moyen Âge*, 88, 1982, pp. 49–76; R. Hilton, *Bond Men Made Free*, London: Temple Smith, 1973, pp. 114–15, 118–19.
3 For example, Mollat and Wolff, *Popular Revolutions*, pp. 283ff; Fourquin, *Anatomy*, pp. 155, 159–60. For early examples of work emphasising the political context of medieval popular rebellion, see R. Cazelles, 'The Jacquerie' and S. Cohn, Jr., 'Florentine insurrections, 1342–1385, in comparative perspective', in R. H. Hilton and T. H. Aston (eds), *The English Rising of 1381*, Cambridge: Cambridge University Press, 1984, pp. 74–83, 143–64.
4 Among pan-European treatments, B. Guenée, *States and Rulers in Later Medieval Europe*, trans. J. Vale, Oxford: Blackwell, 1986; J.-P. Genet, 'L'État moderne: un modèle opératoire?', in J.-P. Genet (ed.), *L'État moderne, genèse: Bilans et perspectives*, Paris: Éditions du CNRS, 1990, pp. 261–81; the volumes in the European Science Foundation 'Origins of the Modern State in Europe' series, under the general editorship of J.-P. Genet and W. Blockmans, Oxford: Clarendon, 1995–2000; J. Watts, *The Making of Polities: Europe, 1300–1500*, Cambridge: Cambridge University Press, 2009.
5 H. Spruyt, *The Sovereign State and its Competitors*, Princeton, NJ: Princeton University Press, 1994; C. Tilly and W. P. Blockmans, *Cities and the Rise of States in Europe, AD1000–1800*, Boulder, CO: Westview, 1994; P. Blickle (ed.), *Resistance, Representation and Community*, Oxford: Clarendon, 1997, esp. Pt 1; T. Scott, *The City-State in Europe*, Oxford: Oxford University Press, 2012.
6 Watts, *Making of Polities*; W. Blockmans, A. Holenstein, and J. Mathieu (eds), *Empowering Interactions: Political Cultures and the Emergence of the State in Europe, 1300–1900*, Aldershot: Ashgate, 2009.
7 Blockmans et al. (eds), *Empowering Interactions*, and see also e.g. B. Kümin, *The Communal Age in Western Europe, c.1100–1800*, Basingstoke: Palgrave Macmillan, 2013; P. Lantschner, *The Logic of Political Conflict in Medieval Cities*, Oxford: Oxford University Press, 2015.
8 For example, J.-P. Genet (ed.), *La légitimité implicite*, 2 vols, Paris: Publications de la Sorbonne, 2015, and other works arising from his ERC-funded 'Signs and States' project; M. C. Erler and M. Kowaleski (eds), *Gendering the Master Narrative: Women and Power in the Middle Ages*, Ithaca, NY: Cornell University Press, 2003; C. Fletcher, *Richard II: Manhood, Youth and Politics*, Oxford: Oxford University Press, 2008; B. Rosenwein, 'Thinking historically about medieval emotions', *History Compass*, 8, 2010, 828–42.
9 B. Stollberg-Rillinger, 'The impact of communication theory on the analysis of the early modern state building processes', in Blockmans et al. (eds), *Empowering Interactions*, pp. 313–18; J. Dumolyn, 'Political communication and political power in the Middle Ages: a conceptual journey', *La Edad Media*, 13, 2012, pp. 33–55.
10 For example, W. H. TeBrake, *A Plague of Insurrection: Popular Politics and Peasant Revolt in Flanders, 1323–1328*, Philadelphia: University of Pennsylvania Press, 1993, pp. 7–8; S. K. Cohn, Jr., *Lust for Liberty: The Politics of Social Revolt in Medieval Europe, 1200–1425*, Cambridge, MA: Harvard, 2006, dust-jacket – 'not the last resort of desperate people, but remarkably common' – and pp. 2, 228; Lantschner, *Logic of Political Conflict*, pp. 5–6.
11 Cohn, *Lust for Liberty*, pp. 8–13; Watts, *Making of Polities*, pp. 276–80; Lantschner, *Logic of Political Conflict*, pp. 4–5, 7–10, and *passim*; J. Dumolyn, J. Haemers, H. R. Oliva Herrer, and V. Challet (eds), *The Voices of the People in Late Medieval Europe*, Turnhout: Brepols, 2014, esp. essays by Herrer and Watts.
12 J. Dumolyn and J. Haemers, 'Patterns of urban rebellion in medieval Flanders', *JMH*, 31, 2005, 369–93, esp. p. 382ff; Lantschner, *Logic of Conflict*, pp. 4–5, 9, ch. 3; V. Challet and I. Forrest, 'The masses', in C. Fletcher, J.-P. Genet, and J. Watts (eds), *Government and Political Life in England and France, c.1300–c.1500*, Cambridge: Cambridge University Press, 2015, pp. 279–316, at 297–300.
13 For the former point, see e.g. Hilton, *Bond Men Made Free*, pp. 13–14, ch. 1 and *passim*; A. Wood, *The 1549 Rebellions and the Making of Early Modern England*, Cambridge: Cambridge University Press, 2007, pp. v, 4, 9–10, 16–18, 55ff, ch. 4 and *passim*; A. Wood, *Riot, Rebellion and Popular Politics in Early Modern England*, Basingstoke: Palgrave, 2002, pp. 5–23; M. Boone and M. Prak, 'Rulers, patricians and

burghers: the great and the little traditions of urban revolt in the Low Countries', in K. Davids and J. Lucassen (eds), *A Miracle Mirrored: The Dutch Republic in European Perspective*, Cambridge: Cambridge University Press, 1995, pp. 99–134.

14 S. K. Cohn, Jr., *Popular Protest in Late Medieval English Towns*, Cambridge: Cambridge University Press, 2012, argues something similar on p. 8 and in ch. 4, though his emphasis is on the opportunities presented by royal weakness, rather than the challenges it presented and the problems of legitimacy that it raised.

15 Hilton, *Bond Men Made Free*, pp. 122–30; C. Dyer, 'The social and economic background to the rural revolt of 1381', in Hilton and Aston (eds), *English Rising*, pp. 9–42, at 14–19; Te Brake, *Plague of Insurrection*, pp. 57–60; Cazelles, 'Jacquerie', pp. 76–7; Wood, *Riot, Rebellion*, pp. 50, 51, 54, 64–5, 66, etc.; C. D. Liddy and J. Haemers, 'Popular politics in the late medieval city: York and Bruges', *EHR*, 128, 2013, pp. 771–805, at 776, 778, 801.

16 See also P. Freedman, *Images of the Medieval Peasant*, Stanford, CA: Stanford University Press, 1999, pp. 258–9ff.

17 See also J. Watts, 'The commons in medieval England', in Genet (ed.), *La légitimité implicite*, 207–22, and 'The pressure of the public on later medieval politics', in L. Clark and C. Carpenter (eds), *The Fifteenth Century IV: Political Culture in Late Medieval Britain*, Woodbridge: Boydell, 2004, pp. 159–80, esp. pp. 176–8; J. A. Solorzano Telechea, 'Protestas del común y cambio politico en las villas portuarias de la España…', in H. R. Oliva Herrer, V. Challet, J. Dumolyn, and M. A. Carmona Ruiz (eds), *La comunidad medieval como esfera pública*, Seville: Publicaciones de la Universitad de Sevilla, 2014, pp. 45–72.

18 Dumolyn and Haemers, p. 46, in this volume. See also C. D. Liddy, 'Urban enclosure riots: risings of the commons in English towns, 1480–1525', *P&P*, 226, 2015, pp. 41–77; Wood, *Riot, Rebellion*, pp. 100–6.

19 I. M. W. Harvey, *Jack Cade's Rebellion of 1450*, Oxford: Clarendon, 1991, pp. 87–8.

20 Examples in Cohn, *Lust for Liberty*, ch. 8. See Firnhaber-Baker in this volume for destruction of castles.

21 J. Dumolyn and J. Haemers, '"A bad chicken was brooding": subversive speech in late medieval Flanders', *P&P*, 214, 2012, pp. 45–86; J. Haemers, 'Filthy and indecent words: insults, defamation and urban politics in the southern Low Countries, 1300–1550', in Dumolyn et al. (eds), *Voices of the People*, pp. 247–67.

22 Cf. the distinction between 'contained' and 'transgressive' forms of contention in D. McAdam, S. G. Tarrow, and C. Tilly, *Dynamics of Contention*, Cambridge: Cambridge University Press, 2001, pp. 7–8.

23 D. Nirenberg, *Communities of Violence: Persecution of Minorities in the Middle Ages*, Princeton, NJ: Princeton University Press, 1996, pp. 5–7, 241–9 and *passim*; H. Skoda, *Medieval Violence: Physical Brutality in Northern France, 1270–1330*, Oxford: Oxford University Press, 2013, pp. 1–2, 232–44 and *passim*.

24 These phrases come from the work of Charles Tilly, e.g. *Regimes and Repertoires*, Chicago, IL: University of Chicago Press, 2006, p. vii. See also the work of Dumolyn and Haemers in this volume and elsewhere.

25 Note the protestation of Cade's rebels in 1450: the men around the king 'calle us risers and treyturs and the kynges enymys, but we schalle be ffounde his trew lege mene and his best freendus' (Harvey, *Cade's Rebellion*, p. 189).

26 Cohn, *Lust for Liberty*, p. 147ff.

27 See also Freedman, *Images of the Medieval Peasant*, pp. 259ff.

28 Cohn, *Lust for Liberty*, pp. 23–4, 156.

29 For organisation, see now S. K. Cohn, 'Enigmas of communication: Jacques, Ciompi and the English', in Oliva Herrer et al. (eds), *Comunidad medieval*, pp. 227–47.

30 See above, n. 8, and, more generally, E. Ikegame, 'The emotions', in U. Rublack (ed), *A Concise Companion to History*, Oxford: Oxford University Press, 2012, pp. 333–53, esp. p. 339ff; J. Plamper, *The History of the Emotions*, trans. K. Tribe, Oxford: Oxford University Press, 2012, esp. pp. 277–81.

31 J. H. Arnold, 'Religion and popular rebellion, from the Capuciati to Niklashausen', *Cultural and Social History*, 6, 2009, pp. 149–69, at 163–5.

32 Lantschner, *Logic of Conflict*, *passim*.

33 These themes are well surveyed for England in C. Dyer, 'The political life of the fifteenth-century English village', in Clark and Carpenter (eds), *Political Culture*, pp. 135–57.

34 TeBrake, *Plague of Insurrection*, pp. 29–34; Cohn, *Popular Protest in Towns*, pp. 83–90; and note the suggestive remarks of P. Contamine on the Leagues of 1314–15: 'De la puissance aux privilèges: doléances de la noblesse française envers la monarchie aux XIVe et XVe siècles', in *La noblesse au Moyen Âge: XIe-XVe siècles: Essais à la mémoire de Robert Boutruche*, Paris: Presses universitaires de France 1976, pp. 235–57, esp. pp. 242–7.

35 J. B. Given, *Inquisition and Medieval Society: Power, Discipline and Resistance in Languedoc*, Ithaca, NY: Cornell University Press, 1997, pp. 5–9, 16–20, ch. 5; P. Linehan, 'Castile, Navarre and Portugal', in M. Jones (ed.), *New Cambridge Medieval History VI, c.1300–c.1415*, Cambridge: Cambridge University Press, 2000, pp. 619–50, at 620–9.

36 V. Challet, 'Au miroir du Tuchinat: relations sociales et réseaux de solidarité dans les communautés languedociennes à la fin du XIVe siècle', *Cahiers de recherches médiévales (XIIIe–XVe siècles)*, 10, 2003, pp. 71–87; Linehan, 'Castile', pp. 648–9.

37 Boone and Prak, 'Rulers, patricians and burghers'; J. Watts, 'Public or plebs? The changing meaning of "the commons", 1381–1549', in H. Pryce and J. Watts (eds), *Power and Identity in the Middle Ages*, Oxford: Oxford University Press, 2007, pp. 242–60.

38 For the under-appreciated example of Sweden, see K. Katalaja, 'Against tithes and taxes: peasant unrest and medieval Scandinavian political culture', in *Northern Revolts: Medieval and Early Modern Peasant Unrest in the Nordic Countries*, Helsinki: Finnish Literature Society, 2004, pp. 32–52.

INDEX

Page numbers in **bold** denote figures.

abuse of power 27–9, 43, 66–7, 116, 131, 133, 137–8, 146, 157–8, 168–9, 171, 173, 175–6, 243, 285, 294–6, 304, 323, 340, 365n32; *see also* customary rights; taxation
Anonimalle Chronicle 58, 81–2, 84–5, 99n61, 272, 287, 290n23, 291n50
Antwerp 44, 105, **107–8**, 113, 115–16, 118; *see also* Flanders
Arab Spring 3, 95
aristocrats, as rebels 28, 130–2, 159–60, 201, 206n80, 218n33, 220, 275; *see also* leadership, of revolts
Aristotelianism 42, 171, 175, 334
arson 64, 65, 74n89, 76, 77, 83, 85, 87, 157, 211, 283, 288, 291n50, 332, **333**

'bad lordship' *see* abuse of power
banditry 19–20, 22, 24, 34
banners 4, 7, 9, 45–7, 60, 68, 71n50, 83–4, 89, 171, 173–5, 179, 180–1, 209, 224, 227, 229, 284, 296, 374; *see also* communication: symbolic; revolt: legality and legitimacy of
Battle of Courtrai (1302) 63, 104, 118–19, 271
Battle of the Golden Spurs *see* Battle of Courtrai
Black Death 6, 55, 155, 156, 167n35, 210, 216, 222, 322, 370
Bologna 138, 143, 168–83, 373
Boudiccan revolt (CE61) 27–8, 32, 33, 273
Bourdieu, Pierre 49, 335
Bruges 39–54, 118, 122–3
Bruges Matins massacre (1302) 119, 209, 210
Burgundy (duchy) 106, 120, 124, 157
Burgundy (dynasty) 43–4, 105–9, **107–8**, 115–24, 146, 237, 279–82, 287; *see also* Charles the Bold; John the Fearless
butchers 41, 46–7, 112, 227–8, 234n52, 234n62, 244, 279–81, 322; *see also* craft guilds

Calle, Guillaume 62, 287
cannibalism 58, 110, 267, 272–3, 275, 282–4, 290n27
carnival *see* festivals
Cassius Dio 32, 35, 273
Charles (dauphin of France) *see* Charles V (king of France)
Charles I (king of England) 212, 341
Charles I (king of Castile) *see* Holy Roman Empire
Charles II (king of Navarre) 56, 59, 60, 272, 287
Charles IV (Holy Roman Emperor) *see* Holy Roman Empire
Charles V (Holy Roman Emperor) *see* Holy Roman Empire
Charles V (king of France) 46, 56–9, 62–4, 67, 283–5, 287
Charles VI (king of France) 279
Charles VIII (king of France) 351, 354–5
Charles the Bold (duke of Burgundy) 44, 107, 114–16, 122–4, 247; *see also* Burgundy (dynasty)
Ciompi Revolt (1378) 2, 60, 94, 175, 181, 211, 221; *see also* Florence
cities: armed conflict between 23, 25, 236, 240–3, 254n16; institutional structure of 140–1, 169–70, 177, 191–200, 228–30, 236–40, 243–5, 296–301, 313–15, 338–9;

381

Index

cities *continued*
  revolt in 156, 321, 349–50; social hierarchies in 245–6, 303, 318, 322; *see also* craft guilds
clerics, as rebels 92, 93, 178–80, 211; *see also* leadership, of revolts
Cohn, Samuel K., Jr. 4, 55, 60, 155–7, 191, 221–2, 293, 365n32
collective action 41; forms of 45–9, 79, 110, 173–4, 193, 195, 199, 209, 226–8, 237–8, 240, 244–5, 251, 320–1, 374; as 'repertoires' 10, 68, 170, 175, 349, 376; terms for 39–49; *see also* craft guilds; revolt; riots and rioting; Tilly, Charles
collective identity 29, 34, 68, 95, 107, 109–13, 120, 135–7, 146, 248, 251, 292, 331, 338–9, 344, 363; *see also* oathtaking
collective memory 3, 8, 10, 41–2, 49, 56, 109, 115, 164, 248, 251, 271, 275, 312, 331, 338, 340, 375; and chronicles 8, 79, 104–5, 116–19, 143, 237
communication: and physical movement 40, 45–7; rebellious speech 8–9, 39–40, 44–5, 209, 228, 232n26, 316, 319, 322, 324; repertoires of 8; sites of 9, 45–6, 141, 209, 285, 316–17, 361; and sound 46, 274, 308n57; symbolic 7–9, 45, 84, 89, 175, 224, 286, 296
coniuratio see oathtaking
conspiracy 31–2, 45–6, 48, 57–8, 136, 139, 211, 226, 244–5, 250–1, 320; *see also* oathtaking; rumour
corruption *see* abuse of power
craft guilds: alliances of 220, 222, 227, 230, 235n66; assemblies of 46–8, 49, 226, 228, 234n52, 251, 297; and collective action 46–8, 197, 203n17, 223–5, 228–9, 233n32, 321, 371; conflict within 200, 227–30, 235n70; participation in revolts 49, 92, 111, 114, 123, 171–3, 181, 220–3, 227–8, 237, 247, 251, 297, 373; privileges and statutes of 44, 170–1, 173, 243, 245, 297, 318, 322 (*see also* rebellious speech); and urban government 113–15, 124, 169, 171, 193, 220, 223–5, 227–30, 239, 245, 248, 252, 297–9; *see also* butchers; textile workers; customary rights
crime and criminality 5, 20, 30–2, 37n31, 43, 57, 59, 64, 74n89, 111, 139, 174, 211, 228, 240, 280, 282–4, 286–7, 313, 316–17; *see also* rape
customary rights 33–4, 45, 88, 133–4, 138, 142, 146, 160–1, 173, 196, 226, 293, 304, 308n59, 340–2, 373; *see also* abuse of power; craft guilds; revolt: legality and legitimacy of; taxation

Damascus 168–70, 175–82

Dampierre, Guy de 39, 104, 119
Davis, Natalie Zemon 58, 213, 215, 305n4
destruction of records 82–5, 94, 288
dissent *see* communication: rebellious speech
Douai 46–8, 209, 216

emotions 8–10, 28, 37n31, 43–6, 57–8, 64, 115, 162, 208, 294, 300, 319–23, 375–6
English Rising (1381) 2, 41, 57, 60, 68, 193, 211, 281, 284, 321, 373; and gender 7; geographic extent of 77, 81–2; and symbolic violence 286–8; terminology of 97n23
execution 63, 76–7, 79, 83–5, 93, 117, 174, 177, 209, 211, 250, 267, 279–82, 284, 287–8, 332, 352, 374 (*see also* violence: against officials); of rebels 91, 101n122, 112, 116, 122, 227, 267–8, 272–6, 281–2, 287–8, 353, 359

feud 12n25, 43, 156, 158, 224–5, 227, 230, 238–40, 244, 248–9, 310n98
festivals 9, 15n63, 39–41, 45, 79, 274, 360, 372
flags *see* banners
Flanders 9–10, 42–3, 47, 68, 74n90, 91, 104–6, 109, 116–24, 156, 159, 221–4, 228–9, 245, 285, 298, 374, 377; *see also* Antwerp; Ghent
Florence 4, 173, 175, 181, 210–14, 297, 349–57, 359–60, 362; *see also* Ciompi Revolt (1378)
Fourquin, Guy 3, 190, 221–2
Frederick I (Holy Roman Emperor) *see* Holy Roman Empire
Frederick III (king of Sicily) 242, 252, 292, 294–6
freeing of prisoners 83, 189, 200, 281, 283, 313, 359
French Revolution (1789) 5, 94, 95, 142, 208
Frisia 28–9, 32, 111, 121, 158, 161, 163
Froissart, Jean 58–60, 64, 67, 78, 82, 105, 273, 282–4, 290n23; *see also* revolt: depictions of in chronicles

German Peasants' War (1525) 241, 271
Ghent 44–6, 106, 109, 113, 115, 118–19, 122–3, 125n17, 229, 244; *see also* Flanders
Guha, Ranajit 20, 35–6

Holy Roman Empire 51n31, 123, 130–3, 159, 162, 238–40, 242, 247, 252, 253n7, 272; Charles IV 238, 240–2; Charles V 239–41, 244, 245, 331, 335, 340, 373; Frederick I 130–47, 247
Hus, Jan *see* Hussites
Hussites 57, 213, 237, 349–53, 357–60, 362

Islam 6, 9, 94, 168–88

Index

Jack Cade Revolt (1450) 40, 193
Jacquerie (1358) 2, 9–10, 41, 48, 267, 272–3, 283; geographical extent 60, **61**, 67; terminology of 55, 60, 64; women and 210, 282
Jean le Bel 57–60, 64, 67, 71n42, 120, 273, 290n23
Jean de Venette 58, 66, 68, 210
John the Fearless (duke of Burgundy) 44, 119, 279–80; *see also* Burgundy (dynasty)
John of Gaunt 76, 79, 89, 92
Justice, Steven 57, 77, 80, 155

Lantschner, Patrick 4–5, 55, 94, 197, 200–1, 223, 225, 233n31, 235n66, 293, 297
Laon 5, 56, 59, 68, 133–6, 156
lawsuits 6, 10, 64, 69n8, 82–3, 87, 157–9, 171, 173–4, 178, 180–1, 191–3, 195–201, 210–11, 223, 238, 244–6, 249–52, 285, 291n49
leadership, of revolts 5–6, 25, 26, 29, 40, 58, 62, 64, 68, 72n60–72n61, 76, 79, 82, 85, 93–6, 109, 136, 160, 163, 177–9, 220–3, 226, 228–30, 267–8, 272–3, 279, 287–8, 303, 337, 354–5, 359, 362, 368n68, 372, 374–5; and women 209–12, 215; *see also* aristocrats, as rebels; clerics, as rebels; craft guilds; 'vertical' alliances
liberties *see* customary rights
London 3, 76–9, 81–9, 91–4, 156, 191, 194–6, 198, 239, 286–7, 311–18, 320–4, 372–3
looting *see* crime and criminality

Marcel, Étienne 2, 56–7, 59, 62–3, 284, 286–7
Milan 132, 134–40, 144, 156, 169, 210, 214–15

oathtaking 28, 29, 44–5, 93, 132, 136, 141–2, 174, 176, 226–7, 230, 245, 247, 251, 260n119, 313, 318, 375; *see also* conspiracy
Owain Glyn Dŵr 40, 91

papacy 140, 147, 158, 169–74, 175, 215, 239, 241, 305n2, 373; Alexander III 132, 136–7, 144–6; Gregory I 158, 171; Gregory IX 162; Gregory XI 172; Innocent IV 62; Julius II 171–4; Leo X 273; Martin V 274, 352; Nicholas V 172; Pius II 167–73, 181
Papal State *see* papacy
Paris 46–7, 56–64, 67–8, 239, 279–81, 283–7
petitions and petitioning 8, 41, 45, 67, 84–5, 88, 101n122, 157, 178, 181, 193, 195, 197–9, 211, 223, 292, 296, 298, 300, 302, 320–1, 331–2, 373–4, 375
popes *see* papacy

rape 27–9, 58, 64, 73n85, 210, 268, 273–4, 280, 284–5; *see also* crime and criminality

rebels: names and terms for 23, 42–3, 47, 79; and negotiations 172, 222–3, 224, 283–4, 292, 301–2; pardon of 56–60, 62–3, 64, 67, 82, 84, 87, 90n89, 91, 101n108, 182, 210–11, 217n22, 280, 282–4, 286, 323, 375–6; punishment of 25, 47, 79, 137, 160, 179, 192, 197, 209, 211, 216, 220, 227–30, 231n2, 283, 302 (*see also* execution; torture); social origins of 84, 85, 91–3, 143–4, 160, 171, 215, 330
revolt: communication in 8, 106, 137, 247, 331, 349–50, 359, 366n35, 369n80; and conflicts with the church 83–4, 88, 158–9; definitions of 4, 11n3, 22, 41, 164n1, 189–91, 313; depictions of in chronicles 8, 10, 40–5, 46, 55–60, 64, 67–8, 78–82, 84–5, 132–7, 155–6, 158–9, 161–2, 168, 172, 176–7, 209–12, 213–15, 234n55, 237, 243–4, 249, 251, 268, 273–4, 280, 282–5, 287, 290n23, 291n50, 333, 346n46, 368n68, 376; legality and legitimacy of 4–5, 30, 45, 49, 60, 71n50, 84, 146, 168–78, 180–2, 190–5, 232n29, 249–51, 281, 287–8, 296, 340–1, 373 (*see also* abuse of power; customary rights; taxation); naming of 7, 19–26, 39–49, 51n31, 55, 57, 78–9, 80; and 'normal' politics 3–5, 55, 120, 156, 170, 173, 175, 223–5, 321, 372–3, 375 (*see also* collective action); and publicity 106, 137, 247, 331; and religion 9, 55, 58, 76, 176, 178, 212
revolt narratives 19–36, 158; *see also* revolt: depictions of in chronicles
riots and rioting 3, 23, 25, 43, 114, 169, 189–91, 197, 211–16, 279, 281, 301–3; and communication 357; and 'contentious politics' 41, 45–6; and elections 193–4, 197; and enclosure 212, 315, 321; and food 208–9, 212–3; and revolt 85, 93, 178, 189–91, 193, 200, 203n9, 208, 211, 294; and vengeance 111; and women 211–16
ritual *see* festivals
rumour 26, 41, 44, 55, 79, 105–6, 111, 189, 232n26, 249, 319–21, 324, 375; *see also* communication: rebellious speech

slave revolt 19, 158
strikes *see* collective action: forms of

taxation 3, 27, 76, 80, 89, 106, 134, 137, 146, 156–7, 164, 176–7, 179–80, 209, 212, 214–15, 238, 239, 245, 252, 261n148, 283, 285–6, 288, 293, 294–7, 299, 301, 303, 304, 316, 320–1, 331–2, 335–6, 340–2, 370; *see also* abuse of power; customary rights; revolt: legality and legitimacy of textile workers: and collective action 45, 48, 180, 245; in revolts 43–6, 78, 89, 105, 119, 123, 209, 244; *see also* craft guilds

Tilly, Charles 215; and 'contentious politics' 11n3, 41, 208; and 'repertoires' 224

torture 58, 64, 209, 267–73, **269**, **270**, 314; *see also* execution

Tuchins 40, 263n171, 267, 272, 287–8, 377

tyranny *see* abuse of power

urban revolt *see* cities: in revolt

'vertical' alliances 6, 144, 160, 220f 337, 343–4, 352

violence: against the church and clerics 74n100, 76, 88–9, 92–3, 101n122, 157, 161, 212, 215, 273; against nobles 57–60, 62–8, 85, 89, 92–3, 111, 157–8, 161, 165n14, 210–11, 240, 267–9, 272–4, 282, 284, 288; against officials 56, 63, 76–7, 85, 89, 93, 116–17, 177, 181, 211, 250, 283, 284, 303, 352 (*see also* execution); against women 58, 62, 64, 66, 198, 268, 279, 280, 282, 290n23; and gender 7, 156; symbolic violence 286–8

weavers *see* textile workers